Anthony Eden

A BIOGRAPHY

David Carlton

ALLEN LANE

ALLEN LANE
Penguin Books Ltd
536 King's Road
London SW10 0UH

First published 1981
Copyright © David Carlton, 1981

ISBN 0 7139 1829 7

Set in Monophoto Photina by
Filmtype Services Limited, Scarborough
Printed in Great Britain by
Richard Clay (The Chaucer Press) Ltd
Bungay, Suffolk

Preface

I have incurred many debts during the decade I have devoted to Anthony Eden. I am able here to record my thanks to only a few of those concerned. My particular thanks are due to Mr Piers Dixon for permitting me to examine and to reproduce passages from the diary and papers of his father, Sir Pierson Dixon, Principal Private Secretary to Eden between 1943 and 1945. He has, moreover, discussed with me at length many aspects of Eden's times, basing himself in part on expertise deriving from having written *Double Diploma*, a fascinating study of his father.

I owe a special debt to Sir Evelyn Shuckburgh. His position as Principal Private Secretary to Eden during most of the latter's third term at the Foreign Office in the 1950s made him uniquely qualified to help me to explain the events of a period still covered by the so-called Thirty-Year Rule relating to official British records. After discussions with me and after reading a first draft of the relevant chapter, he allowed me to read portions of the diary which he kept at that time and to make a number of quotations from it, though it is not his intention that the diary as a whole should be made public in the immediate future.

Extracts from Crown Copyright records in the Public Record Office appear by permission of the Controller of H M Stationery Office. The following are also thanked for consenting to my use of unpublished copyright material: Professor Robert Bowie; Lord Coleraine (formerly Mr Richard Law); Mr Douglas Dillon; Lord Harlech; Mr John Hightower; Mrs Mary A. Homans; Mr Robert Hopkins; Professor A. K. S. Lambton; Admiral W. H. Leahy; Mr Malcolm MacDonald; Mr William B. Macomber; Rev. Livingston Merchant; Mr Drew Middleton; Mrs G. Moon; Dr Alexander Murray; William Collins, Sons and Co Ltd and Mr Nigel Nicolson; Mr Roderic O'Connor; Mr Paul Paget; Mr William Parsons; the Earl of Perth; Viscount Simon; the Beaverbrook Foundation; the University of Birmingham Library; the Master and Fellows of Churchill College, Cambridge; the University of Cambridge Library; the Yale University Library; the Library of Congress; the Rector and Visitors of the University of Virginia; and the House of Lords Record Office. I am also grateful to the *Journal of Contemporary History* for permission to reprint some passages from my article published in its pages in 1971.

I thank the following for granting me interviews on the subject of Eden and his times: the late Lord Allan of Kilmahew, Lord Butler of Saffron

Walden, Sir John Colville, Professor David Dilks, Dr Frank Hardie, Mr Keith Kyle, Mr Malcolm MacDonald, Sir Anthony Rumbold, Lord Sherfield, the late Sir Michael Wright and several former public servants in both Great Britain and the United States who do not wish to be identified.

Fellow-historians who have helped me with particular points include Dr Vaughan Baker, Professor James Barros, Dr Martin Ceadel and Anthony Seldon.

I have been enabled to explore relevant archives in the United States partly as a result of invitations to lecture in numerous American universities. In this connection I owe a special debt to Professor Herbert M. Levine and his colleagues at the University of South-Western Louisiana.

I must also pay tribute to the patience and encouragement of my editors, Mr Peter Carson and Dr Christopher Cook, and to my agent, Mr Hilary Rubinstein of A. P. Watt & Son. For typing I am grateful to Mrs Sybil Everitt and her staff at the Typing Centre of the Polytechnic of North London.

Finally, I must register my particular indebtedness to Professor Robert Skidelsky, now based at the University of Warwick but previously, for all too brief a period, my Departmental Head at the Polytechnic of North London. He read the entire manuscript and offered many constructive suggestions concerning content and style. Remaining shortcomings naturally remain my sole responsibility.

I recognize that, despite my having had access to the diary of Sir Evelyn Shuckburgh and to numerous collections in the United States, my chapters on Eden during the 1950s may suffer from the absence of material from the British governmental archives, which are at present closed under the Thirty-Year Rule. Clearly a more authoritative biography would have been possible had I waited until 1987, the year in which official records relating to the last crisis of Eden's career, namely Suez, will be released. Parts of the present work should therefore be seen as an interim verdict. I intend, however, to publish an expanded and up-dated edition in 1987. I invite those readers who are in a position to throw light on aspects of Eden's life which I have overlooked or perhaps inadvertently misrepresented in this edition to write to me care of my London publishers.

David Carlton
August 1980

1

Early Years
1897–1931

It is ironic that County Durham, which has been in the twentieth century the most loyal to the Labour Party of all counties in England, should have been the birthplace of no Labour leader of distinction but should instead have produced a future Conservative Prime Minister. Robert Anthony Eden was born on 12 June 1897 at Windlestone Hall near Bishop Auckland. He was the third son of Sir William Eden, who owned a substantial estate of 800 acres. The Edens had been prominent in County Durham since the fifteenth century, a baronetcy having been conferred in 1672.

Anthony Eden's father was a remarkable eccentric. An engaging portrait, *The Tribulations of a Baronet*, was published in 1933 by Sir Timothy Eden, his second son. And more recently Anthony Eden himself offered some rather more discreet glimpses in *Another World*, a book of reminiscences about his own early years. Sir William's irascibility was legendary and may at times have verged on insanity. Sir Timothy recalled that 'he took a marked delight in embarrassing those with whom he talked, and he spared no one, neither for their helplessness nor their strength, man, woman or child, peer or peasant, from his sweeping condemnation or his biting ridicule'. He recorded without disbelief that his father had been accused of having bitten a carpet. And he revealed something of the strain faced by Sir William's children when he wrote: 'Nor will anyone readily admit that the whistling of a boy in the street can be a good or sufficient reason for breaking a window with a flower-pot.'[1]

Some of Sir William's temperamental outbursts were not, in retrospect at least, without their amusing aspect. He was, for example, insistent that blue flowers should predominate in his gardens and above all that any of a red variety should be instantly decapitated. And Anthony Eden recalled this anecdote about a day when a meet assembled outside Windlestone Hall:

My father had a fixed obsession that on any day when he wished especially for fine weather, the Almighty would send a downpour to vex him ... On this day the rain was true to tradition, beating down on hounds, huntsmen and loyal followers. As my father came through the front hall to join them, his eye fell on a barometer hanging on the panelled wall. He walked up to it and tapped: it read 'Set Fair'. He tapped again; it still replied 'Set Fair'. He took it off the wall, walked through the front door to the top of the flight of steps and sent it clattering down before the assembled company, saying, 'Go and see for yourself, you damned fool.'[2]

Such an agreeable example of eccentricity must have been exceptional. More often Sir William's behaviour must have been simply boorish and extremely difficult for his children to bear. At the end of Eden's political life, early in 1957, Lord Moran recorded in his diary that he gossiped with the aged Winston Churchill about Eden's unusual early years:

> I asked him [Churchill] if he had read the memoir by Sir Timothy Eden, Anthony's brother, about their father, Sir William Eden. Winston shook his head. It makes sad reading, I told him. Sir William's uncontrolled rages terrified his children, who were always on tenterhooks, fearing that they might say something that would start an explosion. A barking dog might give rise to a terrible tornado of oaths, screams and gesticulations. Sir William was a gifted egoist without any control, so that at any time there might be a terrible scene of rage and tears. Anthony did not inherit his father's instability, but it must have been a handicap to be brought up in such an atmosphere.[3]

Whether any lasting effects can be discerned in Eden's political life, as Moran seemed to suppose, will probably remain a subject for entirely inconclusive speculation.

Anthony Eden's mother, Sybil, was the daughter of Sir William Grey, who had been Lieutenant-Governor of Bengal and Governor of Jamaica. Lord Grey of the Great Reform Bill was her great-uncle and Sir Edward Grey, the Foreign Secretary, was more distantly related. Sybil Eden was in some respects almost as eccentric as her husband but this is less well documented in her sons' reminiscences. Anthony Eden did, however, permit himself one illuminating comment in *Another World*: 'I think my mother preferred the simpler relationship which existed between donor and recipient to the more complicated one between mother and child.'[4] A volume of her own memoirs was apparently suppressed in the 1930s.

From this bizarre background Anthony Eden was despatched at the age of nine to Sandroyd School in Surrey and at thirteen duly entered Eton. Here he achieved little distinction. He appears to have been a reserved and shy boy who made no strong impression on his contemporaries. He recalled in *Another World* that he 'never pretended to like school' and that his years at Eton were 'far from the happiest' in his life.[5] Yet for all his coolness about Eton, he sent his own sons there.

While Eden was still at Eton the First World War broke out. Within three months his eldest brother, John, had been killed – the first of an unusually large number of personal tragedies to befall him. The following February saw the death of his father. Eden was now eighteen years of age and thus qualifies as one of the many British Prime Ministers who lost a parent before achieving his majority. In September 1915 Eden volunteered to join the army. There seems to have been no hesitation about his taking this step rather than proceed, as he doubtless would have done in peacetime, to Oxford. He joined the rifle corps and for most of the war was at the Western

Front. In 1917 he became an adjutant. He was also awarded the Military Cross, reputedly for rescuing his sergeant. Characteristically he made no reference to this act of valour in his otherwise detailed account of his war experiences in *Another World*. In 1918 he became at the age of twenty the youngest brigade major in the army. But none of these experiences may have been as traumatic for him as the loss of his younger brother Nicholas, to whom he had been very close. He died at the end of 1916 in the Battle of Jutland when a mere sixteen years old. It was without doubt the saddest event in Eden's life until the death of his own son in the Second World War. How far his harrowing experiences both at the Western Front and in losing two brothers influenced his later thinking about politics is difficult to assess. But they may well account for his relatively robust approach to many issues, not least in the interwar years when so many of his ministerial colleagues were too old to have seen war at first hand and were thus paradoxically prone to embrace anti-war sentiments. One historian has written:

The Cabinets which governed Britain in the 1930s were composed of men who believed that almost no price was too high to pay to avoid another war. The exceptions, curiously enough, were those who had had first-hand experience of war. Anthony Eden and Alfred Duff Cooper, who knew that, vile as the experience was, it was not utterly intolerable, and there might be others yet worse.

Eden himself chose to recall in *Another World*: 'I had entered the holocaust still childish and I emerged tempered by my experience, but with my illusions intact, neither shattered nor cynical, to face a changed world.' Anthony Nutting, reviewing *Another World*, assumed that Eden's war experience 'explains the dedication that he was later to show as a young Foreign Office minister towards the League of Nations'.[6] But whatever Eden meant by not being cynical and having his illusions intact, he cannot have been implying that he had excessive faith in the League of Nations. For, as will be seen, he only belatedly adopted a political line that appeared to put him in the camp of the internationalist zealots.

At the end of the war Eden considered becoming a professional soldier or alternatively entering the diplomatic service. He deferred a final decision, however, by going to Christ Church, Oxford, at the age of twenty-two. He decided to read for the degree in Oriental languages (especially Persian and Turkish). This unusual choice was partly designed to fit him for a specialized future in the diplomatic service. While he did not in the event become a professional diplomat, he was nevertheless destined to spend much of his life in the Foreign Office. His knowledge of Oriental languages, however, was probably of no particular value in his political rôles there. Yet he was no doubt led by his studies to feel sympathy for Turkey, Persia and various Arab states. Indeed, until the final drama of 1956 he was to be a friend of most of the Middle Eastern nations and hence an anti-Zionist.

13

He enjoyed his time at Oxford more than at Eton. Yet his wartime experiences must have cut him off to some extent from those of his fellow students who had endured no such trauma. He showed little enthusiasm at Oxford for politics but involved himself in cultural activities. He joined with Lord David Cecil, for example, in forming the Uffizi Society for the study of art – an appropriate course for the son of Sir William Eden, who had been a far-sighted collector of modern paintings. This interest remote from politics was to be a helpful diversion in later years on occasions when the strain of public life was unbearable.

On leaving Oxford Eden decided to enter politics rather than the diplomatic service. His family's standing in County Durham made it easy for him to be selected to contest the unwinnable seat of Spennymoor in the General Election of November 1922. The Labour candidate, Joseph Batey, polled 13,766, while Eden narrowly secured second place with only 7,576 votes. In the following year he was successful in being selected as Conservative candidate for a by-election in the safe constituency of Warwick and Leamington. The main interest in the campaign was that his Labour opponent was Lady Warwick, the eccentric former mistress of King Edward the Seventh who had undergone a belated conversion to extreme socialism. By chance she was also Eden's sister's mother-in-law. To complicate matters further Lady Warwick's son, Guy Brooke, who was a Conservative, sent a message of support to Eden. Few doubted that Eden would easily win, though he was quite unable to match Lady Warwick in the matter of publicity. He held unexcitingly orthodox views. Lady Warwick's biographer records that 'he made it clear that he considered fox hunting one of God's gifts to freeborn Englishmen; that as a churchgoer he would resist the disestablishment of the Church of England; and that he opposed undermining the sanctity of marriage by easier divorce'.[7]

The by-election contest was cancelled when polling day was only a week away. For Stanley Baldwin, the Prime Minister, had asked for a dissolution in order to seek a mandate for tariff reform. Hence Eden had to wait another three weeks before being returned to Parliament in the General Election of 6 December 1923. The result at Warwick and Leamington was

Eden (Conservative)	16,337
Nicholls (Liberal)	11,134
Lady Warwick (Labour)	4,015

Eden was to remain MP for this same constituency (with boundary changes) until his retirement in 1957. He was never to have the slightest difficulty in holding it – not even in 1945. Nationally the outcome for the Conservatives in 1923 was less satisfactory. The number of seats obtained by the three main parties was: Conservatives 258; Labour 191; and Liberals 158. This led Baldwin to resign. For although the Conservatives were the largest single party, the other two parties had both supported free trade and hence it was clear that on the central issue of the Election the Conservatives had been denied the mandate they had sought. Thus in January 1924 James Ramsay MacDonald formed the first Labour Government, a minority administration sustained in office by the Liberals. Eden accordingly took his place on the Opposition benches. He was now twenty-six years of age.

The end of 1923 was also of great importance in his private life. For he married Beatrice, daughter of Sir Gervase Beckett. This marriage was not destined to be a success. They had two sons, Simon and Nicholas, and they appeared contented in their early years together. Gradually, however, they drew apart. For Beatrice Eden was not much interested in politics and found irksome her husband's increasing commitments as he rose in office. During the Second World War their relationship appears to have worsened markedly.[8] After the Second World War a final parting became inevitable. In 1946 Beatrice Eden settled in the United States and divorce duly ensued. She died in 1957.

The match was not between people of equal social rank. Eden's whole background for several centuries had lain with the landed élite. His wife's, on the other hand, was less distinguished. Her father was a banker and more nearly resembled the middle-class industrialists who came to dominate the Conservative Party between the wars – typified by Baldwin and the Chamberlains. Harold Macmillan, Eden's contemporary, by contrast, married above himself – to the daughter of the Duke of Devonshire. Eden, then, had scarcely made a traditional dynastic link. Nevertheless his father-in-law was not without importance. For he was a Conservative MP and chairman of the *Yorkshire Post*, a staunchly Conservative newspaper. This was to be helpful to Eden in his early career in that he was assured of an outlet for his first journalistic efforts.

Eden's apprenticeship in the House of Commons lasted from 1924 until August 1931 when he was invited to become a junior minister at the Foreign Office. During these years he followed a shrewd course: he associated himself with his party's leadership while for a considerable period paying lip-service, surprising as it may now seem, to some of the views of the more 'blimpish' section of the Conservative backbenchers. He also decided to specialize. From the outset he concerned himself with overseas and defence questions, with particular reference to the air force, the Middle East and the Dominions. He travelled a good deal in order to see at first hand areas of special interest.

Eden made his maiden speech on 9 February 1924. He chose to intervene in a debate on air policy. He was evidently a strong supporter of the 'hawkish' views of Hugh Trenchard and had scarcely veiled contempt for the neo-pacifist uneasiness felt on the Labour benches. Indeed, so forthright were his expressions that, despite his plea for the customary indulgence given to maiden speakers, he was interrupted. Hansard records Eden thus:

Attack is the best possible form of defence (Hon. Members: 'No, no!'). I expected hon. Members opposite would be a little surprised at that doctrine. I was not suggesting that we should drop our bombs on other countries, but simply that we should have the means at our disposal to answer any attack by an attack. It is a natural temptation to hon. Members opposite, some of whose views on defence were fairly well known during the years of the War, to adopt the attitude of . . . the terrier, and roll on their backs and wave their paws in the air with a pathetic expression.[9]

So controversial a maiden speech was contrary to the traditions of the House of Commons. Hence it is perhaps unsurprising that the next speaker, Captain William Wedgwood Benn, the Liberal MP, responded by withholding the customary courteous words of congratulations. Eden's maiden was, then, something of an embarrassment. But, as with Benjamin Disraeli, whose first effort was an outright disaster, he was destined eventually to capture the attention of the House in very different fashion. Incidentally, his early views on air deterrence had two curious sequels. In the early 1930s he apparently changed his position considerably by becoming, as will be seen, a leading opponent in the National Government of the Air Ministry in the matter of air disarmament. But by 1937 he was again to be found in the air lobby when he argued in Cabinet against the momentous shift, insisted upon by Neville Chamberlain, from bombers and deterrence to fighters and defence.

In October 1924 the Labour Government was defeated in the House of Commons. King George the Fifth consented to a dissolution. Eden thus fought his third General Election in two years. He cheerfully joined in the 'Red Scare' politics which dominated the national contest. The first MacDonald Government had fallen because of the withdrawal of a prosecution of J. R. Campbell of the Communist *Weekly Worker*. But the Soviet Union itself was also an issue, since the Government had granted diplomatic recognition to the Bolshevik regime. And the last days of the contest saw sensational controversy about the Zinoviev letter – a document whose alleged lack of authenticity has in recent years probably been too readily accepted. Eden, whose later attitude towards the Soviets was on occasion markedly less hostile than towards some right-wing dictatorships, was at this time critical of Labour's recognition of the Soviet Government. In his election address he described Labour's Anglo-Soviet treaties, involving recognition and loans, as 'makeshifts hurriedly improvised in response to pressure exercised by extremists in the country'. He went on: 'They embody the principle that the British taxpayer shall guarantee the repayment of a loan to the Bolshevik Government – a government actuated by motives of hostility to the British Empire and all it stands for.'[10] Such are the fluctuations of politics that within twenty years Eden was to play the leading rôle in meeting Soviet wishes not in something as innocuous as granting recognition and loans but by forcibly repatriating vast numbers of anti-Communist Soviet citizens.

The result of the 1924 General Election was a triumph for the Conservatives. They obtained 415 seats. Labour was reduced from 191 to 152, though its total vote surprisingly increased. The real loser was the Liberal Party whose representation was reduced from 155 seats to a mere 42. This meant that henceforth none could reasonably doubt that Conservative and Labour were the two great parties of state and that the Liberals were now doomed to become a minor party. Hence 1924 represented in one sense an electoral victory for Labour even though accompanied by immediate loss of office. Baldwin now formed his second administration and Eden for the first time took his place on the Government side of the chamber. He was quickly given the unpaid post of Parliamentary Private Secretary to Godfrey Locker-Lampson who was Parliamentary Under-Secretary at the Home Office. The Home Secretary was Sir William Joynson-Hicks, the 'Jix' of legendary reactionary reputation. Eden was but little interested, however, in the Home Office. Hence in July 1925 he sought and was granted leave of absence for a five-month Imperial tour. He was in part financed by the *Yorkshire Post* which published a number of pieces containing his impressions. He visited Canada, Honolulu, Fiji, New Zealand, Australia and Ceylon. On his return to London he expanded his journalistic efforts into a full-length book. This work, entitled *Places in the Sun*, was published in 1926 by John Murray. It lacked distinction and revealed relatively little about his developing ideas on international affairs. His judgements were conventional, unoriginal and plainly not intended to give undue offence to any in his own party. He avoided fanaticism on either side of the imperial preference controversy and likewise largely steered clear of the constitutional problems relating to future Dominion status. Possibly his most daring expression of opinion read:

Let it be said, and with emphasis, that it is impossible to visit Australia or New Zealand, or any other Dominion, without being deeply impressed by the need for a closer cooperation in our imperial foreign policy. The need becomes every day more apparent. The affairs of Europe are our preoccupation, those of the Pacific are Australia's, those of Suez and of Singapore must engage us both jointly and continuously with the other partners in our imperial heritage. The mechanism of closer coordination may be difficult to evolve: the form is of less importance than the substance. It is earnestly to be hoped therefore that this all-important subject will, as the result of the Imperial Conference of this year [1926], be brought a stage nearer to an active and happy solution. It is the final link that needs must be forged in the imperial chain.

Another feature of his book was his unfortunate propensity to offer clichés and platitudes on a scale unusual even for a politician – a fault which, according to many critics, was apparent throughout his career. A choice example from *Places in the Sun* reads:

The inter-dependence of all sections of the Empire becomes every day more evident. No individual part can attain its best without the help, the cooperation of the whole ... The helping hand must ever be ready from each to all, unity must be made to live and grow. Unity and cooperation must become so real as to be instinctive, so complete as to be imperceptible. The mutual instincts aroused in times of crisis must be operative always. Then shall this Empire have achieved its true significance, and the British race its allotted place among the nations. Then shall there be peace in the world, and plenteousness in its cottages.[11]

Nevertheless Eden evidently had a sufficiently good conceit of himself and of his book to ask the Prime Minister to contribute a foreword. This Baldwin consented to do but wrote nothing of significance.

Eden was at this stage a supporter of the incumbents rather than any 'reversionary interest' in his own party. He showed himself almost embarrassingly loyal to Baldwin – not least in the Prime Minister's long-running feud with the press barons, Lord Beaverbrook and Rothermere. An opportunity to display his reliability came shortly after his return from his Imperial tour. On 21 December 1925 a Commons debate was held on the vexed question of a League of Nations arbitration on the boundary between Turkey and the territory of Iraq, then under a British mandate. The Government accepted the League's decision but, as this involved a prolongation of the mandate, criticism came both from the anti-colonial left and the isolationist, anti-League right. Using 'blimpish' terminology, Eden defended the continued British presence in Iraq:

... no words, however strong, could exaggerate the harm which we should do to our reputation not only in Iraq, but throughout the East, if we were now to scuttle, like flying curs, at the sight of our own shadow. Hon. Members know that if we pursued a course like that, our name would be a jibe in the mouth of every tavern-lounger from Marrakesh to Singapore. It might take centuries to recover.

I am not myself enamoured of Western forms of government in Eastern lands. With us democracy, whatever its merits or demerits may be, is at least a plant of natural growth. In the East, it is a forced growth, an importation, and foreign to the soil. Consequently, it needs many years more to develop and many more to grow to be understood by the people.

He reaffirmed his general support for Turkey: 'I am not and never have been in favour of a bag and baggage policy.' And he finally rounded on the press barons, whom he saw as being in an unholy alliance with the Soviet Union in their hostility to British policy in the Middle East and in encouraging Turkish irresponsibility: 'Are we to see Bolsheviks perusing the columns of the *Daily Express* and Noble Lords bustling to Fleet Street in Russian boots?'[12]

19

The following year, 1926, saw two major strokes of good fortune for Eden. First, his chief, Locker-Lampson, was transferred to the Foreign Office as Parliamentary Under-Secretary. This took Eden into the department in which he had pre-eminent interest and it marked the beginning of an association that was to last, with interruptions, for almost thirty years. A second stroke of luck came in July 1926 when L. R. Lumley, Parliamentary Private Secretary to Sir Austen Chamberlain, the Secretary of State, decided to resign and forge a new career in the Civil Service. Eden was invited to replace Lumley as aide to Chamberlain. It was an opportunity of which he was to take the fullest advantage.

Chamberlain was a controversial Foreign Secretary and often faced severe criticism from different directions. To his right stood a group of outright isolationists led outside the Government by Beaverbrook and within the Cabinet by Winston Churchill, Leopold Amery and the Earl of Birkenhead. To his left stood an internationalist grouping associated with the League of Nations Union. Within the Cabinet its representative was Viscount Cecil of Chelwood. Outside it drew support from much of the so-called political centre – an influential group of Labour MPs led by Arthur Henderson, some left-wing Conservatives and many Liberals. Henderson, during the last months of the Labour Government, had negotiated the so-called Geneva Protocol which involved the acceptance by Great Britain of compulsory arbitration of disputes and a willingness to operate sanctions against international law-breakers whenever necessary. This policy was in line with the desires of France and her numerous allies, who otherwise threatened in practice to refuse to jeopardize their security by consenting to arms reduction by international agreement. For France, British endorsement of the Geneva Protocol was the symbol of a repudiation of the neo-isolationism which had hitherto characterized British foreign policy after the withdrawal of the United States in 1919 and 1920 from its obligations under the League Covenant and under the abortive Anglo-American guarantee of French integrity. Whether or not the Labour Government would have endorsed the Geneva Protocol is far from clear. For before a decision could be taken the Conservatives had regained office. In the new Cabinet only Cecil favoured the Protocol, which was accordingly dropped. The debate now centred on whether Great Britain should offer to France some more limited arrangement. Eden's chief, Chamberlain, probably favoured an uncomplicated Anglo-French security pact. But this was too redolent of the pre-war alliance systems to be popular with centre opinion. And the isolationists were against all commitments, whether of the old-fashioned variety or under internationalist auspices. Churchill, for example, was reported as arguing that 'all we had to do was to go our own way and in a few years' time we should see France on her knees begging for assistance and allowing us to impose anything whatever on her'.[13] Faced with these divergent pressures, Chamberlain, after threatening resignation, success-fully promoted the compromise idea of a western European regional security arrangement, involving Great Britain, France, Belgium, Germany and Italy. This resulted in the famous Locarno Agreements. The French concurred *faute de mieux*, but had no enthusiasm for extensive measures of disarmament when the British were plainly not prepared to fight to maintain the international Rule of Law in eastern Europe where France had so many commitments. Locarno was thus too limited to please those in the centre of British politics who broadly accepted the French thesis on collective security and went too far for the outright isolationists on the Conservative right. Eden was to adopt, however, a stance of total loyalty to Chamberlain. In his early career, therefore, he was certainly not sym-pathetic to Cecil or the zealots of the League of Nations Union. In the mid and late 1930s many of the latter came to see Eden as one of their leaders but to a large extent they deceived themselves – though he seems at times to have been reluctant to undeceive them. They had in fact only themselves to blame, for his speeches in the late 1920s revealed beyond a doubt that he did not share their internationalist vision and that he was in no sense a reliable ally of Cecil.

Austen Chamberlain's conduct of foreign policy after Locarno continued to be controversial. In particular, on a number of issues he struck attitudes that outraged centre opinion, going far beyond the League of Nations Union grouping. On the other hand, the isolationist right generally found themselves in agreement with him on everything except Locarno. Eden was apparently happy to follow his chief in his move to the right. As one interim biographer wrote: 'he was climbing upon the broad backs of the Diehards'.[14]

The first major controversy to outrage centre opinion was Chamberlain's handling of Germany's entry to the League of Nations. Under the Locarno Agreements Germany agreed to take her place at Geneva. As a traditional great power she naturally expected to be given a permanent seat on the League Council and this was generally agreed. The French Government, however, possibly to soothe anti-German domestic opinion, attempted to humiliate Germany by urging that Poland should also be given a permanent seat. The insult was obvious: Poland was being equated with Germany as a great power. In reality Poland was a French client state and had unsettled border disputes with Germany. If much of British centre opinion was sympathetic to France on the issue of the Geneva Protocol and collective security guarantees, it was decidedly francophobe on matters relating to the treatment of Germany. From at least the time of the invasion of the Ruhr, centre opinion in Great Britain favoured reconciliation with Berlin and wished to see Gustav Stresemann's moderate line given appropriate encouragement. Hence a storm of protest resulted when

Chamberlain appeared to support Aristide Briand's line on League Council membership. In fact Chamberlain was not primarily interested in promoting Poland's claim. Rather he wished, for quite plausible reasons, to take the opportunity to secure a permanent seat for Spain. He explained privately to Viscount D'Abernon, British Ambassador in Berlin, that if the Locarno Agreements were put to the test, the League Council would inevitably also be involved and its judgement would in theory be binding. He continued:

Just consider by whom that decision would be given. There are at present ten members of the Council: add Germany and it makes eleven. Of the eleven six would be interested parties and unable to vote. The decision today would rest with Japan, Spain, Brazil, Sweden and Uruguay. But now suppose the rotation of temporary seats had begun. Japan would remain: Spain's place might have been taken by Portugal, Sweden's by Holland or Norway or even Denmark, Uruguay's by some other of the smaller American states and Brazil's, let us say, by Argentina or Chile. Does anyone think that a decision by a rump of five so constituted would carry the weight which would be required to secure its acceptance? If you find some power not perhaps to be described as a Great Power meaning thereby one not with a world Empire or world interests, but still standing out by its present position and its past history from the ruck of little nations – would it not be well to keep such a Power on the Council permanently, and is not Spain exactly such a Power?'

However cogent this reasoning, it took insufficient account of German susceptibilities. The result was an upsurge of public feeling ably supported within the Cabinet by Cecil. By 4 March Baldwin was compelled to defend Chamberlain in a Commons debate and at the same time give ground to the critics. He conceded that priority at the forthcoming Special Assembly of the League would be given to Germany and that the claims of Poland, Brazil and possibly Spain would have to be resisted. Despite this retreat the Government's majority at the end of the debate was only 100 – less than half the normal margin. The new line came too late, moreover, to make agreement at Geneva possible. Hence the matter had to be postponed until the autumn when an outraged Germany was finally given her way, but only at the cost of the resignation of Spain and Brazil from the League. As Chamberlain himself wrote to one of his critics: 'It was the excitement of public opinion in different countries before we met at Geneva which left the representatives of every country unable or afraid to change his attitude after he got there.'15 What Chamberlain did not appear to grasp, however, was that his own conduct had largely encouraged the various unrealistic claims which had directly led to the 'excitement' of public opinion in different countries'. His critics, not least in the House of Commons, were less myopic and he accordingly had to face a motion of censure on 23 March 1926. He survived, but with a much damaged reputation in the political centre. Only the enemies of the League on the isolationist right were happy. Eden himself may not have been anti-League. But he was certainly not to be found on this issue in the centre. He made a speech stoutly defending the Foreign Secretary. He took the opportunity, moreover, to tilt at the general approach of the partisans of the League of Nations Union:

To expect the League to change human nature in a year or two was an extravagant expectation ... You will not change by one instrument or in one day the passions of nations. It must take time. Far more harm has been done to the League by people with their heads in the clouds and their brains in their slippers than by the most inveterate enemy the League ever had.[16]

He went on to affirm his support for Locarno, from which he was more inclined to draw comfort than he was inclined to be despondent about the weakness of the League. Finally, he went out of his way to attack David Lloyd George – a tactic to which he regularly reverted in a rather transparent bid to secure Baldwin's approval.

There was also great drama at home. Many years of industrial strife culminated in 1926 in the General Strike and a subsequent prolonged continuation of industrial action by the miners alone. Eden was a dutiful supporter of the Government's firm but not wholly extreme stance. He did not, however, involve himself in the controversy, apart from making one somewhat anodyne speech on 8 December, many months after the heat had gone out of the crisis.[17] Foreign policy clearly remained his primary interest.

In the following year, 1927, the Government was again subjected to much criticism for its rôle in international affairs but was again loyally backed by Eden. Now the focus of attention was an abortive naval disarmament conference held in Geneva. The conference was called by President Calvin Coolidge, who hoped to see an extension of the Washington Naval Agreement of 1922, which had successfully limited the capital ships of the five principal naval powers. Coolidge now hoped that cruisers, submarines and destroyers could be likewise dealt with. His enterprise was ill-fated from the outset. First, France and Italy refused to participate, since they wished to link naval limitation to the land and air spheres, concerning which the Preparatory Commission for the World Disarmament Conference was making snail-like progress owing, in part, to British unwillingness to give adequate security guarantees. Then, when the three remaining naval powers – Great Britain, the United States and Japan – actually met at Geneva in June 1927, bitter disagreements were revealed. The points at issue were complex. But in essence the British Cabinet wavered a good deal about whether, and in what sense, it was prepared to agree to parity with the United States in cruisers. Churchill and his allies in the Cabinet were opposed to any agreement. They had, however, to overcome the view of Cecil that it was unnecessary to see the United States as a potential enemy and that Great Britain should therefore readily concede the principle of mathematical parity. Churchill skilfully achieved this not by a frontal assault on Cecil's position but by arguing that the British should agree to 'maritime' as distinct from 'mathematical' parity. The scattered nature of the British Empire and need to protect distant sea lanes meant that 'parity' with the United States could only be achieved by Great Britain having a much larger number of small cruisers. Plausible though this argument was, it made an arms control agreement with the Americans extremely difficult to achieve. Nevertheless, Cecil and William Bridgeman, the First Lord of the Admiralty, worked hard in Geneva to find a formula to reconcile the allegedly conflicting needs of the British and the Americans in the matter of cruisers. They came near to success but were frustrated by astute manoeuvring by Churchill. The conference accordingly broke down amid mutual Anglo-American recriminations. Cecil decided to resign. His somewhat opportunistic action, made public on 30 August 1927, was a plain repudiation of his own country's position in an argument with a foreign state. It was, therefore, accorded much publicity. And such was the pacifistic national mood in Great Britain at the time that much centre opinion, without perhaps following the complexity of the cruiser controversy, assumed that their own Government must be in the wrong. The League of Nations Union exploited the situation with a series of spectacular rallies designed to promote 'internationalism'. And Cecil himself made a vigorous and wide-ranging attack on his former colleagues in a debate in the House of Lords on 16 November 1927. With scant regard for conventions he outlined the whole course of his differences with his colleagues over several years. As he explained: 'No resignation is an isolated act.' He particularly regretted the rejection of the Geneva Protocol and by implication the substitution for it of the limited liability policy embodied in the Locarno Agreements.[18]

A week later a gleeful Opposition raised Cecil's strictures in the House of Commons. Chamberlain and the Government, though in no risk of defeat, were plainly in an unenviable position, now being subject to much criticism of their broad foreign policy both at home and abroad. This was a time for Eden again to show his loyalty to his chief. He did so in a fashion that will surprise those who only remember his later apparent espousal of the principles of the League of Nations and of collective security. He first denounced Cecil, the hero of the League of Nations Union, for his conduct in resigning over the failure of the Coolidge Conference. He argued that Cecil had gone to Geneva 'with the ecstacy of a martyr on his way to the stake'. 'The stake in this case,' he added, 'was unnecessary and entirely self imposed, but it does not affect in any way the genuineness of his martyrdom.' Eden next affirmed his hostility to the Geneva Protocol to which Cecil and his followers attached such importance:

We are told that the smaller nations are supporters of the Protocol. I can readily believe that. If I was a member of a smaller nation I should be a supporter of the Protocol, because the smaller nations get all the advantages and this country has to bear the greater share of the burdens.

Eden was at this point interrupted with the deadly question: 'Is France a small nation?' He was only able to evade and in so doing revealed that he, like Austen Chamberlain, was not quite as strongly pro-French as he later sought to establish. During these years he was only pro-French on matters that happened to be acceptable to the right in British no less than in French politics. That he was hostile to the broader French approach to collective security is clear. He continued his speech thus:

I think we should refuse to bind ourselves to tie our hands in directions where we cannot see what the future may hold for us. I do not believe we can maintain peace in Europe now by handing out a hotchpotch of pledges. I believe that the policy of 1925 is in the long run better and wiser than the policy of 1924.

Finally, Eden made another largely gratuitous attack on Lloyd George. Interrupted with the question whether Lloyd George was to blame for everything he replied: 'Yes, for most things in the world.'[19]

Another example of Chamberlain's capacity for outraging centre opinion and Eden's willingness to endorse his chief's line came in 1928. This concerned the episode known as the Anglo-French Compromise, another development in the long-running quest for arms control, to which nations then attached greater importance than is easily comprehended today. In July the British and the French reached a secret agreement on future arms control negotiating policy. The British would support France against Germany and Italy; in return the French offered to back Great Britain against the United States.

Unfortunately for Chamberlain the nature of the agreement leaked out. It involved four major changes in Great Britain's arms control policy. First, she would abandon her opposition to the French retention of conscription. Secondly, she would cease to advocate in any form the limitation of six-inch gun cruisers of smaller displacement than 10,000 tons – a step which was inevitably extremely unpopular in the United States, especially in the light of the negotiations at the Coolidge Conference. Thirdly, she would end her long-standing leadership of the movement for the abolition of *all* submarines, in which she had received considerable support from the United States. Finally, in what was widely regarded as a precedent for the revision of the ratios for capital ships agreed upon at Washington in 1921 and 1922, she undertook to accept the claim of France to parity with the largest naval power in two classes of fighting vessel, namely in eight-inch gun cruisers and in large submarines – another decision greatly resented by the United States. The first of these four changes in British policy represented a blow to German claims for equality of treatment, since under the Treaty of

Versailles she was not allowed conscription. It was therefore inevitably seen at home and abroad as an endorsement of the most hard-line strand in French public opinion, which was in reality opposed to reconciliation with Stresemann's Germany. The other three modifications in British policy were wholly unacceptable to Washington and all three had been conceded under pressure from Paris at an advanced stage in the negotiations.

It seems obvious in retrospect that the anti-American character of these belated concessions undermined the rationale of British policy, which from the outset of the negotiations with France had been one of offering support to Paris against Berlin on trained reservists in return for French acceptance of the broad Anglo-American view on naval arms control. Whether these moves by Chamberlain were based on a clumsy inability to grasp their implications is a matter for doubt. Possibly he was so eager to forge an old-fashioned *entente* with Paris that he did not much care about the effect on either Germany or the United States. Whatever the truth of the matter may be, he had greatly underestimated the reaction at home. The result was that once again Baldwin had to come to the rescue by announcing the abandonment of the agreement and a repudiation of any exclusive relationship with Paris. On 28 October he stated:

I must contradict the idea that has gained currency in some quarters but for which there is no shadow of foundation, that we have to some extent abandoned our position of impartiality and conciliation which we assumed at the time of the Locarno Pact. That is not so. Our interests and our inclinations alike prompt us to preserve and even strengthen the cordiality of our relations with Germany as well as with France.[20]

Inevitably a parliamentary inquest took place. The Government was much criticized for its ineptitude and its excessive pro-French bias. Ironically, the only enthusiastic supporters of what Chamberlain had attempted were on the extreme right – not because they were pro-French but primarily because they were inclined to be both anti-American and opposed to arms control. It is in this context that Eden's intervention in the House of Commons, on 13 November, has to be seen. He did not, it is true, fully endorse the 'diehard' position. But he gave strong support to Chamberlain against critics of his alleged secretiveness:

Ever since this campaign of misrepresentation began – I will not discuss its origins and causes – various suggestions have been thrown out about undue secrecy, about there being some sinister purpose behind such secrecy ... It would seem that the existence of those charges cannot for a moment be justified in fact.

He added the usual assault on Lloyd George, stressing his difficulties with the French when he had been Prime Minister and offered this explanation:

The French for all the ardour of their patriotism are essentially a practical race.

The Welsh are oftentimes sentimental. The French are essentially masculine and perhaps a little prickly to handle intellectually; the Welsh are perhaps a little more gentle, a little more feminine.

Later, in 1939, Eden published a collection of his speeches, entitled *Foreign Affairs*. Given his prevailing attachment to centre opinion, it is not surprising that he chose to reproduce little from his period as Parliamentary Private Secretary to Austen Chamberlain – nothing at all, for example, from his remarkable anti-Cecil effort of 1927. But he did include a pro-French passage from his speech on 13 November 1928. He used it to suggest that he was a consistent friend of France.[21] Yet his support in 1928 had been in the context of the Anglo-French arms control deal, in which the centre and the internationalists had never seen merit. As Cecil wrote: 'It achieved the almost impossible result of combining against itself the opinion of the United States, of Italy, of Germany and of the great mass of people in this country who take an interest in the subject.'[22]

In May 1929 the Conservatives lost a General Election and MacDonald formed the second Labour Government. Eden returned to the Opposition benches, where for the next two sessions he concentrated on criticizing the foreign policy of Henderson. This was a somewhat unexciting brief. For most political interest centred on domestic policy and on the largely unsuccessful efforts of the Government to grapple with the dislocation caused by the intensifying depression. Moreover, the Labour Government's conduct of foreign affairs, despite differences between MacDonald and Henderson, was generally well received except in extreme right-wing quarters. The character of official Conservative criticism was accordingly somewhat muted. Since Eden by now fully identified himself with the leadership's approach, his attacks on Henderson's actions usually took a ritualistic form. He regretted some of the detail but little of the broad substance of the Government's foreign policy: improved relations with the United States; conciliation in Europe leading to the evacuation of the Rhineland and a reduced reparations burden for Germany; the quest for disarmament allied to increased obligations to accept arbitration in international disputes; a degree of conciliation towards the forces of Chinese and of Egyptian nationalism; and the resumption of diplomatic relations with the Soviet Union.[23]

Eden at this period was also to show himself once again as decisively loyal to Baldwin. This turned out to be a shrewd judgement, for the Conservative leader, who had lost two out of three General Elections, was under great pressure to resign and was unlikely to forget those who did not waver in his support. The Empire Free Trade campaign, led by Beaverbrook, was the vehicle used by Baldwin's opponents to try to oust him. They were on the verge of success in March 1931 when only the victory of Alfred Duff Cooper in a crucial by-election gave the leader a new lease of life. Eden had courageously declared himself an agnostic on the tariff issue in a Commons speech on 16 April 1930. He said:

Perhaps it is true of the younger Members – certainly the young Members of our party – that we are merely opportunists in these fiscal matters. I personally am prepared to plead guilty to the charge. It seems to me that the only useful test which can be applied in these fiscal controversies, which have no academic interest whatever, is the result which is actually achieved.[24]

He was still more unambiguous in his support of Baldwin when he sent a letter to *The Times*, on 6 October 1930, after a number of his colleagues had written in critical terms. He replied:

If the Conservative Party jettisons Mr Baldwin it will sacrifice its greatest electoral asset. But that is not, of course, the sole reason why many of us would deeply regret to see Mr Baldwin relinquish the Leadership of the Conservative Party. So long as Mr Baldwin leads the Conservative Party so long will its 'right' wing be unable to dominate the party's counsels and narrow its purposes – of this the Trade Disputes Bill was a sufficient example; so long also will confidence persist that the Conservative Party can remain truly national, both in the sources of its strength and in the objectives of its policy. Nor, with Mr Baldwin as its Leader, will the Conservative Party ever sink to become the creature of millionaire newspaper owners or a mere appanage of big business.[25]

Eden was equally loyal to his chief when India became a prominent issue. It has been seen that some of his earlier views on 'scuttle' might have predisposed him to support the 'diehards', now led by Churchill, who resisted the official Conservative line of broad support for the Report of the Simon Commission, which opened the way for ultimate Dominion status for the brightest jewel in the Imperial crown. But Eden was now totally committed to Baldwin and gave no hint of agreeing with Churchill.

The first definite reward for Eden came in March 1931 when he was nominated, together with Austen Chamberlain and Sir Samuel Hoare, to represent the Conservative Party on a unique three-party subcommittee of the Committee of Imperial Defence charged with examining the issues involved in the forthcoming World Disarmament Conference. For the first time he sat as a nominal equal with a dozen of the foremost politicians and civil servants of the period; and he was given access to much material normally denied to those outside government. He attended ten meetings between 18 March and 15 July and doubtless absorbed a great deal that was to be of value to him later. He was, however, deceptively modest, making only three brief and unimpressive interventions in the whole course of the ten meetings. He seemed content to allow Chamberlain and Hoare to put the Conservative case.[26]

His reticence was certainly not held against him. For when the National Government was formed in August 1931 Baldwin let him know that he hoped to secure for him the post of Parliamentary Under-Secretary at the Foreign Office. The Conservative leader was somewhat fortunate in obtaining this for him, as the Prime Minister, MacDonald, had originally intended to give this coveted post to his own son, Malcolm. As it was, the younger MacDonald became Parliamentary Under-Secretary at the Dominions Office and never subsequently caught up with Eden in status. If the decision had gone the other way there can be little doubt that Eden's political career would have taken a very different course – with no glittering prize likely to have come his way at least until middle age.

Junior Minister in the Foreign Office
1931–5

At the outset of his ministerial career Eden was particularly fortunate in
that the new Secretary of State for Foreign Affairs, Lord Reading, was in the
House of Lords. Since in those days there were only two political appointees
at the Foreign Office, Eden thus became its sole spokesman in the Commons.
This agreeable arrangement lasted, however, less than three months. For
after the General Election of 27 October 1931, which resulted in a landslide
victory for the National Government, a ministerial reconstruction saw
Reading replaced by the former Liberal lawyer, John Simon, who sat in the
Commons.

To judge by the tone of Eden's memoirs, one might imagine that the
working relationship between him and Simon was marred throughout by
personal coolness and fundamental disagreements. The contemporary
records do not, however, bear this out. Indeed, it might even be argued that
acute and open differences between them did not occur until Neville
Chamberlain's premiership, by which time Simon was at the Treasury. But
the most persuasive explanation is that Eden was entirely loyal to Simon
during 1932, became rather disenchanted in 1933 and evolved during
1934 into a conscious if cautious critic of his chief. Whether this
metamorphosis owed most to growing self-confidence, to vaulting ambition
or to a change in his thinking about basic policy issues is difficult to judge.
Certainly the Eden of 1934 bore little apparent resemblance to the Eden
of the years before 1932. Not only was he far better known by 1934 but
he had definitely come to be associated, unlike Simon, with the
'advanced', if somewhat ill-defined, point of view of the League of Nations
Union, whereas, as has been seen, he had held in his first sessions in
Parliament an entirely contrary position.

The dominant subjects in the first phase of Eden's service under Simon
were the Japanese incursions into China and the World Disarmament
Conference. Eden's rôle was greater in respect to disarmament. But his part
in shaping British policy towards Japan was by no means entirely
negligible. Certainly it is odd that he should have devoted less than one out
of almost 2,000 pages of political memoirs to the subject. His only personal
recollection was: 'I had myself no direct part in these happenings except for
occasionally representing His Majesty's Government on the Committee of
Twelve, which deliberated in private from time to time as the grim events

unrolled.'[1] In fact he regularly answered parliamentary questions on the subject, wrote minutes in the Foreign Office and was even a member of the Cabinet's Far Eastern Committee.

During both the initial Japanese involvement in Manchuria late in 1931 and the subsequent less ambiguous extension of the conflict to Shanghai early in 1932 Eden gave no sign of dissenting from the broad Foreign Office 'appeasing' approach. This should occasion no surprise if his association with Austen Chamberlain is recalled. For his former chief had advised British intervention in China in 1927 on grounds not dissimilar to those now advanced by Japan, namely the chronic lawlessness which prevailed in some areas of China where foreign powers had long-standing trading interests and treaty concessions. Nor, as has been seen, had Eden developed any doctrinaire views about the capacity of the League of Nations to deal with all crises, least of all those involving Great Powers. Moreover, even Cecil was prepared to concede that the absence from the League of the Soviet Union and the United States meant that the Far East was an area of special difficulty for potential coercive peacekeeping directed from Geneva.

An early indication of Eden's approach came in a Foreign Office minute written on 6 October 1931. He warned against 'pressing the only available precedent too far'. This was the Greek – Bulgarian dispute of 1925 which had been settled as a result of League pressure. It bore 'no true analogy to the Manchurian troubles truer than it would to any accentuation of our difficulties with China'.[2] This line was indeed consistent with Eden's earlier opinions on the Greek – Bulgarian issue. For he had told the Commons on 24 November 1927 that he disagreed with a previous speaker who had praised the League's prompt intervention in the dispute: 'On the whole, for my part, I believe that if settlements can be achieved by direct negotiations between the parties without appeal to the Council or to the League, those settlements are much better than settlements arrived at through the intervention of the League.' In the same speech he had asked whether there was 'anyone who wishes this country to act as a special constable, say, in a dispute between Japan and China or between Poland and Russia'.[3]

Eden achieved public prominence in the Sino-Japanese conflict early in 1932 when he was required to answer various parliamentary questions on the subject of non-recognition of changes brought about by force. Henry Stimson, the American Secretary of State, favoured some declaration on these lines as he made clear in a message to Senator William E. Borah. But he and, still more so, President Herbert Hoover were averse to the use of armed force. To the British Government Stimson's approach was un-attractive. For Great Britain's interests in the Far East were both of greater importance and far more vulnerable to Japanese attack than those of the United States. Moreover, the British Foreign Office had no illusions that any Anglo-American collaboration, necessarily limited to vexatious declarations, would be sufficient to cause the Japanese to withdraw from Manchuria. As Sir Robert Vansittart, the Permanent Under-Secretary, minuted on 1 February 1932: 'The conclusion ... would seem to be that we cannot contemplate, in any circumstances, the severance of economic and diplomatic relations, unless we are eventually prepared for war.' It is significant that four days later Eden initialled this minute without dissent.[4] Having neither the capacity nor the desire to wage a single-handed war against Japan for the sake of a disintegrating China, the British Government rejected Stimson's overtures. Eden agreed with this judgement and was at this juncture, if anything, more insensitive to American feelings than Simon. He had the task of indicating to the House of Commons that, instead of endorsing Stimson's letter to Borah, the British Government would prefer the less dramatic rôle of patiently seeking, on a multilateral basis, conciliation and/or pressure through League machinery. Eden was, moreover, unwilling to admit that Japan was in breach of the Nine-Power Treaty of 1922. He told the Commons:

I would remind the House ... that Japan has stated categorically on several occasions that she has no territorial ambitions in Manchuria, and no intention of interfering either with the principle of the open door ... or the provisions of the Nine-Power Treaty. We should certainly not agree to seeing the terms of the Nine-Power Treaty flouted but in the face of the assurance given by the Japanese Government I can see no justification for our assuming that anything of the kind is likely to take place.[5]

Years later Stimson wrote bitterly: 'Mr Eden apparently did not agree with the Borah letter that the treaty had *already* been flouted and his statement must have been consoling to the Japanese Foreign Office; His Majesty's Government was still receptive to assurance.' There can, moreover, be no doubt that Eden had intended to give this impression and judging by his marginal notes on his Foreign Office brief for a session of parliamentary questions it may be confidently asserted that he was in no way a reluctant minister acting on instructions or bound by collective responsibility.[6] Again. Eden went out of his way to attack publicly criticisms of the Government's alleged weakness made by his old *bête noire*. On 18 March he told an audience at Kenilworth, 'Mr Lloyd George would act the rôle of the pugnacious pacifist – characteristically careless of the contradiction in terms. To show his devotion to the Goddess of Peace, he would risk to deluge the steps of her altars with blood.'[7] This public utterance incidentally goes some way to undermine a criticism made of Eden in a recent analysis of British policy in the Manchurian crisis. The writer first cited Leopold Amery's view that Eden 'cheerfully voiced all the popular catchwords'. He then continued: 'From a study of his minutes – within the Foreign Office, where the "catchwords" were somewhat different, there seems no reason to dispute Amery's comment as regards 1931–2.'[8] But the Kenilworth speech shows that there was no inconsistency at this time between his Foreign Office minutes and his words 'outdoors', where indeed the popular 'catchwords' were certainly 'somewhat different', but not those used by Eden.

His line remained much the same throughout 1932 and even to some degree in 1933. On 6 September 1932, for example, he minuted regarding those clamouring at Geneva for harsher measures against Japan: 'We with vital interests at stake must continue to moderate the zeal of those who have none.'[9] In February 1933 he was still able to write private letters to Baldwin which have been characterized by one historian as 'displaying in private a certain long-suffering amusement where the Geneva radicals were concerned'. Yet the same writer also concludes that Eden was at this time susceptible to the atmosphere at Geneva, where since the beginning of 1933 he had been spending much of his time dealing both with the Far East and disarmament. Certainly he sent home some dispatches which reflected deep concern that Great Britain might become isolated from the majority of nations on the Japanese issue, especially about the new Japanese puppet state of Manchukuo. For example on 1 February 1933 he wrote to Simon:

For my part, the conviction grows hourly that our attitude towards the recognition of Manchukuo will prove the touchstone by which our policy will be judged by the League, by China and by the United States of America. I believe therefore that it now becomes the right course for us even to take the lead, if necessary, in a declaration in favour of non-recognition of Manchukuo without condition or qualification. A qualified declaration will not propitiate Japan, but will further alienate China ...

Again, towards the end of February he found himself at odds with Simon over the possibility of Great Britain taking a lead in the direction of an arms embargo covering both Japan and China. On 23 February he telegraphed to Simon from Geneva: 'In all the circumstances I should be reluctant to take the lead but would express readiness to agree to join with all other Powers interested in examination of the problem.' Five days later, however, Simon announced to Parliament that Great Britain would give a unilateral lead on an arms embargo. The implied impartiality of the move was of course unwelcome to the critics of Japan. And for the first time an impression began to grow both at home and in Geneva that Eden was a better internationalist than Simon. The Geneva correspondent of the *Manchester Guardian*, for example, wrote of the arms embargo issue: 'Nobody blames Mr Eden, who has won the esteem of everybody, and whose sincerity and good faith nobody doubts for a moment. Next to Mr Henderson, he is the best representative that Great Britain has had in Geneva for years.'[10]

At this period Eden was fortunate, not for the last time, in that the utterances of some of his superiors were so unpopular that mere silence on his part seemed a sufficient contrast to ensure a good press. Simon of course never fully recovered from the unfavourable reception accorded to his speech of December 1932 when he had, perhaps unintentionally, given the impression of seeking to highlight every criticism of China in the report of the inquiry into responsibility for the outbreak of the Far Eastern crisis, conducted under Lord Lytton's chairmanship.

Eden may have been flattered by the favourable reception he received at Geneva. Or he may have been genuinely converted to a more positive assessment of what the League could mean for the future peace of the world. Or he may have simply decided to seek political advancement by appealing to the centre of the political spectrum at home. But for whatever reason Eden undoubtedly distanced himself during 1933 from the anti-internationalist sceptics who were so numerous among Conservative MPs and to a lesser extent in Whitehall. On 1 October, for example, William Ormsby-Gore, a member of the Cabinet as First Commissioner of Works, wrote to Baldwin from Geneva, 'The man who really has *the* international position here is Anthony Eden. Somehow or another Anthony has got the confidence – nay the adulation – of all these strange animals that live in this zoo. Simon can never get it.'

On the issue of the Far East Eden began to assert himself increasingly strongly against the pro-Japanese sentiments of some in the Foreign Office and, in particular of Sir Francis Lindley, the British Ambassador in Tokyo. Of him he wrote on 28 March:

I confess I do not regard Lindley's dispatches as convincing. It is news indeed that the League has from the first adhered too strictly to its principles. I should rather fear that the criticism of history might be that, had the League at the outset shown the measure of firmness its report eventually contained, the later stages might have been avoided. After all, Japan's conduct has not been impeccable and Sir F. Lindley's apparent dislike of the League leads him too far in defence of the country to which he is accredited . . . The League has its limitations, which a dispute such as this is nicely calculated to lay bear [sic]; but the League has not done so badly, if only because it has not created any of those ills Sir F. Lindley would lay to its charge.[11]

Eden was careful not to become an outright League zealot. He knew that Baldwin and Neville Chamberlain, the Chancellor of the Exchequer, were out of sympathy not only with the leadership of the League of Nations Union but that they were, if anything, inclined to seek an eventual rapprochement with Japan. Both Baldwin and Chamberlain were also bitterly anti-American at this time and, above all, resented the way in which Stimson had largely succeeded in putting Great Britain in the dock on the Far Eastern issue. The Prime Minister, MacDonald, preferred by contrast to seek improved relations with Washington and resisted efforts to re-forge the links with Japan which had been broken at American insistence after the First World War. Simon's position, as on so many issues, was opaque. In this delicate situation Eden was not foolish enough to flaunt any pro-American sentiments he may have harboured. Indeed, their subsequent emergence in 1937–8 undoubtedly came as a surprise to Neville Chamberlain and it is tempting to wonder how deep-rooted they really were.

That Eden had certainly not undergone any absolute transformation of opinion on the Far Eastern issue is demonstrated by his cool remarks in Parliament on 7 November 1933. He quoted with approval the view of Lord Grey that the Sino-Japanese dispute was not a test case for the League because it was not a European question. Eden continued: 'It never seems to me that anyone, judging at once the authority and the limitations of the League, would have anticipated any other course of events, so far as the League was concerned, than actually took place.'[12]

Although the evolution of Eden's views on the Far East are of interest to the historian, it was his rôle in the World Disarmament Conference that was most noticed by his contemporaries and which first enabled him to achieve national prominence. When the Conference opened at Geneva on 2 February 1932 he was almost unknown; his standing had been transformed by the time of its effective collapse in mid-1934. During 1932, however, he had few opportunities to speak at the Conference and was not of great weight in British policy-making. His most notable actions appear to have been to write privately to his patron Baldwin urging him both to press for a radical line on air disarmament and to attend the Conference in person.[13] Baldwin rejected the last suggestion. But he had independently arrived at the conclusion that strong measures on air disarmament were a *sine qua non* for the success of the Conference. He consequently fought hard in Cabinet in May 1932 for a British lead against bombers and bombing. He did not, however, go as far as the French and their allies in the British League of Nations Union, who called for the internationalization of civil aviation or for the creation of an international air force. His prescription was thus arguably far from adequate for reasons once defined by Salvador de Madariaga:

The importance of this problem [civil aviation] is crucial. It flows from the following chain of facts:

The immense majority of nations do not consent to separating land, sea and air disarmament.

Air disarmament is impossible unless something is done to allay the fears of air-disarmed nations lest their rivals use their civil aviation for war purposes.

Therefore, without an adequate solution of the problem of civil aviation, no air disarmament; without air disarmament, no general disarmament.[14]

Nevertheless Baldwin's approach was more radical than that of the majority of the Cabinet. Lord Londonderry, Secretary of State for Air, was allowed by his friend MacDonald to insist on the public enunciation of a reservation that the British could not renounce bombing in 'outlying areas' of Imperial interest. This reservation was seized upon by domestic critics of the British Government. With a possibly mistaken sense of priorities they began a prolonged campaign for its repudiation and hence tended to lose sight of much more vital questions relating to civil aviation. As a result Baldwin and Eden, rumoured to be the leading ministerial critics of the Londonderry reservation, gained a 'progressive' reputation on air disarmament which was not perhaps wholly deserved.[15]

The other principal feature of British disarmament policy in 1932 was the lack of a sense of urgency. Not until July did the British put forward a set of clear proposals and by this time the Government of Heinrich Brüning, the last moderate leader of Germany, had fallen. Some have argued that the British delay in presenting a plan was fatal to Brüning. Others have maintained that his offer of a disarmament treaty made in April 1932 was the crucial missed opportunity. If only, the argument runs, the British had supported Brüning to the extent of insisting that the French Premier, André Tardieu, come to Geneva at that point, the history of the world would have been different. Eden himself went some way to endorsing this view when he revealed in his memoirs that he had written in his diary on 14 October 1933, 'I should not like Simon's conscience about the earlier part of last year when Brüning was still in power. We missed the bus then, and could never overtake it.'[16] The difficulty with this thesis about a 'moment of hope' is that it rests on the assumption that the French, before the rise of Hitler, could have been talked into adopting any serious measures of disarmament without obtaining from the British Government far-reaching security guarantees which would certainly not have been on offer. Indeed, it fell to Eden on 3 February 1933 to spell out at Geneva just how adverse the British were to the French thesis on security undertakings as a precondition to disarmament: 'I can give no hint of encouragement that it will be possible for us to ... undertake new obligations, to which, I believe, the public opinion of my country is unalterably opposed.'[17]

The fact was, therefore, that the British plan of July 1932 was basically unacceptable to the French and this had nothing to do with the fall of Brüning. The key to French acceptance of a disarmament agreement remained in London as it had done throughout the 1920s. But that key, security guarantees, was one that Eden at this stage showed no inclination to urge his superiors to turn. Matters were not, however, made easier when in September 1932 the new German Government withdrew from the Conference and announced that a declaration of acceptance by the other Great Powers of Gleichberechtigung [equality of rights] was the precondition for their return to Geneva. Small wonder, therefore, that the prospects for the conference looked bleak by the autumn of 1932. Eden, however, did not want to abandon hope. In this he seems to have had a different attitude to his chief, of whom Wing-Commander E. J. Hodsoll wrote to Sir Maurice Hankey, the Secretary to the Cabinet: 'Sir John Simon is evidently much exercised in his mind about the situation and would, I gather, in his heart of hearts, welcome a break up of the Conference . . .', an impression Hankey had also gained.[18]

In December 1932, however, Simon played a major part in persuading the new, moderate French Premier, Édouard Herriot, to agree to a compromise formula conceding to Germany equality of rights 'in a system which would provide security for all nations'. But hopes raised by the consequent return of Germany to the Conference and this hint of British recognition of French requirements regarding security were soon dimmed by developments in January 1933. In France the more inflexible Édouard Daladier replaced Herriot, while in Germany Adolf Hitler became Chancellor.

At this sombre time Eden was given a greatly enhanced rôle in the matter of disarmament. On 23 December 1932 MacDonald wrote to Simon:

> Now that the Disarmament Conference has been floated again we ought to decide how we are to handle that very troublesome body. I think it is perfectly obvious that you cannot be expected to live part of the week at Geneva and the rest of the time in London, but as a matter of fact something like that would be required . . . if we are to be anything but a sort of whipping boy at Geneva, we must have an authoritative representative there most of the time.
>
> . . . I believe you will agree with me in dismissing the idea that, however able an Under-Secretary, like Anthony Eden, may be, or a permanent official, like [Alexander] Cadogan [of the Foreign Office], neither, nor both together, carry the weight which we must carry in Geneva.

MacDonald then advanced the names of Cecil and Austen Chamberlain while simultaneously explaining why neither was wholly suitable. He asked Simon's view and then added:

> There is, of course, one thing that will probably be in your mind, which is also in mine, although I have my doubts about it. That is to make Eden Lord Privy Seal, appoint him to the League of Nations and give you a new Under-Secretary. My doubt consists mainly in whether Anthony's guns have got big enough yet for this important position.

On 30 December Simon replied, 'I do not think that either Cecil or Austen would be generally accepted as a good choice.' He continued:

> My own inclination therefore would be rather in favour of a younger man who could join the Cabinet as Assistant Foreign Secretary with standing duties at Geneva. I should be perfectly ready to see Anthony Eden in that position, but of course you would want to think this over very carefully and no doubt S.B. [Baldwin] would have some observations to make.[19]

The upshot was that from the beginning of 1933 the bulk of Simon's Geneva work was delegated to Eden, who nevertheless was not invited to join the Cabinet and remained Parliamentary Under-Secretary.

The chance to shine at Geneva was one that Eden was determined to seize despite his underlying pessimism about the prospects of forging a disarmament convention and despite his earlier lack of *rapport* with the zealots of the League of Nations Union. Initially he was given authority to explore with other delegations the British-sponsored so-called 'programme of work'. He discovered that the French, with a leftish ministry briefly in office, were now apparently less rigidly insistent on far-reaching security guarantees as a basis for at least partial measures of disarmament. For example, Joseph Paul-Boncour, briefly Prime Minister, gave the impression that he might favour a separate air disarmament convention. This hint revived in acute form the controversy in London about the British reservation in the matter of bombing so-called 'outlying areas' as well as posing more fundamental questions concerning civil aviation. Eden recorded in his memoirs his disappointment at the success Londonderry had in defending the interests of his ministry. Moreover, his disenchantment with Simon was apparently growing: 'I was indignant with the Foreign Secretary for making, as it seemed to me, no attempt to defend our work against the Service Departments.'[20] As a result Eden turned more and more towards Baldwin, whom he bombarded with private communications. He evidently saw nothing wrong with attempting by these means to force through decisions which Simon could not be counted on to favour. Normally such disloyalty by a junior minister towards his immediate departmental chief would be unthinkable. But the position in the years following 1931 was complicated by the fact that the Government was a coalition. Since neither the Prime Minister nor the Foreign Secretary belonged to the numerically dominant Conservative Party, Eden may have been justified in having private dealings with his own party's leader, who was incidentally, as Lord President of the Council, much involved in the formulation of Cabinet and Committee of Imperial Defence policy in matters of arms control and defence. Whether and when Simon realized the extent of Eden's dealings with Baldwin is unclear. Certainly personal relations between the two men do not appear to have suffered. As late as 28 June 1934, for example, Simon wrote to Eden '*pro forma*, to say that the Prime Minister has approved the suggestion that you should be one of the delegates to the Assembly in September' and then added this affectionate postscript: 'This is according to Protocol. More briefly "Dear Anthony meet me at Geneva. Yours Cleopatra".'[21] Perhaps there is after all something in his later claim that he was as fond of Eden as if he were his own son.

Eden for his part certainly lacked respect for Simon by 1933, though it seems improbable that he ever spelt this out openly to him. Instead, as indicated, he sought to by-pass Simon through private channels to Baldwin.

Probably the most important example of this came at the end of February 1933 when Eden reached the conclusion that a more radical approach than the 'programme of work' was essential if the Disarmament Conference was to be saved or if Great Britain was to escape being blamed for its collapse. He suggested that the British should put forward a Draft Convention complete in all its details and he frankly recorded in his memoirs: 'I deliberately made my first approach to Baldwin, thinking that he would be more sympathetic.' Two days later he informed Simon.[22]

At the beginning of March Eden left Geneva for London in order to canvass his approach in person. Meanwhile he, Cadogan and General A. C. Temperley had drawn up a draft scheme to present to his superiors. This was certainly a remarkably self-assured step for a junior minister to take. No less ambitious was his conduct on arrival in London. He had luncheon on 2 March with the Prime Minister and Foreign Secretary. When Simon suggested a meeting of the Cabinet Disarmament Committee during the following week, Eden successfully pressed for it to be held without delay. The Committee accordingly met that evening and again on the following day, 3 March. Here Eden almost single-handedly secured approval for his proposals in principle and, moreover, persuaded the Prime Minister to come to the Disarmament Conference with a view to launching the British Draft Convention at a propitious moment. How did Eden thus triumph over the entrenched forces of inertia and the vested interests of the Services? The minutes of the Committee reveal, as his memoirs do not, the skilful nature of the appeal he made:

He did not think that an adjournment [for six months] was the right answer because there was grave danger that Germany would at once proceed to rearm and it was this situation which had inspired our Delegation to attempt to produce a Convention ...

Mr Henderson [the President of the Conference] was known to have prepared himself a Convention which he might bring forward as a last effort. From what was known of the Convention it appeared that the security proposals went too far for us.

Mr Eden emphasized that Mr Henderson had said he would not produce his Convention if any Government was willing to come forward with one of their own. He reminded the Committee also that Mr [Nicolas] Politis [of Greece] and Mr [Eduard] Beneš [of Czechoslovakia] were Mr Henderson's chief officers and obviously any Convention produced under these auspices would be of a very French nature.

Sir Philip Cunliffe-Lister, later Lord Swinton, saw the force of Eden's approach:

... if we took no action, we should have to face not only the fact that the Conference would fail but, also, that Mr Henderson might produce his scheme which was known to have grave disadvantages from our point of view and which we should inevitably have to oppose.

In the end, therefore, we might be leaving the Disarmament Conference in the position of having had to oppose the proposal of the President, and we should be very likely to get a large measure of the blame for the breakdown.

Even Simon saw the point. Henderson's prospective convention 'would, in fact, play up security to a degree to which we could not subscribe', – though 'it might perhaps please the League of Nations Union'.[23] But most decisive for Eden was the support of MacDonald. The Prime Minister was, like most of his colleagues, a dedicated opponent of the French quest for security guarantees. But in his case an additional dimension was surely his long-standing and bitter conflict with Henderson, who in 1931 had led the rebellion in the Labour Cabinet over cuts in unemployment benefit and whose tenure of the Foreign Office between 1929 and 1931 had been marked by many policy clashes with Downing Street. The fact was that Henderson, like Cecil, was an 'internationalist' and endorsed most of the post-Versailles tenets of French foreign policy, whereas MacDonald was a neo-isolationist and usually more sympathetic to Berlin than to Paris.[24] Moreover, since the beginning of the Disarmament Conference both MacDonald and Simon had been harsh critics of Henderson's being simultaneously Chairman of the Disarmament Conference and General Secretary of the Labour Party. This is evident from MacDonald's notes of a telephone conversation with Simon on 24 July 1932. The Prime Minister complained that 'a man who is presiding over the conference' could 'during a holiday from it, go home and direct the affairs of the Party in Opposition in Parliament'.[25] Now in March 1933 MacDonald was determined to prevent Henderson pillorying him on the issue of security. He told the Cabinet Committee that 'we might be put in a very difficult situation if Germany and France did accept Mr Henderson's Convention'. Later he added:

we had got to make our moves on the Chess Board in such a way as to get ourselves into a double and not a single corner. We must face the fact that if we produced a document, it would undoubtedly be criticized and might leave us with no friends. On the other hand a Henderson document might leave us in an even worse fix.[26]

Thus it was decided that MacDonald should present a Draft Convention at Geneva and this he duly did on 16 March 1933. Apart from some modifications on points of detail, it was essentially on the lines drawn up by Eden, Cadogan and, above all, Temperley. The Convention proved unacceptable, needless to say, to France and her allies. Nor did the League of Nations Union leaders at home approve. Gilbert Murray wrote to Cecil: 'I think Ramsay's speech hollow, ranting and inadequate and the Foreign Office scheme rotten as usual. Not a single sacrifice by England: all the reductions to be made by others.' Cecil replied: 'I entirely agree with everything you say about the Prime Minister's speech and about his proposals.'[27]

Eden had thus deliberately instigated moves which prevented Henderson's plan being advanced and which to some extent saved Great Britain from being put in the dock by the French. It was undoubtedly an anti-French manoeuvre; and the French at least would have said that it was also both a pro-German and an anti-disarmament stroke. Criticism of the Convention did not, however, come only from supporters of the French sanctionist thesis. Some on the extreme right in Great Britain were also incensed. In particular, Churchill from his Commons backbench wilderness made a sharp attack on both MacDonald and the Convention. It fell to Eden to rebuke his future leader:

The right hon. Gentleman accused the Prime Minister of being responsible for a deterioration in international politics, in international relations, during the past four years. I do not believe, myself, that anyone who has examined the course of international affairs during that period could regard that charge as other than a fantastic absurdity, though many of those who listened to the right hon. Gentleman's speech this afternoon might have reckoned it more as a mischievous absurdity.[28]

Eden, having been largely responsible for the British adoption of the anti-French Draft Convention, sought in the ensuing months to modify his own handiwork. Having canvassed the idea of a British initiative because too much 'security' would be included in Henderson's alternative, he now urged that parts at least of the French claim for security guarantees and adequate supervision should be met. He also belatedly criticized some of the detailed British claims for particular levels of armaments. On 27 March, for example, he urged Simon to enter into consultations with France 'to see if we could meet them on security' and pointed to 'the weakness of our position in upholding our right to bomb for police purposes in outlying areas'.[29] Again, on 1 May, facing continuing criticism of the British Draft Convention at Geneva, he wrote to Simon (with a copy to Baldwin!):

A strange conjunction of chances is combining to make us look as though we had produced a Convention for our own convenience . . . A hostile critic might even thus sum up our Draft Convention . . . that we maintain our position at sea; that we gain a parity in the air we had not previously enjoyed, and together with our Dominions an unparalleled superiority; that on land we shall possess the most effective striking force in Europe. I know you will not think I am suffering from Geneva fever because I write this. It is only that I must put to you the position as it is seen from this end.[30]

Eden followed up this plea at a meeting of the Cabinet's Disarmament Committee on 12 May. He urged concessions, in particular, regarding the number of tanks required by Great Britain. But his superiors instructed him to refuse to be drawn into discussion of details until the outstanding Franco-German divergence on matters of principle had been settled. A month later Eden drafted a detailed memorandum reflecting an even deeper sense of urgency. He hoped that the British Government would call a Heads of Government meeting on disarmament during the course of the World Economic Conference, then meeting in London. But he stressed that in his view 'the possibility of conversations is dependent on our being able to modify our own attitude somewhat'. He then listed points on which the British found themselves isolated. First, and most significant, was London's attitude towards supervision of the execution of a Convention – an increasing French obsession. Eden wrote:

I understand our present position is that we can make no further concessions in this direction. I think we should be literally alone in this; I can think of no other delegation at Geneva that would make any difficulty about making the provisions for supervision more stringent. We may have the best of reasons for our attitude, but we must realize that we should appear as single-handed obstructors.

Second was 'our present instruction to refuse to extend the "no resort to force declaration from Europe to the world"'. On this 'we ... stand alone in our refusal'. Thirdly, the British declined to agree to a clause defining aggression. 'The French,' Eden wrote, 'and indeed the majority of the Conference set much store by such a definition.' Fourthly, 'in respect of budgetary limitation and private manufacture of arms we have to resist proposals the majority of the Conference would be glad to put into force'. Fifthly, the British were open to criticism with respect to proposed force levels: 'Our tank figure, which I understand is to be 500, shows, I believe, a large increase. Our Dominion air figures will at least give the British Empire twice as large an air force as any of the great Powers.' Sixthly, 'in respect of our reservation for bombing in "outlying areas" we stand almost alone'. Eden concluded, 'When all these circumstances are taken into account it will be seen how unenviable our position is becoming ... The search for the victim will soon begin. It is in an effort to avoid the British Delegation being cast for this part that this paper has been written.'[31]

Eden was invited to defend this paper at the Cabinet Disarmament Committee meeting on 19 June. He ran into great difficulties. The Service ministers were predictably hostile; he received no significant support from Simon or even Baldwin; and he was directly opposed by MacDonald and J. H. Thomas, the Dominions Secretary. The two National Labour leaders were even less 'advanced' than their supposedly more right-wing colleagues in the matter of international disarmament. They could see no value in making concessions along the lines proposed by Eden, since the French appetite was insatiable. A decision was accordingly reached that there should be no further British offers as a contribution to the Franco-German negotiations but that all criticism of the British approach should be met with a formula that promised reconsideration only if 'a real and complete agreement was being held up because of our attitude'.[32]

This formula was by no means to Eden's liking. He skilfully used it, however, to score a point at Londonderry's expense. On 5 July Austen Chamberlain, with all the authority of an elder statesman, made what looked like a pre-concerted intervention in the controversy over the reservation concerning bombings of 'outlying areas'. He stated in the Commons: '... I say to the Government: Can you allow a disarmament conference to break down by your insistence on this? The answer is inevitable.' Given this opening Eden delightedly replied: 'If the occasion arose when the only thing that stood between the signing of the Convention and the agreement on the Convention was this reservation, then indeed a very different situation would have arisen from the situation at the present time.'[33] Londonderry wrote a letter of furious protest at Eden's failure to reaffirm the reservation but was in the last analysis impotent.[34] Eden's victory made no material difference, however, to the attitude of France, for her appetite, if not insatiable, needed more from Great Britain than this one hint at concession. On the other hand, news of his action was favourably received in League of Nations Union circles, where his responsibility for the 'rotten' Draft Convention was either not understood or was forgiven.

Apart from his victory over Londonderry, Eden had at this stage few grounds for satisfaction. He saw that the gap between France and Germany would be impossible to bridge without an active British policy. Moreover, the chance of getting Hitler to abstain from rearmament had gone, if it had ever existed. The choice was now between controlled and uncontrolled German rearmament. Already it was widely acknowledged that infraction of the Versailles disarmament clauses had long been taking place and that in practice neither Great Britain nor even France intended to use force to deal with it. If, therefore, Eden appears in 1933 and 1934 as an outright revisionist, as a vocal and unashamed accomplice of the German unilateral dismantling of Versailles, he was only pursuing a line which almost all his contemporaries had tolerated in silence. On 24 July 1933 he drew up a memorandum explaining his conviction that all hope now rested with France:

... if a Disarmament Convention is to be obtained, it can only be as the outcome of persuading the French to make such an offer as can be reasonably forced down the German throats with an Italian spoon. Do we want such an offer made? Does His Majesty's Government still desire a Disarmament Convention? If so, will we play our part, which must consist in exerting our influence on the French to induce them to agree to measures of disarmament comparable with those contained in our Draft Convention?[35]

In September Eden was accordingly given permission to visit Paris to explore the situation with Daladier and Paul-Boncour. Before his departure he sent a gloomy note to Hankey:

As to the outcome . . . I am frankly pessimistic. I am afraid that French Ministers, having recently returned from contact with their constituents, will be more difficult than ever. They will say, 'How can we disarm while Germany behaves as she is now doing?' I, however, confess that I am still unable to see how France will be better able to control Germany if the Conference breaks down this autumn, or how indeed Germany can in practice be controlled at all except by means of a convention to which she has put her hand. All rather a desperate tangle.[36]

In fact Daladier proved willing, at least in theory, to contemplate controlled German rearmament, but only after a trial period in which Germany did not acquire weapons banned under the Versailles Treaty. Moreover, acceptance of such an agreement by France would be conditional on a British pledge to apply sanctions to any party which violated the Convention. This was of course entirely unacceptable to London. Daladier also stressed France's insistence on adequate verification. In this connection Eden, on 20 September, sent a memorandum to MacDonald and Simon explaining the difference between the British and French position:

The main point of the French amendments [on supervision] is that commissions of investigation should carry on their work in the principal countries by inspection at regular intervals (the French idea is perhaps twice a year). Our proposals only allow investigations on a complaint. The French are also more far-reaching as to the investigation itself and include supervision of the manufacture of arms and war materials.

On the same day, however, the Cabinet decided to offer no concession to France: Great Britain would 'avoid being drawn into questions of detail' but would consider any point if it was the *only* barrier to the successful conclusion of a Convention.[37]

From this point British policy on international disarmament, with Eden's apparent concurrence, assumed a steadily more pro-German character. This was skilfully exploited by Hitler. First, on 14 October, he caused Germany to withdraw from the Disarmament Conference and to resign from the League of Nations in protest against the denial of equality of rights. Then he allowed the impression to be created that he would after all settle for an agreement which would give the French considerable superiority in armaments for a protracted period. Believing controlled and limited German rearmament preferable to the alternatives of coercion or resigned acceptance of unlimited German rearmament, both the British and the Italian governments were tempted into sponsoring compromise plans which were an open endorsement of the revision of Versailles and which had not been approved in advance in Paris. Yet the French, despite much rhetoric, were not eager in practice to use force to reimpose the Versailles levels even on Hitler's Germany. Hence their policy was essentially one of drift and so less realistic than that of Great Britain and Italy.

The new British scheme was published as a White Paper on 31 January 1934. It envisaged the acceptance from the outset of a degree of German rearmament as well as some disarmament by other powers. In particular, Germany was to be allowed an army of 200,000 men together with larger tanks and guns than under the Versailles terms. Germany was also to be permitted to have a small air force within two years and full parity at the end of ten years if agreement on the total abolition of air power had not by then been achieved. Eden, who in the New Year had been appointed Lord Privy Seal without a Cabinet seat, was now instructed to visit Paris, Berlin and Rome to canvass support for this compromise plan.

Paris was his first destination. Here, after the Stavisky convulsions, a new government with a distinctly Rightish flavour had just come into office. The key figure was Foreign Minister Louis Barthou. Eden sent a private letter to Simon on 18 February describing his initial impressions, which more than confirm his recollection in his memoirs that they were 'not favourable':

Politically poor France is in an unhappy state and her troubles are by no means over. This is not a national government in our sense of the word, but a collection of old gentlemen forced to come together by mobs of exasperated, and mostly middle-class Parisians . . .

I will try to give you some impressions of the men with whom we have immediately to deal. [Gaston] Doumergue [the Premier] perhaps you know already. He is a gay and gallant old gentleman who has been uprooted from retirement, and one cannot help feeling, has been a little shaken in the process. He told me that he had never expected in any circumstance to have to return to office and perhaps his chief strength lies in his little liking for it. He is, however, probably past his best work and a little given to reminiscence.

Barthou I did not like. I thought him bristly and foxy. I should think a nasty old man at heart and I do not find it difficult to believe the gossip that is current about him: I hope I do him an injustice. He makes long speeches at one in conversation . . .

So far as our own work goes we may find the present government less likely to listen to the Quai d'Orsay than its predecessor, but not for that reason more constructive or more helpful.

To MacDonald Eden wrote on the same day:

I was glad to have had your warning of Barthou's porcupine tendencies. He was inclined to use his quills, especially in the early stages of our talks. Doumergue was essentially helpful, and I hope that we have at least set him and Barthou thinking upon the lines of our memorandum. They had clearly not studied it closely before . . .

The crux of the whole business is going to be paramilitary training, the problem of the SA and SS. Rightly or wrongly the French regard this question as the touchstone of German sincerity.[38]

The new French Government, as Eden quickly perceived, was unfamiliar with the British compromise proposals, for in its short life the internal crisis had understandably been of surpassing concern. Accordingly he left Paris without any clear French verdict but with every reason to assume that the new government would be even less amenable than its predecessor, under the guidance of the relatively flexible Daladier, had been. Eden arranged, however, to return to Paris after his visits to Berlin and Rome.

Beginning on 20 February Eden had a much more fruitful series of meetings with Hitler and his colleagues. It was the Führer's first meeting with a minister of a Great Power and he behaved with unusual moderation. The two men found that they had in common their having fought opposite one another on the Western Front. If Eden in his memoirs understated the unfavourable impression made upon him by Barthou, he also understated his positive response to Hitler. Even the first meeting, at which the full extent of German concessions on disarmament was not revealed, led Eden to see Hitler in a relatively rosy light. On 21 February he wrote to Baldwin of this first encounter:

We had our first interview with Hitler yesterday afternoon. We were given a grand salute on arrival by a very fine guard of SS (illegal) armed to the teeth (also illegal). Having thus condoned breaches of Versailles, we march through passages greeted by salutes by everyone, even the typists . . .

He [Hitler] is a surprise. In conversation quiet, almost shy with a pleasant smile. Without doubt the man has charm. I am told, however, that we saw him at his best. He did not shout, in part because he had to pause for an interpreter to translate at intervals, and in part because I suppose someone had told him that Englishmen do not like being shouted at . . .

The war seems to have left an indelible impression on Hitler, and no wonder, poor man, since he was badly gassed by us and blind in consequence for three months. None the less he likes to talk about the war, seems to feel friendly to anyone who was in it on whichever side . . . I find it very hard to believe that the man himself wants war. My impression is much more that this country has plenty to do internally to be thus preoccupied for five years to come.

. . . For the moment Hitler seems to me much more like [Engelbert] Dollfuss [the Austrian Chancellor] on a larger and rougher scale than like the Hindenburg types or the von Bülows. It is the last named who are the sinister beings here. They have learnt nothing and forgotten nothing and I am sure they hate us.

On the same day he wrote to Simon:

We had a heavy day of interviews yesterday. Four hours in all. The snags were those you had anticipated, and above all, of course, the air. I cannot tell yet what they may finally have to say as to their attitude to our memorandum . . . if von Bülow has much to do with defining their attitude . . . we cannot be hopeful. Of one thing I am confident, the new Germany of Hitler and Goebels [sic] is to be preferred to the old of Bülow.[39]

By the end of the next day, the position was clearer. Both Eden and the British Ambassador in Berlin, Sir Eric Phipps, were surprised at the extent of Hitler's concessions. For the Führer signified a willingness to accept both a long period of apparent French superiority and severe limitation on his own para-military forces, the SA and the SS. He also reaffirmed the Locarno Agreements as having been freely entered into by Germany. The only important respect in which his approach was incompatible with the British position was his unwillingness to tolerate a total absence of German military aircraft for two years. There was, however, a further German request, namely that the British should take responsibility for sponsoring the proposed German amendments regarding the SA and the SS – a subtle move whose importance Eden may have underrated. That Eden was encouraged by his encounter with Hitler is apparent from his private letter sent to MacDonald from Berlin:

I wish I could be in two places at once and judge of your reaction to the last German proposals. There seem to me to be helpful elements in them. First, this German offer is a firm offer. I think that we can trust the Chancellor [Hitler] not to go back on his word ...

We have always realized, I think, the extreme difficulty that there must be for any German Government to accept to go without military aeroplanes in these two years. It was not only that such a refusal could be considered a denial of equality of rights, but the more formidable fact that Germany has these aeroplanes today and we know it. I confess that when I came here the best result for which I hoped was that the German Government would accept our memorandum subject to being allowed some aeroplanes. Actually the Chancellor has done better than that. Although he has asked for the aeroplanes, as we knew that he would, he has offered some important concessions in compensation. The French are more anxious about the SA and SS than about any present feature of German armament. In this respect I think that you will agree that Hitler's five undertakings are far-reaching and that, short of the actual dissolution of the force [the SS and SA], which politically he could not sanction if his regime is to survive, he could scarcely have gone further.

Then as to disarmament. The Germans themselves, as you know, have never really been eager to press disarmament upon the French, maybe for the reason that if France still had any of the heavier and more offensive weapons at the end of the period of the Convention, Germany would then have a good excuse for asking for them. In these conversations I have, however, insisted that no Convention would be of any use to us which did not contain disarmament, and this ingenious German suggestion is intended to meet our point of view in this respect. The heavily armed Powers will begin to get rid of their material in the latter half of the Convention. This will have real attractions for the French for in truth it gives them once again the two periods in respect of their own disarmament though not in respect of German rearmament.

There will, therefore, be five years during which supervision will be in operation before France is asked to part with any portion of her arms. I need hardly say that I have given the Chancellor no indication that we could accept his proposals and have only emphasized to him the difficulty created by his demands in the air. Nevertheless, I do feel myself, for what my opinion is worth, that there is here a possible basis for a Convention, and I am convinced that the Chancellor has himself made an earnest effort to come to meet us ... Perhaps his concern for agreement is only because he will have, for some years to come, plenty to do internally, but whatever the reason, this may be our very last chance and therefore I feel sure that you will agree that his proposals at least deserve to be carefully examined ...

To sum up, our view here is that the Chancellor's proposals were much better than we expected. Phipps is frankly delighted, though of course the air aspect raises a formidable difficulty. But should not we be much better off with such a Convention than with none at all? Maybe that is the true alternative.[40]

Eden's obvious enthusiasm was not shared in London, largely as a result of a vigorous intervention by Vansittart. The Permanent Under-Secretary, in the absence of Simon from London, wrote to MacDonald about Eden's letter:

Phipps and Eden evidently think much better of these proposals than we do. This letter more than confirms it. Eden is evidently more than tempted and 'Phipps is frankly delighted' ... This is one of the most attractively baited traps I have ever seen – but it is a trap all the same. If we were to father (a very sudden fatherhood) a proposal that Germany should start right off with 1,000 aeroplanes we should (1) get no Convention (2) split with the French, and be considered by them to have betrayed them and (3) at home ... all our critics would attack us ... the Germans must do their own work for themselves ... If France and Italy were both to leap at these proposals coming explicitly from Germany, it is possible that we could reluctantly accept them in order to reach an agreement desired by all others. We cannot contemplate more than that possibility – and it is really an impossibility.

As a result a telegram was sent to Phipps and Eden asserting that London had been 'put in a position of great embarrassment'.[41] This was undoubtedly an undeserved rebuke, for nothing in either the relevant telegrams or Eden's private letters supported the interpretation that he had made any unauthorized commitment to fall in with Hitler's wishes; the Lord Privy Seal had merely expressed his private opinion to his own Government. Moreover, Vansittart's extreme scepticism about the possibility or even desirability of a Disarmament Convention involving Germany was quite unrepresentative of the mainstream of Foreign Office and Cabinet thinking. It would of course be easy to praise Vansittart's prescience and to make jibes at the expense of the youthful Eden on account of some of his remarks about Hitler. But that would be to ignore both that Vansittart was not invariably as uncompromising vis-à-vis Germany as on this occasion and that Eden was by no means alone in 1934 in believing that Hitler sincerely desired a Disarmament Convention – a proposition, incidentally, which even the historian, having the advantage of hindsight, would have difficulty in decisively disproving, especially when it is recalled that a year later Germany actually finalized a disadvantageous naval arms limitation treaty with Great Britain.[42]

The third stopover on Eden's tour was in Rome. It has been the subject of controversy ever since. For according to rumour he was insulted by Benito Mussolini and as a consequence maintained ever after a vendetta of incalculable significance. One interim biographer wrote in 1955:

He [Eden] had never forgiven the dictator for bursting into uproarious laughter when, advancing over the huge polished floor of the dictator's study in the Palazzo Venezia, Eden tripped on a rug. Another report has it that to emphasize his points Mussolini thumped the desk with such effect that ink had been splashed on Eden's immaculate waistcoat.

Such accounts are not persuasive. Eden himself of course categorically stated that 'there is no truth in the legend'.[43] Moreover, most of his senior colleagues evidently did not take it seriously – otherwise they would scarcely have sent him on a special mission to Rome a year later in the early stages of the Abyssinian crisis. On the other hand, it may be that the first Eden–Mussolini encounter, while not a dramatic disaster, was in no way marked by personal warmth despite both men's long association with Austen Chamberlain. There was after all some reason on both sides for a degree of coolness. Eden had gradually emerged during the preceding year as the principal mediator in the disarmament negotiations. He cannot therefore have been best pleased when towards the end of 1933 Italy, never quite a Great Power in British eyes, sought to play a similar rôle and even had the effrontery to put forward rival proposals to those of the British. It was also possible to read Italian conduct as being motivated not by the desire to seek disarmament but by an opportunistic wish to have a balanced position between France and a reviving Germany. Mussolini on his side may have felt slighted at the tepid response to his efforts. Relevant here is a letter, sent on 29 January 1934, to Simon by Sir Eric Drummond, the British Ambassador in Rome. He had gained the impression that the Italians were displeased on receiving the latest British disarmament proposals. His suggested explanation was: 'The Italian memorandum was communicated in its plenitude to us alone. The French and Germans were not given more than the main points. We on the other hand communicated our document more or less simultaneously to *six* powers.'[44] Hence Mussolini's *amour propre* may have been wounded and this may have been on his mind at the time of his meeting with Eden.

The British formal record of the Eden–Mussolini encounter reveals nothing suggesting a quarrel. Instead the impression is given that both men saw that the French now held the key to further progress towards disarmament and that Anglo-Italian differences on the subject were of only marginal significance. According to Eden's recollection, he next decided to leave for Paris a day earlier than planned 'because our discussions had proved so satisfactory'. Perhaps this really was the principal reason. But the possible absence of personal cordiality is indicated by the fact that a

scheduled dinner between Eden and Mussolini was cancelled.[45] The Lord
Privy Seal in fact stayed in Rome for a further day after all but had no
further conversation with the Duce.

On 1 March Eden was back in Paris and had a further meeting with
Doumergue and Barthou. They seemed unimpressed by Hitler's 'moderate'
offer. And they were still unable to give a definite verdict on the British
memorandum, though sanctions against any violator of a Convention were
now increasingly stressed. The French were, moreover, frankly doubtful
whether they desired a Convention at all if it had to be based on any degree
of German rearmament. They accordingly asked for more time, perhaps
weeks, to finalize their response.

Eden thus had to return to London with dimmed hopes of being hailed as
the architect of a World Disarmament Convention. Probably his main
spleen was reserved for the French. But he also sought once again to
persuade his own colleagues to make some gesture to France concerning
security as a means of inducing them to endorse the broad character of
Hitler's proposed amendments to the British memorandum. So exasperated
did he become at the Cabinet's negative response that, to use his own term,
he became 'cheeky'. This was perhaps most clearly the case at a meeting of
the Disarmament Committee on 28 March. On the subject of security only
Neville Chamberlain, interestingly, seemed prepared to consider any radical
departure from the previous policy. MacDonald remained, however,
adamantly opposed to giving any precise commitments. Eden, still not even
a member of the Cabinet, persisted. He continued to think that 'we should,
sooner or later, have definitely to come out into the open'. The Prime
Minister slapped him down by reiterating that he 'was entirely opposed to
answering any hypothetical question'.[46]

On 17 April 1934 the final blow fell. The French Government announced
that it could not accept the British memorandum and would sign no
convention involving any German rearmament. It was the effective end of
the interwar quest for general multilateral arms control. Eden subsequently
contended that a 'firm British offer of guarantees of execution might have
tipped the scale'.[47] But the evidence on the French side does not support this
view. The fact was that a French government of the right was not yet able to
contemplate the affront to domestic chauvinism that would have been
involved in formally consenting to any German rearmament. At the time
Eden was inclined to blame his own colleagues and, above all, Barthou. He
never sufficiently grasped that recognition of German rearmament was not
practical politics in the France of 1934. For that he would have to wait for
the era of Pierre Laval and Pierre-Étienne Flandin.

In the ensuing months Barthou moved decisively towards a policy of
armed encirclement of Germany. It was not a line that appealed to the
British Government and least of all to Eden, who remained basically

sympathetic to Germany's case on disarmament. The French Foreign Minister's first step was to seek to bring the Soviet Union out of isolation. The British Government, with Eden's concurrence, saw no difficulty in endorsing Soviet admission to the League of Nations. But there was no support from Eden or any of his colleagues for a bilateral Franco-Soviet alliance towards which Barthou simultaneously began to move. Tension between London and Paris reached new heights on 31 May when Barthou, speaking at Geneva, poured scorn on the British approach to disarmament and wittily referred to Simon as '*mon cher collègue et presque ami*'. Nevertheless the British Foreign Secretary refused to take offence and now adopted a much more moderate attitude towards the French than Eden favoured. Simon had perhaps a better grasp than his younger colleague of the conflicting pressures operating both in London and Paris and of the extent to which in a period of unusual flux in international politics too doctrinaire an approach could be self-defeating. In particular, he decided to use what influence he possessed to deflect the French from forging a bilateral alliance with Moscow. Hence when Barthou visited London on 9 July 1934 Simon offered an acceptable bargain. This was that the British would look favourably upon but not take part in a so-called Eastern Locarno Pact involving Germany and Poland as well as the Soviet Union and France. The French might hope in return to get Polish participation which would be most improbable without a British blessing. Simon also persuaded Barthou that the French should guarantee Germany against the Soviet Union as well as vice versa. Justifying his policy to King George the Fifth, the Foreign Secretary wrote: 'It has always to be remembered that if the French plan fails, and especially if Britain pours cold water upon it, the outcome may be a renewal of the Franco-Russian alliance, with the result that Europe will, once again, become divided up into opposing camps and indeed French cooperation with this country may be seriously affected.'[48]

It was no part of Simon's deal with Barthou that France would make any concession on disarmament. This clearly irked Eden who would have liked to make this a precondition of British goodwill towards an Eastern Locarno. The position was set forth precisely by Barthou in a speech at Bayonne on 15 July:

> If I had been asked to negotiate disarmament in order to obtain the conclusion of the Eastern Pact I would not have admitted a parallelism, which would have been unjustified ... That [disarmament] negotiations can open as a result of the conclusion of regional pacts, yes; but that they should open as a condition of these pacts, I say definitely no.

Vansittart, Ralph Wigram and Orme Sargent all wrote Foreign Office minutes endorsing this as a correct interpretation of the London talks. But Eden was as anxious as ever to try to force Barthou into a Disarmament

Convention involving German rearmament. He accordingly sent a memorandum to the Foreign Office covering a conversation he had had on 17 July with Hugh Wilson of the United States:

The conversation turned first upon M. Barthou's visit here, and Mr Wilson expressed himself as very much gratified by the turn events had taken. He thought His Majesty's Government deserved much credit for broadening the French proposals from what was in truth a Franco-Russian alliance into a mutual pact of guarantee ... Would it not be possible for His Majesty's Government by all means in their power to encourage the German Government to return a constructive reply to our invitation to them to cooperate in the Eastern Pact. Could it not, for instance, be hinted to them that they might well reply to the effect that they were prepared to discuss the negotiation of an Eastern Pact *pari passu* with discussions of the practical recognition of their equality of rights? This proposal seems to me to have certain attractions.

The reaction of the officials in the Foreign Office was hostile. They correctly saw Eden's proposal as incompatible with the spirit of the London accord with the French. In addition, he was challenged from two incompatible standpoints. Wigram wrote:

If there is now any chance of getting the Germans to accept the Eastern Locarno, will it not rather be by abandoning for the time being the attempt to play middleman between France and Germany? We do not surely hold that their respective positions are equally well-founded and just. Shall we not rather conduce to agreement ... by coming definitely into the open ... on the French side as against Germany, in order to secure acceptance from Germany? Is it not often our doubtful attitude which encourages German resistance?

On the other hand, Lord Stanhope, who had succeeded Eden as Parliamentary Under-Secretary, minuted: 'Are we quite sure that we still require a Disarmament Convention on the terms which France would now insist on – viz. with what *France* considers *adequate* guarantees of execution?'[49]

Simon merely noted these exchanges but plainly did not favour the Lord Privy Seal's plan. Eden's somewhat intemperate rejoinder, dated 1 August, tells us much about his thinking at this period:

The fact is then, as I feared, only the old, old story. When France gets it [the Eastern Pact] she will ask for her next 'want' – as with 'uniformization', 'supervision', 'guarantees of execution' – every other condition that France postulated to enable her to sign a Convention; having got it she will ask for more. In the meantime with perfect loyalty she will seek to saddle us with the blame for not getting a Convention, e.g. M. Barthou's last conversation with Mr Henderson in London. The Bayonne speech made depressing reading.

I cannot shake off the conviction – shared I believe by the great majority of my fellow countrymen – that it is the Barthous of this world who have made Hitler inevitable.

However, there the problem is, and for the moment there is nothing to be done but help M. Barthou to ring round a Germany whose present methods are detestable to us all. But this is no permanent solution, perhaps not even a temporary one, for the closer France draws to Russia, the closer Poland will draw to Germany. We can but wait and watch. No doubt it is my fault for finding the foxy chauvinism of M. Barthou so antipathetic, but I do.

Eden's gloomy mood was momentarily revealed in the House of Commons when on 13 July he stated: '... it is clear enough that the old Adam is not yet dead. At times I wonder whether he is even old.'[50] Given this evidence of his continuing hostility to Barthou, who now only had three more months to live, it is curious to read in Eden's memoirs that despite his unfavourable first impression, 'as I got to know him better I revised my views and grew to admire his courage and brilliant mind, even though his love of epigram must have cost France some friends' and that 'I came to modify my judgement of Barthou, respect his statesmanship and understand that he was often right, even if he seasoned all he had to say with bitter aloes.'[51] Of course it is easy to see that, given Eden's later reputation as an anti-appeaser, his record as a steady opponent of Barthou is superficially embarrassing. For, as one historian has argued, 'Under Barthou, the French at least tried to contain Germany; after his death the negotiations over the Eastern Pact became part of a wider policy of appeasement by the Western Powers.'[52] Yet when France came under his appeasing and less pro-Soviet successors, Laval and Flandin, Eden was no better pleased. But it was not with their policy towards Germany nor with their reservations about the Soviet Union that he quarrelled. On the contrary, he found their European policies much more acceptable than Barthou's. It was their unwillingness to stand firm against Italy in Abyssinia that appalled him. This selective resistance to appeasement must have seemed curious and inconsistent to Laval and Flandin. All the same, Eden's approach was one shared by the majority of the British people and he, in common with them, moved only slowly towards the anti-appeasing line in Europe which Barthou so strikingly represented.

Barthou, western Europe's last anti-appeasing Foreign Minister before the Second World War, was murdered on 9 October 1934 at Marseilles. Also assassinated was King Alexander of Yugoslavia who had just arrived in France for a state visit. It fell to a large extent to Eden to defuse the international crisis that arose out of accusations and counter-accusations of the alleged involvement of Hungary and Italy in the plot of the Croatian terrorists responsible for the outrage.

The crisis was a great embarrassment to the French. For they desperately desired, at a time of evident German resurgence, to improve their relations with Italy. At the same time they had a moral obligation to support their Yugoslav allies. Laval was inclined to give priority to appeasing Italy and he accordingly sought to persuade the Yugoslavs to draw a veil over the assassination. Yugoslavia went some way towards the French position by agreeing to disregard the rôle of the Italians as protectors of Croat terrorists. But in order to appease domestic opinion and to head off extremism the Yugoslav Government deemed it necessary to seek an alternative scape-goat. Hungary was singled out for this part despite the case against her being less strong than that against Italy. E. H. Carr in the British Foreign Office was clear that French pressure had led to 'the concentration of the whole attack on Hungary to the exclusion of Italy'. He added: 'That exclusion is a French, not a Yugoslav interest. And, naturally, it imparts an air of complete dishonesty to the Yugoslav case.'[53]

When the matter came before the League Council in December 1934 Italy, while anxious to prevent her Hungarian ally from being too harshly censured, was in the last resort willing to accept the French line. A third Great Power, Great Britain, was also happy with this approach and accordingly Eden was required to use his good offices to enable the two Latin Great Powers to impose their solution on the smaller states. Eden's main aim was therefore not to seek abstract justice but to prevent the estrangement of Italy and France. He told the Council that he could not pass judgement on the issue of guilt, though in the end as *rapporteur* he produced a formula which involved a resolution criticizing Hungarian subjects but not the Government of Hungary and a speech by himself that went rather further. Despite having a justified sense of injustice. Hungary decided to consent to a settlement involving a degree of censure upon her. With great statesmanship she took refuge in stressing the involved and ambiguous character of the formula prepared by Eden. Kálmán de Kánya, the Foreign Minister in Budapest, told Laval that he found it 'utterly incomprehensible', to which the Frenchman replied, 'Excellent!'[54]

The British Foreign Office was well aware that Italy was more to blame than any Hungarians. Simon, for example, had written to King George the Fifth as early as 26 November reporting that the Yugoslavs had traced the assassin's pistol to Trieste.[55] Thus Eden's rôle in ignoring Italian responsibility and stressing that of Hungary does seem in retrospect to be not particularly high-minded, even if entirely justified in terms of *Realpolitik* and even perhaps the preservation of peace. But, as so often, Eden was fortunate in that the British League of Nations Union assumed his conduct to be based on disinterested concern for justice. As one historian has written, 'the "solution" of the Marseilles incident, acclaimed by many well-meaning people as a "triumph of the League of Nations", was in point of fact a peculiarly discreditable piece of "secret diplomacy"'.[56] At the time, however, Eden received much praise in various quarters both at home and abroad. Not the least warm of his admirers was, moreover, Simon. The Foreign Secretary told the House of Commons that he took 'particular satisfaction in dwelling upon the important part which my right hon.

Friend [Eden], in cooperation with other members of the Council, has played in this matter'.[57]

Possibly the most interesting aspect of the Marseilles episode is that, as one student of the crisis has written, 'what appeared to be a brilliant diplomatic *tour de force* was in reality a pragmatic response to the requisites of appeasement, and at that time appeasement of Italy was perceived as eminently rational by the status quo powers'.[58] Eden evidently had no objection to shielding the Italians from allegations of complicity in the assassination and at this point he shared the basic premise of both the British and French Government, namely that it was worth countenancing a degree of uneven justice in order to pave the way for a Franco-Italian rapprochement. It is, moreover, ironic that Eden's rôle may have been decisive in making such a rapprochement possible. For when it came in January 1935, on the occasion of Laval's visit to Rome, the consequence was the Italian build-up against Abyssinia. Thus Eden may have laid the foundations for the attack on Abyssinia and the destruction of the League of Nations; and these developments in turn led to his obtaining a reputation as anti-Italian and as an anti-appeaser!

Late in 1934 another opportunity arose for Eden to win credit in League of Nations circles. This concerned the problem of the Saar. Under the terms of the Versailles Treaty this territory had been placed under the control of an international commission and its coal mines were handed over to France. But provision had been made for a plebiscite to be held after fifteen years, when the inhabitants would be allowed to choose whether to remain under international rule, whether to return to Germany or whether to be incorporated into France. The crucial vote was to be held on 13 January 1935.

During 1934 tension steadily mounted. In Berlin there were fears that what had hitherto looked to be a certain victory for those favouring a return to Germany might after all not materialize because of anti-Nazi sentiment. Accordingly pro-Nazi elements in the Saar began to apply pressure in such a fashion as to raise doubts among foreign observers, and especially among the French, about whether law and order would be maintained and whether a free plebiscite would in practice be allowed to take place. Some even feared a German putsch. Barthou let it be known that if matters got out of hand French troops would intervene – at whatever cost to Franco-German relations. But his successor, Laval, was more reluctant to contemplate this course and instead hinted that the British and the Italians, under the auspices of the League Council, should intervene if the need arose.

Eden strongly favoured a positive response to Laval's feeler. Simon was less enthusiastic. He doubted whether the threat was as great as had been depicted and he was aware of the strength of neo-isolationist feeling among his Cabinet colleagues. On 5 November he accordingly told the House of Commons at question time that he ruled out any dispatch of British troops. On the same day the Foreign Secretary wrote to the King:

The answer [in Parliament] contains the definite assertion that there is no intention to lend British troops for the purpose of maintaining order in the Saar. This is the first time that this statement has been definitely made and Sir John feels sure that Your Majesty will agree that it is on all grounds important to remove all doubt on the matter. Hints have been thrown out in Paris that the French would appreciate the promise, in case of need, of at any rate a small British contingent, but Sir John has succeeded in forestalling any formal request by making the statement today that this cannot be contemplated.

Simon also sent to the King a Foreign Office memorandum which contained the assertion that 'if an emergency does arise, this [the dispatch of French troops] would seem to be the least unsatisfactory solution'. But the Foreign Secretary plainly did not at this stage consider an emergency probable.[59]

By 20 November, however, Simon was having second thoughts, as fears about the situation in the Saar grew. Now he wrote to Eden:

For your private and personal information. I am wondering whether it is politically possible and internationally preferable for a couple of regiments, British and Italian, to be stationed *inside* the Saar till the plebiscite is over. The plan of waiting till there is trouble and then leaving French troops to enter, seems pretty hopeless. The best course would be to avoid *both* complications because [Geoffrey] Knox [the President of the Governing Commission] estimates he can hold the position.[60]

But by early December Simon had retreated again and refused to back Eden's plea to be allowed to offer the presence of British troops to a meeting of the League Council. Eden responded by appealing to leading figures in his own party, Lord Hailsham, the Secretary for War, Neville Chamberlain and, as usual, Baldwin. Hailsham sided with Simon. But Baldwin exerted himself strongly on Eden's side and at a meeting of ministers on 3 December defeated the Foreign Secretary.[61]

On the following day Eden was in Geneva to make the British offer. At the last moment, however, he received a message from Simon instructing him to insist that the intervention force should consist of a minimum of three and preferably four non-involved powers. As Eden had at that stage only approached the Italians, the new instructions from London had either to be ignored or an unfortunate delay would have occurred. Eden boldly decided to disobey and forthwith announced British and Italian willingness to intervene. Only later were the Dutch and the Swedes persuaded to participate also. The result was that the plebiscite passed off without serious disturbances and an overwhelming majority of Saarlanders opted to rejoin Germany.

Simon cannot have been pleased at his defeat at the hands of Baldwin and Eden although he had at one stage appeared to be privately converted to their policy. The fact was that the Foreign Secretary was on the public record, in his Commons answer, as an opponent of an 'advanced' and 'internationalist' step. Eden, on the other hand, had made the announcement that signified to the world that Simon's line had been abandoned. Once again, therefore, Eden was praised at Geneva and by the League of Nations Union at home. Cecil, for example, wrote to him on 7 December:

> I was immensely delighted over the proposal to send British troops to the Saar and, if I may say so, I thought it the right thing done in the right way. Does it not show that if you use the League in the right way with due regard to publicity and all that, it really is a great instrument of peace?

Eden replied:

> I was, of course, very happy that the Government decided to offer the aid of British troops to an international force ... this has been a real tonic for the League and may have far-reaching consequences.[62]

Here, then, was a measure of Eden's achievement in his short period at Geneva. From having earlier been far apart from Cecil, he was now held in high esteem by the man who at this period was the acknowledged spokesman of the 'progressive' and 'internationalist' Peace Movement. Yet Eden also retained the confidence of Baldwin who remained profoundly unsympathetic towards Cecil – an attitude that was fully reciprocated. For Eden the question was now how long he could continue to maintain his delicate balancing act. The year 1935 was to see him put to a severe test – but one he was destined to pass.

When the year began Eden was still a junior minister in the Foreign Office. By its end he had taken two giant strides towards the premiership: in June he had entered the Cabinet, while in December he was appointed to the coveted office of Secretary of State for Foreign Affairs. His personal good fortune was brought about by his capacity, whether based on instinct or calculation, to keep in step with confused British public thinking on the rôle of the League of Nations. Hitherto, the League had appealed to all men of goodwill, but only because its essential character was open to divergent interpretations. For some of a Panglossian turn of mind it was the Parliament of Man whose very existence was a guarantee that international war could no longer occur and under whose auspices international disarmament would presently be achieved. To others it was a mere forum of the nations which could never be sufficiently cohesive to involve Great Britain in an unwanted war. To yet others it was an embryonic world police force in whose name the British would be willing in the last resort to take the lead in spilling blood in 'waging other people's wars'. And the largest group of all consisted of those who, while maintaining 'loyalty' to the League, had not thought through their positions sufficiently to know which of these irreconcilable views they actually shared. In 1935, however, the reckoning was at hand: Mussolini was to force the British adherents of the League to decide which kind of League they believed in and to put those beliefs to a decisive test.

Possibly, the most charitable explanation of Eden's course in the Abyssinian crisis would be that at the beginning of 1935 he belonged to the category of those who had not fully thought through their positions. In the late 1920s, for example, he had rejected the idea of a sanctionist League, at least for cases outside areas of vital British interest. He had, as has been seen, supported Austen Chamberlain against Cecil in refusing to endorse measures, such as the Geneva Protocol, designed to clarify and extend British obligations to operate a wide collective security system. Instead, he had supported the limited liability thesis which had underlain the Locarno Agreements. Since becoming a minister in the Foreign Office in 1931, however, Eden had apparently drawn closer to the zealots who led the League of Nations Union. He had been a regular visitor to Geneva both to League meetings and to the interminable wranglings of the World Disarmament Conference. He had held 'advanced' positions on issues relating to disarmament and had also succeeded as a mediator in the Marseilles and Saar crises. Moreover, unlike most of his colleagues, especially Baldwin, he evidently found the atmosphere on Lake Geneva congenial. His youth was an obvious asset, while his rhetoric was often suitably idealistic and even woolly. In short, he had developed what one historian has described as a 'habit of deploring the nastier facts of international life'.[63] But on the decisive issue of sanctions against aggression, it was unclear whether or not Eden had become more 'advanced' than he had been in the 1920s. Manchuria had not, of course, provided a real public test for him. For even 'Leagueomaniacs' like Cecil had been circumspect in that particular case when they could not fail to acknowledge that all but one of the Great Powers in the Far East were either opposed to or absent from the League.

In 1935, however, the League was faced with a more searching challenge when Italy openly threatened the integrity, if not the very existence, of Abyssinia. On this occasion the challenger was a Mediterranean, not a Pacific, country and hence it could not possibly be argued that the League's membership did not have the reach or the capability at least to attempt to uphold the Covenant. The question now was whether Great Britain and France had the will to act. Of the two France had superficially a more sanctionist reputation. From the drafting of the Covenant in 1919 to the World Disarmament Conference the French had sought to build up a system of collective security and mutual guarantees and in this endeavour they had placed much stress on Great Britain's obligations under the League Covenant. They had indeed, as has been seen, often vainly sought to draw the British into reaffirmations or amplifications of their commitments. In 1935, however, Laval decided to end the long-standing French declaratory commitment to a sanctionist League and to concentrate instead on the pragmatic course of improving France's external relations on a selective bilateral basis. At times he appeared to favour a direct settlement with Hitler. On other occasions he sought reinsurance against him – in western Europe with Italy and Great Britain and in eastern Europe with the Little Entente and even the Soviet Union. But a crusade for the sake of Abyssinia or for France's erstwhile thesis that peace was indivisible held no appeal for Laval. On the contrary, he virtually offered Mussolini a free hand during the course of a visit to Rome in January 1935.

In the light of this volte-face by France, the British might have been expected to heave a sigh of relief. For had not the large majority of British statesmen of whatever political colour long argued in practice in favour of limiting British commitments to areas vital to the national interest? Why then should any but a fringe of anti-Establishment zealots in the League of Nations Union favour sanctions on behalf of Abyssinia, a country even more remote than Poland, for which few leading politicians seemed willing to risk the life of a British grenadier? After all, no vital British interests were more than marginally involved, as the Maffey Committee was able to confirm in June 1935. Nevertheless, to the amazement of both the French and the Italians, the British Government did indeed slide step by step into the position of replacing France as the leading advocate of fidelity to the sanctionist clauses in the Covenant. In this process, Eden played no small part but his rôle was by no means as decisive as some have supposed.

From the outset of this crisis, sparked by the Wal Wal incident late in 1934, the Foreign Office was racked by divided counsels. Simon, as usual, saw every side of every question and appears to have hoped that it would be possible to avoid choosing between good relations with Italy and a final showdown with the supporters of a sanctionist League at home. Hoare, who succeeded Simon in June 1935, was at times to be almost as optimistic that the circle could be squared. Only Vansittart was consistently prepared to face the facts. 'It is as plain as a pikestaff,' he wrote on 8 June 1935. 'Italy will have to be bought off – let us use and face ugly words – in some form or other, or Abyssinia will eventually perish.'[64] He was clear that Italy would not climb down and no less clear that France would not risk war for the sake of the League. In these circumstances, he was throughout this crisis unequivocally opposed both to trying to bluff Mussolini and to arousing the expectations of the British public that Great Britain alone was in a position to lead an effective sanctionist crusade.

What of Eden's position? He would have us believe, judging by his memoirs, that he was no less clear-sighted than Vansittart, though on the opposite side of the argument. True, he wrote many robust minutes; he wished to warn Mussolini about the folly of taking British acquiescence for granted; and he constantly sought to drag declarations of support for the League from the reluctant French ministers. But he failed to recognize that the League could not be triumphantly vindicated without war; and that in that case Great Britain would be left to do the bulk of the fighting.

In his memoirs he is scathing about the shortcomings and vacillations of Simon and Hoare. Yet, like them, he accepted that Great Britain should not take steps which would involve her in war without the assurance of French support; and he similarly entertained illusions that Mussolini might be persuaded to back down substantially in the face of pressures short of military sanctions. He differed from his two colleagues only in that he was rather more optimistic, and hence probably more unrealistic, about the nature of the steps which could be safely taken without risking war; and in that he was inclined to be more pessimistic than they about the chances of Mussolini actually backing down as a result of friendly, secret approaches as distinct from public pressure through the League. But these were only differences of emphasis. Moreover, like most politicians, he was less consistent than he subsequently supposed. For example, in his memoirs he cited many examples of his gloom about Mussolini's intentions. Yet he overlooked the occasions when he believed the opposite. For example, on 23 October 1935, Eden told the Commons that there was no danger of Great Britain becoming involved in war but he did not concede that the League was impotent to save Abyssinia. Nor was this merely a public front. For in September he minuted his belief that Mussolini was weakening and had lost confidence in his Abyssinian policy.[65] He was thus no more consistent than Simon or Hoare. Yet he emerged from the crisis with an enhanced reputation. This was because he was on balance less realistic in recognizing the truth that effective sanctions involved a war in which Great Britain would have to bear the main burden and he was thus inclined to engage in what must be judged, given his premises, to be ill-considered brinksmanship. Not for the last time, however, such an apparently robust approach appealed to the instincts of large sections of the moulders of public opinion who did not, of course, share or even understand the premises underlying his position.

Public opinion was, moreover, of unusual importance in this crisis, for it surfaced shortly after the League of Nations Union had embarked upon its most successful venture – the organization of the so-called Peace Ballot. Volunteers undertook to put a number of questions to as large a proportion of the electorate as proved feasible. Astonishingly, no fewer than twelve million people responded. The result was announced in June 1935 shortly after Hoare had replaced Simon. It provided a striking fillip for Lord Cecil and the supporters of an advanced interpretation of the rôle of the League. The Peace Ballot has been the subject of much partisan misrepresentation. As recently as 1974, for example, one historian described it as 'notorious' and 'pacifist'.[66] Yet it may be argued that it was not a manifestation of pacifist feeling, but, on the contrary, of a widespread resolve to resist aggression. This was certainly the view of Lord Beaverbrook, himself a critic of the Peace Ballot from a frankly isolationist standpoint. He bluntly described it as the Blood Ballot. Critics of the anti-pacifist interpretation have of course pointed to the endorsement in the ballot of the objective of disarmament. But they do not invariably mention that multilateral and not unilateral disarmament was envisaged, nor do they explain that such multilateral disarmament was not generally assumed to mean 'general and complete disarmament' but rather the more modest goal of arms limitation and an end to the arms race. Those who have sought to present a pacifist interpretation of the Peace Ballot have also sought to belittle the 74 per cent vote for military sanctions by stressing the size of the minority opposed to sanctions in comparison with the smaller number of negative responses to the other less sharply worded questions. Yet even on the eve of war in 1939 Mass Observation estimated that 'one person in three was of the opinion that anything (even a second Munich) would be better than war'.[67] What seems in fact to have outraged Conservative critics of the Peace Ballot, however much they have sought to disguise it, was not the 'pacifism' but the 'internationalism' it revealed. The Peace Ballot marked the highest peak of public support for the vision of Woodrow Wilson: a willingness in the last resort to contemplate waging war not for the national interest but to uphold the Rule of Law in the international community.

It should not, however, be assumed that the importance of the opinions manifested in the Peace Ballot was confined to the days immediately following the announcement of the result. The sentiments of its sponsors had been a force of some significance even in the 1920s and held an intermittent potency throughout the 1930s. The famous Oxford Union resolution that its members would not fight for King and Country was carried in 1933, not apparently solely because of pacifist feeling but because most of its supporters were not prepared to fight under such an old-fashioned banner; many might have favoured participating in a war to uphold the authority of the League of Nations.[68] It may also be argued that but for his belief in the strength of sanctionist opinion Hoare would not have spoken so strongly for collective security in his famous speech of 11 September 1935; that the National Government would not have fought the General Election of November 1935 on the same slogan; and that Hoare would not have been forced out of office in December 1935. It can even be argued that it was the reviving hold of this Wilsonian idealism on public opinion in the period after Munich, and not any careful consideration of the narrow national interest, that was the primary determinant of the British Government's decision to go to war for Poland in September 1939.

It is against this background that Eden's conduct on Abyssinia has to be judged. From the beginning of 1935 the forces which were sponsoring the Peace Ballot made it clear to him that they expected him to fight to uphold the Covenant and he was sufficiently persuaded or sufficiently astute to give them some degree of encouragement both in his private correspondence[69] and public pronouncements. Yet while he appears to have gone with the tide, he was never to drift far from the shore. He had, of course, never been an out-and-out 'internationalist' and had probably obtained the crucial support of Austen Chamberlain in the 1920s for precisely that reason. Now in 1935 he steered a course which avoided giving fatal offence either to the majority of his Cabinet colleagues or to the zealots of the League of Nations Union. He placated the 'internationalists' by seeming always to be somewhat more 'advanced' than his colleagues, while he kept the confidence of his colleagues by loyally accepting apparently unpalatable decisions. On the subject of the Peace Ballot itself he maintained in public at the time and also in his memoirs a prudent reticence. Yet in private he thought the wording of the questions tendentious.[70] A harsh verdict would therefore be that Eden's support for collective security was to a large degree a matter of domestic political calculation and hence more apparent than real.

As early as 8 January in the fateful year of 1935 Eden assumed a declaratory position certain to please the League of Nations Union. In a speech at Edinburgh he said:

We were now going through a period of transition. Almost imperceptibly a change was taking place and a new order in the world was being evolved. In the years gone by the foreign policy of this country was often criticized abroad as being exclusively concerned with the balance of power ... Now the balance of power was no longer our foreign policy. Our foreign policy was based on the League of Nations and on the maintenance of a collective peace system.

This was in truth an immense change of outlook. The Balance of Power meant the maintenance of peace by the nice adjustment of force. The collective peace system meant the abolition of force and the substitution of the rule of law.[71]

But within the privacy of the Foreign Office Eden was by no means inclined to see matters in these simplistic terms. Only three days later he and Simon met Laval and heard of the recently completed secret agreement between France and Italy, which obviously had ominous implications for an equitable outcome of the Italo-Abyssinian dispute. Yet Eden showed only marginally more sense of urgency than his colleagues in the ensuing diplomatic skirmishing. Not until 26 February did Eden produce a memorandum urging that the British Ambassador in Rome, Sir Eric Drummond, be instructed to give the Italians some kind of warning. As he put it: '... unless some hint, and a pretty strong hint, is given to the Italians that we should not view with indifference the dismemberment of Ethiopia ... then this dismemberment will take place ...'[72] But Eden was a long way from seriously contemplating the possibility that Italy would resist diplomatic pressure and hence he made no attempt to promote a study of possible sanctions.

At this stage Simon clearly differed little from Eden for he agreed to the dispatch of a warning to Mussolini. But Drummond, like Vansittart, had a clearer recognition that harsh words alone would not deter the Italians and he accordingly delivered the message to Mussolini in as low-key and friendly a fashion as possible. Eden criticized Drummond for this action in his memoirs. But at the time he seems not to have become particularly excited about it. Instead, during March 1935, he concentrated most of his attention on dealings with other European powers, which may now be conveniently considered.

On 16 March, Hitler carried out his first major ostentatious assault on the Versailles settlement by announcing the adoption of compulsory military service and the creation of German armed forces far in excess of what was permitted. The British had of course long known that Germany was in practice evading the military provisions of Versailles – even the democratic Weimar administrations had done so. But Hitler's move constituted an unprecedentedly blatant challenge. The British Cabinet sent a formal protest but nevertheless decided to go ahead with a planned visit to Berlin by Simon and Eden later in March. Neither Eden nor even Vansittart objected to this course in principle – more evidence that the early so-called appeasement policies had support within a wide spectrum of opinion. The decision to continue with the visit was settled without reference to Paris. But Eden was sent to Berlin via Paris so that he could seek to reassure the somewhat disconcerted Laval. One consequence of this visit to Paris was a decision to hold a British–French–Italian summit to review the new European situation. This took place at Stresa in April.

Meanwhile, Eden went on to Berlin where he and Simon had talks with Hitler. Simon's approach was to adopt a generally passive attitude in the face of complaints from Hitler. Even on the subject of the rearmament announcement the Foreign Secretary was evidently not prepared to offer more than pained but polite dissent. Eden inevitably had to follow this low-key lead. Again, when Hitler claimed incorrectly that Germany had reached air parity with Great Britain, neither British visitor had much to say, although Eden recorded in his memoirs that 'there was grim foreboding in my heart'. [73]

While Simon returned home, Eden went from Berlin to Moscow for talks with Joseph Stalin. He was the first minister from any Western country to be received by Stalin. Eden claims to have been impressed: 'though I know the man to be without mercy, I respected the quality of his mind and even felt a sympathy which I have never been able entirely to analyse.' Much of Stalin's conversation, and still more so, that of the Foreign Minister, Maxim Litvinov, related to the German threat and to doubts about Great Britain's willingness to resist. Stalin stressed his support for collective security, saying: 'We are six of us in this room and if [Ivan] Maisky [the Soviet Ambassador in London] chooses to go for any one of us, we must all fall on Maisky.' Although the Soviets had for most of the post-war era dismissed Geneva as the seat of a 'League of Burglars', Eden agreed to acknowledge the Soviet Union's supposed conversion to collective security. For at the end of his visit he signed a communiqué including this passage: 'They [Eden, Stalin, Litvinov and Vyacheslav Molotov] are confident that both countries ... will govern their mutual relations in that spirit of collaboration and loyalty to obligations assumed by them which is inherent in their common membership of the League of Nations.'[74]

Eden recalled in his memoirs that he was unsure of the attitude of the British Cabinet to his visit:

I also wondered what the reaction of my colleagues was likely to be; unenthusiastic I felt sure. Something would depend on the extent to which they might have been influenced by Simon's report on Berlin. The graver they judged the German danger, the more acceptable our work in Moscow might seem to them. Two points of view were, however, strongly held in the Cabinet and between them they might militate against any effective pursuit of the opening the Moscow visit had created. Some, religious in their views, regarded communism as anti-Christ. Others were brave enough to consider supping with the devil, but doubted whether he had much fare to offer.

Readers of this passage and of his relatively friendly references in the same memoirs to Stalin and Litvinov ('a communist and a loyal Russian, of course, but ... a good European' and 'fair and reliable as an international colleague') might be led to suppose that in the mid-1930s Eden was much more well-disposed toward the Soviet Union than most of his colleagues in the British Government.[75] The reality may have been different. True, he was not a vocal public critic of the Soviet Union in this period – for that would not have been popular with centre and League of Nations Union opinion. But in private his views differed little from those of Baldwin, Neville Chamberlain and other supposedly more anti-Communist colleagues. As will be seen, Eden *privately* disapproved of the Franco-Russian Alliance, was suspicious of Soviet aims in the Spanish Civil War and did not, as long as he was in office, seek to sponsor any British endeavours to involve the Soviets in European collective security arrangements designed to contain Germany. It was not until 1939 that he showed any marked enthusiasm for close cooperation with Moscow – a change of mind that may have been of seminal importance for the whole future of Europe.

Eden completed his European tour by travelling on from Moscow to Warsaw and thence to Prague. He evidently found the outlook of Colonel Joseph Beck rather unpalatable and got on much better with Beneš in Prague, even though he considered the latter's optimism about Czechoslovak relations with Germany somewhat complacent. From Prague Eden set out to fly back to Great Britain but his aeroplane ran into a severe storm and had to land at Cologne. Too ill to continue his journey at once, Eden had for a day to be an unexpected guest of the Third Reich. When he returned to London, he was found to have suffered a minor heart attack on the flight from Prague and was ordered to rest for six weeks.

Eden was thus unable to attend the Stresa Conference with the result that the Prime Minister himself, MacDonald, decided to go. It has often been claimed that this was a fatal development for the Abyssinians in that, in Eden's absence, the British and French statesmen at Stresa allegedly offered no warning to Mussolini. But this line of argument is open to question. For what would Eden, not at that time in the Cabinet, have felt able to say on the subject and, in any case, how realistic is it to suppose that Mussolini could have been deterred by warnings, however vigorous? The importance of the Lord Privy Seal's absence from Stresa may therefore lie not in the effect on the course of events but instead on the reputation of Eden who was thus later given credit for not having been involved in the supposedly unsavoury Stresa affair.

In June 1935 Baldwin replaced MacDonald as Prime Minister and instituted a Cabinet reshuffle. As a long-standing protégé of Baldwin, Eden was confidently expected to become a Cabinet Minister in charge of his own department. Indeed, he was even led by Hankey to believe that he might be made Foreign Secretary. His chances of achieving such a dramatic rise may not, however, have been helped by two messages received by Baldwin: one from Neville Chamberlain doubting his suitability and one from Cecil urging his promotion to the Cabinet on the grounds that he had 'never known anyone in anything like Eden's position who has achieved such universal approval – putting aside the *Daily Express*' and that his exclusion 'would be received with triumph by Beaverbrook and Mussolini'.[76] In the event, Baldwin elevated him to the Cabinet as Minister of League of Nations Affairs but compelled him to remain in a junior rôle in the Foreign Office under Hoare, the new Foreign Secretary. Eden had earlier urged Baldwin not to ask him to continue to serve in such a subordinate capacity, but the Prime Minister insisted, pointing out that it did not fall to many men to be in the Cabinet before the age of thirty-eight. Apart from having the problems arising from continued divided responsibility, Eden was also conscious that he 'had no experience outside the Foreign Office'.[77] But revealingly he had hoped to get such experience as First Lord of the Admiralty – early evidence of that damaging indifference to domestic ministries which was to be a feature of his whole career.

With some reluctance, therefore, Eden agreed to serve with Hoare. He showed an impressive degree of loyalty, making it clear to the House of Commons, in response to a comment by Churchill, that there were 'no two Kings of Brentford on one throne': 'My Right Honourable Friend the Foreign Secretary is king.'[78] Moreover, even in private there appear to have been no really serious quarrels between the two men and differences of view about Abyssinia would seem to have been of a more marginal character than either of them subsequently implied.

The first proof that Eden was by no means a recognized dissenter from the outset on the Abyssinian issue came within a fortnight of his elevation to the Cabinet. For he agreed, at the request of the Cabinet, to go to Rome to attempt to interest Mussolini in a plan whereby Great Britain would cede to Abyssinia territory in Somaliland, including the port of Zeila, in return for Abyssinia ceding territory in Ogaden to Italy. Eden claimed in his memoirs that he was 'not enthusiastic about the proposal'.[79] Nevertheless, he went along with it. When the plan became public knowledge, however, there was somewhat surprisingly no outburst of righteous indignation on the part of the spokesman of the League of Nations Union. Yet, without doubt, the plan represented a willingness to buy off a bully with territory to which he had no legitimate claim. But Eden, in contrast to Hoare six months later, was fortunate enough to escape without significant censure.

While the Zeila plan was tolerated in Great Britain, reaction in Rome was uncompromisingly hostile. Eden was unable to make any impression on Mussolini. There appears to be no firm evidence to confirm the current rumours that the two statesmen had a quarrel any more than is the case with their meeting a year earlier. Nevertheless, their interview lacked warmth and from around that period the Italian press waged a continuous campaign against Eden. As one historian, Mario Toscano, has written:

In a certain sense Eden's mission can be considered a tardy and unfortunate attempt – the first, moreover, of any seriousness of intent – of the British Government to resolve the Ethiopian question peacefully and avoid a crisis in relations with Rome, an attempt which, paradoxically led, thanks especially to the publicity given to the British statesman's trip, to results diametrically opposed to those originally sought.

Whether Eden fully deserved his reputation at this time as an outright opponent of Mussolini is thus a matter for doubt. Certainly when faced with the knowledge that the Zeila plan was unacceptable, Eden was careful not to issue any unequivocal threats or warnings on behalf of the British Government. Echoing the line of Simon, he instead stressed the concern of 'the British people'. But talk of public opinion, in Great Britain or elsewhere, is not something likely to make an impression on a dictator. Moreover, as Toscano has written:

> During his stay in the Italian and French capitals, the British Minister listened with interest to suggestions for a solution of the Ethiopian question which were totally favourable to the aspirations of the Fascist government, thus giving the impression of some degree of uncertainty about the line he would pursue.[80]

Eden journeyed to Great Britain via Paris, which he had also visited on the outward journey. On each occasion he saw Laval. At the first meeting he had had the unenviable task of raising the bilateral Anglo-German Naval Agreement, which had just been signed in complete disregard of the Stresa spirit. Now, at the second meeting, Eden had to explain to Laval the failure of his mission to Rome. Laval was clearly unimpressed, not least by the lack of prior consultation on both matters. Not surprisingly, he revealed no enthusiasm for joining with the British in any serious endeavours to restrain Mussolini.

During the two months following his return to London Eden played a major rôle in the discussions which were to be of decisive importance in shaping British policy concerning Abyssinia. It is difficult to discern much inner consistency in Eden's conduct or even in the account which he gave of this phase in his subsequent recollections. In the space of a few pages in his memoirs he conceded that he was 'deeply uneasy' about Laval; he acknowledged that it was essential 'to align our policies with France'; and yet he claimed that July 1935 was the month for an 'unmistakable warning' to be sent to Rome.[81] From contemporary evidence he did indeed hold all these positions simultaneously and in addition was pessimistic about Mussolini's intentions, yet optimistic that he would back down if only the British Government would indicate its displeasure.

Hoare, too, was inconsistent but probably more consciously so than Eden. The Foreign Secretary's private opinion was probably best expressed at a meeting of the Dominion High Commissioners on 29 July:

> His Majesty's Government might decide to invoke the name of collective security and go so far as to contemplate a call for sanctions. In that case Italy would leave the League: France would refuse to cooperate with Great Britain, who would be left in a position where she could not only be isolated but would incur the odium attaching to a sanctimonious advocacy of methods she could not enforce.[82]

That Hoare should have come within six weeks to express a different view in public in his famous speech of 11 September to the League Assembly was not caused by any fundamental loss of scepticism about the League of Nations and collective security. It was due quite plainly to his assessment of the electoral needs of the National Government in the mood which prevailed after the announcement of the results of the Peace Ballot. This is evident from the minutes of a small meeting of ministers held on 21 August. Hoare declared that the 'only safe line . . . was to try out the regular League of Nations procedure'. As one historian has stressed, Hoare spoke of the only *safe* line 'not the right or the best line'.[83]

Eden, who was present at this ministerial gathering, did nothing to encourage this cynical conversion. On the contrary, he evidently feared that the expectations of the sanctionists might be too hastily raised. He 'hoped that in practice economic sanctions would not be begun until a Committee of the League Council had carefully worked out the methods of their application – that is, until it had ascertained definitely what attitude the non-Member States were going to adopt'.[84] Eden was also unhappy at the stridently sanctionist note Hoare struck at the League Assembly on 11 September even though on the previous evening he and his Parliamentary Private Secretary, Lord Cranborne, had succeeded in persuading the Foreign Secretary to make some softening modifications.[85] In the light of subsequent events, Eden's unwillingness to play party politics with the same ruthlessness as Hoare seems creditable. But a corollary is that it is difficult to see in Eden at this juncture much of the resolute sanctionist of popular legend.

At the beginning of October Italy's invasion of Abyssinia began. The League machinery for imposing partial economic sanctions now moved into operation with surprising speed and efficiency. The spotlight in the Geneva public discussions inevitably fell on Eden, to whom Hoare delegated the task of arranging the details of the sanctions. Eden thus inevitably became the symbol to the British public of resistance to Mussolini and of aid to the Abyssinians. But he was of course merely the instrument of the whole Cabinet. Rumours that he had greatly exceeded his instructions were inaccurate, but were of great value to him a few months later when Baldwin needed to appease outraged sanctionist opinion. The nearest thing to a rebuke that Eden received came in a private letter from Hoare on 16 October:

I write this line to tell you about this morning's Cabinet. As you may imagine, it was held in an atmosphere of great perturbation. Our strongest supporters were seriously shaken by Laval's reservations [about coming to the aid of Great Britain if the latter should be attacked by Italy] and our critics, of course, immensely strengthened. As I knew there was a considerable feeling that you had taken the initiative too much at Geneva I began by pointing out the various misre-presentations in the press, for instance, the statement that you have made the proposal of the embargo upon goods coming into Italy . . . It was clear to me that a good many members of the Cabinet were not entirely reassured. This feeling showed itself later in the expression of a unanimous desire that you should go as slowly as possible and take the initiative as little as possible until Laval has withdrawn his reservation ... if Laval is recalcitrant, the reason for our going slow will have to come out both in Geneva and in London. I cannot overestimate the urgent importance that the Cabinet attach to this recommendation ... The important thing is that we should not remain in the dangerous position of making initiatives whilst we are still running the risk of being stabbed in the back.[86]

The chances of Mussolini being stopped by the League were never good. The British Government wished to undertake only what was essential to avoid losing the impending General Election, while the French Government wished to do only what was essential to avoid having to bear the sole odium for the failure of the League of Nations. Partial economic sanctions were adequate for both countries' objectives. The French blocked the idea of an oil sanction whereas the British Government, with Eden's concurrence, was not prepared to run the risks involved in instituting a naval blockade, or a closure of the Suez Canal. The possibility of military sanctions was not taken seriously either in Paris or London.

If Eden was more 'advanced' than Hoare, it was on relatively marginal points. Eden vainly strove, for example, to end the ban on the export of arms to both belligerents in favour of permission for arms to be sent only to Abyssinia. He was also in favour of an early introduction of an oil sanction, though he was fully aware of French resistance and at no time argued for unilateral British action. On the other hand, Eden made no difficulties about the sending of Maurice Peterson of the Foreign Office to Paris to explore terms for a possible compromise peace. In a sense this line flowed directly from his own efforts in the mission to Rome and his later abortive work on the League-sponsored Committee of Five. But the mood of the British people and of backbench MPs was now changing, under the influence of a combination of the Peace Ballot, Hoare's speech to the Assembly, the outbreak of actual war in Abyssinia and the rhetoric engendered by the General Election campaign. Hence by December, even though the General Election of the previous month had been safely won, the Government could not expect to seek a settlement with Mussolini as if none of these things had occurred. But that of course was what they did, with fatal results for Hoare and with no less delightful if possibly somewhat undeserved rewards for Eden.

Peterson's negotiations with the French, having been conducted at a slow tempo during the November election campaign, had reached a stage by early December that led Hoare to go in person to Paris to seek to finalize matters. The Cabinet was informed on 2 December that he was to go and can have been in no doubt that he intended if possible to bring Peterson's effort to a conclusion. Again, on 5 December, Hoare told the Dominions High Commissioners that 'he was going to see M. Laval ... and if it was possible to reach an agreement with him on joint proposals'.[87] The seriousness of the endeavour was underscored by his being accompanied by

Vansittart. Thus Eden must have known that an agreement was possible but he chose neither to offer any protest at the idea in principle nor to attempt to lay down any conditions. Indeed, he had earlier minuted conditional approval, together with Hoare and Vansittart, of Peterson's message of 25 November which contained a large part of the basis of the famous Hoare–Laval plan. By contrast, two departmental officials minuted their opposition.[88] It may well be that, had Eden been invited to accompany Hoare and Vansittart to Paris, he would also have gone along with them, or he might have done so after wringing from Laval concessions which would have been too insubstantial to make any difference to the public reaction. His non-appearance in Paris was thus probably one of the most fortunate turning-points in Eden's career.

The proposals agreed between Hoare and Laval on 8 December were rather more unfavourable to Abyssinia than Eden had expected. But what Eden, no less than Hoare and the rest of the Cabinet, failed to see at this juncture was that public feeling at home and abroad had been so aroused by preceding events that a Franco-British sponsorship of *any* conceivable compromise peace plan was likely to be unwelcome. The essence, which the British public and world opinion quickly grasped, was that the Italians were to be bought off with something approaching a third of their victim's territory. And there is little reason to suppose that the indignation would have been less if the reward had been only a quarter instead of a third. Hence much of the debate about whether Hoare was careless on territorial detail is irrelevant.

When the British Cabinet met on 9 December they had before them details of the Hoare–Laval Plan but the Foreign Secretary himself was absent, having proceeded from Paris to Switzerland for a holiday. It thus fell to Eden to guide his colleagues. Still apparently unaware that a storm of public protest was about to break, he gave no clear lead: 'while supporting the Foreign Secretary's proposals, he felt bound to warn his colleagues that some features of the proposals were likely to prove very distasteful to some States Members of the League'. His principal tactic, however, was to argue, contrary to Laval's wishes, that the Emperor of Abyssinia must be shown the plan no later than Mussolini. Eden eventually won this relatively trivial point both in Cabinet and in Paris; but he lamely abdicated to Baldwin responsibility for guiding the Cabinet on the substantive issue. The result was that Baldwin backed Hoare and on the following day caused the Cabinet to instruct Eden to support the plan at Geneva. Eden was also required to dispatch a telegram to the British Minister in Addis Ababa instructing him to use his 'utmost influence to induce the Emperor to give careful and favourable consideration to these proposals and on no account lightly to reject them'. Eden complied. Only at the third Cabinet, on 11 December, did Eden show signs of having serious doubts: he hoped that 'he would not be expected to champion the proposals in detail at Geneva'.[89] But by now, the British press, following leakages in Paris, was ablaze with speculation and much indignant condemnation.

Faced with mounting pressure from press, constituents and, most important, MPs of all parties, Baldwin and his colleagues now began the agonizing process of working their way from supporting the absent Hoare to deciding that he must be publicly sacrificed so that they might survive. At the decisive Cabinet of 18 December, Hoare was left with no supporter except Lord Zetland, while no fewer than five ministers, led by Lord Halifax, openly called for his resignation.[90] When it is recalled that ten days earlier the whole Cabinet had endorsed Hoare's plan, his dismissal is a striking commentary on the standards of honour of a Prime Minister and indeed of other colleagues who pretended to believe in Cabinet collective responsibility.

Eden was spared the embarrassment of having to take a direct part in the final destruction of his Foreign Office chief, as he was in Geneva on the crucial day. But he had played some indirect if unavoidable part by letting it be known that the plan was no more acceptable to Geneva than to British public opinion. He had telephoned on 12 December: 'The impression which the Paris proposals have made upon opinion here is even worse than I had anticipated.' He had also persuaded his colleagues, at a meeting of Ministers on the 16th, to allow him to state at Geneva that Great Britain would not wish to pursue the Hoare–Laval Plan further, given the evident absence of agreement by Italy, Abyssinia and the League.[91]

Once Hoare had been required to resign, it was inevitable that Eden would be the beneficiary. As one historian has perceptively written:

He won immense and durable prestige from this crisis simply through not being Hoare, through not having been been at the meeting with Laval in December, through association with Geneva rather than Paris. Baldwin used his reputation as a screen by making him foreign secretary on 22 December. This was effective because he was believed to stand for the League and collective security. So he did, yet the Cabinet and Foreign Office records show that any divergences between himself on the one side and Hoare and Vansittart on the other were expressed with far less clarity and force than outside opinion supposed. Then, as at other times, Eden gives the impression of hesitancy in argument – perhaps the result of indecision in thought.[92]

III

Baldwin's Foreign Secretary
1935-7

Eden at thirty-eight had become the youngest British Foreign Secretary since the second Earl Granville in 1851.[1] Youth was not his only advantage. His handsome appearance and sartorial elegance were undoubtedly an asset both at home and abroad. He was indeed widely thought of as the Noel Coward of international politics. Only in Italy were his good looks generally scorned: there he was known as Lord Eyelashes! But the essential basis of his strength surely lay in his somewhat fortuitously sustained reputation as an all-out supporter of the League of Nations which thus ensured him much public support. Sir John Wheeler-Bennett recalled:

In those years after the war when our enthusiasm and our optimism were still pristine, my contemporaries and I came to look upon Anthony Eden as the one person in public life who represented our ideals. From the moment he entered the House of Commons in 1924 [*sic*] and became PPS to Austen Chamberlain, then Foreign Secretary, Anthony was the Golden Boy, slim, handsome and charming. My generation looked upon him as typifying the generation who had survived the war to become the champion and defender of our pathetic belief in what proved to be ephemeral Wilsonian shibboleths of 'a war to end war' and 'let us make the world safe for democracy'. Though he did not succeed, we knew that it was no fault of his, and he retained our confidence.[2]

Even Eden's more anti-sanctionist Cabinet colleagues found it useful for a time to shelter behind him in the aftermath of the Hoare–Laval débâcle and it was all the easier for them to do this because they knew how little of a zealot he was in private. In his memoirs Eden chose to present a different picture, suggesting that some of his older colleagues were resentful of his rapid rise and making much of the constant interference by the Cabinet in his conduct of foreign policy. He described his manner of appointment by Baldwin as off-hand and unenthusiastic. He added that he knew 'that Baldwin's support would be fitful and lethargic'. Yet scrutiny of the Cabinet minutes reveals little to support this recollection. The broad conduct of foreign policy remained firmly in Eden's hands and he was almost invariably given such support from Baldwin as he needed. The view that the Prime Minister was totally uninterested in foreign affairs simply cannot be sustained. Indeed, according to one historian, such was the harmony between Premier and Foreign Secretary that it is possible to talk of a

Baldwin–Eden approach to foreign policy.[3] Moreover, as will be seen, the two men remained on close terms even after Baldwin's retirement.

Nor was Eden encumbered, as Hoare had been, with another Cabinet Minister based in the Foreign Office. True, Halifax sometimes deputized for him but as Eden himself generously wrote:

> He did not have a room, nor a Private Secretary, or any official position, but he eased some of my burden, especially on my brief spells of leave. We had long been friends and I was grateful for an arrangement which never caused me any anxiety, even when we did not agree about the decisions taken, as happened later.[4]

If there was a sphere in which Eden was sometimes unable to get his way, it was on some aspects of rearmament policy. But this subject was, on a narrow view, primarily the departmental concern of the Service ministers. Moreover, in so far as Chamberlain at the Treasury resisted some demands for rearmament, he was undoubtedly weighing broader considerations of what the country's economy would stand and how far public opinion and the trade unions were ready for greater sacrifice. In strictly foreign policy matters, however, Eden had little cause for complaint in the Baldwin phase. While it is perhaps not surprising, given his later reputation, that he should have strained in his memoirs to magnify any evidence to the contrary, the fact is that on all the great issues, Abyssinia, the Rhineland, and the Spanish Civil War, it was his policy that prevailed in broad essentials.

Within days of becoming Foreign Secretary, Eden made it clear, at a meeting with the Dominion High Commissioners on 24 December 1935, that he did not favour any immediate British campaign for the imposition of an oil sanction against Italy. In some respects this was surprising, for, as he stressed in his memoirs, he had personally pressed for such an approach in November and early December and had only with reluctance given way in order to allow time for Hoare to make his peace bid in Paris. Now with Hoare disgraced and with the Prime Minister desperately needing the shield of his new Foreign Secretary's prestige, Eden could certainly have insisted on being allowed to take an initiative in calling for an oil sanction. That he did not do so was probably the result of several factors. First, Vansittart, who still had much influence within the Foreign Office, was strongly opposed to the idea. Secondly, Eden knew that Laval, after the disappointment of Hoare's fall, was unlikely to be in a mood to respond to any oil sanction initiative and French cooperation was in the final analysis considered to be essential by Eden no less than by his more 'reactionary' colleagues. Finally, Eden now considered there to be no urgency about the situation despite his earlier pleas for immediate action. Thus on 24 December, at his first meeting with the High Commissioners, he reported casually that 'he had not found at Geneva any enthusiasm for proceeding immediately to consideration of the oil sanction and he felt that, for the moment at any rate, it was desirable to pause and take stock'. He gave no indication of disagreement when J. W. Dulanty of the Irish Free State argued that, as a military stalemate might soon result, there was probably no urgency about the question of oil.[5] Nor was Eden's attitude more vigorous on the occasion of his next meeting with the High Commissioners on 16 January 1936. Anticipating the League Council meeting scheduled for four days later, he said that 'he was inclined to think ... that the Committee of eighteen should first arrange for a survey of the existing sanctions'. He was of the opinion, moreover, that 'the Committee should also obtain a report on the practicability of an oil embargo: there was not only the attitude of the League members to be considered, but also the attitude of the United States'. 'The United Kingdom, for their part,' he added, 'were prepared to participate in any embargo imposed by the League, but he did not wish to take the initiative himself in the question.' Charles te Water of South Africa, whose country was now the most hawkish of the Dominions, thought 'it was imperative now to make up their minds as to whether they intended to impose an embargo or not'. He continued: 'Would not the proposal to refer the question for examination by a committee be regarded merely as a means of killing it?' Dulanty then asked how many months' oil supplies Italy now had in reserve. Eden, with remarkable complacency, considered that supplies might last for six or seven months but he expected campaigning to cease in mid-April for the duration of the rainy months. He also drew comfort from the weakness of Italy's gold reserves.[6]

Given this plain statement of intent not to press for an oil sanction and given that he had also urged precisely this line on the Cabinet on 15 January, it is surprising to read in Eden's memoirs this comment on his meeting with Laval on 20 January: 'We ... agreed that experts should examine the efficacy of an oil sanction. I could not get Laval one inch beyond this preliminary exercise, with which I would have preferred to dispense.'[7] Eden's complacency on an oil sanction was no doubt bolstered by a General Staff assessment of 17 January which came near to forecasting an ultimate Italian defeat and particularly stressed the improbability of an Italian victory before April, when the opening of the rainy season was expected to prevent active operations for a period of about five months. A month later the General Staff held the same view.[8] But Eden had by mid-February finally awakened to the danger that Mussolini might be in sight of an early victory, and he began, therefore, to consider the case for an early imposition of an oil sanction. In a meeting of the Dominion High Commissioners on 21 February he advanced the following view:

He had felt when the Report of the Expert Committee [on an oil sanction] was published, that it only remained to give the proposal decent burial and let existing sanctions take their course. But he had been lately thinking that there was something to be said on the other side ... The military position of the Italians had undoubtedly improved. It was not so certain therefore that the Abyssinians and existing sanctions would suffice to prevent Italy being at least partially successful ... There was also the United States to consider. If the League merely washed their hands of the embargo on the grounds that it was useless to impose one without the cooperation of the United States, then it would probably be argued in the United States that they were merely putting it forward as an excuse for doing nothing.[9]

On 26 February Eden accordingly persuaded the Cabinet to allow him to support an oil sanction, though initially he was urged not to take the initiative in public.[10] On 3 March he privately raised the subject at Geneva at a meeting with Flandin, the new French Foreign Minister following the fall of Laval. The French reaction was distinctly cool. But, as so often, the French were unwilling to take their appropriate share of the blame. Flandin, manoeuvring so as to prevent the British putting France in the dock, raised the possibility that Italy would respond to an oil sanction by withdrawing from Locarno. If this happened, asked Flandin, would Great Britain 'be ready to support France even alone in the maintenance of the demilitarized zone'.[11] This was a question to which Eden could give no adequate answer. An oil sanction against Italy was thus ruthlessly linked to the future of the Rhineland. Eden saw at once that an oil sanction was now impossible and he could not even have the satisfaction of publicly putting the blame on the French lest they retaliate with recriminations regarding the Rhineland.

Flandin's pointed question of 3 March about the possible German re-militarization of the Rhineland was more immediately relevant than either he or Eden could have known. For four days later, Hitler unilaterally marched in. Apart from the timing, however, the move was by no means a total surprise either to the British Foreign Office or at the Quai d'Orsay. Indeed, so far as Eden was concerned, the Germans had unilaterally seized what he was in any case prepared to cede, preferably in a negotiated bargain.

If Eden's mild reaction to Hitler's tearing up of both Versailles and Locarno is to be understood, it is essential to appreciate that when he became Foreign Secretary at the end of 1935 he found his officials deeply committed to seeking a permanent settlement with Germany and that he broadly endorsed their approach. Indeed the quest for a settlement with Germany, that is for her 'appeasement', had been pursued by the Foreign Office for many years past. Since at least 1931 there had been no significant faction in the Foreign Office which believed in upholding the Versailles settlement intact. This applied no less to the supposed anti-appeasers, Vansittart and Wigram, than to the rest of their colleagues. It applied also to Lord Cranborne, who was now Parliamentary Under-Secretary and an extremely important influence on Eden at this period. The decisive questions for all the British policy-makers were how far they could persuade Paris, given the supposed difficulties with French public opinion, to accept their view, and how far they could get Berlin, in return for concessions concerning Versailles, to enter voluntarily into agreements designed to promote European stability and secure vital British interests. Neither the rise of Hitler nor that of Eden made any serious difference to what one historian has called 'the essential continuity of British policy towards Germany throughout the nineteen-thirties'.[12] But if there was continuity, there were also, as the same historian has demonstrated, phases of exceptional endeavour on the part of the British. The first of these had come early in 1935, culminating in Simon's and Eden's visit to Berlin notwithstanding the German unilateral announcement of the introduction of conscription. A second major effort was in contemplation when Eden became Secretary of State and he undoubtedly favoured the idea in principle.

If there were disagreements among Eden's advisers and Cabinet colleagues they were almost exclusively concerned at this time with problems of tactics. Should the British enter directly into negotiations with Berlin or consult Paris in the first instance? What kind of pressure should be applied to the French if they were uncooperative? To what extent might the French in certain contingencies act unilaterally, as in the Ruhr in 1923, and to what extent were they actually in favour of yielding to Hitler but anxious to place the whole responsibility on London? What in any case was Hitler's word worth and if, as some came to think, he was unlikely to favour a stable, permanent peace, would it be a British objective to buy time for rearmament with limited concessions? Finally, which concessions could reasonably be made to Hitler in the various circumstances envisaged?

On all these aspects copious minutes were written by the officials of the Foreign Office's Central Department and their superiors in the two months before Hitler's march into the Rhineland. Eden himself was not particularly given to writing down his detailed comments on such minutes – certainly less so than his mentor, Austen Chamberlain. Nevertheless, it is not difficult to reconstruct the broad trend of his thinking on Germany at this time, partly because the subject was also studied both by a Cabinet Committee and by the full Cabinet. As has already been noted, Eden's initial personal impression of Hitler in 1934 had been extremely favourable: moreover, the Germans 'appeared genuinely to desire peace in order to push on with the fifteen years' internal programme which they had in view'.[13] There is no evidence that by the beginning of 1936 he had substantially modified this assessment despite Germany's introduction of conscription in the previous year. Of course Eden was aware that Hitler wanted further revisions in the Treaty of Versailles and even changes in the Locarno Agreements. But he was prepared in principle to permit many of these modifications to come about without resistance. If Eden saw a risk to peace over Germany, it did not seem to him to lie in Hitler's revisionism *per se*, still less in any British rigidity in the maintenance of treaty terms. It lay primarily in the possibility that the French Government, because of pressure from her East European allies or from domestic public opinion, might feel obliged to resist Hitler if he pursued his aims by open threat or by the technique of the unilateral *fait accompli*.

Eden was prepared in principle to make concessions not only to Hitler but also to Mussolini if matters could be so arranged as to involve no loss of face. But whereas he had come to the conclusion by the beginning of 1936 that Mussolini was probably not the man to play this game, he remained cautiously optimistic that Hitler might be. He was, therefore, at least until 1938 much more inclined to be hostile to Italy than to Germany. In retrospect this seems to betoken an odd sense of priorities as apologists for men as different as Vansittart, Neville Chamberlain and Churchill have often stressed. Yet in the years before 1938 Eden was obviously closer than his critics to public sentiment. For nothing done by Hitler in the external sphere during Eden's time at the Foreign Office aroused any public reaction remotely comparable to that which engulfed Hoare over Abyssinia.

Eden clearly saw, however, that if his German policy was to have any chance of success he had not only to worry about what Hitler might do, he also had to win over the French to a policy of step-by-step peaceful revision. And at times he found Paris more resistant to his approach than Berlin. Eden certainly was not an extreme francophile at this period. Though he was perhaps less bitter than in the Barthou phase, his irritation with Paris was often in evidence during his time as Foreign Secretary. He was especially angered at the way in which Flandin used the issue of the Rhineland to block an oil sanction against Italy. This was no doubt increased because he appears to have agreed with his officials' verdict that France was no longer vitally interested in the future of the demilitarized zone. After all, a primary reason for maintaining the zone had been to enable France rapidly to occupy German territory in the event of war between her eastern allies and Germany. But first the construction of the Maginot Line and then Flandin's reported comments in 1935 to the effect that the French alliances in eastern Europe were an embarrassment provided sound grounds for doubting whether the zone *per se* was any longer something for which a French Government would really wish to fight. At the same time, the French Government might have to face difficulties from public opinion. Conscious of all these considerations, Eden resented the cynical use made of the zone by the French in the Abyssinian context and was determined not to let Great Britain be pilloried on the issue. On 14 February he submitted a memorandum to his colleagues on the Cabinet Committee on Germany containing this passage:

M. Flandin's soundings show, I think, that the French Government are themselves uncertain as to what attitude they ought to adopt. They would probably like us to make up their minds for them, and then excuse themselves for not fighting for the zone on the ground that we would not join them . . . it seems unlikely that any French Government would attack Germany merely in order to maintain the demilitarization of the Rhineland.[14]

The last sentence is revealing, for it demonstrates not only Eden's view of the French attitudes but also betrays something of his own thinking. The use of the word 'merely' shows that he did not rate highly the strategic significance of the Rhineland, while his application of the word 'attack' to a possible French response may reveal a possibly unconscious bias against the case for maintaining the sanctity from unilateral repudiation of even the Locarno Treaties, let alone the Versailles settlement.

Clearly Eden wanted France to give way to Germany on the Rhineland as part of a multilateral peaceful settlement. He was also tacitly in favour of Flandin's coolness towards eastern Europe. And he was decidedly against the draft Franco-Soviet agreement being ratified. He was wisely conscious, however, that there were limits to the effective pressures he could apply to Paris. On the issue of the Franco-Soviet Pact, for example, he received on 15 February a memorandum from Wigram and Sargent hoping that it would not be ratified. Eden minuted: 'I too hope, but we can *do* nothing about it.'[15] Incidentally, this provides an illustration of the tricks that memory can play. In his memoirs Eden made flattering reference to the fact that Barthou was the original driving force behind the newest manifestation of 'the traditional policy of many French statesmen, including Clemenceau, calling in the power of Russia to balance the growing threat from Germany'. Eden added: 'The fact that Soviet military power was unproved and that he himself [Barthou] was a man of conservative opinions did not deter him. I think that his decision was justified *and thought so then*, but this policy was not popular with some of my colleagues, particularly the older ones, who were less realistic than M. Barthou.'[16] (Italics supplied.)

So far as Germany was concerned Eden believed that it was worth making a supreme effort at a general settlement. But he was never strikingly optimistic about the prospects, nor did he at any time waver about the need in the meantime to rearm. This was much in tune with Vansittart's approach. If Eden differed from his Permanent Under-Secretary, it was on the matter of what might be offered to Germany. Vansittart was, perhaps surprisingly, keener than his chief on giving away British possessions and interests as distinct from those of other states. In particular, Vansittart favoured the restoration of at least some former German colonies to Berlin. Eden's view was rather different as he made clear at a meeting with his officials on 3 February:

As regards the cession of colonies to Germany, the Secretary of State pointed out the advantage of mandates over full colonial sovereignty. However much the Germans might press for colonies in full sovereignty, he did not see how anything more than colonies in mandate could be ceded. The point was very important as regards the enlistment of black troops and also as regards public opinion in this country. It was pointed out that in the matter of colonies it might be very difficult to give anything more than the Cameroons.[17]

Sargent evidently shared Eden's view rather than that of Vansittart. He wrote a minute on 4 March on the future of the Stresa Front recognizing the vital link between concessions on colonies and concessions on central Europe:

> On the one hand if we are to attempt a general settlement with Germany it may be easier to negotiate in the absence of Italy. If we have to carry Italy with us we will have to put in the forefront of our demands the maintenance of the status quo in Austria; whereas if Italy is out of the negotiations a compromise as regards Central Europe may become much easier. It must always be remembered that the more uncompromising we are as regards Central Europe the more necessary it becomes for us to make concessions as regards colonies in order to obtain a settlement.
>
> On the other hand, an Italy completely unattached in Europe is itself a source of uncertainty and doubt which is bound to react unfavourably on French nerves and make them less inclined to take risks with Germany.

Eden underscored the passages on Italy and on colonies and indicated his general agreement with Sargent that it would be preferable to proceed without Italy.[18]

Eden also came under much pressure from his officials, from Hankey, and from his Cabinet colleagues to decide to what extent to consult France in advance and whether or not to go ahead with bilateral negotiations with Berlin if Paris was discouraging. Eden wavered a good deal but in the end did not contradict his colleague Halifax when he said at a Cabinet Committee on 17 February that 'he would be for going ahead alone' if France was obstructionist. Instead Eden drew comfort from the belief 'that one interpretation of the position was that France would be relieved if we compelled her to face facts'.[19] The 'facts' Eden wished to force on Paris were plainly that France must be prepared to join in a settlement with Germany involving an air pact, a tacit abandonment of her traditional rôle as protector of the rigid status quo in east-central Europe and an early revision of the Versailles and Locarno terms concerning the demilitarization of the Rhineland.

Before this package could be presented in full to Paris and Berlin, however, Hitler took matters into his own hands, marching troops into the Rhineland on 7 March 1936. Eden was naturally dismayed. As he at once made clear to the German Ambassador, he was particularly aggrieved at the unilateral abrogation of the Locarno Agreements into which, unlike the

Versailles Treaty, Germany had freely entered. But he was at no time in any doubt that he wished to avoid war on the issue even if it meant allowing Hitler to get away with his action. Thus on the day of the coup, before consulting either the Prime Minister or the Cabinet, he urged restraint on the French Ambassador. He added: '... we must not close our eyes to the fact that a *contre partie* was offered and that that would undoubtedly have a considerable effect on public opinion. We could not leave this side of the situation unconsidered.'[20] The *contre partie* was Hitler's offers to join an air pact, to sign various non-aggression pacts, to return to the League of Nations, and to enter into negotiations about a new demilitarized zone to which France and Belgium, as well as Germany, would contribute territory.

The French, as Eden had expected, did not act precipitately but agreed to consult with the British and the Belgians. Though Eden could not know it with certainty, this marked the effective end of the risk of war arising out of the Rhineland crisis. From now on it was simply a question of the French manoeuvring to shift the responsibility to the British, whom they must have known would resist war or the threat of war.

The British Cabinet met on 9 March and endorsed the Foreign Secretary's policy of discouraging French action and of seeking to reach vis-à-vis Germany, in Eden's words, 'as far-reaching and enduring a settlement as possible whilst Herr Hitler is still in the mood to do so'. It is clear, moreover, that the initiative for this 'appeasing' policy came from Eden and was in no way forced upon him by the Prime Minister or the Cabinet. The Foreign Secretary even resisted the idea that Germany's action might be effectively dealt with by the League of Nations. As he wrote in his memoirs: '... I thought we must agree to a formal condemnation of Germany's action by the League, but resist any attempt to apply financial and economic sanctions which would be too slow to be effective in this instance.'[21] He did not explain either at the time or in his memoirs why the *speed* with which sanctions became effective was a decisive consideration.

Eden went from the Cabinet to the House of Commons to make a statement. He gave the French no reason to hope for decisive British support concerning the Rhineland but he skilfully reaffirmed Great Britain's Locarno commitment to France and Belgium in the event of 'any actual attack'. To the Germans he administered some public rebukes. But he was also kinder than he chose to recall in his memoirs on the 'positive' aspect of Hitler's position:

One of the main foundations of the peace of Western Europe has been cut away, and if peace is to be secured there is a manifest duty to rebuild. It is in that spirit that we must approach the new proposals of the German Chancellor. His Majesty's Government will examine them clear-sightedly and objectively, with a view to finding out to what extent they represent a means by which the shaken structure of peace can again be strengthened. In the present grave condition of international affairs, His Majesty's Government feel that no opportunity must be missed which offers any hope of amelioration.[22]

Eden next commenced a series of difficult meetings with the French and Belgian leaders. Accompanied by Halifax, he first travelled to Paris. There they found Flandin in an apparently inflexible mood. claiming that he favoured an appeal to the League Council to be followed by sanctions, including, in the last resort, military action. Moreover, negotiations with Germany could not begin until after the withdrawal of her troops. Pressed by the British, Flandin maintained that this line had the united support of the French nation – a great exaggeration, as Eden guessed and as has subsequently been proved by accounts of French Cabinet divisions at this time.[23] Fortunately for Eden, Paul Van Zeeland of Belgium took a somewhat less rigid view, favouring negotiations with Germany and possibly a remodelled version of Locarno. This divergence between Paris and Brussels enabled the British to postpone any decision until the League Council convened in London during the following week.

When the Locarno Foreign Ministers met again, in an informal session on 12 March in London, Flandin had altered his position sufficiently to offer to make a 'quasi promise' to Berlin that German military sovereignty over the Rhineland would be conceded by negotiation if Germany would withdraw at least some of her occupation forces. He was not willing, however, to envisage ultimate German fortification of the Rhineland frontier, as distinct from the presence of troops. Contrary to the impression given in his memoirs, Eden, knowing already from feelers in Berlin that even temporary and symbolic withdrawal was unacceptable to Hitler, from the outset resisted Flandin's new proposal. As he informed various British ambassadors on 13 March:

We pointed out...that the programme which Monsieur Flandin outlined was hardly one which Germany could be expected to accept. If she could not accept it the result might mean war. If the result were war, what would the world have gained? Was it thought that Germany could be taught a lesson by such means? Monsieur Flandin replied that the purpose was not to teach Germany a lesson, and history showed that the Germans were slow learners anyway; the purpose was to show the nations of Europe that international law was strong and the collective system was worth supporting.[24]

When deadlock thus resulted between Eden and Flandin, Van Zeeland undertook to seek a compromise formula and the meeting was adjourned.

On the following day, 14 March, Van Zeeland in effect suggested a reluctant abandonment of the threat of immediate sanctions against the German *fait accompli*. Instead, he favoured negotiations with Germany and as a consolation to France proposed closer cooperation between London and Paris, including the holding of staff talks. Flandin rejected this plan and produced Paul-Boncour to report on the latest state of French opinion which he depicted as hawkish. Neither the British nor the Belgians were impressed and once again deadlock resulted.

On 17 March a desperate Flandin increased the pressure on London. In a private conversation he threatened Eden with the possible substitution for the existing French Government of an anti-British successor, which would make separate terms with Germany. But Eden, strongly encouraged by Cranborne, was unmoved.[25] At a Cabinet meeting on 18 March any faint chance of support for Flandin disappeared. Ministers knew that British public opinion and the parliamentary Opposition were hardening against conflict; and they were aware that the influential Conservative Foreign Affairs Committee, at a meeting on the previous day, had accepted the conciliatory line recommended by Amery and even Austen Chamberlain. In addition they had before them a surprisingly defeatist warning from the armed services: 'From information given by the Service Ministers it transpired that our position at home and in home waters was a disadvantageous one, whether from the point of view of the Navy, Army and Air Force or anti-aircraft defence.' In this situation Baldwin moved decisively, as was his custom at moments of crisis. The Cabinet minutes record:

> The Prime Minister thought at some stage it would be necessary to point out to the French that the action they proposed would not result only in letting loose another great war in Europe. They might succeed in crushing Germany with the aid of Russia but that would probably only result in Germany going 'Bolshevik'.[26]

Baldwin did in fact personally speak with Flandin and probably had much influence on him.

Baldwin's emphasis on the possibility of Communism in Germany is revealing. For it was this fear, rather than an aggressive desire to turn Hitler against the Soviet Union, which lay at the root of much Conservative support for the policies of appeasement in the mid-1930s, before this factor was decisively reinforced after 1937 by consciousness of increasing British military weakness. For example, Hankey wrote on 9 October 1936 that the more he examined the possibility of war with Germany 'the more silly a business does it seem' and that he favoured a settlement with Hitler on the grounds that an Anglo-German war would be so exhausting to both 'that we should probably become a prey to Bolshevism – the very thing Hitler most fears'.[27] Even a so-called anti-appeaser, Harold Nicolson, the National Labour MP, wrote to his wife at the time of the Rhineland remilitarization:

> ... if we send an ultimatum to Germany, she ought in all reason to climb down. But then she will not climb down and we shall have war. Naturally we shall win and enter Berlin. But what is the good of that? It would only mean communism in Germany and France, and that is why the Russians are so keen on it.[28]

Eden was probably more sympathetic to this line of argument than his memoirs suggest. As has already been noted, he was opposed to the ratification of the Franco-Soviet Pact. Now he made no attempt to resist Baldwin's anti-Communist justification for appeasing Hitler. Instead he pointed out to the Cabinet of 18 March 'that at bottom the French nation was very pacifist'. He added presciently that 'what they really apprehended was the outbreak of a serious war in three years time' and he 'shared their conviction as to the danger'.[29]

In these circumstances Flandin finally backed down on 19 March. On British initiative a joint plan was to be put to Germany. This involved negotiations on the Rhineland, including the possible creation of a British-led international force to cover both sides of the Rhine frontier and pacts of non-aggression and submission of the Franco-Soviet Pact (which had been the pretext for Hitler's coup) to the Hague Court for a legal judgement concerning its compatability with the Locarno Agreements. Additionally, however, Eden offered staff talks to the French in return for their concurrence in this plan. Such was the mood in Parliament that there was some doubt whether even this concession might not be going too far in the direction of France. But Eden, with Baldwin's strong backing, crushed Cabinet resistance from Simon and Kingsley Wood, and an effective speech by the Foreign Secretary in the Commons on 26 March served to carry the point for the time being. It cannot be too strongly stressed, however, that if there was any domestic threat to Eden it came not from the anti-appeasers but from the isolationists. Only Cecil seems to have favoured sanctions against Germany. Other so-called anti-appeasers, including those in the Liberal and Labour parties, were silent or openly dovish. Even Churchill, whose anti-appeasing credentials are even now usually thought to be in good order at least in the case of Germany, said in the House of Commons:

Although on the major issue violence has triumphed, no one can deny that but for the existence of the League of Nations there might have been war at this moment. France and the nations associated with her might have attempted to rectify the situation by the sword.

Small wonder, therefore, that on the same occasion Eden said of his proposals to Germany: 'They are not an ultimatum, still less a *Diktat*.' He added the ringing declaration: 'I assure the House that it is the appeasement of Europe as a whole that we have constantly before us.'[30]

Henceforth, Eden was able to use the prospect of cancelling projected staff talks to coerce the French into abandoning all serious resistance to the British line on the Rhineland. When the Germans predictably rejected the substance of the proposals made to them, he was unwilling to allow this fact to be unambiguously stated. Instead, he insisted on 2 April that he would not go to Paris or Brussels 'to say conciliation had broken down'. The

French recognized that the staff talks were at stake and after some hesitation agreed to pretend that further negotations with Germany could indeed be usefully pursued. Thereafter the issue of the remilitarization of the Rhineland was for practical purposes tacitly dropped by all concerned.

In his memoirs Eden came near to expressing regret at his rôle in not resisting the German coup. After relating how formidable the difficulties had been, he concluded: 'If, as Clemenceau tells us, politics is the art of the possible, Hitler's occupation of the Rhineland was an occasion when the British and French Governments should have attempted the impossible.' And it may be that memories of this Anglo-French humiliation at the hands of Hitler was much in his mind in later years – with possibly vital significance in 1956. Yet he was subsequently aware that but for his careful handling of the French, including the offer of staff talks, the outcome might have been worse: Hitler might not only have succeeded in holding the Rhineland but also in fundamentally dividing London and Paris. Eden told Nicolson in 1940 that although Hitler 'scored a great strategical triumph, he did not secure a diplomatic triumph'.[31] It is a verdict few historians are likely to challenge.

If Eden forced the French to abandon even half-hearted protests on the Rhineland, he in turn was sabotaged by Paris on the subject of Abyssinia. There was now no hope of French support for any intensification of existing sanctions against Italy, let alone the introduction of an oil sanction. To make matters worse for Eden, Italian use of poison gas had speeded up the war to such an extent that Addis Ababa seemed unlikely to hold out until the coming of the rainy season. On 6 April Eden told the Cabinet that 'the only effective action at the present stage would be the closing of the Suez Canal'. He did not recommend this and the Cabinet predictably did not urge such a course upon him.[32] Indeed, neither Eden nor any of his colleagues could have done so without abandoning the policy of acting only in concert with France, which they had unanimously made an axiom of their policy throughout the crisis. But Eden initially refused to contemplate the abandonment of existing sanctions even if they proved ineffective. After the fall of Addis Ababa on 5 May, however, he was to change his view on the issue.

As early as 8 May he revealed to the Dominions High Commissioners that he accepted the ending of sanctions in principle but believed tactical considerations should govern the timing. The following extracts from his exchanges with Stanley Bruce of Australia are extremely revealing:

Mr Bruce said that it was necessary to be clear as to what they hoped to obtain by continuing sanctions. He thought that they were agreed that it was hopeless now to think that by continuing sanctions they could do anything to help the Abyssinians themselves. If this was so, were they then to continue sanctions for the sake of the League? The League had never been conceived as an instrument of terrorism, and action by members of the League with this object would not be covered by the terms of the Covenant.

Mr Eden agreed.

Mr Bruce continued that there remained the argument that sanctions should be maintained because they might be used as a bargaining factor. This argument frankly terrified him. They could not contemplate the continuance of sanctions indefinitely, and the time must come when they would have to take them off in return for some settlement which they would then to some extent be obliged to sponsor. This seemed to him an intolerable position. It would be much better to face the criticism of the misguided enthusiasts now than to raise their hopes and anger the large body of responsible opinion in all their countries which was opposed to sanctions. They would later have to face the criticism of both parties, the one because they would consider that they had been twice betrayed, the other because the Government had finally been compelled to capitulate to Mussolini a second time and the prestige of the country had suffered a double humiliation.

Mr Eden said that Mr Bruce's arguments were very strong ... if ... they were to raise sanctions at once, they would certainly be faced with a very strong criticism that they had taken the first opportunity to back out. Another consideration which weighed with him was that if sanctions were raised now, the new French Government would be able next month to turn around and accuse the United Kingdom of having let down the League. He would speak frankly; they all knew that France had tried at every step to prevent or delay the imposition of sanctions, and he felt it would be intolerable that she should now be given the opportunity to turn round and say it was the United Kingdom who had broken the sanctions front. For that reason he would prefer to see any decision on sanctions postponed until June. While therefore he agreed that sanctions would have to be raised, he did think that there were very strong arguments against taking precipitate action in the course of the following weeks.[33]

On 27 May, however, Eden was less forthcoming when the Cabinet discussed the matter, stating that his 'strong inclination, if a good reason could be found, was not to raise sanctions'. By 10 June he was 'rather veering towards the view that if sanctions were to be removed there was something to be said for our taking the initiative' but 'there was no immediate hurry'.[34] It is possible to discern in this wavering and temporizing course not merely calculation about the tactics of national policy but also a reluctance on Eden's part to face up to the unpleasant personal implications of policy decisions which he had already made on an intellectual level. Neville Chamberlain came to feel that this was a trait in Eden's character and was eventually to express great impatience with it. In June 1936, however, Chamberlain and Eden were on good terms and hence when the Chancellor publicly took the initiative on the sanctions issue he did so without apparently desiring to pick a quarrel with the Foreign Secretary. But Chamberlain's speech on 10 June 1936, in which he spoke of the maintenance of sanctions as 'the very midsummer of madness', was a striking example of his self-confident and perhaps selfless willingness to perform disagreeable tasks which others wished to see carried out but hesitated to undertake themselves. He revealed leadership qualities of a high order in being prepared to risk the fate of Hoare if a similar outcry to that of the previous December had ensued. For reasons which may never adequately be explained, backbench MPs and maybe the wider public remained relatively unmoved on this occasion and thus the Cabinet was able on 17 June to agree to Great Britain giving a public lead at Geneva for lifting sanctions.

Eden had not been consulted by Chamberlain and was entitled on that score to feel resentful – something he and others were to make a good deal of in later years. At the time, however, he probably had rather mixed feelings. True, it was a blow to his standing among his colleagues, for, as Swinton, then Secretary of State for Air, wrote: 'A man beaten once in politics at this level can be beaten again. Chamberlain knew from that moment that he had the measure of Eden.' On the other hand, Eden was much the younger man and Chamberlain was the evident heir to Baldwin. More important, Eden was not exposed to the initial risk of repudiation and he was later even able to let it be thought that he was a reluctant conscript to the policy of raising sanctions and thereby retain, for the second time in six months, a rather undeserved degree of credit with the League of Nations Union and centre-left opinion in his own party and beyond it. But, as we have seen, not least from his conversation with Bruce, he was in no sense either a late or a conscripted convert to the principle of abandoning sanctions. It is therefore not altogether surprising that Chamberlain wrote in his diary that Eden had 'been as nice as possible about it'. And to his sister Hilda he wrote on 14 June:

I have only taken after my Pa [Joseph Chamberlain] in committing a blazing indiscretion. But as you say if those who should give a lead won't, someone else must occasionally do so and it seemed to me that this was one of the opportunities which should not be missed. The only person I actually consulted was Sam [Hoare] who strongly approved. I did not consult Eden between ourselves because although I believed that he was entirely in favour of what I was going to say I knew if I asked him he was bound to ask me not to say it! But I sent him a nice note which he has very nicely acknowledged and though I greatly regret that my speech should be a stick to beat him with by the *Daily Mail* I think we can get over that.[35]

It now fell to Eden to defend the lifting of sanctions. It was undoubtedly a disagreeable task but, after Chamberlain's speech, relatively uncontroversial. Only two Conservative MPs, Vivyan Adams and Harold Macmillan, voted against the Government in the Commons. Macmillan refused the Whip for a year. Abroad not even the French, under Léon Blum's Popular Front Government, opposed the policy; nor did they, as Eden had earlier feared, seek to put exclusive blame on the British. Of the Dominions only New Zealand and South Africa made difficulties but, as so often, with no perceptible influence on British policy.[36]

Of his position at this time Eden wrote in his memoirs:

I did not feel called upon to resign, for I had not had control of policy, either in the early stages of the dispute, or during the critical first period in the imposition of sanctions when my own decisions would have been more persistent and far-reaching than those which were taken. Nor would the Abyssinians have remained unarmed if I had had my way.[37]

It is certainly true that Eden's views were at various points in the crisis somewhat more robust than those of his colleagues. But he did not differ from them about the undesirability of moving from a collective to an essentially unilateral approach. This, given the attitude of France, suggests that even if Eden's line had prevailed throughout, the result would in all probability have been the same. Moreover, Eden's position was not at all times consistently hawkish, even within the constraints imposed by France. This was especially the case immediately after he became Foreign Secretary when he was to be surprisingly dilatory and half-hearted in canvassing an oil sanction. We may thus conclude that Eden's attempt in his memoirs to disclaim responsibility for the destruction of Abyssinia and the League of Nations was somewhat too generous to himself and was by implication unfair to most of his colleagues. He might have been on sounder ground if he had argued that he and all his colleagues were at times and in varying degrees insufficiently vigorous but that all their faults paled into insignificance in comparison with those of the French.

In the middle of July 1936 a deteriorating situation in Spain suddenly flared into a full-scale civil war and thus presented various governments with new grounds for developing mutual antagonisms. Eden rapidly concluded that the wisest course for Great Britain was to avoid direct involvement in the conflict. But he was aware that many of his colleagues had ideological sympathies with Francisco Franco rather than with the Madrid Government, which they considered to be susceptible to a Communist takeover. The Prime Minister himself was apparently near to being in this category. According to Thomas Jones, Baldwin remarked on 27 July that he had 'told Eden yesterday that on no account, French or other, must he bring us in to fight on the side of the Russians'. Hoare, now back in office as First Lord of the Admiralty, appeared to believe that British neutrality should be conditional on 'the Russians neither officially nor unofficially' giving 'help to the Communists': 'On no account must we do anything to bolster up Communism in Spain, particularly when it is remembered that Communism in Portugal, to which it would probably spread and particularly in Lisbon, would be a grave danger to the British Empire.'[38] Hankey went even further in a private memorandum. He considered that Great Britain must detach itself from European entanglements and eschew Locarno-type treaties: 'In the present state of Europe, with France and Spain menaced by Bolshevism, it is not inconceivable that before long it might pay us to throw in our lot with Germany and Italy.'[39] On the other hand, the Labour Movement and much of British public opinion supported the Republicans. Hence Eden had no difficulty in persuading his colleagues that neutrality was the only viable option. His own initial private sympathies are uncertain, though in his memoirs he claimed that from the early months of 1937 he would have preferred a Republican victory. At the outset, though clear that official recognition should continue to be given solely to the Madrid Government, he was anxious to halt supplies of British arms to either side. He appreciated, however, that suddenly to refuse arms to a recognized government which had hitherto been at liberty to purchase them presented difficulties. Nevertheless on 31 July he simply minuted to his officials that he hoped that His Majesty's Government would 'be able to avoid supplying [arms] by some means or other' – an objective soon to be achieved. Nor was Eden sympathetic to the Republicans' Soviet backers. On 19 November 1936 he told the House of Commons that 'so far as breaches [of the Non-Intervention Agreement] are concerned I wish to state quite categorically that I think there are other Governments more to blame than those of Germany and Italy'. And as late as 1 June 1937, following the bombing of a German pocket battleship by Spanish Republicans, he told Robert Bingham, the American Ambassador in London, that 'it looked as if the Soviet Government wanted the British to pull its chestnuts out of the fire and would not be disturbed if Germany was at war with England and France leaving Russia with a comparatively free hand on the other side'.[40]

If the British Government was determined to be neutral in word and deed, the same could not be said of other European powers. At the outset Italy and Germany were poised to aid the Nationalists, whereas the Soviet Union and France seemed likely to support the Republicans. This pattern was only partially maintained, however, following the surprising change of attitude on the part of Blum's Popular Front Government in Paris. The modifications in their policy came in three stages. First, on 25 July, they suspended the export of arms to Spain, though they refrained from simultaneously taking the further logical step of banning the export of civil aircraft, which could of course easily be converted for military use. Secondly, on 1 August, France decided to promote an international non-intervention agreement, which, while originally intended only for Mediterranean powers, was subsequently pressed on Germany and the Soviet Union as well. Third, on 7/8 August, the French imposed a unilateral ban on the export of civil aircraft to Spain without previously having received any positive response from Italy and Germany to their non-intervention proposal.

These vital modifications in French policy were and are often attributed by supporters of the Republican side to British pressure. Eden as Foreign Secretary has been singled out in this connection. In order to evaluate his rôle, it is therefore necessary to examine each phase of the development of French policy. The first shift came on 25 July on the question of arms supply to Madrid. In 1960 an American diplomatic historian, basing himself on a telegram from the American Ambassador in Paris, presented the left-wing interpretation under the by-line 'Mr Eden restrains M. Blum from Rendering Assistance to the Spanish Republicans':

On 21 July 1936, Air Minister [Pierre] Cot decided to agree to a request from the Spanish Republicans and to send arms and ammunition to the Madrid Government. On July 22, M. [Charles] Corbin, the French Ambassador in London, called Blum and emphasized that the British were extremely agitated over Cot's decision. Corbin asked Blum to come to London. Upon Blum's arrival in London Eden informed him that the Baldwin Government considered that any assistance lent by the French Government to the Spanish Government might conceivably develop a most critical international situation, especially in view of the Italian and German attitudes. What is more, there were reports of German troop movements on the French frontier. What could the pliable Blum do? He chose to assume that he could not offend his recently acquired ally. Upon Blum's return to Paris on the 25th he immediately called his Cabinet together and the issue was debated. Blum sided with the more moderate members, Daladier, Minister of National Defence, and [Yvon] Delbos, Minister of Foreign Affairs, to override Cot's objections. Finally, a policy of strict neutrality was decided upon and the Spanish Republican Government was 'officially' cut off from its most important source of arms.[41]

The London meeting to which Blum came had long been planned. It had been designed to explore further the future of the Locarno Treaties and, according to the British record of the proceedings, that was in fact all that was discussed. Moreover, there is not the slightest evidence in either the British unpublished records or in the French Foreign Ministry's published documents to support the claim that Blum was summoned or decided to attend at the last minute in order to discuss Spain. We are left, then, with the possibility that the French leader, though in London for other reasons, nevertheless had unofficial conversations on the Spanish question. The substance of Blum's testimony more than ten years later was merely that Eden had said to him of Spain: 'That is your affair; I ask only one thing of you, I beg you, be cautious (*soyez prudent*).' But even this claim finds no confirmation in the British archives, in the published French documents, or in Eden's memoirs. It is not, however, unlikely that Eden made some comment of this kind. Certainly it would be surprising if the two statesmen had not made even casual reference to Spain during informal conversations at the social functions accompanying the conference. Yet even if the accuracy of Blum's claim is accepted, what does it amount to? A casual exhortation to be careful hardly justifies the claim of Blum's biographer that 'the conference was to be an important link in the chain of events that led to non-intervention', and that 'the disapproval with which the British Cabinet viewed plans to aid Spain and Eden's admonitions at a time when the closest Anglo-French cooperation was desirable, played a significant part in the ultimate decision'.[42]

There was, however, one really significant development from Blum's point of view during the London Conference, but it had nothing to do with the British. This was the receipt from the Quai d'Orsay of a telegram containing the message:

M. Cot has telephoned me to say that he is sending to the Department for approval a request presented by the Spanish Government for the purchase of twenty or thirty bombers. The Air Minister added that, being in agreement with the President of the Council and the Minister of Foreign Affairs, and in view of the urgency, he would proceed tomorrow immediately with the delivery of the order, unless countermanded by the President of the Council, even if he had not received the approval of the Department [of Foreign Affairs]. While I was preparing this telegram M. Henri Bérenger telephoned me to point out the strong feelings aroused in the Senate by the news of the possible delivery of any war material to the Spanish Government in the present circumstances because of the precedent which this would create. He believes that he is expressing the almost unanimous opinion of the Committee of Foreign Affairs that an official *démenti* be made.

In these circumstances, I shall await your instructions before drawing up a reply.[43]

This warning proved to be a decisive blow to Cot's policy, which on the return of the French ministers to Paris was quickly repudiated. It seems likely that the main reason why the French Cabinet at their meeting on 25 July decided on this reversal was that a majority of ministers feared that if Cot's policy were followed the Cabinet would either break up or be defeated in the Chamber, with the further possible consequence that France, too, might be plunged into civil war. Foreign policy considerations were almost certainly secondary – and of these fear of a conflict with Germany and Italy may have been more persuasive than respect for what at this stage was a largely undefined British view.

The second stage in the development of French policy was the decision, on 1 August, to propose an international non-intervention agreement. Claude Bowers, American Ambassador to the Republican Government in Madrid, wrote nearly two decades later that 'it is now fairly established' that non-intervention 'was hatched in London and that Blum was practically blackmailed into acceptance'. In taking this line Bowers was frankly disbelieving statements made at the time by both Eden and Blum. On 6

September Blum told a left-wing meeting that he assumed 'complete responsibility' for the non-intervention policy. Then on 29 October Eden told the House of Commons:

> It is suggested that the French Government took their initiative under strong British pressure. Some even go so far as to say that we threatened the French Government with all sorts of pains and penalties if they did not do this thing... It is pure fabrication. The French Government took this initiative on their own account and in doing so in our view rendered very material service to European peace.[44]

Neither the published French documents nor British archival material provide any support for Bowers's interpretation. There appears to have been no ultimatum, *démarche* or even friendly suggestion from the British Government in favour of non-intervention. Moreover, on 28 August Eden sent the following private telegram to Sir George Clerk, the British Ambassador in Paris, after having spoken with the French Ambassador in London:

> M. Corbin asked me whether I had any information as to the attitude of our own Labour Party in the question of Spain. He rather had the impression that they were not very much interested. I replied that I did not think that that was the case, though I had been somewhat amused at the story which one of them brought back from Paris that the suggestion on non-intervention was not originally a French but a British initiative. I had said that there was, of course, no truth in this, though I had always thought M. Blum's initiative a wise one. The Ambassador remarked that so far as he could recollect there had been no discussion of the Spanish problem during our three-Power meeting.

In fact the false rumour seems to have been widely believed in the Labour Party. The only exception was Hugh Dalton who recalled in his memoirs that he had dined with Blum at the beginning of September 1936:

> Speaking as head of the Popular Front Government, he insisted that the policy of non-intervention in Spain was *his* policy. It was he and not Eden, as some alleged, who had first proposed it ... He asked ... [George] Hicks [of the Labour Party National Executive Committee] and myself 'to urge my British comrades to support *my* policy of non-intervention'.[45]

Finally came the French decision of 7/8 August to impose a unilateral ban on the export to Spain of civil aircraft. Concerning this Hugh Thomas, the distinguished historian of the Spanish Civil War, presented the traditional left-wing interpretation in a surprisingly dogmatic fashion:

> ... on August 8 the French Cabinet changed their policy. A *communiqué* announced that from August 9 all export of war material would be suspended. This was explained as being due to the 'almost unanimously favourable' reply the Government had received to its ideas for non-intervention. In fact the previous day Sir George Clerk, the British Ambassador, had almost presented Delbos with an

ultimatum. If France did not immediately ban the export of war material to Spain, and war with Germany were to follow, Britain would hold herself absolved from her obligation to aid France under the Treaty of Locarno. Furthermore by this time, Admiral Darlan had returned with bad news from London. He had seen an old friend, Admiral Lord Chatfield, who had told him that there was no point in making any official approach to the Government through Sir Maurice Hankey, and that Franco was a good patriot. The Admiralty, also, were 'unfavourably impressed' by what they had heard of the murder of Spanish naval officers. Darlan therefore reported that there was no possibility at all of Britain looking favourably on French aid to the Republic and fear of offending England was the reason why the Cabinet was brought, on August 8, to reverse its decision of August 2.

A still more extreme version was offered by Pertinax (André Géraud), who claimed that the Spanish Ambassador in Paris, Juan de Cárdenas, went to the British Embassy to get the British to 'unleash the Rightist press'. The latter's 'howls rose to heaven'. 'Clerk,' Pertinax continued, 'did not mince his words and some of his staff terrified drawing-rooms and editorial offices.'[46]

Again, there exists no evidence to justify these wild claims. First, there is no reason to believe that the rôle of the Admiralty was as important or as sinister as is implied in accounts of the Darlan–Chatfield conversation deriving apparently from the recollections of Blum. On the contrary, if one is to believe Chatfield's own contemporary account to the Foreign Office, he behaved with complete correctness and stated that 'the Admiralty had no policy in these matters'.[47] Secondly, while Clerk undoubtedly did bring pressure to bear on the French, on 7 August he informed Eden that he had made it clear that he was not speaking on behalf of his Government. The British Ambassador's own account of what took place on the occasion of his famous so-called *démarche* deserves to be quoted at some length:

I asked the Minister for Foreign Affairs to see me this afternoon. I told him that my visit was a personal one and made because I was profoundly disturbed about the situation in Spain ... I said that I understood that the French Government, though they were still maintaining their refusal to deliver ammunition or war material to the Madrid Government, had felt they could not refuse to allow five Dewoitine aircraft, which it was said had been ordered before the troubles began, to be delivered, and the departure of the five machines had accordingly been authorized. M. Delbos admitted that that was so. He said that in the face of the already known provision of Italian aircraft to the insurgents and of the despatch of twenty-eight German aeroplanes ... to the same destination ... the French Government considered that it was not possible for them to maintain their embargo. But this showed the urgent need for agreement on the French proposal. I said that, while I could understand the reasoning of the French Government, there were two points that occurred to me. One was, how could he reconcile the despatch of French aircraft to Spain with the holding up in France of British aircraft destined for Portugal? The other point was, was he sure that the Government in Madrid was the real Government and not the screen behind which the most extreme anarchist elements in Spain were directing events? M. Delbos made no attempt to reply to my first question, though he made a note of it. As regards my second point, he said that it might be so in Catalonia, but law and order ruled in Madrid, and the Government was functioning unhampered by the Extremists. I asked him if he considered the forcible entry into a Foreign Legation and the dragging out and shooting of two Spanish gentlemen was an instance of law and order. He had no reply ... I concluded the interview by expressing the hope that the French Government, even though, pending an agreement of non-intervention, they might feel themselves precluded from stopping private commercial transactions with Spain, would do what they could to limit and retard such transactions as much as possible. I asked M. Delbos to forgive me for speaking so frankly, and I repeated all that I had said was entirely personal and on my own responsibility, but I felt that in so crucial a situation I must put before him the danger of any action which might definitely commit the French Government to one side of the conflict and make more difficult the close cooperation between our two countries which was called for by the crisis. M. Delbos said that, on the contrary, he thanked me for speaking so openly and that he and his colleagues wish for nothing more than that the two Governments should act together as closely as possible. He viewed the situation with the gravest anxiety. He had every reason to fear that General Franco had offered the bait of the Balearic Islands to Italy and the Canaries to Germany, and if that materialized, good-bye to French independence. I realize my responsibility in speaking to the Minister for Foreign Affairs as I did without instructions, but I had reason to believe that the Extremists in the Government were putting increasing pressure on M. Blum and I felt sure that what I said might strengthen the hands of the moderate and sober elements.[48]

Clerk was no doubt aware that in thus acting without instructions he was running the risk of angering Eden. In fact, the Foreign Secretary does not appear to have been displeased. The following message was dispatched to Clerk: 'Your language is approved and appears to have had good results.' It is not clear whether Eden or Halifax authorized it. Halifax was in charge of the Foreign Office at this time as Eden was on holiday but it is possible that the latter was consulted by telephone.[49].

The famous British *démarche* was thus nothing more than a personal expression of view by a retiring British Ambassador. As such, it was probably regarded as of no great importance by the French Government, whose course was largely shaped by fear of domestic conflict on the issue. In any case, Clerk's personal views were far less extreme than those attributed to him in left-wing accounts in which threats to repudiate Locarno find a place.

Hence Eden's responsibility for shaping the international character of the initial phase of the Spanish Civil War and for the ensuing farce of 'non-intervention' was of far less significance than has often been supposed. But his importance undoubtedly increased as the war progressed. For it was he who ensured that the intervention of the Italians, in particular, was kept within limits which did not constitute a threat to the long-term territorial integrity of Spain and which did not involve a complete abandonment of British naval prestige in the western Mediterranean. Some of his colleagues in the British Cabinet were so biased in favour of Franco or so anxious to appease Italy that they might well have failed to ensure that these British interests were maintained. There was, however, a price to be paid for Eden's relative robustness concerning the Spanish Civil War: it became impossible to reconstruct the Stresa Front and at times difficult to avoid a continuance of that hostility between London and Rome which had marked the Italo-Abyssinian conflict and which suggested that Great Britain might presently find herself simultaneously fighting Italy, Germany and Japan.

For such an eventuality the Chiefs of Staff and most Cabinet Ministers considered Great Britain singularly unprepared. Eden, while not totally unaware of the risks involved, did not share the sense of priorities of many of his colleagues whether in the field of defence or in the field of diplomacy. This divergence between Eden and most of the policy-making élite only became acute under Chamberlain's premiership but it is possible to discern its origins in the Baldwin era. On the one extreme at this early stage stood Eden; on the other the Chiefs of Staff and Hankey in his rôle as Secretary of the Committee of Imperial Defence. Eden had never been a pacifist, a neo-pacifist or an opponent of British rearmament. But his close links with the League of Nations Union had probably caused him, at least in the early 1930s, to avoid becoming clearly identified with those Service interests which did clamour at times for particular rearmament projects. Cecil and his colleagues in the leadership of the League of Nations Union had also avoided pacifism or calls for unilateral disarmament. But they had urged multilateral arms control measures which had generally run counter to the thinking of most Service opinion. Eden had to some extent taken this same line at the time of the World Disarmament Conference, especially, as has been seen, concerning limitations on air armaments and the problems raised by civil aviation. It was not until 1935-6 that Eden began to give primary emphasis to the need for rearmament rather than to the need to seek multilateral agreements at Geneva; and, according to Hankey's biographer, it was probably not until late in 1937 that he began to adopt a strident tone on the subject.[50]

By contrast, Hankey and most Service opinion were never hampered by a League of Nations constituency or by any commitment to try to make a success of the World Disarmament Conference. But they were realistic enough to recognize that public opinion and the Treasury placed limits on the extent to which Great Britain could rearm. They therefore argued that British commitments must be cut and that precise military obligations to potential allies must be severely limited. They came to stress with increasing clarity that foreign policy must be tailored to correspond to the armed forces available. In practice this led them into favouring appeasement of all Great Britain's potential enemies, most of all where narrow British vital interests were not at stake. They tended to argue that except in a case of supreme national interest Great Britain ought to avoid making war with even a single enemy lest other powers seized the opportunity simultaneously to fall upon her. However valid this thesis was to be later in the decade, it was perhaps unfortunate that Hankey and his colleagues should have taken this line in the most strident fashion at the time of the Abyssinian crisis. For, given the extreme relative weakness of Italy and the apparent indifference of Germany and Japan, they inevitably created the impression on Eden that their counsels of prudence derived more from their political hostility to Wilsonian internationalism than from an impartial evaluation of the military risks. And, despite the valiant attempts of Hankey's biographer to justify their advice in military terms, it is difficult to escape the conclusion that their views in 1935–6 were unnecessarily alarmist and were to some extent a rationalization of their political preferences.[51] Certainly Eden formed the belief at this time that the Chiefs of Staff were politically motivated and he was accordingly to persist in disregarding their largely justified subsequent clamour, in 1937–8, that those responsible for British foreign policy should reduce the number of potential enemies and, if possible, gain time for further British rearmament. But although Eden did not substantially shift his ground as Great Britain's relative military position rapidly worsened, some Cabinet colleagues did – most notably Chamberlain. Even Vansittart felt the need to play for time, not least where Germany was concerned. As he minuted on 31 December 1936:

Time is the very material commodity which the Foreign Office is expected to provide in the same way as other departments provide *other* war material ... To the Foreign Office falls therefore the task of holding the situation until at least 1939 and ... there is no certainty of our being able to do so, though we are doing our utmost by negotiating with Germany, and endeavouring to regain lost ground with Italy ...[52]

In the last months of Baldwin's premiership the divergence between Eden and a growing group of critics was not fully understood or articulated on either side of the argument. But in retrospect it is possible to see it slowly crystallizing towards the end of 1936. In the sphere of defence policy it may be discerned when the Chiefs of Staff were asked by the Foreign Office to give *technical* advice on the value of Belgian cooperation with Great Britain and France in various contingencies. They returned the reply on 25 November that 'our policy should be directed so as to ensure the greatest possible chance of Belgian neutrality', and it was therefore 'undesirable to add in any way to Belgium's existing or proposed commitments', and that 'nothing should be done, in our opinion, to encourage the idea that there is the possibility of staff conversation between us and either the French or the

Belgians, or both'. In Eden's view this reply entirely ignored the technical aspect and instead amounted to an improper attempt to shape foreign policy in a number of respects, including the matter of staff talks with France, which had been the subject of a contrary decision in principle earlier that year. Eden submitted a sharp rejoinder and the matter was debated on 10 December 1936 at the Committee of Imperial Defence, at whose sessions incidentally the Foreign Secretary was an infrequent attender during Baldwin's premiership. Chatfield, the First Sea Lord, in effect rejected Eden's complaints, using the argument that 'there could be no definite dividing line between policy and strategy' and in this he was supported by Duff Cooper, the Secretary of State for War, who observed that 'the discussion had illustrated how impossible it was to draw any hard and fast line between policy and strategy'.[53]

In the sphere of foreign policy the origins of the later divergence may be seen in Eden's leisurely approach to the possibility of improving relations with both Italy and Germany. He was not of course opposed in principle to holding talks with either country – a fact which tended to delay a showdown with his colleagues. But he was imbued with little sense of urgency and little consciousness of the military peril if Great Britain could not win over at least one of her potential European enemies. As so often he found himself agreeing with Cranborne, whose views were embodied in a paper dated 12 November 1936. The precise example about which Cranborne happened to be concerned on this occasion was Italy but the approach was subsequently to be applied to almost the same degree by Eden to possible appeasement of Germany and Japan. Cranborne wrote:

Two propositions may, I think, be broadly stated –
(1) It seems generally agreed that better relations between this country and Italy are, if possible, desirable.
(2) It seems equally to be generally agreed that we must not give to the world, or to Signor Mussolini, the impression that we are running after the Italians.
On these two propositions there is no considerable difference of opinion. It is over the relative importance of them that such differences as there are arise ... Is there a middle line to be found between these two views? I suggest that there is. For this reason it is of the first importance that we should show ourselves strong. We must continue all our preparations in the Mediterranean on a scale with which Italy cannot easily compete. That will impress not only the Mediterranean powers but Germany, and make Italy less attractive in German eyes.
Secondly, let us take every opportunity of making it abundantly clear that we have no aggressive designs in the Mediterranean. For reasons already stated, a definite pact of non-aggression between the two countries might well do more harm than good. But the same arguments do not apply to parallel unilateral declarations of policy, if this would relieve the mind of Sr Mussolini, who, it is suggested, is genuinely suspicious of aggressive designs on our part, by all means let us go so far to meet him, let us also, at a suitable moment, do what we can to eliminate outstanding

causes of friction between us. Let us replace the Legation at Addis Ababa by a Consulate. Let us, in due time, recognize the Italian annexation of Abyssinia. These, I suggest, would not any longer constitute a further blow to the prestige of the League. It would be accepted as a recognition of a fact. But let us go no further. By any appearance of weakness or defeatism we shall merely bring about the very result we are anxious to avoid – the strengthening of Italian prestige and her power of nuisance; and we shall do it under circumstance for which there is in reality no excuse. For there can be none of us who have any real doubt of what the result would be should any conflict between Italy and this country unfortunately arise.

Eden minuted his agreement with this paper: and even in retrospect he wrote in his memoirs that 'while I was always open to any approach from Rome, we had no cause to crave negotiation with Fascist Italy, our navy and air force were far more powerful than hers'.[54] This military assessment of course revealed no recognition of the possibility that Germany and/or Japan might go to war simultaneously with Italy or, alternatively, implied that such interventions could also be successfully resisted. In either case such assumptions were rapidly becoming, even if they had not always been, a somewhat reckless basis for the conduct of British defence and foreign policy.

Eden's bland view of the military risks thus led him to seek agreement with Italy, Germany and later Japan in a take-it-or-leave-it spirit. By the last months of Baldwin's premiership he had very little to show for his endeavours in any direction. So far as Germany was concerned, he had largely lost belief in the urgent quest for a general settlement which had been the Foreign Office's obsession when he had first become Secretary of State. The Rhineland remilitarization had obviously been a traumatic experience. And in its aftermath he was given little encouragement by Hitler to expect much progress. For example, Eden had addressed a questionnaire to Hitler in May 1936 seeking to discover the character of his future intentions but never received a clear reply. Again, the British, French and Belgians, following their meeting in London in August 1936, vainly endeavoured to convene a five-power conference to construct an amended Locarno system. But Eden at this stage was disinclined to go further. For example, he resisted making any serious offer to Germany in the colonial sphere even when pressed to do so by Blum in the autumn of 1936.[55] During the rest of the year Anglo-German relations accordingly drifted along without serious clashes but equally with no moves towards an enduring rapprochement.

Eden's reserved approach appeared at first to be having rather more success with Mussolini, whom ironically he continued to dislike more than Hitler. For he was able to obtain Italian acceptance of a *modus vivendi* concerning naval difficulties in the western Mediterranean arising out of the Spanish Civil War. This was the so-called Gentleman's Agreement of 2

January 1937. It was a mere affirmation of mutual respect for each other's interests in the Mediterranean and a renunciation of any desire to modify the status quo 'as regards national sovereignty of territories in the Mediterranean area'. That the accord was of so limited a character was in large measure due to Eden. When Dino Grandi, the Italian Ambassador in London, first spoke to him about a so-called 'Gentleman's Agreement' (Mussolini's term!), Eden hoped that the Duce did 'not intend anything in the nature of a pact'. When the Italians fell in with this, the Foreign Secretary telegraphed to Drummond that Great Britain was 'not prepared to take any course liable to arouse the fears and suspicions of other Mediterranean countries, nor would we limit the size and location of our military and naval forces in the Mediterranean or the Red Sea'. He refused 'for the present to recognize the Italian conquest of Abyssinia'; and he wished the Italians 'to accept without qualification the territorial status quo in the Mediterranean and renounce anti-British propaganda in the Near East'.[56]

Nor can the Italians have been unaware of the steps taken in the period following their final victory in Abyssinia to strengthen the British diplomatic and military position in the Mediterranean. First, on 20 July the Montreux Convention had been signed – a settlement of the Straits regime which was acceptable to Turkey. Secondly, on 26 August an Anglo-Egyptian Treaty was forged which brought to an end many years of tension between London and Cairo. Eden naturally played a central rôle in both these sets of negotiations. While not present at the Montreux Conference, he effectively arranged advance British diplomatic backing for Turkey. Eden in short reverted to a British nineteenth-century view of Turkey as a bulwark against Great Power expansionism. This served to ensure Turkish friendship during the rest of peacetime and her largely benevolent neutrality during the Second World War which contrasted strikingly with her rôle in the First World War. The Montreux Convention thus constituted one of the most enduring and valuable, if generally underrated, of his achievements.

So far as Egypt was concerned, Eden simply responded to a request from Cairo for a reopening of negotiations for a formal treaty to establish the basis for formal independence. These had earlier come near to success in 1930.[57] Eden now held that, in the light of the strategic situation in the Mediterranean and north-east Africa, it was worth making some possible long-term sacrifice of British interests if Egyptian goodwill could meanwhile be secured. In particular, he agreed that the British entitlement to defend the Suez Canal zone, to which British troops would normally be confined, might be subject to review after twenty years and that if at that time agreement between London and Cairo should prove impossible, a change in British rights could come about following arbitration. This risk of ultimate expulsion from Egypt seemed negligible to Eden but he had to face the vain opposition of both the Admiralty and the legalistic-minded among his colleagues. This created the impression that Eden's approach towards Egypt was wholly liberal and thus has been thought to render his attitude in 1956 all the more remarkable. But Eden was not so much liberal-minded as, at least in this instance, a realistic judge of short- and medium-term power political considerations. This extract from the diary for 5 June of the British High Commissioner (later Ambassador) in Egypt, Sir Miles Lampson, is revealing:

> Meeting with the Secretary of State at 11.00 a.m. – alone. We had a little general talk about the Anglo-Egyptian problem and he asked me whether in the ultimate resort I did not believe that the only fundamental solution of the problem was the inclusion of Egypt in the British Empire? I said that the same question had been in my mind from the first moment that I reached Egypt. So much so that when I had finally put in my report, in accordance with instruction after six months in the country, I had recorded such as, in my belief, the only true solution to the problem. At the same time I had in that report emphasized that there could in my opinion be no question of trying to reach that solution in present conditions. Neither Egyptian nor I imagined British opinion was ripe for it. Consequently I had at that time advised that we should proceed slowly but systematically in an endeavour to tighten the material interests of the two countries in one another ... we now found ourselves faced with the treaty problem. In the circumstances it had been inevitable that the British Government had tackled the request in the only possible way. So much said, I did not myself believe that the conclusion of a treaty, if so be we got one, need necessarily prevent in the long run the other solution but once more I must record the firm opinion that any idea of closer Imperial connection with Egypt at present was not a matter of practical politics. Anthony Eden said that on the whole he agreed but was interested that I should have had the same idea as he. Obviously it was one to keep entirely in reserve.[58]

Whatever may be thought of Eden's ultimate intentions, it may be concluded that his decision to settle with the Egyptians was, like his Montreux policy, of great value to Great Britain in the following turbulent decade.

Nevertheless the news of these developments was certainly unwelcome to the Italians. They may have been contributory factors, together with the continuing coolness shown by Eden towards Rome, leading to Mussolini moving late in 1936 towards alignment with Berlin and, as already indicated, to the extremely limited character of the Gentleman's Agreement.[59] The fragility of the Gentleman's Agreement was indeed demonstrated within days of its announcement. Various naval incidents in the Mediterranean confirmed Eden in his scepticism about Mussolini's good faith and he was thus reinforced in his intentions to maintain a firm line vis-à-vis Rome. This rapidly found expression in his proposal to the Cabinet on 8 January that the British should give a lead towards establishing a naval cordon around Spain. Hoare, now First Lord of the Admiralty, opposed the plan both on the grounds that it was impractical and that it was designed to prevent Franco from winning. The Foreign Secretary was defeated in a meeting of ministers, at which Baldwin unexpectedly argued that 'the difficulties of a naval blockade were insuperable'. Eden chose in his memoirs to depict the occasion as a major setback. He also implied that he was let down by the Prime Minister, whom he alleged had earlier agreed with his plan.[60]

His sense of grievance towards Baldwin over this incident may have been genuine enough for a time and may go far to explain his excessively warm words of welcome for the impending takeover of Neville Chamberlain. Yet this relatively unimportant divergence from Baldwin does not justify a complete endorsement of Eden's verdict, namely that he was severely hampered during his tenure as Baldwin's Foreign Secretary by undue lack of Prime Ministerial support and consequent vexatious interference from other colleagues. For in most matters during this period Eden had got his way and he had had the Prime Minister's backing when it counted. Moreover, any temporary coolness between them was to be overcome within a year of Baldwin's retirement in May 1937. Eden's recollection of his feelings at the end of his working partnership with Baldwin was thus rather less than generous as well as extremely ironic: 'While I was always grateful for Baldwin's personal kindness to me, I looked forward to working with a Prime Minister who would give his Foreign Secretary energetic backing.'[61]

IV

Chamberlain's Foreign Secretary
1937–8

Neville Chamberlain became Prime Minister on 28 May 1937. His succession had long been a foregone conclusion and it was equally predictable that he would ask Eden to remain at the Foreign Office. The relationship between the two men was at this stage certainly cordial notwithstanding the generation gap which separated them. But it is difficult to appreciate what led Eden on his side initially to rate Chamberlain quite as highly as he apparently did. According to his Private Secretary, Oliver Harvey, he thought 'Neville Chamberlain had makings of a really great Prime Minister if only his health held out'. And in his memoirs he recorded that 'before Chamberlain became Prime Minister, I would think it true that he and I were closer to each other than to any other member of the Government, exchanging opinions on many Cabinet matters without any disagreement'.[1] Yet in fact they had already had their differences. For Chamberlain had shown himself more willing than Eden to move rapidly towards the appeasement of both Rome and Berlin.

Chamberlain's view of Eden was undoubtedly less enthusiastic. He saw him as a promising young man but one who at times needed guidance and leadership. True, he had often agreed with Eden rather than with Simon in the early 1930s, especially over British disarmament policy. But Chamberlain had not admired Eden's occasional lack of decisiveness in facing up to unpleasant and unpopular realities. Hence it had been Chamberlain who had proposed lifting the sanctions against Italy and it had been he who had twice forced a diffident Eden's hand in 1936 and 1937 in the matter of exploring colonial restitution with Germany. Moreover, there is no evidence that Chamberlain ever took seriously the idea that Eden might succeed him.

The Foreign Secretary seems to have expected more support from Chamberlain in Cabinet than he had allegedly got from Baldwin, but not to have realized that a concomitant of such 'support' would be a degree of vexatious interference. This illusion was no doubt rapidly shattered. It is also surprising that Eden, given his supposed initial closeness to Chamberlain, should have simultaneously seen the new Prime Minister, according to his own account, as something of a novice in international affairs. In his memoirs, he recalled with evident approval the occasion during Baldwin's last days in office when Austen Chamberlain said to his half-brother,

'Neville, you must remember you don't know anything about foreign affairs' – probably a flippant remark subsequently accorded undue significance. Again, Eden referred to the Prime Minister as being in the summer of 1937 'new to international affairs'.[2] This view of Chamberlain is impossible to defend. Whether or not his policies were sound, they were not based on ignorance or inexperience. True, he inevitably did not have the same detailed knowledge of some specialized areas as Eden who had spent so much of his career in one capacity or another in the Foreign Office. But Chamberlain had played a major rôle in the making of the Cabinet's international policy ever since 1931; and he had acquired an unrivalled broad grasp of the interrelationship between defence, economic strength and foreign policy. Eden by contrast was disappointingly lacking in expertise and ideas in areas technically outside his departmental sphere. For example, he became a regular attender at the Committee of Imperial Defence only in 1937, and, judging by the minutes, was then often out of his depth on matters of quite fundamental importance. Nor did he reveal in Cabinet any grasp of economic questions, domestic or international. It does not necessarily follow that the Prime Minister's overall approach was in practice wiser than the Foreign Secretary's. But it will not do to argue that Eden was the man of experience and Chamberlain the novice.

The partnership between Chamberlain and Eden lasted a mere nine months but has singular fascination. Its history has a somewhat uneven character and may always escape entirely convincing analysis. For while Eden must rapidly have realized that his early hopes for a totally smooth working arrangement had been misplaced, it may be that neither he nor the Prime Minister concluded that an outright break was unavoidable until the last month or even the last days. There is thus a danger that many of the instances of divergence which occurred during 1937 may seem more portentous to the historian than they did to the participants. If, for example, one or other had died at the end of the year it is not clear that their relationship would seem in retrospect to have been marred by sharper differences than quite often occur between colleagues without resignation becoming a serious likelihood. Moreover, as we shall see, they were usually able, at least until the final confrontation, to speak to one another in personally friendly fashion even when frankly acknowledging the existence of differences on policy matters. The relationships between many Prime Ministers and their Foreign Secretaries have been less personally warm without culminating in dramatic resignation. Certainly policy differences existed and their importance should not be minimized. But here again the opposite danger may be the greater; because war occurred within two years of Eden's resignation some writers may be inclined to allow this knowledge to colour their analysis of the events in 1937 and thus possibly to give rather too much weight to relatively marginal divergences of view. F. W. Maitland's warning to historians is apposite: they should not forget that momentous events now far in the past were once in the future.

The difficulty of striking an equitable balance in describing the Chamberlain-Eden partnership may be illustrated by consideration of their rôles in the Imperial Conference which was meeting in London at the time of Chamberlain's succession. It would be possible by selective use of documents to present a lurid but misleading picture of emerging divergences. Three examples will suffice. First, Eden stated that 'the more immediate danger of hostilities came from Italy rather than from Germany' and subsequently elaborated his views in these words:

> It was by no means easy to summarize the attitude of Italy toward this country ... It should be taken for granted that Italy's policy was opportunistic and to a large extent founded on bluff. Her attitude towards this country was based in the first place on the fear that our rearmament policy was primarily designed to enable us in our own good time to administer a knockout blow to Italy. It should be assumed that this fear was deeply, widely and genuinely felt throughout Italy. It arose out of Italian mentality. If Italy had been in our place this is precisely what she would have done to revenge herself for what Italians would have regarded as the thwarting by a hostile power of Italian policies. Secondly, Italy's attitude towards us was based on the dream of a revival of the Roman Empire at the zenith of its power and glory.[3]

While Chamberlain undoubtedly had sympathy with the first part of Eden's analysis of Italian policy, there is no evidence that he or anyone else in the Cabinet took seriously the second possibility and he certainly did not see Italy as more likely than Germany to initiate a war with Great Britain. A second difference between Eden and Chamberlain arose when the former, together with Malcolm MacDonald, wanted to give the Dominion Prime Ministers a detailed account of the Anglo-French debate on colonial restitution to Germany. Following objections from Chamberlain, the Foreign Secretary reluctantly caused the information to be withheld and even incorrectly stated on 4 June that in his recent conversations in Paris Dr Hjalmar Schacht 'had confined his discussions to financial and economic matters'.[4] Thirdly, on 8 June, Eden supported Australia's controversial desire for a Pacific Pact involving Japan. Of this Hankey wrote: 'A.E. chucked a spanner into a most critical situation today, and wrecked the PM's most promising efforts at a solution. The PM is very annoyed with him.'[5]

On the other hand, the records of the same conference may more convincingly be utilized to reveal a good deal of harmony between Chamberlain and Eden. Above all, they were in substantial agreement about the future of the League of Nations, about central Europe and about the recognition of the Italian conquest of Abyssinia. To Harvey Eden sometimes spoke as if he believed in an extreme sanctionist League, even seeming to be a supporter of the abortive Geneva Protocol of 1924.[6] But in the secrecy of the Imperial Conference he expressed the view that the sanctionist clauses in the League Covenant should if possible be abrogated and thus pave the way for the adherence of the United States and others. His 'innermost conviction was that the League would be stronger if it included all nations even though there were no sanctions'. He foresaw great practical difficulties, however, in formally amending the Covenant 'but he did not see why the members of the League should not be brought up against the fact that the League, as now composed, could not apply sanctions to a Great Power – like Germany for example'. 'If the United States of America were a member of the League,' he continued, 'it would be stronger than it was today, even though it could only exercise moral force.'[7] The Foreign Secretary had thus evidently been converted to the same view as Chamberlain, who later in the Imperial Conference said that 'a universal League with diminished powers would be infinitely preferable to a limited League with increased powers'.[8]

Eden and Chamberlain were also required to reveal to the Dominions their thinking on the possible expansion of Germany in east-central Europe. Here Austria was the most pressing issue. Eden revealed that Great Britain 'would not necessarily wish to oppose' an *Anschluss* if the Austrians wanted it, which he chose to doubt. Chamberlain went even further, saying that 'he himself to a large extent sympathized with the desire of *Anschluss*'. But both Eden and Chamberlain evidently agreed on their broad policy towards Germany's *Ostpolitik*. The Foreign Secretary explained his approach:

We might disinterest ourselves altogether in Central Europe and confine ourselves strictly to our vital interests in the Low Countries and Northern France. Such a policy would be most unwise and would most certainly invite aggression. Alternatively we might declare our readiness to fight for Czecho-Slovakia or Austria if they became victims of aggression. That would be going far beyond our obligations under the Covenant and far beyond where people of this country were prepared to go. There could be no greater danger than for the Government to declare themselves in favour of a policy which did not command the general support of public opinion at home. This would only make things infinitely worse. There remained the third possibility, namely, that without undertaking any military commitment we should make it clear that we were interested in events in Central Europe ...[9]

This statement has been sharply criticized by one historian:

As a policy, this was less compromise than compromised. To be 'interested' in Central Europe – whatever that might mean – meant perilously to combine involvement and impotence. It served only to put off the inevitable moment of decision, for sooner or later the English 'interest' in events in Central Europe must either be exposed as bluff, mere wind and paper, or it must be made good. And that could only be done, in the geographical circumstances, by a proclaimed willingness to go to war.[10]

But Eden had offered as good a definition as any of the policy pursued by Chamberlain until Munich and beyond. The fact was that the 'interest' of the British in central Europe was a bluff which they did not much mind having called unless the consequence was to find themselves having to go to war in any case for the sake of France whose survival as a great power *was* a vital British interest. The Eden–Chamberlain line thus probably constituted the only hope of keeping some control over the French who otherwise might have dragged Great Britain into war for objectives not shared by her. Chamberlain carried this line to its logical conclusion at Munich, where, after evincing an 'interest' in the fate of Czechoslovakia, he successfully steered the French into acting in consonance with British aims. Eden had by then opted out.

The two men also collaborated in the Imperial Conference in seeking a free hand to recognize the Italian conquest of Abyssinia. Here the initiative appears astonishingly to have come from Eden, despite his wilder fears about Italian intentions. For as early as 26 April, before the Imperial Conference convened and before Chamberlain became Prime Minister, the Foreign Secretary sent a telegram to the Dominions aimed at preparing the way for this supreme act of appeasement of Mussolini.[11] At the Imperial Conference itself he and Chamberlain jointly persuaded the other Prime Ministers that it would be a mistake either to allow the question to stand over or to refuse to recognize the actual position. Instead on 22 May the Dominion Prime Ministers agreed on a joint approach to be pursued later in the month at Geneva on the occasion of a Special League Assembly. Chamberlain summed up their position thus:

> The course which seemed to be favoured as a result of the discussion was that the Assembly should, if possible, avoid formal resolutions, but should in discussion reaffirm its previous attitude towards the Italian occupation of Abyssinia; that the failure of the action taken under Article 16 of the Covenant should be admitted; that the States members of the League should be free to take such steps as each should deem appropriate to regulate its future attitude towards the Italian occupation; and that advantage should be taken of the opportunity offered of pressing forward with the future of the League of Nations ... There was, however, a general preference that the question should, if possible, be brought before the Assembly from some quarter other than the Members of the British Commonwealth of Nations.[12]

There was, however, one extremely reluctant Dominion Prime Minister, namely M. J. Savage of New Zealand. He held tenaciously to the view that recognition would be immoral and was severely critical of past British policy concerning both Manchuria and Abyssinia. Eden had at this juncture little sympathy. He minuted that the New Zealand Prime Minister was 'very badly and inadequately informed' and doubted 'whether it would be possible to remove by argument Mr Savage's misconceptions and prejudices'.[13] It is fair to add, however, that Eden did not intend to give

Mussolini instant recognition. He told delegates on 21 May that 'he did not say that France or ourselves would recognize Italy right away, but he thought that both France and Great Britain would start negotiations with Italy and insist on certain conditions'. There is no evidence that Chamberlain disagreed with any part of this statement.[14] And in their later quarrel it was Eden, not Chamberlain, who resisted first bargaining and then any talks whatever with Italy.

The British plans for the Special League Assembly were in the event to be thwarted. As Eden told the Cabinet on 2 June:

It has not been found possible to raise the question of the representation of Abyssinia. No Abyssinian representative had attended the meeting and consequently the Credentials Committee had had no ground to deal with the matter. If an Abyssinian representative had been there the result might have been different ... The question was now relegated to the September meeting of the Assembly. Only a strong British lead could have achieved a result.[15]

The pattern of this early phase in the Chamberlain–Eden partnership is thus clear: matters on which they differed were temporarily dwarfed by their willingness to abandon a sanctionist League and their apparent agreement to open negotiations aimed at granting recognition of the Italian conquest of Abyssinia and not in the last resort to resist Germany's aims concerning Austria. Again, Eden had moved towards Chamberlain's outlook by seeking to remove Vansittart from the Permanent Under-Secretaryship. Harvey recorded on 4 May 1937: 'A.E. spoke to Chancellor [Chamberlain] about Van and necessity of replacing him. Chancellor agreed to such action being taken but said that it would obviously be wise to wait a little.'[16] Vansittart was eventually 'promoted' to the less influential post of Chief Diplomatic Adviser on 1 January 1938 and was replaced by Cadogan.

All this represented a notable revision in the largely negative attitude Eden had shown in the last year of Baldwin's premiership. It may have been symptomatic of a sincere desire to work in harmony with Chamberlain even at the price of some surrender of principle. Or it may have been due to a dawning recognition of the changed character of the military balance in the world. For example, the Dominion leaders heard on 3 June that:

Generally, Mr Eden agreed that it was not difficult to find inconsistencies in our foreign policy. If three or four years ago, the United Kingdom Government had been free to arrange matters, events might have been different, but it was impossible to adopt a simple and logical course among the many dangers of the situation, and, above all at a time when the United Kingdom's armaments were weak. This last point was particularly important. If our armaments in recent months had been at the level which they would reach in the summer of 1939, developments in the Spanish situation would have been very different. Meanwhile he felt that it was his duty to adopt policies which would gain time in the interests of peace.[17]

Whatever the reason for Eden's move towards Chamberlain, he had reverted to his earlier approach by the autumn of 1937 and had plainly lost some of his admiration for the Prime Minister. Why this happened is difficult to discern. For in his memoirs Eden glossed over the fact that any change occurred. He did this by largely ignoring the honeymoon period with Chamberlain and, in particular, by revealing nothing of his various statements at the Imperial Conference. It would seem that the first difficulties arose early in July. The issue was Italy. Despite his evident willingness to contemplate recognition of the conquest of Abyssinia, Eden remained suspicious of Mussolini's intentions. His remarks at the Imperial Conference on the Fascist goal of recreating the Roman Empire have already been recorded. And no less interesting as evidence of his extreme hostility to the Italians are the minutes of a remarkable exchange between Savage and Eden on 1 June, less than a month after the alleged German bombing of Guernica:

Mr Savage inquired whether Germany and Italy were genuinely in favour of maintaining the non-intervention arrangements in Spain.

Mr Eden thought that in this matter we must distinguish between Germany and Italy. Germany throughout had cooperated loyally, efficiently and zealously in all the arrangements adopted by the Non-Intervention Committee. There was also good reason to believe that before this regrettable incident [the bombing of the *Deutschland*], Herr Hitler was becoming favourable to the withdrawal of German volunteers from Spain.[18]

None of this had as yet caused difficulties with Chamberlain. But once the Imperial Conference had ended Eden played down his support for appeasing Italy and pressed his anti-Italian approach on his colleagues in even stronger terms. He began at meetings of the CID on 1 and 5 July by urging that Italy be added to the list of potential enemies against whom the Chiefs of Staff should make active preparations. Chamberlain, with the support of Service colleagues, was reluctant to endorse this view and at first sought with a good deal of tact to persuade Eden that he should not get the Italian danger out of proportion. For example, on 5 July the Prime Minister said

he would like to offer some observations on the general question. It seemed to him that we need not be afraid of attack by Italy ... unless she were sure of German support ... The ideal, no doubt, was to be prepared to fight Germany or Italy or Japan, either separately or in combination. That, however, was a counsel of perfection which it was impossible to follow. There were limits to our resources, both physical and financial, and it was vain to contemplate fighting singlehanded the three strongest Powers in combination. He did not leave out of account that we should probably have allies in such a war, notably France, but France at the present time was not in a very strong position to give us much help...

In foreign affairs there were two aspects to be considered, first our preparations for defence and, second, our foreign policy. These two had to be correlated, since each influenced the other. He thought that we ought so to direct our foreign policy that we did not quarrel with Germany. If we could do that, he did not feel that we need fear any sudden attack by Italy. But even on the assumption that we could maintain good relations with Germany, he still thought that we should regard Germany as our greatest potential danger, and should give first priority to defence preparations against that country. In that case defence preparations against Italy should be considered of secondary importance.[19]

Neither Eden nor Chamberlain were as yet inclined to allow their difference of approach to become an open breach. First, Eden told the CID that he agreed with Chamberlain's broad analysis. Then Chamberlain gave some ground on being informed of the contents of an alarming letter from Drummond in Rome in which the Ambassador wondered whether Italian public opinion might not be being prepared for war: the Prime Minister was still sufficiently open-minded about Eden's fear of Mussolini as well as of Hitler to write to his sister, Ida, that 'the Germans and the Italians are as exasperating as they can be and it is rather difficult to reconcile their profession of desire for our friendship with the incredible licence of their press'.[20] Eden for his part was evidently still willing to allow that there might be something to be said for the Prime Minister's thesis that Mussolini might yet be talked round. For on 16 July he wrote to Chamberlain about a conversation he had had with Sir Ronald Graham, a former British Ambassador in Rome. Eden and Graham had agreed that the Italians probably felt threatened by Great Britain. Eden continued:

We then discussed ways and means of trying to better the situation and I gave Graham a number of assurances as to our peaceful intentions which I asked him to repeat to the King [of Italy]. He undertook to do so, I then took the opportunity to put to Ronald Graham a suggestion that Edward Halifax had made to me a few days ago: that I should write a personal letter to Mussolini. Such a course is perhaps excusable in that I have met Mussolini and that he has written to me direct – not lately, but in the early stages of the Abyssinian dispute. Graham was strongly in favour of the idea.[21]

The idea of an unorthodox message to Mussolini thus originated with Eden, and not, as has hitherto been supposed, with Chamberlain. The point is not mentioned in Eden's memoirs!

Eden did not in fact send any personal message to Mussolini but instead, on 19 July, made a reassuring speech in the House of Commons. This was well received in Italy and led Dino Grandi, the Italian Ambassador in London, to request a personal meeting with Chamberlain. Possibly Eden resented being by-passed in this way. At all events, he endorsed a Foreign Office briefing for the Chamberlain–Grandi meeting, prepared by the erratic Vansittart, which was not fully consistent in tone with his Parliamentary speech or his remarks to Graham. Now his emphasis was again on the Italian threat and, in particular, on the movement of two mechanized divisions to Libya. Sir Horace Wilson, Chief Industrial Adviser and close confidant of Chamberlain, minuted on 26 July: 'This is not my idea of a basis for a genial conversation – it suggests an undercurrent of annoyance which, even if we feel it, should not be displayed tomorrow.'[22]

At the meeting Chamberlain followed Wilson's rather than the Foreign Office's advice. He concentrated on establishing his goodwill towards Italy, and to that end purloined Eden's idea of a personal message to Mussolini. As he wrote to his sister, Hilda:

> My interview with Grandi seems to have made a good impression in Italy and I see they have now 'revealed' that I sent a personal letter to Mussolini. I made it appear that it was a spontaneous idea arising out of the conversation but of course I had made up my mind to do it beforehand. But I thought it would make a better impression if Grandi could report that I had sat down and written it in his presence without any consultation with anyone else and I hear that Grandi himself was delighted and reported that Italy and England had been divorced for two years but were now going to be remarried! I believe the double policy of rearmament and better relations with Germany and Italy will carry us safely through the danger period, if only the Foreign Office will play up. I see indications that they are inclined to be jealous. . .

Later, after Eden's resignation in February 1938, Chamberlain wrote in his diary that he 'did not show my letter to the Foreign Secretary, for I had the feeling that he would object to it'.[23] In common with many historians, Eden, in his memoirs, made a good deal of Chamberlain's reluctance to consult him. He contrasted his conduct unfavourably with that of the allegedly more considerate Churchill, though not, it is fair to add, with his own treatment of Selwyn Lloyd![24] The plain implication has hitherto been that Chamberlain thought that Eden would oppose the sending of a message on policy grounds. But the evidence already adduced shows that Eden had suggested that *he* send an unorthodox personal message. Thus Chamberlain may have decided that the message would come more appropriately from him, since Mussolini was also a Prime Minister, but avoided consulting Eden in advance lest the latter find a pretext for objecting that would in practice be a cloak for offended *amour propre*. Indeed it is no secret that Eden was thought by some of his contemporaries to be unusually touchy and even somewhat conceited. For example, Hankey wrote, on 21 November 1937, that 'at bottom he is vain and doesn't like anyone else to get any credit in Foreign Affairs'.[25] Possibly, then, some similar thought rather than consciousness of a major policy divergence caused Chamberlain to send his message to Mussolini without consultation. Moreover, as Eden made no complaint at the time but only in retrospect, it is clear that too much has in any case been made of the significance of Chamberlain's alleged delinquency concerning this incident.

During August further evidence emerged that Eden was likely to make difficulties about opening serious negotiations with Italy. Spending much of the month on holiday on the Solent, Eden left day-to-day control of the Foreign Office in the hands of Halifax, to whom it fell to supervise the drawing up of plans for early conversations with Rome. On 18 August Halifax journeyed to the Solent to seek the Foreign Secretary's views on the resulting detail. The following day Halifax sent Chamberlain a letter explaining that he had found Eden, as he had expected, 'rather apprehensive about the procedure proposed in the long office discussion'. He continued:

The principal heads of his anxiety might, I think, be summarized thus:

(1) He was very sensitive on the point of our appearing to make recognition of the Italian conquest part of a bargain against advantages that we hoped to receive for ourselves.

(2) He was dubious about the value that we should be likely to get in return and feared that having once given Mussolini the thing he principally wanted, our relations would in a short time, with Spain and other complicating factors still on our flank, be no better than they had proved to be after the Gentleman's Agreement of a few months ago.

Eden 'recognized, however, that having reached the point at which we now stood it was not possible to stand still'. He therefore agreed to negotiations in principle but suggested such stringent conditions that Halifax recommended to Chamberlain that the matter be postponed until after the meeting of the League Assembly at which Abyssinia's status might be considered.[26] After a meeting with Eden and Halifax, Chamberlain agreed to this course but hoped that the delay involved would be minimal. When, therefore, Eden returned to the Foreign Office towards the end of August a precarious harmony with the Prime Minister still existed. But Chamberlain had already been given reason for irritation at temporizing tactics which became more striking as each month passed. More than a year later, after Munich, he was to reject the idea of restoring Eden to office on the grounds that 'he would do what he did before, always agree in theory, but always disagree in practice'. And Hankey wrote in February 1938 that Eden was 'always chopping and changing, blowing hot one day, cold the next', especially concerning Italy.[27]

If Chamberlain and Hankey were justified in later concluding that Eden was not consistently sincere in desiring negotiations with Rome, it may be presumed that he was delighted at a series of French feelers made between 26 and 30 August. Foreign Minister Delbos suggested cooperation against submarine activity off Spain, which had led to a number of neutral merchant vessels being sunk. The perpetrators were described as 'unknown' but few had any doubt that Italy was responsible. (In Paris the Boulevard des Italiens became known as the Boulevard des Inconnus.) Eden now seized on the opportunity presented by Delbos to press his own case for a robust approach towards Rome and by implication for a further delay in *de jure* recognition of the conquest of Abyssinia. He was no doubt bolstered in this resolve by a memorandum dated 30 August from Cranborne, his closest ministerial confidant: 'I was in favour of granting *de jure* recognition. I now tend to be against it. Mussolini's motives are too transparently dishonest ... the advantages likely to accrue do not seem likely to outweigh the odium we shall incur.'[28]

The Prime Minister was on holiday in Scotland when the French messages on piracy were received. Eden demanded his early return to London. Chamberlain's Private Secretary, Osmund Cleverly, deplored this attempt to disturb a well-earned rest and with surprising frankness for a civil servant of the period wrote to his chief on 31 August that he did not judge an early meeting necessary and that 'Mr Eden was in an excitable mood.'[29] This patronizing reference to the Foreign Secretary suggests that Cleverly may have already had conversations with Chamberlain encouraging him to believe that such a description would not be resented by the Prime Minister. The outcome was that Chamberlain declined to return until 7 September but meanwhile contacted Eden on the telephone. Alarmed by talk of submarine activity, the Prime Minister yielded to Eden's desire to concert with the French and was still sufficiently open-minded to say that 'Mussolini must not think he had a free hand to do what he liked just because we had made some friendly remarks to him.'[30]

The way was thus open for Eden to promote with Delbos an international conference to consider the piracy in the Mediterranean. This duly convened on 10 September. So eager was Eden to secure the holding of this anti-Italian gathering that he gave ground to the French on some points of procedure and, in particular, on the matter of which powers should be invited. He wished to confine attendance to Mediterranean powers and, above all, to exclude the Soviet Union – more evidence of his continuing private hostility to Moscow. But this was unacceptable to the French and Eden reluctantly capitulated. As a result both Italy and Germany refused to attend the Nyon Conference; hence, unlike the Non-Intervention Committee, it assumed a one-sided anti-Franco and anti-Italian character. It was precisely this kind of division of Europe into ideologically opposed blocs that Chamberlain feared. On this occasion, however, he had allowed the initiative to be seized by Eden. The Foreign Secretary now forged with Delbos a plan for their two countries to patrol the Mediterranean in order to ensure that submarines should only proceed on the surface of the Mediterranean and to counter-attack any molesters of neutral shipping.[31]

The Nyon Agreement was undoubtedly a severe warning to Mussolini, who henceforth proceeded with greater circumspection regarding piracy. Chamberlain congratulated Eden on his achievement. At the same time he privately told his sister, Ida, of his concern about the effect on the Italians of the Nyon Agreement which 'fairly wrings their withers'. 'It would be amusing,' he added, 'if it were not also so dangerous.' But Anglo-Italian relations had 'gone right back'. Chamberlain was not particularly critical of Eden. He wrote: 'Anthony has I am sure done his best to keep Italy quiet though he has never really believed in Mussolini's sincerity but the Italians have been just as difficult as could be and at the moment I don't know what we can do to improve the situation.' To his other sister, Hilda, he had earlier written that while he was unhappy about the Foreign Office as a whole he had found Eden 'awfully good in accepting my suggestions without grumbling'.[32]

On 1 November Eden made another anti-Italian move without consulting Chamberlain. The Foreign Secretary took the opportunity, in the course of a speech to the House of Commons, to reply to some recent blustering by Mussolini:

> I have noted of late a tendency to use as part of the diplomatic machinery methods which are highly dangerous. There is an inclination to threaten, to issue orders from the house-tops, to proclaim what is virtually an ultimatum and call it peace. Such methods will never have any response here. Such orders will never be obeyed by the British public. We are ready enough to discuss difficulties and issues with those concerned, but we are not prepared to stand and deliver at anyone's command.[33]

Chamberlain had sent a message beforehand that he hoped Eden 'would say nothing to upset the dictators' but J. P. L. Thomas, the Foreign Secretary's Parliamentary Private Secretary, had failed to deliver it. Chamberlain was thus predictably vexed as he confided to his sister, Hilda:

> All my plans seem to be going agley at the moment. Anthony's speech in the House of Commons was a great personal triumph for him but it contained some unfortunate passages, from my point of view, and shows again a characteristic of the Foreign Office mind which I have frequently noticed before. They never can keep the major objects of foreign policy in mind, with the result that they make obstructions for themselves by endeavouring to give smart answers to some provocative foreign statement. On this occasion Mussolini had been more than usually insolent with his offensive remarks about 'bleating democracies' and his outrageous allusion to the Colonies. But Anthony should never have been provoked into a retort which throws Germans and Italians together in self-defence, when our policy is so obviously to try to divide them. It was perhaps fortunate that Grandi was lunching with us next day and I found an opportunity of whispering a few words into his ear to show my attitude was unchanged.[34]

Meanwhile a new opportunity had arisen to sound out Hitler: Halifax, in his capacity as a Master of Foxhounds, had been invited to visit Germany. Chamberlain explained to his sister, Hilda:

> A little while ago Halifax told me that he had received an invitation to attend an International Sporting Exhibition in Berlin in connection with which there were to

be 'hunting' expeditions in the forest ... As one form of hunting was to shoot foxes Edward was much amused and sent on the invitation to Anthony saying that he was going to select that particular kind of sport for his day out. It seems, however, to have occurred to him that it might possibly be desirable to take it more seriously so he had a talk with Anthony and Van, at which the former said he would be 'quite happy' if he went while the latter strongly argued that he should not go as he would certainly be asked awkward questions. When Edward told me all this I was really horrified. I said another opportunity to be thrown away. I can't allow that. And I appointed a meeting with Edward and Anthony and it is now fixed that Edward will go ... But really, that FO! I am only waiting my opportunity to stir it up with a long pole.[35]

What this letter did not anticipate was that Eden, after raising no initial objections, would have second thoughts and would make many difficulties. While abroad in Brussels Eden was informed on 11 November that information about the projected Halifax visit had leaked into the press. Still more serious, in his view, was the news that Hitler would not come to Berlin for a meeting but would require the Lord Privy Seal to visit Berchtesgaden. Eden was understandably nettled. Even so he may have given too much attention to his Foreign Office 'hawks', Harvey and Thomas, who were with him in Brussels. The extreme views of Harvey may be gauged from this extract from his diary for the day in question:

We have (Malcolm MacDonald, Cadogan, Jim Thomas and I) discussed it with A.E., who finally and reluctantly agreed to the visit taking place in these circumstances, but said that he must have time to discuss with the PM and H. on his return what latter is going to say to Hitler. Owing to leakage, to have refused now and so stopped visit would have caused a fresh German grievance and made more bad blood just at the moment when we are anxious to make a fresh start with Germany. Nevertheless, the precipitancy with which the PM and Halifax have pressed on with this visit in A.E.'s absence, knowing that A.E. did not favour it, shows shocking lack of solidarity and even of common decent behaviour. A wobble of this kind following A.E.'s firm speech last week may undo all the good then done.[36]

Chamberlain and Halifax scarcely deserved such strictures for the Lord President had undoubtedly sought and obtained Eden's initial consent in principle. Eden, however, was probably 'bounced' by his aides into trying to downgrade the Halifax visit in a fashion that was bound to irritate Chamberlain. For example, it was somewhat provocative to use Cranborne, possibly the most abrasive member of the Government, as a channel of communication to Chamberlain. No doubt Cranborne in London relayed the Foreign Secretary's reservations about the Halifax visit in the most uncompromising tone. Then, after his return to London, Eden completely lost his temper after another newspaper leakage. Harvey's diary for 16 November is eloquent:

This morning's newspapers (especially *Times* and *Daily Telegraph*) contained the most exaggerated account of scope of Halifax visit . . . A.E. (who had been in bed with slight 'flu since Monday) was extremely annoyed and got up to come down to FO to see Halifax at 11.30. H. was himself much worried at press accounts and felt it made his visit extremely difficult owing to the great expectations which had been aroused. A.E.'s interview with the PM, as he put it, couldn't have gone worse, although the Prime Minister also deplored exaggerated press accounts and undertook to see the Press himself and correct them. The PM also expressed annoyance at the Brussels Conference. A.E., who was evidently fairly roused, also spoke of slowness and lack of imagination shown in rearmament by colleagues and their departments. PM for his part advised A.E. to go back to bed and take an aspirin![37]

Later in the day an unrepentant Eden wrote to the Prime Minister:

. . . When I spoke to Edward [Halifax] this morning, I found him equally anxious to reduce the significance of the visit in the Press as much as possible. I am sure that this is indeed imperative if we are not to run risks of a serious setback owing to exaggerated expectations. While I have always thought that there were advantages in informal contact such as this, the risks inevitably become greater when the visit does not take place in Berlin and when there is no very definite invitation to Berchtesgarden. If on top of these risks the press magnifies the affair to the proportions of anything in the nature of a negotiation, we run grave danger of doing more harm than good.

I am sorry if you thought me 'feverish' on the subject of rearmament this morning but I do feel we are passing through a most critical period when our own rearmament may prove the decisive factor. Papers like that submitted by the Air Ministry recently are, therefore, of profound significance for they show that, despite comforting speeches, we are not in truth getting stronger vis-à-vis Germany at least.

This was the first major personal quarrel between Eden and Chamberlain. It was certainly more serious than the earlier incident about the Prime Minister's personal telegram to Mussolini, whose significance Eden and many historians subsequently exaggerated. Why did Eden lose his temper? There can be little doubt that he had been subject to much pressure from the Cranborne–Harvey–Thomas coterie. And there is no reason to doubt that he genuinely resented the excessive build-up of Halifax and his mission. But perhaps most important was his sensitivity to the supposed machinations of the press and those with access to it – something which was to be a recurring feature of his whole political career. Yet for whatever reason he had allowed Chamberlain, over a relatively trivial matter, to see too much of the tempestuous side of his character which was so at odds with his suave public image. The Prime Minister had himself too authoritarian and too brittle a personality easily to overlook being the subject of such treatment and may thereafter have been resolved to make fewer allowances in future on the grounds that Eden was surrounded by 'misguided' advisers. It was on this same day, 16 November, that Eden wrote a Foreign Office minute that has led one historian to conclude that this was the point at which he became 'really committed to a collision course' with Chamberlain over Italy. Vansittart and Sargent had written minutes urging rapid steps to dissuade Mussolini from moving closer into alignment with Berlin. But Cranborne now took the view that *de jure* recognition of the conquest of Abyssinia constituted too high a price to pay:

> Are we willing to grant it? Will British public opinion allow us to grant it? Will the small Mediterranean Powers consider us justified in granting it? Only if we have reason to suppose that there is some change of heart in Italy. But I can see none – Italian troops remain in Spain – Italian pronouncements, and especially the pronouncements inspired by Signor Mussolini himself, remain as truculent and as deliberately offensive to Great Britain as ever. In such circumstances I believe it would be a political blunder of the first water to grant recognition of the annexation of Abyssinia...

Eden, reversing the line he had taken earlier in the year, minuted: 'I am in entire agreement with Lord Cranborne's minutes.'[38] Yet he did not inform Chamberlain that this was now his view and indeed, as will be seen, took the opposite line with the French later in the month. It may be, therefore, that the minute of 16 November was written in the heat of the moment and even now did not represent a settled conviction. But 16 November was probably a decisive turning-point all the same. For it was probably the day when Eden's personal relationship with Chamberlain underwent a transformation which thereafter ensured that policy differences were likely to assume magnified significance. Oddly enough, Halifax's visit to Germany, rather than the Italian issue, had served as the catalyst for their probably vital altercation.

In the short term, however, both men made an effort to repair their relationship. An exchange of letters couched in friendly terms was followed on 23 November by what even Harvey called a 'satisfactory talk'. Halifax's visit to Hitler had meanwhile taken place on 19 November. It had no remarkable results, though Eden subsequently came to believe that Halifax had not been sufficiently vigorous in discouraging Hitler from adventures in east-central Europe. Possibly this later reflection was related to his not having received at the time as full an account from Halifax as he should have had.[39] But it must also be recognized that Eden had long preferred to appease Hitler in east-central Europe rather than with colonial restitution and that he at no point contemplated armed British resistance to a German *Anschluss* with Austria, however brought about.

The temporary improvement in Eden's relationship with Chamberlain was to reach its highest point on 29 and 30 November on the occasion of a visit to London of the French Premier, Camille Chautemps and his Foreign Minister, Delbos. But it was Eden, not Chamberlain, whose attitude had once again modified. The Foreign Secretary played a full part in persuading the French not to object to the opening of direct British negotiations with both Italy and Germany. He also left the French with the impression that he was in complete harmony with Chamberlain in the detailed discussions which centred primarily on Germany. Both British leaders made it clear that they would not underwrite any French actions in east-central Europe. Their French opposite numbers agreed that Austria would in the last resort have to be abandoned to her fate. But concerning Czechoslovakia the French were adamant that their treaty commitments would be honoured. Chamberlain asserted that 'there was a strong feeling that we ought not to become entangled in a war on account of Czechoslovakia, which was a long way off and with which we had not a great deal in common'. Eden did not contradict this statement which so remarkably anticipated Chamberlain's famous words in September 1938 about 'a far-away country'. Instead the Foreign Secretary urged that the Sudeten German grievances should be redressed while adding that 'there can be no question of our asking France to reconsider her obligations, or our asking her not to carry them out, nor, indeed of our failing to fulfil our own'.[40] More discussions followed on colonial restitution, about which Eden had long temporized both within the Foreign Office and at Cabinet. Now he put up no resistance as Chamberlain explored with Chautemps the basis of an extensive redrawing of the map of Africa for possible use in the context of a general settlement with Germany. After the visit, on 1 December, Eden told his Cabinet colleagues that 'the conversations had enabled them to take an indispensible first step in the direction of some dealings with Germany over colonies and the views of the two Governments had proved to be identical'. Eden also expressed pleasure that the French Ministers did not wish to join a 'left bloc' in Europe nor 'to be in any way under Russian influence'. This echoed what Chamberlain wrote privately about Chautemps: 'I myself liked the little man very much ... He did not conceal his dislike for Soviet Russia and it was evident that his sympathies were with the right rather than the left wing of the Front Populaire.'[41]

Eden and Chamberlain found themselves at odds again, however, at a meeting of the CID on 2 December. Before them was a memorandum from the Foreign Secretary, dated 26 November 1937, on the subject of an earlier paper from the Chiefs of Staff who had advocated general appeasement of the dictatorships and, in particular, speedy diplomatic action to reduce the number of potential enemies. Eden's memorandum set forth the clearest statement he was ever to make while Foreign Secretary of the philosophy which lay behind his distinctive approach to foreign policy. Essentially he favoured what he called 'unheroic cunctation', which Simon not unfairly later defined as 'marking time'. Others have variously defined it as 'keeping the dictators guessing', 'supine delay', 'carping hesitation' or as 'so unconstructive as to leave no alternative but a stalemate followed by war'. Eden wrote:

> It would ... be a mistake to try to detach any one member of the German–Italian–Japanese bloc by offers of support or acquiescence in the fulfilment of their aims. The aims of all three are in varying degrees inimical to British interests and a surrender to one might well be the signal for further concerted action on the part of all three powers.

So pessimistic was Eden that he wrote of tolerating, 'for the time being at any rate, the present state of armed truce' while simultaneously acquiescing 'in more than one *fait accompli*'. Acquiescence after the event was thus obviously more acceptable to Eden than acquiescence in advance: '... it would be ... a mistake ... to risk opening the floodgates of territorial change by open and express acquiescence, in German, Italian or Japanese expansion before it occurs'.[42]

In effect, then, both Eden and Chamberlain recognized that they might be unable to prevent at least intermittent expansion by the dictators. Eden was inclined to pursue a policy of keeping them guessing as to British intentions and then remaining inactive in many cases where a *fait accompli* actually occurred. Chamberlain, by contrast, saw this as too close to a policy of bluff for comfort, especially in the complex European theatre. He believed that it was desirable to anticipate coups and, if possible, arrange for changes to be carried through by civilized negotiations in cases where Great Britain did not intend to have recourse to armed force. He saw this to be of particular importance in Europe because of the risk that otherwise France would be compelled by her public opinion to offer unilateral resistance. He believed, moreover, in the possibility that Mussolini and maybe also Hitler might have limited objectives which could in due course be fully met by peaceful procedures.

The divergences between Eden and Chamberlain were in the short run papered over. Once again it was Eden who wavered. Under pressure from his colleagues in the CID meeting, he conceded that Great Britain 'should make every possible effort to come to terms with each or all of our potential enemies, but not by conduct which would lose us our friends, both actual and potential'. Chamberlain seized on these remarks to devalue Eden's more forthright memorandum: the Prime Minister summed up by stating that the *oral* statement of the Foreign Secretary 'took proper account of the situation'. For his part Chamberlain made a small gesture to Eden by repudiating 'methods that would shame us in the eyes of the world' but he nevertheless called for 'active diplomacy'. Incidentally, the British authorities have capriciously chosen to deny historians access to this particular item in the collection of CID minutes held at the Public Record Office.

Fortunately, their efficiency is as questionable as their judgement, for a copy of the forbidden minutes is available in the Foreign Office records.[43]

How wide, then, was the gulf between Eden and Chamberlain at this stage? In practice it was still relatively narrow. For Eden had shown that he was prepared to go a long way to get agreement with Germany. And on 9 January the Foreign Secretary wrote to Chamberlain that he considered an agreement with Germany 'might have a reasonable life'.[44] Again, the two men differed little concerning Japan. Ironically Chamberlain no less than Eden now saw little hope of appeasing Japan and accordingly 'unheroic cunctation' rather than 'active diplomacy' prevailed vis-à-vis Tokyo.[45] Only concerning Italy were their differences of great practical importance – because Eden believed, at least intermittently, that recognition of the conquest of Abyssinia would indeed 'shame us in the eyes of the world' and, perhaps more important, in the eyes of centre opinion at home. Chamberlain, already at the top and nearing seventy, cared little for the susceptibilities of those whom he considered sentimentalists. For him the main domestic constraint lay in the trade unions whose hostility to too rapid rearmament and conscription could not in his view be safely ignored.

Defence policy in general was also to be a cause of occasional friction between Eden and Chamberlain. Yet here again the Foreign Secretary was at times teasingly imprecise and vacillating. He certainly favoured rearmament in principle but by 1937-8 this was common ground among members of the National Government. The arguments thus related to priorities and to detail. The policy which emerged in this period was largely the work of Chamberlain, Simon and Sir Thomas Inskip, the Minister for Coordination of Defence. They accepted three premises which Eden was reluctant to endorse. First, they saw a considerable risk of being simultaneously faced with war against Germany, Italy and Japan. Secondly, they had no confidence in Great Britain being able to defeat such a combination. Thirdly, they were in any case forced to recognize that victory against Germany, whether or not she had allies, was unlikely to be swift. This third premise led to the judgement that economic and financial strength over a long period would be of decisive importance and that accordingly rearmament in peacetime should not be pursued with such vigour as to undermine Great Britain's still precarious economy. It flowed from this logic that there must be limitation on the pace of rearmament and hence priorities must be defined both between the Services and within them. During 1937 and 1938 a series of decisions was taken which in effect further downgraded the army relative to the other two Services. This involved a cut in contingent commitments – in practice the ruling out of the dispatch of a major expeditionary or field force to the Western Front. Another major shift came in the air force: the construction of defensive fighters was to have priority over bombers. This reduced the credibility of the air deterrent to aggression but the fighters were nevertheless of great. even decisive, value in the Battle of Britain.

Eden was uneasy about these developments. He doubted, for example. whether there was much risk of a simultaneous war with three Great Powers. As late as 31 January, 1938 he wrote to Chamberlain that he considered it very unlikely that the German–Italian–Japanese bloc would 'hold together so strongly as to come into a war against us'. This view is all the more remarkable in the light of his pessimism about the prospects for 'positive diplomacy' and the gloomy assumptions involved in 'unheroic cunctation'. Secondly, he argued on at least one occasion, in a letter to Chamberlain of 9 September 1937. that even in the worst case Great Britain's strength, particularly at sea, was relatively much greater than in 1914. to which Chamberlain retorted that 'the proposition that our foreign policy must be, if not dictated, at least limited by the state of the National Defence remains true'.[46] Such optimism by Eden may have underlain his periodic resistance to negotiations with the dictators and especially Italy. It may also have led him to describe the Chiefs of Staff as 'defeatist' and to have sought to dismiss their clamour for the use of 'positive diplomacy' to reduce the number of potential enemies as a rationalization of their desire. as he put it to Chamberlain in a letter dated 31 January 1938. 'to clamber on the band wagon with the dictators, even though the process meant parting company with France and estranging our relations with the United States'. He went on in the same letter to stress his confidence in France as an ally: 'I believe, moreover, that there is a tendency among some of our colleagues to underestimate the strength of France ... I am myself convinced ... that the French Army is absolutely sound ...'[47]

Eden also had reservations on points of detail. These were perhaps best expressed on 22 December at a Cabinet discussion of Inskip's seminal memorandum, 'Report on Defence Expenditure in Future Years'. The Foreign Secretary opposed the defensive emphasis of some of his proposals. He criticized the switch from bombers to fighters. He further disapproved of the degree to which the limited liability doctrine was embraced. He had 'some apprehension as to the stated inability to assist allies on land'. questioning whether the Maginot Line gave an absolute guarantee that an enemy could not take the Channel ports – a prescient line but not perhaps entirely consistent with his not so prescient view about the soundness of the French army. While not in the last resort prepared to resist Inskip's order of priority, he urged that France be informed and talks held to consider their mutual defence problems. Later, in February 1938. he had a stiff and largely successful contest with the Chiefs of Staff on this last issue – probably in retrospect the most creditable of his interventions in the area of defence policy. The force of all this criticism was much reduced, however, by Eden conceding that he found the general character of Inskip's long-term approach, with its stress on economic strength, 'irresistible'. Hence later the Cabinet approved the whole memorandum without substantial amendment. One writer has commented: 'There might have been a case for [Eden] resigning over defence limitation and the Chamberlain proposal for reducing air striking power ...'[48] But it seems unlikely that such a course could have been seriously entertained by the Foreign Secretary and his advisers. First, he had not developed a sufficiently distinctive line on defence. Secondly, and more important, his natural base of support in the nation, the liberal centre, would not have been enthused by a resignation on either the principles or the details of defence policy.

A case for threatening resignation had indeed already been put in Eden's mind by Harvey as early as 7 November 1937, but it rested on the broad issue of the conduct of foreign policy: 'You are the only Foreign Secretary in sight. If you left the Cabinet the Government would fall. The Government is living on your reputation; you are not only entitled to but you are able to impose your terms.'[49] At the turn of the year, however, Eden was still apparently unprepared to offer a central challenge to his colleagues. After capitulating on the Inskip defence policy, he indicated to Chamberlain that despite misgivings he was willing in principle to enter into talks with Italy. Indeed, before leaving for a holiday on the French Riviera, he caused his officials to draw up two alternative approaches to such negotiations. Moreover, he twice wrote to Chamberlain in surprisingly friendly terms. On 31 December he thanked the Prime Minister 'for your unvarying kindness and help to me this year'. 'I really find it hard,' he continued, 'to express how much I have appreciated your readiness at all times to listen to my problems and help in their solution, despite your many other preoccupations.' On 9 January 1938 he wrote:

> I do hope that you will never for an instant feel that any interest you take in foreign affairs, however close, could ever be resented by me. I know, of course, that there will always be some who will seek to pretend that the Foreign Secretary has had his nose put out of joint, but this is of no account beside the very real gain of close collaboration between Foreign Secretary and Prime Minister which, I am sure, is the only way that foreign affairs can be run in our country.[50]

Within days, however, Chamberlain took an interest in foreign affairs in such a way as to arouse Eden's resentment as never before. This was on the occasion of President Franklin D. Roosevelt's secret inquiry of Chamberlain, received in London on 12 January, about the desirability of his calling together the whole Diplomatic Corps in Washington to urge governments to work out principles designed to improve international relations. The President required a positive reaction from London by 17 January as a precondition. Chamberlain did not welcome this vague proposal, since he believed it would further delay the serious bilateral negotiations he hoped to enter into with both Italy and Germany. He also feared that Roosevelt's reference to 'removing such inequities as may exist by reasons of [the] nature of certain settlements reached at [the] termination of [the] great war' would 'encourage Germany to pitch her colonial claims very high indeed'. He accordingly replied to Roosevelt suggesting that he withhold his initiative for the present. As the Prime Minister recorded in his diary:

> I was in a dilemma. The plan appeared to me fantastic and likely to excite the derision of Germany and Italy. They might even use it to postpone conversations with us as if we were associated with it they would see in it another attempt on the part of the democratic bloc to put the dictators in the wrong. There was no time to consult Anthony for in view of the secrecy on which Roosevelt insisted in emphatic terms I did not dare to telephone. Therefore after consultation with H. Wilson and Cadogan I sent a reply deprecating immediate publication just when we were about to enter on conversations with Germany and Italy and in very guarded terms indicated a possibly hostile reception. This produced a somewhat sulky acquiescence in postponement and some strongly worded warnings against shocking public opinion by giving de jure to Italy.[51]

Eden was summoned back to London on Cadogan's initiative, but owing to the impossibility of using the telephone and to his missing a messenger at Marseilles, he did not have any notion of the Roosevelt–Chamberlain exchange until met by Cadogan and Harvey at Folkestone on 15 January. The Foreign Secretary was justifiably piqued to learn of the Prime Minister's decision to send a reply as early as 13 January when the deadline, on Eden's arrival, was still two days away, namely the 17th. Chamberlain's somewhat unconvincing excuse to Cadogan for deciding that it was not possible to await Eden's return was that he had desired to allow time for a further message from Roosevelt before the deadline expired.[52] But Eden was in any case angered by the rejection of the Roosevelt initiative, whose value he seems greatly to have exaggerated.

Eden had for some months been trying to establish Anglo-American cooperation in the Far East. In July 1937 the so-called Marco Polo Bridge incident had marked a resumption of conflict between Japan and China, which continued with varying intensity throughout the year. It was rapidly recognized that Japan was bent on conquest and that verbal representations from the West would be worthless. Yet nobody in the British Government favoured the unilateral imposition of sanctions of any kind. But had the British any possible collaborators? Since the Chiefs of Staff were opposed to cooperation with the Soviet Union, as that might 'result in the spread of some form of communism through China and the establishment of Soviet influence up to the borders of India and Burma', only the United States was taken seriously as a possible partner for sanctions.[53] Eden tried unceasingly to interest the Americans in common action. But they were elusive, partly because those like Norman Davis who wanted to fall in with Eden's requests underrated the Congressional constraints upon Roosevelt. The fact that the immediate Japanese threat seemed to be directed primarily at British interests in Shanghai rather than any American equivalents only strengthened the case of the isolationists in Washington. Neither Roosevelt's famous 'Quarantine' speech of 7 October 1937 nor American participation in a subsequent conference held in Brussels nor the sinking of the American *Panay* made any serious difference. By this time Eden was virtually alone in the Foreign Office and in the Cabinet in thinking that the Americans were in the last resort likely to take any decisive step. On 9 January 1938, for example, he informed Cadogan that in his view it was unlikely that the United States 'would sit with folded hands and watch [the] British Empire in jeopardy if it really came to that'.[54] But Eden was able to persuade his sceptical Cabinet colleagues to allow him to pursue the Americans by using the argument 'that it was important to avoid putting the American Government in a position to say they could have cleared up the situation but for our unwillingness'. The parallel with Stimson's criticism of Simon over Manchuria made this line more than usually persuasive, not least to political survivors from the early period. At the same time Eden was careful to stress that he did not want the League of Nations involved and that he recognized the futility of the partial sanctions employed against Italy. Eden had told the Cabinet on 13 October 1937: 'He himself would never agree to the imposition of sanctions without the agreement of the United States of America and the other signatories of the China Treaty to support those sanctions by the use of force if need be.'[55]

By the end of 1937 Eden was still hoping desperately for a joint Anglo-American naval demonstration and welcomed Roosevelt's dispatch of Royal E. Ingersoll of the US navy to London for informal talks on possible contingencies. On 9 January 1938 Eden even wrote to Chamberlain of his hopes 'of effectively asserting white race authority in the Far East'.[56] Chamberlain tolerated Eden's efforts, for he had no rooted objections if, against all his expectations, the Americans responded positively. But he would not have done so if he had not by 1937 essentially come to share Eden's view that the only alternative was 'unheroic cunctation' against a remorseless and probably unappeaseable Tokyo. Eden's optimism and Chamberlain's pessimism about the United States's ultimate intentions thus led to no serious divergence between them about British Far Eastern policy *per se*.

Their respective assessments mattered much more, however, when in January 1938, Roosevelt launched his vague appeal principally affecting not the Far East but Europe. Here Chamberlain did believe that appeasement was both possible and desirable and he was not willing to put it at risk for what he considered to be an extremely remote chance that the United

States would ever intervene with more than words. Eden took the opposite view. On the evidence available both at the time and subsequently there seems to be much to be said for Chamberlain's assessment of the American position: 'It is always best and safest to count on nothing from the Americans...'[57] By contrast it is difficult to see much merit in the case later argued both by Eden and Churchill, namely that Roosevelt's initiative represented a last chance to bring the Americans into the European equation and thus avert war. The fact is that Churchill and Eden, who both gambled heavily between 1937 and 1941 on the American unwillingness to see Great Britain sink, were only substantially 'vindicated' by courtesy of Hitler, who gratuitously declared war on the United States in December 1941. This was undoubtedly Hitler's greatest service to the cause of liberal democracy in Europe both in the short-term and in the longer run. But it was not a move that either Eden or Churchill could possibly have anticipated and without it their judgement on the Americans would have been widely seen to have been less acute than Chamberlain's. For both Eden and Churchill expected to receive from the Americans direct military assistance, particularly in 1940, going far beyond what was actually forthcoming, namely such inadequate, inequitable and self-serving gestures as Roosevelt's destroyers-bases exchange.

Indeed Eden's case for giving priority over all other considerations to Roosevelt's vague initiative in January 1938 was of such an exaggerated character that it may well have led Chamberlain to wonder whether his Foreign Secretary was not using it as an excuse, as was his wont, to delay once more the opening of talks with Italy. Certainly in this context Eden made the maximum possible use of Roosevelt's not particularly considered reference to *de jure* recognition of the conquest of Abyssinia. This was made clear at a meeting at Chequers between Chamberlain and Eden on 16 January, the day following the Foreign Secretary's return from France. Chamberlain's diary is eloquent on that meeting and its sequence:

... Anthony got back from France and hurried to Chequers. He did not like my reply and without consulting me sent a fresh wire to R. Lindsay in Washington saying I had not exactly meant what I said. He proposed to me that we should at once call off the idea of Italian conversations lest we should offend USA. But I objected and as we could not agree I summoned the Foreign Affairs Committee of the Cabinet and laid the position before them. As a result we agreed on a compromise reply in which we elucidated our position and made it clear that *de jure* was only to be given as a factor in general appeasement. Subsequent dispatches from Lindsay showed that this had the effect desired by me. The course proposed entirely met the President's views and there was no reason why we should not proceed. During the discussions on the matter A. had suggested resignation but I had pointed out the impossibility of doing this since Roosevelt had enjoined complete secrecy upon us.[58]

Some comments on this account are in order. First, the Foreign Affairs

Committee and Chamberlain in effect surrendered to Eden rather than 'agreed on a compromise' in the matter of Roosevelt's initiative and this would have gone ahead if the President had not changed his mind for reasons which are still obscure. On the other hand, Chamberlain correctly saw that Eden had lost his chance of halting the talks with Mussolini with the news from Sir Ronald Lindsay, the British Ambassador in Washington, that according to Sumner Welles, the Under-Secretary of State, the 'statement of conditions in which it is intended to grant recognition (in the Prime Minister's message of January 22nd) substantially meets the point made by the President'. Lindsay continued: 'My last words as I left were "then I assume my Government may go ahead with their conversations with Rome and Berlin" and his (Welles's) answer was "I can think of no reason whatever why they should not do so".'[59] Chamberlain might thus have expected that this message would lead Eden to drop his opposition to talks with Italy. But Roosevelt's attitude on Abyssinia probably weighed less with Eden than he had initially contended in January 1938. It has been seen, for example, that in the spring of 1937 the Foreign Secretary had taken the lead in preparing the Dominions for recognition of the Italian conquest. Yet he had been aware of Roosevelt's general hostility towards recognition of conquests since at least the previous November.[60] Now in February 1938, with Roosevelt apparently after all not opposed to the approach to Italy, Eden was not for long to be deflected from pursuing his obstructionist course.

Before the Italian issue came to a head, however, the question of colonial restitution to Germany assumed new importance. On 24 January a meeting of the Foreign Affairs Committee heard details of Chamberlain's plan for a new international colonial zone to cover much of central Africa. In its administration Germany would be given a prominent but not an exclusive rôle. Eden argued that the idea was not being sufficiently tied to a general settlement with Germany. Since Chamberlain had all along stressed that this link was vital, Eden's line suggested captiousness or inattention. Finally, however, he appeared to agree with Chamberlain that the colonial plan should be in 'the forefront' of an immediate approach to Germany. Sir Nevile Henderson, the British Ambassador in Berlin and incidentally an Eden appointee, was summoned to the next meeting of the Foreign Affairs Committee on 3 February to discuss the matter in greater detail. Ironically, it fell to Eden to draw up Henderson's instructions in the last week before his resignation. The Foreign Secretary telegraphed that 'As regards the colonial question, you might say that you had found [in London] a real disposition to study this question in all its bearings and to make progress if possible' and that he should hint at 'a new regime of colonial administration' in unspecified areas of Africa. Eden added that the French were to be told only after the approach to Germany had been made – a strange line in the light of the cordial meeting with French Ministers less than three months before. Referring to these developments concerning Germany, Chamberlain wrote in his diary, shortly after Eden's resignation, that 'there was no criticism of all this by the Foreign Secretary though he did not make any constructive contribution'. Yet he concluded in a letter written at much the same time that 'I have gradually arrived at the conclusion that at bottom Anthony did not want to talk either with Hitler or Mussolini'. This view is, however, not entirely consistent with the evidence. More judicious may be the verdict of one historian: 'So long as relations with Germany were the chief preoccupation, Eden was able to keep pace with the Prime Minister.' This is supported of course by the exclusive stress placed on Italy in Eden's various resignation statements. Moreover as late as 21 January he had agreed, against Vansittart's wishes, to Hermann Göring being invited to Liverpool to attend the Grand National.[61]

The fact was that Eden had an unalterable bias only against Mussolini and was, moreover, conscious of it. As Harvey recorded in his diary: 'He [Eden] told me when we lunched together on December 23rd that he always felt that he must be particularly careful to prevent his personal prejudices in regard to Musso from colouring his attitude too much. He said he regarded Muss as anti-Christ!' Ironically, Eden in his memoirs used the same terms in a disparaging reference to some of his colleagues in the pre-war National Government. 'Some,' he wrote, 'religious in their views, regarded communism as anti-Christ!' Eden, for his part, had now decided that in the last resort he preferred Stalin to Mussolini even though, as we have seen, he had hitherto been, particularly in private, much more anti-Soviet than his memoirs suggest. He also preferred Hitler to Mussolini at least until Munich. Geoffrey McDermott, formerly of the Foreign Office, wrote in the course of an intemperate polemic on Eden:

> The occasion of his resignation was not some great question of principle. It was a question of timing and methods limited to only one aspect of our foreign policy. As Vansittart remarked, it was not even the most important aspect. He considered, and rightly, that Italy was a minor front and that the main front remained Berlin.[62]

Against this endorsement of the Vansittart line, it must be stressed that most centre opinion in Great Britain at the beginning of 1938 shared Eden's assessment of Mussolini as more repugnant than either Hitler or Stalin. It had after all been the Duce, not Hitler or Stalin, who had decisively destroyed the League of Nations, whose creation had seemed to so many to justify the suffering in 'the War to end Wars'. In due course public opinion, faithfully accompanied by and to some extent led by Eden, belatedly turned against first Hitler and then Stalin. It evidently did not prove easy to focus on more than one anti-Christ at a time!

The final drama between Eden and Chamberlain came in February 1938.

After the defusing of the conflict between them over the Roosevelt initiative and the apparent acceptance by the President of the Prime Minister's case for *de jure* recognition, there appeared to be no further obstacles to talks with Rome. On 25 January Eden visited Paris and secured French acquiescence in principle to a general settlement with Rome. As he put it in his memoirs: 'Great Britain, I said, could only grant *de jure* recognition of the conquest of Abyssinia as part of a general settlement, which would include propaganda, Spain, the Italian garrison in Libya, the Red Sea and possibly some demilitarization in the Mediterranean itself.' Some of Eden's advisers, however, counselled him against granting *de jure* at all. Harvey wrote in his diary on 14 January: 'I talked to Bobbety [Cranborne] who was rather worried and feels that A.E. may have committed himself too far on the principle of *de jure* as a result of continuous and wearing discussions in Committee. I rather feel so too.' Cranborne, whose opposition to *de jure* recognition in the previous November has already been noted, followed up on 4 February with a memorandum for Eden which concluded:

To sum up; I do not think that an agreement with Italy involving *de jure* recognition is at the present time necessary: I do not think that it is desirable; and I think that it might easily be disastrous to the structure of peace that is being so laboriously built up. Let us proceed, as rapidly as may be, with our negotiations with Germany. Let us do all that is in our power to promote cooperation with the United States. It is in these directions that we must, I suggest, seek a solution to our difficulties.[63]

Eden did not on this occasion openly endorse this view but sent a copy to Chamberlain. Cadogan recorded in his diary, however, that this memorandum had impressed Eden. He continued:

Horace W. [Wilson] rings me up that PM wants A. [Eden] to fix a meeting with Grandi for Tuesday to begin conversations. A. now digs his toes in. This is all wrong – he has agreed in principle to talks with Musso, and nothing has happened to change situation fundamentally ... A. is silly on this question – he doesn't like the medicine, and makes no bones about it; but then he seems to agree to take it, and uses every excuse – clutches at it – to run out. This makes very bad impression.

But by 8 February Cadogan could write: 'A. [Eden] more hopeful of Italian conversations since his interview with Grandi ... Thinks he can get something on propaganda and Spain and so slide easily into "conversations". Maybe ... !'[64]

At this point Eden's hawkish advisers and maybe Eden himself had a stroke of luck. On 8 February Harvey wrote in his diary:

A.E. complained of the constant obstructiveness and indeed, double crossing of his colleagues. He feels that there is a really fundamental difference between him and the PM as to policy. He was particularly annoyed to hear from Perth [formerly Drummond] that Lady [Ivy] Chamberlain [widow of Sir Austen] had again been hobnobbing with Muss and [Galeazzo] Ciano [the Italian Foreign Minister], reading to them letters from the PM implying that we are passionately anxious for a settlement 'and negotiations are to begin in February'. He wrote to the PM objecting strongly to this and asking him to tell Lady Chamberlain not to engage in any further such conversations which could only confuse the position ... I told him I thought he must insist on getting his way on what he regarded as important or go ... Whenever he took a firm line, the Cabinet gave way because they couldn't face his resignation.

Chamberlain had not authorized his sister-in-law to show his letters to the Italians, though he should have realized that his letters would in any case have been likely to be opened and read by the Italian authorities. Yet Eden himself had apparently earlier given Ivy Chamberlain encouragement to 'hobnob' with leading Italians. She wrote to the Prime Minister on 16 December 1937:

... he [Eden] told me that anything I could do to help towards better relations between our two countries he would be grateful for, and when I said to him that I understood that they don't like you in Italy and feel you are working against them he replied, 'I know but you can say that when we had our conversations with the French it was I who pleaded with them for better understanding with Italy – not the Prime Minister.'

Instead of drawing this to Eden's attention, Chamberlain's reaction to his Foreign Secretary's complaint was uncharacteristically conciliatory. On 8 February he sent Eden a letter agreeing to ask his sister-in-law to desist from her activities. But he added: '... don't let us in our anxiety not to be over-eager, give the impression that we do not want to have conversations at all. That might have very unfortunate consequences.'[65] Chamberlain's diary recounts the sequel:

Unfortunately this episode seemed to produce in Anthony only further suspicion. If the Italians wanted talks there must be some catch in it, and we had better hang back. Early in February Grandi came back from his holiday and asked to see me and the Foreign Secretary. It was some time before the latter informed me and even then he did not suggest that I should meet his wishes ... He did however see him himself ... Anthony discussed subjects of conversations including *de jure* about which he did not appear to think there would be any difficulty or delay in 'getting League sanction'. Yet still no date was fixed for contact and this time it was suggested that we must first get further with the settlement of the Spanish situation and the withdrawal of volunteers. At last there came another surprise from Germany ... Schuschnigg, the Austrian Chancellor, was suddenly summoned to Berchtesgaden, where he was outrageously bullied by Hitler and faced with a series of demands to which he was obliged to yield, since on this occasion Mussolini gave him no support. Very soon afterwards Ciano told Perth that he had instructed Grandi to press for an early start of the conversations in view of 'possible future happenings' ...
Perth had reported that he had been unable to get any explanation of these

mysterious words though we might be more fortunate with Grandi. To me they seemed clear enough. Hitler had made his coup and Mussolini was furious about it. He wanted to know where he stood with us for if he had to regard us as a potential enemy he would have to make the best terms he could with Hitler ... At any rate remembering that Grandi had asked to see me I suggested that now was the time when we should interview him. This was on Thursday morning the 17th. Anthony agreed and said he would ask Grandi to call at No. 10 next morning when we might try to extract from him the real meaning of Ciano's words. Both A. and I lunched that date with P. Sassoon. Before I left Downing Street for lunch I received a message that the Foreign Secretary would speak to me at lunch. I suspected that this meant another change of mind and so it proved. A. who sat next me explained that Cadogan had suggested that it might be better that A. should see Grandi alone and if necessary bring him afterwards to see me. I resisted this as I was convinced it was intended to prevent me seeing Grandi lest that should bring the conversations nearer ... I succeeded in staving off this attempt. In the course of the evening however a final effort was made by Anthony who sent me a note begging me very earnestly not to commit us to any talks when I met Grandi.

This note convinced me that the issue between us must be faced, and faced at once ... I told Horace Wilson ... that I was determined to stand firm, even though it meant losing my Foreign Secretary. After this events moved swiftly to a crisis. Grandi met Eden and myself in the Cabinet room at 11. He fully confirmed my interpretation of Ciano's words to Perth and Ivy Chamberlain ... He declared that Mussolini was ready to discuss anything we chose to mention which might affect our relations. Spain would not be a serious difficulty nor would propaganda. In view of Anthony's note I said finally to Grandi that he had better leave the Foreign Secretary and myself to talk and return at 3 o'clock ... When he had gone I said at once that I had no doubt what we ought to say ... We should say that conversations should begin at once and we would get Perth back for instructions. Anthony however objected. Since Mussolini was so ready for conversations this was a reason for withdrawal on our part ... He believed there was a German Italian agreement ... If Italy was in earnest she would at least make a gesture, she might indeed have accepted the British formula for the withdrawal of volunteers [from Spain] ... I asked if Italian acceptance now of the formula would overcome his scruples. He had made a lot of the want of any sign of good faith but rather inconsistently now declared that acceptance would make no difference whatever. There was no accommodation possible and for the first time I could not refrain from reproaches. I told A.E. that he had missed one opportunity after another of advancing towards peace ... It was all in vain; I could not move him.

The die was cast. Grandi was asked to postpone his second call until the following week. At this critical point the Ambassador sent a revealing dispatch to Rome:

Chamberlain and Eden were not a Prime Minister and a Foreign Secretary discussing with the Ambassador of a foreign Power a delicate situation of an international character. They were – and revealed themselves as such to me in defiance of all established convention – two enemies confronting each other, like two cocks in true fighting posture . . . Eden wishes to continue with his policy of hate and vendetta, to pave the way for war with Italy at some date sooner or later and to pose – as he is now doing – as a sort of new Pitt facing the Napoleon of Italy. To say that Chamberlain will have an easy task would be inexact. Eden has on his side the man in the street, or the 'historical beast' which is always lurking in a large section of the British people, the left-wing Parties, French anti-Fascism and Masonry, who all see in him the head of the future British Popular Front . . .[66]

The Cabinet was now summoned to deal with the split between Chamberlain and Eden. The Foreign Secretary had not one outright supporter on the merits of his stand, although a number of colleagues, dismayed at the news that he intended to resign, sought to dissuade him or to find a compromise formula to save his face. Walter Elliot forecast 'the end of the Government' and Oliver Stanley spoke of the resignation as a calamity and he himself offered to quit. After a second inconclusive Cabinet meeting, a small group of ministers sought to promote a reconciliation. But as Chamberlain wrote in his diary: 'They made no attempt to induce me to alter my views, their efforts were directed to convincing Anthony that the differences were less than he had made out and that he could with a clear conscience accept the Cabinet's decision and proceed with talks merely *warning* Grandi that a Spanish settlement was essential to an agreement . . .' This made no difference to Eden. Nor did the late news that the Italians were prepared to accept the British formula for the withdrawal of volunteers from Spain – to which Eden earlier in the month had appeared to attach great significance. The Cabinet finally gave up the attempt to retain him on the evening of 20 February 1938 and he accordingly resigned.[67]

What lay behind Eden's decision? First, we may dismiss as a factor Chamberlain's alleged contacts with Grandi behind the Foreign Secretary's back. Highly coloured accounts of intermediaries in Conservative Central Office and the Prime Minister's Office having dealings with the Italian Ambassador have been given much prominence by post-war writers of the anti-appeasement school. But even though such channels of communication certainly existed they made little or no difference to Chamberlain's broad approach and moreover were entirely unknown to Eden until after the war when Ciano's diplomatic papers were published. Hence even if Chamberlain is judged as having been at fault or even as having behaved dishonourably, this factor can have no bearing on Eden's decision to quit. Essentially, then, his departure sprang from an unwillingness to treat with Mussolini. Yet Eden was an ambitious politician and it is therefore safe to assume that high-minded opinions on policy went hand in hand with calculations about the implications for his own future. He was nearly thirty years younger than Chamberlain and might have much to lose from too close an association with a policy that might be extremely unpopular both in the immediate short-term and also in the longer run. Nor need such a personal reluctance to be 'compromised' have been based solely on narrowly selfish or ignoble calculations about the future. He may have anticipated the likelihood of war and recognized that he ought to hold himself in reserve as a figure who could help to unite the country in that contingency. As Eden put it in his memoirs with respect to his thoughts in 1937 when chided that he was not 'sharp enough' with the Opposition: 'I thought that Foreign Secretaries ought to be as far as possible above the battle: I always had it in mind that one day I might have to go down to the House of Commons and tell the nation that it was at war.'[68]

Eden may also have had more strictly personal considerations in mind at the time of his resignation. Maybe he felt too ill to continue in office. Simon believed or affected to believe that this was the case and on 18 February told Thomas that he had realized that Eden was 'both physically and mentally ill'. He urged that Eden, of whom he was 'as fond as if he had been his own son', should take six months' holiday. He had also asked Eden himself whether he was 'certain that you're all right'. Eden, according to his memoirs, assured him that he was 'in perfect health'.[69] But an independent witness to the possibility that Eden was ill has now emerged. Malcolm MacDonald recalls:

Late in the afternoon of the day when Cabinet meetings had failed to reconcile the difference of view between Chamberlain and Eden, and when the efforts of a group of other ministers to persuade Eden to change his mind about resigning from the government had also failed, Chamberlain suggested to me that I should have a talk with Eden in a final attempt to dissuade him from his proposed course. I agreed to do this. Eden and I were cordial personal friends and ministerial colleagues who had often cooperated together in the context of the government's international policies.

I went to the Foreign Office to see Eden and invite him to dine with me that evening in my house in Hampstead, where we could talk relaxedly and in confidence together. When I entered his private secretary's room Oliver Harvey looked at me with some concern. He expressed the hope that I was not going to try to persuade the Secretary of State to withdraw his threat, and he made it clear that he himself had urged the minister to maintain it. I knew Harvey quite well, and liked him; but I disapproved of this intrusion by a civil servant into such a critical political matter.

Eden gladly came to dinner with me. Through the meal and for a long time afterwards as we sipped drinks we discussed the current problem. I expressed the reasons why I thought that he should not resign on the issue which had arisen. He re-stated the reasons why he thought he should do so; and we exchanged arguments and counter-arguments in a very friendly way. Sometimes he agreed with a point which I made, but then he shifted his comments to another aspect of the subject. Usually he stayed firm in his opinion, but just now and then he appeared perhaps to be prepared to reconsider his decision, and to continue serving as the Foreign Secretary. Then, at one of those moments, he suddenly shook his head rather desperately and said that although there was much to be said for my point of view he could not continue working as a Minister because he did not feel fit to do so; he felt physically unwell and mentally exhausted. (I do not now remember the exact words that he used, but that was the substance of his remark.)

He might have been making this an excuse for not being persuaded by me to alter his decision; but by then I did not think this was the reason for his sudden somewhat emotional outburst. During our talk I felt increasingly worried about the state of his mind. His thoughts seemed to be less clear and reasonably coherent than they usually were, and his statements were occasionally somewhat confused. I began to wonder whether he was well enough to continue performing the difficult tasks of his supremely important office through the critical times which lay ahead. When he made that remark I decided that it would in fact be better if he did resign.

Before the Cabinet met the next morning I went to see the Prime Minister in 10 Downing Street. I told him that my efforts to persuade Eden to change his mind had failed – and that indeed by the end of my talk with him it was I who had changed my mind. I said that I thought that he was too mentally and physically exhausted to continue working wisely and well in his high office, and that in the circumstances, however regrettable, it would be better if he did resign.

Chamberlain smiled and said that he had 'slept on the matter' and had come to the same conclusion.[70]

Another possibility is that Eden's attitude towards the Prime Minister had been decisively coloured, perhaps subconsciously, by their altercation in the previous November and at the time of the Roosevelt overture. He had also been repeatedly urged by Harvey to take a stand against his colleagues on the grounds that without his support the Government would certainly fall. Cranborne, Thomas and Eden's wife, Beatrice, also took this line if somewhat less dogmatically. Again, as we have seen, two Cabinet colleagues. Elliot and Stanley, evidently held the same view. Further and perhaps decisive evidence to tempt Eden into overplaying his hand may have come from a meeting of backbenchers held on 17 February, on the eve of the final dramatic meeting with Chamberlain and Grandi. Eden recalled:

On the morning of February 18th, I read the record of a meeting held the previous evening by the Foreign Affairs Committee, which was composed of Members of Parliament supporting the National Government. They had shown themselves robust. Mr Harold Nicolson had said that any nervous advances to Germany or Italy would suggest fear and this was not a moment to show the slightest move in the direction of de jure recognition of Italy's conquest of Abyssinia. This last remark was cheered by the Committee, which appeared to be unanimous against attempting to buy Italian friendship on this condition.[71]

It is possible, then, that Eden hoped that his resignation would have a short-term pay-off – much as Lord Randolph Churchill at much the same age had once calculated that he could topple Lord Salisbury. If so, Eden, like Churchill, was to be taught a severe lesson. In Churchill's case there was indeed to be no recovery, so extreme was his reaction to the disappointment of losing his battle with the Prime Minister. Eden at least knew when to stop. As Goethe put it: '*In der Beschränkung zeigt sich erst der Meister.*'

V

In the Wilderness
1938–9

It is difficult to be sure whether in the immediate aftermath of his resignation Eden expected that Chamberlain would have difficulty in continuing in office. Superficially and with the benefit of hindsight, it might appear obvious that Eden could only have had long-term objectives in mind. For was not Chamberlain one of the strongest and most determined peacetime premiers of modern times? And how could Eden possibly have imagined that Chamberlain might be unable, in the short term at least, to survive a resignation which had not been on the face of it about an issue of any great substance and which had not been supported by any of his Cabinet colleagues? Yet that Eden may indeed have overestimated his indispensability is suggested both by a reading of the entries in Harvey's diary for this period and by evidence that he was involved, shortly after his resignation, in intrigues with Baldwin which may have been based on the assumption that Chamberlain might feel compelled to resign, a contingency which could lead the King to recall Baldwin to the premiership on a stopgap basis with Eden as the heir apparent. In Eden's case such hopes, if seriously entertained, may seem to a later generation to have been the product of his relative inexperience and youth – for he was still only forty. But it was not as fashionable in 1938 as it is today to believe in the near-impossibility in practice of a Prime Minister being removed against his wishes between general elections. On the contrary, contemporaries appear to have believed that Baldwin had survived the Hoare–Laval débâcle of 1935 only because the Conservative Party's elder statesman, Austen Chamberlain, had been persuaded (or been deceived) into speaking in his favour. And there were no doubt many who were influenced by the knowledge that Baldwin himself, together with Andrew Bonar Law, had brought down Lloyd George in 1922. It is not therefore quite out of the question that Eden had had serious expectations that his resignation would plunge Chamberlain into an immediate battle for survival. But if this was the case, he had been deluded. For by 21 February, when Eden appeared in the House of Commons to make his resignation speech, it had become apparent that there would be no backbenchers' revolt and that the press and the general public were unlikely to be fired with a feeling of emotional outrage such as had engulfed Hoare in 1935. On 24 July 1942 Harvey wrote of the 1938 resignation: 'if only he [Eden] had been in closer touch with some of his colleagues his resignation might have provoked theirs and the Government would have been overthrown. As it was, the colleagues were ill-informed and bewildered.'[1]

Having, then, possibly overplayed his hand in resigning, Eden now overreacted in the other direction. His resignation speech was low-key and involved no attempt to broaden the basis of his differences with Chamberlain. Equally unsensational was his explanation to his constituents at Leamington. Even Chamberlain was moved to write to Eden:

After reading your speech to your constituents I should like to send you a few friendly words. You had a difficult task. You had to say enough to justify your resignation, and to vindicate your views, and the easiest, and perhaps the most popular, way would have been to emphasize differences and to call for support ... Anyhow, whatever the temptations, you have resisted them, and the dignity and restraint of your speech must add further to your reputation.[2]

From this time onward at least until the summer of 1938 Eden was to maintain a surprisingly low profile. He deliberately sought to avoid setting himself up as a figure in total conflict with Chamberlain by standing for diametrically opposed policies on a range of subjects. To have done so would no doubt have involved, given his earlier record when in office, some mental gymnastics and would have brought innocuous accusations of inconsistency. Yet a politician of the front rank who chooses to resign from an administration can usually be counted on to behave in this fashion after a barely decent interval. Why, then, did Eden begin his period in the wilderness so quietly? Maybe he actually was mentally and physically unwell, as Simon and MacDonald believed. Perhaps he had temporarily lost his nerve as a result of the modest consequences which had flowed from his resignation. Possibly he did not wish to place himself in a fast-moving situation beyond hope of recall to office. Again, he may have been conscious of the danger, stressed by Baldwin, of becoming too closely identified with Churchill, who had arguably already established himself as the foremost exponent of outright Conservative onslaughts on the Chamberlain Government.[3] Perhaps, too, Eden, relatively impecunious and with a family to support, may have feared that he might have difficulties with his Leamington Constituency Association if he went as far as Churchill, whose own Constituency Association at Epping came close to rejecting him as its member. For some or all of these reasons, Eden, with Baldwin's private encouragement, practically hibernated for several months. Not only did he make no controversial speeches, he even neglected to spend much time at the Palace of Westminster and thus lost an opportunity to build up his influence behind the scenes.

Eden was even largely silent on the main developments in foreign affairs in the months after his resignation. In the case of Hitler's annexation of

Austria in March 1938, his reticence is understandable, for while in office
he had been warned that the *Anschluss* might occur at an early date and he
had agreed with his officials that Great Britain would be in no position to do
anything about it. And, as has been seen, he had in effect argued against
any British intervention both to the Dominion Premiers and to the French
leaders during the course of 1937. He had even told Ribbentrop in
December 1937 that the Austrian question was of much greater interest to
Italy than to England, 'whose people recognized that a closer connection
between Germany and Austria would have to come about sometime'.[4] More
difficult to understand is Eden's failure to offer vigorous public condemnation of the conclusion of the Anglo-Italian Agreement of April 1938
which included *de jure* recognition of the conquest of Abyssinia. This, to be
sure, was not to come into force, according to the terms, until the
outstanding questions on Spain had been settled. Nevertheless the announcement of a conditional agreement of this sort gave Eden an ideal
opportunity to belabour the Government on the issue on which he had
apparently differed most acutely from Chamberlain. True, Churchill also
kept a low profile on this subject. As he wrote to Eden on 18 April:

> ... I feel that considerable caution is necessary in opposing the agreement bluntly. It
> is a done thing. It is called a move towards peace. It undoubtedly makes it less likely
> that sparks from the Mediterranean should light a European conflagration. France
> will have to follow suit for her own protection, in order not to be divided from
> Britain. Finally, there is the possibility that Mussolini may be drawn by his interests
> to discourage German interference in the Danube basin.[5]

On the other hand, Churchill, by no means the consistent anti-appeaser of
legend, had, unlike Eden, never been inclined to treat Italy as Great Britain's
principal enemy.

Next came the beginning of the crisis over Czechoslovakia. In May 1938
the British and French Governments became seriously alarmed that Hitler
was about to use armed force to deal with the alleged persecution of the
Sudeten Germans. The first phase of the crisis culminated in a German
climbdown after a warning by the British that they could not be counted on
not to intervene. About these events Eden said nothing of note either at the
time or in his memoirs.

At this juncture, however, he was not averse from engaging in private
parley with Chamberlain. According to his own account, Eden was sounded
about a possible return to the Government once the Anglo-Italian
Agreement had come into force. He reserved his position on the grounds
that 'we had better see first how all this works out'. In his memoirs he
professed to be embarrassed by these advances but added somewhat
disingenuously that he 'did not want to be rude in the face of an invitation

which was obviously friendly in intention'. If Eden had not altogether closed the door on the possibility of a return to the Government, he was, on the other hand, willing to associate openly with a number of Chamberlain's moderate critics. During the summer of 1938 he began to emerge from isolation and to mix not only with Cranborne and Thomas, in whose company he had resigned, but also with such figures as Macmillan, Nicolson, Mark Patrick, Paul Emrys-Evans, Richard Law, E. L. Spears, Anthony Crossley and Ronald Cartland. By the end of 1938 there were between twenty and thirty MPs said to belong to the 'Eden group' and occasional informal meetings were held.[6] The importance and cohesiveness of this group may well have been exaggerated by historians. For the fact is that when put to the test in the crisis over Czechoslovakia in September 1938 the so-called group offered no united resistance to Chamberlain and thus did not make itself a serious factor in his calculations. Moreover, though Eden gradually emerged from the silent isolation that had marked the first months after his resignation, he continued to avoid close public involvement with the more unequivocal Conservative opponents of Chamberlain, namely Churchill, Brendan Bracken, Duncan Sandys and Robert Boothby. This may not have derived merely from fear on Eden's part of being associated with the reputation for irresponsibility which attached to Churchill as a result of his record on India and the Abdication. The explanation may simply have been that even now he was not as convinced as Churchill that war with Germany was becoming inevitable.

The personal relationship between Eden and Churchill was also doubtless of significance. It cannot be too strongly emphasized that at this period they were rivals and equals. Only after Churchill became Prime Minister did the gap in their ages lead people with short memories to assume that Eden was Churchill's protégé or that they had a father-and-son relationship. Eden's real patrons, as has been seen, were first Austen Chamberlain and then, more importantly, Baldwin. Churchill, for his part, heartily disliked Baldwin and thus was not likely to be a warm admirer of one of his acolytes. Moreover, Eden had rebuked Churchill in 1934 for his attack on the 'boneless wonder', MacDonald, over disarmament. It is not surprising, therefore, that Churchill wrote in December 1935 that he had no confidence in Eden's appointment at the Foreign Office and later that he considered him to be a lightweight. Relations between the two men improved during 1937 when Eden's differences with Chamberlain became known; both were unhappy, for example, with aspects of defence policy. Yet they were far from being in close alliance. Thus Churchill was in no way responsible for or even apparently consulted about Eden's decision to resign. Indeed, shortly after Eden's resignation, he signed a backbench round-robin expressing confidence in the Prime Minister and his policy. For

Churchill's priorities were the reverse of Eden's: his concern was with Hitler, not Mussolini. It would thus be surprising if Eden's departure came as a severe blow to his future chief. Yet, writing in 1948, Churchill's recollection was:

... my heart sank and for a while the dark waters of despair overwhelmed me ... During all the war soon to come and in all its darkest times I never had any trouble sleeping ... But now on this night of February 20, 1938, and on this occasion only, sleep deserted me. From midnight till dawn I lay in my bed consumed by emotions of sorrow and fear. There seemed one strong young figure standing up against long, dismal, drawling tides of drift and surrender ... he seemed to me at this moment to embody the life-hope of the British nation ... Now he was gone. I watched the daylight slowly creep in through the windows and saw before me in mental gaze the vision of death.[7]

Could this famous passage possibly contain an element of hyperbole?

The reality of the divergence between the two men was brought out clearly in the Czechoslovakian crisis of September 1938. Eden, as has been seen, had played no significant part in the first major Czechoslovak scare in the preceding May but during the ensuing months of relative calm his mind must gradually have begun to focus on the subject. Should he argue that there was a difference in principle between the Austrian *Anschluss* and a possible change in the status quo in the Sudetenland? Should he cling to the traditional line that Great Britain had no vital interests in east-central Europe worth a major war? In March 1937 Eden himself had told Basil Newton, the British Minister in Prague, that the British Government was 'not prepared to take the responsibility for counselling Dr Beneš to negotiate a settlement of whose terms they are quite unaware, and which might, indeed, entail dangerous or humiliating concessions' – in short a British refusal to get involved in what Eden already saw was more than just a minority problem.[8] And in November 1937 he had even gone so far as to suggest to Delbos that Great Britain and France might 'concert with Germany in seeking to find a satisfactory solution to the problem'.[9] In June 1938 Eden's position still remained equivocal. On the one hand, he told his Leamington constituents:

Nobody will quarrel with the Government's wish to bring about appeasement in Europe. Any other intention would be as foolish as it would be wrong. But if appeasement is to mean what it says, it must not be at the expense either of our vital interests or of our national reputation or our sense of fair dealing. Appeasement will be neither real nor lasting at such a price. It would merely make real appeasement more difficult at a later stage.[10]

At the same time however, Eden maintained a studied silence about the possibility of giving a British guarantee to Czechoslovakia. Probably, then, he desired, as in the case of Austria, to avoid if possible dramatic involvement in the Sudeten dispute lest Great Britain's 'national reputation' should be sullied by having to give advice to Beneš which might 'entail dangerous or humiliating concessions'.

Chamberlain and his Cabinet colleagues would no doubt have been happy to adopt the same reserved approach if they could have relied upon the French either to become totally disinterested or to bully their Czech allies into making whatever Sudeten concessions Hitler required. They were driven to the conclusion, however, that there was a serious risk, as in 1914, of the French Government going to war over an eastern European quarrel and thereby causing a conflict in western Europe from which the British could not afford to remain aloof. Accordingly Chamberlain gradually and reluctantly came to take charge of the crisis. First came the Runciman mission to Czechoslovakia. Then, during September, the British Prime Minister assumed the responsibility of negotiating with Hitler and coercing the Czechs into surrender.

Eden's attitude during these events was to accept that Great Britain was now, for good or ill, involved in the Czechoslovak affair. He accordingly adopted a declaratory position which was throughout marginally more resolute than that of Chamberlain. Yet he was careful at every stage not to urge wholly reckless steps and still less to demand a declaration or threat of war. He may have hoped that if Chamberlain adopted a rather more vigorous approach, Hitler would have been deterred from carrying out his threat to solve the Sudeten issue by force. But if he had actually believed, as Chamberlain correctly did, that Hitler was not bluffing, it is questionable whether he would really have favoured dispatching an ultimatum. Churchill, on the other hand, certainly did favour war in the last resort.

Eden's first divergence from Churchill came at the outset of the September crisis. Returning from a holiday in Ireland, Eden paid two visits on 9 and 11 September to Lord Halifax, his successor at the Foreign Office. They discussed what should be done in the light of Czechoslovakia's offer, in the face of German threats, to enter into serious negotiations with the Sudeten leaders. Halifax was able to tell Chamberlain that Eden 'expressed complete agreement with the line taken'. In particular, Eden endorsed Halifax's view that Hitler should be urged to press the Sudeten Germans to respond favourably and that a warning should be given that a war in central Europe could not be localized. In fact no formal warning was given to Hitler following objections by Henderson in Berlin. But Eden, with the concurrence of Halifax and Chamberlain, published a letter in *The Times* of 12 September. He drew attention to British friendship and solidarity with France and argued that a conflict could not be limited to central Europe. At the same time he obviously favoured negotiations: 'The Czechoslovak Government in their most recent proposals have shown their sincere desire to go very far to meet the grievances of the Sudeten Party. It should not be

impossible to evolve from these proposals a settlement acceptable to all.'
Churchill, by contrast, preferred a bolder course. According to Harvey, he
telephoned Halifax on 10 September and urged the need for an immediate
ultimatum to Germany.[11]

On 15 September Chamberlain left London for the first of his three visits
to Germany. He met Hitler at Berchtesgaden and for the first time explored
the possibility of the transfer of the Sudeten area to Germany. The Prime
Minister returned to London on the following day to consult his colleagues
and the French about a practical plan for implementing this idea. At this
stage Eden maintained a discreet silence. On 18 September, however, he
dined with Harvey who found him 'miserable'. According to Harvey, 'A.E. is
determined to go for the Government over this when the House of Commons
meets.' By implication, therefore, he was not prepared to act *immediately* by
issuing a public statement. Eden next wrote to Halifax 'to tell him how
deeply disturbed' he was at press reports of the outcome of the Anglo-
French consultations. He added: 'Nothing official has appeared and I can
only hope that what the press has published is not accurate, for if it is, I can
only look to the future with increased apprehension.' Eden privately, then,
was still not prepared to go so far as to advocate an ultimatum to Hitler and
still less war. Nor did he apparently intimate to Halifax what he had told
Harvey, namely that he would eventually make an attack in Parliament on
his party leaders. Indeed, Nicolson recorded in his diary on 19 September
that Eden 'doesn't wish to lead a revolt or secure any resignations from the
Cabinet'. Churchill, by contrast, had meanwhile taken the drastic step of
going to Paris to try to influence French opinion against agreeing to the
Berchtesgaden plan.[12]

Chamberlain now returned for his second meeting with Hitler, on this
occasion at Godesberg. He brought with him substantial British, French and
even Czech concurrence to the Berchtesgaden plan. But to his dismay, he
discovered that Hitler's price had now gone up. The Führer insisted that
both the scope and the timing of the dismemberment of Czechoslovakia
would have to be drastically modified, to the detriment of Prague. Once
again Chamberlain decided to consult his colleagues and he duly arrived
back in London on 24 September.

On the previous evening Eden had spoken in his Leamington constituency. Once again he reiterated his earlier public view but in rather
vague language:

Nobody will quarrel with the Government's wish to bring about appeasement in
Europe . . . But if appeasement is to mean what it says, it must not be at the expense
either of our vital interests, or of our national reputation, or of our sense of fair
dealing.

For our own people the issue becomes clarified . . . They see freedom of thought, of
race, of worship grow every week more restricted in Europe. The conviction is

growing that continued retreat can only lead to ever-widening confusion. They knowing that a stand must be made. They pray that it be not made too late.[13]

On 25 September Eden took his most drastic step in the whole Czechoslovak crisis: he sent Halifax a private message urging the rejection of Hitler's Godesberg proposals. This action, together with similar pressure from Cadogan, may have helped to push Halifax into diverging from the Prime Minister, who favoured in effect surrendering to Hitler. But whatever the reason, Halifax's decision to lead a Cabinet revolt caused the British Government to hold back from actually recommending the Godesberg terms to Prague. Neither the Czechs nor the Germans were now expected to make any move to break the deadlock.

War seemed inevitable in a matter of days and on 28 September Chamberlain accordingly began to explain to the House of Commons the full gravity of the situation. Then, in the middle of his speech, he received a message that Hitler, instigated by Mussolini, had issued invitations to a four-power conference in Munich. Wild cheering ensued on all sides of the chamber with only a small number of MPs ostentatiously remaining seated and silent. Eden avoided outright commitment by leaving the chamber, though even this action plainly separated him from the bulk of ministerial supporters.

Eden's judgement and perhaps courage were put to the test in more dramatic fashion on the following day, 29 September, after Chamberlain had departed for Munich. A meeting of the anti-appeasing Focus Movement was held in the Pinafore Room at the Savoy. Lady Violet Bonham Carter recalled:

I ... suggested that during the afternoon, a few of us should draft a telegram to the Prime Minister adjuring him to make no further concessions at the expense of the Czechs ... The telegram was to be signed by Winston, Lord (Robert) Cecil, [Clement] Attlee, Archie Sinclair, Eden and Lord Lloyd.
... Cecil, Lloyd, and Archie Sinclair were eager to sign.
Eden, to whom we telephoned, refused – on the grounds that it would be interpreted as an act of hostility to Chamberlain. (Was he not hostile to his policies?) Attlee, with whom [Philip] Noel-Baker pleaded urgently ... refused to sign without the approval of his party ...
The telegram was not dispatched and one by one our friends went out – defeated. Winston remained, sitting in his chair immobile, frozen, like a man of stone. I saw tears in his eyes. I could feel the iron entering his soul ...
I spoke with bitterness of those who had refused even to put their names to principles and policies which they professed. Then he spoke: What are they made of? The day is not far off when it won't be signatures we'll have to give but lives – the lives of millions. Can we survive? Do we deserve to do so when there's no courage anywhere?[14]

Eden apparently had no subsequent recollection of this episode, though

Lady Violet's account has been supported by several other participants in the Focus meeting.

Chamberlain's final meeting with Hitler culminated in a midnight agreement which to some degree represented a retreat by Hitler and an improvement on Godesberg. Nevertheless the Czechs were virtually compelled to accept a collective *Diktat*. According to Harvey, Eden telephoned on the following day to protest against *this aspect* of it.[15] This was surely a less than heroic or thorough-going reaction.

Chamberlain returned to a hero's welcome and spoke unwisely of peace for our time and peace with honour. A three-day debate was then held in the House of Commons. Given the public's mood of euphoria, Eden's intervention was awaited with interest, not least by some of his anti-appeasing friends. He chose the path of equivocation. As he understandably recalled in his memoirs, he threw in some implied criticism of the Government. For example he said: 'Surely the House will be agreed that foreign affairs cannot indefinitely be conducted on the basis of "stand and deliver". Successive surrenders bring only successive humiliations, and they, in their turn, more humiliating demands.' But simultaneously, as he equally understandably failed to stress in his memoirs, he went far to neutralize these criticisms by heaping compliments on many of the architects of the destruction of Czechoslovak integrity. He praised Lord Runciman, 'whose efforts in this difficult time and whose services are beyond all praise – for he did a truly wonderful piece of work under the greatest of difficulties'. He endorsed the Prime Minister's praise of Halifax: 'I feel sure that the noble Lord is richly deserving of that tribute.' He paid a somewhat patronizing tribute to the hapless Czechs who 'have laid all Europe under an obligation to them by having made the greatest contribution to the preservation of peace'; while the worst he could find to say about Great Britain's rôle in pressing the dismemberment proposals on Prague was that it was 'unpleasing'. Above all, he went out of his way to salute Chamberlain himself: 'We all owe him and every citizen owes him a measureless debt of gratitude for the sincerity and pertinacity which he has devoted in the final phase of the crisis to averting the supreme calamity of war.' Eden later added: 'The influences which finally contributed to averting war were many. It is probably too soon to attempt to analyse them, but one of them was certainly the Prime Minister's refusal to give up hope.' By contrast, Eden paid only a formal tribute to Duff Cooper, who had resigned from the Cabinet in protest and had earlier addressed the House of Commons in unequivocal terms: 'Whatever our views may be, there cannot have been one of us who was not impressed by the manifest sincerity of that speech.' Eden appears to have thought that the divergence of outlook between himself and the Government was not as to the morality of Munich but 'whether the events of the last few days do constitute the beginning of better things ... or whether they only give us a breathing space, perhaps six months or less, before the next crisis is upon us'. 'I should very much like to take the more optimistic view.' he continued, 'but this year we have had many optimistic forecasts and they have all been falsified.' Yet Eden was far from resigned to the certainty of war. 'It is the duty of each one of us,' he argued, 'to devote what time we can to stocktaking and to considering how it was that Europe came thus to the very edge of the abyss; to considering what we can do to see to it that such a state of affairs shall never occur again.'[16]

The contrast between Eden's speech and Churchill's could not have been more marked. Churchill heaped no praise on Chamberlain. Instead he said: 'If I do not begin this afternoon by paying the usual, and almost invariable, tributes to the Prime Minister, it is certainly not from any lack of personal regard.' Nor did Churchill leave any doubt that he was an unqualified pessimist about the future. He concluded his speech with this ringing declaraction:

And do not suppose that this is the end. This is only the beginning of the reckoning. This is only the first sip, the first foretaste of a bitter cup which will be proffered to us year by year unless by a supreme recovery of moral health and martial vigour, we arise again and take our stand for freedom as in the olden time.[17]

Although a superficial reading of subsequent events would appear to justify Churchill's line, there was much to be said at the time for Eden's less dogmatic reading of the prospects. Was not Churchill merely guessing in 1938 when he assumed that Hitler would wish to expand beyond the German-speaking areas of Europe, which had hitherto constituted the limits of his territorial expansion? How could he be sure that Hitler was basically motivated by an obsessive desire to subjugate the British Empire? Would he not have taken a different line if he had concluded that such ambition as Hitler had lay primarily in eastern Europe? How could he know whether favourable diplomatic consequences would flow from the Government's policy of pressing ahead with rearmament?

The divergence between Churchill and Eden almost led to a public split among Conservative critics of the Government. Harvey recorded that Eden's friends were 'disappointed, not to say shocked' at his speech.[18] Then there were differences about how to vote at the end of the Commons debate. Some, like Churchill, wanted to vote against the Government. But a majority favoured abstention. On the other hand, Eden and Amery, who at this time was possibly his closest ally, were apparently almost persuaded to vote with the Government as a result of Chamberlain's summing up. But in the end all the rebels settled for a collective abstention. Nevertheless, Amery wrote to Chamberlain at once to inform him that 'your speech moved me very deeply, and very, very nearly persuaded both myself and Anthony Eden to vote'.[19]

Eden, then, was far from an unequivocal opponent of Munich. His carefully chosen words in his memoirs sum up his position: 'I have never blamed the British and French Governments for not supporting Czechoslovakia to the point of war, though I think it would have been to their nations' advantage to have done so.'[20] The first part of this sentence is obviously consistent with the attitude he adopted at the time. The last half seems, on the other hand, to be a judgement based on hindsight. For at the time he does not seem to have favoured war. On the contrary, he remained equivocal about the extent to which the British should enter into commitments relating to eastern Europe. Possibly he would have agreed with Amery's verdict recorded in his private diary entry of 8 October 1938:

> We may be giving Germany much greater power in Central Europe, but on the other hand our position becomes psychologically and strategically much simpler. Fundamentally it is a policy which I have always favoured; my difference on this occasion has been, not with the policy itself, but for adopting a different policy up to the last moment and then abandoning it under panic conditions, which are only likely to increase Hitler's annoyance.[21]

Again, Eden *at the time* was not unsympathetic to the argument that Munich won valuable breathing space for the democracies. As he wrote to Baldwin on 30 September: 'I think that Munich has given us time at least, at the expense of the unhappy Czechs.'[22]

Judging by his memoirs, then, Eden came to feel some subsequent doubts about the correctness of his course at the time of Munich. But it may also be argued that his record was neither particularly dishonourable nor in itself in the least remarkable. If anything is surprising it is that he appears subsequently to have felt under the entirely unnecessary obligation to perpetuate a mythical image of heroic consistency long after it had lost any practical political value for him.

In the aftermath of Munich Eden was faced with a substantially changed political situation. For the dramatic surge of enthusiasm for Chamberlain's achievement raised the possibility that his foreign policy might be made the dominant issue in an early General Election and that those Conservative MPs, like Eden, who had abstained in the Munich debate, might be placed in an almost impossible position. Had this happened immediately, Eden himself was apparently reconciled to having to fight as an independent Conservative. But he understandably hoped to avoid this necessity and was accordingly unwilling to take any steps which would give the Prime Minister an added incentive or pretext to go to the country. As Harvey recorded in his diary:

> What should A.E. do? Should he break away from the Party and lead a crusade in

the country? Or should he stay just inside the Party, pressing rearmament? Too firm a stand now might force the PM to have an immediate election which he might win. There must be an election within a year – a policy of attrition from within, damaging speeches from the backbenchers, may be more effective in breaking the hold of the Party machine and securing a more easy change-over from the PM's regime to a wider Government. I gather the balance of opinion of A.E.'s supporters in the House of Commons is in favour of less heroic course.[23]

A factor reinforcing Eden's inclination to adopt this approach was undoubtedly the emergence of Halifax as a potential critic of Chamberlain. The Foreign Secretary had established his independence from the Prime Minister by persuading his colleagues not to recommend the Godesberg terms to Prague; and he had subsequently urged Chamberlain not to use the debate on the Munich settlement to launch an immediate General Election. Now in the aftermath of Munich Halifax drew close in private to Eden and began to urge the broadening of the National Government, including as a first step the return of Eden to the Cabinet. The reasons for Halifax's new attitude are a matter for speculation. Perhaps he really had lost sleep, as he claimed, about the fate of the Czechs. Perhaps he was genuinely more pessimistic than Chamberlain concerning Hitler's intentions, though even the Prime Minister was by no means as complacent as might have been suggested by some of his euphoric remarks made at the time of his hero's welcome on returning from Munich. Perhaps Halifax was primarily concerned to see the Conservative Party win the next General Election and saw Eden's support either for the existing Government or a reconstructed version as essential to reducing the chances of an outright Labour victory. But perhaps, above all, Halifax – 'Holy Fox' to his enemies – saw himself as strengthening his own chances of obtaining the premiership if he seemed to stand half-way between the 'Eden group', and the out-and-out supporters of the increasingly abrasive Chamberlain. But, whatever may be the truth about Halifax's motives, one result was that Eden was offered a potential lifeline back into the centre of events and in the ensuing months he showed himself increasingly careful not to put this at risk.

Eden thus adopted an extremely cautious public stance. First, he refused to have anything to do with attempts in October by Macmillan, one of his most hawkish supporters, to create an alliance between the Conservative dissenters and the Labour and Liberal parties – 'a 1931 in reverse'. Dalton recorded in his memoirs that Macmillan proposed that the two of them should have a meeting with Attlee, Herbert Morrison, Duff Cooper and Churchill to arrange some tentative basis for the coordination of their criticisms of the Government. Dalton wrote, 'But even this modest programme evaporated. Macmillan sounded Duff Cooper, who would not come without Eden, and Eden would not come at all. Churchill was quite willing to come, but in view of the refusal of the others, we on our side thought it best to call a halt.'[24] Many may be tempted to assume that subsequent events proved Churchill wiser then Eden in thus moving towards a realignment. Yet would a Labour-dominated Coalition Government, if this had emerged from a subsequent General Election, as a result of Conservative defections, have proved particularly effective in facing up to the Fascist threat? Would it, for example, have introduced conscription as early as Chamberlain and would it have used the post-Munich period for promoting rearmament to anything like the same extent?

Another example of Eden's prudence was his unwillingness late in 1938 to support Amery in the creation of a pressure group calling for the immediate compilation of a national register of the whole population and for the introduction of some form of national service. But even Churchill declined to participate.[25] No doubt the known hostility of the Labour Party was of significance in the calculations of both men. Churchill diverged from Eden, however, in a Commons debate about the desirability of creating a Ministry of Supply to facilitate rearmament. Churchill spoke and voted against the Government's view that such a departure was unnecessary whereas Eden voted as the Whips directed. Even Harvey, who by now was generally showing an understanding attitude towards the policy of caution, on this occasion regretted Eden's decision.[26]

Again, Eden disappointed some of his more ardent supporters by the vague and uninspiring character of his address to a major rally of the League of Nations Union at the Queen's Hall at this period. It was left to Lady Violet Bonham Carter to rouse the enthusiasm of the audience. She told Basil Liddell Hart that 'she had to propose the vote of thanks – and she felt more like proposing a vote of censure on the speaker'. 'I cannot help thinking,' she wrote subsequently, 'that what I would prefer to call his tepid impartiality is due to a not unnatural human desire to return to office.' Cranborne and Nicolson were also inclined to be critical. Nicolson wrote in his diary of 15 November 1939, 'Have a drink with Bobbety Cranborne. I tell him to persuade Anthony to be just a little less cautious. The whole youth of the country is waiting for a stirring lead and all Anthony is [doing] is to repeat flabby formulas. He agrees.' And on 22 December the same diarist obtained confirmation that the question of Eden's return to the Cabinet was indeed still open; 'We ask whether after [Chamberlain's visit to] Rome he will join the Government. He says that he has not yet been asked. I see the two wings coming closer together.' In later years, incidentally, Eden found these diary entries distressing. He wrote to Paul Emrys-Evans on 13 August 1965: 'I have been in correspondence with Nigel Nicolson, and he assures me that his father now thinks that I was right and he was wrong in the line we took from the moment Bobbety and I resigned, i.e. that while we expressed our opinions as forcibly as need be, our purpose was to convert the Party rather than to break it asunder.' Eden also wrote to Nigel

Nicolson to deny that he 'would have rejoined the Government if asked'.[27] This was probably a case of selective recall in old age. For while this was his stand at certain points between February 1938 and September 1939, he was also intermittently inclined to favour the other view. Probably he was at no time absolutely opposed to rejoining Chamberlain's Cabinet but, reasonably enough, regarded the terms to be insisted upon as of decisive importance.

Meanwhile what of the majority of the so-called 'Eden group', or 'the Glamour Boys' as they were known to the Whips? In the last months of 1938 the bulk of its members were apparently no more resolute than its supposed leader. On 9 November Nicolson recorded that at a meeting of eleven sympathizers it was decided that 'we should not advertise ourselves or even call ourselves a group'. Nicolson continued in terms that are surprising in the light of what he had said to Cranborne only six days later:

> We should merely meet together from time to time, exchange views and organize ourselves for a revolt if needed ... Obviously they do not intend to do anything rash or violent ... It was a relief to me to be with people who share my views completely, and yet who do not give the impression (as Winston does) of being more bitter than determined, and more out for a fight than reform.

On 23 November Nicolson added: 'We still do not really constitute a group, and Anthony still hesitates to come out against the Government.'[28]

For Eden, as stated, the greatest difficulty was to decide whether or not to be prepared, if invited, to re-enter a Chamberlain Cabinet and, if so, on what terms. Very soon after Munich he appears to have decided that he would indeed return if the price was right; and that price appears to have slid steadily lower over the ensuing months. There were several possible elements in calculations about the price. First, how far should he insist on places for his loyal friends, and particularly for Cranborne who had resigned with him? Secondly, had he a duty to insist on particular policy pledges? Thirdly, should he insist on the creation of a truly national coalition and, more important, how should that be defined?

As late as 6 January 1939 Eden spoke to Harvey of not being able to return alone to the Government. Thereafter, however, this line appears to have been quietly dropped – except for occasional references to Churchill. On specific policy points he was also at first inclined to adopt a rather strong stand. For example, he told Nicolson on 21 November 1938 that he could not agree to serve in a Government whose policy was 'still directed towards a Four-Power Pact'.[29] But with the passage of time such conditions also became less prominent, possibly because Eden had convinced himself that Chamberlain's basic policy had already undergone a fundamental change. To the end, however, Eden continued to talk of the necessity for the creation of a truly national government. But what exactly did this mean? Would it be unfair to wonder whether the minimum definition of this was not at times simply his own inclusion in the Cabinet?

Chamberlain's own attitude to the return of Eden also underwent a change after Munich but in a contrary direction. It will be recalled that, shortly after Eden's resignation, Chamberlain had vainly tried to persuade him of the desirability of rejoining the Cabinet. Now, late in 1938, the Prime Minister was unenthusiastic when Halifax urged this course on him. For he cannot have been unaware that, after the Foreign Secretary's revolt over the Godesberg terms, the balance of power within the Cabinet was no longer so decisively in his own favour that he could risk the inclusion of so weighty a potential critic as Eden. Chamberlain rationalized his position as follows:

What makes him [Eden] think it possible to get unity is my insistence on the necessity for rearmament, and the news that I didn't like Hitler personally. He leaves out, or chooses not to see for the moment that the conciliatory part of the policy is just as important as the rearming.

He also believed that Eden's departure had had its advantages. On 5 November he wrote:

... the reflection must have come to many that if Anthony Eden had had his way I could never have made my appeal to Mussolini, he would never have intervened to persuade Hitler to accept negotiation and many a man who is happily living with his family today would be dead or mutilated.[30]

Eden meanwhile decided to widen his appeal both nationally and internationally. First, towards the end of 1938 he embarked upon a tour of special areas and trading estates. This was designed to enhance his reputation for domestic liberalism which would be an asset in any future broad coalition. He was also no doubt conscious, then as at other times in his career, that his almost exclusive specialization on international politics left him open to considerable criticism if he should ever make a bid for the premiership.

Eden also saw the need to keep his name before the broad international community. He accordingly undertook a visit in December to the United States. It was his first experience of the American mainland, though he had once stayed in Hawaii. He travelled to New York by the *Queen Mary*. Judging by a letter sent to Baldwin, he was acutely nervous about his reception, though evidently with little cause; 'I was in a fever how to deal with reporters' questions ... on arrival. Having said my piece I was asked one question: "How many children have you?" I was so flustered I couldn't remember.' He later made formal speeches in both New York and Washington. He also had private talks with numerous public figures including Roosevelt himself. The President conversed with him for three-quarters of an hour. The topics were varied but treated in a general way. But they avoided reference to the initiative of the previous January, though it must have been in the minds of both men. Eden conveyed his impressions of his visit as a whole to Baldwin:

I was horrified at the atmosphere I found. Poor Nancy [Astor] and her Cliveden set has done much damage, and 90 per cent of the US is firmly persuaded that you and I are the only Tories who are not Fascists in disguise. Certainly HMG have contrived to lose American sympathy utterly.

... I can assure you that while I was there most of my time was spent in asserting that Neville was not a Fascist, nor John Simon always a 'double crosser'.

You see how American I have become. I hope that I have not perjured myself too often, on J.S.'s behalf.[31]

Soon after Eden's return the post-Munich tranquillity in European affairs ended. On 15 March 1939 Germany entered what remained of the Czech lands – a move which involved the tearing up of the Munich Agreements and the incorporation of the first non-Germans into the Third Reich. But although this constituted a severe setback to his hopes, Chamberlain's initial response in the House of Commons was surprisingly mild and did not appear to presage any dramatic shift in British policy. Even more surprising was that Eden's speech on the same occasion was equally low-key. He made no attack on Chamberlain; on the contrary, he went out of his way to defend him against a Labour charge of having spoken of the Czechs without feeling. Nor did he call for conscription, still less for war. He confined himself instead to a vague appeal for national unity. It is not therefore surprising that even Henry 'Chips' Channon, Parliamentary Private Secretary to R. A. Butler at the Foreign Office and an ardent supporter of Chamberlain, recorded in his diary that Eden was 'not hostile to the Government and took me by the arm at one moment'.[32] It is difficult not to conclude that Eden was signalling his essential pliability in a bid to get back into office.

At this point Chamberlain's public attitude to foreign policy was to change considerably. On 17 March the Prime Minister, at a meeting in Birmingham, spoke in strong terms of Hitler's bad faith and warned that there were limits beyond which Great Britain would not go for the sake of peace. Then, on 31 March, after much high-speed diplomatic activity, the Government announced the famous 'guarantee' of Poland. Shortly afterwards Greece and Romania were given similar undertakings of British support. This momentous shift owed nothing to any immediate or direct pressure emanating from Eden. But this does not mean he and his group were not a major factor in determining the Cabinet's thinking. It was almost certainly Halifax who played the immediately decisive rôle in that he is thought to have indicated to Chamberlain that the Conservatives were heading for electoral defeat unless they moved towards the Centre of British politics and that meant essentially reversing the traditional line of abstaining from threatening military resistance to Germany in east-central Europe.[33] The Prime Minister reluctantly agreed. But why was Halifax able to convince him of this necessity? Was it not primarily the existence of Eden and his followers? Their lack of enthusiasm for Munich had already done much to turn undecided opinion against a neo-isolationist foreign policy. And despite Eden's caution and irrespective of whether or not he came back into the Cabinet, the possibility of his adopting a stance of outright disloyalty to Chamberlain at some future date could not be ignored. Moreover, Eden's position on the left of his party gave him a potentially pivotal position in British politics that was an additional worry for Chamberlain and Halifax. For, unlike Churchill, who was still widely considered to be a figure of the extreme right, Eden might with credibility have thrown in his lot at any time with a moderate electoral coalition of Liberals and Socialists. Eden, then, was a lion barring Chamberlain's path to continued appeasement – even if his roar was generally muffled. It is not therefore unreasonable to claim that Great Britain's eventual declaration of war for the sake of Poland probably owed more to Eden than to any other British politician. If he had not resigned in 1938 but had continued in office with his earlier views on not offering military resistance to Germany in east-central Europe, the destiny of his country and indeed of all Europe could have been entirely altered. There would have been no comparably significant left-wing Conservative pressure on Chamberlain to change course; British public opinion might have remained broadly pacific apart from brief outbursts of indignation; Hitler might have absorbed Poland without resistance; and the next war in Europe could have been between Germany and the Soviet Union with the Western Powers neutral and steadily rearming.

In the face of the shift away from appeasement for which he was so largely responsible, Eden tried to underline his commitment to the belief that little now need separate the so-called Conservative rebels from Chamberlain. While joining with Churchill and others on 29 March in signing a Commons Motion declaring in favour of national unity and, at last, even of national service, he stated on 31 March, in a speech at Newcastle upon Tyne, that it was 'unadulterated nonsense' to suggest that there was dissension in the Government ranks over foreign policy. On 1 April he wrote to Chamberlain:

I was sorry not to be in the House yesterday afternoon for I should have liked to have had a chance to say how completely I agreed with the statement you made ... It may perhaps interest you to hear that a very big meeting at Newcastle cheered to the echo an endorsement of what you had said. I have seldom seen such enthusiasm. There is no doubt of the mind of the North.

Then, on 3 April, he spoke in the Commons welcoming the new

developments in foreign policy and praising Chamberlain personally. He was no less warm towards the Government in a speech nine days later.[34]

Harvey's view of these developments was ambiguous. He regretted the almost undignified haste with which Eden appeared to be giving Chamberlain full support. Yet he endorsed Eden's desire to return to office at an early date and eagerly discussed the prospects with him.[35] Chamberlain, however, was not to be tempted, despite renewed entreaties from Halifax.

On 19 May Eden joined in clamour in the House of Commons for the Government to supplement their new east European policy with a Soviet alliance. He said:

> I have never been able to see any reason why, on any part of the earth's surface, the relations of this country – the British Empire – and the Soviet Government should come into conflict. If there is one country that has surely got plenty to do at home, that country is Russia . . . No country in the world has a greater need for peace . . . I really cannot understand why we should hesitate to come to an arrangement.[36]

In June, recalling his earlier visit to Stalin, he even offered to go to Moscow to negotiate on behalf of the Government. Halifax was prepared to agree. But Chamberlain, while he was compelled to consent with evident distaste to an attempt being made to reach agreement with Moscow, successfully blocked the idea that Eden should play any part and ensured instead that relatively unknown emissaries were dispatched. In the event no alliance with Moscow materialized in 1939 – much to the Prime Minister's relief. But he and his colleagues were sufficiently compromised by the attempt that they had in practice no alternative but to ignore the Soviet share in the aggression on Poland in the autumn. The further logic was that Stalin, despite acts of aggression no less blatant than those of Hitler, would be embraced in 1941 as an ally and that many of his crimes would be officially denied or condoned by London. It was perhaps poetic justice that Eden, who had played so large a part in creating the mood which led Great Britain to fight a war on the basis of such double standards, should have had to take the main public responsibility for covering up for Stalin and should eventually have been faced with the awesome but probably unavoidable duty of returning large numbers of innocent people to assumed execution in the Soviet Union. Ironically, Eden, as has been seen, had earlier manifested no enthusiasm for collaboration with Moscow. In this he was unusual among anti-appeasers and might therefore have been expected to find his subsequent rôle as a Soviet apologist all the more unpleasing. As late as May 1937, for example, he had successfully persuaded the French to abandon plans for Franco-Soviet conversations at the level of military attachés (which they saw as essential for the defence of Czechoslovakia) and into agreeing instead 'to reduce to the smallest possible compass any further developments of the Franco-Soviet Pact'. Eden had told Delbos that 'he much regretted' the intended conversations. 'To many,' Eden continued, 'who disliked and feared the diplomatic influence of the Soviet Government in Europe the extension of Franco-Russian collaboration would be interpreted as restricting in a new and dangerous way the libsrty of action of the French Government in European politics.'[37] Within two years, however, Eden, was ready for even Great Britain to abandon her liberty of action. It may be argued that in fundamentally revising his attitude to the Soviet Union he was wiser than Chamberlain. After all, the pro-Soviet policy led, after many vicissitudes and some luck, to the elimination of the threat posed by Nazi Germany both to British interests and to western civilization. But the price was high – just how high in the longer term is even now impossible to assess. It was certainly a price Chamberlain would not have wished to pay; and, if he had lived he might have derived some wry satisfaction from seeing Eden in office having to grapple with the more disagreeable consequences: the need during the war to condone Soviet crimes; a post-war Europe destined to be dominated by two essentially non-European superpowers; and an exhausted, impoverished and declining Great Britain.

In 1939 Eden cannot of course have fully appreciated the momentous character of the transformation in British policy for which he was so largely responsible. Hence as the year proceeded he contined to follow his chosen path. For example, in early June he and his followers were involved in a newspaper campaign, spearheaded by the *Daily Telegraph*, for the widening of the National Government. But this was a disappointment to Eden. For not only did Chamberlain resist the advice, but the newspapers involved rather surprisingly made it clear that they saw the inclusion of Churchill, and not Eden, as the most important symbol of a change in the direction of British policy – a somewhat perverse and unthematic preference for an opening to the right rather than to the left.[38]

Even now Eden did not change his tactics. He was still determined to give no new overt offence to Chamberlain and in no way to rival Churchill as a critic. This was well illustrated when some of Eden's friends sought to persuade him to oppose the Government's decision to move a two-month Parliamentary adjournment on 2 August. Nicolson, in particular, was discouraged at Eden's attitude – 'he is missing every boat with exquisite elegance' – and contemplated breaking ranks and casting an opposing vote with Churchill: 'I cannot let the old lion enter the lobby alone.'[39] In the end even Churchill drew back from voting with the Opposition, though he, unlike Eden, spoke out in the debate.

Eden meanwhile had decided to rejoin the Territorial Army. While in camp late in August he was actually awakened in his tent with the news that the Molotov–Ribbentrop Pact had been signed in Berlin. This was the signal for Germany to bring the simmering Danzig crisis to a head. On this occasion Hitler decided to invade Poland without giving the other powers time to organize a second Munich Conference beforehand. The choice facing Great Britain and France was thus either to declare war at once or to try to arrange an international conference while those whom they had 'guaranteed' were actually being overrun. Despite the supposed revolution in British policy in the previous March, Chamberlain opted for delay partly to explore the chances of negotiation and partly to obtain agreement with France on a common ultimatum. On the other hand, he was now extremely pessimistic about the prospects and he accordingly made plans for constructing a small War Cabinet and sounded Churchill about becoming First Lord of the Admiralty.

The decisive day for war or peace was 2 September 1939 when the House of Commons was recalled. Chamberlain astonished many of his supporters, including several ministers, by delivering a speech which appeared to leave the door open to a negotiated settlement. At this point Arthur Greenwood, Acting Leader of the Labour Party, spoke in more vigorous terms and was strongly cheered by many supporters of the National Government. Eden had at this point yet another chance to speak out, but, despite prompting by Duff Cooper and others, continued to sit in impassive silence.[40] Chamberlain, however, in view of the atmosphere in the Commons and an ensuing revolt by a number of junior ministers, finally determined to send an ultimatum to Germany. This was delivered at 9 a.m. the following day, 3 September, and was timed to expire two hours later.

Meanwhile, on the previous evening, Eden had seen Churchill, who had been offered a seat in the War Cabinet. He indicated that Eden would also be invited to join the Government but he could not be certain that he would have War Cabinet status. On the following morning, 3 September, while waiting for the expiry of the ultimatum, Eden met a group of his friends at Ronald Tree's house. Nicolson recorded: 'Some people think he [Eden] must refuse to join except as a member of the War Cabinet. Anthony wriggles and writhes, from which I gather he has already committed himself to join, and does not relish all these suggestions.'[41] In the event the Prime Minister did not send for Eden until the afternoon of 3 September, after war had been formally declared. He offered him the Dominions Office without a seat in the War Cabinet.

Surprisingly Eden accepted this humiliating offer. After overestimating his position early in 1938, he now greatly underestimated his unique popular strength. His position, however, was made no easier by Churchill, who proved less loyal to Eden than Eden may have expected. Churchill, it is true, had written to Chamberlain pressing Eden's claims to a seat in the War Cabinet but he had not done so to the point of refusing to serve. Ironically, Eden had told Harvey on 16 April 1939 that 'he would not go back without Winston and he did not think Winston would go in without him'.[42] Possibly the fact that Eden was at least given second-rank office and the special circumstances of war provided justification, if any were needed, for Churchill's conduct. Yet it is clear that Eden's short-term chances of obtaining the premiership were severely damaged and Churchill's much enhanced by the different status now accorded to each of them. Churchill himself must have realized the extent to which Chamberlain and even he himself had outmanoeuvred Eden. Later in the war he, Eden and Beaverbrook had a revealing conversation on the matter. According to Eden:

Max girded at me for not understanding my strength when I resigned and for coming back as Dominion Secretary. He said that had I played my hand strongly, I must have succeeded Neville. Winston said I was right to take Dominions Office. My own feeling about it all was that I do not truly believe my own contribution at any time to be so overwhelmingly good as to be prepared to drive it *à outrance*.[43]

Perhaps, then, Eden differed from Churchill in that he had at least a tendency to behave like his mentor Austen Chamberlain, of whom it was well said that he always played the game and always lost it. Had he acted differently, Eden, not Churchill, could well have had the privilege of giving the 'Lion's Roar' in 1940.

VI

European War
1939–41

The period from the outbreak of war to the fall of Neville Chamberlain on 10 May 1940 was probably the most frustrating of Eden's career. True, he was a Minister and had charge of a Department. But for a former Foreign Secretary it was humiliating to be denied Cabinet status, particularly when such a relative nonentity as Leslie Hore-Belisha had full membership. Nor can it have been much comfort that he was in practice allowed to attend every Cabinet in order to act as a means of communication with the Dominions. For if his presence was so necessary why should he not have had full Cabinet rank which would have carried with it the right to speak out on all issues and not merely those involving the Dominions? Clearly Chamberlain was to some extent afraid of him. Yet by joining the Government outside the Cabinet Eden got the worst of all worlds. For he could neither set himself up as an alternative Prime Minister from within the administration nor mobilize backbench critics from outside. Churchill was thus enabled to assume the first rôle while Amery took over from Eden as leader of the 'Glamour Boys'.

Eden must also have feared that the war would peter out after the fall of Poland. His whole political future now clearly rested on the opposite occurring and hence on his supposedly courageous anti-appeasing stand appearing to have been justified. Unfortunately for him, however, the Dominions were inclined during the period of the so-called 'Phoney War' to flirt with the advocates of a compromise peace. He was thus obliged to convey views to the Cabinet with which he must have privately disagreed. Again, his scope for handling problems involving the Dominions was limited by the appointment of Lords Hankey and Chatfield, two supporters of Chamberlain, to oversee his work through the means of a small Cabinet Committee. And a further limitation on his power to deal with the Dominions primarily through the High Commissioners, most of whom he had known when Foreign Secretary, came with the decision to invite each Dominion to send a Cabinet Minister to London for a series of meetings with Chamberlain and other key ministers. When this grouping assembled in October they were thus open to influence from the more appeasement-minded elements in the Government. In some cases the Dominions ministers needed little encouragement to adopt an unheroic line and indeed to go even further than their hosts.

The question of a compromise peace first arose in acute form on 6 October when Hitler offered a general settlement. In effect he asked of the West the abandonment of any interest in eastern Europe and the restoration of Germany's former colonies in Africa. France was, however, entirely opposed to any early settlement. She wished to crush Germany and subject her to the severest possible terms. All the Dominions, on the other hand, opposed a Carthaginian approach and called instead for a Declaration of Allied War Aims along 'Wilsonian' lines. They were, moreover, vague about the preconditions they would require before favouring negotiations with Berlin. Certainly no Dominion urged the restoration of the *status quo ante* with respect to Polish frontiers, let alone those of pre-Munich Czechoslovakia. Nor was the fall of the Nazi regime or even of Hitler made a specific requirement. This sharp divergence between France and the Dominions was clearly awkward for London. Moreover, there were some differences of emphasis even within the British Cabinet: Churchill was sympathetic to the French outlook, whereas Chamberlain and Halifax, particularly in their private views, leaned towards the Dominions. Chamberlain's solution was to try to maintain a temporary unity among the divergent elements by publishing a deliberately vague rejection of Hitler's overture. On 10 September he had written to his sister, Ida, that he anticipated early changes in Germany that would make possible a peace conference. Now, in the light of Hitler's offer of 6 October, he was driven to write to the same sister: 'I must say that I see no sign yet of any move which would or could be acceptable to us.' Yet by 5 November he felt that the war would nevertheless be over by the spring. That his requirements for a settlement were not particularly far-reaching, however, is proved by his subsequent private statement, in the following March, that Welles of the US State Department had 'appreciated our vital need for security and that if Hitler did not disappear he would have to agree to give up most of what Nazidom stands for'.[1]

Eden seems never to have contemplated favouring such an outcome to the war. All the same, he had the disagreeable task of conveying such sentiments from the Dominions to the War Cabinet. On 10 October, for example, he had to report that the Dominions thought that even Chamberlain's draft reply to Hitler 'went too far in the direction of "slamming the door" on further discussion'. Mackenzie King of Canada had even cabled to urge that 'the United Kingdom and France should put their own positive programme of basis upon which war could be terminated, framed in such broad terms as to win the support of the United States and other neutral countries'. On 11 October the Dominions Secretary had to point out to his colleagues that the Australians were opposed to a settlement merely on the basis of 'the status quo of the conditions of the Versailles Treaty' – possibly a critical reference to the Polish frontiers that had provided Hitler with his ostensible grounds for going to war. Next, on the following day, Eden had to report that all the Dominions had endorsed an idea canvassed by Jan Christian Smuts of South Africa, namely that of calling a conference of neutral powers which would be invited to determine the boundaries of any restored Poland or Czechoslovakia.[2] True, none of these proposals proved acceptable to Chamberlain – but his attitude was in large part determined by his unwillingness at this juncture to have an open conflict with Paris.

The arrival of the Cabinet Ministers from the Dominions enabled Chamberlain and Halifax to explain privately the thinking that lay behind their approach to the war. Indeed, so much was said at the first of their meetings on 1 November that the record constitutes as good a brief apologia for the policy of so-called appeasement as can be found in any contemporary document. In the presence of a silent Eden, Halifax stressed how much better Great Britain's position now was than would have been the case if war had broken out in September 1938 when 'Germany, Italy and Japan were acting in close concert and Spain was likely to be more readily available for Axis purposes'. 'On the other hand,' the Foreign Secretary continued, 'we might at that time [1938] have had the somewhat doubtful advantage of the cooperation of Russia.' In fact Halifax's central premise was that the changed rôle of the Soviets was a decidedly positive development. He evidently saw merit in Chamberlain's alleged initial reaction to news of the Molotov–Ribbentrop Pact: the more gentlemanly authoritarian states might now be detached from the vulgar Fascists in Berlin and it might even be possible for the former to ally with the democracies in a new anti-Comintern pact directed against Hitler and Stalin, both of whom might now be characterized as 'National Bolsheviks'. As Halifax told the Dominions ministers:

Today the Anti-Comintern Pact had been shaken to its foundations by the Russo-German Agreement. The Japanese were feeling aggrieved, and were now susceptible to pressure from other quarters. The attitude of Italy was very much different from what it had been a year ago, and was much more favourable to our cause than it had been even two months ago. Italy had no desire to go to war, certainly not on the side of Germany ... There were many forces in Italy now working in our favour, particularly the Royal House and the army. The recent changes in the Italian Cabinet had been all to the good. So far as Spain was concerned, General Franco only wanted to keep out of the war and carry on with the construction of his country.

Halifax continued to examine the implications of the British having lost out to Hitler in the quest for Stalin's favour:

It was very questionable, however, whether Herr Hitler would obtain any positive advantage from the Agreement. We could, he thought, have had an agreement with Russia in the summer if we had been willing to acquiesce in encroachment by Russia upon the Baltic States such as we had witnessed in the last month. Acquiescence in such actions would, however, have been against all our principles. We hoped that history would show that we had been right in our action in regard to Russia, and that Herr Hitler had taken the wrong road when he turned toward Russia. Germany had already suffered serious losses, both strategical and political, in Russia's encroachment on the Baltic States.

But, most strikingly, Halifax, hitherto such a weather-vane between the Prime Minister and Eden, had now evidently been converted to one of the former's fundamental foreign policy aims: at all costs to prevent Communism moving into the western end of Europe. Both men asked themselves whether Hitler, despite his earlier posturing as an anti-Communist, might not, as a result of his agreement with the Soviets, open the way to such an outcome. And if, as both Chamberlain and Halifax believed, there was a serious risk of this, should the British go to war with the Soviet Union as well as Germany? Halifax presented his verdict to the Dominion ministers:

One important result of the [Molotov–Ribbentrop] Agreement was the danger of Bolshevism spreading to Western Europe. Time would alone show whether Herr Hitler would lead this movement, or whether it would result in his extinction. It was a danger, however, which we had to face, and we had to make up our minds whether we should tackle it by drawing apart from Russia or even declaring war upon her. If we did that we might throw Russia more into the arms of Germany. The alternative policy was to concentrate first on the German menace, and it was this policy which the United Kingdom Government had decided to adopt. It was hoped that we should be able to avoid open hostilities with Russia, which might have serious repercussions in the Middle East and in India.

The implication of stating that the British should 'concentrate first on the German menace' was that Moscow's turn might yet come. That the Soviet Union was at this stage seen as an enemy and that the reason for not declaring war on her was purely tactical is supported by some words addressed by Chamberlain to the Dominions ministers: 'Even ... if matters went badly in the West it did not follow that Japan would come into the open against us. For one thing, Japan was extremely unlikely to enter war *on the same side as Russia.*'[3] (Italics supplied.) These various arguments must have been anathema to the silent Dominions Secretary who had recently invested so much political and emotional capital in opposing the Fascist Powers, especially Italy, and in seeking an alliance with the Soviet Union.

No less unwelcome to Eden must have been the tone of a subsequent meeting on 16 November. Now the question of an early peace conference was raised. It was the New Zealand Deputy Prime Minister, Peter Fraser, who took the most appeasing line. This was somewhat surprising in the light of his country's robustness at the time of the Abyssinian crises. But in calling for 'a general conference' of belligerents and neutrals he was speaking with full authority. For his Prime Minister, Savage, had cabled to Robert Menzies, Prime Minister of Australia, on 5 November:

... good does not come out of a peace imposed by a victor on the vanquished. We should therefore not wait until the exhaustion and bitterness of war has rendered impossible a peace on equal and rational terms, but rather take the earliest opportunity of making an attempt to bring about sincere and constructive peace discussions. It should also be made clear to the French that the Commonwealth cannot be party to an ungenerous peace.[4]

Chamberlain's response to the New Zealand appeal was by no means as resolute as Eden would have wished: he did not desire to 'exclude the possibility of a conference at some time' but he considered that there was no prospect of a useful conference in the near future. He continued that the Germans 'were not yet convinced the game was up, and until they did feel that, it was hard to believe that Hitler would give way'. Fraser, however, was unconvinced and reiterated 'New Zealand's desire for a conference before enormous casualties had taken place on both sides'.[5] The other Dominions did not go as far as New Zealand but probably only on tactical grounds. Bruce of Australia, for example, had cabled to Menzies on 8 October:

Difficulty I see is that it is impossible to see what terms we could lay down for *immediate negotiation* save ones so drastic as to be absurd without creating the impression that we were weakening. We would also open door to counter-proposals which might lead us into an impossible position.[6]

These, then, were depressing days for Eden. He must indeed often have wondered whether the 'Phoney War' would peter out altogether, leaving his own prospects in ruins.

This was also a testing time for his group of left-wing Conservative followers. They met regularly but only rarely had direct contact with their leader. Instead his interests were represented by his close friend, Thomas. That spirits were sometimes low is shown in Nicolson's diary:

In the evening we have a dinner of the Eden Group at the Carlton Hotel ... There are present Amery, Duff Cooper, Harold Macmillan, Louis Spears, Hubert Duggan, Paul Evans, Ronald Cartland and Jim Thomas. We begin by discussing the foreign situation but agree that it is too speculative at present for us to come to any decision. The general view is that the whole problem is whether the Russo-German alliance is positive or negative, if the former we may have to try a compromise before it is too late.[7]

Nor were Eden's relations with Churchill particularly warm at this period. He would have been more than human if he had not felt pangs of jealousy at being so clearly overtaken in the premiership stakes by the ebullient First Lord. Moreover, while the Dominions Secretary found the experience of again serving Chamberlain irksome – 'If it had not been for the emergency of war, nothing would have induced me to return'[8] – Churchill was often in a euphoric mood about the change in his fortunes. The First Lord also succeeded in getting on to good personal terms with the Prime Minister, whereas Eden was unwilling or unable to do the same. And further strain was put on Eden's relationship with Churchill by a major policy divergence, namely with respect to Eire. Under the leadership of Éamonn de Valera, Eire was the only Dominion to proclaim herself neutral on the outbreak of war. Initially this raised a difficult constitutional point: could she remain a member of the Commonwealth if she would not declare war on the King's enemy? But behind this argument lay naval fears: Dublin evidently intended to deny to the British the right to use Irish territorial waters, while, on the other hand, she might in practice turn a blind eye to German violations of Irish neutrality. Eden favoured a flexible and temporizing response. On 18 September the Cabinet endorsed this line and agreed to send Sir John Maffey to Dublin to seek a *modus vivendi* on matters likely to cause friction. Churchill found this 'profoundly unsatisfactory'. Maffey's talks with the Irish were only partly successful. He secured private expressions of sympathy for the Allied cause; he was able to deal with the problem arising from Irishmen who had volunteered to serve in the British army appearing in Eire in British uniforms by the simple expedient of having stocks of civilian clothing available at British ports; and he secured de Valera's support for a compromise agreement whereby the British envoy to Dublin was called a Representative rather than either a High Commissioner or an Ambassador. But Maffey could not persuade de Valera to grant any privileges to the British navy or even to agree to call for British assistance if Germany violated Irish territorial waters. The Irish leader declared, 'If ... facilities were voluntarily afforded in breach of neutrality, his Government could not live. No other Government which might endeavour to meet our request could survive for twenty-four hours.'[9] Eden concluded that this was no less than the unalterable truth. As he minuted to Halifax on 20 October, 'I fear that it becomes everyday clearer that it is scarcely possible for "Dev" to square neutrality with the grant of the facilities for which the Admiralty ask. And at least 80 per cent of the Irish people favour neutrality. Altogether a pretty problem.'[10] He was accordingly prepared to accept that London would have to manage without Irish naval cooperation, though the cost to British shipping through U-boat attacks might prove grievous. And he held that any response to a German violation of Irish neutrality should be determined only if the eventuality arose.

To Churchill the Government's Irish policy seemed inexcusably invertebrate. He could not forgive the move, made as recently as 1938, to hand over to the Irish the so-called Treaty Ports reserved for British use at the time of Partition. And, unlike Eden, he favoured seeking the reversal of this decision by threatening the use of force, particularly with respect to securing the use of Berehaven. To bolster this policy he developed the argument that Eire could not constitutionally abstain from war. As he minuted to Halifax, 'So far as "legality" counts, the question surely turns on whether "Eire is to be regarded as a neutral state" . . . Legally I believe they are "At war but skulking." '[11]

The implications of this doctrine for relations with other Dominions were dramatic. For though all had declared war on Germany, none had acted as if she had had no constitutional right to make a choice. Eden was horrified at this irresponsibility and fought out the matter with Churchill at the Cabinet on 24 October. The result was a victory for the Dominions Secretary, though the First Lord was to some extent humoured by a decision to call for reports on what the consequences of expelling Eire from the Empire would be.[12]

Churchill appears to have borne no permanent grievance against Eden on this account – though he never forgave Malcolm MacDonald for having negotiated the Treaty Ports Agreement of 1938. Indeed, at the beginning of 1940 he gave the appearance of wanting to help Eden. For when Hore-Belisha was dismissed from the War Office, he suggested him as a successor. This would have brought Eden into the War Cabinet and would have given him tasks that would have provided an adequate outlet for his energy. But it may be that Churchill was making only a token gesture in the certain knowledge that in any case Chamberlain would not want a dangerous rival to have full Cabinet status. The first year of the war was in fact to be a period in which the self-interests of Churchill and Chamberlain often lay in the same direction – with Eden and Halifax being cast as rivals to be kept at bay. In the event, therefore, Stanley became Secretary of State for War and Eden remained at the Dominions Office.

Churchill's policy towards Eire and his failure to secure promotion for him may even have affected Eden's attitude to the possibility of Churchill's becoming Prime Minister. On 1 October Nicolson formed the impression that 'he [Eden] evidently thinks that if the real war comes (as come it must) we must have a coalition under Winston'. But by 30 October, according to Harvey, Eden was 'beginning to doubt whether Churchill could ever be PM so bad is his judgement in such matters [Eire and India]'. And on 6 January 1940, the day of Stanley's appointment, Nicolson recorded, 'He [Eden] believes that in the end Halifax not Winston will become Prime Minister. He says that Halifax "will clear out the dead wood" even more effectively than Winston would. The latter is rather more sentimental about people.' In 1966, it is fair to add, Eden found this last passage 'puzzling'. 'I certainly did think this before the war broke out,' he wrote, 'but after it, Winston seemed the inevitable choice, and was certainly mine.'[13]

During these grim months Eden thus had little to console him in the world of Whitehall and Westminster. One of his officials, Saville Garner, recalled:

... he chafed at not being included as a full member of the War Cabinet and at working in what he regarded, after he had been so long in the Foreign Office, as the lesser Department of the DO; above all his restless energy could not be tamed to endure the futile inactivity of this strange period. He gave an impression of superficiality with no profound interest in the problems of the Commonwealth.

It must therefore have come as a relief to him to be able to pay an official visit to France in November in the company of the ministers from the Dominions. The visitors were not impressed by what they saw at the Front. On returning to London they made representations about various weaknesses, Deneys Reitz of South Africa even going so far as to tell Chamberlain that 'the Germans will go through there like a knife through cheese'.[14]

Always diverted by a 'jaunt', particularly if it involved inspecting armed forces, Eden followed up his visit to France with one to Egypt, Palestine and Malta in February 1940. His principal purpose was to greet forces arriving in Egypt from Australia and New Zealand. The occasion had later significance in that he met for the first time General Sir Archibald Wavell. The two men struck up a friendship which was to survive a severe test the following year.

Returning to London, Eden had again to endure being passed over for promotion to the War Cabinet when a new reshuffle took place in April. Churchill now canvassed his name for the Air Ministry but instead Kingsley Wood was appointed. Clearly a new foreign trip was called for. This time he was ambitiously determined to visit each Dominion in turn. But this plan was nullified by the sudden end of the 'Phoney War'.

Ironically, primary responsibility for the sharpening of the conflict lay with the Western Powers. They began the process by raising expectations that they would join the so-called 'Winter War' in which the Soviet Union invaded Finland. In Paris and London those whose principal motive was hatred of Moscow combined with others who wished to intervene in the north to deny Germany iron ore supplies from Sweden. But the mixed motives caused such delays in Western planning that the pretext was to be removed before any expedition could be launched, Finland reaching a compromise peace with the Soviet Union on 12 March 1940. But a momentum had been created that made some action in the north unavoidable. Hence the British Cabinet, on Churchill's urging, decided to mine Norway's offshore waters as a means of reducing the flow of iron ore to Germany. This, however, involved a violation of Norwegian neutrality and led Hitler to take pre-emptive action by invading both Denmark and Norway on 8 April. The British duly came to Oslo's aid with a landing at Narvik. But this gesture proved futile and was followed by a humiliating retreat. Now the moment had come for Chamberlain's enemies to combine against him. Eden, as a member of the Government, had to give token support to the Prime Minister, while Churchill, a prime mover in the Narvik expedition, even presented an outright defence in the subsequent inquest. But Eden's supporters on the backbenches were less inhibited. On 7 and 8 May they organized a major revolt, in speech and vote, during a crucial two-day Commons debate. On the first day Channon recorded: 'The "glamour boys" are smacking their lips but their full strength is not yet known.' On the following day, after Amery had invoked the Deity in urging the Prime Minister to quit, the Government's majority fell from the normal 240 to a mere 81. Channon now saw that the end for Chamberlain was near. In the lobby he had seen Eden and Thomas both of whom 'looked triumphant'. As for the Prime Minister:

Neville appeared bowled over by the ominous figures, and was the first to rise. He looked grave and thoughtful and sad: as he walked calmly to the door, his supporters rose and cheered him lustily and he disappeared. No crowds to cheer him, as there were before and after Munich – only a solitary little man, who had done his best for England.[15]

Many of Chamberlain's colleagues now made it known that the Labour Party must be invited to join a Government of National Unity. And soon it became apparent that the Labour leaders would serve, but only under a new Prime Minister. Chamberlain thus had only one remaining task: to recommend his successor to the King. His final choice fell on Churchill rather than Halifax. This was not, however, inevitable from the outset. For the Labour leaders would have served under either man. Nor need Halifax's membership of the Lords necessarily have been vital: the King himself suggested that this could have been 'placed in abeyance for the time being'.[16]

Why, then, was Churchill chosen? The traditional view is that he and Halifax settled it between themselves in a meeting with Chamberlain. The background to this was that Wood, now Lord Privy Seal, had surprisingly warned Churchill, in Eden's presence, that Chamberlain would want him to agree to Halifax's succession. But Wood advised Churchill to let Halifax do the talking. Hence in the crucial encounter Churchill remained silent for two minutes after which an allegedly embarrassed Foreign Secretary capitulated. This may be true as far as it goes. But it does not constitute a sufficient explanation. If, as has usually been supposed, Chamberlain wanted Halifax to have the post, why did he convene such a meeting and act so far out of character as effectively to abdicate? Why did he not, knowing that Attlee and his colleagues were prepared to serve, simply advise the King to send for Halifax? One possibility is that he actually preferred Churchill but did not wish it to be known. This would explain

Wood's conduct in giving helpful advice to Churchill – something which left Eden 'shocked . . . for he had been so much Chamberlain's man'.[17] But why should Chamberlain have preferred Churchill? A clue to the answer may lie in the former's diary entry for 9 September 1940 by which date he had had a major operation: 'I have still to adjust myself to the new life of a practically crippled man which is what I am. Any ideas which may have been in my mind about possibilities of further political activity and even a possibility of another Premiership after the war have gone. I know that is out of the question.'[18] This provides a reminder that Chamberlain, at the time of handing over the premiership to Churchill, retained the leadership of the Conservative Party. It also makes it clear that he contemplated recovering the premiership at the end of what he may still have believed would be a brief war. In the meantime as Lord President of the Council he expected to remain in charge of running the home front. As Chamberlain may have seen it, Churchill's unpopularity with Conservatives and his advanced age made it unlikely that he would be able to retain the premiership in peacetime, whereas Halifax might have proved a more formidable rival. It may indeed be, therefore, that Chamberlain and Churchill reached a tacit understanding about the future and that Wood was at that time the only person privy to it. This would be consistent with Churchill's subsequent promotion of Wood to the War Cabinet. It would also explain the contradiction between a letter written by Chamberlain to his sister, Ida, suggesting that he had Halifax 'in mind' and the following record which survives in Beaverbrook's papers, headed 'Kingsley Wood, Question and Answer':

'Did you decide that Chamberlain ought to be supplanted by Churchill? and if so when did you start working to that end?'

'Quite soon after the start of the war Chamberlain himself told me he would have to give way to Churchill. He never intended that Halifax should be Prime Minister, he always intended Churchill to be his successor. By the end of the year it had become obvious that the change was not far off, and I started negotiations with Churchill which resulted in the change.'[19]

It may even be that Chamberlain, Wood and Churchill were more deeply in league than Eden was permitted to know. For in some respects Eden stood to suffer almost as much as Halifax from collusion between Chamberlain and Churchill, since the outgoing Prime Minister's disapproval of Eden was such that he was likely to insist in any deal that his successor must deny him significant advance. Concern about offending Mussolini, who was still neutral, was no doubt also a factor that Chamberlain could be relied upon to stress. Yet Churchill plainly could not leave him at the Dominions Office after earlier having told him that he had twice suggested his name to Chamberlain for other posts. His solution was to make him the offer of the

War Office but to blunt its importance by excluding him from membership of the War Cabinet. Moreover, Churchill made himself Minister of Defence and Chairman of a newly constituted Defence Committee, thereby circumscribing Eden's freedom of action.

Eden, however, was entirely happy with the new arrangement and he evidently convinced himself that Churchill had a positive attitude towards him. In any case he had little time to brood. For on entering the War Office on 12 May he found himself facing a series of unparalleled crises for the British army. The Germans had attacked the Low Countries on 10 May and within a fortnight were within sight of outright victory on the Western Front. Churchill and the War Cabinet, together with the Chiefs of Staff, took most of the major decisions. But Eden's rôle was not negligible. On 14 May, for example, he was asked to broadcast to the nation calling for so-called Local Defence Volunteers – and received an overwhelming popular response. It is fair to add, however, that the plan had been drawn up before he went to the War Office, while it was Churchill who decided that the 'Home Guard' would be a more appropriate title. On 13 May Eden called for British bombing to be concentrated on the advancing German forces rather than on their communication lines. But his pleas were rejected. This presaged the War Cabinet's decision, made in circumstances of some controversy, that no further squadrons could be committed to the Continent without seriously jeopardizing the capacity of Great Britain to fight on alone if France should collapse.

By the last days of May more critical decisions had to be taken. Some were on the political level. Should the British, in response to the appeals of the Premier, Paul Reynaud, join France in asking Mussolini to explore the terms that might be on offer in a European Peace Conference? Churchill and Halifax differed on this subject in the War Cabinet. The Prime Minister, according to Chamberlain, thought that 'it was incredible that Hitler would consent to any terms that we could accept though if we could get out of this jam by giving up Malta and Gibraltar and some African colonies he would jump at it. But the only safe way was to convince Hitler that he couldn't beat us'. Halifax, supported by Chamberlain, argued 'that there could be no harm in trying Musso and seeing what the result was. If the terms were impossible we could still reject them.' According to the Cabinet Minutes, Churchill confirmed that 'if Herr Hitler was prepared to make peace on the terms of the restoration of German colonies and the overlordship of Central Europe, that was one thing', but he concluded that 'it was quite unlikely that he would make any such offer'.[20] Thus Churchill, unless it is to be presumed that he was deceiving his colleagues, was at this stage not opposed *in principle* to a settlement with Hitler but merely considered that acceptable terms would not be on offer. It is questionable whether Churchill's judgement of Hitler's attitude was correct. For the Führer may well have been interested in establishing a neutral West that would leave him a free hand in the East. Whatever the truth about Hitler's aims, a tentative feeler which Halifax put out to Rome through Roosevelt came to nothing because Mussolini was unwilling to be bought off, still less to act as intermediary in Berlin. Instead he belatedly decided to go to war at Hitler's side. The possibility of a compromise peace with Berlin thus ceased to be practical politics. For Eden this was more good fortune in that it marked the last echo of Chamberlain-style 'appeasement'. Moreover, the War Secretary had not been invited to attend the crucial War Cabinet meetings at which compromise peace had been discussed. He was thus enabled to emerge from the Second World War with in one sense a more 'heroic' record even than Churchill, whose remarks in Cabinet, if taken literally, were in striking contrast to his public stand. The historian, if he so chooses, can indeed argue that the collapse of prospects for a compromise peace may have been based on a mere failure of communication between London and Berlin and not, as is usually supposed, on Churchill's resolve, as Dalton recalled it, to lie 'choking in his own blood upon the ground' rather than contemplate 'parley or surrender'.[21] No such controversy about Eden's attitude to compromise peace is possible.

The Secretary of State for War was, by contrast, much involved in some of the vital military decision-making in the last days of May. On the 25th he ordered Brigadier Claude Nicholson to hold Calais at any cost. He considered this a painful necessity if the rest of the British Expeditionary Force (BEF) was to have a chance of reaching the Channel ports to the east of Calais. By the 29th the War Cabinet, with Eden's support, finally ordered Viscount Gort to evacuate all British forces. Thus began the epic of Dunkirk. In the ensuing hectic days Eden was fortunate to have at his side a new Chief of the Imperial General Staff (CIGS) in whom he had complete confidence. This was John Dill, who had replaced Edmund Ironside on 27 May. The Secretary of State and the CIGS could reasonably claim to have timed the operation successfully. To have delayed longer would have cost the country most of the BEF. To have moved even a few days earlier might have given the French genuine grounds for complaint that they were being deserted before all hope was gone. Reassuring the French was in any case no easy task. The War Cabinet was to some extent able to do this by claiming that they were engaged on a tactical withdrawal and intended to redeploy the BEF in western France. They also adopted a declaratory position that trapped French troops would be given the same opportunity for evacuation as their British counterparts. Indeed, Eden in his memoirs, continued to stick to this line by writing: 'I asked him [General Harold Alexander] to give French troops equal facilities with our own to get away.' But he did not reveal that on 31 May he had told the War Cabinet that Gort had asked 'whether he ought to hold on as long as possible, in order to evacuate as many French as possible, or whether when he judged that it was not safe to delay any longer, he should order the withdrawal of the remaining British troops' and that he had replied that 'the second was the course which we wished him to pursue'.[22]

The need to assess whether continuing French resistance in western France was likely to be worth supporting led Churchill to visit Reynaud and his principal colleagues at Briare, near Tours, on 11 June. He asked Eden to accompany him. The two men, after protracted conversations, returned home on the following day convinced that the complete military defeat of France was close at hand. Now the critical question was whether Reynaud should be encouraged to seek the best terms available or move his Government overseas and leave others to accept a military armistice. Eden wrote to Churchill:

You will keep in mind the vital distinction between armistice and peace. The former is military, the latter political. We could consent to France asking for the former under military duress. We could never agree to her making *peace*. Holland has not made peace nor Norway.[23]

Matters were complicated, however, by the possibility that the French fleet, and particularly the part of it based at Toulon, could fall into German hands. At a crucial War Cabinet on 16 June Churchill and his colleagues were influenced by this factor into agreeing to release Reynaud from his obligation not to enter into separate negotiations with the enemy: they said he might make inquiries about armistice terms provided he forthwith ordered the French fleet to British harbours. Eden was the most reluctant of those present to consent to this course. As one historian has written:

It may be that the British Cabinet erred in thus giving its consent to a French request for terms. [Georges]Mandel [Minister of the Interior] had been in favour of an uncompromising reply, and it is possible that Reynaud too would have preferred a straightforward negative, so that he could take a firm stand based on British intransigence. Spears thought that a dangerous door had been opened to the French defeatists. A few days later, on 22 June, Vansittart wrote that it was 'an expensive error ... It set us on a downward path up which we have never been able to climb again.'[24]

The French Government thus did not go overseas, and Reynaud soon gave way to Marshal Philippe Pétain. Above all, the French fleet was not ordered to British ports. Churchill's gamble must therefore be judged a failure. Eden's approach, if tried, could scarcely have had worse results. But he loyally abstained from spelling out in his memoirs the extent to which his more robust line was overruled by Churchill. At this period, too, the War Cabinet decided to make the abortive offer to Paris of an Anglo-French Union. Eden's views were not recorded, though he was surprisingly to show interest in reviving the idea during the Suez crisis of 1956.

With Great Britain alone and effectively excluded from continental Europe, Eden now focused his attention on two main theatres: the Home Counties in case a German invasion should be attempted and the Middle East where British forces were contesting the future of north Africa with the Italians. He was privately inclined to believe that Hitler would try to secure outright victory by crossing the Channel. Indeed, on 27 July he confidentially told W. P. Crozier, the editor of the *Manchester Guardian*, that 'it was at this moment the considered opinion of our General Staff that the attempt was coming'. Together with Dill and his new Commander-in-Chief, Home Forces, Sir Alan Brooke, Eden visited the troops and engaged in endless contingency planning for the event which never materialized. Eden was naturally alarmed at the desperate lack of available equipment. But, while he cannot have been too hopeful about the prospects, he did not permit himself to brood or show any trace of defeatism. At one depressing moment Churchill helped to keep up his spirits by saying: 'About time No. 17 turned up, isn't it?' This referred to a pre-war occasion at the casino at Cannes. The two men had won handsomely at roulette by backing No. 17. In the summer of 1940 they were again in luck.[25]

Eden's special involvement in military developments in the Middle East stemmed from Churchill's suggestion to Eden on 11 July that he should become Chairman of a Middle East Committee. This new responsibility for Eden was to involve him in a series of clashes with his chief relating both to policies and personalities. The first arguments came very early. For by late July Churchill was agitating for the removal of Wavell as Commander-in-Chief, Middle East; and when Dill supported Wavell, the Prime Minister also began to criticize the CIGS. Eventually Eden and Dill were driven by the Prime Minister's attacks on Wavell, in the presence of other ministers, to consider resignation. Churchill, however, backed down and agreed that Wavell should continue. But he was never subsequently to change his mind about the unsuitability of both Wavell and Dill for their senior posts; and after Eden's departure from the War Office, he duly removed both of them.

Churchill's hostility to Wavell and Dill did not apparently damage relations between the Prime Minister and his War Secretary. For late in July Eden had a friendly discussion with his chief about whether the dying Chamberlain's imminent departure from the War Cabinet might provide the opportunity for promotion. No doubt he wished to be in the War Cabinet but, as always, was not eager to serve on the domestic front. The Foreign Office was plainly his goal. But Halifax was unlikely to wish to move. Matters came to a head late in September when Chamberlain finally resigned. Halifax was indeed reluctant to take over as Lord President and might well have left the Government rather than give way. That Churchill did not even risk such an outcome was probably due to one final intervention by Chamberlain against Eden's interests. In a conversation with Wood, he referred to rumours that Eden would replace Halifax: '... the change at the Foreign Office would be taken to mean a change of policy and a condemnation of my policy'.[26] Churchill could scarcely afford at this stage to alienate Chamberlain and hence he told Eden on 30 September that he did not want Halifax to depart 'at the moment when Neville is leaving'. He could therefore at present offer him a choice only of the Lord Presidency with a seat in the War Cabinet or continuation at the War Office. Eden chose the latter. He must, however, have found it galling to see John Anderson (Lord President), Ernest Bevin (Minister of Labour) and Wood (Chancellor of the Exchequer) promoted to the War Cabinet ahead of him. But Eden had the consolation that a grateful Churchill told him that 'the succession must be his' and that he would 'not make Lloyd George's mistake of carrying on after the war'.[27] Eden evidently at this stage believed both these statements. And certainly his prospects were much enhanced by Chamberlain's retirement and early death and by the consequent election of Churchill as Leader of the Conservative Party. Like two earlier leaders of coalitions, Lloyd George and MacDonald, Churchill had begun his premiership without a major party behind him but, unlike them, he had now succeeded in taking one over. Arguably it was this event rather than the resignation of Chamberlain from the premiership which marked the beginning of the so-called Social Democratic Age. In such an era Eden could expect to prosper and he soon became the obvious heir to Churchill. His wait for the succession was, however, to be longer and more exasperating than he could then have guessed. For it was Churchill even more than Eden who profited from Chamberlain's retirement and death. A jaundiced foreign observer, Josef Goebbels, also came to see in Chamberlain's demise a decisive turning-point. He wrote in his diary on 12 March 1945:

I have sensational news from neutral sources about Chamberlain's timely death. After the Polish campaign Chamberlain had advocated an attempt at a compromise peace with Germany. The real enemy of Europe, he said, and therefore of Britain's position as a world power, was not the Reich but the Soviet Union. If the war were continued, it would certainly turn into a war of attrition. Germany might perhaps go down in this war of attrition but England certainly would. This forecast of Chamberlain's was dismissed by the Churchill clique at the time as the idle talk of a tired and senile man. It has turned out to be true to an astonishing degree. People on the British side even suspect that Churchill commissioned the Secret Service to administer poison to Chamberlain. I do not believe this but it is a fact that Churchill was not particularly downcast at Chamberlain's death.[28]

Immediately after it had been confirmed that Eden would remain at the War Office, he was asked, on 6 October, to undertake a mission to the Middle East. For weeks he and Churchill had been in disagreement about the degree to which equipment and manpower should be diverted from the Home

Front to north Africa. At this stage Eden was inclined to doubt whether a German invasion would be attempted and favoured shoring up the British position in Cairo. Churchill, on the other hand, was unenthusiastic and in any case unsure about the best means of helping Wavell. It was thus to be Eden's task to form a first-hand impression of the war in the Middle East. Arriving in Cairo on 16 October, he found himself once more in broad sympathy with Wavell and tended at this stage to fall in with the military assessments given to him. Together they toured Palestine and Transjordan as well as spending much time in Egypt. Wavell was confident that an early offensive against the Italians was possible if adequate reinforcements could be provided. Whether the Prime Minister would have fully endorsed Wavell's requests must, however, remain problematical. For towards the end of October the situation was transformed by evidence that Mussolini intended to attack Greece, war actually breaking out on the 28th. Now Churchill became a sudden convert to overseas adventure. But while Eden and Wavell wanted to concentrate on attacking Italy in the Sahara, Churchill preferred to offer assistance to Athens. Initially the War Cabinet wished to tell Greece that the best way to help her was for Great Britain to defeat Italy but not necessarily to make the Balkans a principal theatre. This would have meant that only a limited number of British fighter aircraft would have been sent to Athens. But by the beginning of November Churchill had persuaded his colleagues that more direct help was desirable, including land forces. He later talked of the loss of Athens being 'as serious a blow to us as the loss of Khartoum'.[29]

In Cairo Eden and Wavell were unimpressed by Churchill's approach. Eden wrote in his diary on 1 November: 'We are both apprehensive lest the cries from Greece should result in our being asked to divert any part of our very small resources from here.' For, as has been seen, Wavell had it in mind to launch an early attack on the Italians in north Africa and this was not yet known in London. The next days saw the frantic exchange of many telegrams between Eden and Churchill. The War Secretary wished to return home to press his point of view, while the Prime Minister affected not to see any reason for this. Both men, in their memoirs, gave the impression that, because of security considerations, Eden did not explicitly refer by telegram to the decisive factor of Wavell's impending offensive. Yet on 3 November, after sending earlier circumlocutory hints, Eden dispatched to the Prime Minister by personal cypher a quite unequivocal statement:

Entirely for your own information Wavell is having plans prepared to strike blow against Italians in Western Desert at the earliest possible moment, probably this month. He is particularly anxious to keep secret his intention which is at present known only to very few senior commanders and staff officers who are drawing up plans. Plan involves certain risks and requires all trained and fully equipped troops in Western Desert and Reserve in Egypt. Margin is small and any withdrawal of troops or equipment would mean cancelling plan and remaining on defensive. It is of this plan that I wish to speak to you on my return.[30]

Churchill was not influenced by this message. Nor did he tell the War Cabinet about it. Instead he persuaded his colleagues on the following day to approve significant aid being sent to Greece. Eden naturally disapproved. He had written in his diary on 3 November:

The weakness of our policy is that we never adhere to the plans we make. If we had ever thought to help Greece, we should long since have laid our plans accordingly. Instead of which we took a deliberate decision not to do so, and then go back on it ...

On the following day he wrote: 'These new commitments have an uncanny habit of growing despite all promises that they will not.'[31]

Forced to accept Churchill's instructions to weaken the forces available in north Africa, Eden was at last permitted to return home. He left Cairo on 6 November and arrived in London two days later. This was when Churchill, according to his memoirs, first discovered that Wavell planned an offensive:

Here, then, was the deadly secret which the Generals had talked over with their Secretary of State. This was why they had not wished to telegraph. We were all delighted. I purred like six cats. Here was something worth doing.

But, as one historian has commented:

Why did Churchill wait until 8 November before allowing himself to purr like six cats? He knew five days earlier what was planned in North Africa. Why did he pretend that he did not? Why, nearly ten years later, when no security reason inhibited him from setting out the facts, did he tell his readers that he had to wait for Eden's return to learn that Wavell was about to mount an offensive? It looks like a deliberate attempt to conceal his knowledge of the proposed offensive both at the time, and when he was writing *The Second World War*; but if this is true it is difficult to understand what his purpose was.

The same writer is also puzzled that Eden, too, in his memoirs, ignored his explicit telegram of 3 November and wrote merely of 'telegraphing hints but not proclaiming our plans'.[32] The explanation may be that Churchill was conscious, when writing his memoirs, that he had deliberately concealed from his colleagues Eden's extremely relevant telegram and that knowledge of this might well have led survivors, including Attlee, to accuse him of dictatorial conduct. The fact that Eden had enjoined secrecy upon the Prime Minister might not have seemed sufficient reason for not informing at least the members of the War Cabinet. Eden's *suppressio veri* in his memoirs can in turn best be explained as a chivalrous action designed to avoid depicting Churchill in an exceptionally unfavourable light. He seems to have behaved with equal loyalty in November 1940, despite his disagreement with the Prime Minister. For he did not allow the existence of his personal telegram of 3 November to become known to any colleague in the Government.

This willingness to submit to Churchill's will did not go unrewarded. First, on 5 December Churchill surprisingly offered Eden the Middle East Command – presumably involving his ceasing for a time to be a minister. Despite having had fantasies in his youth about a military career, Eden was too shrewd to risk his whole future in such a venture and may even have wondered about the Prime Minister's motives in making the suggestion. But his doubts must have been dispelled by Churchill's next offer: a return to the Foreign Office and full membership of the War Cabinet. A reluctant Halifax was to be virtually ordered to go to Washington as British Ambassador. Eden's return to the Foreign Office was accordingly announced on 23 December. As Churchill wrote, he was like 'a man going home'.[33]

As 1941 began Great Britain's position looked already much less desperate than six months earlier. The threat of a German invasion had receded. Meanwhile Wavell's desert offensive, which had gone ahead despite the Greek diversion, had brought a success over the Italians at Sidi Barrani. And the Greeks, with limited British support, had also done unexpectedly well against the Italians. In the early months of 1941 Greece was indeed to become a dominant concern for Eden. For signs began to appear that Hitler might decide to come to the rescue of his embarrassed ally. This in turn might open the way to a total German victory in the Balkans and even possibly permit a thrust through Asia Minor into the heart of the Middle East. For all his lofty rhetoric in support of a country guaranteed by Great Britain in 1939, Eden was bound to view the German threat to Greece in this wider context. He was in any case undoubtedly more sympathetic to and concerned about the fate of Turkey. Hence the suspicion must remain that he was not particularly scrupulous in his handling of Athens. For example, he did nothing to encourage proposals for a compromise settlement between Greece and Italy and refrained from passing on to the Greeks hints from neutral sources that provided she behaved with prudence Hitler might by-pass Athens in any *Drang nach Osten*. Eden's aim seems to have been to use the Greeks to draw both Yugoslavia and Turkey into collective resistance to Hitler. His hopes, however, proved vain, being based on unrealistic assessments of Turkish and Yugoslav intentions and capabilities. Thus a broadly unfavourable verdict on his general Balkan policy during this period would appear to be justified. Moreover, Greece was required to pay an unnecessarily high price for this flawed diplomacy.

Early in 1941, Eden, fearing heightened German influence over Bulgaria and Romania, became eager to increase the British military presence in Greece. This was a sudden reversal of his earlier hostility to Churchill's policy of diverting at least some aid to Greece from the north African theatre. But the rationale behind Eden's metamorphosis was fear that the

Greeks might reach agreement with both the Axis powers and lapse into neutrality. Turkey and Yugoslavia would then be open to German pressure to follow suit or even join the Axis. Moreover, even Crete would cease to be available to the British. As Sargent minuted on 7 January, this 'would mean that she would have to insist upon our evacuating any naval and air bases which we had occupied on Greek territory ... We might of course defy the Greek Government ... but if we did so our position would politically be an invidious one.'[34] On the following day the Defence Committee decided to ask the Greeks to allow British forces to be moved into Salonika. Wavell was accordingly ordered to Athens to try to win over the Greeks. But the Government of John Metaxas, seeing this move as likely to be provocative to Berlin, refused. The British were disappointed but as Cadogan wrote in his diary: '... we can't force assistance down Metaxas's throat'.[35] By early February, however, the mood in Athens was changing. Metaxas had died suddenly on 29 January and had been replaced by the much less authoritative Alexander Koryzis. At the same time, the German threat was thought to be increasing. This led the Greek Commander-in-Chief, General Alexander Papagos, to assume a position of increasing influence with King George II and with his enfeebled Government. Yet Papagos had evidently not fully thought through his position. He appears to have favoured resistance to the Axis powers, including even a German invasion. Yet any slight chance of successfully repelling such an attack had to rest upon substantial British support being present in advance, even if that should be seen as 'provocative' in Berlin. This Papagos appeared not to grasp. Churchill and Eden concluded that a major effort should therefore be made to get the Greeks to modify the rather negative line they had taken with Wavell. But whereas Churchill saw aid for Greece as practically an end in itself, Eden was much more interested in hopes of influencing Turkey into resisting Germany. In the face of all the evidence of Turkish intentions, he persisted in the belief that he could persuade Ankara to accept a major British presence. On 29 January, for example, he wrote in his diary: 'Turkey is the key and we must intensify our efforts there. We [Eden and Churchill] discussed my going to Turkey.'[36] On 8 February, however, the Greeks indicated a willingness to accept British forces in principle and also to discuss the details. Accordingly Churchill and the Defence Committee decided to send Eden and Dill to Athens. There remained, however, an important difference of emphasis between Eden and Churchill. The former was primarily anxious to aid the Greeks, if at all, as a means of bringing Turkey into the conflict; the latter was more pessimistic about Turkish intentions but saw merit in giving aid to Greece in any case.

On 12 February Eden, Dill and a small number of aides travelled by rail to Plymouth to begin a lengthy and perilous journey to Cairo. First, bad weather delayed the departure of their aircraft. Then their flight to Gibraltar almost ended in disaster when a fuel shortage seemed likely to force them to land in Spain, a development that could have led to the Foreign Secretary's internment. After stopovers in Gibraltar and Malta, they at last arrived in Cairo on 19 February. *En route* Eden was allowed to open his sealed orders which required him to decide how best to help Greece and gave him liberty of action in an emergency. This sealing of orders was, incidentally, a decidedly eccentric action on Churchill's part. As Eden recalled:

> I had 'sealed orders' which the Prime Minister had entrusted to me with solemnity and relish when I left, with the injunction that I must not open them while I was still in the country. I broke the seals at Gibraltar, which was not so dramatic as it sounds because I had discussed the contents at length with Mr Churchill during the previous days.[37]

At this stage of the war, however, Eden's relationship with Churchill was exceptionally good and hence the Foreign Secretary took no offence at the Prime Minister's bizarre behaviour. But in later years when quarrels intensified, Eden may have recalled this incident, along with many others, as an attempt to humiliate him.

Having arrived in Cairo, Eden and Dill spent two days in lengthy consultations with Wavell and his local Service Commanders-in-Chief. Dill, hitherto sceptical, was impressed by the strength of the military advice in favour of making a major British effort in Greece. The capture of Benghazi on 7 February had evidently made Wavell and his colleagues less obsessed with north Africa than hitherto. Eden was ill-equipped to challenge this policy on military grounds – though he would probably have made the attempt if his instincts had so prompted him. But the military advice was reinforced in the political sphere by the presence in Cairo of Colonel William Donovan, Roosevelt's special envoy to the Mediterranean region. In a brief meeting with the Foreign Secretary, Donovan urged British resistance to German encroachment upon the Mediterranean, not least on the grounds that a passive attitude would be unfavourably received by American public opinion. As has been seen, Eden had long been optimistic regarding the extent to which the United States might be drawn back into European affairs and hence he was only too ready to give disproportionate weight to Donovan's counsel. The British team in Cairo accordingly invited themselves to Athens for a secret meeting to be held on 22 February and privately decided to offer substantial assistance to the Greeks. But in view of the subsequent controversy about the terms on which help was to be given, it is necessary to stress that on the eve of his departure for Athens, Eden telegraphed to Churchill:

> We should all have liked to approach Greeks tomorrow with a suggestion that we should join with them in holding a line to defend Salonika but both [Arthur]

Longmore and [Andrew] Cunningham are convinced that our present air defences will not allow us to do this. Dill and I are not prepared to take a final decision until we have discussed the matter with the Greeks.[38]

Clearly, then, the possibility of abandoning Salonika was already in the Foreign Secretary's mind but he had not yet made a final decision.

Arriving in Athens on 22 February, Eden, Dill, Wavell and their aides were taken to Tatoi, the Greek monarch's country palace. A series of meetings was held and records were subsequently made by Pierson Dixon of the Foreign Office. The Greeks also kept notes but these have apparently disappeared. The problem for the historian is that Papagos's later account of what was agreed diverged fundamentally from that of Eden (and of Dixon).[39] The Greeks were anxious in principle to make plans to receive British assistance but did not readily accept the suggestion that Salonika should definitely be abandoned, since it would involve pressure being taken off the Italians. Nor did they at first agree that significant numbers of British troops should be sent to Greece at once lest the Germans be provoked. Papagos, in particular, was probably undecided whether his first priority was the optimum resistance to the Germans or a prestige-motivated denial to the Italians of any serious share in the Axis defeat of Greece if such an outcome could not be prevented. Naturally he did not put it this way to the British. But he stalled on the timing of the arrival of British reinforcements and argued that, provided the Yugoslavs agreed to help Greece, Salonika need not be written off. The British military representatives replied that the Yugoslav attitude was uncertain and that the pressure of time made it desirable to take the more prudent course of rapidly concentrating on the so-called Aliakmon Line, which involved the abandonment of Salonika. Papagos, however, though not openly disagreeing, placed great emphasis on needing to know with certainty that Belgrade would not help.

In a private meeting of the British representatives, held at 7.45p.m. on the evening of the 22nd, it was agreed that 'unless we can be sure of the Yugoslavs joining in, it was not possible to contemplate holding a line covering Salonika; in view of the doubtful attitude of Yugoslavia, the only sound plan from the military point of view was to stand on the Haliacmon [Aliakmon] line'. It was further decided that the Greeks 'should be told that in our view it was essential to put in motion at once the movement of British troops from Egypt to Greece'.[40] These points were conveyed by Wavell to the Greeks at a full plenary meeting which assembled at 10.45 p.m. in the presence of the Greek King. At first Papagos appeared to have been won over both to the need for British action at the earliest possible date and to concentration on the Aliakmon Line. For Wavell presented the British view without equivocation and Papagos offered no objection. At this point, however, Eden intervened. Possibly the lateness of the hour, following the strenuous character of his travels during the previous week, affected his grasp of what had been agreed in the private British meeting earlier in the evening. Possibly he secretly disagreed with abandoning Salonika, in that it would have signified a loss of hope of drawing into the conflict Yugoslavia and, beyond her, Turkey. But, for whatever reason, he greatly complicated the discussion. Dixon's minutes read:

The Secretary of State said that it was clear that the British and Greek military representatives were in agreement on the military plans. There remained however, one or two political questions.

PREPARATIONS ON THE HALIACMON LINE

Firstly, the attitude of Yugoslavia made it desirable from the military point of view, to organize the Haliacmon line at the earliest possible moment. Thus, whatever attitude Yugoslavia adopted, work on roads, etc. should be pressed forward as rapidly as possible, especially the work needed to enable our mechanized forces and our medium artillery to be used to the best advantage.

The President of the Council agreed.

WITHDRAWAL OF THE GREEK FORCES TO THE HALIACMON LINE

Continuing, the *Secretary of State* said that, secondly, military requirements demanded an immediate withdrawal of the Greek forces in Eastern Macedonia to the Haliacmon line.

From the political aspect there were three possibilities:

(i) To withdraw the troops without waiting for Yugoslavia to declare herself.

(ii) To begin the withdrawal concurrently with an approach to the Yugoslav Government.

(iii) To wait until Yugoslavia had made her intentions clear.

He was not hopeful as things were of obtaining a satisfactory indication of the Yugoslav Government's attitude in a hurry. He was, however, prepared, if the Greek Government wished it, to send a Staff Officer to Belgrade to discuss the position with the Prince Regent. It was questionable how much the Prince Regent should be told of our plans. It might be desirable to tell him that His Majesty's Government, in agreement with the Greek Government, intended to send a British force to Greece, and to explain that the choice of a line for the Anglo-Greek forces must depend on the attitude of Yugoslavia; if we could be certain of Yugoslavia joining in upon a German attack on Greece, it would be possible to constitute a line to defend Salonika; so long as we were uncertain of the Yugoslav attitude we could only contemplate holding a line West and South of Salonika. It must, however, be borne in mind that, in revealing our intentions to Prince Paul, we ran the risk of them being passed on to the Germans.

General Papagos suggested that Prince Paul should merely be told in general terms, without going into details, that British forces were being sent to the help of Greece, and that, if the Yugoslavs were prepared to come in, this would naturally have an effect on the dispositions of the Anglo-Greek forces. Prince Paul should also be told that we were aware that Yugoslavia, like Greece and Great Britain, had a capital interest in Salonika.

The Secretary of State suggested that decisions should now be taken on the following three points:

1. Whether a British Staff Officer should be sent to Belgrade to see Prince Paul.
   It was agreed that this should be done ...
2. Whether preparations should at once be made and put into execution to withdraw the Greek advanced troops in Thrace and Macedonia to the line which we should be obliged to hold if the Yugoslavs did not come in.
   It was agreed that this should be done.
3. Whether work should at once be begun on the improvement of communications in Greece in order to facilitate the deployment of our mechanized forces.
   It was agreed that this should be done.[41]

Eden's remarks stood in stark contrast to the line taken by Wavell. They left Papagos with some freedom of manoeuvre. For, pending word from Belgrade, he felt entitled to prepare for withdrawal to the Aliakmon Line rather than actually move any troops. Eden himself, after all, had said that 'work on roads, etc. should be pressed forward as rapidly as possible' but had not specified that any given number of Greek troops should be redeployed by a particular date. Yet when Eden returned to Athens on 2 March and discovered that no troops had yet been withdrawn, he at once protested that this had not been his understanding of what had been agreed. Who, then, was to blame for the 'misunderstanding'? It has been claimed that Papagos's subsequent stress on the word, 'preparations', as enshrined in the second point of the Tatoi decisions, was sharp practice.[42] And it seems probable that he had deliberately disregarded what he knew to be Wavell's wish to see an immediate withdrawal to the Aliakmon Line. Yet Papagos's opportunism does not exonerate Eden from the charge that his intervention at Tatoi was ill-timed and a good deal less precise in support of immediate withdrawal to the Aliakmon Line than he later claimed. That he really did intend to keep open the option of defending Salonika and that his stress on 'preparations' in relation to the Aliakmon Line was quite intentional appears to be confirmed, moreover, by extracts from the text of a telegram sent to Churchill immediately after the fateful meeting:

From the ensuing discussion between the CIGS, Commander-in-Chief Middle East and Air Officer Commanding on the one hand, and General Papagos on the other hand, it emerged that in view of the doubtful attitude of Yugoslavia the only line that could be held and would give time for withdrawal of troops from Albania would be a line west of the Vardar–Olympus–Veria–Edessa–Kajmakcalan. If we could be sure of Yugoslav moves it should be possible to hold a line further north from the mouth of the Nestos to Beles covering Salonica. It would be impracticable, unless Yugoslavia came in, to hold a line covering Salonica in view of the exposure of the Greek left flank to German attack.

In full agreement with the Greek Government the following detailed decisions were reached:

a In view of the importance of the Yugoslav attitude as affecting the redeployment of troops in Greece, it was agreed that I should make a further effort to attempt to persuade the Yugoslav Government to play their part.

b That the Greeks should at once make, and begin the execution of, preparations to withdraw the advance troops to the line which we should have to hold if the Yugoslavs were not willing to come in.

c That work should immediately be started on improving communications in Greece to facilitate the occupation of the line.[43]

The existence of this telegram is not mentioned in Eden's memoirs. And Sir Llewellyn Woodward, the official historian of British foreign policy in the Second World War, even saw fit to summarize the Tatoi proceedings in this distorted fashion:

... M. Koryzis stated formally that the Greek Government accepted the British offer and approved the detailed arrangements reached in the military conversations.

The most important of these arrangements was that the Greeks should withdraw most of their advanced forces from Thrace and Macedonia in order to join with the British forces in defending the so-called Aliakmon line ... The British representatives agreed that if we could rely on Yugoslav help we might subsequently go beyond this line and defend Salonika, but that there should be an immediate withdrawal to the shorter and more defensible position to the south-west. According to the British record (though General Papagos stated later that this was not his view of the decision) the Greek representatives agreed.[44]

Yet it would be wrong to assume that Eden was necessarily insincere in his subsequent protestations that he was in no way to blame for Papagos's failure to withdraw troops to the Aliakmon Line. Perhaps this was because both Wavell and Dixon endorsed his criticism of Papagos. On 23 December 1951, for example, in the context of the drafting of the official military history by General I. S. O. Playfair, Eden wrote:

There was, of course, no real misunderstanding – our documents were quite clear and so was Lord Wavell with whom I have often discussed this point. I know that Lord Wavell was critical of General Papagos's book on this count, and on others.[45]

Dixon's own recollection, dated 12 December 1951, was also made known to both Playfair and Eden:

... we were absolutely taken by surprise and indeed horrified to find on our arrival for the second time in Athens that nothing had been done. After the Tatoi meeting we had thought that an absolutely clear understanding had been reached. Subsequently General Papagos maintained that it had been agreed at the first (Tatoi) meeting that the move from Macedonia should not begin until the reaction of the Prince Regent of Yugoslavia had been ascertained. But in my mind there was no doubt that what had really been agreed was that we were going to stand on the Haliacmon line (the Greek Macedonian divisions being moved down to it) except in the eventuality (which both we and the Greeks thought remote) of the Yugoslavs being ready to come in. If the Yugoslavs were ready to come in then we might consider defending a line further north, i.e. covering Salonika. We all thought at the time that General Papagos had invented the alleged misunderstanding.[46]

Dixon's diary also has a passage that supports this line. (The relevant parts of his entry for 22 February were, as he himself scrupulously recorded, written on about 11 April after his return home.)[47]

On the other hand, the head of the British military mission in Athens, Major-General T. G. G. Heywood, did not interpret the Tatoi decisions in the same spirit as Eden and Dixon. For between 23 February and the Foreign Secretary's return to Athens on 2 March he made no protest to Papagos nor did he send messages of warning to London or Cairo concerning Greek inaction. Having been asked about this by Playfair, Dixon wrote in a memorandum dated 12 December 1951:

As to the lack of news about the Greek change of front, I told General Playfair that my recollection was that we were surprised that General Heywood had not given us some earlier warning, and had not discovered and reported that the anticipated move of the Greek divisions from Macedonia had not been put in hand.[48]

In Papagos's account, published after the war following Heywood's death, he naturally argued that Heywood's silence constituted support for his interpretation and even claimed that he had regularly asked the British for news of the soundings in Belgrade and had received no word.[49] Nothing has so far been discovered in the British archives to disprove this claim. Probably, then, both Heywood and the British Ambassador in Athens, Sir Michael Palairet, had failed to grasp Eden's alleged intentions or at least his alleged sense of urgency in the Tatoi conversations. True, none of this shows Eden to have been guilty of trying to deceive posterity in the many subsequent inquests. But it does suggest that he was careless in his choice of words at Tatoi and did not give Palairet and Heywood sufficiently precise instructions. The nearest he came to recognizing this was when he wrote in his memoirs:

On reflection, I have no doubt that it was the political implications of withdrawing Greek troops from Macedonia which proved too much even for the stalwart intentions of the Greek Government. Possibly, if we had foreseen them, *we could have dotted the i's and crossed the t's more fixedly* at Tatoi; but I doubt if this precaution would have had the necessary consequences. [Italics supplied.][50]

His speculation that Papagos would in any event have refused in practice to withdraw to the Aliakmon Line is interesting but obviously cannot be proved.

Following the Tatoi meeting and the apparent agreement with the Greek Government, Eden returned to Cairo. His next mission was to Turkey, where he arrived on 26 February. He received a friendly reception and was congratulated on the wisdom of his decision to assist Greece. But his hosts were no more willing than before to promise any immediate aid to Greece. They held out vague hopes, however, that they might concert with the Yugoslavs if Belgrade so desired. Dixon recorded in his diary: 'The conversations were not satisfactory, since the Turks profited by our admission that most of our available resources were going to Greece to recede from their obligation to declare war if Greece was attacked.' But Eden, obsessed by his belief in Turkey as the key to his whole policy, refused to draw a similarly realistic conclusion. Instead he sent a complacent telegram to London:

The upshot of these discussions is that Turkey undertakes in any event to enter the war at some stage. She will of course do so immediately she is attacked. But if she is given time by Germans to re-equip herself she will take advantage of it, and will then make war at a moment favourable to the common cause, when her weight can be used with real effect.[51]

Some in London were not deceived, as these extracts from Cadogan's diary illustrate:

28 February 1941
Telegram from A. at Angora [Ankara], which puzzles me. It is couched in jaunty and self-satisfied terms, talking of the 'frankness' and 'friendliness' and 'realism' of the Turks. The 'reality' is that they won't do a damned thing. Has he had his head turned by crowds of hand-clapping Turks? And what is he now to say to the Yugoslavs and Greeks? The former will now of course curl up, and we shall be alone with the Greeks to share their inevitable disaster . . . To A. they [the Turks] appear to have said quite flatly that they will only fight if attacked (which of course they won't be – yet). But he seems quite happy. What's bitten him?

1 March 1941
Glad to find PM has sent a sobering telegram to our temperamental Secretary of State, saying 'You appear to have got nothing out of the Turks.' And that is true: he is on a lemon-gathering expedition, and he has only got that ninny Dill, with him . . . This stunt trip is a most disastrous one. And A. seems quite gay about it . . . It's a diplomatic and strategic blunder of the first order.

3 March 1941
He [Churchill] authorized me to read to the Cabinet A.'s raspberry from Ankara. Which I did, and left them all looking rather blue-nosed . . . Everyone's reaction is the same – how *can* one account for the jaunty tone of a recital of *complete* failure.[52]

Meanwhile the War Cabinet had endorsed Eden's agreement with the Greeks. Members were much influenced by three considerations. One was the surprisingly optimistic tone of the military prognostications of Dill and Wavell with respect both to Greece itself and to the British position in north Africa, the latter being assumed to be not unduly at risk if troops were diverted to the Balkans. A second factor was a recognition that Greece had been the recipient of a specific British guarantee and could not honourably be left to fight alone. Finally, Churchill was conscious of having received a paper from Donovan which appeared to constitute semi-official American advice. It included this passage:

It is a truism to say that the will of her [Germany's] people must be broken and her armies must be at some point thrown on the defensive and beaten in the field. The Balkans offer perhaps the only place for such a defeat. The British must then retain a foothold there . . .[53]

Meanwhile Eden in Ankara had received news on 27 February from Yugoslavia. The regime dominated by Prince Paul was already moving in the direction of Hitler and accordingly sent a cold reply to the British attempt, following Tatoi, to obtain undertakings to come to the aid of Greece. Two days later Bulgaria joined the Axis and invited German forces into her country. Cadogan wrote in his diary: 'A real answer to A.'s [Eden's] silly antics.' The German threat to Greece had now become immediate. Hence Eden's return to Athens on 2 March was arranged as a public spectacle designed to boost the morale of the Greek people for the inevitable ordeal. But on arrival Eden and Dill were informed, as has been seen, that no Greek troops had been withdrawn to the Aliakmon Line. Moreover, Papagos now argued that the German move into Bulgaria meant that there was no longer time to carry through the total redeployment that the British desired. Recriminations about the 'misunderstanding' were pointless. Hence Wavell, having been summoned from Cairo, joined with Dill in intense discussion with their Greek counterparts. Reluctantly the British recognized that, in the new situation, their original plan would have to be modified, with the only alternative being a complete British withdrawal. Eventually Dill and Wavell reached a compromise with Papagos: British forces would concentrate on the Aliakmon Line and be joined there by three Greek divisions, while the rest of the Greek army would have to remain in more exposed positions. Astonishingly, Dill and Wavell expressed the view to London on 7 March that, even with depleted Greek support, there nevertheless remained a fair hope of holding the Germans on the Aliakmon Line. As Woodward the official historian, wrote: 'It is remarkable that neither General Wavell nor General Dill had gone to see the ground before coming to the conclusion that there was a good chance of holding the Aliakmon line.'[54]

Churchill and his colleagues in London were understandably alarmed and repeatedly pressed Eden for detailed justifications. These were not forthcoming. And the Foreign Secretary also ignored the Prime Minister's clear message to him that he should not feel inhibited from calling off the operation. Thus the two men had completely reversed their positions since the previous November. Now it was Eden who was reckless. True, before making a final recommendation, he held two conferences with his advisers in Cairo and to the second he invited Smuts from South Africa. But all were unanimous that full-scale aid to Greece should still go ahead. On 7 March the Cabinet in London reluctantly endorsed the decision. But they did so in a different spirit to the team in Cairo. For the Cabinet the decisive factor was now the alleged need, because of neutral opinion, to be seen to stand by an ally and to share some of her anguish. As for the military case, those in Cairo no longer carried weight. Menzies of Australia, present at the British War Cabinet, tartly remarked that the arguments given by Eden and his military advisers 'told against, rather than in favour of, their advice'.[55] In Cairo, on the other hand, there was wholly misplaced optimism that the enterprise might turn out to be militarily sound. They disliked a justification solely based on what Eden later called *noblesse oblige*. Judging by the formal record, this mood was created by Dill and Wavell, Eden being a recipient of their expert advice.[56] But if the personalities of those involved are taken into account, it may reasonably be contended that Eden was actually the moving force behind the policy. The fact is that Dill and Wavell owed their survival in their posts to Eden and were on extremely friendly terms with him. They were, moreover, men generally judged as lacking the Foreign Secretary's strength of character. It seems possible, therefore, that they offered military advice palatable to Eden. Moreover, when the Greek campaign had ended in disaster, Eden showed no resentment towards his two friends for giving him bad counsel. Indeed, he consistently defended every aspect of their military advice to such an extent as to suggest that it was as much his line as theirs or even more so. But if this interpretation is correct, it must next be asked why he adopted such an approach. Why did he not seize on the German move into Bulgaria and the Greek failure to withdraw in time to the Aliakmon Line as a good reason for abandoning the perilous enterprise? Cadogan believed that his head was turned 'a little'.[57] But this is not a sufficient explanation. The fact was that he was to a large extent a prisoner of his public reputation, not entirely deserved, for vigour and valour in politics. To have been seen to take the main responsibility for leaving the Greeks to their fate would have been damaging to that reputation and, maybe more important, to his own ego. He also no doubt was able to rationalize his recklessness by clinging desperately to the hope that British-supported Greek resistance might somehow change hearts and minds in Turkey and Yugoslavia.

That Eden had still not despaired of Ankara is shown by his decision to invite the Turks to a further meeting. Even Wavell was initially sceptical about the value of another encounter but was inevitably won over. On this occasion the Turks preferred to come to Cyprus and accordingly on 18 March Eden received his counterpart, Sükrü Saraçoglu, there. The Turks proved to be a little more forthcoming than hitherto, for they hoped to dissuade the Yugoslavs from joining the Axis. Saraçoglu undertook to ask

Belgrade to enter upon discussions with a view to concerting measures of collective defence – though in the event he did not do so. Meanwhile Eden was anxious to exert his own influence on Belgrade. He accordingly sent a personal message to Prince Paul but also urged the British Embassy to give every encouragement to anti-German subversives of the Yugoslav Government. On 25 March, however, Prince Paul signed a pact with Germany. Eden's efforts seemed to have failed.

On 27 March Eden arrived in Malta *en route* for London. Here to his delight news reached him of an anti-German *coup d'état* in Belgrade. Eden at once decided to return to the Balkans and arrived on the following day in Athens. The fall of Prince Paul was the first and only real success for Eden's personal policy during the whole of his protracted Mediterranean odyssey. For, as he rightly claimed, 'the presence of British and Dominion forces in Greece had directly influenced events in Yugoslavia'.[58] In London Churchill was no less elated and would undoubtedly at that moment have withdrawn most of his reservations about the wisdom of the course taken by his Cairo team. King George the Sixth, too, was delighted. 'So glad,' he telegraphed to the Foreign Secretary, 'to think that your strenuous efforts to deal with the Balkan situation have, in spite of all difficulties, had such fruitful and encouraging results. My congratulations to you and Dill.'[59] But unfortunately for Eden the new Yugoslav Government was to prove less pro-British than he expected. At first the Yugoslavs offered to see both Eden and Dill in Belgrade but by 31 March had had second thoughts. Receiving Eden would be too provocative to Germany. Instead Dill alone was invited. He soon returned to Athens with the news that his hosts had been elusive. Nothing if not persistent, Eden succeeded in next arranging for a secret meeting just inside Greece between himself and a Yugoslav general, Radivoje Janković. This took place on 3 April and was predictably inconclusive. With the Yugoslavs so reserved, the Turks, too, were easily able to evade continuing efforts by Eden to draw them into concerting moves for collective defence. Thus when Germany attacked both Greece and Yugoslavia on 6 April British plans were still in disarray. The *coup* in Belgrade had after all made no decisive difference: military disaster for the Greeks and the Yugoslavs was now inevitable and British forces were ignominiously withdrawn from the Balkans within three weeks. Meanwhile General Erwin Rommel had taken advantage of the weakening of the British position in north Africa to achieve a significant victory at Benghazi. Thus when Eden arrived back in London on 10 April his mission appeared to have been a depressing failure. Nor was he consoled by Churchill's immediate reaction. Cadogan recorded in his diary: '. . . had a talk with A. in his flat. PM had been rather tiresome to him – saying he had never wished to help Greece! I said that it must be his mood: no one could have supported A. more stoutly and consistently in his absence than PM had done.'[60] The

Prime Minister eventually backed Eden both in Cabinet and in the House of Commons. But Eden, as he himself said, had lost some 'tail feathers'. His defence in the House of Commons was heard quietly but without enthusiasm. And Harvey noted in his diary some glee among his enemies in the press, in the City and among the supporters of Chamberlain in Parliament.[61]

Eden appeared, however, to have the last laugh at the expense of his critics. For after Hitler had attacked the Soviet Union in June 1941, he proved unable to reach Moscow before the winter set in. This allegedly fatal failure was supposed to have been caused by the loss of time involved in conquering Greece and Yugoslavia. Eden accordingly wrote in his memoirs: 'Although we could not know it then, this in itself justified the suffering of Greeks and Yugoslavs, British and Dominion troops in the final reckoning.' But even this *ex post facto* argument is now open to question. For one authority on German policy has claimed that Hitler's timetable was not decisively affected by Eden's mission.[62] So the Foreign Secretary's critics not only had the better of the argument at the time but seem even in retrospect to have a respectable case.

VII

Global War
1941–5

Soon after his return from the Mediterranean, Eden began to receive intelligence reports suggesting a sharp deterioration in German–Soviet relations. By 2 June 1941 he found the portents sufficiently serious to justify alerting Maisky to the possibility of a German attack – a warning not apparently taken seriously by Stalin. On 19 June the War Cabinet considered the line to be taken in the anticipated eventuality. Churchill went no further than making clear his intention to describe Hitler 'as an insatiable tyrant that had attacked Russia in order to obtain material for carrying on the war'. His prospective attitude towards the Soviet Union was left vague. While the War Cabinet clearly intended to give Moscow assistance by, for example, increased air action in the West, they were not at this stage asked to face the political problems involved in forging an open alliance with or even in expressing friendly sentiments towards the Soviets.[1]
The British Government had after all gone to war in defence of Poland, one of whose attackers had been the Soviet Union. Moreover, Soviet acts of aggression against Finland, Latvia, Lithuania and Estonia were all fresh in the public memory. True, the Cabinet no longer contained any weighty anti-Communists in the Chamberlain–Halifax 'appeasing' tradition. But this did not necessarily mean that a pro-Soviet *volte face* could be attempted without risk. For the majority of Conservative backbenchers had probably not abandoned their basic convictions even if most of them might increasingly find it prudent not to express them volubly. And many Labour MPs, not least those in the War Cabinet, were in varying degrees anti-Communists who had perhaps felt more high-minded indignation about the attack on Finland than their more worldly Conservative counterparts. Hence Churchill decided to confer with Eden about the Soviet question and duly summoned him to Chequers on the weekend of 21–2 June.

On the Sunday morning Eden awoke to find a cigar from Churchill and news that 'Barbarossa' (the code name for the German invasion of Russia) had been launched. Both men were no doubt exultant as they spent the day considering the terms of a radio broadcast which the Prime Minister was giving that evening. Speaking without War Cabinet authority, Churchill risked angering his anti-Soviet colleagues by offering the Soviets a full working partnership. Moreover, there is no evidence that Eden 'bounced' him into doing so. But whereas the Prime Minister's enthusiasm for

Moscow was to prove a passing emotion, the Foreign Secretary entered upon a prolonged phase of near-infatuation.

Churchill, reminded of his anti-Bolshevik past, retorted that if Hitler invaded Hell, he would at least make a favourable reference to the Devil. At the time he was probably genuinely convinced that Nazism represented a more serious threat to the British Empire than Communism – and in this he no doubt had the support of the majority of the population, who had been subjected during the previous eighteen months to real fears of a German invasion. On the other hand, the German attack on the Soviets and the flight of Rudolf Hess to Scotland might have led some of the 'Municheers' in the Conservative Party to revive in élite circles discussion about possible terms for a compromise peace as the best means of serving British long-term interests. Churchill, possibly in some apparent contrast to a year earlier, showed no interest in such an outcome, for now, apart from any other consideration, it would have decisively undermined his standing as Prime Minister. The 'Municheers' were thus presented with a *fait accompli* of a speedy commitment to cooperation with Stalin and in the event they did not rebel. Yet it was a step whose later consequences Churchill found in some respects unpleasing: he came to see that the effect of his broad strategy on the eventual fate of the British Empire and of Europe might put his reputation in some jeopardy. For example, Boothby produced this revealing recollection:

He [Churchill] once talked to me, when the war was over and he was out of power, about the position he would ultimately occupy in history; and I said that nothing could take from him the fact that he had saved Britain in 1940. He then said, rather sadly: 'Historians are apt to judge war ministers less by the victories achieved under their direction than by the political results which flowed from them. Judged by that standard, I am not sure that I shall be held to have done very well.'[2]

Eden had fewer doubts and such as he had developed later than those of Churchill, whose actions within months of Barbarossa revealed the uneasiness he felt at the assistance he was giving to the cause of Communism. Eden, at least until 1944, appears to have seen the Soviet Union as a genuine ally of liberal democracy and an agent of 'progress'.

Eden's attitude was symbolized by his reappointment of Harvey as Principal Private Secretary. Having meanwhile already served at the level of minister in the British Embassy in Paris, Harvey by reverting to a relatively humble if influential rank took an unusual step by Civil Service standards. The eccentricity of his willingness to serve in such a post in his late forties was matched by the outlandish character of his views. Always unusually opinionated, he was now close to being an apologist for the Soviet system. On Christmas Eve of 1941, for example, when accompanying Eden on a rail journey from Murmansk to Moscow, he observed without apparent pity part of Stalin's 'Gulag Archipelago'. He saw the ruthlessness involved as the price to be paid for the modernization of the Soviet Union.[3] Harvey's admiration for the Soviets was matched by scorn for the United States. 'America', he wrote on 7 January 1942, '[is] far more old-fashioned and anti-Russian than Great Britain – a hundred years behind us in social evolution.'[4] About the future of British politics his views were also radical. His detestation of the 'Municheers' knew no bounds. He also saw little merit in the British press or its supposed freedom.[5] His vision of the post-war future for Great Britain was also unusual. If Churchill adopted too anti-Soviet a position there would be revolution. If not, then the prospect would be for a two-party system based on a Conservative–Labour coalition opposed by a Communist grouping.[6]

It is highly unlikely that Eden was quite as extreme in his private opinions as Harvey. But his hatred of the followers of Chamberlain and his increasing difficulties with Churchill over Soviet issues caused such an over-reaction as to leave him for a few years much further to the left than at any other period of his career. This led him to find Harvey a congenial aide and he clearly tolerated while not necessarily wholly sharing all his opinions. Moreover, Eden's own view of the future was certainly remarkable for one who was still nominally a Conservative. As early as 15 January 1941, according to Harvey, he indicated that in the post-war era he might move over to the left. By 6 June 1941 the same source noted that Beatrice Eden had told him that her husband had ceased to feel like a Conservative and was getting on particularly well with Ernest Bevin. On 25 August 1942 Harvey recorded in his diary:

A.E. had previously had a most useful dinner with Bobbety [Cranborne] who was most sympathetic to his ideas. He too spoke of the importance of drawing younger men together as a nucleus for a future party ... he thought they should work with Labour (Bevin and Co.) and leave the opposition to the Communists. This is also an idea of A.E.'s.[7]

Churchill shared Eden's suspicion of at least some of the 'Municheers' but, unlike Eden, he only reluctantly made himself the agent of social democratic causes at home. Similarly, he did not for long share his Foreign Secretary's desire to fall in with many of Moscow's aims for the post-war world. Perhaps the Prime Minister's initial attitude to Stalin was based on expectations of an early Soviet defeat and calculations that friendly words would thus at little cost minimize potential ideological divisions at home. Perhaps he became increasingly jealous of Stalin as Soviet military achievements came to outshine those of Great Britain. Or maybe early evidence of Stalin's ruthless ambitions for the post-war future revived his long-standing hatred of Bolshevism. But, for whatever reason, he soon found himself differing sharply from Eden. True, there were subjects other than the Soviet Union about which they quarrelled. These included France, Portugal, Spain, India, Japan, the future of Germany and various Bulkan issues. But the relationship with Moscow was without doubt the principal cause of the clashes between them.

Eden was at first successful in imposing his will concerning Soviet questions on the War Cabinet. For example, he was able to forge an interim Anglo-Soviet arrangement for mutual cooperation early in July 1941 and later in the same month to persuade the Polish Government-in-Exile to re-open diplomatic relations with Moscow on terms which did not guarantee the restoration of the Polish frontiers of 1939. During August he success-fully canvassed a Soviet plan for a joint ultimatum to the neutral Iranians requiring the removal from their country of large numbers of German citizens. When Teheran refused, British and Soviet forces invaded and in effect partitioned Iran. Harvey saw this as 'a credit to A.E., without whom the PM and the Chiefs of Staff would never have moved'. But the same diarist noted: 'Our first act of "naked aggression". A.E. rather ashamed of himself, so too is PM. But I tell him it is essential for us to get our base and the oilfields secure while the going is good.'[8]

Churchill soon began to put up stiffer resistance to Eden's plans. Nothing, for example, came of the Foreign Secretary's desire to incite the Spanish Communists to revolution against Franco. And he was equally unsuccess-ful in campaigning for more aid to the Soviets. The Prime Minister found reasons not to mount diversionary air attacks on German-held Western Europe; he argued cogently that the dispatch of war material to the Soviet Union must be severely limited by the shortages still affecting Great Britain's own war effort; and, most tellingly, he refused to send even a token force of British troops, let alone the twenty-five to thirty divisions demanded by Stalin, to fight alongside the Soviets on the Eastern Front. On 27 October Harvey recorded:

PM is disquieting A.E. by giving very evident signs of anti-Bolshevik sentiment. After his first enthusiasm, he is now getting bitter as the Russians become a liability and he says we can't afford the luxury of helping them with men, only with material. No one stands up to him but A.E. – not even the Labour Ministers who are as prejudiced as the PM against the Soviets because of their hatred and fear of the Communists at home.[9]

More differences arose between Eden and Churchill towards the end of 1941 concerning Finland, Romania and Hungary. All were in a state of war with the Soviet Union, though not with Great Britain. Stalin insisted that the British should show solidarity with him by themselves declaring war on Hitler's collaborators. Since in the cases of Finland and Romania, the Soviets had been the original perpetrators of aggression, this was no easy demand to meet. Eden, however, favoured doing so. But when the question came before the War Cabinet on 11 November he was rebuffed. According to Harvey, he had only the support of Beaverbrook, but he was opposed by Bevin and Greenwood, whose attitude to the Soviet Union was determined by their anti-Communism. A week later Harvey tried to help his chief by briefing J. H. Martin, a Labour backbencher, about the stance adopted by Bevin and Greenwood. Martin hoped to bring pressure to bear on his leaders through Labour Party channels.[10] This was certainly irregular conduct by a civil servant whose clear duty was to treat his knowledge of Cabinet discussions as top secret.

Churchill's problems in resisting Eden intensified towards the end of November, when Sir Stafford Cripps, the British Ambassador in Moscow, threatened to resign unless more was done to meet Soviet wishes. And Stalin, near to having to withdraw his Government from Moscow, sent more violently worded messages demanding the dispatch of British forces and equipment. Perhaps in part motivated by fear of a separate Soviet-German peace, Churchill moved for a time towards appeasing Stalin. At first he hoped to get away with sending Generals Wavell and Bernard Paget to explain in military terms the impossibility of sending more assistance for the present. But Stalin, having already had conversations with Beaverbrook limited to supply questions, replied that he would receive the British generals if they were able also to discuss the post-war future of Europe. Believing that only a politician could undertake such a task, Churchill decided to send Eden to Moscow at an early date, though with instructions to give no concrete pledges. But this in turn gave the Foreign Secretary some leverage: he could in effect refuse to go without some concession to offer Stalin. Unable to obtain Churchill's consent to an immediate increase in aid and equally forbidden to fix post-war frontiers, Eden at least was able to secure by stages declarations of war on Finland, Romania and Hungary. At one point, 25 November, Churchill had received a message from Stalin accepting that a British declaration of war against Finland would be sufficient for the immediate future; 'with regard to Hungary and Romania we can perhaps wait a little while'.[11] But by 5 December Eden had persuaded the War Cabinet to authorize war being declared on all three countries. A delighted Harvey noted in his diary on the following day the reluctance with which Churchill had consented.[12] A day later Eden left Euston for Scotland, whence he was to sail to Murmansk: he would now learn for himself whether this 'positive appeasement' had led to his country being more warmly regarded by Stalin.

Meanwhile divergences between Eden and Churchill had also arisen concerning the Far East, although during the first two years of the European war neither was able to devote more than a small part of his time to the subject and neither was wholly consistent in his approach. Eden was usually more inclined than Churchill to strike heroic postures in the face of Japanese threats. Both were, however, in broad agreement about the desirability of trying to draw the United States into war with Japan and in pursuit of that end were prepared to risk a degree of increased hostility towards Great Britain from Tokyo. They assumed, without much evidence, that the Americans' involvement in a Pacific war would also serve to bring them into the European war. They thus rejected the view that in the event of an American–Japanese war Roosevelt, whatever his private wishes, might not be able to obtain from Congress a declaration of war on Hitler and that as a consequence aid being sent from the 'arsenal of democracy' to Great Britain might actually have to be reduced in deference to a 'Pacific first' clamour. True, this did not happen. But it must remain a matter for speculation whether this would have been the case had Hitler not obliged the British by declaring war on the United States immediately after Pearl Harbor. During 1939 and 1940 Chamberlain, the Chiefs of Staff and Butler (then Parliamentary Under-Secretary at the Foreign Office) were more willing than Eden and Churchill to give credence to the possibility of the Americans becoming less rather than more involved in the European war. Butler, for example, considered that it might be a British interest to tempt the Japanese to expand at the expense of the Soviet Union rather than in areas of direct British concern. On 22 September 1939 he wrote:

Russia and Japan are bound to remain enemies, and with our position in India and the East it would pay us to make a return to the Anglo-Japanese alliance possible. It does not appear that there are the makings of a war between America and Japan; the American interests in the Far East are insufficient to justify a major war. I do not believe it will pay us to keep Japan at arm's length and distrust everything she does for the sake of American opinion.[13]

This line flowed logically from Chamberlain's and Halifax's reported preference for establishing a true anti-Comintern pact directed against the two 'National Bolshevist' states, Germany and the Soviet Union. The fall and death of Chamberlain, the removal of Halifax and the German attack on the Soviet Union effectively destroyed Butler's hopes. By the summer of 1941 British policy was in large measure in the hands of a Foreign Office team which believed in giving priority to supporting the Soviets and to somewhat recklessly jeopardizing short-term British interests in east Asia in an all-out bid for American involvement in global war. Churchill was nearer to Eden than to Butler. For he, too, was willing to gamble much in the effort to draw Washington into war with Berlin. But he was at times sufficient of a realist to put a brake on his Foreign Secretary. While generally underrating Japanese power and resolve, he nevertheless grasped that there was some risk of the British finding themselves attacked by Japan with the United States remaining neutral. In 1940, for example, he had agreed to the closing of the Burma Road, the main means of supplying China. But while this was a sufficient act of appeasement to postpone a confrontation with Tokyo, it clearly fell short of the general settlement advocated by Butler. In the summer of 1941 Churchill similarly restrained Eden without satisfying Tokyo. For he agreed to support and encourage the new American policy of imposing severe economic sanctions on Japan, while preventing Eden from moving ahead of the Americans in provocation of Tokyo. The principal difference between Eden and Churchill concerned the Dutch East Indies. The Foreign Secretary was anxious to offer a public guarantee of military assistance to the Netherlands Government-in-Exile in the event of a Japanese attack on their colonial possessions. He affected to believe that such a guarantee would effectively deter Tokyo. He also held, with characteristic optimism, that in any case the Americans could now be counted on to declare war if the British should be called upon to honour a guarantee of Dutch possessions. In retrospect Eden saw this line as 'bold but perhaps not unwise'. Churchill was more cautious. As he told the Cabinet on 21 July: 'It might well be that, even if Japan encroached on the Dutch East Indies, the right policy would be that we should not make an immediate declaration of war on Japan.'[14] This same disagreement persisted until the beginning of December when Roosevelt resolved it by at last agreeing to recommend American military support in the case of any direct attack on the British or the Dutch.[15]

Thus Eden and Churchill agreed that war in the Far East was desirable if the Japanese and the Americans could possibly be embroiled with one another. They received no assistance, however, from Sir Robert Craigie, the British Ambassador in Tokyo. On 30 September 1941 he reported to Eden his opinion that 'a very considerable – though not yet a radical change – has occurred in the political situation here' and warned against the Americans' policy of using economic sanctions to try to force on Tokyo a detailed agreement which 'bids fair to wreck the best chance of bringing about a just settlement of Far Eastern issues which has occurred since my arrival in Japan [1937]'.[16] The American Ambassador in Tokyo, Joseph Grew, held much the same opinion and sought to persuade the State Department to modify its policy. Eden refused to follow Craigie's advice to add a British voice to that of Grew. To the War Cabinet he piously claimed that 'a display of firmness is more likely to deter Japan from war than provoke her to it'.[17] Yet the reality was that both he and Churchill welcomed Pearl Harbor when it came (7 December 1941) because it at last made the United States a belligerent. As Churchill exulted 'So we had won after all!'[18] It is not surprising that, given this outlook, neither Eden nor Churchill did anything to help the Japanese when they showed signs of wishing to back down in the face of continuing Western economic sanctions. They declined to rise to hints from Tokyo that the British might attempt to act as mediators or as a channel of communication with Washington. Finally, late in November Churchill and Eden severely discouraged the Americans from showing interest in a Japanese proposal for a so-called *modus vivendi*. Cordell Hull, the American Secretary of State, initially wished to explore terms that would have involved an end to sanctions in return for a Japanese retreat from southern Indochina. But Stimson, now Secretary for War, wanted to insist also on an end to the 'China Incident'. So, too, understandably enough, did Chiang Kai-shek. Hull, recognizing that such a line would be entirely unacceptable in Tokyo, sought British support for less exacting terms. But Churchill, almost certainly prompted by Eden, telegraphed to Roosevelt on 26 November urging that Chiang's interests should not be neglected. Hull now admitted defeat: all negotiations between Washington and Tokyo were effectively terminated. Unable to face a future of continuing Western economic sanctions, the Japanese now committed themselves to making a desperate bid for Pacific supremacy. Their attack on Pearl Harbor followed on 7 December. In 1943 Craigie produced a final report on his mission in which he questioned the wisdom of British policy in not supporting Hull. Churchill and Eden were dismayed and refused to permit any wide circulation of the report. The Prime Minister minuted:

It was ... a blessing that Japan attacked the United States and thus brought America unitedly and wholeheartedly into the war. Greater good fortune has rarely happened to the British Empire than this event which has revealed our friends and foes in their true light, and may lead, through the crushing of Japan, to a new relationship of immense benefit to the English-speaking countries and to the whole world.[19]

As one authority has commented:

Historians will argue for ever whether the subsequent course of Anglo-American relations has justified Churchill's hopes and whether the cost in lives, hopes and treasure paid by Britain and her citizens and subjects in the Far East and South-East Asia was not too high.[20]

On the 'Day of Infamy' Eden found himself in Scotland about to leave for Murmansk. This should have been a moment of unalloyed triumph: he had won another retrospective victory over Chamberlain. But his pleasure was somewhat marred by two irritating developments. First, he had contracted gastric influenza and, according to Cadogan, awoke on the morning of 8 December 'feeling like nothing on earth': he was clearly not in the best of conditions to face a long voyage across tempestuous seas.[21] Even more depressing was a telephone call just before sailing from the Prime Minister who told Eden he intended to visit Washington as soon as possible. This had several unwelcome implications for Eden. First, Churchill's trip would distract attention from Eden's – and even the devoted Harvey recognized that his master, no less than the Prime Minister, was a *prima donna* anxious for maximum publicity. More important, Eden naturally feared that Churchill would make commitments to Roosevelt without his approval. True, the Prime Minister would need to refer back to London from time to time – but if the Foreign Secretary was in Moscow there would probably be no War Cabinet member willing to stand up to him. Cadogan tried to persuade Churchill to abandon his plan on the grounds that the Prime Minister and the Foreign Secretary should not simultaneously be abroad in different places. But Churchill replied: 'That's all right: that'll work very well: I shall have Anthony where I want him.'[22] Eden also tried to block Churchill's plan by telephoning to Attlee and to Gilbert Winant, the American Ambassador in London. But the Prime Minister got his way.

On 13 December *HMS Kent* safely docked in Murmansk. Eden, now somewhat recovered in health, prepared to make the long train journey to Moscow. He had with him from the Foreign Office both Cadogan and Harvey. All three men kept diaries. It is, therefore, of some interest to compare their first reactions to wartime Russia. All were struck by the gaunt beauty of Murmansk in the half-light of the Arctic winter. But Harvey at least, as has been seen, noticed also Stalin's 'Gulag Archipelago'. The published extracts from the diaries of Eden and Cadogan contain no mention of its existence, still less any hint of moral concern. Cadogan, however, found room to write: 'Good food on the train. And good vodka. But much disappointed by the compressed caviar, which has no taste.'[23]

Eden's train arrived in beleaguered Moscow during the late evening of 15 December. The following day he had his first meeting with Stalin, who at once put forward some precise proposals. The Soviet Union wished to sign two treaties with Great Britain. One would be a formal military alliance, the other a detailed and secret arrangement concerning post-war frontiers. Eden wanted, instead of two treaties, merely a generalized declaration. Stalin replied: 'A declaration I regard as algebra, but I prefer practical arithmetic . . .' By this he meant a bilateral agreement on post-war frontiers and maybe even far-reaching spheres of influence. First, he mentioned the Soviet Union frontiers of 1941: Great Britain would have to accept the incorporation of the Baltic States; the amended frontiers with Romania and Finland which had been achieved during the period of the Soviet-German collaboration; and the Curzon Line of 1919 with Poland. Next he wanted the right to establish bases in the remainder of both Finland and Romania. He further suggested the breaking up of Germany. In return the British would be tacitly given a free hand in western Europe. Perhaps they might care to establish bases in Denmark and Norway or even in Boulogne and Dunkirk? Eden was prevented by his instructions from agreeing to any of these proposals. For Churchill and Roosevelt in their meeting at Placentia Bay in August 1941 had signed the Atlantic Charter whose idealistic terms, in the American view, ruled out, in advance of a Peace Conference, any secret arrangements for the transfer of territories without the consent of their populations. Eden privately regretted the acceptance of this interpretation but duly informed Stalin that he was unable at that stage to negotiate a bilateral Anglo-Soviet agreement involving future frontiers. On 17 December Stalin retorted that if the Soviet frontiers of 1941 could not be recognized he would rather have no agreement at all. Even Harvey deplored this: 'Stalin is rejecting a golden opportunity. A.E. is the one man in England who is ready to put their case.'[24] But Eden's labours to obtain British declarations of war on Romania, Hungary and Finland had clearly been insufficient to dispel Stalin's suspicions. And Eden was unable to offer any additional military aid. For Cabinet authorization of a promise to dispatch ten air force squadrons at some unspecified future date had had to be withdrawn. In these circumstances, fearing that his mission would end in spectacular failure, Eden decided somewhat to exceed the spirit of his instructions and he now left Stalin with the impression that frontier concessions would soon be forthcoming. He promised that on his return to London he would raise with Churchill and the War Cabinet the possibility of going some way to meet Soviet wishes. He also undertook, on Harvey's suggestion, to try to organize a tripartite conference at an early date to obtain American acceptance of some of Stalin's demands. For none of this did he have authority from London.

Stalin responded benignly: on 20 December he proposed a draft communiqué couched in friendly terms which Eden was delighted to accept. There then followed a reception in the Kremlin lasting from 10 p.m. to 5 a.m. There was much feasting and drinking of pepper vodka. No fewer than thirty-six toasts were offered. On this convivial note Eden's mission ended. He returned home by the same means as he had come and was back in London by 30 December.

During the first half of 1942 Eden set about securing from the War Cabinet and from Washington some of the terms demanded by Stalin. On 5 January the Foreign Secretary telegraphed to the Prime Minister, still in Washington, urging him on grounds of 'stark realism' to present to the Americans the case for 'immediate recognition' of the Soviet frontiers of 1941. Churchill sent a crushing retort three days later:

> Your telegram surprised me ... We have never recognized the 1941 frontiers of Russia except *de facto*. They were acquired by acts of aggression in shameful collusion with Hitler. The transfer of the peoples of the Baltic States to Soviet Russia against their will would be contrary to all the principles for which we are fighting this war and would dishonour our cause. This also applies to Bessarabia and to Northern Bukhovina and in a lesser degree to Finland which I gather it is not intended wholly to subjugate and absorb...
>
> You suggest that 'the acid test of our sincerity' depends upon our recognizing the acquisition of these territories by the Soviet Union irrespective of the wishes of their

peoples. I, on the contrary, regard our sincerity involved in the maintenance of the principles of the Atlantic Charter to which Stalin has subscribed ...

When you say ... that 'nothing we and the US can do or say will affect the situation at the end of the war' you are making a very large assumption about the conditions which will then prevail. No one can foresee how the balance of power will lie, or where the winning army will stand. It seems probable, however, that the US and the British Empire, far from being exhausted, will be the most powerfully armed and economic block [sic] the world has ever seen, and that the Soviet Union will need our aid for reconstruction far more than we shall need theirs.

... there must be no mistake about the opinion of any British Government of which I am the head; namely, that it adheres to the principles of freedom and democracy set forth in the Atlantic Charter and that these principles must become especially active whenever any question of transferring territory is raised. I conceive, therefore, that our answer should be that all questions of territorial frontiers must be left to the decision of the Peace Conference.[25]

Eden refused to retreat. He contacted Dalton in the hope of securing support in the Labour Party. And Harvey kept Martin informed.[26] Next, on 28 January, the Foreign Secretary, in defiance of the Prime Minister's wishes, circulated a memorandum to his War Cabinet colleagues spelling out the 'stark realism' that led him to favour appeasing Stalin:

On the assumption that Germany is defeated and German military strength is destroyed and that France remains, for a long time at least, a weak power, there will be no counterweight to Russia in Europe ... Russia's position on the European continent will be unassailable.

This argument, as he recorded in his memoirs, was based on the belief that 'Russian forces would end the war much deeper into Europe than they began it in 1941' and that 'it therefore seemed prudent to tie the Soviet Government to agreements as early as possible'. He further recalled:

The United States Government were not, at this stage of the war, so convinced. On the contrary, they became more tolerant of Soviet demands as Russian military victories developed and the likelihood of sharper Soviet appetites grew.[27]

He might have added that Churchill also unsurprisingly became more amenable to Soviet desires when, during 1944, he reluctantly recognized that he had no effective means of resisting them. In that same year, however, Eden perversely began to talk for the first time of resisting the Soviets. Eden's zeal to surrender to Soviet expansionism thus took a surprising form: he showed greater deference towards Stalin when he was weak than when he was strong. In one sense he had shown the same attitude towards Hitler: he blocked military resistance to a weak Germany in 1936 but favoured issuing reckless threats against her in 1939. There was, however, a contrast as well as a parallel between Eden's pre-war and wartime approaches to appeasement. In the 1930s it was Chamberlain who had generally favoured 'positive' appeasement and Eden who had believed in the tactics of keeping others guessing, followed by acquiescence if one's bluff should be called. Now, in 1942, it was Eden who favoured 'positive' appeasement of Stalin, while Churchill wanted to pursue a policy of 'cunctation' or even resistance.

The crisis between Eden and Churchill over Soviet frontiers came to a head at a meeting of the War Cabinet on 6 February. The Foreign Secretary wished to inform the Americans that Great Britain favoured granting Stalin's desires. He had the strong support only of Beaverbrook – an ironic development in view of their mutual hostility during the interwar years. Attlee, on the other hand, argued no less firmly against betraying the high-minded principles enshrined in the Atlantic Charter. Morrison, in a surprising move for so resolute an anti-Communist, leaned towards Eden's line. Perhaps he had hopes that Eden would soon be Prime Minister and that he might be rewarded with the Foreign Office. Other colleagues remained silent or spoke in ambiguous terms. So angry were the exchanges between Attlee and Beaverbrook that each in turn threatened to resign. For Churchill this was no doubt particularly distressing at a time when his own leadership was increasingly under challenge from a variety of sources. He accordingly subordinated his own view of the Soviet issue to the need to keep his Cabinet intact: he successfully proposed an ingenious compromise whereby the Americans would be informed of the British dilemma in a 'balanced' presentation. By 9 February it had been agreed that Roosevelt should be asked whether he preferred to meet outright the Soviet demand for immediate recognition of their territorial claims or whether, at this stage, the Soviets should merely be offered bases in and control of the foreign and defence policies of the Baltic States.[28]

Roosevelt proved predictably unenthusiastic. He refused to endorse either of the British suggestions and proposed instead to raise the subject on a bilateral basis with Moscow. Domestic political reasons led the President to wish to avoid being committed to deals involving the post-war fate of eastern European peoples. He accordingly hoped to persuade Stalin to leave such matters until the Peace Conference. But Roosevelt would clearly have to offer the Soviets some attractive bait if they were to comply. Some in London came to fear that this might take the form of American pressure on the British to make an early attempt at establishing a Second Front in France. This possibility of a Soviet–American bargain, however, lent support to Eden's pleas to Churchill to yield to Moscow in a bilateral Anglo-Soviet deal. The Foreign Secretary was also able to point to an order of the day issued by Stalin on 23 February to the Red Army. This could be read to imply that Stalin's aim was the liberation of Soviet territory rather than the overthrow of Hitler. Churchill was thus faced with two contradictory threats: a separate German–Soviet peace or a bilateral Soviet–American deal to dictate Allied war strategy. On 7 March he accordingly bowed to Eden's wishes and sent an unambiguous appeal to Roosevelt:

> The increasing gravity of the war has led me to feel that the principles of the Atlantic Charter ought not to be construed so as to deny Russia the frontiers she occupied when Germany attacked her ... I hope therefore that you will be able to give us a free hand to sign the treaty which Stalin desires as soon as possible...[29]

The Americans ignored the British request and instead entered upon talks with the Soviets. But, in the absence of an American willingness to give formal recognition to Stalin's frontier demands, no progress ensued.

On 17 March Harvey recorded in his diary: 'On the whole A.E. favours our going on with the Anglo-Russian Treaty on our own. It is noticeable that opinion seems to be veering more and more in favour of meeting the Russians ...' An example of the change in mood had come four days earlier when the agile Butler, now Minister of Education, had sent a surprising letter to Eden:

> Our future relations with America are always going to be interleaved with instances where we take a closer interest in European affairs than they do. We may just as well, therefore, start our relations on a realistic basis and not confine them to the rarefied atmosphere of the Atlantic Charter. We have suffered greatly in the last twenty years through taking on wide and idealistic commitments beyond our strength. I, therefore, hope that we shall not be prevented by generalized statements from pursuing what might, from time to time, suit our own interests.
>
> In my opinion, our own interests at the present moment lead us to come to an agreement with the Soviets that they may attain their 1941 frontier. I am sure that our refusal to concede their claim to certain territories in Central Europe – the future of which without them we are unable to influence – will tend to maintain that atmosphere of suspicion which has for so many decades affected Anglo-Soviet relations.[30]

On 24 March Eden definitely resolved to by-pass Roosevelt.[31] Two days later the War Cabinet authorized Eden to inform Washington of the British intention to deal directly with Moscow. Roosevelt's response was frigid: he would have to state in public that he had been told of the British action, would try to say no more, but would not be able to indicate approval and expected that his silence would be taken to imply disapproval. But the War Cabinet allowed Eden to go ahead. By 23 April Stalin was sufficiently encouraged to agree to send Molotov to London to draw up details of an Anglo-Soviet Treaty – ominously linked, however, to the need to discuss plans for a Second Front. But by now Eden was facing unexpected resistance to his policy from a variety of quarters. Christian leaders were among the first to protest. They included the Bishops of Gloucester and Derby, the Dean of Chichester, and the Cardinal Archbishop of Westminster. The Bishop of

Gloucester, Chairman of the Church of England Council on Foreign Relations, wrote to Churchill on 31 March:

> On 17 June 1940 large masses of Russian troops crossed the frontiers [of the Baltic States]. The National Governments were overthrown. Very soon religious persecutions began ... Religious instruction was forbidden in all schools. All Church property was taken away. During 1941 the persecution became more severe. Three clergy were put to death – at least seventeen were deported to Russia. Churches were destroyed. Those who remembered the horrors of the Bolshevik revolution in 1917–18 are agreed that the activities of the GPU this time were much worse, much more systematic and carried out with greater thoroughness and refinement of cruelty. The Inspector of the Latvian police was tortured till he went mad. A former Latvian Cabinet Minister had sharp needles driven between his nails.
>
> In April 1941 the campaign of mass arrests and mass murders began. Train loads of prisoners were sent to the interior of Russia. Boys who wore the Latvian flag in their coats were arrested. It is credibly asserted that 49,000 men were either murdered or deported – a large proportion out of a total population of two millions.
>
> I venture to represent to you ... that great indignation would be aroused in the country if these nations were finally to lose their freedom.

The Prime Minister sent this letter on to Eden with the comment: 'You ought to read this.' But the Foreign Secretary was unmoved. He wrote to the Bishop of Derby on 17 April:

> The successful prosecution in close alliance with us and the United States of America of the present struggle against our common enemy may, I sincerely hope, bring about a change in the Soviet outlook upon this question of religious freedom and upon other matters in which public opinion in this country and the United States is closely interested. In the meantime, we must ... concentrate on the common interest of the two countries in the prosecution of the war and for the time being avoid raising contentious matters.[32]

More ominous for Eden, however, were the protests of politicians. On 17 April Victor Cazalet wrote that he had 'never felt so deeply moved about anything, even about my Jews'. 'Surely,' he added, 'it is a kind of inverted Munich.' Cazalet proceeded to organize resistance in the Conservative Foreign Affairs Group. Harvey recorded in his diary on 22 April:

> Victor Cazalet is flapping about the H of C stirring up opposition to our Soviet Treaty because of the Baltic States. This is part of the Polish offensive but it threatens to assume serious proportions. There is only too much anti-Soviet feeling about in influential quarters on both sides of the House to make trouble easy. The Chief Whip [James Stuart] is by nature on that side, the Cabinet itself is lukewarm, even or especially the Labour members. But Cripps is now back, thank goodness, and I hope Stalin doesn't make matters difficult by haggling. If he does he won't get his treaty.[33]

Eden was initially inclined to dismiss his critics as followers of Chamberlain. But soon enemies of the former Prime Minister joined the protesters. On

22 April Duff Cooper, now Chancellor of the Duchy of Lancaster, wrote to Eden:

... there was no more brutal and indefensible act of aggression than Russia's occupation of [the Baltic States] ... Germany's interference with Czecho-Slovakia, where there was a large German population and with Poland, where the Corridor created an extremely difficult position, were far more excusable actions than that of Russia against the Baltic States.

... it seems to me to be playing straight into the hands of Laval, who is trying to persuade the French that the only alternative to German domination, from which they are suffering, is Russian domination, which would be far worse. He will be able to say that our recognition of Russia's conquests in Europe, during the war, before we have recognized any other changes, proves that we are reconciled to Russian control of the Continent.

... such an act on our part would tear into ribbons the Atlantic Charter and brand us as the arch hypocrites of the world.

Two days later Nicolson wrote in similar vein. He threatened: 'I ... would certainly vote against the agreement and might also speak against it.'[34] On the same day George Harvie Watt, the Prime Minister's Parliamentary Private Secretary, sent the Prime Minister a report of the views of the Foreign Affairs Committee. Churchill forwarded this account to his Foreign Secretary: '... many members are making adverse comments to the effect that ... [it is] Munich over again but worse ... The subject was discussed at the meeting of the Foreign Affairs Committee, when deep concern was expressed.' On 28 April Eden sought to persuade the Prime Minister to disregard the agitation:

I think this account is exaggerated. The Foreign Affairs Committee had been heavily lobbied by Cazalet and others. There were only 30 present. Opposition so far comes mainly from the most ardent supporters of Munich, but I agree it may become serious. Munich was a collapse before a foe, and the betrayal by France of an ally. It has, of course, no resemblance to the present project.[35]

On 8 March Simon, now Lord Chancellor, joined in the controversy: 'I really do not know how, if such a transaction came to be debated in the House of Lords, I could defend it ...' Now Churchill felt strong enough to revert to his earlier position. Moreover, the Soviets had suffered some recent military setbacks at the hands of the Germans and hence were less well-placed than earlier to forge a separate peace with Germany. On 13 May the Prime Minister accordingly wrote to Eden:

As this raises fundamental issues it would be imprudent not to carry important Ministers with you. I do not want to face a bunch of resignations. The Lord Chancellor and Mr Duff Cooper from very different angles have expressed the strongest objections.

On 22 May Stuart, the Chief Whip, added his decisive weight to Eden's critics:

While nothing is known generally about the matter, a limited number of Members have some knowledge of a proposed Treaty with Russia affecting the Baltic States. While my own information on the subject is very limited and while the Foreign Secretary may be able to show that the Treaty is essential for the prosecution of the war, I am disturbed about its political repercussions and feel it my duty to mention the matter to you . . .

I am afraid the impression may be given that our pro-Russian sympathies have carried us away to an extent which will disturb American and Polish opinion, while our determination to help the Russians, who did nothing to help us until Germany forced them into the war, is proved by our deliveries of war material to them at great risk and considerable cost to ourselves . . .[36]

Meanwhile on 21 May Molotov had arrived in London. He at once confirmed to Churchill and Eden that the Soviets would not be satisfied with recognition of their incorporation of the Baltic States. As Eden put it to Harvey, they were 'opening their mouths very wide'.[37] But Eden had been in touch with Maisky for weeks past and surely cannot have been surprised that Molotov also wanted acceptance of a western frontier with Poland that was far beyond what it had been in August 1939 and guarantees of effective Soviet control of the external policies of Romania and Finland. The Foreign Secretary now saw a chance to use these Soviet demands to slide out of even the limited frontier agreement which threatened to make him so many enemies in Parliament. Clearly Churchill favoured this course. But even within the Foreign Office such counsels were gaining strength. In particular, Cadogan urged Eden to offer an alternative draft treaty that would omit all territorial references, including the Baltic States, but would merely commit Great Britain and the Soviet Union in vague terms to twenty years of alliance and to mutual support against future German aggression. This was tentatively put to Molotov. But Cadogan was at first doubtful whether the Foreign Secretary would really fight for it if the Soviets continued to demand a territorial settlement. On 23 May he wrote in his diary: I '*think* he'll be all right. But he is subject to temptation and that ass Harvey's advice.' On the following day he was depressed when the Soviets began to retreat from their extreme demands. 'Unfortunately,' he confided to his diary, 'they [the Soviets] had come a long way on the Polish frontier question and it will be difficult to break on that!' Harvey was meanwhile pushing Eden in the opposite direction. By 24 May he wrote sadly in his diary:

A.E. getting hesitant about the treaty because of . . . American opposition coupled with that of elements in the H of C. Even Cardinal [Arthur] Hinsley has written to express abhorrence of it. A.E. now obviously eager to get away from the old treaty and on to the new. I tell him it is no use listening to Catholics, they are on the side of darkness anyway. As for the H of C opposition it is of the worst and wettest elements.[38]

On the same day Cadogan also noticed a distinct change in Eden's attitude: 'A. now longing to get out of his promise about frontiers. (Winant has been twisting his tail.) But it's a bit late for that now!'[39]

Fortunately for Eden, however, it was not too late. For on the next day, 25 May, Molotov suddenly agreed to study Cadogan's draft treaty and within twenty-four hours had obtained permission from Moscow to accept it. Probably decisive was a meeting between Molotov and Winant. The American Ambassador announced that Roosevelt was adamantly against any Anglo-Soviet treaty involving territorial pledges. The fact that Molotov was scheduled to proceed from London to Washington to discuss the Second Front issue presumably caused the *volte face* of his acceptance of Cadogan's plan. If the military pressure on Moscow had been less severe he would no doubt have given priority not to the Second Front but to post-war frontiers. In that event Eden would have been gravely embarrassed. But such were the domestic pressures that he might well have been forced by Churchill to renege on his offer concerning the Baltic States and break off negotiations with the Soviets. Certainly the Prime Minister came to believe that Eden had agreed in principle to retreat. For on 6 October 1943 he wrote to his Foreign Secretary reminding him that they had sheered off agreeing to Stalin's territorial demands because of 'the perfectly clear menace of very consider-able division of opinion in the House of Commons'.[40] Molotov's sudden capitulation to American pressure had thus saved the Foreign Secretary from humiliation. Eden was at times a decidedly fortunate politician.

Eden's prolonged tussle with Churchill about the recognition of Stalin's conquest of the Baltic States had been accompanied by other differences relating to the Soviet Union – some profound, some apparently trivial. For example, between June 1941 and January 1942, they had quarrelled about the desirability of broadcasting 'The Internationale' on the BBC, given that the anthems of other allied states were regularly played. Eden had finally triumphed.[41] Again, Eden had differed from Churchill about the practica-bility of creating a Second Front. While less fanatical on this subject than Beaverbrook, the Foreign Secretary nevertheless dissented from Churchill's cautious approach to attempting a landing on the Continent in response to Soviet demands. For example, on 23 March 1942 he wrote to Churchill that '... our effort this year should include an attempt to seize and to hold some part of the enemy's long and exposed coast-line'.[42] With the Americans gradually emerging as champions of an early invasion of western Europe, Eden was thus to find himself increasingly at odds with his chief on the central issue of war strategy.

There were also many other policy differences dividing Eden and

Churchill during the remainder of the war. France, Portugal, India, the Balkans and the future of Germany were from time to time to cause great friction. But as well as pure policy arguments, there were two other major reasons for a deteriorating relationship. First, there was a growing sense of irritation on Eden's part about the Prime Minister's methods of conducting the war and his tendency to interfere capriciously in the running of the Foreign Office. Secondly, there was also to some extent a mutual recognition that Eden might in certain contingencies be tempted into making a bid to replace Churchill as Prime Minister.

As is well known, Churchill, like Hitler, kept extraordinary hours. He regularly detained his colleagues until 2 or 3 a.m. and cared little about the effect of this on those who had large departments to run and who thus could not easily spend half the daylight hours in bed as he was able to do. Eden was in constant demand for these nocturnal sessions. Sometimes meetings of a formal character were held during the night but more usually the Prime Minister would hold forth to a small captive group on all manner of subjects of little immediate relevance to the conduct of the war. Eden could not always even keep sacrosanct his weekends, which he liked to spend at his country cottage at Frensham. He would be disturbed with repeated telephone calls about trivial issues – sometimes in the early hours. And he could not even be sure that he would not be arbitrarily summoned to wait upon the Prime Minister in person. Harvey recorded one such disrupted weekend:

A.E. . . . had been over to Chequers on Saturday . . . it was like a Russian play. He arrived at 6 p.m. having motored at speed from Frensham to get there in time for Defence Committee to find PM and [General Claude] Auchinleck sitting in two chairs in the garden. PM said 'I'm afraid you will be very cross with me but I've put off the Defence Committee till after dinner, as I think I'll now go off and have a sleep!!' When dinner came, PM suddenly said, 'I don't want to do any more tonight. I want to see that film again of Nelson and Lady Hamilton!' It was then found that the film unit had already set off back to London. PM said it must be got back and so telephoning went on at intervals through dinner which was very prolonged. 'Put people across the road to stop them!' However, the film unit slipped through the net and there being no cinema the PM finally and reluctantly settled down to work at midnight and they worked solidly up till 2 a.m.; A.E. getting back to Frensham at 4 a.m.!

Formal meetings, particularly of the Defence Committee, to which Eden belonged, were often as wearing as the unofficial sessions of Churchillian reminiscences. Harvey's diary is eloquent:

1 August 1941
A.E. very cross today after again spending five hours in Defence Committee – completely wasting time while PM discoursed on strategy to Auchinleck. A.E. finds PM's views on strategy disastrous: he pressed Auchinleck to undertake an immediate offensive in the Western Desert which Auchinleck refused to do as he hadn't got enough tanks. PM very rude but General very calm and answered well . . .

The meeting broke up in some confusion, PM grumbling and growling – purple in the face and with streaming eyes. A.E. is really worried at the PM's management or lack of management – feels he is wearing out Chiefs of Staff to no purpose.

3 August 1941
A.E.'s accounts of his [Churchill's] conduct of the Defence Committee are disturbing – a monologue – any opposition treated as factious – policy and operations decided by impulse – no proper planning ...[43]

All attempts by Eden and others to persuade the Prime Minister to become more considerate and less verbose proved vain. The pattern continued unchanged throughout the war.

That there was a bond of underlying mutual affection between the two men is clear. Yet the possibility of a decisive quarrel was always present. For Churchill, despite his unusual propensity in a Prime Minister for forming emotional links with some of his political colleagues, was in the last resort capable of ruthlessly defending his own position at whatever cost to friendship. For example, despite his long-standing affection for Beaverbrook, he recognized that a parting of the ways between them might have to come. Told by Eden in October 1941 that Beaverbrook might be planning a campaign against him, the Prime Minister expressed his doubts but added that, if so, 'it would mean war to the knife against him'. So too with Eden. Churchill probably had at this period more respect for him than for any other Cabinet colleague, not even excluding Beaverbrook. And he sometimes even heeded his advice. But the importance of this should not be exaggerated. For the competition usually did not amount to much: the Prime Minister had deliberately surrounded himself with mediocrities. As he told Eden in January 1942, 'I'd rather have a Cabinet of obedient mugwumps than of awkward freaks.' So Eden's position vis-à-vis Churchill was only enviable in that he alone, for most of the war, was the only Cabinet Minister to have much influence on him in the international sphere. But the cost was to have to put up with treatment that must have been vexatious in the extreme for a man of Eden's standing and self-esteem. His later claim that Churchill's conduct towards him was better than Chamberlain's is not easy to endorse. For when every allowance has been made for the exigencies of wartime, the Prime Minister's behaviour was often as cavalier as it is possible to imagine. He maintained from the outset of the war a private correspondence with Roosevelt. Then in 1941, to Eden's dismay, he began additionally to by-pass the Foreign Office in communicating with Stalin. And, needless to say, he quixotically interfered in many lesser matters. Eden was often tempted to quit but his earlier resignation from Chamberlain's Cabinet may have served as a deterrent. As early as 10 July 1941 Harvey recorded:

Very tiresome Cabinet last night over Russian proposal. A.E. says PM most arbitrary and insisted on replying personally to Stalin. (It is just like Neville and Musso! A.E. said) ... A.E. very fed up with PM's monopolistic tendencies. I told him we can't have him resigning from Winston's Government.[44]

This evidence of continuous unhappiness on Eden's part must lead historians to ask whether he ever contemplated the alternative solution to escape or resignation, namely the organization of a political coup against Churchill. Did he in short ever see himself acting as Lloyd George had towards H. H. Asquith during the First World War? If such a possibility existed at all, it was during 1942. This was the year of the disastrous loss of Singapore, of the fall of Tobruk and of the famous Motion of Censure in the House of Commons. The first threats to Churchill's position came in February 1942. A newspaper campaign demanded substantial Cabinet changes and the appointment of a separate Minister of Defence. But Churchill was not prepared to remain Prime Minister if he could not also remain Minister of Defence. He clearly saw that Asquith's position in the First World War had been decisively undermined by giving in to demands that deprived him of the central direction of the war.

Eden's sympathies lay with the critics. On 12 February 1942 Harvey recorded in his diary:

Further talk today with A.E. about PM ... A.E. feels he is more and more obstinate and at the same time losing his grip. I spoke of the rising of public opinion at successive disasters and failures which we both agreed was entirely justifiable. There might be an explosion which would sweep the whole Government out. The War Cabinet is now quite ineffective and so is the Defence Committee. A most disturbing situation which can't last. A.E. hesitates to say more to the PM who knows his views well enough.[45]

On the following day Harvey wrote to his chief arguing that if Churchill would not create a separate Minister of Defence he must be got to go. On receiving this note, Eden telephoned Harvey and told him that he agreed with it. On 16 February Eden held a discussion with Harvey, Thomas and Richard Law, the Parliamentary Under-Secretary at the Foreign Office. According to Harvey, Law at least believed that Eden would soon become Prime Minister. Harvey's diary continued:

A.E. had discussed with Ned Grigg over weekend how things were worked in Lloyd George's time ... The press is strongly urging a separate Ministry of Defence. I thought the crisis might come in 2 stages if PM yielded now – a stage with Winston and a separate M of D, and then a later stage when Winston faded out. Dick said country had lost all confidence in the Government and A.E. should tell PM so and if he didn't make change, then it would lose all confidence in him (Churchill). Jim Thomas ... confirmed this – A.E. agreed and said he would say this and urge appointment of a separate M of D ... As regards [Alexander] Erskine Hill [of the 1922 Committee]. A.E. was most anxious not to lend himself to any intrigue. He proposed to say we must all rally round PM and try to strengthen the Government.[46]

In these dangerous circumstances the Prime Minister showed both resolution and resourcefulness. Faced with Eden's arguments, he conceded that Cabinet changes were needed but would not agree to a separate Minister of Defence. He now moved swiftly to win Attlee's support by offering him the Deputy Premiership and he also raised the possibility of making the dynamic Cripps Leader of the House. None of this was to Eden's liking. As Harvey recorded: 'A.E. expressed doubt about Attlee becoming Deputy PM as giving some blessing to the idea of him [Attlee] as a successor – also, as PM confesses, the whole thing is eyewash leaving Minister of Defence as before.'[47] On 17 February Eden met Lloyd George. Harvey recorded that Eden had been impressed by the former Prime Minister and declared that, if he formed a government, he would give him a War Cabinet post.[48] On the following morning Eden again saw Churchill and may have expressed unhappiness at the prospect of Cripps as Leader of the House. For the Prime Minister now decided to tempt Eden by offering him the Leadership of the House as well as the Foreign Office. Eden's initial reaction was hesitation: 'I said I would like to think about it an hour or two.' The two men agreed to meet again at 5.30 p.m., as the Prime Minister claimed to need his afternoon rest. But for once Churchill did not go to sleep after his luncheon. Instead he summoned Cripps. At 5 p.m. Cripps met Eden and told him that he had accepted Churchill's invitation to join the Government. 'Good,' replied Eden, 'in what capacity?' 'Leader of the House. Unless you want it ...' Harvey wrote in his diary:

A.E. rather annoyed at PM offering it to Cripps before he had had A.E.'s views and rather bitten now with leading H of C as a stepping stone to being PM later. He doesn't want Cripps to groom himself for PM ... [Eden] felt PM had bowled him a quick one.[49]

Eden's punishment for pressing unwelcome changes on Churchill had thus been to face the rapid build-up of both Attlee and Cripps as potential long-term successors. Nor had the Prime Minister yet run out of resources in his vigorous campaign to discourage Eden from moving against him. Having on several previous occasions told Eden that he was his heir in the event of his sudden death, Churchill now let him know that he could not after all count on succeeding. This thrust was delicately combined with apparent words of reassurance about the significance of Attlee's promotion. According to Harvey, Churchill said that 'although he would make Attlee Deputy Prime Minister, this didn't mean he had any claim on succession, as PM must be a Tory and because if the PM fell down dead, he had told the King that he should choose either A.E. or [John] Anderson and that he should wait 4–5 hours to see which way opinion went'.[50]

Eden was understandably disturbed. Urged on by Law, Cranborne and

Thomas, he decided to try to gain at least some face-saving advance: he would make a determined bid for the Leadership of the House, which both Churchill and Cripps had apparently acknowledged was open to him if he insisted upon it. But late on the night of 18/19 February even this was now denied to him. According to Harvey:

> A.E. had pressed his preference for Leadership but Attlee didn't back it and Chief Whip was clearly opposed to it. PM said to A.E. 'You are a man of action and not of talk and I can't think why you want it' ... Dick and Jim very shattered at this ...
> A.E. rather sore and feeling, I think, he hadn't pressed half enough.

Churchill had thus survived Eden's first tentative assault upon his position. As he wrote in his war memoirs: 'I should not of course have remained Prime Minister for an hour if I had been deprived of the office of Minister of Defence. The fact that this was widely known repelled all challenges ... I must record my gratitude to all who helped me to succeed.'[51]

Eden's next step was to draw close to Cripps. This was perhaps surprising after he had sought to prevent his becoming Leader of the House and in view of the verdict he had expressed to Harvey about him in Moscow in December 1941, namely that he was a clever fool. Harvey's diary reveals a rapid change of attitude:

25 February 1942
Cripps and A.E. are getting together. I'm glad ... Cripps told A.E. that he and himself (C.) were the only people who had any hold over the country and they must see to it that the PM agreed to what they said. They must pull the machine together and drive it along. A.E. very pleased at this and realizes obvious importance of these two pulling together. I'm thankful. I was afraid he might resent the assumption of equality.

27 February 1942
A.E. told me he would be quite happy to see Cripps at No. 10, if he himself could be Minister of Defence and run the war side. This surprised me ... Of course if Cripps were PM now, A.E. could become the Tory PM when parties divide again ... We are all convinced that the PM cannot last much longer ...

2 March 1942
It is fantastic that there should be no War Cabinet meeting daily to deal with the war, but only an occasional defence committee meeting at 10 o'clock at night once or twice a week at the whim of Winston. A.E. doesn't believe PM will ever agree to give up anything.[52]

But before the Eden–Cripps alliance could make any impact, Churchill sent the Leader of the House on a mission to India. During his absence, however, Eden contemplated the possibility of dramatic action on his return. On 2 April Harvey recorded: 'A.E. worried as usual over PM's methods of running the war. He is convinced it cannot go on and says when Cripps returns a frontal attack must be made.'[53]

No such joint attack ever materialized. Even with Churchill's health giving increasing cause for concern and with the possibility of further military setbacks on the horizon, Eden appears instead to have settled down to play a waiting game. Moreover, Churchill restored Eden to his earlier place as sole heir apparent, having on 16 June on the eve of a visit to the United States formally written to the King in this sense. By the second half of 1942 Cripps was thus in effect on his own. His performance as Leader of the House had not served to strengthen his claims to the premiership, a development that now gave Eden some satisfaction. In fact Eden had become extremely cautious where challenges to Churchill were concerned. Harvey recorded on 13 August:

> Winterton [a Conservative MP] came to see A.E. today, worried about the future of the Conservative Party and of the Government. He said he thought PM would have to go sooner or later and A.E. should take his place. Would A.E. be prepared to do so? A.E. said he would do no plotting against Winston, now or ever, and he would be ready to serve under any of his colleagues.
>
> I took him to task rather for his passive attitudes but he said he didn't wish to appear in any way as intriguing. He thought his position was pretty secure in actual fact in the country and also owing to the PM's famous testament which he had left with Alec Hardinge [Private Secretary to the King] recommending that the King should send for him if anything happened to himself ...
>
> He feels he hasn't any serious rival. Cripps no party and no experience, Lyttelton no experience, Anderson ridiculous, Attlee and Bevin unthinkable.

Cripps became so disillusioned at Churchill's conduct of the war that he began to talk of resigning. The support he received from Eden was now rather limited. Harvey's diary is revealing:

22 September 1942
A.E. said Winston favoured letting Cripps go, but he A.E. would be reluctant to lose him as an ally; but if he went, then he would try to get Bobbety [Cranborne] into the War Cabinet. A.E. said that when he sees the PM again tonight he would stake out his claim for the leadership [of the House].

1 October 1942
PM had accused him [Cripps] of trying to upset the Government and said he must have an answer as to whether he was going or staying within 24 hours ... A.E. is uneasy himself because he agrees with much of Cripps's criticism.

2 October 1942
He [Eden] found the PM in a great state of anger, rolling out threats and invectives against C. [Cripps] and declaring it was a conspiracy. A.E. set about calming him and reasoning with him. When W. [Churchill] started shouting, A.E. said 'I thought we were fighting the Germans!' He said he must see that Cripps had a case and that it really was not a conspiracy. A.E. finally persuaded him, and it was no small

business, that he should not try and drive C. out but should offer him either the Washington Supply job or MAP [Ministry of Aircraft Production]...

[Later when alone, Cripps] asked if A.E. would then join with him in insisting on a change of method. A.E. declined to promise this because, as he said to me afterwards, he couldn't enter into a bargain about this.

Cripps agreed to stay for a brief period as a major north African assault was near. But on 22 November he left the War Cabinet to become Minister of Aircraft Production; Eden succeeding him as Leader of the House. As he wrote in his memoirs of Cripps: 'Some such solution was the only outcome possible after Cripps's express criticism of the Prime Minister's conduct of the war.'[54]

Thus Eden's own challenge to Churchill had never gone very far. Now, with Cripps's fall, he was compelled to wait for illness or military disaster. But no more setbacks comparable to Singapore or Tobruk occurred. Churchill himself had told his colleagues before the north African landings: 'If Torch fails, then I'm done for and must go and hand over to one of you.'[55] Torch succeeded and so Eden's chances of becoming wartime Prime Minister faded. Why had he not made a bolder bid in 1942; Did the memory of the lack of impact of his resignation in 1938 cause him to adopt an ultra-cautious attitude? Or was it in the last resort that, despite all their differences, a feeling of affection and admiration for Churchill led him to stay his hand? The truth may never be known.

Eden's acquisition of the Leadership of the House strengthened his long-term claim to the succession. But during 1943 the only effect was to weaken his grip on the conduct of foreign policy. The need to be regularly in the Commons inevitably reduced the time he could spend on briefing himself for policy clashes with his chief. Churchill took full advantage of this and played an increasingly dominant rôle in shaping British relations with both the Americans and the Soviets. Symbolic of this was the Casablanca Conference of January 1943 between Churchill and Roosevelt. Neither Eden nor Hull was permitted to attend. No doubt Roosevelt's waning confidence in his Secretary of State was the main reason for this decision. But it is doubtful whether Churchill was as reluctant to agree as he maintained to Eden.

The principal issues at Casablanca concerned future military actions, relations with the Free French and the terms of which the capitulation of Germany and Japan could be accepted. The occasion is remembered, above all, for Roosevelt's determination to commit the Western Allies to 'unconditional surrender'. Conscious of the problems created for Wilson by accepting an Armistice in 1918 and anxious for electoral reasons not to be drawn into prematurely giving precision to any future territorial settlements, Roosevelt took refuge in this bombastic formula. Churchill was less enthusiastic possibly because he was already worried that such a line would ultimately benefit the Soviets. But he half-heartedly recommended it to his Cabinet by telegram in the belief that the matter would remain secret for some time. He was therefore dismayed when Roosevelt, without prior consultation, proclaimed their joint commitment to unconditional surrender at a press conference. Eden, however, was markedly less disturbed than his chief at the President's line. From London he even sought vainly to have the formula extended to cover Italy as well as Japan and Germany.

Less acceptable to Eden was Roosevelt's policy concerning France. For at Casablanca the President evidently hoped to build up General Henri Giraud instead of General Charles de Gaulle as a post-war leader. Eden, on the other hand, had long held that de Gaulle, for all his arrogance towards his British hosts, must be sustained. But Churchill wavered. For, while only intermittently sharing the Americans' extreme prejudice against de Gaulle, he was not prepared in the last resort to quarrel with Roosevelt on his behalf. The Prime Minister, for example, had even been willing to condone the Americans' deal with Darlan, a Vichyite renegade, in the aftermath of the north African landings of 1942. Eden had protested vigorously but vainly, Churchill even arguing at one moment that 'Darlan is not as bad as de Gaulle anyway'. De Gaulle himself recognized that Eden was genuinely on his side and recalled that the Foreign Secretary had been 'moved to the point of tears' over the Darlan deal.[56] No doubt, therefore, Eden was much relieved when Darlan was assassinated in mysterious circumstances on 24 December. Now at Casablanca, with Eden absent, Roosevelt still showed little enthusiasm for de Gaulle's claims. The President was willing, however, to hold a meeting with de Gaulle and Giraud. De Gaulle, then in London, was therefore summoned to the Conference. According to Harvey, he was at first unwilling to comply for fear of being 'Muniched'. But Eden, on Churchill's instructions, bullied him into flying to Casablanca, on pain of being totally repudiated by the British Government. In the event de Gaulle was not 'Muniched' at the Conference, but he was nevertheless forced into a partnership with Giraud in the knowledge that the Americans' long-term aim was to see him outmanoeuvred.

For Eden a further humiliation followed Casablanca when Churchill insisted on visiting Turkey before returning home. This clearly constituted a personal attempt to bring Ankara into the war. Churchill's mission failed. But the divergence of aim between the Prime Minister and his Foreign Secretary was to have considerable long-term significance. Whereas Eden had fought hard to secure a Turkish declaration of war early in 1941, he now disapproved of such a policy following the fall of Greece and Yugoslavia. He accordingly persuaded the War Cabinet to send a remonstrance to Churchill, who duly ignored it. The key to Eden's new approach was his concern for Soviet susceptibilities. Harvey recorded:

> We all hate this plan. First, it will alarm the Turks and make them go backwards. This would not matter in itself if it were no more than that, for we shall be better without the Turks in this war. It will however make an unpleasant effect on the Russians who will see in it an attempt to nip into the Balkans with their old enemy Turkey before they can get there themselves.[57]

Eden thereafter believed that Churchill's diplomacy and military strategy were to a considerable extent motivated by hostility to Moscow and a desire to save as much as possible of east-central Europe from post-war Soviet influence.

This view of Churchill's aims was widely accepted by commentators in the years following the Second World War. Most notably, Chester Wilmot endorsed this interpretation and further claimed that Roosevelt's gullibility about the Soviets effectively frustrated Churchill. The increasing American insistence on priority being given to a Second Front in France rather than to the Mediterranean symbolized for Wilmot this divergence between Roosevelt and Churchill on attitudes towards Moscow. Recently, however, many historians have rejected this interpretation of Churchill's motives. Much has been made, for example, of Fitzroy Maclean's account of a conversation with Churchill in 1943 about Yugoslavia: '"Do you intend," asked the Prime Minister, "to make Yugoslavia your home after the war? ... Neither do I. And that being so, the less you and I worry about the form of Government they set up, the better. What interests us is ... doing most harm to the Germans."' Again, evidence has emerged suggesting that fear of vast casualties was Churchill's principal reason for opposing any early attempt at an invasion of western Europe. And Michael Howard, a British official war historian, has pointed to the narrow chauvinism of Churchill and has alleged that at times his main concern was merely to see Generals Alexander and Bernard Montgomery riding in triumph through Rome. He has also stressed the pragmatism of the British Chiefs of Staff. An American scholar has even gone so far as to write: '... we now know ... that responsible British leaders never advocated an Allied invasion of the Balkan peninsula and that the "Balkan versus western Europe" controversy referred to by many post-war writers is a myth.'[58] Yet the recent opening to inspection and partial publication of Harvey's diary provides some support for the formerly fashionable view that Churchill was indeed intent from at least the beginning of 1943 on 'nipping into the Balkans' before the Soviets could get there. Clearly Harvey gained his impression of the Prime Minister's outlook from Eden, who probably had a clearer insight into his chief's thinking on these matters than any other contemporary. For Churchill liked to settle differences with his Foreign Secretary in private meetings in the early hours of the morning. But once they had decided upon a course they did not invariably explain their reasoning with complete candour to the War Cabinet, to the Chiefs of Staff or to their Allies, still less to insignificant actors like Maclean. It is therefore not surprising that historians have found only scanty formal evidence of anti-Soviet motivation in Churchill's attempts to shape Anglo-American Grand Strategy. Harvey's diary, on the other hand, may take us nearer to the truth simply because Eden was Churchill's closest confidant. But though Eden probably had the privilege of having the best insight into his chief's thinking on Grand Strategy, it did not follow that they were in general agreement. On the contrary, the Foreign Secretary did a good deal to undermine the Prime Minister's approach. For his attempt to prevent Churchill's visit to Turkey was, as will be seen, only the first of several moves during 1943 to that end.

Eden's discomfiture at being excluded from the Casablanca Conference was partly reduced by Roosevelt agreeing to see him in Washington soon afterwards. After a delay caused by Churchill's illness, the Foreign Secretary departed on 11 March for the United States where he was to remain for almost three weeks. He had no narrow agenda and no precise mission other than to explore a variety of Anglo-American concerns with all the leading policy-makers. From the outset he was struck by the lack of harmony in the American camp. Harvey recorded on 13 March:

A.E. feels it is all rather like a mad house. He said to me he felt more at home in the Kremlin. There at least they meant business. Here all is confusion and woolliness. President jealous of Hull, Winant and Welles at cross purposes. It is not possible here, imagine, to discuss our problems with Roosevelt, Hull and Welles altogether. Each has to be addressed separately and it is doubtful if one will tell the other what he has said.[59]

Eden wisely perceived, however, that Harry Hopkins of the White House staff was now Roosevelt's unchallenged favourite and hence counted for much more than anyone in the State Department. He accordingly spent much time with him and the two soon got on to excellent terms. This was fortunate, since Hopkins's initial impression of Eden when they had first met in London in January 1941 had been unfavourable. As he had written privately to Roosevelt:

This morning ... I drove to the Foreign Office to see Eden – sauve, impeccable, unimportant. The words were quite right but carried no conviction for I am sure the man has no deeply rooted moral stamina. A goodly number of soft Britishers must like him and his hat and I fancy Churchill gives him high office because he neither thinks, acts, much less says anything of importance.
... I gained the impression that Mr Anthony Eden had little more to do with the prosecution of the war than the Supreme Court. But they put on a good show and

the old foreign office crowd showed me in and out in the best tradition – and Mr Eden took me to my car where the photographers were conveniently and no doubt spontaneously waiting.[60]

Now Hopkins formed a different view of Eden. He accordingly urged Roosevelt to give his visitor every sign of approval. After their first meeting for dinner on 13 March the President repeatedly found time for further discussions. They dined together on both the 14th and 15th; took tea on the 17th; and had a further meeting on the 19th. By the 15th Harvey could even note in his diary: 'Roosevelt is developing a passion for A.E. "*On ne se quitte plus*".'[61] So good an impression had Eden made that he was presently given the unusual honour of being invited, once he had returned from engagements outside Washington, to move from the Embassy into the White House for the last three days of his stay.

It was obviously to Eden's advantage at home that he had got on to such good terms with the President. Halifax reported to the Prime Minister on 31 March: 'Anthony has just left for Canada ... From the first he clicked with everyone from the President downwards, both in private and in public. He has never put a foot wrong.' And Hopkins wrote to Averell Harriman: 'Anthony's trip here has been good. Everyone likes him and we have made a thorough and frank exploration of everything with which the United Nations are concerned.'[62]

Eden's personal success did not mean, however, that he had been as much in agreement with Roosevelt as he allowed him to think. He disapproved, for example, of some of the President's ideas for the post-war world. These included setting up a four-power world directorate to consist of the United States, Great Britain, the Soviet Union and China. And in Europe at least no other state would be allowed to have armaments. This would clearly have constituted savage treatment of France. Equally unacceptable to Eden was the idea that the Allies should themselves initially run a liberated France. He was also privately scornful about Roosevelt's desire to break up Yugoslavia and to create a new state of Wallonia comprising parts of Belgium, Luxembourg and France. In his memoirs he wrote somewhat patronizingly about these suggestions:

Roosevelt was familiar with the history and geography of Europe. Perhaps his hobby of stamp-collecting had helped him to this knowledge, but the academic yet sweeping opinions which he built upon it were alarming in their cheerful fecklessness. He seemed to see himself disposing of the fate of many lands, allied, no less than enemy. He did all this with so much grace that it was not easy to dissent. Yet it was too like a conjurer, skilfully juggling with balls of dynamite, whose nature he failed to understand.[63]

This was Eden's way of saying that he would have found it extremely easy to dissent but that he had not found it politic to do so.

Even more ominous for Anglo-American relations was the President's line on the future of colonial empires. Basing himself on long-standing American anti-imperialist doctrines and on the high ideals enshrined in the Atlantic Charter, he underlined his commitment to establishing an alternative system of trusteeships throughout the world. The matter had long been under consideration in both London and Washington. But Churchill had made it clear from the outset that the Atlantic Charter should not be taken as applying to British possessions and on 10 November 1942 he had declared: 'We mean to hold our own. I have not become the King's First Minister in order to preside over the liquidation of the British Empire.' It had thus been hoped in Great Britain that the Americans would agree to a relatively vague declaration as a means of reassuring world opinion that her colonial policy would take an en-lightened form without raising hopes that independence would be an automatic right. Now in Washington Eden learnt that this would not satisfy Roosevelt, who even proposed, for example, that the British should give up Hong Kong. According to Hopkins, 'Eden dryly remarked that he had not heard the President suggest any similar gestures' on the part of the United States.[64] The divergence in outlook between Washington and London continued throughout the war, though Churchill felt more passionately about it than his Foreign Secretary.[65] Eden's turn to feel bitter at American posturing on so-called 'colonialism' came in the 1950s when, as will be seen, both Democratic and Republican Administrations refused, partly on such grounds, to help to defend British interests in the Middle East.

Eden found himself in greater agreement with Roosevelt on the future of Germany. The President definitely favoured dismemberment at this stage of the war. Eden accepted this in principle, though perhaps without en-thusiasm. He wrote to Churchill: '... on the whole I favoured the idea of dismemberment as you have often spoken to me in favour of it'. But all details were left for later consideration. Eden was also apparently in broad agreement with Roosevelt on Soviet intentions. He recalled in his memoirs:

The big question which rightly dominated Roosevelt's mind was whether it was possible to work with Russia now and after the war. He wanted to know what I thought of the view that Stalin's aim was to overrun and communize the Continent. I replied that it was impossible to give a definite opinion. Even if these fears were to prove correct, we should make the position no worse by trying to work with Russia and by assuming that Stalin meant what he said in the Anglo-Soviet Treaty.[66]

For Eden the importance of Roosevelt's intense interest in the future of Germany and of the Soviet Union was that it provided reassurance that those in Washington who wished to give priority to the war with Japan were gaining no ground. A letter from Hopkins to Eden shortly after the end of the visit provided confirmation:

The shooting of our fliers in Tokyo has started all the isolationist papers promoting the war in the Far East as against Germany. I notice one of the Hearst papers said this morning that, after all, Hitler was not nearly so bad as [Hideki] Tojo. All that crowd, of course, would make a separate peace with Hitler tomorrow if they could get away with it, but I don't think they have any real public opinion behind them. Nor do I think that the Australians or Mme Chiang can change our strategic policy.[67]

One issue raised during Eden's conversations in Washington illustrates the unsentimental strand in his approach to foreign affairs. This concerned Hitler's treatment of European Jewry. On 17 December 1942 the Foreign Secretary had made known to the House of Commons the contents of an Allied Statement condemning Hitler's 'barbarous and inhuman' conduct. In the ensuing questioning these exchanges had taken place:

REGINALD SORENSEN: Having regard to the widespread abhorrence of all people regarding these crimes, could attempts not be made to explore the possibility of cooperation with non-belligerent and neutral governments to secure the emigration of Jews, say to Sweden or some other neutral country?

EDEN: My hon. Friend will see that it is only too clear, from what I have said, what is going on in these territories occupied by Germany. Naturally I should be only too glad to see anything of the kind, but the hon. Member will understand the circumstances.

To another questioner Eden replied: 'It would clearly be the desire of the United Nations to do everything they could to provide wherever possible an asylum for these people, but the House will understand that there are immense geographical and other difficulties.'[68] The interlude ended with a spontaneous demonstration by the Commons: the Members stood in silent tribute to the Jewish martyrs. In Washington, however, Eden, despite his Parliamentary answers, showed little interest in giving refuge to Hitler's victims. Hopkins recorded that on 27 March, in the presence of Roosevelt:

Hull raised the question of the sixty or seventy thousand Jews that are in Bulgaria and are threatened with extermination unless we could get them out and, very urgently, pressed Eden for an answer to the problem. Eden replied that the whole problem of the Jews in Europe is very difficult and that we should move very cautiously about offering to take all Jews out of a country like Bulgaria. If we do that, then the Jews of the world will be wanting us to make similar offers in Poland and Germany. Hitler might well take up any such offer and there simply are not enough ships and means of transportation in the world to handle them.

Eden said that the British were ready to take about sixty thousand more Jews to Palestine, but the problem of transportation, even from Bulgaria to Palestine, is extremely difficult. Furthermore, any such mass movement as that would be very dangerous to security because the Germans would be sure to put a number of their agents in the group...

Underlying Eden's policy, however, was a desire not to offend unduly the

Arabs, whose oil he judged to be of indispensable value. Moreover, while never an anti-Semite, he was personally less sympathetic to Jews, and especially Zionists, than Churchill. In this respect he diverged from Harvey, to whom he had minuted in August 1941: 'Let me murmur in your ear that I prefer Arabs to Jews!'[69] But those who wish to argue from this evidence that the fate of European Jewry must to a certain extent be attributed to Eden personally have to face the difficulty that Churchill, who would never have expressed a preference for Arabs over Jews and who greatly regretted the decision of Chamberlain's Government in 1939 to issue a White Paper repudiating partition, was driven to embrace, for the duration of the war, essentially the same Palestinian policy as his Foreign Secretary: Great Britain was simply not in a position to put her oil supplies at risk.[70]

Eden's visit to the United States in 1943 had its lighter moments. He was able, for example, to spend two days in one of his favourite pastimes: inspecting parades of the armed services. And on 26 March he was invited to address the State Legislature of Maryland in Annapolis – a symbolic choice in that his ancestor, Sir Robert Eden, had been Maryland's last colonial governor. Following a brief visit to Canada, Eden was back in London on 4 April.

On the following day the *Völkischer Beobachter* launched the claim that the Germans had discovered the mass graves of over 10,000 Polish officers at Katyn near Smolensk – a figure later reduced to 4,510. In ensuing days the German media gave the story increasing prominence and categorically stated that the Soviets had been responsible during 1940 when they had controlled the relevant territory. For Eden this was a sombre development. Relations between the Soviet Union and the Polish Government-in-Exile were already at a low ebb because of Polish unwillingness to accept the permanency of the loss of any territory seized by the Soviets in 1939. Now the Poles were predisposed to believe in the accuracy of the German charges regarding Katyn as, notwithstanding the resumption of Polish–Soviet diplomatic relations in 1941, prolonged attempts to locate Polish officers captured by the Soviets in 1939 had failed. The Polish Government appear to have raised Katyn with Eden for the first time on 16 April at a luncheon for Allied Foreign Ministers. But they did not explain that they intended to make a public appeal for the truth of the German claim to be investigated by the International Red Cross (IRC) – a step they took on the following day. Had they done so, Eden would have discouraged them on grounds of *Realpolitik*. During May Cadogan minuted: 'I cannot recall that they mentioned the appeal to the IRC.' Eden added: 'Nor can I. They only mentioned that they must reply and I argued, as did Sir A. Cadogan, that they should throw doubt on the German story.'[71]

Did this mean that Eden actually believed that the Germans and not the

Soviets had committed the atrocity? A British official historian, Woodward, eager as always to defend his country's reputation, later wrote:

> In a long report of 24 May, 1943, examining the evidence then available, Mr [Owen] O'Malley, British Ambassador to the Polish Government, considered that the evidence led to the conclusion that the responsibility for the executions lay with the Soviet Government. The Foreign Office had at first inclined to think, as the Prime Minister had said to General [Wladyslaw] Sikorski, the German statements were propagandist lies. They agreed later with the conclusion reached by Mr O'Malley ... the weight of opinion has continued to attribute the responsibility to the Russians. It should be added that, in view of the fearful atrocities committed by the Germans against the inhabitants of Poland, the British and United States Governments had good reason for thinking, at first, that the Germans had carried out the mass executions at Katyn.[72]

But it is not established that Churchill told Sikorski that he was inclined to think that 'the German statements ... were propagandist lies'. For according to Eduard Raczyński, the Polish Ambassador in London, the Prime Minister said as early as 15 April: 'Alas, the German revelations are probably true. The Bolsheviks can be very cruel.' He also minuted on the same day: 'I may observe however that the facts are pretty grim.'[73] And within the Foreign Office no less a figure than Cadogan wrote in his diary as early as 26 April that he saw the Soviet reaction as 'indicative of a bad conscience'. Eden also made no attempt to dissuade the Poles from provoking Moscow on the grounds that the Germans were lying: tacitly his appeal for discretion was on the basis of political calculation. On 19 April Eden told the War Cabinet that he was trying to persuade the Poles to treat Katyn 'as a German propaganda move'. But this, as one historian has commented, 'was different from saying it was untrue'. But by the 27th Eden was frankly informing his colleagues that he feared that the London Poles' reaction to Katyn might give Stalin a pretext to set up an alternative Polish Government under 'Soviet influence'. Already Stalin had 'interrupted' diplomatic relations with the London Poles in retaliation for their appeal for a Red Cross investigation. Churchill for once agreed with Eden. 'There is no use,' he minuted to his Foreign Secretary on 28 April, 'prowling morbidly round the three-year-old graves of Smolensk' – incidentally, another endorsement by the Prime Minister of the German claim that the massacre occurred in 1940.[74]

It was on this same day, 28 April, that Churchill wrote to Stalin:

> Eden and I have pointed out to the Polish Government that no resumption of friendly or working relations with Soviet Russia is possible while they make charges of an insulting character against the Soviet Government and thus seem to countenance the atrocious Nazi propaganda.

He added that he had taken steps to control the unofficial Polish press in

London and he had persuaded the Polish Government to drop their request for a Red Cross investigation. He accordingly hoped that diplomatic relations would be resumed and that Polish forces in the Soviet Union would be allowed to leave. Abasing himself at the feet of a regime he believed guilty of mass murder of prisoners of war, Churchill added the sentence: 'We hope earnestly that ... you will consider this matter in a spirit of magnanimity.' His appeal was unsuccessful. And the Soviets never again had diplomatic relations with the London Poles.[75]

A similar humiliating task awaited Eden on 4 May. He was required to answer parliamentary questions about the Katyn allegations. His principal statement read:

His Majesty's Government have no wish to attribute blame for these events to anyone except the common enemy. There is no need for me to enter into the immediate origin of the dispute; I would only draw attention, as indeed the Soviet and Polish Governments have already done in their published statements, to the cynicism which permits the Nazi murderers of hundreds of thousands of innocent Poles and Russians to make use of a story of mass murder, in an attempt to disturb the unity of the Allies. From the outset His Majesty's Government have used their best efforts to persuade both the Poles and the Russians not to allow these German manoeuvres to have even the semblance of success.[76]

This statement, and indeed the whole Katyn episode, find no place in Eden's memoirs. It must therefore be presumed, in the absence of evidence to the contrary, that his words were a conscious cover-up of what he knew beyond reasonable doubt to be a Soviet crime. Later in May O'Malley produced a full-scale analysis demonstrating the overwhelming case against the Soviets. He concluded:

We have in fact perforce used the good name of England like the murderers used the little conifers, to cover up a massacre; and in view of the immense importance of an appearance of Allied unity and of the heroic resistance of Russia to Germany, few will think that any other course would have been wise or right ... since no remedy can be found in an early alteration of our public attitude towards the Katyn affair, we ought, maybe, to ask ourselves how, consistently with the necessities of our relations with the Soviet Government, the voice of our political conscience is to be kept up to concert pitch. It may be that the answer lies, for the moment, only in something to be done inside our own hearts and minds where we are masters.

Cadogan at least was moved to minute:

This of course raises terrible problems, but I think no one has pointed out that on the purely moral plane, these are not new. How many thousands of its own citizens has the Soviet regime butchered? And I don't know that the blood of a Pole cries louder to Heaven than that of a Russian. But we have perforce welcomed the Russians as Allies and have set ourselves to work with them in war and peace ... the other disturbing thought is that we may eventually, by agreement and in collaboration with the Russians, proceed to the trial and perhaps execution of Axis 'war criminals' while condoning this atrocity. I confess that I shall find that extremely difficult to swallow.[77]

Eden, however, judging by the silence in the diaries of Cadogan and Harvey, showed no comparable disquiet. It would appear that not until 1944 was his conscience to be stirred by the degradation involved in being in alliance with the Soviets. Perhaps his hostility to Fascism and, maybe still more, his hatred of the anti-Communist followers of Chamberlain had caused his heart to harden. Churchill, on the other hand, felt keenly the disagreeable aspects of collaborating with Stalin. Yet he, like Eden, had been in large measure the author of his own fate. Their conduct between 1938 and 1941 had effectively caused the British to select the Soviets as their allies. Churchill had said after Munich:

... do not suppose that this is the end. This is only the beginning of the reckoning. This is only the first sip, the first foretaste of a bitter cup which will be proffered to us year by year unless by a supreme recovery of moral health and martial vigour, we arise again and take our stand for freedom as in the olden time.[78]

Now from a different quarter a bitter cup was still being proffered. And between Katyn and Potsdam Churchill and Eden were repeatedly required to drink from it at least as deeply as Chamberlain. True, during the remainder of the War, Churchill laboured hard, though largely in vain, to mobilize American support against the continuing violation of his values. Eden, on the other hand, gave his chief no consistent support to this end. But his critics are left to speculate whether this was principally due to failure of intellect, imagination or character.

On his return to London from Washington Eden found no relief from an almost intolerable burden of duties. From the end of 1940 he had had to attend numerous meetings of the War Cabinet and the Defence Committee and regularly to endure Churchill's rhodomontades until the early hours as well as run a great Department of State. Within the Foreign Office, moreover, major administrative change had to be overseen, culminating in the so-called 'Eden Reforms' of 1943.[79] Now, however, he was compelled in addition as Leader of the House to spend large parts of his working day on the Front Bench handling an infinite variety of topics. On 24 November 1942, shortly after Eden had assumed this new rôle, Cadogan recorded in his diary:

Met A. in [St James's] Park and asked what we were to do about FO work now that he was leading the House. He said we could go on as before. But we can't! He leaves London lunch-time Fri: gets back lunch-time Mon., and will now have to spend Tues., Wed. and Thurs. in the House. Quite impossible!

216

By 19 January 1943 even the faithful Harvey wrote in his diary that Eden was often inadequately prepared for his meetings and that he was equally unable to delegate responsibility.[80]

Now after his return from Washington Eden faced still more problems. For interest in domestic policy issues was increasing, involving more pressure on the Leader of the House. In particular, the publication of the Beveridge Report on 17 February signalled the beginning of intense debate within and outside the Government on the post-war future. Eden sympathized with the more 'advanced' elements in the Government, favouring not only the Beveridge Report but also such symbols of post-war collectivist planning as the retention of rationing. Churchill, by contrast, became increasingly conservative. Eden thus had a large share of responsibility for pushing the Conservative Party towards acceptance of the post-war consensus now known as the 'Social Democratic Age'. This did not endear the Foreign Secretary to Conservative Party activists. Nevertheless, in the absence of Churchill in Washington in May 1943, he was obliged to make the principal speech to the Conservative Party Conference – yet another example of the excessive burdens now falling to him. Harvey recorded:

... he said 'I dislike speaking to the Conservative Party. That is not where my supporters come from. The Conservative Party only has me because it must!' I agreed and said his supporters lay among the general mass of opinion in this country, which was not strongly party-minded.[81]

Overwork combined with the strain of collaborating with Churchill caused Eden at this period to contemplate becoming Viceroy of India. The prestigious nature of the post, soon about to fall vacant, had the further advantage that the public would not assume that he had resigned from the Foreign Secretaryship on policy grounds for the second time in five years. In his memoirs he wrote that the suggestion may first have been made in April 1943 by Amery, the Secretary of State for India. But, according to a horrified Harvey, it was Eden himself who first mentioned the idea as early as 16 November 1942:

A.E. disturbed at the differences between himself and the PM over foreign affairs, 'just like with Neville Chamberlain again' ... [He] spoke of going to India himself! I said that was nonsense. No one going to India now could ever be PM. He could resign again if he must but he must remain in England.

The matter became a live issue when Churchill took it up the following spring. After initially having rejected the idea, as a result of consultations with Buckingham Palace, the Prime Minister changed his mind and began to press Eden to go. The Foreign Secretary was entirely aware that his chief's motives might not be disinterested. 'A.E. said,' wrote Harvey on 26 April 1943, 'that he felt part of the PM's eagerness to see A.E. Viceroy was due to his own growing desire to handle foreign affairs himself.'[82]

Eden was nevertheless sorely tempted. Initially he may have been much influenced by the thought that by appearing to take it in earnest he would, as he told Harvey, 'show the PM that he is not so eager to succeed him as he may think'. Gradually, however, Eden's interest in the post became wholly serious. Harvey's diary tells the story:

24 April 1943
I see how A.E. feels himself. The East and India have an immense pull on him. He has so often said to me half longingly in jest that he believed India was his fate. At the same time now he feels the future closing in on him if he remains here, no escape from No. 10, and he shrinks from it, as well he may. But the combination of these two reactions, the lure of the East and escapism from the West, added to the PM's pressure which makes it all look like duty, is very strong indeed.

11 May 1943
He [Eden] is feeling tired and defeatist and full of self-pity ... The truth is he quails before continuous battling with the PM. He fondly believes India will be a rest-cure from which a grateful country and H of C will summon him back to take over in two or three years' time.

18 May 1943
Jim [Thomas] had ... given me S.B.'s [Baldwin's] account of the conversation [between Eden and Baldwin]. B. had been very fatherly but had made it clear that if he went to India, he would never come back to be PM. A.E. had pleaded that it was so difficult to know what was his duty. To this S.B. had replied, 'when in doubt between two duties, it is wise to choose the most unpleasant' ... He [Eden] said he loathed the H of C and hated the thought of years more of it combined now with battling with the PM. 'I should love to go to India and have a show of my own.'

This mood of escapism eventually passed. By 7 June, according to Harvey, he took the view that 'the PM wanted him to say that he himself felt he should go' but 'he declined to do that and said it was a matter for the PM to decide, and that embarrassed the PM very much'.[83] The plan was accordingly dropped and instead Wavell was appointed.

Within five weeks of Eden's renunciation of the Indian option an acute crisis in his relations with Churchill had once again developed. Now he was faced with a stark choice between resignation and capitulation to the Prime Minister's will. At issue was the American attitude to the Free French. As early as March 1943, on the occasion of his visit to Washington, Eden had indicated to Roosevelt and Hull, in one of his rare moments of frankness, his inability to share their hatred of de Gaulle. But Churchill, in Washington two months later, was more willing to fall in with the Americans. Believing the matter to be one of relatively subordinate importance in the context of his attempts to shape the Grand Strategy for the remainder of the war, Churchill telegraphed to his War Cabinet for their concurrence in an Anglo-American decision to 'eliminate de Gaulle as a political force'. Eden bravely instigated his colleagues to return a unanimous refusal. The Prime Minister bowed to their verdict and appeared at first to forgive Eden. For example, he invited the Foreign Secretary to join him in Algiers early in June to help carry into effect a compromise policy of trying to cement relations between de Gaulle and Giraud. But the rebuff rankled with Churchill who was invariably envious of the almost unlimited powers possessed by Roosevelt. On their return to London, therefore, Churchill began to prepare for a reckoning with Eden on the French issue. On 14 June Harvey recorded:

Roosevelt is determined not to let de G. control the French Army and to keep [Pierre] Boisson [the Governor inherited from Vichy] at Dakar. PM is supporting him in this and has sent a stream of angry telegrams to Macmillan [in Algiers] in this sense. A.E. is much annoyed at this intervention in foreign affairs ('I gave up India so as to be Foreign Secretary!').

A week later the War Cabinet discussed a new plea from Roosevelt for a break with de Gaulle. With Churchill back in the chair, Eden found it less easy to win support from his colleagues and hence he had to settle for an ambiguous reply being sent to Washington.[84]

Eden was even less successful when in the ensuing weeks he tried to secure a unilateral British announcement of formal 'recognition' of the French Committee of National Liberation (FCNL). On 2 July he circulated a Cabinet Paper urging this course without obtaining Churchill's approval. It was an attempt to repeat the coup he had staged against his chief early in 1942 on the issue of meeting Soviet frontier requirements. Churchill minuted to Eden: 'I did not know you were going to bring this matter before the Cabinet formally. I think what you proposed ... is altogether premature ... I hope that you will not press for a decision ... at the present time.' A crisis was temporarily averted, however, by news from Algiers that the leading Americans there, General Dwight D. Eisenhower and Robert Murphy, were thought to favour American recognition of the FCNL. Churchill and Eden accordingly agreed that the Prime Minister should telegraph to Roosevelt in these terms: 'This is rather sudden. I should like to know your reaction. Our Foreign Office would also like to go ahead and recognize. My chief desire in this business has been to keep in step with you.' Roosevelt, however, merely rebuked his subordinates: 'You are not to recognize the Committee under any condition without full consultation and approval of the President.'[85]

Eden now returned to the idea of forcing through the War Cabinet agreement to unilateral British recognition. But Churchill was now ready to take revenge on his Foreign Secretary for earlier acts of disloyalty. He felt confident that he could humiliate him. On the evening of 12 July, according to Harvey:

A.E. dined ... at No. 10 ... He went full of misgiving as the PM has been intolerable of late ... after the guests had left, he and the PM had a set-to till 2.15

a.m. I gathered the broadsides were pretty hot! ... on the question of immediate recognition, he [Churchill] was adamant and said menacingly, 'I will fight you to the death. You may get some support, but it won't last long!' The PM was in a crazy state of exultation ... The quantities of liquor he consumed – champagne, brandies, whiskies – were incredible.

The following day Churchill drafted a remarkable paper for the War Cabinet clearly intended to be the basis for forcing his colleagues to choose between him and Eden. He discerned 'a decided United States policy which is not likely to be altered by the interchange of dispatches between the Foreign Office and the State Department'. He continued:

If it is to be changed at all within the lifetime of the present United States Administration, which may conceivably be prolonged, it can only be by time and events ...

At the time of de Gaulle's visit to Syria and his interview at Brazzaville in 1941, I formed the opinion that he was anti-British, and this is confirmed by every British officer or official abroad who has had to deal with him. Wherever he went he left behind him a trail of anglophobia ... I have therefore for some time regarded him as a personage whose arrival at the summit of French affairs would be contrary to the interests of Great Britain, which, after all, it is our prime duty to guard.

The personality of de Gaulle is no less detrimental to what I believe to be the main interests of France. He is animated by dictatorial instincts and consumed by personal ambition. All those who have worked with him know that he shows many of the symptoms of a budding Führer ... There is no doubt in my mind that he would bring civil war into that country and he himself has spoken, according to General Giraud, of the need for a 'révolution sanglante' in France. He would, have no doubt, make anti-British alliances and combinations at any time when he thought it in his interests to do so, and he would do this with gusto ... I am convinced that we should be wrong to quarrel with the Government of the United States for the sake of such a man.

Still more important, I am resolved never to allow de Gaulle or his followers to cloud or mar those personal relations of partnership and friendship which I have laboured for nearly four years to develop between me and President Roosevelt by which, I venture to think, the course of our affairs has been most notably assisted. I must ask my colleagues to face this position squarely, as it is fundamental so far as I am concerned. I believe that if I fully explained it to Parliament or by broadcast to the nation, I should receive a full measure of support. Whether this be so or not would make no difference to what I conceive to be my duty.[86]

Eden, probably unaware that this formal document had been prepared by his chief, sent to Downing Street a memorandum of his own. Now Churchill could humiliate him. Eden's diary is revealing:

July 13th:
Sent Winston my memorandum at lunchtime as agreed. Surprised to get further letter from him, rather formal. Went over to see him at 7 p.m. and asked him why. He said he didn't like my paper and thought we might be coming to a break.

The Prime Minister's 'rather formal' letter read:

I have just read your paper ... and it is quite clear that both our points of view may have to be placed before the Cabinet. I am having my own paper printed ... If after having read my print you are in the same mind, both papers can be circulated tomorrow ...[87]

Eden no doubt realized that he had been outmanoeuvred: if Churchill chose to make the matter one of confidence he would certainly carry the War Cabinet. Rather than resign, the Foreign Secretary abjectly yielded. He agreed that neither memorandum should be circulated to the War Cabinet. Recognition of the FNCL would have to await discussion at the Anglo-American summit to be held in Quebec more than a month later. Churchill thus had his revenge for earlier Cabinet defeats at Eden's hands. Thereafter the Foreign Secretary continued to oppose his chief on a variety of issues but he was driven to use subtler tactics. Meanwhile Churchill in victory was magnanimous: he would permit some limited exploration with Washington of the recognition issue. This Eden misleadingly portrayed to his Private Secretary as something of a defeat for the Prime Minister. Harvey's diary entry for 14 July read:

A reconciliation! I'm beginning to know the form now. Frightful row, nervous exhaustion on both sides, then next day a rather contrite PM seeking to make up, like a schoolboy who knows he's been naughty, rather shamefaced, needing much face-saving. Rather winning ...

PM said 'I dislike having to argue with you in Cabinet. I'd much rather fight it out with you like this in private.' Yes, but at the cost of what nervous exhaustion!

However, as a result of all this, the PM has agreed to A.E. answering in good forthcoming terms a PQ ... about recognition ... All this is good going. I remarked to A.E. what a triumph this was for him, that it was the artistic temperament in the PM which made him react in these contradictory ways. He said 'yes – but there is a bit of artistic temperament on both sides!'[88]

The reality was that Eden had been taught a sharp lesson by a Prime Minister whose position was now growing stronger with increasing military success in the Mediterranean and with signs that Germany was unlikely to defeat the Soviet Union.

Churchill's overriding preoccupation during this phase of the war was with Grand Strategy. In May 1943 he had gone to Washington to try to win over Roosevelt to the view of the British Chiefs of Staff that the Mediterranean should continue to have priority in practice over preparations for a cross-Channel assault. His personal aim was to conquer Italy and thereafter to concentrate on the eastern Mediterranean and the Balkans. Fear of post-war Soviet domination of east-central Europe was, it has earlier been argued, a primary though not exclusive motivation. But he did not at this stage find it prudent to spell out his anti-Soviet views to the Americans.

Indeed, he even argued that a long period of Anglo-American inactivity between the conquest of Sicily and a cross-Channel attack, which would have been the consequence of adopting the strategy favoured by Stimson and Chief of Staff George Marshall, 'would have a serious effect on the Russians', whom he depicted as desperately in need of continuous Western military pressure on the Axis. Roosevelt went some way but not the whole way to meet Churchill. He agreed to a compromise worked out, with much difficulty, by the Combined Chiefs of Staff. Sicily would be followed by such Mediterranean operations 'as are best calculated to eliminate Italy from the war and to contain the maximum number of German forces', but Western forces were to be limited and preparations for a cross-Channel assault in May 1944 were to go ahead. Churchill, much to the annoyance of his military advisers, argued for a definite commitment to an invasion of Italy. And he also still clung to the hope that the Balkans might follow. As he put it to Roosevelt: 'Operations in the general direction of the Balkans opened up very wide prospects . . .' In the end, however, he accepted the compromise, no doubt with the mental reservation that as events unfolded he would have new opportunities to upgrade the importance of the Mediterranean and to downgrade what came to be known as 'Roundhammer' and then 'Overlord'. He also persuaded Roosevelt to allow him to take Marshall with him on an immediate visit to the Mediterranean theatre commanders in Algiers.[89]

Arriving in Algiers on 29 May, Churchill summoned Eden to join him. He might not have done so had he realized that his Foreign Secretary had given encouragement to Stimson and Marshall on the Second Front controversy during the course of his visit to Washington in March. Stimson had then recorded in his diary:

. . . he [Eden] came around . . . At this talk . . . it . . . turned out that Eden was worried about the delay in respect to Bolero [the build-up to a cross-Channel assault]. I told him I was too and after I had gotten back from my trip . . . Marshall on March 25th told me of the conversation he had had with Eden in the meanwhile . . . [Eden] brought up to Marshall in the same way that he had to me the delay in Bolero. Marshall gave him no sympathy but pointed out that Eden was partly responsible when as a member of the War Cabinet he had voted for the African expedition against Marshall's warning that that would necessarily delay Bolero. So between us Marshall and I put the finger of responsibility for that sad situation directly upon the British government itself where it belongs.

In a later entry Stimson added:

. . . I went to a dinner given by Secretary Hull for Anthony Eden . . . I had a few words with Eden who was highly enthusiastic about his visit to our troops. He said this had been the highlight of his trip. I said to him, 'Do you now understand why we were so anxious to have Bolero?' and he said he did.[90]

Now in Algiers on 31 May Eden struck a different note but no more helpful to Churchill. In the presence of Marshall the Foreign Secretary emphasized that the British aim was to enter not merely Italy but also 'the Balkan area'. Turkey, he added, 'would become much more friendly when our troops reached the Balkan area'. This was also no doubt Churchill's private hope but in Washington he had found it prudent to go no further than canvas an invasion of Italy and this remained his tactic in Algiers. Eden's intervention, whether by accident or design, was thus extremely untimely. It must be borne in mind, moreover, that five months earlier Eden had tried to prevent Churchill meeting the Turks and had deplored what Harvey had called 'an attempt to nip into the Balkans' with the Russians' old enemy Turkey 'before they can get there themselves'. An American historian has recounted the sequel:

> On 31 May, he [Churchill] interrupted Eden 'to observe emphatically that he was not advocating sending an army into the Balkans now or in the near future'. But the damage had already been done and Marshall continued to insist that the final decision [on Italy] await the results of HUSKY [the Sicilian invasion] and the looming battles on the Eastern front. On June 3, the Prime Minister was forced to agree.[91]

Eden's display of excessive loyalty to his chief was repeated on 12 July when Stimson was in London. The War Secretary recorded in his diary:

> He [Churchill] criticized our American system of fixed presidential terms ... He commented that in this way we might be deprived of the immense asset of Mr Roosevelt's leadership. I at once rejoined that I agreed with him as to the danger involved in such a contingency and pointed out to him in detail how that danger might be accentuated by getting the United States involved in a theatre like the eastern Mediterranean in which our people were less intelligently interested and would be undoubtedly subjected to campaign arguments to the effect that we were being made to fight for interests which were really those of the British Empire; in other words that the war leadership in that respect was not good.
>
> I told him that the American people did not hate the Italians but took them rather as a joke as fighters; that only by an intellectual effort had they been convinced that Germany was their most dangerous enemy and should be disposed of before Japan; that the enemy whom the American people really hated, if they hated anyone, was Japan which had dealt them a foul blow. After setting out the details on which my conclusion was predicated, I asserted that it was my considered opinion that, if we allow ourselves to become so entangled with matters of the Balkans, Greece and the Middle East that we could not fulfil our purpose of Roundhammer in 1944, that situation would be a serious blow to the prestige of the President's war policy and therefore to interests of the United States.
>
> The PM apparently had not had the matter presented to him in that light before. He had no answer to it except that any such blow could be cured by victories. I answered that that would not be so if the victories were such that people were not interested in and could not see any really strategic importance in them. Towards the

end he confined his position to favouring a march on Rome with its prestige and the possibility of knocking Italy out of the war. Eden on the other hand continued to contend for carrying the war into the Balkans and Greece. At the end the PM reaffirmed his fidelity to the pledge of Roundhammer 'unless his military advisers could present him with some better opportunity' not yet disclosed.

Ten days later Stimson had another meeting at Downing Street, recording in his diary afterwards:

He [Churchill] ... broke into a new attack on Roundhammer ... I directly charged him that he was not in favour of the Roundhammer operation ... On this he said that, while he admitted that if he was C-in-C he would not set up the Roundhammer operation, yet having made his pledge he would go through with it loyally ... I stressed the dangers of too great entanglement in an Italian expedition and the loss of time to Roundhammer which it would involve. He then told me that he was not insisting on going further than Rome unless we should by good luck obtain a complete Italian capitulation throwing open the whole of Italy as far as the north boundary. He asserted that he was not in favour of entering the Balkans with troops but merely wished to supply them with munitions and supplies. He told me that they were doing magnificently when only being supplied ten tons a month. ... In these limitations he thus took a more conservative position than Eden had taken at the dinner of July 12th.[92]

The Second Front controversy again dominated Anglo-American discussions when Churchill and Eden met Roosevelt and his team at the Quebec Conference which opened on 14 August. But Churchill eventually drew even nearer to the position of Stimson and Marshall. The date for the cross-Channel assault was reaffirmed as May 1944 but now precision was given to the number of divisions to be transferred from the Mediterranean theatre by 1 November. This was designed to limit Churchill's Mediterranean ambitions to the capture of Rome. Crossing the Alps or major operations in the Balkans were effectively excluded. Perhaps Churchill finally yielded at Quebec on the cross-Channel issue because for the first time the Americans defended it in part on the grounds that its early implementation would enable the Western Powers, in Roosevelt's words on 23 August, 'to be ready to get to Berlin as soon as did the Russians'.[93] Clearly a Mediterranean strategy might enable the West to reach Vienna or various Balkan capitals ahead of the Soviets. But what if that merely allowed Stalin instead to dominate the plains of northern Europe? Churchill did not wholly accept this analysis. Yet he was much happier to defer to Roosevelt when the underlying premises of their discussion had an anti-Soviet content. Certainly both Churchill and Roosevelt were in apparent agreement at Quebec, perhaps for the last time, that Stalin's demeanour was alarming. Both the Prime Minister and the President, according to Harriman, resented the tone of Stalin's communications to them. Churchill even declared to Harriman that there would be 'bloody consequences in the future' and that Stalin was an 'unnatural man'. 'There will be grave troubles,' he added. Again, according to Harriman, the Prime Minister 'ticked off Anthony when Anthony suggested it was not so bad, saying "There is no need for you to attempt to smooth it over in the Foreign Office manner."'[94]

Eden, on the other hand, disagreed in this respect with Churchill and Roosevelt. On 30 August, for example, Harvey recorded in his diary: 'He [Eden] has had frightful tussles with the PM and F.D.R. over Stalin whose rude messages have infuriated them. The PM, he thinks, is now getting dangerously anti-Russian.'[95] It was, therefore, all the more ironic that Churchill and Roosevelt should have tentatively agreed at Quebec that their Foreign Ministers should seek a meeting with Molotov to explore the strained state of Allied relations. For it gave Eden an opportunity to undermine his chief, and, above all, to try to persuade leading American personalities to adopt a less anti-Soviet position. While at Quebec Eden also spent much time seeking a settlement of the FCNL 'recognition' problem. Hull remained, however, bitterly opposed to de Gaulle and may never have forgiven Eden for his persistence on the subject. Roosevelt and Churchill finally resolved the matter by agreeing that the British would grant 'recognition' but that the Americans would use a more ambiguous formula. For the Foreign Secretary this was as satisfactory an outcome as he could reasonably have expected.

Once back in London Eden began to prepare for the Conference of Foreign Ministers which eventually opened in Moscow on 18 October. He found Churchill's anti-Soviet attitude unhelpful and on 5 October, according to Harvey, even threatened not to go to Moscow. Churchill was insistent that 'we mustn't weaken Germany too much – we may need her against Russia'.[96] Eden was accordingly given little of substance to offer to the Soviets. Moreover, Churchill and Stalin were also at cross-purposes at this period about the number of Arctic convoys being sent from Great Britain. Hence Eden arrived in Moscow with some fear that his mission would be an obvious failure. But much to his delight Stalin and Molotov adopted a relatively friendly attitude throughout his stay.

Eden clearly desired that the watching world should receive an impression of Allied harmony from the Moscow Conference – no doubt in part because it would reflect credit on himself. Rather than put this at risk he was prepared to pay a considerable price on issues of long-term importance. For example, he had hoped to obtain a clarification of Soviet intentions concerning Poland. But Hull regarded this as a 'piddling' issue and Eden therefore allowed the Soviets to evade it rather than bear the sole burden of pressing it. Again, he hoped to make definite arrangements about the future of Yugoslavia, where two rival resistance forces, Communist and anti-Communist, appeared to be more interested in fighting each other than in inconveniencing the Germans. But Molotov easily escaped from making any commitment by pleading ignorance. Earlier in 1943, on 11 January, Sargent had sent a minute on Yugoslavia to Eden:

I assume that HMG are definitely opposed to the policy advocated by Professor [E. H.] Carr in *The Times* that we should tacitly disinterest ourselves from Central and South-East Europe, and that now and at the peace settlement we should recognize all this part of Europe as falling within the exclusive Russian sphere of influence.

The Foreign Secretary had indicated his agreement with Sargent.[97] Now at Moscow he was unwilling to incur Soviet hostility by plain speaking. This approach was similar to that which he had adopted towards German ambitions in east-central Europe in 1937 when talking to the Prime Ministers of the Dominions: as has been seen, he opposed 'disinteresting ourselves altogether in Central Europe' but was also against 'declaring our readiness to fight for Czechoslovakia or Austria if they became victims of aggression'. One historian characterized this policy as 'perilously to combine involvement and impotence'.[98]

The same criticism may be made of Eden's attitude during the Moscow Conference to Soviet–Czechoslovak relations, an extremely important subject entirely ignored in his memoirs. From the time of Molotov's visit to London in 1942 Eden had argued that the Great Powers should avoid forging bilateral pacts with individual minor states and he believed that he had won Soviet consent to a so-called 'self-denying ordinance'. During 1943, however, Beneš of the Czechoslovak Government in London eagerly sought a separate understanding with the Soviets. Eden deplored this suggestion, both because of the precedent involved and because it made it less likely that a Federation of Central European states could be created. At the Moscow Conference he had intended to put pressure on the Soviets not to renege on their earlier acceptance of the 'self-denying ordinance'. But having raised the matter with Molotov, he wavered when he realized that the Americans were not with him. Harriman, the American Ambassador in Moscow, recalled: 'As the restiveness of the American delegation grew steadily during this essentially bilateral discussion, Eden slipped a note to Hull explaining his purpose: "I am sorry to take your time, but behind all this is a big issue: two camps in Europe or one."' But when this effort to convince the Americans failed, Eden suddenly capitulated. The news was not well received in the Foreign Office though Cadogan philosophically minuted: 'no doubt the Foreign Secretary found it necessary to give way ... in view of wider considerations'.[99]

What were the 'wider considerations'? Important no doubt was Eden's desire not to wreck the chances of receiving the favourable personal publicity that would result from a harmonious outcome to the Conference. But he may also have seen great value in two 'concessions' made by the

Soviets. First was their agreement to the establishment in London of a European Advisory Commission. Eden hoped that this body would come to possess great powers in settling the shape of the post-war world and that, being based in London, it would be particularly sensitive to his own wishes. But in practice neither the Soviets nor the Americans permitted it to develop along these lines. It was accordingly to be of only limited significance and certainly not worth the price Eden paid to the Soviets at the Moscow Conference. A second Soviet 'concession' at Moscow was agreement to a Declaration on General Security which presaged the establishment of the United Nations Organization with a provision for leadership to come from four Great Powers – the three participants in the Moscow Conference together with China. It seems probable, however, that Anglo-American willingness to pay a price for Soviet agreement to the principle of a world organization was unnecessary: Stalin had nothing to gain by retreating into isolation and gave no indication that he intended to do so. Probably Eden rated this matter less highly than his American counterpart but he nevertheless saw its value in helping to give the impression that his 'show' in Moscow had been a great success. In any case Eden seems to have had little genuine respect for the woolly-minded Hull who had given him no support on several crucial European issues. Hull, for his part, was privately critical of Eden. Breckenridge Long of the State Department wrote in his diary on his chief's return:

Eden made a poor impression and Hull reports that Stalin sort of waived [sic] him aside – paid little attention to his proposals or recommendations. This was so to the extent that Hull thought it wise to write Eden an effulgent letter about his work at Moscow – fearing he would react unfavourably towards the United States after his return home.

Some of those with Hull ... obtained a very poor impression of Eden and said that even members of his own delegation allowed their unflattering opinions to be known to the members of our delegation. They gave the impression they felt Eden was trying to use the Conference to further his personal political ambitions at home to become Prime Minister. It was that atmosphere which warned Hull he should try to placate a disappointed Eden so he would not turn against the United States to cover his failure in Russia.

Eden sat between two astute poker-players – and got outplayed.

The terms of Hull's insincere letter to Eden are thus of some interest:

Now that the Conference has drawn to a close, I wish to express my great admiration for the splendid contribution made to our deliberations by yourself and the members of the Delegation of Great Britain. At the same time, the members of the Delegation of the United States and I want you to know of our real appreciation for the many kindnesses which we have received at your hand. It has been a real pleasure to all of us to have had the privilege ... of being associated with you.[100]

Few historians would now be likely to endorse the claim that Hull qualified as an 'astute poker-player' at Moscow. But nor, on that occasion, was Eden. The only winner was Molotov. As one historian has written:

> Among the other wartime gatherings of the three Allies, the Moscow meeting stands out as the only one where issues were clearly defined, systematically discussed, and disposed of through genuine bargaining. Furthermore, no foreign conquests by the Red Army had as yet cast a shadow over the deliberations ... The Russians were the party playing a weak hand, but they played it well. Molotov was at his very best at Moscow – a compliment which can hardly be made to his British, much less his American, counterparts.[101]

Eden's rôle at Moscow may also have been vital in influencing Roosevelt's general attitude towards Soviet ambitions. For during his time there Eden was so much annoyed by two moves made by Churchill in London that he sought to mobilize members of the American Delegation to undermine his chief's anti-Soviet policies. First came a telegram from Churchill instructing Eden to inform Stalin that the promised cross-Channel operation for the spring of 1944 might again have to be postponed. The Prime Minister had seized upon a pessimistic message from Alexander indicating that the needs of the Italian campaign might be greater than originally expected. Much to Eden's relief, Stalin took the news with surprising aplomb. Perhaps he no longer felt the same need for a Second Front now that the risk of a Soviet defeat had virtually disappeared. Maybe, too, he saw that his chances of dominating central Europe after the war would be greater if the cross-Channel attack was delayed. On the other hand, he urged Eden to try to draw Turkey into the war. As a result Eden, immediately after the Moscow Conference, journeyed to Cairo to meet leading Turks in a vain bid to oblige Stalin. This was an ironic turn of events, for, as has been seen, the Foreign Secretary had earlier in 1943 been opposed to Churchill's wooing of Ankara lest the Soviets be alarmed.

If Stalin took the threat to Overlord with equanimity, the Americans certainly did not. General John R. Deane at once informed Washington of Churchill's use of Alexander's message. He held that it would 'carry the inference to the Soviets that Overlord will be delayed or possibly abandoned because of the Italian situation'.[102] Stimson's reaction was extreme. On 28 October he wrote in his diary:

> Jerusalem! this made me angry because there was nothing to show that Eisenhower's comments on Alexander's pessimistic statement had been sent up too by Churchill and therefore Stalin would not have seen the counter comment of Eisenhower showing that he was not pessimistic at all. But when I got at Marshall I found that he had already been busy and that our Joint Chiefs of Staff had sent a message over to Deane to be sure that it got to Stalin to the effect that the Joint Chiefs of Staff of the United States did not think there was any chance of having Overlord delayed, not to say abandoned. It was perfectly ridiculous. But this shows how

determined Churchill is with all his lip service to stick a knife in the back of Overlord and I feel more bitterly about it than I ever have before.

On the following day he first saw Hopkins: 'I talked over with him the action of Churchill in regard to Overlord and he felt just as strongly as I did.' Next he met Roosevelt:

I then told him what we had done in regard to rebuffing Churchill's intervention at Moscow against Overlord ... The President seemed quite in accord with our views in respect to that. He intervened to tell me what his views were in regard to the Balkans. He said he would not think of touching the Balkans unless the Russians get to a position in their invasion of Germany where they wanted us to join and act side by side with them.

On 4 November Stimson again spoke to the President, describing Churchill's conduct as 'dirty baseball'. Roosevelt, according to the War Secretary, 'at once acquiesced saying it was an improper act'.[103]

Meanwhile in Moscow Eden had made it known to Harriman that he disapproved of Churchill's action. Harriman responded by informing Eden of the existence of Eisenhower's dissenting commentary on Alexander's report. Harvey wrote in his diary on 30 October:

PM, we discover, in sending Alexander's gloomy report on Italy, suppressed Eisenhower's covering report which did not support it and said only some more landing craft were needed. Pretty hot! Fortunately A.E. had taken Harriman into his confidence and the latter showed him the Eisenhower report. But the PM's action might have wrecked our conference, if Stalin had chosen.[104]

A second move by Churchill was also unwelcome to Eden. Harvey's diary for 29 October is eloquent:

This morning [General Hastings] Pug Ismay heard that the PM had invited the President to meet him near Casablanca about November 20th to discuss military matters, that the President had agreed and had urged that the Russians should be invited to send a general too, but that the PM had objected to this.

A.E. is aghast at this. The PM has deliberately refrained from letting A.E. know his intentions. To exclude the Russians from a military conference now would torpedo all the results of our present conference and make A.E.'s position impossible. Public opinion in Russia, as at home, would be outraged at an exclusive Anglo-American meeting fixed up behind A.E.'s back while he was in Moscow and he could not possibly defend it.

Eden again informed the Americans that he disapproved of his own chief's policy. Harvey recorded in his diary on 30 October:

Hull has now been pressed into the task of ensuring the Russians are not excluded from the PM's military conference. He has telegraphed to the President to urge that the meeting be delayed until he has returned. A.E. has telegraphed to the PM to insist on the importance ... of inviting a Russian representative to any future military discussions. The PM is set on keeping them out if he can and he is quite unscrupulous in his methods ...[105]

The effect of Churchill's conduct on Roosevelt was soon to be evident. The President in effect refused to meet the Prime Minister alone for any considerable period in advance of the three-power Summit at Teheran which opened on 28 November. And such time as they spent together in Cairo was marked by distinct coolness. Roosevelt insisted that Chiang Kai-shek be present and would have had Molotov there too if he had not been too busy to leave the Soviet Union. Moreover, Roosevelt had now clearly abandoned the anti-Soviet sentiments which had apparently united him with Churchill at Quebec. Hopkins, whose influence had now been much strengthened, said to Moran: 'Sure we are preparing for a battle at Teheran. You will find us lining up with the Russians.' To Churchill he offered a clear, written rebuff to pleas for advanced coordination of Anglo-American tactics to be deployed against Stalin: 'We, my dear sir, are playing poker – and years ago I learned that three of a kind beat two pair.[106] Churchill was equally unsuccessful in renewed attempts to obtain Roosevelt's consent to increased emphasis in military planning on the Mediterranean at the expense of Overlord and potential campaigns in Asia. Admiral William D. Leahy, the President's Chief of Staff, recorded in his diary:

The Prime Minister used every artifice of his charm to induce the President to assist in obtaining from the Chiefs of Staff approval of the British proposal that the Burma Campaign be reduced in order that naval, air and ground forces may be made available for the seizure of Rhodes and other islands in the Aegean Sea. Mr Eden did little to assist him and the President persisted in his stand that promises made to Chiang Kai-shek be fully carried out.[107]

Thus Churchill and Eden arrived in Teheran to find Roosevelt eager to cooperate with the Soviets. Stalin rapidly perceived the strain in the Churchill–Roosevelt relationship. He accordingly recovered an enthusiasm for a cross-Channel operation and thereby finally settled the Second Front controversy in favour of Washington. And he happily joined the President in teasing the Prime Minister about the shortcomings of the British Empire. Churchill's bitterness was noted by Moran. On the first day the Prime Minister sought to have luncheon à deux with the President but was refused. Churchill told Moran: 'It is not like him.' Then, after luncheon, Roosevelt sought out Stalin with the Prime Minister pointedly excluded. Moran recorded in his diary:

Until he came here, the PM could not bring himself to believe that, face to face with Stalin, the democracies would take different courses. Now he sees he cannot rely on the President's support. What matters more, he realizes that the Russians see this too. It would be useless to try to take a firm line with Stalin. He will be able to do as he pleases. Will he become a menace to the free world, another Hitler? The PM is appalled by his own impotence.[108]

Teheran was a brief and badly organized Conference. Few formal decisions were taken about the character of the post-war world. All the same it marked a turning-point. For now even Churchill had to recognize that the Soviets would emerge from the war with the upper hand in much of Europe and that the Americans were unlikely to take effective steps to prevent it. There was a sense in which this was a victory for Eden. For the dramatic change in Roosevelt's attitude towards Churchill and his anti-Soviet warnings had at least in part flowed from the events at the Moscow Conference. No doubt Churchill was tactically foolish to have reopened the Second Front controversy with the provocative use of Alexander's message. But Eden's criticism of his chief to the American delegation may well have encouraged American over-reaction. Of even greater direct consequence were his pleas to Hull to prevent Churchill manoeuvring Roosevelt into an Anglo-American meeting without the Soviets, though in his memoirs he surprisingly wrote that he 'could not fathom the apparent American unwillingness to make ready with us for the Conference in advance'.[109] If Churchill's isolation at Teheran was partly Eden's work, the Foreign Secretary did not for long relish the consequences. While Churchill rapidly adjusted to the changed position and during 1944 sought to forge a cynical 'spheres-of-influence' understanding with Stalin, Eden became more and more inclined to protest against some of the unpleasant implications. Certainly the Foreign Secretary soon became much less well-disposed towards the Soviets. In part this was no doubt caused by the increasing accumulation of evidence of the extent of Soviet ambition. But he may also have found his opinions changing once he ceased to be under the influence of the pro-Soviet Harvey, whom he released from the post of Private Secretary at the end of 1943. Harvey's successor was the calmer and less opinionated Dixon who had accompanied Eden to the Balkans in 1941.

It was thus Churchill rather than Eden who usually gave a lead during 1944 in the appeasement of Moscow. As late as 6 October 1943 the Prime Minister had favoured reserving territorial questions for a general settlement at the end of the war.[110] But at Teheran he had raised with Stalin the idea of seeking to persuade the Poles to accept the Curzon Line in return for compensation in the West at Germany's expense. Roosevelt, conscious of the importance of the ethnic vote during the 1944 Presidential Election campaign, was unwilling to give public support to pressure on the Poles but equally indicated in private that he would take no steps to dislodge Stalin from disputed territory. On 16 January Churchill accordingly raised with Eden the question of Polish frontiers and also those other territorial demands raised by Molotov in 1941 and 1942:

... the Russians may very soon be in physical possession of these territories, and it is absolutely certain that we should never attempt to turn them out. Moreover, at Teheran when Stalin talked about keeping East Prussia up to Königsberg we did not say anything about the Baltic States, which clearly would be comprised in the Russian Dominions in any such solution.

We are now about to attempt the settlement of the eastern frontiers of Poland, and we cannot be unconscious of the fact that the Baltic States, and the question of Bukovina and Bessarabia have very largely settled themselves through the victories of the Russian armies.

Eden replied:

I am convinced ... that we should agree to all these claims (Russo-Finnish frontier; Russo-Rumanian frontier; the Baltic States). But in the case of the Baltic States, we should maintain our decision not formally and publicly to recognize them before the peace settlement ...

I am inclined to think that we should prepare the Russians as to the line we are going to take publicly before their nearer approach to the territories which they claim provokes public discussion. Otherwise we might have an explosion from Moscow or at least in the Soviet press. We could assure Stalin that we had no intention of disputing the Soviet claims, but explain our difficulties and warn him in advance of our intention to go on saying that these territorial matters were all for final settlement at the Peace Conference.[111]

Poland was another matter for Eden. Maybe he had a bad conscience, for on 21 April 1942 he had written to Sikorski that 'His Majesty's Government do not propose to conclude any agreement affecting or compromising the territorial status of the Polish Republic.'[112] But, for whatever reason, he informed the War Cabinet, before going to Teheran, that any assurances to the Soviets about the Curzon Line would have to be matched by Soviet pledges to allow the London-based Polish Government unfettered control over the rest of Poland – a precondition presently abandoned in its turn by Great Britain. Moreover, Eden throughout 1944 revealed more sympathy than his chief for the obstinate London Poles. While Churchill was inclined to try to bully them into compromises with Moscow on frontiers and later even on power-sharing with the Committee of Communist-dominated Poles established at Lublin by the Soviets in the summer of 1944, Eden tried only intermittently and hesitantly to cajole them into 'realistic' conduct.

Throughout 1944 the Foreign Secretary repeatedly revealed his disquiet on the Polish issue. Two entries from Dixon's diary are illuminating:

7 February 1944
PM, who had seen the Poles on Sunday [6 February], sent over a draft message to U.J. [Stalin] in which he handed out all the trumps, gave the Poles up for lost, and proposed to reinsure heavily against an Anglo-Russian quarrel. Arranged meeting to discuss this after dinner in the Office. A.E. dictated a firm minute urging a stay of 2 or 3 days ... Went over late to No. 10 with it, and obtained PM's agreement. A.E., at

his best during this meeting, collected, resolute and clear-headed. O'Malley tells me his obvious sincerity impressed the Poles, who are seemingly convinced that we are doing all we can for them (though I think we ought to do more, or rather we fatally gave away our case and theirs at Teheran). The PM astonishingly childish, for a politician and leader, in his approach to the Russians, not comprehending that plain-speaking and hard bargaining produces far better results with them ...

9 *March 1944*
A.C.K. [Archibald Clark-Kerr, the British Ambassador in Moscow] didn't like his instructions about the Poles and wanted to make them more conciliatory. After a somewhat stormy discussion, A.E. tore up the Department's attempts to meet Archie half-way and told me to draft a minute to the PM saying that we must stand firm.

Equally interesting is an entry for 10 March from the diary of Harvey, who now saw much less of Eden:

PM and A.E. both in very anti-Soviet mood – rather dangerously so, I think. We mustn't wed ourselves too much to this Polish Government which after all is an exile Government out of touch since 4 years with opinion in Poland ... There may be more genuine pro-Soviet feeling than we suspect.[113]

Eden also wrote fierce though private minutes of impotent disapproval of Soviet conduct. Receiving a Foreign Office paper putting up a case for Stalin, Eden minuted: '... I confess to growing apprehension that Russia has vast aims and that these may include the domination of Eastern Europe and even the Mediterranean and the "communizing" of much that remains.'[114] Churchill had had such fears for much longer but he was now primarily concerned not to bewail the fate of Eastern Europe but to rescue whatever was possible. He could not afford to be sentimental about what he judged could not be saved. Nor could he be too scrupulous in the methods he used in trying to outmanoeuvre and tie down Stalin. Generally the Prime Minister had the rather tepid support of his Foreign Secretary. But it seems clear that if Eden had been Prime Minister British policy would have been less decisive during the remainder of the war. It would presumably have more nearly resembled that of the United States, which, at least during the remainder of Roosevelt's life, was ostensibly high-minded but simultaneously ineffectual in limiting Communist expansion.

The case of Yugoslavia provides another illustration of the difference between Churchill and Eden. Both came to the 'realistic' view that right-wing Draza Mihailović would have to be dropped and the obviously more successful Josip Tito, a Communist, recognized. But Eden lacked his chief's sense of urgency. Both wanted to use King Peter as a means of strengthening Western influence with Tito, but Churchill believed that there was insufficient time to permit lengthy negotiations to take place and hence he could not agree to this being made a precondition for the de-recognition of Mihailović. As one historian has written:

... Churchill and Eden spent a surprising amount of time and energy in January and February 1944 fighting one another on the question whether the British should first break with Mihailović and then ask Tito to receive King Peter at his headquarters, as Churchill wanted, or the other way round, as Eden wanted. They were both chasing a chimera since Tito would not have the King at his headquarters and, if he had done so, the King would have been quite incapable of exercising power and authority.[115]

Eden eventually lost this argument: Tito was recognized unconditionally. But all Churchill's subsequent efforts to get King Peter established at Tito's court proved futile. As early as 16 February 1944 Dixon reflected Eden's view when he wrote in his diary:

PM is making the mistake habitual to him in foreign affairs of (a) rushing his fences (b) attributing the characteristics of an English gentleman to the other party (in this case an upstart Balkan politician still hardly able to credit that the British PM is ready to woo and flatter him).[116]

But this divergence over Yugoslavia also revealed a mistake habitual to Eden: a tendency to accept in principle the need for appeasement of a person or a government but then to show no sense of urgency in carrying out the policy, the character of his approach towards both Italy and Germany during his spell as Chamberlain's Foreign Secretary providing the most obvious precedent.

During the early part of 1944 Eden again contemplated giving up the Foreign Secretaryship. The burden of combining the post with the Leadership of the House was simply proving intolerable. Neglect of his Foreign Office duties was unavoidable on days when he had to sit for long periods on the Front Bench. Cadogan noted in his diary on 5 January that 'he [Eden] doesn't like it if one sends him too many papers, but is always ready to complain if *one* slips past him ...' and on 21 February he added: 'Don't know how A. does it [his work]. Suppose he doesn't.' Dixon's diary reveals similar concerns:

2 March 1944
Anthony had to intervene 3 times as Leader of the House, and just pulled the Government through. The sitting went on till 10.15 p.m. – another day completely lost for foreign affairs.

3 March 1944
Had 10 minutes with Anthony early and pushed through the really urgent decisions. He then disappeared to the House and telephoned after lunch to say he was stuck, as another crisis was developing over the Pensions Bill. Went over to the House about 3 and managed to get a little work through in the intervals of A.E. darting into the Chamber or having discussions in his room with the PM and the Chief Whip ... Back to the Office at 4.30, and a great scramble to get through before A.E. left for the country soon after 5.

Eden himself was well aware of his problem as is clear from Dixon's diary:

15 February 1944
A.E. on our morning walk told me he had put it to the PM last night that he couldn't carry the two jobs – FS and Leader of the House. The PM had said 'You can be in no doubt which one you will have to keep', which I interpreted as meaning the House. Anthony said he didn't know which he meant, but he must clearly leave it to PM to decide.

23 February 1944
A.E., walking in the Park, reverted to the idea of giving up the FO, saying that all were agreed that he could not do both jobs, that the home front was important, and that it was a mistake for him to be merely a specialist on foreign affairs. I urged him to consider the importance of having a great department of state at his back, and that foreign affairs covered practically all our great problems. I think his mind turns on leaving the FO when he is tired.[117]

Eden's uncertainty bore a similarity to the crisis of the previous year when he had almost become Viceroy. There was, however, a big difference: Churchill was now anxious to keep him at the Foreign Office. Perhaps this was because the two men had in private drawn rather closer together on the central issue of Soviet intentions. But for the Prime Minister there was the further difficulty that Eden hinted that he was only prepared to leave the Foreign Office if Cranborne could succeed him – a prospect unwelcome to Churchill. According to Harvey, Churchill, rather than accept Cranborne, even contemplated taking on the Foreign Office himself – the only great office of state to elude him. Moreover, according to Cadogan, 'any reshuffle presents a difficulty in that Attlee demands more places for his party'.[118]

The matter was settled for a time early in April. Dixon's diary is illuminating:

4 April 1944
Climax of discussions about A.E.'s future. The press today spoke of his leaving the FO as a matter decided, especially the *D. Telegraph* in an article on the first page which, as we learnt later, had been written by Camrose himself after dining with B.B. [Brendan Bracken].

The PM put Anthony off last night and asked him to come at 7 this evening.

1½ hours debate on the question this afternoon with J. Thomas and Dick Law. The first question was, could he do the 2 jobs? Answer no, with a rider from me that much of his paper work could be done by another junior minister. Second question: if he gave up the FO, should he insist on being 1st Lord of the Treasury, or become Lord President in Attlee's place. The PM was now doubtful about giving up half his functions – there would be constitutional difficulties, and there was a question whether the PM would be left with any salary at all. As Lord President, he would have a machine, a house (No. 11) and a Committee, and it would thus be able effectively to control the Home Front. Against it, it would look mouldy succeeding Attlee, and would be hard to convince public opinion that he was not being demoted. And would Attlee agree? And if he did, and became Dominions Secretary in Cranborne's place, would not this be bad in view of the imminent Conference of Dominions Premiers?

5 April 1944
A.E. on the walk told me that he had had two long sessions with the PM before and after dinner, and the PM finally turned everybody else out of the room and made an appeal to him to keep the FO and the Leadership a little longer. His avowed reasons were that changes would be bad so soon before coming events [Overlord?] and the meeting of Dominions premiers. But I think his real reasons were that he can't face working over foreign affairs, in which he is increasingly interested, with a new man especially if he is to be C. [Cranborne] . . . PM begged A. to take 3 weeks holiday and get himself fit, and then think again.

During the morning Jim [Thomas] and B. B. [Bracken] hotted A. up and urged him to press PM to release him from the FO . . . all through the afternoon A. was in a painful state of restlessness . . .[119]

Eden finally accepted Churchill's suggestion. He accordingly was on holiday during most of April and returned to his duties much refreshed. Fortunately for him pressure in the House of Commons was also to ease during the remainder of 1944, permitting him to spend long weekends in the country. Dixon's diary entry for 3 July provides the explanation: 'These prolonged weekends, besides being very good for A.E., are now quite manageable owing to the quietness of the House. This in its turn is due to the [flying bombs], which lead members to prefer their constituencies to London.' True, Eden at times still contemplated giving up one of his posts. On 28 June Harvey wrote in his diary: 'He [Eden] told me he thought he had decided to give up leadership of H of C to R. A. Butler after this session and do FO only.' But Harvey had earlier noted: 'As to H of C [Leadership] they [Churchill and Eden] profess that there is no one else but A.E. who can do it. I don't believe this. R. A. Butler or Stanley could do it or try to do it. But they don't want them to try in case they succeed.'[120]

Another factor prompting Eden to continue to bear his double burden was his expectation that the premiership would soon be vacant and that he might not succeed without a struggle. On three occasions during 1944 Harvey noted Eden's concern for Churchill's health and on 6 September the Foreign Secretary even expressed the view that his chief was actually dying.[121]

During Eden's holiday in April 1944, Churchill took charge of the Foreign Office. Dixon recorded that he was said 'to be enjoying his new toy'. But in the absence of Eden he also brought to the conduct of Anglo-Soviet relations a greater degree of decisiveness than hitherto. Matters came to a head when the Soviet news agency gave support to the pro-Communist mutineers among Greek forces in Egypt. On 16 April Churchill wrote to Molotov: 'This is really no time for ideological warfare. I am determined to put down mutiny . . . I wish you all success . . . in your Romanian negotiations in which ... we consider you are the predominant power.' On 23 April the Prime Minister repeated to Molotov that 'we regard you as leaders in Romanian affairs'.[122] The Soviets took the hint and protested at the presence in Romania of British officers from the Special Operations Executive (SOE). The way was now open for a spheres-of-influence bargain involving Greece and Romania. During May, after Eden's return from holiday, terms for an agreement along these lines were formally discussed between London and Moscow. Surviving British records do not, however, conclusively show whether Eden was wholly in agreement with Churchill about the implications. Possibly the Foreign Secretary saw the Greek–Romanian deal at this stage as being limited to the immediate phase involving military action, whereas Churchill may have realized that Romania was in all probability destined to be permanently Sovietized. Nor did Churchill move towards a spheres-of-influence deal without occasionally thinking aloud about an alternative course, namely that of confronting Moscow. But this was at least as much 'dreaming' as his contemplation of a major Balkan invasion had been during the previous year. His dreams could not be turned into reality without American support, which was not on offer. Hence Churchill's quest for a bilateral bargain with Moscow was pursued with some urgency and a fair degree of consistency during the summer months of 1944.

The Soviets proved surprisingly willing to do business. Their only reservation, reasonably enough, concerned the Americans. How far would any bargain struck with the British be accepted in Washington? Churchill accordingly sought American agreement to the Romanian–Greek arrangement. But the 'high-minded' Roosevelt made great difficulties and eventually consented only with reluctance to a three-month experiment in Anglo-Soviet management of affairs in Greece and Romania. The Soviets were not particularly enthusiastic about this temporary solution but they did not definitely reject it. It was thus now a matter of some urgency for the British to put the 'understanding' with Moscow to a practical test. Hence in July 1944 Eden became almost as anxious as Churchill to prevent Greece, then about to be liberated from German occupation, falling into Communist hands. Dixon recorded on 12 July the crucial moment:

An exhilarating day, during which the plunge was taken which we ought to have taken long ago to support [Georgios] Papandreou and extirpate EAM [Communists] in Greece. In a very racy interview with the Greek Ambassador A.E. asserted our whole-hearted support for the Greek Government and promised that we would if necessary withdraw our support and men from EAM, though we 'didn't want to break all the crockery at once'.

In the ensuing months Moscow's reactions on the subject of Greece were ambiguous. Soviet propaganda was muted. But eight Soviet officers were flown in to advise the Communist ELAS forces, leading Eden to minute on 3 August: 'On the face of it this may be a Russian attempt to complete domination of the Balkans and I think we should make it pretty plain that we are not standing for it in Greece.'[123]

If Eden and Churchill had drawn closer together in their approach towards Soviet ambitions in east-central Europe, this did not mean that all was now harmony between them. In particular, during the summer of 1944 they quarrelled once more about de Gaulle's rôle. The Anglo-American compromise about 'recognizing' the FCNL reached at the Quebec Conference of 1943 had not endured. For in November de Gaulle had precipitately proclaimed the establishment of a Consultative Assembly which elected him as President and he simultaneously downgraded Giraud. This caused Roosevelt to resolve not to hand over liberated France to the FCNL but to retain Allied administration of the country until free elections could be held. As usual Churchill was not prepared to oppose Washington for de Gaulle's sake. Eden, however, took the FCNL's part and argued bitterly with his chief on the subject.[124] Even on D-day itself, 6 June 1944, the two men quarrelled incessantly about the extent to which American views should be disregarded. Eden recorded in his diary:

Again soon after midnight W. [Churchill] rang up in a rage because Bevin and Attlee had taken my view. Argument continued for forty-five minutes, perhaps longer. I was accused of trying to break up the Government, or stirring up the press on the issue. He said that nothing would induce him to give way ... F.D.R. and he would fight the world.[125]

More distress for Eden on the subject of de Gaulle came in the ensuing days when Marshall took him to task in undiplomatic language in the presence of Churchill. Stimson later reconstructed the scene:

Marshall just turned himself loose on Eden at a house party that they were both at at Chequers. Eden was trying to push Churchill into recognition of de Gaulle and finally Marshall broke loose. He said he couldn't talk politics but he said he knew more about the Army and he knew more about the people of the United States than Eden and that, if Eden went on in this way and the things that happened from de Gaulle's course came out in the news in full ... it would make a wave of indignation in the United States which would swamp the whole damn British Foreign Office. He said that Eden got very angry, his face flushed, and he finally left the room and went upstairs and stayed away from the rest of the conference ...[126]

Only in October 1944 was the problem resolved. Such had been the spontaneous rallying by the liberated French to de Gaulle and the FCNL that even Roosevelt was moved to change his mind. With scant regard for British feelings he accordingly ordered unilateral recognition of de Gaulle's Provisional Government before informing London. Eden had thus been vindicated but found it galling to have to grant recognition merely in the wake of Washington. Churchill, on the other hand, had what one historian has called 'a most forgiving nature where Roosevelt was concerned'.[127] Put another way, the Prime Minister grasped more clearly than Eden that concern for the susceptibilities of de Gaulle must take second place to the need to maximize American support for wider objectives throughout Europe.

During the summer of 1944, however, Churchill's careful wooing of Washington brought few positive benefits. In the run-up to the Presidential Election Roosevelt became less and less willing to depart from 'high-minded' rhetoric. While in practice unwilling to resist by threats Soviet designs in east-central Europe, he was also averse from striking bargains with Stalin intended at least to set limits to Soviet expansion.

It was at this critical juncture, with the future of the tentative Anglo-Soviet spheres-of-influence arrangements in doubt and with the Americans in a relatively unworldly mood, that Eden had to face the daunting problem posed by the capture of Russians fighting in Hitler's army. Following the successful establishment of the Second Front, advancing British forces found a surprisingly large number of Russians wearing German uniform. Eventually several million fell into British hands. Some were captured Soviet citizens who had willingly enlisted on the German side; some were Soviet citizens who had donned German uniforms only to avoid being shot; while yet others were anti-Soviet Russians who had left their native land at the time of the Bolshevik Revolution, who had never claimed Soviet citizenship and who had from the outset been eager allies in the struggle to overthrow Stalin. Moscow asked the British Government to return all, whether willing or unwilling, to the Soviet Union. From the outset and indeed even before the Soviet request was formally made, officials in the Foreign Office were clear that compliance would in practice be unavoidable and also that those repatriated would probably face a grim fate, for Soviet soldiers were expected to die rather than surrender. Patrick Dean, assistant legal adviser in the Foreign Office, wrote on 24 June: 'In due course all those with whom the Soviet authorities desire to deal must ... be handed over to them, and we are not concerned with the fact that they may be shot or otherwise more harshly dealt with than they might be under English law.'[128]

The subject came before the War Cabinet on 17 July. Eden favoured repatriation in principle but hoped that the Soviets would agree that implementation must await the ending of the war 'in order not to discourage surrender on the part of others impressed by the Germans'.[129] Whether Eden had at this stage given much thought to the problem may be doubted. But he received a jolt on 21 July from Lord Selborne, the Minister of Economic Warfare and head of SOE, who wrote:

As you may know, one of my officers has during the past four weeks interviewed a number of Russian prisoners, and in every case their story is substantially the same. In the first place they were subject to incredible hardship and treatment on being taken prisoner [by the Germans]. They were marched in many cases for several days without any food. They were placed in concentration camps under appalling sanitary conditions and were starved. They became infested with vermin, they were victims of loathsome diseases, and starvation was carried to such a point that cannibalism became prevalent. In more than one instance the Germans filmed cannibalistic meals for propagandist purposes.

Selborne was concerned at 'the prospect of sending back many thousands of men to die, either by execution or in Siberia ...' He concluded: 'I ... suggest that, in the interests of humanity, we keep our hands free as to what to do with these Russian prisoners after the war. If their number is not too great there should be no difficulty in absorbing them in some of the under-populated countries of the world.' Eden promptly scribbled across this letter: 'Dept. what do you say to all this? It doesn't deal with the point, if these men don't go back to Russia, where are they to go? We don't want them here.'[130] This may seem in retrospect to constitute an almost incredibly callous response. But it must be remembered that he rarely had time, because of his duties in the House of Commons, to treat any Foreign Office letter or memorandum to more than a cursory glance. Again, he had had with both Selborne and his predecessor, Dalton, many difficulties arising out of the SOE's activities which were often poorly coordinated with Foreign Office policies. For example, only a few weeks earlier Selborne had rebuked Eden for pusillanimous 'appeasement' of the Soviets in Romania without apparently understanding the central place of Romania in the wider context of the quest for an Anglo-Soviet arrangement that would save Greece from Communism. Eden's response had been to describe his colleague's intervention as 'gross impertinence'.[131] Thus Eden's initial response to Selborne's new protest, though unwise for a man who cared greatly about his future standing at the 'bar of history', should not be taken as constituting his considered position on forcible repatriation. For that it is necessary to turn to the defence he sent to Churchill on 2 August after the Prime Minister had shown momentary sympathy with Selborne's plea.

Eden did not retract his view that 'we don't want them here', a line consistent with his earlier policy of not encouraging mass emigration of Jews. But this argument was buttressed by two further extremely powerful considerations. First, he was conscious that many British troops were falling into the hands of the Soviets as they liberated German prisoner-of-war camps in the east. Eden wrote:

It is most important that they should be well cared for and returned as soon as possible. For this we must rely to a great extent upon Soviet good will and if we make difficulty over returning to them their own nationals I feel sure it will react adversely upon their willingness to help us in restoring to us as soon as possible our own prisoners ...

He thus did not argue, as some of his critics in the 1970s appeared to suppose, that the Soviets would have reacted to a rejection of their request for forcible repatriation by an outright refusal to return British prisoners. But he clearly desired that his own compatriots should not undergo delay and discomfort in order to prevent much greater suffering being imposed on the Russians then in British hands. However difficult such an approach may be to justify in abstract ethical terms, few of the relatives of the British prisoners of war would at the time have disagreed with their Foreign Secretary. Probably even more important, however, in shaping British policy was a further argument deployed by Eden:

To refuse the Soviet Government's request for the return of their own men would lead to serious trouble with them. We have no right whatever to do this and they would not understand our humanitarian motives. They would know that we were treating them differently from the other Allied Governments on this question and this would arouse their gravest suspicions.[132]

During the furore over this matter in the 1970s one of Eden's severest critics, Nikolai Tolstoy, appeared at one point to acknowledge the strength of this argument when he wrote that 'any act which might seriously endanger the alliance between Britain and the Soviets would clearly be dangerous to contemplate at this critical juncture of the war'. But elsewhere he wrote:

This was no cynical policy of *Realpolitik*. Eden and his advisers were not postponing an inevitable confrontation; they sincerely believed in Stalin's goodwill. Eden himself felt for Stalin strong affection and admiration. These sentiments were shared by his permanent officials ...[133]

Another critic of Eden's policy on repatriation even went so far as to write:

Throughout his career he [Eden] was cast for that perennially tragic role, 'the boy hero who cannot grow up', the man who spends his life unconsciously obsessed by the strong, dominant 'Father' to whom, at the depths of his own psyche, he cannot imagine himself succeeding. After the war, Eden spent years in the shadow of one such 'Father-figure', Churchill ... And in Stalin Eden (like so many others similarly afflicted, e.g. Bernard Shaw) found the hypnotically fascinating 'Father-figure' whom he would seek to placate to the ends of the earth.[134]

In reality Eden by mid-1944 was, as has been seen, by no means an unqualified believer in Stalin's goodwill. True, he permitted documents to be circulated to the Cabinet, on 14 June and 8 August, which held out hopes for post-war collaboration. But he was also by now privately close to sharing Churchill's wary pessimism. Again, not all officials in the Foreign

Office felt strong 'affection and admiration' for Stalin. No doubt some of the junior officials, especially in the Northern Department, held naïve or even fellow-travelling opinions about the Soviet Union. And the over-zealous implementation of the subsequent repatriation policy was to some extent in such hands. But Cadogan, for example, cannot possibly be placed in this category. His private hostility in 1943 to the Soviets over Katyn has already been noted. Then on 17 January 1944 he wrote in his diary of the Soviets: 'They are the most stinking creepy set of Jews I've ever come across.' And a year later he wrote to his wife: 'How can one work with these animals?' Yet even the anti-Soviet Cadogan's response to Selborne's protest was to be 'reluctantly driven to the conclusion that we shall have to hand these men back to the Soviet, if the latter demand it'.[135]

On 4 September the War Cabinet again discussed repatriation with Eden's considered memorandum before them. Neither Churchill nor even Selborne persisted in their doubts about his policy. Selborne indeed had gone so far as to write to Eden that 'the reasons you give are very weighty, and some of the points you stress cannot be gainsaid'.[136] Thus the policy was adopted and in subsequent years ruthlessly implemented. Clearly it was not Eden's personal policy but that of the War Cabinet as a whole. What was unusual, however, was the clarity of mind and the decisiveness which he had shown in supporting so unpleasant a necessity. For once he had behaved with the vigour of a Churchill, while the Prime Minister, equally uncharacteristically, had shown a tendency to waver worthy of his Foreign Secretary. But both ultimately united on a policy of recognizing that repatriation was a *sine qua non* for any bargain with Stalin over the future of east-central Europe. Conscious of British military impotence in the region and of Roosevelt's indifference, they did not feel able to forgo the chance of such an arrangement. The price paid in human suffering and hence in the long run in terms of British self-esteem was clearly appallingly high. Yet if, as seems likely, the alternative was the loss of Greece into the Soviet orbit, the decision may possibly have constituted the lesser of two evils.

Another opportunity for Churchill and Eden to discover whether Roosevelt might not after all be persuaded to interest himself in the fate of the Balkans presented itself in mid-September 1944 when they met him in Quebec. The essentially negative conclusion they reached was reflected in their decision to suggest to the Foreign Office that not only control over Romania but also now of Bulgaria should be offered to Stalin in return for the British being allowed to take the lead in Greece. Officials in the Foreign Office objected to this proposed further concession to Moscow and subsequently persuaded Eden to put up more of a fight for Bulgaria than Churchill thought prudent.

The main subject at Quebec, however, was not the fate of the Balkans but the future of Germany. Roosevelt endorsed the famous plan of Henry Morgenthau, his Secretary of the Treasury, for her pastoralization. Churchill, though privately unenthusiastic, was unwilling to quarrel with the President on the matter. But Eden, with his tendency to overrate British power and influence, wished to resist. The Foreign Secretary sought to draw Hull into the argument, for he was known to be opposed to pastoralization. This led to a violent altercation between Eden and his chief. As he wrote in his memoirs: 'This was the only occasion I can remember when the Prime Minister showed impatience with my views before foreign representatives. He resented my criticism of something which he and the President had approved, not I am sure on his account, but on the President's.' Stimson recorded in his diary the account given to him by Morgenthau:

When Eden came in and was informed of Churchill's decision, he broke out into violent opposition, reminding Churchill that both he and Eden had publicly taken an entirely different position before their people. Churchill retorted, in words, as I remember Morgenthau's account, that he was going to prefer the interests of his own citizens to those of the enemy. Churchill also warned Eden not to go back to London and line up the War Cabinet against him, Churchill. The paper was then initialled by Churchill and Roosevelt.

Once again Eden gave way rather than resign, though in the event opposition in Washington persuaded Roosevelt to abandon the idea. Dixon recorded Eden's feelings in Quebec at having lost his temper: 'A.E. on drive to airport regretted lack of unexcitability, but agreed that unless you live on your nerves you miss the things your nerves tell you.'[137]

Once back in London, Churchill resolved to clinch with Stalin a bilateral arrangement for the future of as much of east-central Europe as possible. Such was his sense of urgency that in his view nothing less than a summit would suffice. Hence on 9 October he and Eden arrived in Moscow. The famous 'percentage agreements' resulted.

Eden initially sought in Moscow to resist Churchill's desire to strike a bargain with Stalin on whatever terms he could get. In contrast to his line on repatriation, the Foreign Secretary now reverted to his habit of overestimating British power and of hesitating to take unpleasant steps. Hence Churchill told Moran: 'The Foreign Secretary would be obstinate, he must be told that there is only one course open to us – to make friends with Stalin.' On two issues, however, Eden continued to resist. One concerned Poland. Dismayed by the Soviets' unwillingness in the previous month to help the rising in Warsaw of the non-Communist Polish forces, he was not in a mood to yield much to Stalin on Poland's future. On the contrary, according to Moran, he told Churchill: 'We've got to bring up this Polish question at once and tell Joe that Russia has enemies and they could make out quite a case against her in the last few weeks.'[138] A second issue was

Bulgaria. Stung by criticisms in the Foreign Office of the 'appeasing' line he and Churchill had agreed upon at Quebec, the Foreign Secretary reversed his position. Because of Bulgaria's proximity to Turkey and the eastern Mediterranean he wished to see Great Britain have a larger say in her fate than in the case of Romania, with which he was determined that she should not be equated.

Once in conference with Stalin and Molotov, however, Eden in contrast to his conduct at Quebec, made no serious attempt to prevent Churchill handling matters as he wished. At their first meeting the Prime Minister chose to tackle Stalin with a remarkable bluntness. According to the first draft of the minutes taken by Clark-Kerr:

Prime Minister then produced what he called a 'naughty document' showing a list of Balkan countries and the proportion of interest in them of the Great Powers. He said that the Americans would be shocked if they saw how crudely he had put it. Marshal Stalin was a realist. He himself was not sentimental while Mr Eden was a bad man. He had not consulted his cabinet or Parliament.

Churchill's precise proposals were:

Romania	
Russia	90%
The others	10%
Greece	
Great Britain (in accord with USA)	90%
Russia	10%
Yugoslavia	50–50%
Hungary	50–50%
Bulgaria	
Russia	75%
The others	25%

Churchill, in his memoirs, claimed that Stalin simply 'took his blue pencil and made a large tick upon it, and passed it back to us'. 'It was all settled,' he added, 'in no more time than it takes to tell.' In fact the discussion was more complicated. For, according to Clark-Kerr's minutes, 'Marshal Stalin reverted to the Balkans and asked for the figures about Bulgaria on the "naughty document" to be amended and suggested that our [British] interest was not as great as the Prime Minister claimed.' There was also some debate about the future of the Montreux Convention which Churchill was in principle willing to see revised; and Stalin tacitly agreed to use his influence to restrain the Italian Communists. Nevertheless Churchill was substantially correct to recall that a rapid understanding was reached at his first direct encounter with Stalin.[139]

It was probably never intended by Churchill and still less by Eden that a bilateral Anglo-Soviet treaty on post-war arrangements should be drawn up in view of American susceptibilities. But Churchill did consider sending a formal letter to Stalin, of which a mere copy would have gone to Roosevelt. Even this, however, he decided not to do after Harriman had warned him that it would be badly received in Washington. With the 'percentages agreement' thus remaining a wholly informal arrangement too much should not be made of the ensuing Eden–Molotov discussions on details which were in any case technically inconclusive. But they were of some importance in that they convinced the Foreign Secretary that Soviet ambitions were more extensive than he had imagined. Molotov, for example, tried to persuade Eden to accept that the Soviet 'share' in Bulgaria should be increased to 90 per cent as in the case of Romania. Since Churchill's 75 per cent formulation represented a concession by the Prime Minister to Eden's pleas, the Foreign Secretary was unwilling to give way. But, since it was unclear how 75 per cent could in practice have been less decisive than 90 per cent, Eden's stubbornness on this point seems rather academic. On the other hand, he did not discourage Molotov from raising the question whether, if the Soviets agreed to 75 per cent for Bulgaria, they might not increase their 'share' in Hungary from 50 to 75 per cent. But, as stated, these discussions had no decisive or formal outcome.[140] What probably mattered much more was Molotov's clear indication that, though the British and the Americans would be allowed to sign an armistice with Romania and Bulgaria on equal terms with the Soviets, in the post-Armistice phase Soviet troops would remain in exclusive occupation of these countries with a Soviet chairman permanently heading a three-power control commission. That Eden grasped how potentially decisive this was is clear from what he wrote to his Foreign Office critics in London:

as it now appears that the Soviet government intend to maintain forces in Bulgaria so long as the Control Commission operates, and as neither we nor the Americans are in a position to send troops to the country, I fear we must simply accept the realities of the situation, however disagreeable.[141]

Eden had thus been brought round, as so often happened, to accepting Churchill's realism.

Much the same happened in the matter of Poland. Churchill, fearing that the Soviets would set up a puppet government, insisted that the leader of the London Poles, Stanislaw Mikolajczyk, should come to the Moscow Conference to try to reach a settlement with Stalin. The Prime Minister was quite clear that the Poles would have to accept the Curzon Line as their eastern frontier and, in addition, yield to Stalin on most other disputed points. Mikolajczyk stubbornly resisted on the grounds that his colleagues would repudiate him if he agreed to these demands. In particular, he absolutely refused to consider Stalin's demand for the town of Lwów.

Churchill accordingly bullied him mercilessly but without result. Eden's anguish was noted by Thomas Barman, then serving in the British Embassy in Moscow:

> Eden himself became emotionally involved in the question of Lvov. He felt it would be wrong if the British Government were to give way to the Russian demand for this ancient Polish town. He seemed unhappy and uneasy. One evening he came back to the Embassy very late after a long session with Molotov and the others. He seemed exhausted and depressed as he came into the Ambassador's room, where one or two of us sat talking over the day's events . . . He strode up and down the room for a while . . . Suddenly he stopped: 'If I give way over Lvov,' he said, 'shall I go down in the history books as an appeaser?' He did not wait for an answer. First he put the question to the Ambassador, and moved on. Then he came to my colleague and put it again, and moved on. Then he put it to me. At no time did he wait for an answer. Perhaps he didn't want an answer. It was clear to me that he was plagued almost beyond endurance by the need to make what he regarded as an unreasonable and unjust concession.

But he had no answer to Churchill's view, recalled in his memoirs in explanation of his failure to react strongly to Soviet cynicism at the time of the Warsaw Rising, that '. . . terrible and even humbling submissions must at times be made to the general aim'.[142] Eden was accordingly a helpless spectator as Mikolajczyk had to declare his inability definitely to accept Stalin's terms and was thus left facing a grim future. True, the Polish Prime Minister undertook with little expectation of success to try to persuade his colleagues in London to modify their intransigent stand. His effort merely led to his resignation on 24 November.

Depressed though Eden was at the evidence of Soviet intentions for the future of Poland, he nevertheless still had ambivalent feelings about the general prospects for post-war cooperation. For example, he steadily refused to endorse the view of the Chiefs of Staff that circumstances might arise in which 'we should require German assistance against a hostile USSR'.[143] He was also no doubt flattered to remain the Soviets' favourite British statesman. Dixon recorded in his diary on 10 October: 'The popularity of Anthony [at the Moscow Conference] was clear, and the Russians fussed round him even more than round Churchill.'[144]

His consciousness of having a special standing with Stalin may have led him to settle the repatriation issue with none of the anxiety that had affected him on the Polish issue. Certainly his report to the Foreign Office had a remarkably self-satisfied tone to it:

> At dinner last night [11 October] my conversation with Marshal Stalin turned for a moment on the Russian troops whom we had in England. The Marshal said he would be extremely grateful if any arrangements could be made to get them back here. I said we should be glad to do anything we could to help . . . The Marshal repeated that he would be deeply in our debt if we could arrange matters for him

about this. I replied that he could be sure that we would do all we could to help and in return I felt sure that his Government would give all the help in their power to our prisoners in Germany as and when the Red Army reached German prison camps in which they were located. The Marshal said at once that certainly this would be done. He would make this his personal charge and he gave me his personal word that every care and attention would be given to our men ...[145]

Some analysts may discern a similar ambivalence in Churchill during the last months of the war. Moran, for example, wrote in his diary on 30 October:

All this havering, these conflicting and contradictory policies, are, I am sure due to Winston's exhaustion. He seems torn between two lines of action: he cannot decide whether to make one last attempt to enlist Roosevelt's sympathy for a firmer line with Stalin, in the hope that he has learnt from the course of events, or whether to make his peace with Stalin and save what he can from the wreck of Allied hopes. At one moment he will plead with the President for a common front against Communism and the next he will make a bid for Stalin's friendship. Sometimes the two policies alternate with bewildering rapidity.

As evidence of Churchill's capacity for optimism the minutes of the post-Yalta War Cabinet may be cited:

So far as Stalin was concerned, he was quite sure that he meant well to the world and to Poland. He did not think that there would be any resentment on the part of Russia about the arrangements that had been made for fair and free elections in that country ... Stalin, at the beginning of their conversation on the Polish question, had said that Russia had committed many sins ... against Poland, and that they had in the past joined in the partitions of Poland and in cruel oppression of her. It was not the intention of the Soviet Government to repeat that policy in the future. He felt no doubt whatever in saying that Stalin had been sincere. He had very great feeling that the Russians were anxious to work harmoniously with the two English-speaking democracies.

Dalton recorded in his diary on 23 February that the Prime Minister had said: 'Poor Neville Chamberlain believed he could trust Hitler. He was wrong. But I don't think I'm wrong about Stalin.'[146] But Churchill's hopeful words probably did not represent his settled conviction about the Soviets. Rather he may have been putting the best face on the bargains struck with Stalin for the benefit of those colleagues who would otherwise have had difficulty in accepting the need for disagreeable surrenders. What Moran saw as 'havering' and 'conflicting and contradictory policies' were merely a reflection of his desperation when faced with the reality of Great Britain's relative military weakness. Indeed on one reading Churchill showed a fair degree of consistency. Three quotations from the Prime Minister during the last year of the war illustrate the argument:

Churchill to Eden, 8 May 1944
I fear that very great evil may come upon the world. This time at any rate we and the Americans will be heavily armed. The Russians are drunk with victory and there is no length they may not go.

Churchill to Cranborne, 3 April 1945
Always remember that there are various large matters in which we cannot go further than the United States are willing to go.

Churchill quoted in Moran's diary, 22 July 1945
The Russians have stripped their zone [of Germany] and want a rake-off from the British and American sectors as well. They will grind their zone, there will be unimaginable cruelties. It is indefensible except on one ground: that there is no alternative.[147]

Eden differed from his chief not so much about the character of the Soviet threat, which, at least intermittently, he had come to accept, but about whether east-central Europe could be saved without American support. He had to be constantly reminded by Churchill of the limits of British influence, as for example when the Prime Minister minuted on 17 June 1945:

It is beyond the power of this country to prevent all sorts of things crashing at the present time. The responsibility lies with the US and my desire is to give them all the support in our power. If they do not feel able to do anything, then we must let matters take their course.[148]

In Churchill's view only one substantial prize could be secured by the exertions of Great Britain alone. This was Greece. Hence following his return to London from Moscow the Prime Minister during the remainder of 1944 treated her future as of supreme importance. Eden, while not opposed to trying to save Greece from Communism, showed no comparable sense of urgency. This led Churchill to write to him on 7 November:

In my opinion, having paid the price we have to Russia, for freedom of action in Greece, we should not hesitate to use British troops to support the Royal Hellenic Government ... We need another eight or ten thousand foot-soldiers to hold the capital and Salonika for the present Government ... I fully expect a clash with EAM, and we must not shrink from it, provided the ground is well chosen.[149]

The simmering crisis in Athens, which had been liberated on 14 October, erupted into civil war on 4 December. A Communist takeover appeared imminent. Churchill held that the situation was too urgent to allow time to consult the Americans or even his War Cabinet. He accordingly took drastic action on his own initiative with only the rather passive consent of Eden. Dixon wrote in his diary in an account somewhat at variance with that in Churchill's memoirs:

Crucial decisions today over Greece. The climax not reached till after dinner ... we discussed a statement to be made by the PM in the House the following day, and while this was going on telegrams came in from Rex [Leeper, British Ambassador in Athens] saying that the situation was deteriorating and Papandreou [the Greek Prime Minister] about to resign. We drafted a telegram and a statement which I then took over to No. 10 ... [and]showed him [Churchill] the Greek telegrams and our proposed instructions to Leeper. He thought them not nearly strong enough, and held that the time had come to order General [Ronald] Scobie to take over law and order and to disarm the ELAS by force. He cleared this on the telephone with Anthony, who was going to bed, and then settled down to draft his instructions, sitting gyrating in his armchair and dictating on the machine to Miss Layton, who did not bat an eyelid at the many blasphemies with which the old man interspersed his official phrases. He was in a bloodthirsty mood, and did not take kindly to suggestions that we should avoid bloodshed if possible – though I couldn't agree more that force must be used if required. Rex was told that there must be no Cabinet-making till order had been restored. Having sent off these tremendous telegrams, he turned to the statement. This, with other matters, took till 2.30 a.m.[150]

Thus Churchill alone drafted the famous telegram to Scobie which soon rapidly leaked through American channels into the press: 'We have to hold and dominate Athens. It would be a great thing for you to succeed in this without bloodshed if possible, but also with bloodshed if necessary.'[151]

Even Churchill conceded in his memoirs that this telegram was 'somewhat strident in tone'.[152] It led to bitter recriminations in the House of Commons and, more importantly, to a quarrel with the Americans. Edward Stettinius, now Secretary of State, issued a pointed statement deploring British interference in the internal affairs of Italy and also, by implication, in Greece. This caused Churchill to rebuke Roosevelt, who in turn effectively endorsed Stettinius's line. In the Foreign Office Eden and his officials now became uneasy about Churchill's Greek policy. Dixon's diary is revealing:

5 December 1944
I confess I felt increasingly anxious about the wisdom of our midnight plotting, and was further shaken by a tiresome statement put out by Stettinius condemning our interference in Italian and Greek internal affairs. The actual military situation in Greece is, as expected, more disquieting every hour. It has yet to reach its climax, which can only be an armed clash between Greek and Briton, unless the Elas capitulate.

6 December 1944
A.E., very calm, but a bit worried about the PM's position if things get worse in Greece.

11 December 1944
After brooding on Greece during the weekend ... returned to the FO convinced that we must, without signs of weakening, find some way out before we are really locked in battle with EAM. Found that Moley [Sargent] and the Department's minds were working on the same lines. When A.E. came up at midday we put this to him and he took a plan over to the PM who, however, would agree to no instructions going to Athens for fear ... of crossing the wires now Harold Macmillan and FM Alexander

have gone there to find a solution. I feel unhappy about this, as we have given them no lead and with each hour that passes we are more deeply committed to an unnecessary struggle with the Greek irregulars.

19 December 1944
News from Athens no better ... The great debate is whether there should be a Regency in Greece. There is a divergence on this point between A.E. and the PM, the former considering that our military force is not enough to settle the issue and that a political solvent is needed. The PM on the other hand believes that our forces should be allowed to settle the matter, and that raising the constitutional issue would result in a dictatorship or a communist regime. He underrates the ELAS force, overrates our force, ignores the risk to the Italian front of a festering and unpopular crusade in Greece, and above all is swayed by the wish to maintain the King of Greece in power. The feeling is growing ugly in the country, where people see the simple fact that British troops are being made to fight friends. Whether the Regency would help much is perhaps doubtful, but it would help a little, and our situation is so serious that every contribution should now be thrown in.[153]

Churchill, however, kept his nerve and was soon rewarded with the news that the Communists had clearly failed in their bid to take over by the use of armed force. On Christmas Eve the Prime Minister suddenly decided that the time was ripe to visit Athens to investigate at first hand Eden's claim that the establishment of a Regency under Archbishop Damaskinos would best serve British interests. For Eden this presented a painful dilemma: should he accompany his chief or should he spend Christmas with his family, including his elder son who was on leave from the air force? He decided that his family must, as so often, take second place. He and Churchill thus arrived on Christmas Day in Greece where they slept aboard *HMS Ajax*. Next day they met a wide range of Greek politicians, including some Communists. The outcome was Churchill's conversion to Eden's view that Damaskinos could be trusted. It was accordingly agreed that the Greek King should invite him to serve as Regent and the Communists tacitly consented in return to end their armed resistance. Both Churchill and Eden thus departed for London on 28 December believing that they had by their differing contributions done much to bring a degree of stability to the country for which they had sacrificed so much to Stalin.

Eden's next expedition came at the end of January 1945 when he accompanied Churchill to the Crimea for the Yalta Heads of Government Summit. The Foreign Secretary was inevitably dwarfed by his chief, who in turn was overshadowed by Roosevelt and Stalin, both of whom now visibly deployed military might far in excess of that of Great Britain. Hence Eden's rôle at Yalta was not of great importance. Moreover, as at Teheran, the Conference was too brief and too badly prepared to permit many issues to be definitely settled. Here it is appropriate to consider a few themes as they affected Eden.

First, the controversial repatriation arrangement, agreed earlier, was formally signed by Eden and Molotov. Next, Eden concurred in an American-inspired declaration on colonial trusteeship that went far, at least on paper, to undermine Churchill's insistence, adumbrated earlier in the war, that British possessions could not be subject to outside in-vestigation or interference. One historian concluded that this was largely the result of clumsy diplomacy on Eden's part and that in the subsequent inquest he tried to cover up the extent of his responsibility.[154] But if Eden had proved unexpectedly accommodating to the Allies on this issue, he favoured an unyielding stance when they brought forward a declaration, secretly drawn up between them, on the future of the Far East. Churchill also disliked the terms, which took no account of Chinese susceptibilities and which were clearly intended to exclude the British from increasing their influence in east Asia. But he felt obliged to sign the declaration rather than have an open divergence from his allies. He overruled Eden's objections.

Another issue at Yalta concerned the future of Germany. No firm decisions were reached either on the nature of her proposed dismember-ment or on the level of reparations. This owed something to Eden's unwillingness to submit to over-persistent pressure from Molotov. But it may have derived more from a long-standing uncertainty on the Foreign Secretary's own part where the future of Germany was concerned. As one historian has written: Eden 'may have suffered from genuine indecision on the question . . . It is hard to explain his conflicting statements on the matter in any other way.'[155] Eden did, however, welcome one Soviet gesture on the subject of Germany: the French should be allowed to play a part in her post-war control.

The dominant issue at Yalta, however, was Poland. On this subject, as has been seen, Eden felt strongly. On the eve of the Conference he sent a minute to Churchill:

The essential thing for us is that there should be an independent Poland. The danger is that Poland will now be insulated from the outside world and to all intents and purposes run by the Russians behind a Lublin screen. It is possible that the Russians, realizing how unrepresentative Lublin is, may not be averse from strengthening the Lublin Provisional Government with representative Poles who are in favour of collaboration with Russia. It might even be possible to persuade the Russians to add M. Mikolajczyk and one or two others from London.

But this of itself would not guarantee independence. We and the Americans would have to be represented in order to see for ourselves, and there should ultimately be free elections with British and American observers as well as Russian.

This may seem a tall order. But something of the kind we must get from the Russians if Poland is to be really independent and if Anglo-American-Russian relations are to be possible on that basis of cordiality necessary for the future of peace of Europe.[156]

There were other aspects of the Polish question to which the Foreign Secretary attached subsidiary importance. One was the eastern frontier. For he still hoped that Roosevelt would try to secure at least Lwów for Poland. But on that issue the President quickly gave way to Stalin. Another concern was the amount of German territory to be given to Poland in compensation for her losses in the East. Eden hoped to confine the Polish gains to the line of the eastern rather than the western Neisse lest the Poles incur such permanent enmity in Germany as to drive them into total dependence on Moscow. On this no formal agreement was reached at Yalta but the Soviets seemed poised to use their control of the relevant territory to impose *de facto* the solution they favoured – and this eventually happened. But, as stated, ensuring the independence of the Polish Government was now Eden's principal aim. As he had forecast, the Soviets insisted that the Lublin Committee should form the core of the Polish Provisional Government but for the sake of appearances they agreed to have discussions about adding some further names 'from within Poland and from abroad'. Eden fought hard to secure better terms in a confrontation with Molotov but he was effectively defeated when Stettinius refused to back him up. Everything now rested on whether free elections would be held under international supervision. The Soviets agreed to elections in which 'all democratic and anti-Nazi parties shall have the right to take part and put forward candidates'. They also signed a document, produced by Roosevelt, entitled 'Declaration on Liberated Europe', which contained vague commitments to the establishment 'through free elections of governments responsive to the will of the people' and to 'the right of all peoples to choose the form of government under which they will live'. But the Soviets' real intentions for Poland were revealed by their refusal to agree to arrangements for Western participation in the supervision or even observation of elections. Churchill wrote in his memoirs that this was 'the best I could get'.[157]

Clearly he and Eden could insist on nothing more with Roosevelt and Stettinius in so irresolute a mood. But perhaps Roosevelt, too, believed that nothing more could be achieved by diplomatic means. Leahy, for example, claimed that he told the President that the agreement on Poland was 'so elastic that the Russians can stretch it all the way from Yalta to Washington without ever technically breaking it'. Roosevelt is said to have replied: 'I know it, Bill – I know it. But it's the best I can do for Poland at this time.' This has led to speculation that Roosevelt was tacitly of the same opinion as Churchill had been at Moscow in October 1944: suspicious of the Soviets but reconciled to a spheres-of-influence deal. Yet his position also surely differed from Churchill's. First, he had not seen the need to crush the

Communists in Greece. Secondly, he had much more military strength at his disposal than Churchill but was quite unwilling to make even the most limited use of it in diplomatic bargaining. On the contrary, at Yalta, in a moment of unparalleled feebleness, he volunteered the information that American forces would leave Europe within two years. Certainly Churchill did not respect Roosevelt's attitude at this time. On 13 March, for example, he wrote a minute to Eden deploring 'the weakness of the United States diplomacy'.[158] Thus Churchill and Eden left Yalta with few positive achievements – but the principal fault was clearly not theirs. The 'bitter cup' had still not been drained.

If Churchill and Eden were disappointed, they did not immediately reveal it to their colleagues. As has been seen, the Prime Minister spoke optimistically to the War Cabinet. He and Eden also defended the Yalta arrangements in the House of Commons, where vocal opposition came from a number of Conservative backbenchers, including the future Prime Minister, Lord Dunglass, later Sir Alexander Douglas-Home. Nicolson recorded in his diary: 'Winston is as amused as I am that the warmongers of the Munich period have now become the appeasers, while the appeasers have become the warmongers.'[159]

That Churchill did not set much store by the Yalta Declaration or on the promised elections in Poland is, however, clear from his private minutes to Eden. He remained convinced that the British should try to hold the Soviets to the 'percentages' arrangements of the previous October even at the cost of condoning Stalin's breaches of the Yalta Declaration in the Soviet sphere-of-influence. Eden, on the other hand, was more hopeful that, with American support, the British might yet induce the Soviets to respect the Declaration and hence not seek the Bolshevization of Poland or even of Bulgaria and Romania. He was thus anxious to engage in active diplomacy contrary to the spirit of the 'percentages' agreement when, soon after Yalta, dramatic developments occurred in Romania. Pro-Communist elements, with the support of the Red Army, began openly to persecute and intimidate their rivals. Eventually King Michael agreed, under direct Soviet pressure, to dismiss the Prime Minister, Nicolae Radescu, thereby opening the way for a Communist takeover. Churchill, unlike Eden, wished to keep a low profile. Indeed, even before Yalta the Prime Minister had shown remarkable concern for Soviet susceptibilities so far as Romania was concerned. On 19 January, for example, he had informed Eden that he positively favoured the Soviets being allowed to deport Romanian citizens to the Soviet Union as forced labour:

We seem to be taking a very active line against the deportation of the Austrians, Saxons and other German or quasi-German elements from Roumania to Russia for labour purposes. Considering all that Russia has suffered, and the wanton attacks made upon her by Roumania, and the vast armies the Russians are using at the front at the present time, and the terrible condition of the people in many parts of Europe, I cannot see that the Russians are wrong in making 100 or 150 thousand of these people work their passage. Also we must bear in mind what we promised about leaving Roumania's fate to a large extent in Russian hands. I cannot myself consider that it is wrong of the Russians to take Roumanians of any origin they like to work in the Russian coal-fields, in view of all that has passed.[160]

He conveniently forgot how reluctant he had been to make a British declaration of war on Romania in 1941. Now, after the fall of Radescu, the Prime Minister again rebuked Eden, on 5 March, for the excess of zeal in support of the Yalta Declaration shown by the Foreign Office and by British representatives in Bucharest:

We really have no justification for intervening in this extraordinarily vigorous manner for our late Roumanian enemies, thus compromising our position in Poland and jarring upon Russian acquiescence in our long fight in Athens. If we go on like this, we shall be told, not without reason, that we have broken our faith about Roumania after taking advantage of our position in Greece and this will compromise the stand we have taken at Yalta over Poland. I consider strict instructions should be sent to all our representatives in Roumania not to develop an anti-Russian political front there. This they are doing with untimely energy without realizing what is at stake in other fields.[161]

Eden's response underlined his naïve obtuseness. He pointed out that the Americans had protested at developments in Romania and had 'invoked the Yalta Declaration'. 'It seemed to me,' he continued, 'the best we could do was to support the Americans.' Ignoring power political considerations, he piously reminded Churchill that the Yalta Declaration 'applies indifferently to lesser Allied countries which have been liberated and to ex-enemy countries which have been occupied by the Allies'. He concluded:

Although our percentage of interest in Roumania and Bulgaria is small, surely that does not prohibit us from appealing for consultation between the three Powers in accordance with the Yalta Declaration ... ? If we are not allowed to do this in respect of Balkan countries, I fail to see what interpretation we can put on the Declaration or what answer we are to give in public if asked why we did not act in accordance with the procedure laid down in the Declaration ...

I realize of course, that if we invoke the Yalta Declaration in respect of Roumania, we may expect the Russians to do the same in regard of Greece or elsewhere. But you have already offered Russia full inspection in Greece, and I do not think that we have anything to fear, at least so far as Greece is concerned ...[162]

This argument appeared to be based on the assumption that the Yalta Declaration had miraculously made it safe for Great Britain to abandon the spirit of the 'percentages' agreement. Churchill was unimpressed. For he grasped that over-reliance on the Yalta Declaration, accompanied by a tacit repudiation of the 'percentages' agreement, might lead not to the salvation of Romania but to the loss of Greece. On 13 March, for example he minuted to Eden:

We must remember
(a) Roumania is an ex-enemy state which did great injury to Russia;
(b) That we, for considerations well known to you, accepted in a special degree the predominance of Russia in this theatre;
(c) That the lines of the southern Russian Army communications pass through Roumania;
(d) The weakness of the United States diplomacy.[163]

Eden had to face similar disillusionment with the effectiveness of the Yalta Declaration in the case of Poland. The Soviets showed no sign of being willing to establish an independent Polish government or to arrange for free elections to be held. And sixteen non-Communist Poles who had gone to Moscow for discussions with the Soviets were rumoured to have disappeared. By 23 March the Foreign Secretary wrote in his diary that he took 'the gloomiest view of Russian behaviour everywhere'. 'Altogether,' he added, 'our foreign policy seems a sad wreck and we may have to cast about afresh.'[164] His old ally Cranborne felt the same way and even considered resignation if Eden went to San Francisco to take part in establishing a world organization which in the circumstances he thought foredoomed to be a farce. Above all, he was angered that at Yalta the British had accepted in principle a Great Power veto on coercive actions by the new organization. He held that the Soviets' failure to fulfil their obligations under the Yalta Declaration presented an opportunity to renege on that concession. On 9 April he wrote to Eden:

On Thursday [5 April] I urged you, even at this late hour, to try and get the Conference at San Francisco put off, until the situation was clearer and there was some chance of building on firm foundations. You said that it was too late, and very likely you are right; and you sketched out an alternative line of action which you thought would safeguard us from any charge of hypocrisy. As I understand it, your idea is, first, to make in Parliament, before you leave, a frank unvarnished statement about the position over Poland. Then when you get to San Francisco and the actual Yalta proposal on voting in the Security Council comes up for discussion you will, while supporting it, make clear that its success depends on a determination on the part of the Great Powers, to respect, scrupulously, the rights of their small neighbours. You will add that you cannot say in all honesty that that attitude is at present being universally adopted by all the Great Powers, and that the agreement of HMG to the proposal must therefore be conditional and subject to revision.

Cranborne added that the result would be 'only a mongrel affair, bred of opportunism and appeasement, disliked by all, distrusted by all'.[165]

Whether Cranborne would have resigned and whether Eden would have spoken out in Parliament or at San Francisco must remain speculative. For the whole world scene was drastically altered on 12 April with the death of Roosevelt. The new President, Harry S. Truman, rapidly showed signs of reversing his predecessor's acquiescent attitude to Soviet action in eastern Europe. He sent friendly replies to telegrams from Churchill urging united pressure on Moscow; and on 23 April he fiercely attacked Molotov in person for not sticking to agreements. Clearly Eden could not now strike an independent note at least until he saw how the new American Administration's policies evolved. From 25 April to 13 May he accordingly played a relatively muted rôle during the San Francisco Conference. In the circumstances he found it extremely frustrating to be away from home for the celebrations following the announcement, early in May, first of Hitler's death and then of Germany's surrender.

On 3 May Eden was given a chilling reminder of the portents for Poland. Dixon recorded:

> A Polish day and a very bad one. A.E. came back after dinner with the news that the Russians have arrested the 16 Polish leaders whom they had invited to talk. This Polish shadow has been overclouding the Conference since the failure of Yalta, and though I don't think it will bust the Conference, it well might.[166]

Next day Eden privately rebuked Molotov. 'I said ...,', the Foreign Secretary telegraphed to Churchill, 'I was amazed to hear that they would be accused of terrorism because we knew them to have been good patriots all through the period of German occupation and democrats who favoured good relations with Russia ...' This was as far as Eden could go. For with a new American President he could not make a unilateral public attack on the Soviets. But the Americans in San Francisco proved disappointingly indecisive. True, Stettinius privately endorsed Eden's remarks to Molotov. Yet Dixon recorded in his diary: 'The Americans were divided on Poland between those who, like ourselves, thought the Russian behaviour over the 16 Poles outrageous, and those who thought that firmness on our part on that issue might wreck the Conference.'[167] And gradually it emerged that Truman, despite his initial robustness, intended to avoid open clashes with Moscow. The President, for example, rejected pleas from Churchill and Eden to occupy Prague ahead of the Soviets. He also declined to try to hold on to German territory hitherto designated for Soviet occupation. And on the Polish issue he agreed to send Hopkins, usually well-disposed towards the Soviets, to Moscow in an attempt to reduce tension. By the time Eden had returned to London on 17 May British hopes that the Americans would give a decisive lead against Stalin had thus faded. But meanwhile the United Nations Organization had been launched in a form acceptable to the Soviet Union.

The fighting spirit which had marked Eden's attitude towards Moscow

With Foreign Secretary Sir Samuel Hoare after a Cabinet Meeting on Abyssinia, August 1935

members of Neville Chamberlain's War Cabinet, November 1939. *From left to right, standing*: Sir John Anderson, Minister for
e Security; Lord Hankey, Minister without Portfolio; Mr Leslie Hore-Belisha, Secretary of State for War; Mr Winston Churchill,
Lord of the Admiralty; Sir Kingsley Wood, Secretary of State for Air; Mr Anthony Eden, Secretary of State for Dominion Affairs;
dward Bridges, Secretary to the War Cabinet. *Left to right, seated*: Viscount Halifax, Secretary of State for Foreign Affairs; Sir John
n, Chancellor of the Exchequer; Mr Neville Chamberlain, Prime Minister; Sir Samuel Hoare, Lord Privy Seal; Lord Chatfield,
ster for the Coordination of Defence

Above, inside the War Office, December 1940
Below, with Molotov and Cordell Hull at the Moscow Foreign Ministers'
Meeting, October 1943, according to *Punch*

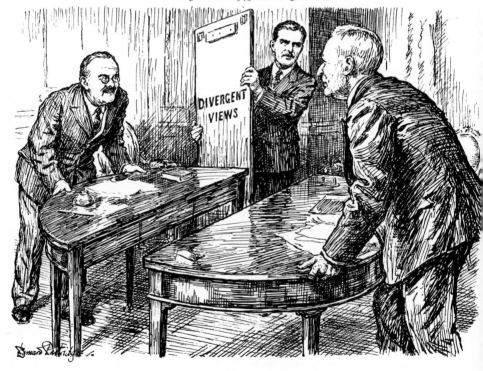

THE RUSSIAN ROUND TABLE

"Let's sit closer together."

...ve, with Dean Acheson,
...erican Secretary of State,
... United Nations meeting, November 1951

Norman Mansbridge

...ht, Punch view of Eden's role
...he Geneva Conference on Indochina, May 1954

Punch view of Eden's impatience
to succeed Churchill, November 1954

Above, taking over the Premiership from Sir Winston Churchill, April 1955
Below, with John Foster Dulles, American Secretary of State, and Christian Pineau, French Foreign Minister, at the Suez Canal Users' Association meeting, September 1956

Gaitskell and Eden at cross-purposes during the Suez crisis. *Punch*, September 1956

Punch view of Eden's Suez enterprise on the day after the announcement of a ceasefire, November 1956

Punch view of the prospects of Eden,
Macmillan and Butler a week before
Eden's resignation as Prime Minister,
January 1957

Leaving No. 10 Downing Street for Buckingham Palace
to tender his resignation as Prime Minister, January 1957

between the Yalta and San Francisco Conferences subsided. He now had, moreover, other preoccupations. First, he knew that a General Election was to be held on 5 July following the break-up of the wartime Coalition Government. Secondly, he fell ill towards the end of May with a duodenal ulcer and spent most of June at Binderton. He was only able to play a token part in the Conservative Election campaign, màking one radio broadcast on 27 June. This period was also one of deep anguish for Eden because of news that his elder son, Simon, was missing after a flight in Burma.

By 15 July Eden was sufficiently recovered in health to accompany Churchill to Potsdam for the final wartime summit with the Americans and the Soviets. For the Foreign Secretary the personal strain at this time was no doubt almost unbearable. Because of the need for servicemen's votes to be collected from around the world, the result of the General Election would not be known until 25 July, three weeks after polling day. So Eden did not know at Potsdam whether he would remain a world statesman or be reduced overnight to relative obscurity. And, dwarfing everything else, he still had no confirmation of his son's fate, though hope was rapidly fading. In the circumstances he showed great courage in continuing to carry out his duties in the glare of world attention.

Potsdam was a summit at which few agreements were finalized. In some cases endorsement was given to decisions already reached in advance; in others definitive arrangements were allowed to await the Peace Conference or a meeting of Foreign Ministers to be held later in the year. Poland was one substantial subject on the agenda. But the recognition of an expanded Lublin Committee as the legitimate Polish Government and the de-recognition of the London Government-in-Exile had been accepted in principle by Churchill before Potsdam as a result of Hopkins's visit to Moscow having persuaded Truman that this should happen. Eden had thus no serious hope at Potsdam of securing effective application of the Yalta Declaration to Poland, though he paid lip service to that ideal. He was inclined to see in Churchill's conduct both in this and in other respects – such as his willingness to see the Soviets have free access to the Mediterranean – evidence that the Prime Minister was 'again under Stalin's spell'.[168] But this revealed on Eden's part an inclination once again to exaggerate the extent to which the British alone could influence developments. An example of Eden's stubbornness concerned the western frontier of Poland and in this he had for once Churchill's backing. He insisted that it should run along the eastern, not the western, Neisse. The Americans were prepared, however, to agree to a *de facto* arrangement involving Polish occupation up to the western Neisse while leaving the definitive settlement to the Peace Conference. It eventually fell to Attlee and Bevin to accept the American approach. Technically, then, Eden and Churchill did not surrender on this point. But had they stayed in office they surely would have had to yield to the joint pressure of Truman and Stalin. On the future of Germany much the same pattern emerged. When the Americans favoured a compromise on reparations Churchill and Eden had to agree. But when Truman desired postponement of various issues to the Peace Conference, the British leaders were equally obliged sooner or later to echo him.

The British had clearly ceased to be equal partners of the Soviets and the Americans and hence were rarely decisive in shaping policies, though often politely consulted. An example of consultation concerned the use of the atomic bomb on Japan. Churchill and Eden raised no objection. But had they done so, it seems improbable that Truman would have changed his mind.

On 20 July Eden received confirmation that his son had perished in Burma. He reacted with stoic courage. Moran wrote that he was warned by Churchill in advance of a dinner that Eden had just heard the news: 'They talked until midnight as if nothing had happened. I wonder if I could have behaved with the same quiet dignity ... ?'[169]

On 25 July Churchill and Eden left Potsdam for London to be on hand for the General Election results the following day. Eden was in his Warwick and Leamington constituency to hear that he had easily been returned with a majority over Labour of 7,634. But in the country as a whole the outcome for the Conservatives was catastrophic: they obtained a mere 213 seats compared to Labour's 393. Depressed at the loss of his son and weary of working with Churchill, Eden was not greatly distressed at the result. He no doubt assumed that after so striking a defeat Churchill would soon retire and thus enable him to lead the Conservatives into the next General Election. Churchill evidently had the same expectation. For in the Cabinet Room after holding his last Cabinet he said to Eden: 'Thirty years of my life have been passed in this room. I shall never sit in it again. You will, but I shall not.[170] Churchill's failure to stick to this line was to cast a shadow over the next decade of Eden's life.

VIII

In Opposition

1945–51

The Labour Party's victory in the General Election meant that neither Churchill nor Eden returned to the Potsdam Conference. Indeed, this marked the beginning of a phase in which both men showed little interest in seeking public attention. Exhaustion, disappointment at the ingratitude of the electors and, in Eden's case, personal tragedy, made such an attitude understandable. And his wife, anxious about his health, pressed him to spend most of his time at their country home. On 25 September Stettinius visited the Edens at Binderton and wrote in his diary:

I had a private conversation with Mrs Eden while walking in the fields. She stated that ... Anthony was really picking up and his stomach ulcers were pretty well cured. While he had to be careful, she said, she was sure he was on the road to full recovery. She said she was very anxious for him not to get back into active life and wanted him to take things easy in the country, only going into town for a day or so when Parliament was in session.

Mr Eden stated he had an opportunity to do some writing and had been approached by a publisher, but after looking at his tax returns there was no incentive whatsoever. If he did get a large fee, he wouldn't get any of it so he was not going to do any writing ...

Eden had an old mare and very fine thoroughbred he was planning to breed in order to raise a colt. He also had three cows he was very interested in ...

To the small band of Conservative backbenchers, however, their leaders' other preoccupations seemed to symbolize a lack of fighting spirit. In consequence Churchill and Eden had to face a critical meeting of the 1922 Committee on 19 November 1945 at which they were urged to promise more frequent attendance and more vigorous opposition.[1]

Eden at least responded to the pressure to some degree with a major speech on foreign affairs in the House of Commons on 22 November. But Churchill defiantly announced that he intended to go to the United States for several months' holiday and on 19 December invited Eden to act as Leader of the Opposition in his absence.[2] It may have been this decision that led to widespread Conservative expectations that Churchill, now seventy, would soon retire altogether. Eden as heir-apparent was more sceptical. He realized, moreover, that if Churchill decided to remain the difficulties in the way of dissuading him would be formidable.

In these circumstances Eden came to be tempted by the secretary-generalship of the United Nations. The episode bore similarities to that involving the viceroyalty of India in 1943. On both occasions he was unhappy at the prospect of having to continue to serve under Churchill, while not feeling able to have an open breach with a second consecutive Conservative leader. And in 1945, as in 1943, Churchill made no serious attempt to dissuade his colleague – and potential rival – from leaving British politics. So depressed was Eden in 1945 that he would probably have accepted the UN post if it had been definitely offered to him. He wrote in his memoirs: 'I took no step to promote my candidature, but if this offer had been made to me, it could hardly have been refused.' According to Trygve Lie, the Norwegian to whom the appointment eventually went, it was Attlee's Government that 'was not favourably disposed' and hence no formal offer was made to Eden.[3]

Cranborne commented on 12 February 1946 to Paul Emrys-Evans, who had been a member of the so-called Eden Group of MPs in the late 1930s, that he could not understand Churchill's motives in advising him to consider the UN post.[4] He might have done so if he had realized, as he was soon to do, that another major policy divergence was arising between Eden and his chief. As had so often been the case during the war, the issue related to the Soviet Union. On this subject Eden's early peacetime speeches, unlike Churchill's, revealed no dramatic break with his public wartime line. Eden thus stayed broadly in line with Bevin, the new Foreign Secretary. He continued to speak of the Soviet Union as an ally while criticizing in fairly mild terms particular features of her foreign policy. Difficulties were acknowledged to exist but they were mainly attributed to fear of a revived Germany and to excessive concern with national security. That a fundamental ideological difference might lie at the root of the East–West tensions, even over free elections in eastern Europe, was not at this stage given public credence by either Bevin or Eden. Indeed, both continuity and bipartisanship were never more in evidence in British foreign policy than in the pronouncements of the principal Labour and Conservative foreign affairs spokesmen during the last months of 1945. For example, on 20 August Eden went out of his way in the House of Commons to refer to Bevin as his 'Right Honourable Friend'. He drew attention also to their wartime harmony: 'He and I served four years together in the War Cabinet ... During that period there were many discussions on foreign affairs, but I cannot recall one single occasion when there was a difference between us. I hope I do not embarrass the Foreign Secretary by saying that.' Bevin cheerfully replied in the negative. Small wonder that one Labour MP was reported to have remarked 'Hasn't Anthony Eden grown fat?'; while another view was that Bevin had dropped nothing from his Conservative predecessors' policies except the aitches. The cooperation was, moreover, gradually made more definite with Dixon, now Bevin's Private Secretary, acting as a link between the two men and on occasion supplying Eden with confidential information.[5]

Eden's public attitude towards the Soviet Union is perhaps best captured in these passages from a speech delivered in the House of Commons on 22 November 1945 in the aftermath of the failure of the first post-war Foreign Ministers' meeting:

Nobody here will deny that recently there has been an increase of suspicion and mistrust between the Soviet Union and the other two great partners in victory, the United States and ourselves. We all deplore that, and if I make some remarks upon it I hope it will be understood that they are made by one who has always been and is still convinced that the future peace of the world depends upon an understanding between ourselves, the United States and Russia ... We want the fullest Russian participation in all world affairs on equal terms. That is the object of our policy. Let us look at the Western *bloc*, as it is called – I think wrongly. Many times Russian statesmen have spoken to me ... of their need for security and of the necessity they feel for friendly relations with their neighbours. We have never disputed that. The Russians have gone very far in making arrangements with all their neighbours ...

Against whom are all these Russian arrangements being aimed? I know the answer; they have given it so many times. They are being aimed against the possible resurgence of German plans for the domination of Europe ... Any arrangements which the right hon. Gentleman [Bevin] may make in Western Europe are for precisely the same purpose ... We know that Russia's arrangements are not aimed against us. We can surely ask her to believe that our arrangements are not aimed at her either.

I have said that there continues to be in this country, among virtually all sections of the people, a deep desire for friendship with Russia, as close and cordial a friendship as we have with the United States of America. But there is another unhelpful influence which militates against this ... It is the difficulty of getting information out of Russia and out of territories controlled by the Soviet Union ... I would beg our Russian friends to believe that they could make no greater contribution to real understanding between our countries than to allow the foreign correspondents in their territories, or territories under their control, the same freedom as is allowed to Russian correspondents here. We have got to get to know each other and that involves freedom to speak and freedom to comment across frontiers. Drop these barriers of censorship and you will blow away in one gust much of this black fog of suspicion.

In the same speech Eden went on to regret Soviet conduct in Iran in using Russian troops, present by agreement with the British since 1941, to prevent the Iranian Government from dealing with domestic disturbances in the north-west of the country. But he avoided condemnation and instead called on 'our Russian allies' to take steps to remove suspicions. He had taken much the same line on 20 August in complaining about the failure of the authorities to hold free elections in Poland or Bulgaria.[6] He adopted the same tone in another speech to the House of Commons on 21 February 1946:

> It has been said many times in this Debate – and I think with truth – that it is difficult for us to understand the profound impression that has been made upon the minds of the Soviet Government and the Soviet people by the wide and deep invasion of their land by the German armies ...
>
> I am convinced that it is the scourge of that invasion – and not the only one in that country – which is the dominant motive in Soviet foreign policy ... The determination not to allow Germany to be in a position to do this again ... resulted in a Soviet determination to have as friendly neighbours as they can ...
>
> It often happens that those whom the Soviet Government think they can trust among their neighbours are not those whom the majority in those countries wish to govern them ... Inevitable friction results ...
>
> I believe that the Soviet Union is sincere when they say to us that they want to collaborate with ourselves and the United States ... But here comes the rub. While Russia wants this collaboration ... she appears only to want it on her own terms. That will not work. Sooner or later, that must land us all in difficulties.[7]

Eden's generally conciliatory approach, which was in rather marked contrast to the private views he had expressed between the Yalta and San Francisco Conferences, proved increasingly unacceptable to Churchill, who had now become more hawkish both in private and in public. As early as 16 August the Leader of the Opposition had dwelt in a House of Commons speech on the 'police governments' in much of Europe:

> President Roosevelt laid down the four freedoms and these are extant in the Atlantic Charter which we agreed together. 'Freedom from fear' – but this has been interpreted as if it were only freedom of fear of invasion from a foreign country. That is the least of the fears of the common man. His patriotism arms him to withstand invasion or go down fighting; but that is not the fear of the ordinary family in Europe tonight. Their fear is of the policeman's knock. It is not fear for the country, for all can unite in comradeship for defence of their native soil. It is for the life and liberty of the individual, for the fundamental rights of man, now menaced and precarious in so many lands, that people tremble.[8]

But the gap between Churchill and Eden only became manifest on 5 March 1946, when at Fulton, Missouri, in the presence of Truman, the Conservative leader delivered his famous 'Iron Curtain' speech. True, he paid lip service in terms that Eden could not have faulted to the desirability of extending the twenty-year Treaty of Collaboration and Mutual Assistance with the Soviet Union; he acknowledged his 'strong admiration and regard for the valiant Russian people and for my wartime comrade, Marshal Stalin'; and he stated that 'we understand the Russian need to be secure on his western frontiers from all renewal of German aggression'. But some other passages in his speech went far beyond anything Eden, or Bevin, or perhaps even Truman, found prudent. He referred, for example, to the delicate question of the American monopoly of nuclear weapons:

It would ... be wrong and imprudent to entrust the secret knowledge or experience of the atomic bomb ... to the world organization, while it is still in its infancy. It would be criminal madness to cast it adrift in this still agitated and un-united world. No one in any country has slept less well in their beds because this knowledge and the method and raw materials to apply it are at present largely retained in American hands. I do not believe we should all have slept so soundly had the positions been reversed and some Communist or neo-Fascist state monopolized for the time being these dread agencies. For fear of them alone might easily have been used to enforce totalitarian systems upon the free democratic world with consequences appalling to the human imagination. God has willed that this shall not be, and we have at least a breathing space before this peril has to be encountered; and even then, if no effort is spared, we should still possess so formidable a superiority as to impose effective deterrents upon its employment, or threat of employment by others.

Then, still more boldly, Churchill spoke of the threat of Communist tyranny and of Soviet domination in Europe:

From Stettin, in the Baltic, to Trieste, in the Adriatic, an iron curtain has descended across the Continent. Behind that line lie all the capitals of the ancient States of Central and Eastern Europe ... The Communist Parties, which were very small in all these eastern states of Europe, have been raised to pre-eminence and power far beyond their numbers and are seeking everywhere to obtain totalitarian control. Police governments are prevailing in nearly every case, and so far, except in Czechoslovakia, there is no true democracy.

... in a great number of countries far from the Russian frontiers and throughout the world, the Communist fifth columns are established and work in complete unity and absolute obedience to the directions they receive from the Communist centre.

He drew the conclusion that to aim at mere balance of power would be insufficient: 'We cannot afford if we can help it to work on narrow margins, offering temptations to a trial of strength.' To this end he proposed a special relationship between the British Empire and the United States, not based on generalities but on 'the continuance of intimate relationships between our military advisers' and 'the joint use of all naval and air bases in the possession of either country all over the world'. He was not modest in assessing the weight of the potential British contribution to such a partnership:

Let no man underrate the abiding power of the British Empire and Com-monwealth ... do not suppose that we shall not come through these dark years of privation as we have come through the glorious years of agony or that half a century from now you will not see 70,000,000 or 80,000,000 of Britons spread about the world and united in defence of our tradition, our way of life and of the world cause we and you espouse.

He concluded:

> If the population of the English-speaking Commonwealth be added to that of the United States, with all that such cooperation implies in the air, on the sea, and in science and industry, there will be no quivering, precarious balance of power to offer temptation to ambition or adventure. On the contrary, there will be an overwhelming assurance of security.
>
> If we adhere faithfully to the Charter of the United Nations and walk forward in sedate strength, seeking no one's land or treasure or seeking to lay no arbitrary control on the thoughts of men, if all British moral and material forces and convictions are joined with your own in fraternal association, the high roads of the future will be clear, not only for us but for all, not only for our time but for a century to come.[9]

The reaction in London to the Fulton speech was generally unfavourable. For example, *The Times*, while seeing merit in Churchill's platitudes that sounded relatively friendly towards Moscow, editorialized:

> Mr Churchill was perhaps less happy in the passages in his speech in which he appeared to contrast 'Western Democracy' and 'Communism' as irreconcilable opponents dividing, or attempting to divide, the world between them today. Yet it would be an assumption of despair to hold that they are doomed to a fatal contest. Indeed, a clearer recognition of two points might well serve to mitigate on both sides some of the asperities of recent exchanges. The first is that there are many forms of government intermediate between western democracy and Communism and some of them may be better adapted at the present stage of development to the requirements of Eastern Europe or the Middle or Far East. The second is that, while western democracy and Communism are in many respects opposed, they have much to learn from each other – Communism in the working of political institutions and in the establishment of individual rights, western democracy in the development of economic and social planning.[10]

The Labour Government, too, was unenthusiastic. Bevin, in particular, eventually asked in Cabinet for agreement to outright dissociation from the Fulton speech. Attlee, however, was prepared to go no further than pointedly to abstain from endorsing it. The following exchanges took place at question time in the House of Commons on 11 March:

Mr [William] Warbey: Would my right hon. Friend make it clear that His Majesty's Government entirely disapprove of the tone and temper of the speech of the right hon. Gentleman the Member for Woodford [Mr Churchill]?
The Prime Minister: His Majesty's Government are not called upon to express any opinion of a speech delivered in another country by a private individual. The policy of His Majesty's Government has been laid down perfectly plainly in the House by the Foreign Secretary.
Mr [T. E. N.] Driberg: The Leader of His Majesty's Opposition surely has something more than the status of an ordinary private citizen? Will my right hon. Friend not explicitly repudiate the dangerous doctrine contained in the speech?[11]

Many Labour backbenchers were more outspoken than Attlee. A motion was tabled in the following terms:

... this House considers that proposals for a military alliance between the British Commonwealth and the USA for the purpose of combating the spread of Communism, such as were put forward in a speech at Fulton ... are calculated to do injury to good relations between Great Britain, USA and the USSR, and are inimical to the cause of world peace; and affirms its view that world peace and security can be maintained, not by sectional alliances, but by progressively strengthening the power and authority of UNO to the point where it becomes capable of exercising, in respect to world law, order and justice, the functions of a world government.

Among the signatories was the future Prime Minister, James Callaghan.[12]

Eden's public response to the Fulton speech was a studied silence. But in private he was critical of his leader and, as so often, sympathized with Bevin. Moreover, he had apparently received inadequate advance warning of Churchill's intentions. On the eve of the Fulton speech, for example, he had taken part in a foreign affairs debate in the House of Commons and had felt obliged to reply to references by John McGovern to

rumours ... that ... Mr Churchill ... is making a sensational speech in America tonight. In that speech, according to those who claim to know, he is to put Russia 'on the spot' and the attempt is to be made to draw up a closer union between the United States and this country ... for the national defence of those countries.

Eden retorted:

The hon. Gentleman said that ... Mr Churchill was going to make a speech this evening, in which he was going to put Russia on the spot. I do not know where he got that information. I certainly have not heard anything of the kind from my right hon. Friend, and, may I add, I do not believe it for one single moment. If the hon. Gentleman will cast his mind back to the speech which the right hon. Gentleman the Member for Woodford made on the night when Russia was attacked and to a number of other speeches, and to events since, he would know that there is nothing in which my right hon. Friend is more sincere – and I think I can claim to know him in these matters – than in his regard for good relations with the Soviet Union.[13]

That Eden actually disagreed with Churchill is apparent, however, from a letter written on 14 March by Cranborne to Emrys-Evans. Both Eden and Cranborne differed from their chief on largely tactical grounds, whereas during the war they had at times been more fundamentally at odds with him. But in British politics disagreements about tactics may generate as much heat as the most far-reaching divergences of view about fundamentals. In the case of Fulton Eden was apparently anxious about the effect on the prospects for forging a western pact in Europe, whereas Cranborne feared that Labour backbenchers would so object to Churchill's extreme anti-Soviet tone as to make it more difficult for Bevin to express his more measured criticisms of Moscow.[14]

The Fulton affair seems to have inaugurated a sustained period of intrigue within the Conservative Party about the future of Churchill's leadership. Some members of the Shadow Cabinet urged that he should simply retire; others hoped to ease him out by persuading him to share the leadership for a period with Eden. But what if Churchill refused to agree to either of these courses? In the absence of any formal constitutional machinery for leadership elections, how could he be coerced? Probably nothing short of a public resolution signed by the majority of his colleagues would have sufficed. In the event no such drastic step was to be taken. Eden, as the only possible successor to Churchill, was placed in a difficult position. He clearly hoped to take over but, as in 1942, vacillated between loyalty and disloyalty. On the one hand, he undoubtedly gave private encouragement to the anti-Churchill manoeuvres of friends such as Cranborne and Thomas. On the other hand, he held back from an outright declaration of war on his chief, preferring not to associate himself openly with the critics. Instead he had periodic private encounters with Churchill during which he seems to have hoped that his charm would work where the half-hearted intrigues had failed. Such methods were entirely inappropriate as a means of dealing with a man of Churchill's robust character. He had but little difficulty in riding out the rebellion. At the same time, such respect as he felt for Eden can only have been diminished by his approach, which was close to being that of willing to wound, but afraid to strike. Churchill's retention of the party leadership until 1955 may even have been deliberately prolonged, at least in part, in revenge for Eden's conduct in the immediate post-war phase.

Churchill's initial response to the intrigues against him was to offer to discuss a division of functions with Eden. But Eden found this unattractive, for he was under no illusion that his chief would actually yield any powers that he wished to retain or that he would hand over the premiership if the Conservatives should win a General Election. Thomas, now Vice-Chairman of the Conservative Party and still close to Eden, wrote to Emrys-Evans on 26 March 1946:

(1) Boss [Churchill] is horrified at the thought of leading daily the House of Commons and is prepared to give it up at Easter to A. [Eden].
(2) Fully intends to go on leading the Party for a year or two!! He says he still has much to offer while A. establishes his position.
(3) He intends to lead an anti-Communist campaign
and
(4) an anti-capitulation Indian campaign so we are back to 1930–33.

Evidently referring to Churchill's plan to offer to Eden leadership functions in the Commons without yielding the party leadership, Thomas wrote: 'A. [Eden] today is quite firm that he will not accept one without the other as there is no sign of a fixed date of retirement.'[15] By 22 April Thomas recorded that Eden had been to see Churchill: 'Anthony went in calm but determined mood. The old 'un is not pleased with him and is snooty.' Later the same source reported: 'Position bad. Winston grasping anything and A. [Eden] more and more disgusted. But W. [Churchill] looks ill'; and then later still: 'Anthony is no further with Winston who has mercifully not mentioned the division of the leadership again. Anyhow A. is disinclined to say yes. I hear that he [Churchill] said "All my most intimate friends recommend retirement and I will fight the lot till the bitter end and challenge them to sack me".'[16]

Eden's own sense of frustration and indecision was made clear on 8 August 1946 in a letter to Halifax, now a Conservative elder statesman:

I am to spend a night with Winston about 20th [August] to decide our plans. He still wants me to take over Leader of Opposition [in the Commons, but not of the Party] in the autumn (unless he has changed his mind again). I am reluctant for many obvious reasons. On the other hand if I have to argue with him I am better placed to do so if I have some official status and you can guess the present position – where one still has to argue! – is not too comfortable either. At the moment he is in the mood to proclaim, as he did last time we discussed the business, that he would lead us at the next General Election.

I have been asked by Chiang to pay a visit to Nanking and I am tempted to accept, to go on to Malcolm [MacDonald, the Governor-General of Malaya, Singapore and British Borneo] and to Australia, leaving in October and being away two months. This would enable Winston to announce at Blackpool [at the Conservative Party Conference] that I would take the leadership of the opposition [in the Commons] on my return. He may not agree to all this, but it might be a good plan for we should then not overlap so much. He could go abroad after Christmas as I am sure that the doctor will insist, though at the moment Winston says he won't.

All this is very disjointed, but I set it down in the hope that you may be moved to comment.

The whole business is so exhausting that one is seriously tempted to accept pleasant city tasks that would allow one a leisured life with headquarters here [Binderton]. Winston is like a porpoise in the bath and one of uncertain moods.

Nothing came in the event of the plan for a formal division of functions. By 16 October Bracken reported to Beaverbrook that 'Winston is in very good fettle and determined to continue to lead the Tory Party until he becomes Prime Minister on earth or Minister of Defence in Heaven!'[17]

The Conservative Party's divisions were not only about Churchill's continued tenure of the leadership and Fulton. For as the full measure of the 1945 landslide was appreciated and as the range of Socialist measures unfolded, Conservatives were naturally uncertain whether stoutly to resist the apparent national mood – reaffirmed in disappointing by-election results for the Opposition – or whether themselves to move towards a more social democratic stance. Eden showed curiously little appetite for striking attitudes on either side of this debate. Given his wartime sympathy for the left and his contemplation of a political realignment in which he and Bevin would find themselves in the same team, he might have been expected to be a Conservative extreme left-winger in the immediate post-war phase – and the more so as Churchill would probably have been on the other side of the argument. He may have realized, however, that the sheer size of the Labour majority made realignment or coalition improbable for a number of years. Whatever the truth of this may be, he was content to allow others, notably Macmillan and Butler, to outflank him to the left on domestic issues.

The first ploy of the Conservative left in the spring of 1946 was to clamour for the formulation of a positive policy statement. Churchill preferred, however, that the Conservatives should lie low and avoid commitments. Eden initially supported him, saying that he was against an 'industrial policy which can be summed up in one word or even one phrase'. He further asserted that Conservatism was 'neither a watered-down form of Socialism, nor is it a doctrinaire opposition to Socialism'.[18] But by October 1946, when the Conservative Party Conference assembled at Blackpool, pressure for a policy statement was so intense that Eden, together with Oliver Stanley, persuaded their chief that some concession was necessary. Churchill accordingly proposed that a statement be prepared – but he was studiously vague at that stage about its scope. The outcome was a rather narrowly-based document, entitled *The Industrial Charter*, which was published in May 1947 and which was in large part the work of Butler. Eden blunted its impact, however, by dutifully stressing Churchill's thesis that it was not intended to be 'a detailed programme'.[19]

Even less successful than Butler in his left-wing agitation was Macmillan. As we have seen, he had wanted in 1938, according to Dalton, 'a 1931 in reverse' and the suspicion must be that in the immediate post-war years he remained in favour of a social democratic realignment. But, if so, he misread both the mood of the Conservative Party and the degree of underlying unity which prevailed on the Labour benches. His wildest excess was to propose on the eve of the Conservative Party Conference of 1946 that his own party should change its name – a tactic adopted thirteen years later by some Gaitskellite Labour MPs after their party's severe defeat in the 1959 General Election, ironically at the hands of Macmillan. The Conservative Party in conference in 1946 was as unimpressed as the Labour Party in 1959. Bracken wrote a right-winger's appreciation of the 1946 Conference to Beaverbrook:

The Tory Conference is over. It was an interesting affair.

The neo Socialists, like Harold Macmillan, who are in favour of nationalizing railways, electricity, gas and many other things, expected to get great support from the delegates who are supposed to be greatly frustrated by the result of the General Election and successive by-elections.

Rab Butler and the other moles engaged in research to produce a 'modern' policy for the Tory Party believed that Blackpool would be a paradise for the progressives.

It turned out that the neo Socialists were lucky to escape with their scalps. The delegates would have nothing to do with the proposal to change the Party's name. They demanded a real Conservative policy instead of a synthetic Socialist one so dear to the heart of the Macmillans and the Butlers, and it gave Churchill one of the greatest receptions of his life.[20]

Eden was enough of a politician to rejoice at the discomfiture of Macmillan. Thomas wrote to Emrys-Evans: 'Harold – you are right – is speaking too much and has blotted his copybook – to A.E.'s great delight! – by renaming the party and there is fury among the colleagues.'[21] Eden could also reflect with satisfaction that his own middle-of-the-road speech to the Conference in favour of a 'nation-wide property-owning democracy' had been well received.[22]

If Eden kept fairly well in step with his chief on domestic policy at this stage, he continued to be, for whatever reason, much less alarmist than Churchill in his statements about the deteriorating relationship with the Soviet Union. On 22 September, for example, Bracken wrote to Beaverbrook: 'Eden has been showing W.S.C. a speech on foreign affairs which he is to fire off tonight. It has infuriated our friend who calls it "lousy and Wallacey".'[23] (A reference to the pro-Soviet Henry Wallace, who had just been compelled to resign from his post as Secretary of Commerce in Truman's Administration.) In the speech, delivered at Watford, Eden revealed a naïve appreciation of the rôle of ideology in Soviet policy and even of the nature of Communist ideology; and appeared to believe that exhortations to Stalin were still worthwhile:

In three great conflicts the Russian and British people have been allies. After two of them we fell away with unhappy consequences for mankind. We do not want that to happen again; yet it is happening now before our eyes with no benefit to anyone. Let us see if we can make any constructive contribution to mend this state of affairs ... I am sure that the overwhelming majority of the people of this country has desired and still desires the most friendly relations with the Soviet Union. Nobody who knows the British people should doubt that for a moment. We have not forgotten, we never can forget, Russia's glorious contribution to the common victory. We know how heavy were her losses in men and material. We have a Twenty Year Treaty of Alliance with the Soviet Union. We have expressed a willingness to prolong that Treaty. We want to work with the Soviet Union, as with our other allies, in peace as in war.

If our Soviet Allies are building their foreign policy on any other premises than our friendship, as I fear that they now are, then they are building on a false reading of the facts. The British people are not fickle friends. But there is only one foundation for enduring friendship in international as in domestic affairs, and that is sincere cooperation based on mutual understanding. Can Soviet statesmen truly feel in their hearts that they have been acting in that spirit recently towards ourselves and towards our allies? ... Nobody in this country contests for an instant the right of the Soviet Union to any form of government she likes. We prefer our own, but the fact that Russian soldiers are Communist does not cause us to value any the less their magnificent fighting qualities or to forget that they played their full part in tearing the guts out of the German Army. There is no reason why two ideologies should not live together in peace if both will accept not to back their fancies in every other land. Restraint may be difficult to practise, but surely this is not too much to ask as the price for enduring peace. If we found it possible in war, in order that we might defeat a common enemy, to relegate ideological differences to a secondary position, why cannot we make a like contribution in order to secure an enduring peace? ...

Surely it must be plain to all that we cannot continue as we are now without consequences which may be fatal to all. What is required is a new spirit and a new approach.

Eden also offered some detailed criticisms of Soviet actions, particularly in the Balkans, but he blunted the force even of his limited assault on Moscow by offering a balancing criticism of the Americans for recent unfriendly references to 'British Imperialism'.[24] A few days later Eden noted that Stalin had made a conciliatory speech. This he eagerly proclaimed 'a new opportunity, which we all welcome, for allied diplomacy'.[25]

If Eden remained something of a 'dove' vis-à-vis Moscow, there was one foreign policy issue at this time that provoked in him an almost jingoistic response. This concerned Egypt. On 24 May 1946 he for once revealed a measure of disagreement with Bevin, who had undertaken to attempt to renegotiate the Anglo-Egyptian Treaty of 1936. With all the pride of paternity Eden insisted in the House of Commons that the Treaty must be maintained at its essential point, namely British rights relating to the Suez Canal. These he compared with Soviet rights to bases in Finland and to the American position with respect to the Panama Canal.[26] Privately he wrote to Halifax that the Government had blundered: reliance on Palestine as an alternative regional base was politically impossible, apart from being strategically inferior to Benghazi.[27] As it happened, the 1946 crisis in Anglo-Egyptian affairs was temporarily defused by a British withdrawal from the wartime occupation of Cairo – to which Eden had no objection – no definitive re-negotiation of the 1936 Treaty proving possible.[28] But a biographer of Eden cannot fail to be struck by the firm tone of his 1946 views on Egypt which differed so little from those of a decade later: rigid attachment to the sanctity of treaty rights and a conscious proclamation of Great Britain's equal status with the Soviet Union and the United States in the matter of vital strategic interests overseas. If such assumptions were not anachronistic in 1946, they had certainly become so by 1956, but Eden seems only dimly to have grasped the extent to which his country's position was changing in the post-war world.

The end of 1946 and the beginning of 1947 brought more unhappiness for Eden: his wife deserted him and the attempts to oust Churchill petered out. His parting from Beatrice came during an extensive tour of the New World. Both went to the United States but she chose to remain permanently in New York. Eden went on alone to Barbados, to Trinidad and to Brazil. The development was not only disturbing on a personal level but was also, in the pre-permissive era, a potential blow to his career. Though many adulterers had hitherto been Prime Minister, no divorcee, even a so-called 'innocent party', had reached Number Ten. For Eden the dilemma was painful: should he remain merely separated or should he seek a divorce that would enable him to remarry? Fortunately for him by the 1950s the climate had changed sufficiently for a politician to be divorced and to remarry without drastic repercussions. The same, however, did not apply to royalty. While Eden was serving as the country's first divorced Prime Minister, Princess Margaret was compelled to renounce Peter Townsend!

The agitation against Churchill's leadership revived during the first part of 1947 but was doomed to fail. According to the Chief Whip, James Stuart, eight leading Conservatives, not including Eden, met at Harry Crookshank's house in Pont Street and asked Stuart to convey to Churchill their view that he should quit. This the Chief Whip did, but Churchill 'reacted violently banging the floor with his stick and implying that I too had joined those who were trying to displace him'.[29] On another occasion in 1947 plotting took a different form. The hope of some Conservatives was now to persuade Bevin to head a Coalition Government, thereby by-passing Churchill. Dixon, Bevin's Private Secretary, wrote in his diary: 'I don't believe A.E. is in this.'[30]

Eden's caution and the silence of some other colleagues may have improved Churchill's chance of survival. Cranborne at least believed Eden's lack of decisiveness to be of crucial importance. He wrote to Emrys-Evans lamenting that Eden's grumbling to his friends would achieve nothing unless he himself was prepared to face up to the disagreeable task of giving a lead against Churchill and involving all leading colleagues.[31] Evidently he thought that willpower on Eden's part was all that was needed. But Cranborne may have over-estimated the strength of Eden's hand. Macmillan's memoirs reveal that his assessment was not universally shared in the Conservative Party: 'Any attempt to remove a man whom the whole nation knew to be the greatest Englishman of this or perhaps of any time would have been deeply resented by the country and proved fatal to the party's hopes.'[32] Against so unorthodox and determined a fighter as Churchill, Eden may indeed have been wise to behave in the last resort with prudence. But, if so, it might have been expedient for him to have shown more positive loyalty to his chief. His half-threatening attitude, following that manifested in 1942, must have been apparent to Churchill and can have done little to smooth the path for future cooperation.

Differences between the two men in fact continued to multiply. Early in

1947, for example, Eden saw little merit in Churchill's decision to found a 'non-party' United Europe Movement. David Maxwell Fyfe (later Lord Kilmuir), Macmillan and Stanley were among leading Conservatives to be nominated to serve on this body, from which Eden ostentatiously remained aloof. This was the beginning of a conflict in Conservative politics destined to have repercussions for many years. The argument was not whether Europe should be federal or confederal, or whether Great Britain should abandon old associations for an exclusively European future; the essential question was merely whether the Conservatives should seek to appear more 'advanced' than the Labour Party's leaders in European matters. Bevin was neither able nor willing to employ rhetoric designed to pander to the visionary European pressure groups. His problem was to carry with him the bulk of the Labour Party for more immediately vital and practical policies – a course which duly facilitated the signing of the Anglo-French Treaty of Dunkirk, the successful implementation of the Marshall Plan and the formation of the North Atlantic Treaty Organization (NATO). Eden, recognizing Bevin's problems with some of his own isolationist, neutralist, anti-capitalist and anti-American followers, did not wish to complicate the Foreign Secretary's task by urging European declarations that would be even more unpalatable to much of Labour's rank-and-file.

Eden also strove throughout 1947 to keep in line with Bevin on the subject of the Soviet Union. During the first half of the year the atmosphere steadily worsened and it may be claimed that the Cold War really began at this time. Many critics of American policy have blamed Truman for this development, arguing that the so-called Truman Doctrine, enunciated in March, was an unprovoked denunciation of Stalin, who had hitherto stood by the tacit power political bargains struck during the war. In fact the American move was intended to bolster up the seemingly threatened countries of Turkey and Greece, neither of which in the wartime discussions had been allocated to the Soviet Union either for military liberation or as a longer-term Soviet sphere of political influence. Moreover, there had emerged growing evidence of Soviet bad faith even before Truman's démarche of March 1947. True, not all of it was of an unambiguous character. For example, some in the West made much of the failure to hold the promised free elections in Poland. Yet Poland had at times been tacitly recognized by the wartime leaders as tied to enforced friendship with Moscow. Similar arguments applied to Romania and Bulgaria. Equally controversial were developments in Yugoslavia, Greece and Iran, for in none of these countries was Stalin's control over left-wing revolutionary forces incontestably evident. But one unambiguous case of Soviet bad faith *before* the enunciation of the Truman Doctrine concerned Hungary. In the percentage discussion between Churchill and Stalin in 1944 a fifty-fifty share of influence had been suggested; and after the war, in contrast to the cases of Romania, Bulgaria and Poland, free elections had duly been held. But at the beginning of 1947 the Hungarian Communists, who had won only 16 per cent of the popular vote, set out, with the obvious support and knowledge of the occupying Red Army, to Bolshevize the country. Above all, it is clear that Mátyás Rákosi, the Communist leader, was no Tito, able and willing to act without Stalin's approval.

The drama in Hungary began on 20 January 1947 with the arrest by authority of the Red Army of Béla Kovács, General Secretary of the Smallholders' Party, and of seven others among the party's Members of Parliament. All were eventually charged – after delays relating to parliamentary immunity – with complicity in a plot against the Government. The Government was a coalition in which the Smallholders understandably held a majority of posts as they had won 57 per cent of the popular vote in the General Election. By early June the Smallholder Prime Minister, Ferenc Nagy, had sought asylum in Switzerland, agreeing to resign in return for his child being allowed to join him in exile. Within a year the cowed remnants of the Smallholders and the Social Democrats had effectively handed over all power to the Communists. The discovery of the 'plot' of January 1947 thus marked the beginning of a deliberate Soviet plan to break wartime understandings about the future of Hungary. The whole drama was of course played out under the supervision of the Red Army – a presence that rendered any attempt at a right-wing coup too implausible to take seriously. Rákosi himself showed his hand as early as 20 January when he made it clear that he did not wish to see the issue of the 'plot' tested in a new General Election. *The Times* reported:

Speaking at a weekend Communist and Socialist demonstration M. Rákosi ... said that the plot had ramifications throughout the country's economic and political life: it had supporters in the army and also abroad. The plotters wanted, in the first place, to make use of the Smallholders Party, and the peasants could now see what sort of people were in control of the party that had represented them. The two workers' parties were quite ready to go on cooperating with the democratic wing of the Smallholders' Party, but anyone who had any part in the plot must disappear from public life. The argument that there would be no stability in Hungary until general and secret elections had been held must be changed now to the argument that there would be no calm until the last remnants of revolutionary reaction had been uprooted.[33]

These developments were noted with alarm by American diplomats and they undoubtedly did much to discredit the supporters of Wallace.[34]

In London, however, the Labour Government did not react with any equivalent to the Truman Doctrine or with the kind of vigorous rhetoric that had become commonplace by the time of the Korean War. In this restraint they had the support of Eden. While many will be tempted retrospectively to criticize the 'new appeasers' and to make unfavourable comparisons with the more robust Churchill, it is necessary to remember that Bevin had to carry with him party supporters and a general public who only eighteen months earlier had emerged from years of hearing one-sided official wartime propaganda in favour of 'Uncle Joe' and 'our gallant Soviet allies'. Certainly pro-Soviet sympathies at the beginning of 1947 were by no means confined to the ranks of the extreme left. We may consider, for example, Denis Healey, then Head of the Labour Party's International Department. According to his biographers, he had joined the Labour Party in 1937 and had joined the Communist Party 'soon after the beginning of the Spanish Civil War'. Having left the Communist Party in 1940, he was now at the age of twenty-nine a moderate ally of Bevin in handling the Labour Party National Executive Committee's approach to foreign policy.[35] He had visited Budapest as a Labour Party representative at the Hungarian Social Democratic Party Conference, 1–3 February 1947, just a week after the arrest of the prominent Smallholders. On his return he wrote about his visit in *Tribune*. He appears to have had no doubts about the existence of 'the plot which the Communists brought to light a month ago' and which had 'intensified the Government crisis'. His criticism was directed at the Smallholders: 'Had the Smallholders' leaders acted with greater resolution, they might have seized the initiative and prevented the Communists from turning the plot to their own advantage.' He foresaw the possibility of some realignment within the Government Coalition in which the Smallholders would lose their majority stake:

... in fact a coalition of the Left Bloc [the Communists and Social Democrats] with the Left-wing Smallholders, leaving the rest of the Smallholders in opposition, however unwelcome to some of Horthy's friends in the West, would be no more undemocratic in principle than Britain's National Government in 1931.

Notwithstanding the presence of the Soviet Red Army, he evidently took seriously Communist talk about the risk of 'counter-revolution' in Hungary:

The Hungarian 'White Terror' of 1919 and the recent example of reaction in power in Greece, have probably exaggerated Hungarian Left-Wing fears of counter-revolution. But in a country like Hungary, which has just emerged from 25 years of dictatorship, the existence of reactionary conspiracies is more than probable. The danger, above all, preserves the present unity of action between the Socialist and Communist parties.

He saw only an unhappy future awaiting the Smallholders but not for reasons related to Soviet designs:

The Smallholder Party is unlikely to survive for long. With the achievement of the land reform its *raison d'être* has largely disappeared. Its leaders are undistinguished, its supporters heterogeneous; it lacks a political dynamic ... Mindzenthy, the

Primate, is lying low at the moment, but his influence is universally felt and he may hope to become the Seipel of Hungarian clerical reaction. In many ways the conditions for this are more favourable in Hungary today than they were in Austria in 1918.[36]

If such naïve views could be expressed by a leading Transport House official, was this a climate in which Bevin could be expected overnight to denounce Soviet conduct unequivocally? If not, Eden, too, given his assumptions about bipartisanship, was bound to tread no less carefully.

Only on 7 June 1947 did Eden venture to speak out strongly about Hungary. After expressing 'grave concern' about the fate of Kovács and Nagy, he continued: 'The action recently taken by the Soviet authorities results from attempts on the part of the Communist minority to undermine and overthrow the majority party.' But he blunted the force of his remarks by continuing:

There is another aspect of Anglo-Soviet relations to which I must refer. We are all glad to hear the account recently given . . . of the opening of trade negotiations with Russia, and we wish every success to these negotiations. There is no reason to lose all hope of success on account of political difficulties alone. On the contrary, economic progress is one of the surest remedies for political aches and pains.[37]

Five days later Hector McNeil, the Minister of State at the Foreign Office, made a Government statement on Hungary in the House of Commons. He concentrated his criticism of the Soviets on Molotov's refusal to answer British questions about the situation there as being contrary to wartime engagements:

His Majesty's Government regret our Ally's response to our inquiries. For it was because His Majesty's Government desired to avoid possible misunderstanding, that information was sought. We made no accusations against our Ally. We were asking for information of what was happening in Hungary in order that His Majesty's Government might form a just and accurate opinion on the position . . . Because we are co-signatories of the Armistice Agreement, and because also of our Treaty of Friendship with the Soviet Government, we shall continue to press both our Ally and the Hungarian Government for the full information on developments in Hungary, to which we are entitled.

Eden replied: 'I think that the House will have heard the statement . . . with concern and with regret, but also, I think, with general approval of its tenor.' The minuet ended when McNeil responded: 'I must compliment the right hon. Gentleman upon the restrained manner in which he has addressed himself to this matter.' It is of some interest that the Government's restraint, faithfully followed by Eden, had been urged upon them by Healey on 5 June following another visit to Hungary. He had written to Christopher Mayhew, Parliamentary Under-Secretary at the Foreign Office:

In general unless there is an imperative cause for joint intervention, I think it might be a good opportunity to distinguish our attitude to the Hungarian crisis very sharply from that of the Americans. The main fear among genuine Socialists in Eastern Europe since the Truman doctrine is that the Americans will pursue a clumsy, heavy handed and indiscriminate campaign against the new regimes in Eastern Europe which will intensify polarizations of opinion in those countries and drive the Communists to more and more extreme measures. Even if this type of campaign were successful, it could only lead to a counter-revolutionary white terror in which the Socialists would go down with the Communists. I think that by showing more discretion and understanding in such matters we can do a great deal to destroy the Communist-fostered impression that we are simply junior partners in a world offensive of dollar imperialism.[38]

On 19 June Eden spoke out a little more forcefully:

... I believe – this is my forecast – that we now see in Hungary all the usual Communist preparations for rigged elections. I hope I may be proved wrong ... I do not believe that in the long run we do any good to Anglo-Soviet relations if we pretend to accept replies which, in our heart of hearts, we find it impossible to believe ... for those of us who do really want to see Anglo-American-Soviet friendship, it really would be hypocritical to pretend that confidence is unshaken or that good relations are unimpaired ... I know something of the terrible price Russia paid in life for the Allied victory, and there is in our minds always – and it is true today that there still is – an immense fund of good will in this country towards the Soviet Union, but that good will can now be evoked only on the basis of sincere partnership and mutual respect.[39]

If both Eden and Bevin still talked more in sadness than in anger about their Soviet 'allies', they were no less in agreement in giving a positive welcome to increased American involvement in European affairs. On 15 May, referring to Truman's offer of aid to Greece and Turkey, Eden told the House of Commons:

This policy spells the end of isolation – and is there anyone who is not fervently relieved to see such a development? As for the reactions ... upon our other Allies, I submit to the House that it is a profound delusion to suppose that by getting further away from the United States one necessarily gets any closer to the Soviet Union.[40]

Even more warmly welcomed by Eden and Bevin was the Marshall Plan for bringing economic aid to Europe. For this initiative, embodied in a speech given on 5 June at Harvard University by the American Secretary of State, was shrewdly worded so as not in theory to exclude eastern European countries from the proposed benefits, though the realities of power politics meant that in practice only countries outside the Soviet sphere would be able to accept. Consequently Eden and Bevin could strongly support the American move without having to advance an anti-Soviet justification and they found it easier to avoid alienating much of the Labour Party and parts of a wider public. On 19 June Eden spoke out: 'That momentous offer by the

United States Secretary of State, made in his Harvard speech, has brought new hope to Europe and the world. It is, indeed a generous action, and one which deserves to rank with "the most unsordid act in history".'[41] And on 5 July, after the expected Soviet hostility to the Marshall Plan had materialized, he made this appeal in a speech at Leeds:

> In these circumstances the duty of our statesmen is clear. They must go straight ahead in collaboration with our French friends and all the other nations who are willing to come in and make a plan in response to Mr Marshall's historic offer. The essential is that the response to the offer should not be delayed.[42]

Nor was there delay. Bevin and the Foreign Office seized their chance to bring the United States into the centre of the fight for the future of Europe and did so with such skill that the maximum embarrassment to Moscow was caused. There is indeed much to be said in justification of the Bevin–Eden line as it had evolved since the end of the war. If anti-Sovietism had been adopted more rapidly and more stridently, as Churchill appeared to desire, the results might have been counter-productive. Moreover, Bevin and Eden were helped to a great extent by the actions of the Soviets. If Stalin and Molotov had been prepared to allow their intentions and attitudes to become known more slowly and had not wantonly thrown away the goodwill felt by a beguiled public in many Western countries, they might well have been faced with a vulnerable western Europe by the 1950s. None of this, however, exonerates Eden from his share of responsibility for the handing over of half of Europe to Communism. But such responsibility as he had lay in the period 1938–43 and was in any case shared to a large degree by Churchill. By the end of the war there was no way in which Great Britain alone could undo the consequences of those earlier decisions to make Fascism the sole enemy. Hence it might be contended that Eden played out the hand he had dealt himself with more dignity than Churchill. For Eden's method of trying to save what could be saved for Western Democracy between 1945 and 1947 was probably more thoughtful and more effective than that favoured by his flamboyant and self-centred chief. Churchill no doubt hoped that his Fulton speech would enable him to pose at the bar of history as being as sound an anti-Fascist as Eden and as sound an anti-Bolshevik as Neville Chamberlain. But British power had been too limited for that to be possible, as Churchill himself had shown in his dealings with Stalin during the last year of the war. Fulton came much too late: Churchill, no less than Eden, had contributed significantly to the spread of Communism in Europe and mere speeches as late as 1946 could not undo the earlier deeds. The relevant question for Churchill and Eden in the immediate aftermath of the Second World War was not how by irresponsible posturing they could cover up that responsibility but how best and how quickly any further spread of Soviet control could now be resisted. Judged by this test,

Eden's conduct in loyally supporting Bevin may seem more meritorious than that of Churchill.

Eden's differences with Churchill led him to give only half-hearted attention to day-to-day affairs at Westminster. If his chief was determined to be a part-timer, spending much of his time in travel and writing history, Eden was no less resolved not to do his job for him. Hence in the last years of Attlee's first term he became increasingly tempted to undertake diverting foreign visits of his own. These were, moreover, rather sad and lonely years, with his wife still in the United States. And an unusual number of unpleasant incidents occurred at this time. For example, in June 1947 he was sent, from Italy, a letter bomb, which Scotland Yard successfully intercepted. In August he was slightly injured in a car accident. Then, in mid-March 1948, he underwent an operation for appendicitis. December 1947 saw the death of his mentor, Baldwin, whose reputation was then at its nadir. Eden was obliged to pay a Commons tribute to him but ungraciously made no reference at all to his foreign policy, speaking vaguely of his rôle as an industrial peacemaker.[43] There is added piquancy in his silence on the foreign policy aspect given that he had a deserved reputation for never passing up even half a chance to switch from domestic to international matters in his speeches. Certainly as a tribute it was strikingly less courageous and less noble than Churchill's famous oration on Neville Chamberlain.

All these tribulations for Eden were interspersed with travel. In January 1948 he visited the Middle East accompanied by his surviving son, Nicholas. He concentrated on Saudi Arabia, Bahrein and, above all, Iran, which had of course been an area of particular cultural as well as political interest to him since his Oxford days. Among Iranians he made a striking impression by speaking their language. In Ryadh he was a guest of King Ibn Saud who at the end of the visit presented him with a gold watch and a jewelled dagger. Eden unwisely asked the King what he could get for him in return. As a result he was obliged to spend 200 guineas on a sporting gun.[44] In early March he was travelling again: to France as leader of a Parliamentary delegation.

May 1948 saw Eden in The Hague – at a Congress of the European Movements of various countries. This represented a compromise with Churchill and a marginal divergence from Bevin. For the Labour Party's National Executive Committee, with the tacit support of the Foreign Secretary, regretted the convening of this Congress and spoke of the danger that the concept of European unity 'might be corrupted in the hands of reaction'. Plainly most Labour MPs were either isolationist or believed in utopian nostrums about a socialist United States of Europe. If Eden's presence in The Hague was in these circumstances surprising, he took care not to show enthusiasm. His approach to the European issue at this time is evident from a speech made on 30 April, which he later failed to re-publish in the relevant volume of his collected speeches:

Any form of international organization [*The Times* reported], said Mr Eden, must involve some merger of sovereignty, and the same was true of any military plans made jointly by several powers. The conception of a merger of sovereignty did not alarm him, but it should be recognized that it was impossible to build a united Europe or western union without the nations concerned merging in a larger authority certain individual attributes ... The practical difficulties could not be ignored. The most formidable in the public mind was that the first consideration of the United Kingdom must always be the welfare of the Commonwealth ...

He was convinced that there was no fundamental clash between the conception of Britain as the centre of the Commonwealth and as a member of a Western European union; any dilemma was largely artificial.[45]

If Eden remained vague about Europe, he became steadily more precise during 1948 and 1949 about the Soviet Union and Communism. On 6 May 1948, for example, he began to focus on the ideological aspect of Soviet policy. As have been seen, he had earlier maintained that there was no unavoidable conflict between the Western and Soviet ways of life. Now he spoke of the Soviet doctrine about the 'inevitability of war'. And he touched also on the fact that it had 'always been part of the Communist ideology that what they call the capitalist world ... is tottering to its fall'. He found it hard to believe that the men in the Kremlin could really believe that but he nevertheless had to ask himself whether it might be so. By early October, at the Conservative Party Conference, he went so far as to say:

Over a large part of Europe hangs an iron curtain. Behind it Communism rules. In some other lands Communism challenges the authority of the free parties. To me, and no doubt to this Conference, the whole Communist creed is utterly abhorrent and odious. It is ruthless, soulless and without mercy. I hate Communism for its materialism and I hate it for its intolerance, because tolerance and not material gain is surely the hallmark of civilization. But it is not enough to say that we hate Communism. We have to recognize that those who hold that creed, hold it with a fervour that is almost religious. If we are to defeat them we must, therefore, believe just as fervently in our faith and in ourselves.

Later in the same month he referred to 'the problem of the hidden army, the fifth column, the Communist parties, controlled by Moscow, bent on sabotaging economic recovery in the remaining free countries of the world'. He wanted all to close their ranks 'against those fifth columns wherever they appeared, in the field of industry or politics'.[46] On 26 October he told the House of Commons that 'it seems clear enough that the objective now being followed by the Kremlin is what used to be called the Trotskyite principle of world Communism'.[47]

That Eden's speeches on the Soviet Union had become so much more robust no doubt owed much to the changed climate of opinion. Following the subversion of Hungary, Czechoslovakia had slid into Communism in March 1948 and the blockade of West Berlin had followed. Nor was the struggle confined to Europe. In Malaya a Communist insurgency began and in China chaos was serving as a prelude to the Communist takeover in the following year. In the face of these developments both Bevin and Eden became tougher and only the boldest of Communists and their sympathizers continued to offer universal excuses and justification. For example, Healey, author, as has been seen, of a startlingly naïve or fellow-travelling piece on Hungary in 1947, penned in April 1948 a no less extreme denunciation of the Communists. Writing in Chatham House's journal, *International Affairs*, he referred to the nucleus of every Communist Party as having an 'inhuman character' and as being 'a secret army of intelligent and courageous robots, a religious society without God'. Whereas in 1947 he had discerned favourable conditions in Hungary for the success of 'clerical reaction', he now saw in retrospect the importance of the Red Army throughout eastern Europe:

> In Eastern Europe the Communist policy was to obtain, through National Front governments, the assistance of non-Communists in building the machinery of a State. Then when an adequate administrative apparatus was in operation, and they had consolidated their control of the police and the armed forces, the Communists eliminated each of their allies in turn – the bourgeois parties by suppression, the Socialists by fusion ... The initial presence of the Red Army, or the active intervention of Soviet representatives, was an essential element in Communist success in every country in Eastern Europe, except perhaps Yugoslavia, where from the outset the Communists possessed a large army and police force of their own.[48]

Perhaps Healey's metamorphosis was so rapid and total as to be rare, even unique. Nevertheless there were many others whose views of the Soviet Union underwent at least a degree of change at this period. Hence Eden's bolder tone may be readily understood. At the same time his own private views were probably also hardening. For although he may have retained into the immediate post-war years at least some of the pro-Soviet notions, pressed upon him between 1941 and 1943 by Harvey, by mid-1948 any lingering sympathies were certainly over.

Eden's contribution was not, moreover, limited to general warnings. He gave strong encouragement to the Labour Government's practical measures to resist Communism. On Malaya he told the House of Commons on 15 September:

> Here we are faced not with terrorist gangs, as we occasionally read in the newspapers. I do not think that is an accurate description. What we are faced with is a determined Communist attempt to seize power, an attempt which is integrated with the Communist insurrection in Burma, and with Communist activities across

the border in Siam. It is all of a pattern, as I do not think the Foreign Secretary would deny, and has as its objective the overthrow of law and order throughout South-Eastern Asia – which Lenin I think once called the backdoor of the capitalist and imperialist powers – and, as a result, the complete disruption of the economy of that area. Unless the Communist attempt is successfully met and overcome at an early date, the whole security of those vast areas will be jeopardized ... For our part, we shall give unqualified support to the Government in all steps that may be necessary to quell this rebellion ...[49]

On Germany, too, he was forthright. The Berlin Airlift had his full support. And he took a lead, as befitted an architect of the wartime agreements, in urging that nothing should be allowed to prevent the economic recovery of the western zones of Germany. As early as 21 October 1947 he told the House of Commons:

The Potsdam Agreement, in my judgement, can no longer be regarded by us as having any validity in so far as it concerns the economic treatment of Germany. I say that because the basis of the Potsdam Agreement was ... that Germany should have been treated as an economic whole ... That has not been possible. It must be frankly said that the fact that it has not been possible is not the fault of His Majesty's Government ... As the result of the Soviet Government's action, we have to settle these matters now, so far as our zones in the West are concerned, on the basis of what is best for the future peace of Europe. I have no doubt that what is best is that Germany should make the fullest possible contribution to her own economic recovery, but that she should not be put into a position again to re-arm and thereby to endanger the peace of Europe. About that I think there is no disagreement.[50]

He was of course later to change his mind about German rearmament.

Throughout these years Eden rarely made any other than routine references to domestic policy. As Stuart, the Conservative Chief Whip commented:

... when we were in Opposition, Churchill suddenly asked me why I didn't like 'my Anthony'. The question no doubt arose from some criticism I had made, because at that time – as deputy Opposition leader – he was having to speak on economics, housing, fuel and the rest. I answered Winston by explaining that while Eden might be first-class at the Foreign Office, I feared that he lacked knowledge of other important matters such as I have mentioned.[51]

As has been seen, Eden sought to appear vaguely progressive but not as extreme in that respect as Macmillan or even Butler. This meant clichés about property-owning democracy. It also meant carefully worded expressions of concern about each of the frequent financial crises which culminated in the devaluation of 1949. Yet neither he nor any of his leading colleagues attempted any systematic analysis of the country's problems from a traditional Conservative economic and financial standpoint. Certainly there was no challenge to the broad social democratic and 'welfareist' ideology that had emerged from the Second World War. Even on nationalization he was cautious. On 8 June 1949, for example, he offered this not particularly ringing declaration:

A Conservative government would call a halt to further nationalization, and if steel has been nationalized by the date of the General Election they would take steps to denationalize it. Where practicable they would seek to denationalize other industries. This applied to large sections of the road transport industry.

Where it was not practicable to denationalize, they would decentralize. He did not claim that methods of decentralization were anything but a poor substitute for free enterprise 'but once the eggs have been scrambled, it is not at all easy to get them back in their shells'.[52]

In 1946 Eden, like Churchill, had shown no great enthusiasm for the drafting of a detailed policy programme. But, as has been seen, they had had to permit Butler and his friends to produce a rather limited effort, namely *The Industrial Charter* of 1947. By 1948 pressure for a new and more detailed survey was mounting. Accordingly the Shadow Cabinet established a working party and on this occasion Eden, mindful of his status in the party and of talk about his lack of experience in domestic policy matters, chose to become chairman. The outcome of the working party's endeavours was, in 1949, *The Right Road for Britain*, on which the Conservatives fought the General Election of 1950. But it is not evident that Eden played much part in shaping the document. On the contrary, the enthusiasm came from the same coterie which had produced *The Industrial Charter*. Eden was also abroad a good deal during 1948 and 1949 and so can scarcely have given the party's domestic programme his undivided attention. It seems therefore unreasonable to give Eden any special credit for *The Right Road for Britain*. In any case its vote-winning qualities, like those of other party political pamphlets, were probably less considerable than is usually supposed.

From 21 January to 31 March 1949 Eden undertook an exhausting world tour of 40,000 miles, concentrating principally on the Dominions. He was accompanied by the youthful Conservative MP, Allan Noble. He headed first for Canada. Here the main event was his challenging speech to the Toronto Board of Trade on 24 January. Again the ideological basis of Moscow's policy was accorded full recognition:

We must not underrate the challenge. We are dealing with a dynamic and fanatical ideology in which Communists believe with a fervour that is almost religious. If we are to prevail, we must match their frenzy with an even deeper devotion to the faith we hold.[53]

On 29 January Eden left Vancouver and headed via Seattle to New Zealand. By mid-February he was in Australia where he received the most enthusiastic reception of his tour. Most of his speeches were without lasting significance. But in Sydney he revealed what was to become his settled view on Europe: 'For us Empire ties must always come first, but, if by a Western Union we can help to create more settled political conditions on the European continent, that will be a contribution to the peace of the world.'[54]

An echo of problems at home came at Hobart, Tasmania, where he was bluntly asked about the Conservatives' leadership problem. According to *The Times*, 'Mr Eden was asked today at a Press conference: "In view of Mr Churchill's increasing age, is there any possibility of his being deposed as Conservative leader?" Mr Eden replied emphatically: "I am a loyal supporter of Mr Churchill and always will be."'[55] This was a tactful public answer. But at home, according to Macmillan, new efforts to oust Churchill were being made.[56] They came to nothing.

From Australia Eden slowly returned home. He first visited Singapore. Next he was in Delhi where he was invited by Pandit Nehru to address a closed session of the Indian Parliament on 23 March. His final visit was to Italy where he was received by Alcide de Gasperi and the Pope. He then made a broadcast to the Italian nation, whose *bête noire* he had for so long been.

Home again, Eden resumed the familiar round of Parliamentary duties and weekend speechmaking. With a General Election approaching and with financial and political difficulties facing Attlee, Eden now knew that Churchill could not be superseded. He must have had mixed feelings at the thought of the possibility of returning to office but once again in a subordinate rôle. Thus his enthusiasm in the last months of the 1945–50 Parliament was not noticeable. Moreover, he was beginning to pay a physical price for his years of endeavour and restlessness. On 11 June 1949 he even collapsed in public. *The Times* reported:

> Mr Eden was near the end of his speech when he fell backwards, but was caught by other people on the platform. After a few moments he attempted to continue, but had spoken only a few more words when he began to fall forward over the table. He fulfilled a public engagement at Leamington Spa later in the day.[57]

As an example of his lack of partisan spirit even on the eve of a General Election we may cite his complimentary remarks, made in the course of a speech at Bristol on 2 December 1949, on the efforts of the Trade Union Congress (TUC) to exercise restraint in wage claims:

> He had watched the recent discussion of the TUC and the efforts they were making deserved sincere respect. It must be an unpleasant task for them to have to explain to their followers the urgent need for restraint in wage demands, particularly at a time of rising prices like the present.
>
> They had to do all they could to prevent rising costs, while at the same time they were rightly concerned to preserve traditional differentials and to safeguard the position of the skilled workers. In trying to face this situation they were living up to the high traditions of British trade unionism, and if they were successful in their

efforts they would further enhance the status of the trade union movement as an essential part of our industrial life.[58]

Just over a month later Attlee announced that a General Election would take place on 23 February. Eden played a largely routine rôle in the electioneering that followed. His standard speech criticized further nationalization and called in vague terms for public expenditure cuts. Pressed for details, he showed extreme caution: the Conservatives would not, for example, abolish food subsidies. In a radio broadcast on 6 February Eden turned, probably with some relief, to talking mainly about foreign affairs.[59] But as there were no significant differences between him and Bevin, the effect on the electorate can hardly have been momentous.

The General Election of 1950 resulted in a Government victory. Eden held his own constituency, which had significantly altered boundaries, with a majority of 8,814 in a straight fight with Labour. Nationally Labour held 315 seats, the Conservatives 298, the Liberals 9 and others 3. The others consisted of two Irish Nationalists and the Speaker. Hence the Government's practical overall majority was at least six and its majority over the Conservatives was seventeen. It now seems rather surprising that this outcome was not seen as an outright Conservative defeat. But after the large majorities of 1931, 1935 and 1945, the impression was rapidly given by the media that the result was indecisive and that consequently a new General Election at an early date was inevitable. Most of the Labour leaders proved willing to endorse this assessment. This was fortunate for the Conservatives and, above all, for Churchill who was now seventy-five. On 10 January 1950 Bracken had written to Beaverbrook:

Winston is painting in Madeira. I spent a day with him before he left. He was in high spirits and seemed to be in remarkable physical health. He ardently hopes to be back in Downing Street at the beginning of spring. He says if we lose the election he will promptly retire and spend the rest of his life enjoying himself.[60]

After the February election, with universal expectations of a new contest at an early date, Churchill changed his mind about prompt retirement and renewed pressure for a change in the Conservative Party leadership did not arise. Thus Eden's hopes were again frustrated. If Attlee and his colleagues had manifested the same resolve to govern for a full Parliament as Labour Party leaders showed after the equally 'indecisive' result of October 1974, Churchill would surely have had to retire.

The period between the General Elections of February 1950 and October 1951 was one in which Conservative optimism grew. But it was not a period when the Conservative projection of its alternative programme was markedly more successful than it had been before February 1950. For Churchill continued to rely on a personal appeal almost totally above detailed policies and Eden remained half-hearted in his interventions on most subjects other than international affairs.

In the field of foreign policy Eden was of course as active as ever. Now, however, he revealed an increasing tendency to break away from the almost automatic bipartisanship which had been so evident since 1945. His first major divergence from the Foreign Office line came in June 1950 over the Schuman Plan. This was not, however, from personal choice but represented a collective Shadow Cabinet decision. The problem arose when the French Foreign Minister, Robert Schuman, made a sudden public call for the pooling of French and German coal and steel resources accompanied by invitations to other west European states to join in. This move was intended to embarrass Bevin and to try to force the British to endorse a step along a road leading away from sovereign independence. The Labour Government reacted with stubborn hostility and refused even to cloak their resentment. They offered to enter into token negotiations only on terms which were clearly unacceptable to the Europeans – namely that even the supranational principle itself should not be accepted in advance. For the bulk of the Conservative leadership this was too anti-European a line. Few were out-and-out Federalists, but a majority was sufficiently sympathetic to the evolving European experiments, which after all fell far short of federalism, to wish to oppose Bevin's policy. Probably crucial here was Macmillan's influence on Churchill, who had been much flattered by the reception his various earlier forays into Europe in the immediate post-war years had received. Once again Eden diverged from Macmillan.[61] On the face of it, however, the differences between them were not great. Eden was not wholly hostile to European experiments provided Great Britain was not tightly bound in; and Macmillan was no Federalist visionary. There was nevertheless a genuine gulf, apart from any personal antipathy. At root Eden was an Atlanticist with a view of Great Britain as a world power whose aspirations had scarcely altered since the interwar years. He was also eager to support Bevin, who was one of his few personal friends in politics. Above all, he did not wish to diverge from the Foreign Office, which certainly commanded more of his loyalty and affection than the Conservative Party was ever able to do. Macmillan, on the other hand, was rather less of an Atlanticist and saw Great Britain's future as lying increasingly in a European context. In retrospect it is clear that he showed greater flexibility of mind than Eden in recognizing relatively early that Great Britain's rôle in the world could not continue as it had traditionally been. And over the Schuman Plan he was successful in persuading Churchill to coerce Eden into criticism of the traditionalists. It was, however, to be his last major victory on a European issue until after Eden's retirement in 1957.

When it became clear that the British would not be joining the talks on the Schuman Plan which were attended by six nations (France, West

Germany, Italy, Belgium, the Netherlands and Luxemburg), the Conservatives put down this Motion for debate in the House of Commons:

> That this House requests His Majesty's Government, in the interests of peace and full employment, to accept the invitation to take part in the discussions on the Schuman Plan, subject to the same condition as that made by Netherlands Government, namely, that if the discussions show the plan not to be practicable, freedom of action is reserved.

It fell to Eden to move the Motion. He did so in the mildest tones. He avoided any vigorous criticism of the Government. And on the crucial issue of sovereignty he sought to minimize the departure involved in the Schuman Plan by skilfully pointing out that some derogation from full sovereignty had been involved in the Baruch Plan for controlling atomic energy, in the Marshall Plan and in the formation of NATO. He then referred to Schuman's call for 'a common high authority' for the coal and steel community and sought to imply that this might mean little in practice:

> Already the conception of a high authority seems to have been considerably modified. Most of us with any experience of international negotiations could have been fairly sure that that was precisely what would happen. But still, I admit there is a question which must be faced, and I propose to face it. Would we be prepared to enter discussions as a result of which a high authority would be set up whose decisions would be binding upon the nations who were parties to the agreement? My answer to that question would be, yes, provided – [Hon. Members: 'Ah'] – that we were satisfied with the conditions and the safeguards.

His speech closed with a half-hearted appeal to the Government to reconsider their decision. Churchill's speech at the end of the debate was a striking contrast: he poured scorn on the Government and then made a ringing declaration against the idea that national sovereignty should be inviolable, even claiming that the heroism of the British in 1940–41 was 'not purely from national motives' but was based on the conviction 'that it was not only our own cause but a world cause for which the Union Jack was kept flying ...'[62]

Eden was able to return to bipartisanship, however, on the issue of the Korean War which broke out on 25 June 1950. He warmly welcomed both Truman's rapid and vigorous response through the United Nations and the endorsement this received from the Labour Government. According to *The Times*:

> Describing the action of the United Nations as 'the blast of the policeman's whistle in the international sphere', he [Eden] said that if its authority could be upheld we should have taken the most decisive step in our power to ensure peace ... To condemn aggression and then look the other way may be a more damaging course; all recent history goes to show that it is also a futile one.[63]

Then, in a major speech in Parliament on 5 July, Eden addressed a personal appeal to Stalin:

I recall a conversation ... which I had with Marshal Stalin at a very grim period of the war, in December 1941 ... One night, after our discussions about the immediate situation were over and we were conversing more discursively, we spoke of Hitler ... We discussed his character and I remember that Marshal Stalin made this comment, 'we should not underrate Hitler. He is a very able man, but he made one mistake. He did not know when to stop.' ... I suppose I smiled. At any rate Marshal Stalin turned to me and observed, 'You are smiling, and I know why you are smiling. You think that if we are victorious, I shall not know when to stop. You are wrong. I shall know.' Tonight, I am wondering whether the time has not come when it would be well to stop.[64]

Later in 1950 Eden went through a surprising 'hawkish' phase. On 26 October he was reported as favouring 'placing us very nearly on a semi-war footing'.[65] Next, in a speech to the House of Commons on 29 November following a visit to Washington where he had been received by Truman, he spoke warmly of General Douglas MacArthur and made an uncompromising attack on China, whose 'volunteers' had just entered the Korean conflict:

I have read many opinions in the last few months that China's Communism may ultimately take on a Titoist complexion. Well that may be so one day. I cannot tell. But I have never felt ... that that was a basis on which we could found our immediate policy ...
When we look outside Korea how can we pretend that we see Communist China adopting essentially pacific courses? What about Tibet? And Indo-China? And Malaya?

Evidently satisfied that both China and the Soviet Union had been equally instrumental in causing the original North Korean aggression, he set his face against any idea in such circumstances of allowing the Chinese to take a seat on the United Nations Security Council. He ended with this plea, which reads oddly in the light of his later quarrels with Washington: 'If Russia were to succeed in splitting the Anglo-American alliance, the whole of the free world would lie open to forcible subjection to Communism. That is the supreme consideration which must ever be present in our minds.'[66]

A fortnight later, after Attlee's visit to Truman, Eden again addressed the House of Commons in an uncompromising mood. He was opposed to abandoning the goal of uniting the two halves of Korea under Western auspices:

The communiqué which the Prime Minister signed with the President talked about a free and united Korea. That, I presume, means all Korea. That, I suppose, also means that we are not prepared to return to partition. That must surely be right, because to return to partition would merely mean to perpetuate the very dangers with which we have already been confronted, and all the efforts so far made would then have been in vain.

And he further argued that any settlement must cover 'all the territories in the Far East':

... suppose a compromise could be arrived at merely covering Korea and Formosa for the time being, that might only shift the weight of anxiety further south. This would be disadvantageous to us, to put it mildly. But, apart from our own interests, on the broader grounds, I cannot think that it would make for peace. Someone made a reference to Munich just now. That, of course, would be much more like Munich than anything that has happened so far.

He spoke sympathetically of France's troubles in Indo-China. 'There ought to be,' he concluded, 'an overall strategic concept, which has now got to be wider even than the Atlantic zone of defence.'[67] Perhaps most of this was rhetoric designed for once to please his party zealots. For it is certainly difficult to reconcile much of this talk with his policies relating to the Orient after he had returned to the Foreign Office.

One argument deployed by Eden at this time which did have later echoes was on the subject of Egypt. Threats from Cairo of unilateral repudiation of the 1936 Treaty led him to take a different line from Bevin and, unlike the case of the Schuman Plan, there is no evidence that his hand was forced by colleagues. He told the House of Commons on 29 November 1950:

... our contention is that ... we should suspend the supply of arms to Egypt. I will say why, and I can say it with more freedom than a Minister of the Crown. It is because that country has itself challenged the Treaty [of 1936], because it has not adhered to the United Nations Resolution in respect of Korea, and because it still stops our tankers, [bound for Haifa] going through the Suez Canal as they are legitimately entitled to do.[68]

Eden's tendency to diverge increasingly in foreign affairs from the Labour Government was intensified after the enforced resignation of the dying Bevin. The new Foreign Secretary, Morrison, appointed on 9 March 1951, had never been a friend of Eden, whom in 1937 he had described as 'worth his weight in gold as a shopwalker in one of the West End stores'.[69] During the war, when they had been colleagues, Morrison had even vainly sought to persuade Churchill that he should replace Eden at the Foreign Office. Now in 1951 Eden could not see in Morrison a worthy successor to Bevin and to himself. Morrison, on the other hand, in no way approved of Eden's reverence for the Foreign Office as a Department of State of unique standing and told him bluntly in the House of Commons that he did not share his 'superior view'.[70]

Mutual reproaches began almost at once. On 15 March Eden joined Churchill in criticizing a financial agreement reached with Egypt, asking why an end to the blockade of Suez Canal traffic to Haifa had not been made a precondition. Morrison replied that there seemed 'to be some competition between' Churchill and Eden 'to make mischief between us and a foreign country'.[71]

More serious was the conflict between a supposedly 'hawkish' Eden and a supposedly 'dovish' Morrison over the Iranian oil crisis which dominated foreign policy debates between April 1951 and the fall of the Labour Government. Ironically, the differences between the two men may at root have been less serious than they were made to appear. For Morrison privately favoured a tougher policy than the Cabinet would sanction,[72] and Eden, though his language was often robust, carefully avoided an unequivocal call for a military intervention. Indeed, Eden's initial reaction to news of Mohammed Mussadeq's decision to nationalize both the oil wells and the British-owned installations was strikingly pacific. He wrote in the *Daily Telegraph*:

What then can be done? Nothing I think in a hurry. Some opportunity must be given for the present over-heated atmosphere to cool. In present circumstances merely to dispatch British forces would provide no solution. It might even so inflame Persian feeling as to damage the prospects of negotiation. And this is the only way finally to settle the business.[73]

This tone was rapidly altered, whether as a result of changing conditions or under backbench pressure. On 21 June Eden said in the House of Commons:

What should our present action be? In my view evacuation [of the installations] would be disastrous. It would be an abject surrender to force. The Government have taken – and, I think, rightly taken – the legal issue to The Hague Court. The issue they have taken is not the question of who owns the oil in Persia – it has never been disputed by us that it is Persian oil: the issue they have taken is whether the Persians have a right unilaterally to take over our installations. They have now asked for an interim injunction about this.

Meanwhile, while The Hague Court is considering that, it is clear that the British staff must stay. It is as much a Persian as a British interest that they should do so. But if these men are being asked to stay, then it is the inescapable duty of the Government to take any steps that may be necessary to protect them.

This was greeted with loud 'Hear, Hears!' from the Conservative back-benchers. When Morrison replied by speaking of Tory imperialism, Eden was provoked into writing in *The Sunday Times* that 'there has never been in my judgement a speech more unworthy of the office'.[74]

By 9 July Eden was taunting Morrison with a question about a newspaper report that an unnamed member of the British Embassy in Teheran had stated that 'there is a good chance that the lads [at Abadan] will be home for Goodwood'.[75] That the newspaper in question was the *Daily Herald* only provided added piquancy. Yet it is difficult to believe that Eden would have deliberately sought to embarrass the Foreign Office in such a fashion if Bevin had still been in charge. Further vigorous language came from Eden on 14 July. *The Times* reported that he said

that evacuation from Persia would now run counter to the injunction of The Hague Court. We had the duty to carry out the court's recommendations.

Mr Eden said that the Persian crisis should never have been allowed to arise if there had been judgement and foresight and if our Government had possessed a coherent Middle Eastern policy. As it was the situation had become highly inflamed. Even so, he believed it could still be cured if we understood what we were about and showed patience and firmness.

It was to be hoped that all concerned would clearly understand that the issue was not only one of oil ...

'If the revenues from oil cease to flow ... the one steady contributory factor to Persia's national income will lapse,' continued Mr Eden. 'Persia's shaky economy can never withstand such a blow. The result will be disintegration and the triumph of Communism. Should this happen you can picture for yourselves the influence on Persia's neighbours of a Communist satellite state stretching from the Caspian to the Persian Gulf.

'Here is, in very truth, a vital strategic issue. Such a transformation concerns the whole free world. Potentially the threat for the free world is infinitely graver here than it is in Korea ...'

Mr Eden said that much of the argument which appeared to be going on in America and Britain about nationalization seemed to him beside the point. Nobody ever denied that ownership of the oil belonged to Persia. But the installations did not; and these included the largest refinery in the world, built by British capital and enterprise. The Nationalization Act was, in fact, a measure of expropriation.[76]

The dispute dragged on up to and beyond the General Election of October 1951. No doubt it did some small amount of damage to the Labour Government's prestige and it may have been fatal to Morrison's hopes of succeeding Attlee. For Eden, on the other hand, it did much to win increased support among more right-wing Conservative backbenchers who had hitherto doubted his soundness as a defender of narrow British interests. The crisis remained on the agenda, however, after his return to the Foreign Office and it may be that some of his utterances in Opposition made it difficult for him to respond to American pressure in favour of reconciliation with Teheran.

The last months of Opposition also saw Eden developing unexpectedly robust views on Great Britain's world rôle. His principal audiences were not, moreover, domestic ones. For he spent five weeks in the summer in North America, accompanied by Robert Carr, the Conservative MP who was destined to become his Parliamentary Private Secretary. His remarks to various American audiences are worth quoting at some length, for they are of much interest in the light of his later conduct in office. At Denver on 6 August Eden said:

It is not, I think, an exaggeration nor a mark of self-righteousness, to say that the free nations look to the British Commonwealth and the United States to give [a] lead.

The boundaries of British responsibility and influence may seem to have shrunk in recent years, but are they so changed after all? It does not seem so when we look, even now, at the dispersal of British forces in Korea, Hong Kong, and Malaya, in the Middle East, in Austria and Trieste, and nearer home, in Germany. In all this I do not suggest for a moment that the British effort is at its peak. But it is a salutary reminder, none the less, to those who underestimate our present endeavour.

At San Francisco on 10 August he described the British recognition of Communist China as 'a diplomatic step taken with bad timing, because it placed Britain in a position of being out of step with the Commonwealth and the United States'. Finally at Chicago on 20 August he said:

Do not, I beg of you, underestimate the part that my country, and still more the Commonwealth and Empire, can play to guide and strengthen the free world in the pursuit of peace.

The Commonwealth and Empire family may be taking new shapes and forms. But it is my conviction that the opportunities now opening before it to contribute to the wealth and leadership of the world are greater than they have ever been. The world sadly needs examples of the free association of nations. The Commonwealth and Empire is such a partnership. It can render golden service to guide and inspire mankind.

But let us make no mistake about this. It is upon us – the United States and the British Commonwealth – that the chief responsibility for leadership must fall. We have a common language, not only in our words, but in our hearts which beat as one. If we falter or fall apart, all will be lost. If we stand and work together, we can surmount the dangers of the next few years and open a new vista of hope to the world.[77]

The tendency to exaggerate the extent of British power and influence was a striking feature of his position and one that endured until his retirement. As during the premiership of Neville Chamberlain, he appeared unable to distinguish adequately between commitments and capabilities. By contrast, his emphasis on the need for harmony with Washington was something he either chose or felt forced to abandon when back in office. Perhaps his exaggerated estimation of British influence made it impossible for him to seek solidarity with the United States other than on more or less equal terms. It is interesting to speculate whether Dean Acheson, John Foster Dulles or Eisenhower ever later felt tempted to quote back to him his appeals for English-speaking unity.

Eden returned home on 5 September. Twelve days later Attlee called a General Election for 25 October. Once again Eden set out on a round of electioneering. He also broadcast both on radio and on the new political medium, television. His contributions on domestic policy bordered, as so often in his career, on the banal. We may cite two examples of his style from speeches given on 22 October. At Wellington he said that 'the present situation was far too serious to make any promises, but we must have opportunity and incentive at home and peace and stability abroad'. Then he spoke at Northfield, Birmingham. According to the solemn record of *The Times*:

> Of the cost of living, Mr Eden said that the Conservatives had no patent medicine. He was no conjurer and had no hat to bring a rabbit out of. First, Government expenditure had to be reduced for it was inflationary. We had got to bring free enterprise competition into all purchase of food and material from abroad.[78]

All too often his speeches contained what Bevin is said to have described as 'clitch after clitch after clitch'. In another context one aide, having seen the cliché-ridden draft of a speech on a particular subject, daringly said to his chief that it could only be bettered by a declaration of intent to leave 'no stone unturned in the search for agreement'. Eden, however, cheerfully expressed his gratitude and promptly adopted the suggestion.[79]

He was naturally more authoritative when speaking on foreign affairs and, unlike the General Election of 1950, there was now some scope for partisan polemic in this sphere. First, he was able to criticize Government policy regarding Iran and particularly the withdrawal of British subjects from Abadan, which had by now occurred. But he cautiously avoided making precise pledges. Instead on 6 October he proclaimed that 'a further prolonged period of dilly-dally will be disastrous'.[80] Secondly, he was able to capitalize on Egypt's decision on 15 October unilaterally to abrogate the Treaty of 1936. He was again careful not to spell out precise details of possible Conservative responses. But he had no difficulty in maintaining a more 'patriotic' posture than the hapless Morrison. For example, he gave an unequivocal pledge that under the Conservatives the Sudan would be protected from Egyptian ambitions.[81] Morrison countered by endeavouring to represent the Conservatives as having shown themselves eager in the space of a mere ten days to involve Great Britain in two wars – one against Iran and one against Egypt. On polling day, in urging its readers to vote Labour, the *Daily Mirror* asked whose finger was on the trigger. It is difficult, however, to believe that the balance of these exchanges was electorally advantageous to Labour, though such matters are obviously beyond the realm of proof.

The poll resulted in 320 Conservatives being elected as against 295 Labour and six Liberals. Eden's own majority at Warwick and Leamington in a straight fight with Labour increased to 9,803. Churchill thus found himself returning to Downing Street with an overall majority of seventeen. But for neither Churchill nor Eden could there be much sense of having earned their success by the character of their endeavours and persuasive arts in Opposition. For the Conservative Opposition from 1945 to 1951 was one of the least enterprising and admired of modern times – symbolized by its failure to win even one by-election in a Labour-held constituency and by its receiving marginally less of the popular vote than the Labour Party even in the General Election of 1951. The eventual return of the Conservatives to office was thus in part attributable to the boundaries of constituencies. But another precondition was a loss of confidence on the part of the Labour Party after February 1950. Both Bevin and Cripps had been lost through illness and rapid death; Aneurin Bevan and Harold Wilson resigned in a bout of fratricidal dispute with the new Chancellor of the Exchequer, Hugh Gaitskell; and thereafter what remained of Attlee's ageing team seemed to lose the appetite for office and power. Thus Churchill may be accounted somewhat fortunate that his negligent and often inept leadership of the Opposition did not end in personal humiliation but saw him instead restored to the premiership. Eden was no less unfortunate in having to return to office still under Churchill's vexatious leadership. But both men had played their part in making the Conservative period of Opposition so unsatisfactory, though Churchill certainly deserves the larger share of criticism. It is difficult not to endorse the verdict of Richard Law, shrewd son of the former Conservative Prime Minister, when he wrote on 1 January 1950:

What a deplorable opposition we have been. It is Winston's fault – I mean largely because of his very qualities, he's hopeless as leader of an opposition. You can't have a Field Marshal leading an opposition: what you want is a company commander who is on the job every day ... Of course Winston had to be leader; there was no alternative. But what a tragedy it has been.[82]

Churchill's Foreign Secretary
1951–5

No doubt Eden felt a gnawing sense of frustration at again becoming Foreign Secretary nearly sixteen years after first obtaining the post. But his position was immensely strong. For he was now the undisputed heir to the premiership and was still only fifty-four; Churchill, now approaching his seventy-seventh birthday, could scarcely hope to lead the Conservative Party into another General Election. His reputation had never stood higher. He was widely admired in the country as a moderate in domestic matters and he stood to benefit both at home and abroad from his somewhat undeserved image as a heroic and consistent opponent of Chamberlain and 'Appeasement'. In Parliament he was held in respect on all sides. As a speaker he was invariably competent and occasionally dominating, but had so far avoided antagonizing any significant number of MPs by abrasive partisanship. Probably no major politician had fewer enemies.

Eden's strength was reflected in his standing in the Cabinet. As the obvious successor to an aged Prime Minister he could rely on most of his colleagues not daring to cross him, though it would seem that he rarely used his weight to sway opinion on domestic matters. He even persuaded Churchill to recommend that he be made Deputy Prime Minister, as this extract from the diary of Evelyn Shuckburgh, Principal Private Secretary at the Foreign Office under Morrison and then under Eden, reveals:

... at 4 Chesterfield Street [Eden's London home], we found Eden having a heated telephone conversation about whether or not he was to be described as Deputy Prime Minister ... He did not seem to be getting very far ... There was a pause and Winston came to the 'phone. At once he agreed and there was a great deal of 'thank you, dear' ...

In the event, however, objections from Buckingham Palace caused this idea to be abandoned. Nevertheless he was the most powerful subordinate any modern Cabinet has seen. Certainly on foreign affairs he possessed, in the words of Home Secretary David Maxwell Fyfe, later the Earl of Kilmuir, 'a silencing authority'. Kilmuir recalled:

... I am not sure that his great authority and knowledge of foreign affairs was not a defect in the Government. Winston was determined not to oppose his successor, and none of the other members had the knowledge or experience to question or contradict Eden's policies. I doubt if a Foreign Secretary has enjoyed quite so much independence since Lord Rosebery – in very different circumstances – reigned at the Foreign Office in 1892–4. This entrusting of a vital aspect of government to one man, however competent, was in a sense an abrogation of the rôle of the Cabinet . . .[1]

In fact Churchill *was* prepared to oppose his successor. But, as in wartime, their differences were usually settled in private rather than in Cabinet, and the story of their stormy relationship in the period 1951–5 may therefore never be told in full. But merely because Eden got his way in relation to more major issues than had been the case between 1940 and 1945, it would be an error to suppose that he had relatively few difficulties with Churchill. On the contrary, Sir John Colville, Churchill's Private Secretary, testified that the differences between the two men were 'more serious' than during the war! Of course Eden in his memoirs minimized the difficulties whether in war or peace. He quoted his chief as saying 'you could put each of us in a separate room, put any questions of foreign policy to us, and nine times out of ten we would give the same answer'. He also wrote:

It may be irritating to have one's elbow jogged too much; it is much worse to feel that what one is trying to do is not understood. In all the years that Sir Winston Churchill and I worked together, it was this comprehension at the end of the wire that was most remarkable. I suppose that it was in part the result of our lifetimes' experience of world affairs.

Moran, Churchill's doctor and intimate friend, noted in his diary that 'the PM always claims that Anthony and he agree on most things in the field of foreign affairs'. But Moran added: 'it is not very noticeable'.[2] Indeed, as will be seen, the diary of Shuckburgh provides much evidence to the contrary. One example may suffice here:

Attlee put down a PNQ [Private Notice Question] to the PM this morning, about Molotov's note. A.E. determined to take it himself, and had me send a message to No. 10 to that effect. Result – a message that the PM thinks 'as it is addressed to him, he should answer it'. The news, telephoned to A.E. . . . . caused an outburst – 'my nerves are already at breaking point', and he rushed over to No. 10 to beard the PM in person. Won his point, but after he had got back to the FO, the PM sent a message that he would rise himself and say 'I will ask my Rt Hon. Friend to reply'. This caused another fury – 'treating me as if I needed a nurse' – and I succeeded in getting Jock [Colville] to have it withdrawn. By that time, Jock was saying the PM never wanted to make the statement, couldn't care less, etc.[3]

After Churchill's major stroke in June 1953, their relationship was exacerbated by Eden's extreme and understandable impatience to succeed to the premiership and by Churchill's tantalizing and perhaps dishonourable prevarications concerning the date of his retirement. At times their mutual antagonism became noticeable to others. Churchill, in particular, evidently took malicious pleasure on occasion in the use of wounding expressions towards the sensitive and highly-strung Eden. Witnesses of the frequent scenes between the two men were often either amused or embarrassed. An example may be mentioned. Dean Acheson, the American Secretary of State, is said to have found himself in their presence when Churchill began to compliment him on his handsome bearing and sartorial elegance. Turning to Eden, now showing distinct signs of being middle-aged and in less than perfect health, Churchill repeatedly urged his colleague to observe Acheson's appearance, saying, 'Dean looks like you are supposed to do.'[4] Such jibes evidently distressed Eden to an abnormal extent but also suggest an element of sadism in Churchill's attitude towards him. On the other hand, there was by now undoubtedly an unusual degree of underlying affection between the two men. Their relationship was to be further complicated, however, in 1952 when Eden married Clarissa Churchill, his chief's niece, whom he had known for many years.

Eden's relations with the Chancellor of the Exchequer, Butler, were also at times strained. At the outset of the administration, for example, the Foreign Secretary made one of his rare but decisive interventions in domestic affairs to the great discomfiture of the Chancellor, who clearly was not the 'Butskellite' of popular legend. Shuckburgh's diary reveals the details:

At the height of this visit to Lisbon there came out from London Eric Berthoud [of the Foreign Office] with very grim news about the UK balance of payments and a really alarming plan worked out by the Bank of England and accepted by the Chancellor for dealing with the situation. In brief the plan, so far as A.E. and I could understand it, was to block the Commonwealth and other sterling balances (except for limited amounts which would be released) and to make sterling convertible. The effect and object of this would be to throw the burden of the adverse trade balance off the reserves (which were rapidly running right out) and on to the home economy and the standard of living. It would have meant abandoning the policy of full employment and a controlled economy to which both parties had been pledged at the election...

Berthoud made it clear to us that the plan was strongly favoured by the Prime Minister and the Chancellor and also by a great section of the economic planners and senior officials in the Treasury. Lord Cherwell and Lord Swinton were said to be very doubtful about it ... It was clear it was a bankers' plan: logically unassailable, but open to the very gravest political objections ... I suggested to A.E. that the only possible way of putting it across would be for the Government to announce the plan and go to the country on it. They could not possibly put it through with their small majority, in defiance of their election policy. A.E. agreed with this and for a time was quite keen on the idea of an appeal to the country. He had little doubt the Government would lose the election, but at least then they would have told the people the truth and prescribed the honest remedy.

The more he thought about it, however, the more A.E. became doubtful about the premises on which it was based ... A.E.'s inclination was to distrust the automatic character of the plan and to think that the proper course would be to cut back the rearmament programme very substantially, reduce imports further on a selective basis and see whether this could not suffice to restore confidence in sterling without sacrificing the controlled economy and the policy of full employment.

... when we got back to London it became clear that there was a strong body of opinion which felt this way. The Treasury was sharply divided ... The position in the Cabinet, we were told, turned entirely on what A.E. would do, and he went into the fray to kill the plan ... After a series of evidently very stormy meetings, the Cabinet rejected the plan. It was impossible not to be sorry for Rab Butler, but Whitehall as a whole was profoundly relieved. In the event, the Budget was remarkably well received in the country and abroad, and the position of sterling dramatically strengthened ... it seems possible that we may get by.

A.E. rightly takes credit for these developments. It has, however, left a scar on his relations with the Chancellor ...

By a curious twist, Rab's successful Budget started off a series of suggestions in the press that he had taken the lead over A.E. in the Cabinet and was a serious rival for the succession to Winston ...[5]

Later in the year Eden was the subject of more hostile press comment in the succession context. Shuckburgh recorded:

November 1952
There is a suspicion in the Party that the PM's intimates, e.g. Randolph Churchill, Duncan Sandys, [Christopher] Soames etc., and even possibly the PM himself are behind the press attacks. Certainly the PM has done nothing to disown them. The calculation may be that by blackening the one possible successor they may keep the old man longer in office. Or they may be genuinely thinking they can groom Rab Butler for the succession.

16 December 1952
Lunched with Bob Dixon ... He said: 'I suppose you are aware how strongly Winston and all his entourage feel against Anthony getting the succession?'

19 January 1953
Went to Buckingham Palace to see Alan Lascelles [Private Secretary to the monarch] ... I was surprised to be told, 'if Winston were to die tomorrow there is no doubt at all The Queen would send for Anthony. But by the end of this year there will be doubt, if present trends continue. There might be at least 50% opinion in the Party and in the City by that time in favour of Butler' ... I expressed astonishment and am unconvinced.

A.E. obviously feels that this sort of thing is growing. He is very depressed this evening. He doesn't think the Old Man will ever go. There are more attacks on him in the Beaverbrook press. There is no doubt that Rab is coming along fast ... I suddenly thought of myself in the character of Griffith (page to Katherine of Aragon in King Henry VIII) consoling my master in his collapse.[6]

Eden's return to the Foreign Office in 1951 was generally welcome to the officials. For he provided a marked contrast in style and efficiency to

Morrison. But it seems doubtful whether he was as popular as Bevin had been. Partly this was because he considered himself, with some justice, to be too much of an expert on detail to need to respond to the promptings of his officials. For he had more first-hand experience of international affairs than even his Permanent Under-Secretaries, first Sir William Strang and then, from 1953, Sir Ivone Kirkpatrick. But he was undoubtedly becoming increasingly opinionated on subjects with which he was not wholly familiar. Another reason for criticism in some quarters lay in his aversion from long-term planning. According to Gladwyn Jebb, later Lord Gladwyn, Eden was discouraging about the work of a committee set up by Bevin which had evolved into a long-term planning body and hence it gradually faded out.[7] But perhaps the most forbidding aspect of Eden from the officials' point of view was his growing irascibility and restlessness. Sir Roderick Barclay, who had been delighted to serve as Private Secretary to Bevin, was relieved to escape from having to act in such a capacity with Eden. He wrote: 'I do not think I should have been well equipped to look after him ... his impatience and irritability, partly no doubt due to ill-health, tended to make life very difficult for his closest associates during the next few years.' Shuckburgh, who succeeded Barclay, recorded in his diary a number of incidents that illustrated how well-founded this judgement was:

21 November 1951
Another attack in the night, this time at Rome. A good deal worse, and I was fairly sure it must be an ulcer. However, a Sunday in bed and a series of drugs seemed to clear it up. Once again it was the prospect of a speech, I think, which brought it on and the agitation which seems to be inseparable from these occasions. In this case we were not helped in keeping him calm by Victor Mallet [the British Ambassador in Rome], who seemed to have a knack of saying the irritating thing ... There was trouble because he was received by a guard of honour and had not been warned. He had no hat, and as ill luck would have it, neither I nor the detective nor the Ambassador could produce one.

Mid-February 1952
... easily the worst scene I have so far had with A.E. The chauffeur and detective [in Lisbon], thinking they knew better than our instructions, had taken us off to the American [instead of the French] Embassy ... Being already late ... this extra delay seemed intolerable, and the annoyance was for some minutes uncontrolled. It developed into a physical struggle between me trying to shut the window between us and the driver, so that the lower classes might be insulated from these troubles, and A.E. leaning forward to wind it down so that he might call them bloody fools! All ended amicably as usual.

15 January 1953
He is like a child. You can have a scene with a child of great violence with angry words spoken on both sides and ten minutes later the whole thing is forgotten. This is not possible with grown-ups, but it is the regular thing with A.E.

26 April 1954

... A.E. was in a very excitable and increasingly impatient mood. He kept complaining about the procedure [at the Geneva Conference], wanting things to go faster, and making me and Dennis Allen, who could of course do nothing about it, very uncomfortable. Then unfortunately the car was badly held up ... and everyone was roundly cursed, the driver, the detective, me, Lord Reading [Minister of State at the Foreign Office], the United Nations and the entire Swiss people. It was a glorious sunny day, so I said why don't we walk, and Reading said why don't you come and see the villa where the delegation works? Both these suggestions were unfortunate, for when we got to the villa A.E. flew into a rage to see the delegation offices surrounded by green grass, chestnut trees and sunshine, while he was forced to live and work in a filthy hotel, noisy, smelly, uncomfortable, insecure etc. etc.[8]

For all his faults, however, Eden was undoubtedly held in respect by most officials in the Foreign Office, including the Private Secretaries, and by the bulk of his ambassadors. For he was industrious, knowledgeable and probably unmatched in the techniques of conference negotiation. Certainly claims by some in John Foster Dulles's circle that he gave the impression of not having done his homework do not find general endorsement among British politicians and officials who worked with him.[9]

When Eden returned to the Foreign Office the principal issues of the day were Korea, Iran, Egypt and German rearmament. Yet none could be seen in isolation. On the contrary, all four were arguably merely elements in one overriding problem facing the makers of British foreign policy, namely the nature of the post-war relationship with the United States. In Eden's first period as Foreign Secretary, the American factor was of only marginal significance, notwithstanding his attempts to make use of Roosevelt in his dispute with Chamberlain. During his second tenure the United States came to have more and more importance, but Eden did not feel the full force of this, partly because Churchill himself handled much of the diplomacy involving Roosevelt, partly because bilateral relations with the Soviet Union were almost as important. Now, in 1951, Eden had to adjust to the full implications of the United States having become far and away the most active and the most powerful state on the democratic side of a divided planet. He certainly found the process of adjustment difficult. It may even be that his unwillingness to accept the rôle of a junior partner was the most significant feature of the rest of his political career. If so, it was poetic justice. For no British politician in the late 1930s had so yearned for an active United States and no British politician, apart from Churchill, had a greater responsibility for shaping the character of the Second World War as a result of which the future of Europe came to depend on two essentially extra-European superpowers.

In his memoirs Eden plaintively drew attention to the sacrifices expected of Great Britain by Washington in the 1950s. 'Sometimes,' he wrote, 'I would take action which I believed would bring our policy into line with that of the United States ... only to find that the policy had not the significance it had been declared to have ... The lesson may be that allies should subordinate their interests more closely to the opinions of their stronger partner, but an alliance does not gather strength that way.' He complained about lack of consultation on Far Eastern matters, though clearly the Americans had the major presence in that region. 'The Americans,' he lamented to Sir Roger Makins, the British Ambassador in Washington, 'may think the time past when they need to consider the feelings or difficulties of their allies. It is the conviction that this tendency becomes more pronounced every week that is creating difficulties for anyone in this country who wants to maintain close Anglo-American relations.' He felt still more strongly about American policies in the Middle East. As early as 1953 he saw 'an apparent disinclination by the United States Government to take second place even in an area where primary responsibility was not theirs' and he discerned 'Americans, at least locally [in Cairo], withholding support which their partner in NATO had the right to expect ...'[10]

Churchill was more willing to face the realities of the reduced British rôle in the world and hence when the Americans showed sufficient signs of having made a firm choice on a policy question, he was usually more prepared than Eden to subordinate British views to theirs. Ironically, the Americans were willing to humour Churchill on some issues about which he felt strongly, provided they were even marginally undecided: for his legendary wartime achievements and his age led to an understandable unwillingness to cause him distress. Eden, by contrast, was accorded no such sentimental consideration. Moreover, when the Americans could not bring themselves to give ground to Churchill, they were inclined to treat him gently and sought to win him over by the indirect means of putting pressure on his Foreign Secretary.[11]

In his memoirs Eden gave an account of Anglo-American relations in the 1950s which placed particular stress on the unreliability of Dulles and even appears to have sought to make him a scapegoat for almost everything that went wrong. This, however understandable in the aftermath of the Suez crisis, was an essentially distorted picture. It meant, for example, that Eisenhower was given less than his share of responsibility for what was done by his Administration. For though Dulles was a strong Secretary of State, he was by no means wholly dominant over his President. Thus even in the case of the Suez crisis, it was probably Eisenhower more than Dulles who caused the crucial post-ceasefire humiliation of Great Britain – something Eden may have felt inhibited from bringing out in his memoirs, Full Circle, published in 1960 when the President was still in office. Eden's choice of Dulles as principal scapegoat for the Suez débâcle also probably led him to exaggerate the extent of their earlier difficulties. In this respect his relationship with Dulles was uncannily similar to that with Neville Chamberlain. True, their earlier differences were not negligible. But there were periods of harmony on policy as well as of hostility. Nor were their personal relations invariably as frigid as has often been supposed. Friendly personal letters and telegrams were on occasion exchanged, and contemporaries have testified to both men having expressed unsolicited private tributes about the other. For example, Livingston Merchant, then serving in the State Department, recalled:

> ... my sadness over the bitterness toward Foster Dulles which crept into Anthony Eden's memoirs. He attributed to Foster a dislike of himself, which I am satisfied never existed. Foster Dulles was genuinely fond of Anthony Eden ... the Suez Crisis was a very disillusioning and bitter one, and I think from 1956 on, the summer of 1956 on, there were reservations beyond doubt in Foster Dulles's mind. But of course Eden remained in public life only a matter of days or weeks after the resolution of the Suez Crisis ... But I felt that Foster Dulles – and this cropped up many times – attesting to it – was genuinely fond and admiring of Eden. And certainly if Eden was suspicious and distrustful of Foster Dulles, as apparently he was from what he says in his memoirs, then Mr Eden was also a remarkable dissembler, because in all their private and semi-private personal as well as public relations, the attitude was one I thought on both sides of great respect and great liking, and many, many hours I was alone with the two of them and had ample opportunity over the years to judge the relationship.[12]

Eden, for his part, according to Iveragh McDonald of *The Times*, said privately on 8 December 1953 of Dulles: 'I came to like him more and more.'[13] Thus it may be that if either man had retired or died at the end of 1953 or even perhaps as late as the summer of 1956, their relationship would not seem to be one of exceptional difficulty in the inevitably somewhat uneven history of Anglo-American relations. A similar argument, as has been seen, can be deployed with reference to the Eden–Chamberlain relationship before January 1938.

A further consequence of Eden's obsession in his memoirs with Dulles's allegedly mischievous rôle was that he saw fit to minimize his differences with Acheson, who served as Secretary of State during Eden's first fifteen months as Churchill's peacetime Foreign Secretary. Acheson no doubt also had his own reasons for echoing Eden's line and hence his memoirs, too, contain many expressions of esteem but tend to gloss over divergences. Eden, for example, wrote of Acheson:

> Despite a natural courtesy, his gifts can edge him to intolerance. He does not suffer fools gladly, which suffering is a large part of diplomacy. Yet Mr Acheson is above all

a loyal colleague. I would never hesitate to go tiger-hunting with him. If there were occasional squalls in our dealings, our relations usually gained from them ...

He never forgot what was due to an ally and worked in the spirit of an equal partnership, even though the United States carried so much the heavier load ...

Acheson, for his part, wrote:

Eden and I worked easily together, agreed on basic matters, where he was a resourceful and strong ally. In some cases, however, as in Iran and in approaching European integration, he was more cautious than I in departing from traditional policies, quite understandably as he had been far more deeply involved in making them.[14]

Moreover, the two men and their wives kept in touch after their retirement and a genuine friendship ripened; and even if the Suez crisis had not occurred it seems improbable that any similar personal rapport between Eden and the austere Dulles could have developed. Yet there is evidence that the differences between him and Acheson as foreign ministers, both on policy and personal levels, were on occasion as severe as any involving him and Dulles before the Suez crisis. Thus Eden's inability to accept the changed nature of the Anglo-American relationship was not fundamentally attributable to Dulles. On the contrary, the continuity and variety of his difficulties with Washington clearly cut across individuals and Administrations.

Eden's first full-scale encounter with the Americans came at the beginning of January 1952 when he and Churchill made an extended visit to North America. This followed two months of reading himself into his post in the midst of much hectic travel. According to McDonald, 'in his first five weeks he had only eight days fairly stationary in London' – evidence perhaps that his wartime restlessness and need for diversion, as noted by both Harvey and Cadogan, had not left him.[15] In November 1951 he had addressed the UN General Assembly and had attended NATO Conferences in Paris and in Rome, while in December he and Churchill had met French leaders in Paris as a preliminary to their visit to the United States. Once in Washington Eden was quickly made aware of the large range of subjects on which American policies differed from his. We may now conveniently consider each of these in turn.

Korea constituted one major problem. Since July 1951 armistice talks between the North Koreans and the United Nations Command had been in process and, despite some remaining differences, agreement appeared to be in sight. But the Americans feared that the Communists might use an armistice as a mere respite and cynically break it whenever convenient. Acheson accordingly wanted to issue a public warning about the severe consequences to be expected in such an eventuality and had pressed Eden on this point in Paris in November. The United States had in view the bombing of military targets in Manchuria and a naval blockade of China.

Eden was unenthusiastic. True, he wanted an armistice and was now, in contrast to his line in Opposition, willing to accept the reality of a permanently divided Korea. But he wished to minimize the risk of Great Britain becoming involved in war with China – partly because he was apprehensive that this might lead to Soviet retaliation in the European theatre, partly because of the vulnerability of Hong Kong, and partly because, like most in London, he did not see the world primarily through ideological spectacles. He had inherited from Morrison, however, a commitment to support in the last resort the bombing of Manchurian airfields provided prior consultation took place, and he did not feel able to repudiate this. On the other hand, he resisted a naval blockade of China and urged that any public proclamation should be in the most general terms. His tepid line was unwelcome to Acheson, who wanted to issue a more strident warning not only to deter the Communists but also to appease the 'China Lobby' in Congress. In Washington Eden was given little support on this issue by Churchill. Moran recorded in his diary for 5 January 1952: '"I do hope," said the PM, "that Anthony will meet the Americans over China, which really does not matter to us. Then they in turn might meet us about Egypt or Persia, which matter a lot. After all, what Conservative in England is in favour of Chinese Communists?"'[16] But Acheson was unable to persuade Eden to go beyond Morrison's position.

The 'China lobby' in Congress also prompted Acheson to bring up the problem of Japan's relationship with Peking. Dulles, acting as a special representative, had earlier negotiated a Peace Treaty with Tokyo now due for ratification in Congress. In agreement with Morrison, Dulles had initially given the Japanese freedom to choose, *after ratification*, whether to recognize the Communists in Peking or Chiang Kai-shek in Formosa as the legitimate Chinese Government. But fearing difficulties with Congress, Dulles had subsequently obtained a letter from Shigeru Yoshida, the Japanese Prime Minister, indicating that Japan would choose Chiang. Acheson hinted to Eden in Washington that it might be necessary to publish this letter to influence Congress – a course that was bound in turn to cause difficulties for Eden with the Labour Opposition, which could be expected to argue that he had failed to keep the Americans to the spirit of the Morrison–Dulles agreement. Hence Eden, according to his own account, withheld acquiescence. The Americans decided to publish, however, without further consultation and thereby occasioned Eden surprise and embarrassment on his return to London. Acheson subsequently found it prudent to apologize to Eden for the timing. But the matter continued to rankle. Eden, for example, claimed in his memoirs that Acheson's reference in Washington to the possibility of utilizing the letter was imprecise and that he was not shown the text. Acheson, on the other hand, while admitting some lack of clarity, stated that Sir Oliver Franks, the British Ambassador, had had a sight of the letter and thus implied that Eden knew or ought to have known about its contents.[17] A further consequence of this incident was that Eden judged Dulles to have been guilty of sharp practice. Exceptionally he took Morrison's part and on these grounds later allegedly urged Eisenhower not to give the State Department to Dulles.

Another divergence about the Far East concerned the Pacific Pact involving the United States, Australia and New Zealand (ANZUS), which had been negotiated before the Conservatives returned to power, but which had not yet been ratified. Eden opposed this pact unless Great Britain could also be included. Australia and New Zealand, while prepared to support a British presence, proved willing to bow to Washington's insistence to the contrary.[18] Some have unconvincingly attributed this snub to the malign influence of Dulles.[19] In fact both Truman and Acheson were fully aware of Eden's resentment and deliberately chose to maintain the policy.

Another major area of Anglo-American differences in the Washington conversations of January 1952 related to the Middle East. Throughout the years to Eden's retirement in January 1957 there was to be on both sides of the Atlantic infirmity of purpose and divided counsels on this subject. This in turn was the cause of much mutual misunderstanding. American policy towards the Middle East certainly contained many strands. One was a traditional dislike of British 'colonialism'. Another was a crude desire to advance American commercial interests in the region at the expense of the British. But while a number of elected politicians, advisers and businessmen took one or another of these positions, the leading American decision-makers usually viewed the world in this period primarily in terms of the challenge of international Communism. They were therefore inclined to ask how crucial parts of both the Far East and Middle East could best be preserved for the 'Free World'. Calculations about narrow national interest, whether American or British, were of comparatively little account. They came to the conclusion that Communism was on the march in the Far East. But they did not as yet see a similar threat to the Middle East, provided that in certain cases indigenous nationalism was given an early opportunity to thrive. This inevitably meant that they desired a gradual diminution of the British physical presence, especially in cases where the broad consent of the host nation was not apparent. But what if, as happened, the British resisted this advice? Here there was no consistent American position. Some in Washington favoured direct pressure on London to conform; others, pessimistic about the chances of success in converting the British by such means, believed that an attempt must be made *faute de mieux* to share control of parts of the region in collaboration with the British. Matters were further complicated by variations in the degree of American influence in particular countries and at particular junctures. For example, they had little or no say in Iraq or Jordan at any time before Eden's retirement. On the other hand, they were never without influence in Egypt; while their rôle in Iran grew in importance with the passage of time; and their relationship with Saudi Arabia was always exceptionally close, notwithstanding her having a more feudal and reactionary regime than any under British influence. These facts inevitably gave to American policies in the Middle East an uneven and unpredictable character that Eden eventually found impossible to forgive.

British policy towards the Middle East also had its complications. Churchill, for example, at times talked like an old-fashioned imperialist, reluctant to withdraw British forces from Suez, opposed to independence for the Sudan and privately critical of the Labour Government for having 'scuttled and run from Abadan when a splutter of musketry would have ended the matter'.[20] But on other occasions he appeared to believe that the Middle East as a whole no longer had the same strategic importance for narrow British interests as in the past. He told Moran, while in the United States in January 1952:

'Now that we no longer hold India the Canal means very little to us. Australia? We could go round the Cape. We are holding the Canal not for ourselves but for civilization. I feel inclined to threaten the Americans that we will leave the Canal if they don't come in.'[21]

The idea that Great Britain's main task was to defend 'civilization' did not appeal to Eden. Never a wholehearted internationalist and only a belated and relatively unenthusiastic convert to anti-Communism, he was more conscious of narrow British interests, and particularly access to oil. He was therefore usually less keen than Churchill about endeavours to draw the Americans into an active and equal partnership in the region; and he was also more opposed than his chief to giving reciprocal open support to robust American moves in the battle for 'civilization' throughout the Far East. Eden did not favour a joint Anglo-American global crusade along ideological lines but rather an old-fashioned spheres-of-influence arrangement: the Americans should accept British predominance in the Middle East and give moral support only when invited, while in the Far East it should be the British who generally would keep a low profile, particularly vis-à-vis Communist China. In the Washington conversations, therefore, it was Churchill who pressed hardest for an active global partnership in defence of 'civilization'. He failed, however, fully to grasp that the Americans thought 'civilization' in the Middle East could best be defended by selectively encouraging independent nationalism rather than by placing the whole region under Anglo-American tutelage. But on 5 January at their Washington meeting, Acheson did his best to enlighten Churchill:

The Middle East presented a picture that might have been drawn by Karl Marx himself – with the masses a disinherited and poverty-stricken proletariat, no middle class, a small and corrupt ruling class pushed about by foreigners who sought to exploit priceless resources, whether oil or canal. Was there ever such an opportunity to invoke inherent xenophobia to destroy the foreigner and his system and substitute the Communist solution? Anglo-American solidarity on a policy of sitting tight offered no solution, but was like a couple locked in a warm embrace in a rowboat about to go over Niagara Falls.[22]

Churchill gave little sign of appreciating the strength of American opposition to his approach. He continued to urge that a token American brigade should be sent to Suez, presumably without regard to Egyptian opinion. Indeed, he went so far as to embarrass his hosts by mentioning the idea in public on the occasion of his address to Congress on 17 January. In his memoirs Acheson described this as 'unwise' after the 'cold reception' his plan had received in private. The furthest that Truman and Acheson were prepared to go was to take part, provided that Egyptian consent was forthcoming, in a Middle East Command involving also Turkey, Australia and New Zealand. This scheme had originated when Morrison was Foreign Secretary and had the positive support of the Pentagon. Truman and Acheson, however, had supported it only because 'there seemed to be no practicable alternative'. Moreover, they correctly believed that the Egyptians, having just abrogated the Treaty of 1936, would not be interested. The scheme was thus formally endorsed in the Washington conversations of January 1952, but to Acheson it was 'a forlorn hope'.[23]

Eden was probably at this stage less interested than his chief in canvassing American support for dramatic and far-reaching initiatives in the Middle East. For he was more optimistic that the British could retain control in the region provided only that the Americans did not positively undermine them. He accordingly sought to deal with Acheson on a severely practical basis and this meant that in Washington their main encounter related to Iran. The two Foreign Ministers had previously discussed the subject in November in Paris. The Americans, fearful lest worse befall, had invited Mussadeq to Washington with a view to providing him with aid to shore up an economy almost ruined by the rupture with Great Britain. This had caused resentment in London. Eden had informed Acheson on 4 November that 'the United Kingdom is unable to accept the American view that the only alternative to Mussadeq is communism ... and that if Mussadeq should fall there is a real possibility that a more amenable government might follow'. Acheson's comment to Washington was that 'the same incompetents who allowed AIOC [Anglo-Iranian Oil Company] to lead the United Kingdom into disaster are still the source of United Kingdom policy' and that the British would prefer that Iran 'fall to Communism than that they set a precedent for other losses in the Middle East'.[24] The argument was resumed in earnest during the Washington conversations. Acheson recalled:

... I argued that the policy of sitting tight in solidarity offered little promise for British interests in Iran and considerable danger for ours elsewhere in the Middle East; indeed, I pressed this point on Mr Eden with such asperity and impatience as to require subsequent amends, which were good-naturedly accepted.[25]

In fact the exchanges were probably as personal and bitter as any between Eden and Dulles. According to an American student of Acheson's diplomacy, Eden

accused Mussadeq of being little more than a rug merchant who ought to be brushed aside as he deserved. With that Acheson exploded. It was the British who were behaving like a bunch of rug merchants, haggling over financial terms when they ought to be focusing on the bigger issue of how to resolve the crisis without impairing Britain's access to oil. Eden's feelings were so badly hurt that Acheson had to tread easy for a few days.[26]

Another account has it that Acheson not only blamed the Iranian Crisis on insensitive conduct by the AIOC but implied that the British Government should have taken a more active interest:

Eden said it was not the responsibility of the Foreign Office to get involved with practical details – prices, production, transportation etc. Again Acheson disagreed. He made some sharp observations to the effect that the business of the Foreign Office was far broader than it had been in Palmerston's time. The next day Ambassador Franks told Acheson that he had hurt Eden's feelings.[27]

Rumours of the rift even reached the press and so tendentious an account appeared in *Newsweek* that Acheson subsequently sent Eden a conciliatory letter which brought a reply in kind.[28] By this time, however, Eden could afford to make light of the personal clash. For on the main issue he had made progress: the Americans reluctantly agreed for the time being to withhold aid from Iran pending a settlement of the dispute with the British.

Eden had little practical support from Churchill in the Washington discussions. Any notions that the aged Prime Minister could establish the sort of intimate and equal relationship with Truman that he had had at times with Roosevelt proved illusory. He talked mainly in generalities and was otherwise obsessed by one essentially minor issue: whether an American or a Britisher should be NATO Supreme Commander in the Atlantic. That an American should have the post had been agreed by the Labour Government and not even the Admiralty was now anxious to re-open the matter. But Churchill was adamant. Moran wrote in his diary:

Leslie Rowan [of the Treasury] complained that Winston could no longer see things in perspective ... One day he was ready to fight to the last ditch to get his way about the Atlantic Command ... the next day he did not appear to care what four hundred million Chinese thought of England; the ferment in the Middle East hardly seemed to interest him.[29]

Eden was not much concerned about the Atlantic Command and contemptuously made no reference to it in his memoirs. But, with so much else at stake, he must have found Churchill's obsession trying in the extreme. Moreover, the Americans, without yielding on the point of substance, went out of their way to humour the Prime Minister and finally offered him a formula extending British home waters to the hundred fathom line. This he gratefully accepted. As Acheson patronizingly recalled, he and Truman were determined that Churchill 'should return home in a good mood'.[30] No such solicitude was shown to Eden. In addition, Churchill angered his Foreign Secretary by selfishly seeking to monopolize all the publicity involved in the visit, not even allowing him to answer in public questions on foreign affairs. The two *prima donnas* were also at odds about the terms of the official communiqué. Moran recorded: '"Every paragraph," Eden complained, "begins 'The Prime Minister ...' or 'The Foreign Secretary was instructed ...' No one instructs me. The Prime Minister and I are colleagues." ... So it was changed.'[31]

A final subject to which Eden had to devote much attention in Washington was the Anglo-American divergence about West German rearmament and European defence. The background lay in a proposal made on 24 October 1950 by René Pleven, then the French Prime Minister, that German rearmament should take place only within a supra-national framework. This was to be known as the European Defence Community (EDC) project. The American and British Governments were at first sceptical about its desirability or practicability. But Truman and Acheson came to appreciate that French Parliamentary and public opinion would certainly not endorse unfettered West German rearmament and might indeed even reject the safer EDC plan. They accordingly decided that the EDC should have American support to whatever extent was necessary to enable the majority in the French Assembly to be won over. British Labour Ministers had been less enthusiastic and clearly set their faces against active participation. The furthest they would go was to offer to send an observer to the resulting discussions in Paris; and eventually, in September 1951, after provisional agreement had been reached among the six nations which had formed the Coal and Steel Community, they expressed a desire 'to establish the closest possible association with a European continental community at all stages of its development'. This cautious approach was one that Eden personally favoured. Acheson, on the other hand, would have preferred the British to join the EDC and had some momentary hopes that the new Conservative Government would agree to do so. He, and others, were probably misled by statements made in Opposition by Churchill and Eden. For example, Churchill, prompted by Macmillan, had declared at Strasbourg on 11 August 1950:

We should now send a message of confidence and courage from the House of Europe to the whole world. Not only should we reaffirm ... our allegiance to the United Nations, but we should make a gesture of practical and constructive guidance by declaring ourselves in favour of the immediate creation of a European Army under a unified command, and in which we should bear a worthy and honourable part.[32]

But this vague and ill-considered statement pre-dated the Pleven Plan, which had features mysteriously repugnant to Churchill. Certainly once back in office the Conservative leader held an insufficiently 'advanced' position on the EDC to please Macmillan. Again, Eden in his Opposition phase had, on 12 February 1951, falsely roused the Americans' hopes by calling in a Parliamentary debate for delegates, not observers, to be sent to Paris to discuss the details of EDC.[33] Once back at the Foreign Office, however, he prevented any modification in the Labour Government's policy.

Ironically he was to some extent assisted in this by a leading American, namely Eisenhower. For at first he had had to compromise a little with the Cabinet's 'European' faction led by Macmillan, now Minister of Housing and Local Government, and by Maxwell Fyfe, the Home Secretary. The latter was given instructions to speak in Strasbourg along lines designed to leave the door slightly ajar so far as the British attitude to the EDC was concerned. Some interested parties, however, have by selective quotation succeeded in creating an impression that this speech, made on 28 November, was more forthcoming than it actually was. For example, Macmillan in his memoirs quoted only these extracts: '... I cannot promise full and unconditional participation but I can assure you of our determination that no genuine method shall fail for lack of thorough examination which one gives to the needs of trusted friends ... There is no refusal on the part of Britain ...' But what Macmillan did not admit was that the speech as a whole was open to an interpretation that did not please the non-British 'Europeans'. For example, Peter Calvocoressi, in the authoritative Chatham House *Survey* of the year 1952, wrote that Maxwell Fyfe

told the Consultative Assembly that it was quite unrealistic to expect Great Britain to join a European federation and held out no hope that Great Britain might establish anything more than some minor form of association with a European Defence Community. A promise to station a permanent British delegation at the headquarters of the High Authority of the Coal and Steel Community did little to take the chill off these announcements.[34]

What has caused the British 'European' faction to place so much positive stress on Maxwell Fyfe's statement was that Eden chose to make a parallel pronouncement on the same day in Rome where he was attending a meeting of the NATO Council. The Foreign Secretary's words at a press conference did not differ greatly from the Home Secretary's but they had not received advanced approval from the Cabinet and were widely interpreted as an attempt to snub his party's 'European' group and even to sabotage the EDC. A telegram of implied criticism, signed by a number of Conservative delegates at Strasbourg, only added to the impression of a serious rift. Eden's misdemeanour was simply to reiterate Morrison's doctrine that the British favoured 'the closest possible association' with the EDC but to add bluntly that this meant that 'British units and formations would not participate in a European army, but that there might be some other form of association.' His excuse to his colleagues for executing this subtle coup was that he was only acting in line with American policy. In fact he had opportunistically seized upon words spoken to him in Rome on the previous day by Eisenhower, then Supreme Commander of NATO. Eden quoted Eisenhower as stating that it would be 'a mistake' for the British to offer to enter the EDC because of the complication this would cause.[35]

Such was the violence of the reaction in France, however, that Eden had to make some amends in the week that followed. In particular, he and Churchill felt obliged to visit Paris before going to Washington to meet the Americans. They offered the French promises of links between NATO and the EDC that had not previously been under consideration. And it was further steps in this direction that were now pressed upon Eden in the Washington conversations of January 1952, since the more radical course of urging Great Britain to join the EDC was clearly now unacceptable. Acheson is even said to have told Eden that 'the American intention of maintaining troops in Europe depended upon making the EDC effective',[36] a sentiment that anticipated Dulles's later talk of an 'agonizing reappraisal'. Faced with this pressure, Churchill was at this juncture to cause more difficulties than Eden, for he had become obsessed with the futility of mixed-manning. He chose to believe that this would be a feature of the EDC down to the smallest unit and he stubbornly declined to accept correction. Eden was more reasonable. While at times probably both hoping and believing that the EDC would never finally be ratified, he agreed wholeheartedly to commend the scheme provided that the prior commitments and the sacrifices of sovereignty expected of Great Britain could be kept to a minimum. As Acheson put it: 'The British were nudged closer to positions towards Germany that made possible the contractual arrangements of the following May.'[37] Eden was not prepared, however, to leave the world in any doubt that he remained opposed to the British actually joining the EDC or any other supra-national European arrangement. He accordingly spoke bluntly on 11 January in the course of delivering the Gabriel Silver Lecture at Columbia University:

The American and British peoples should each understand the strong points in the other's national character. If you drive a nation to adopt procedures which run counter to its instincts, you weaken and may destroy the motive force of its action ... You will realize that I am speaking of the frequent suggestions that the United Kingdom should join a federation on the continent of Europe. This is something which we know, in our bones, we cannot do ... For Britain's story and her interests lie far beyond the continent of Europe. Our thoughts move across the seas to the many communities in which our people play their part, in every corner of the world. These are our family ties. That is our life: without it we should be no more than some millions of people living on an island off the coast of Europe, in which nobody wants to take any particular interest.[38]

The defiant tone rather than the actual content of these remarks inevitably caused many in Europe to believe that the British might become as lukewarm about their continental commitments as their pre-war predecessors. But a recrudescence of neo-isolationism was not what Eden had in view. He wished rather to see his country playing a global rôle and holding a unique linking position between the western Europeans and the United States. These aims proved unattainable because of inadequate economic resources and because the majority of Americans saw Great Britain's long-term future as just one more European state. For example, even Eisenhower, whose remarks had led Eden to undertake his so-called 'Rome coup' in November 1951, began to retreat: by late January 1952 he could say of the EDC that 'the attempt to include Britain *immediately* would be a stumbling block rather than a help'.[39] The tragedy was that at this period the Europeans took Eden's grandiose vision seriously and feared it might involve neo-isolation from the continental theatre, whereas the Americans did not believe in the vision but were usually too polite to say so explicitly. The British thus got the worst of all worlds. Ineradicable suspicion of London now prevailed in western European capitals with the result that more and more demands were made for binding guarantees of British military support. On the other hand, the Americans during the next three years became steadily more impatient with British pretensions to exceptional world status and step by step bullied a reluctant Eden into meeting European and particularly French demands. In European matters, therefore, Eden can be said to have been his own worst enemy: his somewhat provocative remarks in Rome and at Columbia University were the direct cause of subsequent humiliations.

Churchill and Eden followed their visit to the United States with a brief stay in Canada. The Foreign Minister, Lester Pearson, sent Acheson his impressions:

The Old Gentleman was in good form here, but takes, as you no doubt found out, some time and some champagne to reach that form. When he gets there, however, he is about as brilliantly Elizabethan as ever. There certainly is no one quite like him, and possibly for the problems of 1952, that is just as well. I have always had the impression that the only atmosphere in which he thrives and produces is that of conflict . . .

. . . I have seen a great deal of him in the last few days, and I got the impression . . . that it won't be very many months until Eden takes over. I suspect that you will have mixed feelings about that prospect. I have a high regard myself for Eden's knowledge and experience and good sense in foreign affairs, but his temperament and mannerisms at times make me a little uneasy; especially when he refers to me as 'dear' or 'my dear'. I prefer Ernie Bevin's 'my boy' . . .

The only respect in which the Prime Minister and his Foreign Secretary seemed to differ . . . was on the Far East, and I am aware of that difference only because I had separate talks with Eden. When they were together before our Cabinet, no divergence of view was indicated. However, it is quite clear that Mr Churchill would go further in support of your present attitude towards Communist China and Japan's relation to Chiang Kai-shek than Eden himself is willing to go. You may already know this yourself. They are also very preoccupied with Middle East questions, and here I think Mr Churchill would go a little faster and further in trying to enlist your active cooperation than Eden would . . .

Mr Churchill's chief personal concern . . . was . . . with the North Atlantic Naval Command . . .

You will be amused to learn that the only other matter about which he pestered us here was the restoration of 'Rule Britannia' as the official hymn of the Canadian Navy . . . However this weighty problem was resolved by agreeing to play 'Rule Britannia' whenever a British Admiral boards a Canadian ship and by playing 'Rule Britannia' last night at the State Dinner when Churchill took his place. In return for these concessions, we expect the British to reduce their demand for economic help from, say, a billion dollars to $999 million.

[On EDC] he told me that what he himself had in mind for such an Army was, as he put it, a bunch of faggots bound together, stronger as a bunch than as individual sticks, but each retaining its individual characteristics in the bunch. Pleven's European army, he says, is a 'bucket of wood pulp'.

Acheson replied:

I was much amused at your reference to his [Eden's] mode of address. When I first encountered this in Paris, I expressed considerable alarm to Luke Battle at the consequences which might flow from rugged members of the press overhearing our conversation. I agree with you that old Ernie Bevin had the better approach.

On the EDC, Churchill remained unreconstructed to the last . . . Oliver [Franks] and Eden both assured me that in his address to Congress Mr Churchill would say something helpful on this subject. As I listened to his speech, I could see the struggle clearly portrayed. It began with the good words which his collaborators had induced him to accept and ended with a glimpse of the Old Adam showing through.[40]

Back in London Eden faced renewed pressure on the European issue. The first phase lasted until May 1952. Acheson tackled Eden on several occasions following the end of the Washington conversations: in London on 16 February on the day following the funeral of King George the Sixth; in Lisbon later in the same month; and in May in Bonn. For the British Foreign

Secretary these were months of steady retreat. At the beginning of February he visited Paris and offered the French Foreign Minister, Schuman, a statement that 'His Majesty's Government are resolved to maintain armed forces on the continent of Europe for as long as is necessary, having regard to the requirements of the EDC as well as to their obligations to NATO and their special responsibilities in Germany'. But Schuman found this too vague and feared that as a result the EDC scheme would be rejected in the French Assembly. By mid-February Acheson had persuaded Eden to agree to a joint Anglo-American declaration of guarantee of the EDC from internal or external threats. But this, too, proved inadequate for French purposes. Now the Europeans demanded a formal Anglo-American treaty of guarantee, as distinct from a declaration, though Eden had earlier informed Schuman that he could not support such a departure. Again, the British Foreign Secretary hesitated but by April yielded in principle. Further delays were occasioned by haggling over the length of the guarantees and about other details. Still more minor concessions were wrung from the British in conferences in Bonn and in Paris late in May. Finally agreement between the various governments was reached on the 26th. This was not, however, the last of Eden's troubles over the EDC. For ratification by the French Assembly was still in doubt. In the event this was to be refused in the autumn of 1954, when, as will be seen, still more concessions were to be dragged from the reluctant Eden. It is thus possible that less would in the end have been required of him if his rhetoric had been more conciliatory in tone.

The British partial retreat on the EDC in the early part of 1952 was not matched by any *quid pro quo* from Washington. In particular, repeated British requests that the NATO Council should have a permanent home in London were firmly rejected. Here there was further evidence that the Americans did not believe in Eden's vision of Great Britain as a bridge between the United States and the European members of NATO. But he stubbornly refused to acknowledge that Washington wanted two pillars not three. Moreover some critics have argued that by pursuing the chimera of a unique British rôle he largely created that suspicion of London in western European capitals which lasted until the 1970s and which allegedly caused lasting British impoverishment; while his reluctant concessions, made at American insistence, far from appeasing the Europeans, only served to underline the 'unsoundness' of his other attitudes. Thus men like Jean Monnet and Paul-Henri Spaak became fanatically determined to exclude the British from future European cooperative ventures. Such arguments have merit. Yet it is fair to add that Eden met with little opposition at home. The Cabinet, his own backbenchers, the Labour Party, the press, and the Foreign Office for the most part shared his global vision. And even Macmillan and Maxwell Fyfe found it prudent to remain largely silent in the

Cabinet when these matters were on the agenda. Hence Eden may have been guilty of monumental misjudgements but, if so, many others of his generation deserve to be co-defendants in the same dock.

Soon after his return from the Washington talks of January 1952 Eden was also facing intensifying difficulties with the Americans on the subject of Egypt. Acheson's view was that the British should in effect accept the Egyptian repudiation of the 1936 Treaty, which provided for a British military presence at Suez, and of the 1899 Treaty, which had established an Anglo-Egyptian condominium over the Sudan. As has been seen, the American Secretary of State rejected the idea of a token American presence at Suez and regarded the Middle East Command idea as a forlorn hope unless the British first restored full Egyptian sovereignty. But in the Washington conversations he had not pressed the British unduly. His fears that chaos would otherwise prevail were much strengthened, however, when a major riot occurred in Cairo on 'Black Saturday', 26 January. This followed a major punitive exercise by British troops on the previous day at Ismailia where forty-three Egyptians had been killed in an arguably excessive response by General George Erskine, who had been plagued by saboteurs of British water supplies. Mobs in Cairo attacked the Turf Club and killed nine British subjects. They also committed the near-sacrilege of setting fire to Shepheard's Hotel. On the following day Acheson sought out Franks: 'Speaking very personally the Secretary said that it did not impress him that the operation at Ismailia had been carried out with "unusual skill". He said the "splutter of musketry" apparently does not stop things as we had been told from time to time that it would.'[41]

Eden determined to support Erskine and, fearing that matters might get completely out of hand and require British intervention in Cairo and Alexandria, asked for American support. This was in effect refused. Fortunately, however, the Egyptian authorities succeeded in restoring order without British assistance. But the crisis caused King Farouk to dismiss his government and this in turn made him look increasingly vulnerable to a coup. To the Americans the obvious way to strengthen the regime was for the British to negotiate on Suez and to recognize Farouk as the Sudanese monarch. This did not appeal to Eden. In particular, he was unwilling to give ground on the issue of the Sudan. There had been, it is true, a long tradition in British policy of not permitting the unification of the Nile Valley unless this met with the approval of the Sudanese people – a line that had certainly been motivated in part by high-minded beliefs in rights of self-determination. But the views of the Sudanese people were unclear and Eden showed little enthusiasm for putting them to the test – a course frequently urged upon him by the Americans, and particularly by Jefferson Caffery, their assertive Ambassador in Cairo. Eden even rejected the idea of allowing Farouk to be proclaimed King of the Sudan provided the Sudanese gave subsequent ratification. He recalled:

Endorsement by us of such a title, even provisionally, would be taken by many in the Sudan to mean that we were no longer interested in the matter, and that we acknowledged the King of Egypt as the future ruler of the country. They would conclude that it was no use their resisting this decision and they would vote for the King of Egypt. This would not be a true expression of Sudanese opinion.[42]

This would seem to have been carrying disinterested concern for 'true' Sudanese opinion to such excessively noble lengths as to be somewhat out of character for a man as used to the demands of *Realpolitik* as Eden. The principal reason for his attitude may in reality have been that the Sudan provided a plausible excuse for not finalizing an agreement with Farouk on the Suez question, about which he was in theory prepared to negotiate. And Farouk, for his part, may also have secretly favoured the deadlock. Anthony Nutting, then Parliamentary Under-Secretary at the Foreign Office, subsequently argued that his claim to the Sudan effectively blocked a deal on Suez and this in turn kept the British on hand to help him save his throne if revolution should be attempted.[43] Acheson's pressure on both Farouk and Eden was in these circumstances doomed to failure. But so too was the Farouk–Eden policy of unconstructive prevarication.

The end came late in July 1952. A bloodless coup by young army officers, led by General Mohammed Neguib and Colonel Gamal Abdel Nasser, overthrew Farouk and established a radical nationalist dictatorship. There was no resistance by monarchist supporters, no anti-British violence and hence no pretext for British intervention. According to Nutting, Farouk asked the American Ambassador to obtain British help. But inevitably the State Department used its influence to resist any possibility of action, despite 'urgent consultations between London and Washington'.[44] Now at last the end was in sight for the British military presence at Suez. The stage was being set for Eden's *Götterdämmerung*.

Meanwhile more Anglo-American differences arose in connection with Iran. In June 1952 the International Court in The Hague decided by nine votes to five that it had no jurisdiction in the dispute, since the Anglo-Persian arrangement of 1933, ironically in part the work of Eden himself, did not constitute a formal treaty covered by the provisions of the Optional Clause.[45] This was a severe blow to London and led Churchill to offer to make concessions in an attempt to prevent the United States from pursuing a policy wholly hostile towards British interests. Acheson proposed in July the following compromise: an American grant of ten million dollars would go to Iran; the British would take the oil then stored in Iran at a near-market price; and in return the Iranians would be asked to allow international arbitration of compensation due for the act of nationalization. Eden's initial reply was unhelpful. In particular, he wanted arbitration on whether nationalization itself should have occurred and not merely to determine compensation. Acheson stated that this attitude was 'related and relevant to our proposal ... only by being expressed on paper by means of a typewriter'.[46] Some in Washington were so outraged at Eden's stubbornness that they began to advocate a separate American deal with Teheran at the expense of the Anglo-Iranian Oil Company even though, surprising as it may seem, the American oil companies were known to be reluctant to be party to such a cut-throat policy. Churchill, rightly or wrongly, thought he perceived danger signals and hence in August, while Eden was on leave, agreed to the substance of Acheson's plan being put to Mussadeq in his name and Truman's. Eden disliked this move towards appeasement and may therefore have felt relieved when the Iranians turned it down and broke off diplomatic relations with Great Britain. Moreover, the Americans had now been placed in an embarrassing position: they could not so lightly contemplate a bilateral deal with Teheran. Nevertheless, the last months of the Democratic Administration saw further tentative moves by Acheson both in the direction of demanding more concessions from London and in preparing contingency plans for by-passing the British. For he was obsessed with the fear that the British policy of 'rule-or-ruin' would push Iran behind the Iron Curtain and he frankly recognized that his approach was bound to stir up 'turgid waters' in London. In conversation with Eden on 20 November Acheson stated:

We would in any event always consult with them [the British] and strive for the solution which would be most acceptable to them. In the last analysis, however, the US Government may have no alternative but to move forward in a manner best designed in its opinion to save Iran.

Eden, for his part, refused to be panicked into further appeasement and believed that the West would 'be better occupied looking for alternatives to Mussadeq rather than trying to buy him off'. As will be seen, the new Republican Administration soon acquiesced in the substance of Eden's approach. If, however, Acheson had remained at the State Department, it seems likely that Anglo-American relations on this subject would have rapidly worsened. The extent of his bitterness is revealed in recollections taped in 1954:

The Foreign Office view – that is Eden's personal view – of things was that he, Anthony Eden, understood and knew the Persians. He had taken a trip after he resigned in 1935 or '36 over the Ethiopian issue [sic]; he had gone to Persia as a private citizen and on a visit. And like so many people who have been briefly in a part of the world, his whole knowledge was colossal as a result of that one visit. He knew the Persians; he had been there and in his view they were rug dealers and that's all they were. You should never give in; they would always come around and make a deal with you if you just stayed firm. As far as there being any danger that the Persian economy would go to pieces, it was always in pieces, and it couldn't be much worse than it was and it didn't make any difference. It was a matter of unimportance to anybody ...

I was strongly impressed by the influence of the British Treasury ... It impinged on me, chiefly through Leslie Rowan, who succeeded in making me quite furious. I have never had the difficulty of having one person get between me and the subject as completely as Leslie Rowan did. His view was very clear, very crisp and very absolute. It was that this Iranian action here was an attack on British foreign investments and that the whole British position depended upon its foreign investments which furnished the invisible items in its balance of trade; that if the British permitted any dent to be made in the sanctity and the security of their foreign investments, they were finished ... And so their chief attitude ... towards this effort at nationalization was that it had to fail and had to fail publicly and disastrously and it had to be punished ... [Faced with the argument that] Iran might dissolve and end up behind the Iron Curtain – he was quite unmoved by that. It was perfectly all right; if that was what happened, well, that was what happened. But they had to be punished, and one way of punishing them might be to put them behind the Iron Curtain. And then they would be sorry that they ever interfered with British foreign investment. And this was adamant – you couldn't make any impression on it whatsoever.[47]

Eden's showdown with Washington might thus easily have come over Iran rather than Egypt. If so, perhaps Acheson rather than Dulles would have been the villain of Eden's memoirs.

More difficulties arose between Eden and Acheson on Far Eastern matters. The underlying difference concerned the Communist Chinese, whom the British were more reluctant than the Americans to provoke. For Eden faced a very different public opinion and opposition party from those confronted by the Democratic Administration in Washington. The Labour front bench tried to maintain bipartisanship but needed help from Eden in view of the growing tide of Bevanite criticism. Nor was Eden's caution vis-à-vis Peking solely a matter of domestic politics. He feared that a Sino-American conflict would lead to Soviet retaliation in Europe and maybe even to nuclear attacks on Great Britain. The United States could afford to be more bold, since in the early 1950s her territory was out of range to Soviet bombers. Eden, once in office, accordingly urged Acheson not to go to extremes, either over Korea or over the newly emerging crisis in Indochina. But the Indochina issue was complicated by France's rôle as a major European power that might wreck Eden's hopes of seeing the West Germans playing a full part in deterring Soviet expansion. In May 1952, for example, he felt obliged to support Acheson in making to Schuman vague offers of help in Indochina. This did not represent any real commitment to out-and-out internationalism in the face of a world Communist threat. It flowed instead from Eden's fear that Schuman would not otherwise play his part in presenting clearly unacceptable preconditions for negotiations with the Soviets on German reunification. For Konrad Adenauer could not have hoped to get the EDC plan accepted in West Germany if the French Government had raised hopes, as they were tempted to do, that the Soviets might be genuinely interested in creating a united, neutralized Germany. Western unity in the face of skilful Soviet overtures was only preserved with difficulty – and the price for Eden was a more vigorous endorsement of Franco-American plans in Indochina than he would otherwise have preferred.

More tension arose when, on 23 and 24 June, the Americans for the first time bombed power stations on the Yalu River. These were not on China's territory but supplied her airfields. The British Government, which had not been consulted, was subjected to Opposition criticism. Eden and Churchill, while compelled to admit that they had had no advance warning, reluctantly supported the *fait accompli*. Eden privately rebuked Acheson, who happened to be in London and more or less obliged him to apologize for the discourtesy to a specially convened private meeting of Parliamentarians at Westminster.

In August 1952 Eden had a welcome break from politics: he married Clarissa Churchill at Caxton Hall and went for a honeymoon to Portugal. The *Church Times* led a campaign of protest, maintaining that a generation previously the Foreign Secretary would have had to quit rather than be allowed to re-marry while his first wife was still alive. Drawing a parallel with Edward VIII, it concluded: 'Mr Eden's action this week shows how far the climate of public opinion has changed for the worse ... the world is openly rejecting the law of Christ in this as in so much else.'[48] But the climate of public opinion clearly had changed and the Edens were but little troubled by the criticism.

Eden's new wife was thirty-two, twenty-three years his junior. But, as Churchill's niece, she had already a wide circle of acquaintances in public life and was certainly not politically naïve, having served in the Foreign Office during the Second World War. So, despite her youth, she was a major public asset to Eden during the rest of his political career. But of much more significance for him was her continuing devotion during the twenty years of their twenty-four year marriage which they were to spend out of politics. As a much-assailed and ailing man, he might have suffered greatly during the frustrating years of retirement. To the extent that he did not, this was due to his good fortune in having the care and love of a singularly selfless wife.

In late September 1952 Eden flew to Yugoslavia at the invitation of Tito. It was the first visit to Belgrade by a leading Western statesman since the end of the Second World War. In retrospect this seems surprising, for Tito had broken with Stalin as long ago as 1948. The long delay in any Western attempt to court the dissident regime thus constitutes clear evidence of a degree of ideological rigidity not easily understood in a later era. But it is perhaps significant that it was Eden who first demonstrated a wholly flexible approach to the emerging phenomenon of Communist polycentrism. His talks with Tito had no dramatic result, although the two men discussed the long-running dispute between Yugoslavia and Italy over Trieste. Partly as a result of establishing this contact, Eden was able, as will be seen, to play a major rôle during the following years in reaching a solution and thereby reducing the chances of war in the Adriatic. On leaving Yugoslavia, Eden next visited Austria. This country was still divided into occupation zones but negotiations with the Soviets over possible reunification were under consideration and hence his brief presence in Vienna enabled him to appreciate at first hand the character of Austrian aspirations.

The last months of 1952 saw more sharp conflict between Eden and Acheson. At issue were the terms for a Korean armistice. The principal remaining stumbling block was the Communists' demand for automatic and forcible repatriation of prisoners of war. For Eden this represented an uncanny replay of the moral dilemmas he had faced in the closing stages of the Second World War. He had to balance the claims of anti-Communist would-be refugees against the need to liberate British servicemen in Communist hands. He also had to ask whether the humane cause of giving refuge to potential defectors from Communism was worth putting at risk wider objectives. In 1944-5 he had not felt able to jeopardize the chances of good Anglo-Soviet relations; now he had to ask whether risking failure to obtain an armistice might not increase the threat of a world conflict in which Great Britain might be vulnerable to nuclear attack. But the issue in 1952, unlike the earlier case, was widely discussed, for much of the argument about repatriation was carried on in the United Nations General Assembly. Eden therefore had to make several public statements. These were strongly humanitarian in tone and gave no hint of the claims of *Realpolitik*. For example, on 7 May 1952 he said in the House of Commons:

I am sure the House will feel that the United Nations Command has had no alternative but to resist the forcible repatriation of communist prisoners of war who have shown such a strong determination to remain in the free world. I will not dwell on the practical difficulties of forcibly repatriating more than 62,000 men, many of whom could be expected to commit suicide on the way. It would, I think, clearly be repugnant to the sense of values of the free world to send these men home by force.

Lord Bethell, a severe critic of his wartime rôle, was even led by these remarks to write in 1974: 'It would be heartening to think it was his experience as the architect of forcible repatriation in 1944 that brought

Eden to this noble conclusion and that, to this extent at least, the dismal story has a happy ending.'[49] Eden's private diplomacy, however, was a good deal more equivocal than his public statements would imply.

Eden played a particularly important rôle after 8 November when he arrived in New York for the seventh session of the UN General Assembly. His Minister of State, Selwyn Lloyd, had already spent nearly a fortnight in feverish and complicated negotiations aimed at presenting a resolution on prisoners of war which might open the way to an armistice. One key figure was Krishna Menon of India, who had put himself forward as a mediator between the West and the absent Chinese with whom New Delhi had diplomatic relations. He claimed that a formula could be found that might prove acceptable in Peking but which would not necessarily involve forcible repatriation. He was, however, imprecise about his plans for those prisoners not wishing to return: he evidently envisaged their indefinite retention in captivity until agreement could be reached on their release by a commission whose composition and voting procedure was not clearly defined. This ambiguous approach maddened Acheson, who believed that the result for the prisoners would be that the 'only escape from captivity would be repatriation'. 'It was,' he wrote to Truman, 'as they say in strike lingo, giving us the words and the other side the decision.'[50] But the same ambiguity appealed to the majority of the United States' allies, precisely because it seemed to represent the best hope of securing an armistice. There was, moreover, the further argument that the Communist Powers might reject even the Indian approach and thereby isolate themselves from the sympathies of the growing non-aligned group in the United Nations. And for the British there was yet another consideration: the need to maintain some semblance of Commonwealth unity on this as on other issues. This was of course becoming an increasingly daunting task as the White Dominions were gradually supplemented by states of the so-called New Commonwealth, but one that Eden, in particular, could not ignore after he had indulged for so long in high-flown rhetoric on Great Britain's new world rôle. Hence for all these reasons Lloyd, together with Canada's Foreign Minister, Pearson, then President of the General Assembly, took the lead in trying to lure the Americans into going along with Menon while simultaneously seeking to persuade the latter to accept amendments that would make the ultimate fate of the anti-Communist prisoners look a little more rosy.

Eden claimed in his memoirs that he had 'much sympathy with the American position'.[51] This did not mean that he entirely agreed with it. For the diaries of both Pearson and Shuckburgh reveal that great friction arose between Eden and Acheson during the course of a number of personal encounters in New York. On 13 November Pearson attended a meeting with representatives of France, New Zealand and Australia as well as Eden and Acheson. Only Percy Spender of Australia agreed with the American Secretary of State and even he was opposing his own Government's line. According to Pearson, 'Eden seemed to agree with me, though he was careful not to intervene in the discussion either very often or very emphatically.' But by 19 November Acheson was determined to force Eden's hand. On the previous evening Menon had flatly refused to accept a ninety-day limit to the retention in captivity of prisoners resisting repatriation on the candid grounds that it would be unacceptable to the Communists. Now Acheson offered for the first time to support Menon's plan provided that the proposed commission to handle the prisoners should have a neutral chairman with executive powers and not subject to veto; and that there should be an alternative to repatriation other than indefinite imprisonment. But he added a further brutal condition: Eden must agree openly to support him in these demands. This the British Foreign Secretary initially felt unable to do but was, not surprisingly, embarrassed. Pearson recorded:

Eden had just come from a very tough and not too pleasant hour with Acheson and was a little shaken by the stiff and uncompromising attitude he encountered towards the Indian resolution ... The Americans ... have put Eden 'on the spot'.

Shuckburgh wrote in his diary of this same day:

The climax of the unpleasantness with Acheson took place this evening in A.E.'s room when Acheson and [John] Hickerson [US Assistant Secretary for UN Affairs] came down from a cocktail party ... and proceeded to make a most extraordinary scene. Selwyn Lloyd was there. Half-bantering, half-serious, Acheson said S.L. was not to be trusted. Had misled and twisted the Americans for weeks. Was a Welsh lawyer, etc., etc. Selwyn gave as good as he got and A.E. seems to have sat back astonished. Acheson said that unless the US and UK were in line over this Korea resolution (i.e. unless we agreed with them) there would be no NATO, no Anglo-American friendship, etc. Which side were we on? Hickerson actually said: 'Anthony, which will you choose: the United States or India?' They were probably both a little tight. Also chagrined by the general support of Krishna Menon's resolution and the way it has been improved to meet every objection they have raised. Acheson called Pearson 'an empty glass of water' and said that Canada should be brought to heel by the United States. He said that in his speech next week he would tear the Indian resolution apart. He also used the phrase 'debagging that Swami'.

Acheson admitted for the first time that if the armistice talks failed the Americans had plans for a major offensive.

A.E.: 'But you haven't enough troops!'
A.: 'We have four divisions we could send.'
A.E.: 'Why didn't you tell us this before?'
A.: No answer.

As he left, A. said, 'Don't you ever appoint a Welsh lawyer as your Minister of State again!' He then added, 'All lawyers are failures in foreign policy. Look at myself and John Simon.'

Eden tried to outmanoeuvre Acheson by contacting Eisenhower, who had just won the Presidential Election but who was not due to take office until January 1953. But Acheson and Truman had also had the same idea and by meeting with Eisenhower had effectively neutralized Eden's efforts – at least for a time.[52] The Americans further retaliated by ruthlessly leaking to the New York press accounts of their differences with Eden that put him in as unfavourable a light as possible.

Pearson, writing in his diary, provided evidence that the differences between Eden and Acheson were now assuming a personal character: 'He [Eden] is not looking forward to his talk with Acheson, who seems to inspire a certain amount of apprehension in him. These are two people who shouldn't be left alone in the same room to argue . . .' On 22 November Eden and Lloyd met with Pearson and agreed to continue to try to move Acheson and Menon towards each other. But Pearson recorded, 'We also decided, however, that if the worst comes to the worst and the American amendments went too far to be acceptable to the Indians, we would vote for the Indian proposal as it stood, come what may.' Thus Eden was preparing for an open break with the United States on the subject of repatriation. On the same afternoon the Americans increased the pressure. According to Pearson:

. . . a strange incident occurred. [Ernest] Gross [the American Ambassador to the UN] called on Eden having previously informed the press that he was going to do so, and having given the impression that his visit was a critical one, and that he was going to give the British something in the nature of an ultimatum. Eden was intensely annoyed at this way of conducting delicate diplomatic negotiations. He told me about it afterwards and indicated that it would have the contrary effect on him to that which the Americans desired.

Shuckburgh recorded on the same day:

The battle continues . . . Acheson was heard saying to his staff that they will have to 'fight their way out', which gives a pleasant picture of the American tough guy shooting his way out of an awkward position and scattering his friends on every side. The fact is that, when you scratch this elegant and civilized Acheson, he turns out to be just another tough guy.

. . . Gross asked to come and see A.E. Before he had arrived, the AP [Associated Press] had the story that he was coming to tell A.E. from Acheson where to get off. We confronted him with this. He was speechless and spoke of pressure upon him from the Pentagon and from Washington.

. . . The Russians are beginning to say that the Americans are mad not to support it. We are determined to do so whatever happens. A.E. is feeling 'as he did about Mussolini' and says he would not mind if he had to resign over this. Surprisingly enough, Winston is sending telegrams which indicate no doubts about the line we are pursuing.[53]

The Anglo-American crisis was suddenly defused, however, on 24 November when Andrei Vishinsky of the Soviet Union made a singularly clumsy attack on Menon and his plan. This achieved what Eden had been unable to do: it drove Acheson and Menon closer together. Within a week they had agreed on a three-month maximum period for post-armistice retention of prisoners by an international commission. Remaining disagreements about individual cases would then be determined by a political conference or by the United Nations itself. This formula was approved by the General Assembly by fifty-four votes to five and was eventually accepted by the Communists when the armistice was finally signed in the following summer. Thus a major Anglo-American quarrel in public was again narrowly averted. But the episode provides further evidence that the Eden–Acheson relationship was far from smooth and that had the Secretary of State not retired in January 1953 he would probably have turned into one of Eden's *bêtes noires*.

The advent of Eisenhower's Republican Administration brings us once again to the question of Eden's relationship with Dulles. We have already seen that Merchant, of the State Department, did not believe that his chief felt any strong or consistent hostility towards Eden at least until the Suez crisis of 1956; and that he doubted whether Eden was actually as suspicious and distrustful of Dulles as he chose to imply in his memoirs. Opponents of this interpretation will of course make much of Eisenhower's allegation that Eden had the temerity to advise him not to appoint Dulles – an allegation denied by Eden.[54] But even if Eisenhower's testimony is believed, it is not as decisive as it might appear. For Eden scarcely knew Dulles at first hand and may thus have been merely relaying the opinion of some of his officials and of Morrison, who remained the Opposition's chief foreign affairs' spokesman and who could not forgive the alleged deception involved in the Yoshida letter affair. True, Eden had no high opinion of Morrison. Yet he attached great importance to retaining the support of Labour's front bench for his foreign policy and on these grounds alone may have hoped for a different Secretary of State.

The two men's first encounter after Dulles's move into the State Department came early in February 1953 in London. Shuckburgh recorded in his diary: '. . . a visit from Dulles and [Harold] Stassen who made a good impression on our ministers, rather unexpectedly in the case of Dulles, against whom we had been prejudiced'. But, according to Julius Holmes, then in the American Embassy, who was also present:

They didn't get off to a very good start. There was a little bit of sparring back and forth. Obviously these two men were not sympathetic, one to the other. But after a time – Eden was very forthcoming – and he finally turned and said, 'We're going to work together here – our nations do – and I would like to have an intimate relationship with you. Most of my friends call me by my first name, and I'd like to have that arrangement with you.' And Dulles agreed to it, although it was awkward for him to agree. It was perfectly clear that this surprised him a little bit.

Certainly Eden's style differed greatly from that of his austere and puritanical opposite number. Roderic O'Connor, Dulles's Special Assistant in the State Department, recalled:

> Every time I saw Eden I always felt an overwhelming sense of personal vanity. And Dulles was exactly the opposite. Dulles may have had intellectual vanity, but he had no personal vanity at all. He was as plain as a stick ... Just personality-wise, they just weren't destined to work very well together ... his [Eden's] image ... the Homburg and all the rest – and his rather calculatedly lazy manner, which is one of the upper-class manifestations of the old English aristocracy, wasn't Dulles's dish of tea.[55]

If Dulles had been taken aback by Eden's suggestion that they refer to each other by their Christian names, we may presume that he would have been even more surprised to encounter the latter's habit of addressing members of his own sex as 'my dear'. While evidently by no means uncommon among members of the British élite of his age group, it was probably even more uncongenial to Dulles than it had been to Acheson.

While personality differences were clearly significant, they do not serve as a sufficient basis for assuming that major policy divergences were inevitable. In fact such conflicts as occurred during Dulles's first year were about issues that had arisen under the Democratic Administration and it is even arguable that the heat was taken out of most of them as both sides tried to achieve an improvement in Anglo-American relations. Iran was a case in point. Eden, visiting Washington in March 1953, found an initial inclination on the Americans' part to urge the British to make still more concessions. But he courageously challenged the underlying assumptions of this approach, which had been inherited from Acheson. In particular, he stressed again that allowing the Iranians to be seen to succeed in 'theft' would weaken the West's position throughout the Middle East and that, though obviously undesirable, Iran's disappearance behind the Iron Curtain would be a lesser evil than that. Moreover, he did not believe that if the Americans supported the British any such Communist victory in Teheran was likely. He also made clear 'the deplorable effect on Anglo-American relations' that would result from any American decision to send American technicians to the Abadan refinery, which would not otherwise be able to function. Faced with these pleas, Eisenhower and Dulles yielded; and it is perhaps a measure of the honeymoon nature of the relationship at this stage that even Eden felt obliged to write in his memoirs that 'Dulles reasonably accepted that, if our proposals of February 20th were rejected [they were], we should let the whole question of the oil issue be suspended.'[56] It may be doubted whether Acheson would have been so 'reasonable'.

Eden, for his part, gave ground to the Americans concerning Formosa. Eisenhower, as a move in Korean War diplomacy, had declared that the mission of the Seventh Fleet in the Formosa Strait was no longer even-handedly to interpose itself between the Communists and the Nationalists to prevent hostilities. Some read this as a threat to encourage an attack by Chiang on the mainland. Eden told the House of Commons on 3 February that he feared the statement would have 'unfortunate political reper-cussions without compensating military advantages'. But after his talks with Dulles he told the Commons two days later that he did not expect 'grave results' to ensue from the President's move.[57]

Another issue on which at least a degree of reconciliation proved possible was Egypt. In part this resulted from developments arising from the change of regime in Cairo. In particular, the Sudan was ceasing to be the bone of contention that it had been under Farouk, whose claim to the Sudanese throne had been as unacceptable in London as it had been acceptable in Washington. Neguib's position was more flexible: while not abandoning hope of the unification of the Nile Valley, he was prepared to allow elections to take place in the Sudan on terms that Eden had previously advanced without expecting them to be acceptable. With the precondition about the throne now redundant, Neguib was prepared to take the risk that the elections might result in a demand for Sudanese independence rather than unification with Egypt. For, whatever the result of the election, the British would have to leave Khartoum and hence negotations on Suez could proceed without the Sudanese complication. This move had caused some consternation in London, particularly in Downing Street. Shuckburgh's diary is eloquent:

20 January 1953
Prime Minister returned from his holiday in Jamaica passionately interested in the Egyptian situation. No-one seems to know how he had become convinced ... that a great deterioration had set in ... There were Questions down in Parliament about this ... and he wanted to see the drafts of what A.E. would say. The latter much upset: 'If he has so little confidence in me, I had better go.'

29 January 1953
... Jock Colville came round to see me in a great state of agitation. He said there was going to be a row. He had gone overnight to Southampton and travelled up with the PM. The latter was in a rage against A.E., speaking of 'appeasement' and saying he never knew before that Munich was situated on the Nile. He described A.E. as having been a failure as Foreign Secretary and being 'tired, sick and bound up in detail'. Jock said the Prime Minister would never give way over Egypt. He positively desired the

talks on the Sudan to fail, just as he positively hoped we should not succeed in getting into conversations with the Egyptians on defence which might lead to our abandonment of the Canal Zone.

... In the event, A.E. told me, nothing happened at all. There was no confrontation. The conversation was quite amiable but equally no decisions were taken. These two always shy away from a quarrel at the last moment.

30 January 1953

A Cabinet in the afternoon on Egypt. Expectation of more fireworks, but none took place. I spent a very uncomfortable half-hour with the Private Secretaries at No. 10, during which Colville, [David] Pitblado and [Anthony] Montague Browne all attacked A.E. and the Foreign Office for their policy on Egypt ... they thought it ridiculous that we should not be able to cope with the Egyptian army with the eighty thousand men we have in the Zone. The Chiefs of Staff, they said (obviously quoting the Prime Minister) always say that the force available in any emergency is insufficient. You have to prove the contrary. If we go out of the Sudan and Egypt it will be another stage in the policy of scuttle which began in India and ended at Abadan. It will lead to the abandonment of our African colonies ... [Colville] tells me that the PM is very bellicose against A.E. 'If he resigns, I will accept it and take the Foreign Office myself.'[58]

But Eden felt unable to renege on his declaratory commitment to self-determination for the Sudanese and he carried the bulk of the Cabinet for his view. He accordingly defied Churchill and a number of Conservative backbenchers and set in motion a process that culminated in Sudanese elections. These eventually gave an apparent victory to pro-Egyptian groupings. But factional disputes led to the unexpected conversion of some of those initially elected on a pro-Cairo mandate and hence the Sudan opted for independence which, after a transitional phase, came about in January 1956. But when Eden appeared in Washington for his first meeting with the new Administration the eventual outcome in the Sudan was not clear. What mattered, as already stated, was that the subject could no longer be presented as a stumbling block to a negotiated settlement of the Suez problem. Also welcome in Washington was the decision in December 1952 by the British Cabinet, with the support of the Chiefs of Staff, that changing circumstances meant that Suez could cease to be a principal Middle East base; Cyprus was chosen as a substitute.

Plainly the ground was being prepared for a British retreat. But Eden insisted on some minimum concessions from the Egyptians in return: they should join a Middle East Defence Organization (MEDO) and their partners, in practice the British, should have the right to return to the Canal Zone in certain eventualities. A variation on this plan had earlier been tepidly endorsed by Acheson, but had been rejected by Farouk. Now Eden believed that, with the Sudanese issue on the way to solution and with a new American Administration in office, a new effort was desirable. Where

Eisenhower and Dulles were concerned, his hopes were not misplaced. In their first Washington conversations with Eden they were most forthcoming, endorsing the MEDO plan and agreeing that provision should be made for a return to Suez in the event of attacks being made on MEDO members. This scheme was wrecked, however, by Neguib's refusal to consider Egypt joining MEDO before agreement was reached on ending the British military presence at Suez. In his memoirs Eden argued that the Americans could have done more to show solidarity with London and that, in particular, they could have pressed harder for an equal share with the British in the negotiations in Cairo about Suez 'without being accused of gatecrashing'.[59] This is debatable. But what is clear is that Dulles did his best to persuade the Egyptians to enter upon serious negotiations with the British and that he was strongly in favour of MEDO, as he was later to be of most other anti-Communist defence pacts. Moreover, he aroused much hostility in Cairo by refusing, pending an Egyptian settlement with London, to honour earlier American commitments, dating from the Democratic Administration, to provide armaments on a considerable scale. His visit to Cairo in May 1953 was therefore by no means an unqualified success from the Egyptian point of view.[60] It was on this occasion, however, that Dulles presented Neguib with two silver-engraved pistols as a gift from Eisenhower. This was interpreted by some in London as a symbol of American disloyalty to British interests. But no student of Eisenhower's straightforward personality will believe that so subtle a snub was intended. On the contrary, American policy on Egypt was closer to that of Great Britain in the first year of his Administration than it had ever been in the Truman–Acheson era. But Eden did not see fit, understandably enough, to emphasize this in his memoirs.

In the spring of 1953, shortly after his return from Washington, Eden's ill-health became acute. He had suffered from internal pains for some time and had also had an attack of jaundice in the previous year. Now on 2 April gallstones were diagnosed. According to Shuckburgh, three days later: 'Five doctors, huddled round the case history and the photographs, eventually concluded there would have to be an operation. [Sir Horace] Evans made the remark: "It is hard to assess the degree of pain when dealing with a highly-strung thoroughbred."' Soon a funereal atmosphere enveloped Eden. According to Shuckburgh, he received 'a letter from Selwyn Lloyd which included the phrase, "I have so enjoyed working with you." Added to this, a messenger from A.E.'s solicitors arrived with a little note pointing out that his Will was not in proper shape.' The operation, carried out on 12 April, did not in the event have quite the gloomy outcome these portents appeared to foreshadow. But it was not a success. And a second operation was carried out on 29 April with no better result. Probably Eden would have been wise to recognize from the outset that his country's decline was not confined to international affairs and should have tried to get medical advice elsewhere. But after two failures even he and his British doctors were obliged to consult an American authority, Richard Cattell of Boston. Shuckburgh was told by Evans why Cattell had superior experience: 'It seems that since the war, the English suffer more from ulcers owing to lack of fats, while the Americans are constantly having gall trouble.'[61] Whatever the truth of this may be, Cattell presently undertook to try to rectify what had gone wrong, namely that Eden's bile duct had been severely damaged in the course of the earlier operations. While willing in the last resort to operate in London, he much preferred Boston, even though this involved a difficult journey for a man who was by now in a much weakened condition. Eden accepted the advice and, after a period of rest at Chequers, made the transatlantic journey. For this purpose he was lent the aeroplane of the Governor-General of Canada. A third operation was duly performed and proved to be a relative success. While a complete cure proved impossible – probably as a result of what had been done to his bile duct in the London operations – he was to have a respite from pain, fevers and jaundice for a sufficient period to enable him to obtain the premiership which he must at times have thought likely to elude him. After months of recuperation at Newport, Rhode Island, and cruising in the Mediterranean, he was able to return to active politics in October 1953.

Eden's removal from the scene had inevitably given Churchill an increased degree of influence in shaping British policy. Initially, moreover, the Prime Minister decided that he himself should take charge of the Foreign Office. Though undoubtedly anxious about Eden's state of health, he cannot have found unwelcome the stimulus of the free hand he now had in foreign affairs. Confirmation is provided in the diary of Dixon of the Foreign Office:

3 May 1953
Lunched with W.S.C. at No. 10. In A.E.'s absence he has taken charge at the FO, and is taking a lively interest in its day to day work ... We lunched alone with a Private Secretary (Jock Colville). The PM was wearing a very well cut boiler suit in blue serge with a white pin-stripe. We lunched in the small dining-room. The lunch lasted for 3¼ hours. A varied and noble procession of wines with which I could not keep pace – champagne, port, brandy, cointreau: W. drank a great deal of all, and ended with two glasses of whisky and soda. The champagne was Pol Roger 1928, which he said he liked more than any other; he had managed to buy up most of the stocks in London.

Indo-China. The Communists invaded Laos, one of the Associate States, last month. Should its King be advised to leave the capital, Luang Prabang? W. complained that he had been able to remain ignorant about these areas all his life; it was hard that they had come to tease him in his old age.

Persia. I was explaining a point, and I mentioned Musáddiq. He interrupted me. 'I call him Mussy Duck.'

The FO. Telegrams too verbose and too many of them. The Ambassadors should be made to encypher their reports themselves. The FO too prone to appease.

20 June 1953
Sent for by W.S.C. at 5.20. [Earl] Alexander [of Tunis, Minister of Defence] and Selwyn Lloyd also there. Worked in the Cabinet room till past seven, and another hour's work for me in the FO to finish everything off.

Mentally he [Churchill] is more alert than he was towards the end of the war. As always, he did all the work himself in the sense of dictating the telegrams himself after reaching his decision.[62]

This must surely have been the last occasion when anyone could consider Churchill 'more alert than he was towards the end of the war'. For three days later he had a serious stroke. His speech was slurred, he could scarcely walk and was unable to concentrate on business for any prolonged period. It was at first thought that he would have to quit and it is possible that if Eden had been fit he would have been talked into doing so. But he was able to argue that he should cling on a little longer in order not to rob his Foreign Secretary of the supreme prize. This argument was a little threadbare, for he could have recommended that Salisbury serve on an interim basis rather than put forward Butler, who would otherwise have been the obvious choice. Nevertheless, his decision in the circumstances to persevere was understandable enough, especially as in the summer months he could avoid public appearances.

By the autumn, however, faced with Eden's recovery, Churchill had to find a new reason for staying in office and this turned out to be his belief that there would soon be a summit meeting with the Soviet and American Heads of Government at which his matchless prestige and experience would be needed. This was clearly in part the rationalization of a selfish man, in most respects no longer fit to hold office. He had, moreover, sent messages to his Foreign Secretary which had led the latter to believe that the premiership would be his as soon as he was fit to take it on. The sequel may be judged from Shuckburgh's diary:

22 July 1953
Jock Colville came round to see me to express his anxiety lest A.E. ... assume too much readiness on the PM's part to retire shortly and hand the baton to Anthony. It seems the old man has made a miraculous recovery from his stroke and is far from thinking of throwing in the sponge. Yet A.E. has been led to believe the end was near ...

23 July 1953
After consulting William Strang, decided to write A.E. warning him of PM's mood and condition and am rather apprehensive of the result and see impatient days ahead.
... Met Norman Brook [Secretary to the Cabinet] who approved of my action in writing to A.E. and asked me to tell him ... that the PM feels he is doing very well by A.E. in managing to tide over the period between now and Parliament's return in October, when A.E. will be fully recovered. So he [Churchill] won't like to be asked when he is going to die.

28 July 1953

I went to Lord S's [Salisbury's] house ... Talked about A.E.'s ambitions and his intention to beard the PM about the handover at Chequers next weekend [during the course of a brief spell in Great Britain before leaving for further rest in the Mediterranean] ... He seemed inclined to agree with Jock Colville that A.E. would be ill-advised to voice the matter even now. 'I have been through all this a hundred times. The fact is that the PM is much tougher than Anthony. He soon brings Anthony to the point beyond which he knows he will not go and then he has won the day.' S. does not believe the PM will commit himself to any date for retirement ... I said I was afraid that I had been witnessing in the last two years the slow unfolding of a Greek tragedy; that A.E. would never in fact get the Premiership, which has so often seemed near his grasp. S.: 'Perhaps his real rôle is to be a great Foreign Secretary.' I: 'But that is not how he sees it.' S., the aristocrat: 'That is the trouble with them all. They are so ambitious.'

4 August 1953

S. told me all about the weekend at Chequers. He formed a poor impression of A.E.'s state of health. Thought him 'fragile'. PM in no mood to discuss retirement and they did not raise it. Jock Colville went so far as to speak of Winston carrying on until June 1954 when The Queen comes back from Australia.

1 October 1953

Called on A.E. at 10.45 at Carlton Gardens and drove with him to Downing Street for his first interview with Winston [since his return from convalescence]. He was obviously not looking forward to it. His doctor has said he can do any job except Foreign Secretary; yet he knows the PM wants him to do that and he is afraid to refuse in case it looks as if he is not fit. I advised him not to take the FO, to swallow his pride and to take life easily for a week or so. But I fear his resolution to confront the PM with awkward decisions is ebbing.

At 12.30 he was back ... It was clear he had got no change out of the PM in regard to the future. The old man determined to carry on, first to the Party Conference speech on October 10, then to face Parliament on October 17. Thinks he can do it but promises A.E. that if he finds he cannot 'fully do his duty' he will quit. Does not want A.E. to take a sinecure and act as deputy because this would give the impression he himself is being bolstered up by A.E. ...

After luncheon A.E. kept Rab, Monckton and Salisbury back and they had a consultation together on what is to be done. All profoundly disturbed at PM's determination to carry on ... All agree he [Eden] has only two choices, to acquiesce in the PM's wishes or to refuse to serve in his Government and this they do not think he can do. In short, they are stymied by Winston as usual.[63]

From October 1953, therefore, Eden had an added grievance against his chief, namely that he had reneged on a promise. Relations accordingly plummeted to new depths in the remaining eighteen months of Eden's period as heir apparent.

When Eden returned to politics in October 1953 his annoyance was not confined to the question of the succession. For he found that Churchill had used his period of unfettered power over foreign policy to make a public demand for a Heads of Government summit. This question had long divided the two men. For even in Opposition Churchill had let it be known, in a speech at Edinburgh on 14 February 1950, that once returned to office he would want to revert to the wartime pattern established at Teheran, Yalta and Potsdam. Truman and Acheson were horrified and brought unmistakable pressure to bear on Churchill between October 1951 and January 1953 not again to adopt this approach in public. Above all, the Democratic Administration feared that Churchill would favour a new spheres-of-influence deal with Stalin. An interdepartmental steering committee, advised by the Joint Chiefs of Staff, submitted to Truman and Acheson a paper in preparation for Churchill's and Eden's visit of January 1952 containing this judgement:

... by virtue of a complex of factors, of which its geographic position and its special history in European power relationships are perhaps predominant, the UK may differ with us over the tactical methods to be followed in realizing our objectives. In sum, the UK may tend (1) to put a more optimistic interpretation on the imminence and extent of the Soviet threat than we do; (2) to place more faith in the feasibility and desirability of making arrangements with the Soviet bloc in the 'spheres of influence' tradition; and (3) consequently to place more emphasis on the value of direct negotiations with Soviet leaders.

Another paper from the same committee is also of interest:

The British will tend to question the necessity or desirability of political warfare operations. They are inclined to accept the present *status quo* in Eastern Europe and do not desire to engage in activities which they consider not only will be calculated to increase East–West tension, but which might even provoke the Kremlin to acts of aggression. The British, in short, appear to believe that the immediate dangers of provocation over-balance the long-term deterrent results of political warfare carried on within Moscow's own orbit ... The Soviet Union ... is endeavouring to create disunity, tensions and weakness in the free world. In the face of this massive attack, we believe we cannot adopt a defensive and passive position but rather must counter-attack by political warfare activities directed against the USSR itself and against the Soviet satellites of Eastern Europe with the objective of increasing the discontent, tension and divisions known to exist in the Soviet orbit. The Iron Curtain must be pierced to bring home to the Kremlin's subject peoples the fact that they have friends and allies in the free world. In addition, such activities are designed to form the political bases and operational nuclei for resistance groups which, we hope, would weaken the Soviet regime in case of armed conflict.

We consider that, on balance, this positive activity will operate to deter rather than to provoke the Soviet Union to military aggression ...

The Americans thus clearly saw Churchill's desire for summit talks with the Soviets as likely to undermine these policies. Eden, however, was no less opposed than the Americans to a summit – though for rather different reasons. First, he did not at this stage take as optimistic a view of the vulnerability of the Soviet system as his chief, whose eccentric opinions were noted by Adenauer on the occasion of a visit to London in December 1951: 'The Soviets were more afraid of British friendship than of British hostility. Contact with Britain would cause the Soviet system to collapse. Any contact of the inhabitants of the Soviet Union with the West would mean the end of the accursed system.'[64] Secondly, Eden disliked the idea of a summit in which he would have to play a subordinate rôle to Churchill. This was no doubt attributable in part to mere jealousy between the two *prima donnas*. But the Foreign Secretary had good grounds for believing that his aged chief might give too much away because of lack of command of detail – as had, in Eden's view, even to some extent been the case during the wartime summits.

If the combination of Eden, Truman and Acheson deterred Churchill once in office from even openly canvassing his plan, the situation was to change in the Prime Minister's favour during 1953. First came the change of American President, with Eisenhower initially prepared at least to consider a summit in Sweden. Next came the death of Stalin in March which enabled Churchill opportunistically to argue that the new Soviet rulers were probably more reasonable and should be brought into contact with himself and Eisenhower as soon as possible. Finally came Eden's illness and the consequent removal of any effective domestic constraint. The result on 11 May 1953 was the Prime Minister's public demand for a summit. Eisenhower's response, under Dulles's influence, was unenthusiastic but not as negative as that of his predecessor. On 25 April Eisenhower had cabled to Churchill:

> There is some feeling here also for a meeting between Heads of States and Governments, but I do not think this should be allowed to press us into precipitate initiatives ... This is not to say, of course, that I do not envisage the possible desirability at an appropriate time that the three Western Powers and the Soviets come together. We should by all means be alert.

Churchill next proposed a meeting between Eisenhower and himself at which the issue of meeting the Soviets could be explored. The President agreed but insisted, in a telephone conversation on 3 June, that the French also be invited. This displeased Churchill, who had hoped that memories of his wartime dealings with Eisenhower would ensure that the so-called 'special relationship' became more real and more exclusive than it had been under Truman. As early as 5 January 1953 he had sought to impress this upon Eisenhower, then President-Elect. The extent of his failure is evident from these extracts from Eisenhower's diary:

> Mr Churchill is as charming and interesting as ever, but he is quite definitely showing the effects of the passing years. He has fixed in his mind a certain international relationship he is trying to establish – possibly it would be better to say

an atmosphere he is trying to create. This is that Britain and the British Commonwealth are not to be treated just as other nations would be treated by the United States in our complicated foreign problems. On the contrary, he most earnestly hopes and intends that those countries shall enjoy a relationship which he thinks will recognize the special place of partnership they occupied with us during World War II ...

Winston is trying to relive the days of World War II.

In those days he had the enjoyable feeling that he and our President were sitting on some rather Olympian platform with respect to the rest of the world, and directing world affairs from that point of vantage. Even if this picture were an accurate one of those days, it would have no application to the present. But it was only partially true, even then, as many of us who, in various corners of the world, had to work out the solutions for nasty local problems, are well aware.

In the present international complexities, any hope of establishing such a relationship is completely fatuous ...

Much as I hold Winston in my personal affection and much as I admire him for his past accomplishments and leadership, I wish that he would turn over leadership of the British Conservation [sic] Party to younger men.

The President's attitude to Churchill was, moreover, known to Eden. For, according to Shuckburgh, when the Foreign Secretary had met Eisenhower in November 1952 he had been told, 'You and I, Schuman and Adenauer can work together', with the pointed omission of Churchill. Eden had commented to Shuckburgh: 'It is rather like Queen Mary. Glad she is there, dear old thing.' Churchill was thus compelled to settle for having the French included in a Western summit scheduled to be held in Bermuda in July 1953. But he even had to give up this limited success as a result of his stroke. Instead a meeting of Western Foreign Ministers took place, with Salisbury representing Great Britain. The idea of a meeting of the Big Four was discussed but the consensus was that this should be at the level of Foreign Ministers and not that of Heads of Government. The three Western Heads of Government, however, would meet as soon as Churchill was fit enough to go to Bermuda. This was a disappointing result for Churchill. But as it did not finally close the door on a summit with the Soviets, he resolved to continue his campaign. To the returning Eden in October this constituted a challenge: he was no less determined than before to thwart Churchill's plan. Indeed, his last words to his Parliamentary Under-Secretary, Nutting, before going to Boston for his operation had been: 'Don't let the old man appease the Bear too much in my absence.'[65] Now he could once again personally take charge of the resistance to Churchill. But it was unlikely to be easy, as Shuckburgh noted in his diary on 5 October: 'Fact is A.E. is scared of the popularity of the PM's project and cannot see any effective rôle for himself in the House of Commons until it has been "decently buried". I fear the burial service may revive the corpse.'[66]

On 16 October Dulles came to London for further discussion about a possible meeting with the Soviets. He was faced with French and German arguments that a final effort to reach agreement with Moscow on German reunification was a precondition for ratification of the EDC plan and he accordingly agreed in principle that a four-power meeting should take place early in 1954. But he successfully resisted a Soviet demand that China should be present. He also blocked Churchill's plea that the meeting should be at the level of Heads of Government and not Foreign Ministers. In a meeting with Churchill, Eden and Salisbury, he claimed that Eisenhower could not easily leave Washington for a prolonged summit. Churchill now began to talk of meeting Georgi Malenkov without Eisenhower and was reminded by Dulles that this would give the impression that Great Britain was shifting from ally to intermediary. Eden and Salisbury evidently did not succeed in concealing from Dulles that they agreed with him rather than with their own chief.[67]

The next battle between Eden and Churchill came over the content of a speech due to be delivered by the Prime Minister in the House of Commons on 3 November. According to Moran, he (Churchill) 'said there had been a dispute. Anthony did not want him to talk about a change of heart in Russia. He and the Foreign Office do not believe that there is any evidence that anything of the kind has happened there.' He agreed to tone down his original draft but in his speech defiantly reaffirmed his belief in the desirability of a Heads of Government summit. Two days later Channon found Eden in a 'highly nervous state':

He was affectionate, but in a sudden burst of nerves and revealed to me that he is on bad terms with Winston. 'I get all the knocks; I don't think I can stand it much longer,' he suddenly said. We talked for some time and I had the feeling that he was fed up and almost hysterical.[68]

Churchill followed up his Commons speech with a direct appeal to Eisenhower to hold forthwith a Heads of Government summit involving the three Western Powers. This had been virtually promised to him during the summer. It was to be held as soon as he was fit to travel. Yet, according to Winthrop Aldrich, the American Ambassador in London, some of Churchill's colleagues hoped that Eisenhower would find means of evading the commitment:

At lunch today Eden told me of latest Churchill proposal for Bermuda meeting. Although he himself said nothing about it, I am sure from other conversations that many members of the Government and probably Eden himself are very much disturbed over Churchill's initiative and hope that some way may be found to avoid meeting. It is now obvious that Churchill is determined to make one last gesture toward world peace, that he is acutely aware that his time is fast running out, and that he is therefore taking actions that are really against his own best judgement.

It occurs to me that a Heads of State meeting now just when note exchange with Soviets has reached point which may well leave way open for ratification of EDC would provide exactly the pretext needed by EDC opponents to postpone ratification. It would seem to me that this argument is of sufficient importance so that it could be used in reply to Churchill without risk of seriously antagonizing him. In any event, avoidance of proposed meeting would have full support in influential quarters here.[69]

Walter Bedell Smith, Under-Secretary at the State Department, telephoned Eisenhower with the contents of this message, but did not 'see how we can possibly turn him [Churchill] down'. On the following day, 7 November, Eisenhower accepted Bedell Smith's advice and accordingly offered to go ahead with the three-power Western summit in Bermuda early in December.[70]

Eden thus accompanied his chief to Bermuda with a heavy heart. As he had expected, Churchill used the occasion to put unrelenting and embarrassing pressure on Eisenhower to agree to a Heads of Government summit with the Soviets. But Dulles proved a good ally to Eden and bolstered the President in his resolve not to yield. Moran recorded Eisenhower's sharp retort: 'It appears that when he [Churchill] pleaded with Ike that Russia had changed, Ike spoke of her as a whore, who might have changed her dress, but who should be chased from the streets. Russia, according to Ike, was out to destroy the civilized world.'[71] The decision was accordingly taken that only the three Western Foreign Ministers should meet the Soviets in Berlin in January 1954.

An interesting Anglo-American divergence at Bermuda arose with respect to declaratory policy on nuclear weapons and colonialism, as Shuckburgh's diary reveals:

5 December 1953
... A.E. came in very gloomy and concerned from the dinner with Eisenhower. They had been talking about atomic war and risks of renewal in Korea by China. Ike said the American public no longer distinguished between atomic and other weapons – nor is there logically any distinction ... The development of smaller atomic weapons and the use of atomic artillery makes the distinction impossible to sustain ... A.E. said the 'prospects are too horrible to contemplate' and was in a rather dramatic post-prandial mood.

6 December 1953
This morning PM and A.E. still most anxious about what they heard from Ike about Korea. A.E. ... told me ... to make sure the PM, when he sees Eisenhower before lunch, puts in a reservation about the reference to atomic weapons in his draft speech for next week at UNO which has been shown to us. The speech is not very clever, pretends willingness to internationalize atomic weapons, coupled with the threat to use them. Our object seems to be to get the threat removed. But personally I am more in sympathy with the American inclination to say out loud what they may

do if the enemy makes an aggression, than with our own desire never to say anything unpleasant ...

During the course of the day PM and A.E. decide they must dissociate themselves from two passages ...., one of which spoke of the escape of colonial states from bondage and the other of the threat to use atomic weapons in Korea if the truce is broken by the other side ... Eisenhower willingly made the corrections we asked and it is held that in this we have definitely had a success in restraining the Americans, not only perhaps over the speech but on actual policy.[72]

The other principal issue at Bermuda concerned French doubts that the EDC could be ratified. Here a large burden fell on Eden and Dulles. For their chiefs were not willing to get down to detail. Moreover, the French leaders were exasperating. Premier Joseph Laniel fell ill and seems to have made the most of his indisposition, remaining in bed for much of the Conference. The Foreign Minister, Georges Bidault, on the other hand, pleaded inability to speak for his chief, with whom he was said to be constantly quarrelling. Eden felt obliged in order to secure a communiqué to try to reconcile the two French leaders and this involved visiting the petulant Laniel's sick-room. 'Never again' was Eden's reaction. Bidault for his part exuded resigned pessimism about the chances of securing ratification of the EDC, which he described as a leap into the abyss, since it would involve France alone among the Western Powers in submerging her armed strength in a wider collective. He spoke as if unaware that the EDC had originally been a French idea. His only other contribution was to insist on still more binding pledges of future support from the British and the Americans. Eden, who, as has been seen, had been forced to make concession after concession to Paris in 1952, now felt that it was insulting to be continually asked 'to re-pledge ourselves as if the old pledges were no good'. Eden privately told McDonald of *The Times* that 'he could never agree to the French request ... that we should give a guarantee to keep X number of troops on the continent for Y number of years'. Churchill, too, was angered at French conduct but left to Eden and the Americans the task of talking in detail to the 'bloody frogs'. He had now at last, however, decided to support the EDC and said to Eisenhower: 'Mr President, you are quite right. The French must be called to their duty. They must be spoken harshly to ... But not by me, Sir. By you. Not by me, because I hope to spend a portion of my declining years in the South of France.' Such diffidence did not, however, prevent the Prime Minister from showing Laniel a special mark of disfavour. Robert Bowie of the State Department recalled:

... he [Churchill] had some sort of hearing aid which was rather a cumbersome thing, which had an earphone but also a little box in front of him which he could turn on and turn off. I remember he used to express his displeasure at times by ostentatiously turning off the hearing aid, when he disagreed with what was being said. He rather insulted Laniel, as I remember it at one point, by this gesture.[73]

The Americans were even more disturbed than the British at the French performance at Bermuda. Dulles told them bluntly that the 'new movement in Europe will not lead to disassociation of US from Europe' but 'if old Europe went on she might disassociate'.[74] And a fortnight after the end of the Bermuda Conference he decisively reinforced this warning: while attending a NATO Council Meeting in Paris he told a press conference that if the EDC was not ratified at an early date the United States could not avoid an 'agonizing reappraisal' of its rôle in Europe. This blunt threat was badly received in France where it was widely seen as interfering in her internal affairs. Eden stated in his memoirs that he 'did not like the method' employed by Dulles. But at that time the Foreign Secretary appears privately to have had a different opinion. Moran recorded Churchill as saying on 17 December:

'Anthony and I generally seem to come to the same conclusions. We sent telegrams to each other, which crossed, approving Dulles's warning to France. He was quite right to tell them bluntly that if they don't swallow EDC soon there will be a drastic change in American policy.' 'Dulles', the PM added, 'was better at Bermuda than we expected.'

Clearly Eden's relations with Dulles were at this stage more satisfactory than they had often been with Acheson and so far they had had no serious quarrel. Indeed, according to McDonald, Eden said of Dulles at Bermuda: 'I came to like him more and more.'[75] On the other hand, Eden's empathy with Dulles on the EDC did not cause him to give public endorsement to the 'agonizing reappraisal' statement. For, as Chamberlain had discovered in the 1930s, Eden was sometimes happy to allow others to canvass opinions with which he agreed but which might cause unpleasant controversy. Dulles, like Chamberlain, was cast in a different mould.

Eden's first major venture in 1954, a year according to some writers destined to be his *annus mirabilis*, was to visit Berlin for the four-power Foreign Ministers' Meeting. This lasted from 25 January to 18 February and proved to be a depressing failure. Whether Eden much regretted this, however, is doubtful. For Molotov's conduct was so obstructive as to offer no support to the Churchillian view that new faces in the Kremlin meant changes in policy. Eden did little to encourage the Soviets to compromise on German reunification, which was the main item on the agenda. He seems to have accepted Dulles's opinion that the West should give no scope to the Soviets for lengthy negotiation that would encourage the French to delay ratifying the EDC. Hence the so-called Eden Plan for Germany called for all-German free elections followed by a peace treaty which would leave a united Germany free to rearm and join either bloc. This plan was in fact more American than British in origin. Merchant recalled:

... we had prepared a plan which became known as the Eden Plan because by the accident of rotation Mr Eden was almost by lot chosen as the Western foreign minister to present the plan in outline, to unveil it before Molotov and the Soviet delegation. But in fact the Eden Plan, whereas it had been worked out and refined in working parties with the British, the French and the Germans, had had really its intellectual genesis in the American Department of State, though, . . . it emerged as a consciously agreed policy and a policy to which many contributed in the final refinements and details.

Here, then was further evidence of the general improvement in Anglo-American relations during Dulles's first year in office. Even O'Connor, his partisan supporter in the later quarrels with Eden, recalled of the Berlin Conference: 'At that stage of the game I didn't detect any particular friction.' And Eden in his memoirs wrote of their 'being able to keep closely in touch with each other' at Berlin.[76]

The Soviets could scarcely be expected to accept German reunification on the terms suggested by the West. Perhaps they would not have been seriously interested on any terms – even assurances that Germany would remain neutralized or disarmed. But that this was not seriously put to the test by the West could scarcely have come as a surprise to Moscow. The Soviets, on the other hand, could have indicated their willingness for the beginnings of *détente* when the second major issue, that of an Austrian peace treaty, came before the Conference. For on this subject the Western Foreign Ministers had accepted amendments to their draft along lines proposed at an earlier stage by Moscow. But Molotov now chose, somewhat unexpectedly, to link the Austrian case to that of Germany, a departure which dismayed the Austrian Government and which ensured an unfavourable world press for the new Soviet rulers.

The only concrete result from the Berlin Conference was an agreement to summon a five-power meeting with the Chinese. While this had long been a Soviet aim, Dulles had hitherto resisted it because he did not wish to give any degree of recognition to the Communist regime in Peking. Now Eden and Bidault put strong pressure on him. The French, in particular, were losing heart in their struggle in Indochina and hoped to reach an agreement by talking to the Chinese. Dulles reluctantly recognized the political difficulties involved in remaining intransigent and began to fight for terms that would enable him to save face at home with his 'China lobby'. He accordingly agreed to a five-power conference on the condition that its agenda was confined to Far Eastern questions with the possibility of a Korean Peace Treaty being nominally the grounds for American participation. This decision was probably the fatal concession that lay behind all his subsequent embarrassment at his partial involvement in the French surrender to Communism. And it was probably pressure from Eden that turned the scales. For at this time Dulles and his advisers were still relatively well-disposed towards him and thus found themselves, against their better judgement, making apparently minor concessions which occasionally, as in this case, led inexorably to a major capitulation. Merchant subsequently offered these reflections:

... he [Eden] performed ... with great skill at Berlin. He had had by then of course an almost unique experience as a foreign minister, as a negotiator, as a political figure in Europe and in the world and he was a stout and valued partner ...

Eden was quick, he was skilful, he was eloquent in debate. His rather languid manner concealed a lively, imaginative, perceptive mind. He had an underlying characteristic which I detected in every British statesman with whom I've had any dealings or had any knowledge with the sole exception of Winston Churchill; he [Eden] had that almost inbred, instinctive effort, in any conflict, in any collision, great or small, to find a compromise solution ... the British do have and have had, ever since their power quite patently was on the decline, from the battle of the Somme on, I suppose, have had the realization that their rôle was not of a determiner, not as a dictator of events but as a negotiator, as a compromiser, as a mediator ... in the crunch Eden was always to be counted on, but it had to be very clearly a true crunch. Anything short of that, he was always willing to give away ... a little bit of the United States's position, in order to propitiate the Soviets. I may be unfair ...

If we'd gone into ... negotiations with the original American position, in many cases there would have been concessions that could have been made to the Russians before arriving at the bone. But these concessions were extracted from us by our friends before we ever got to the green baize table with the Soviets. Now this of course was a problem that was peculiar to us. It was not a problem of the Soviets.

Shuckburgh too was uneasy, recording in his diary on 17 February:

I am worried about A.E.'s attitude towards the Far East business. He is so keen to get a conference, so as to have some 'success' to go home with, that he seems to forget how terribly dangerous this topic is for Dulles. Dulles has come a very long way in agreeing to meet the Chinese at all ... We, too, have to be careful not to give a boost to the Communist Chinese – Malaya etc.[77]

Indochina provided a classic example of the British Government, and Eden in particular, successfully restraining the Americans from carrying their anti-Communist containment strategy to its logical conclusion. He was of course now faced by a difficult choice: should he play the noble internationalist and give first priority to the interests of the West as a whole or should he connive at a significant but not final weakening of the anti-Communist forces in the world because his own country would be infinitely more vulnerable in a world war than the United States and thus had narrow and short-term interests that did not coincide with the overall cause of the West? In practice Eden's choice was to put first his perception of his own country's interest as lying in avoiding even a small risk of world war. This inclination was reinforced by the French no longer consistently demanding British support for hard-line resistance in Indochina as a condition for progress on the EDC. But Eden did not frankly explain his position to the Americans: they were left to discover it for themselves in instalments.

Eden's rhetoric on Indochina had at one time been all that Dulles could have desired. As has been seen, he had expressed, while in Opposition, much sympathy with France. And he had even said that to compromise with the Communists over Korea and Formosa at the expense of shifting the weight of anxiety further south would be similar to a repeat of Munich.[78] Now, in 1954, he effectively resisted repeated suggestions from Washington for taking practical steps to prevent the Communists gaining territory in Indochina, but usually only after hesitation or in such a way as to leave open the tantalizing possibility that he might concur in some scheme if certain vaguely defined conditions were met.

Dulles's first move came on 29 March. Faced with the news from Paris that the key fortress of Dien Bien Phu in northern Indochina was about to fall, he spoke publicly of the need for 'united action' to prevent 'the imposition on South-East Asia of the political system of Communist Russia and its Chinese Communist ally, by whatever means'. This might involve serious risks but 'these risks are far less now than would face us a few years from now if we are not resolute today'.[79] By stressing 'united action' he was trying to exclude the possibility of isolated American support being given to the French in the narrow context of Dien Bien Phu. He explained on 5 April to the Committee on Foreign Affairs of the House of Representatives that 'the threat is a grave threat to many countries and our judgement is that it should be recognized as such by them and I would hesitate to ask for action by the United States alone'. His reasons for trying to arrange so ambitious a reaction to the Dien Bien Phu crisis have been much discussed. No doubt he hoped to be able by internationalizing the response to reduce the criticism that the Americans were supporting 'colonialism' in Indochina. With luck the French could then be eased out of their rôle without the Communists taking over. Dulles, too, had to reckon on Congressional difficulties if at least token internationalization did not take place. But probably his main motive was the straightforward one of desiring to build a major long-term anti-Communist regional alliance.

Eisenhower backed Dulles wholeheartedly and sought the support of Congressional leaders on 3 April. They agreed that intervention in south-east Asia should depend on the support of other nations, particularly of France and Great Britain. Accordingly, on 4 April the President sent Churchill a dramatic personal letter: '... we failed to halt Hirohito, Mussolini and Hitler by not acting in unity and in time. That marked the beginning of many years of stark tragedy and desperate peril. May it not be that our nations have learned something from that lesson? ...' He proposed 'the establishment of a new, *ad hoc* grouping or coalition composed of nations which have a vital concern in checking Communist expansion in the area'. They should consist of the United States, Great Britain, France, Australia, New Zealand, Thailand, the Philippines and the three so-called Associated States of Vietnam, Cambodia and Laos.[80] Dulles followed up this suggestion with a precise proposal that these states should issue a warning to Peking about her continued support for the Vietminh guerrillas and be prepared to back this up both by armed intervention in Indochina and by naval and air action against China.

Eden's response to these proposals was muted. He opposed unequivocally any strikes against Chinese territory unless her intervention in Indochina should take a more direct form. On the other hand, he was not ostensibly opposed in principle to the creation of an anti-Communist coalition in south-east Asia. But he came to require that a number of conditions be met. First, he wanted the coalition to come into being only after the Geneva Conference, at which he hoped to see a compromise settlement with the Chinese, involving a partition of Vietnam. Secondly, he did not wish negotiations for an anti-Communist coalition to reach a conclusion and maybe not even begin until after Geneva for fear of wrecking the chances of a deal with Peking and Moscow. Thirdly, he wished to see India consulted about and perhaps involved in the negotiations for an anti-Communist coalition. But he refrained from openly spelling out these conditions to the Americans. Instead he permitted Dulles to come to London on 11 April with only the certain knowledge that the British definitely opposed an immediate threat of action against China. The American Secretary of State obligingly dropped this suggestion and concentrated instead on plans for an anti-Communist coalition. According to one interpretation, he was at fault in not realizing that Eden was opposed to immediate action designed to create such an organization or to any action being taken in Indochina before the Geneva Conference.[81] In fact Eden's memoirs reveal that, though he mentioned doubts, he did not expressly rule out such developments:

If there was to be any question of Allied intervention, military or otherwise, or of any warning announcement before Geneva, that would require extremely careful consideration ... I said I could agree to no more than to engage in preliminary discussions on the possibility of forming a mutual security system in South-East Asia ... I told Mr Dulles that British public opinion, with the Geneva Conference in prospect, would be firmly opposed to any present commitment to become involved in war in Indo-China.[82]

Terms like 'careful consideration', 'preliminary discussion' and 'British public opinion' (which the Americans, like Mussolini in 1935, may have thought of as different from the opinion of the British Government) were sufficiently imprecise to give Dulles the impression that his mission had been a substantial success and that he could go ahead with his preparations. Perhaps Dulles also got some encouragement from Churchill, who was usually more willing than Eden to fall in with American wishes. More important in the long-term was a difference of view about India. Eden believed she must be 'given every opportunity to participate' in the proposed coalition and that she should in any event 'be kept fully informed'. Dulles lightheartedly countered Eden's suggestion by proposing Formosa's inclusion. The result, according to Eden, was that they 'reached no final decision on the matter'.[83] Probably at this stage Dulles did not take this aspect of his talks with Eden particularly seriously, for the presence of India in an anti-Communist coalition was ludicrously implausible. Hence the Anglo-American talks concluded on a note of apparent harmony with the issue of a communiqué, which made no reference to Indian participation or to the Geneva Conference having to precede either talks about or the actual establishment of a regional organization for collective defence. The Americans could feel reasonably satisfied.

Dulles now journeyed to Paris in order to explore French thinking. But on his arrival on 13 April, he was at once made aware that Eden had placed a public gloss upon their agreed communiqué in terms that amounted to a subtle but unmistakable act of sabotage of American plans. Eden's 'betrayal' of Dulles lay in his telling Parliament not only that all he was committed to was 'an examination' of the possibility of collective defence but that 'we could not possibly have gone further' and that 'the effective outcome of that examination, in its turn, will be greatly influenced by what happens at Geneva'. 'I hope,' he continued, 'that those critics who thought that we were going to issue some fulminating declaration before the Geneva Conference took place will realize that we are as anxious as they are – and perhaps more so – to see the Geneva Conference succeed.' This plainly implied that no British action in Vietnam was even possible before the outcome of the Geneva Conference was known. In Dulles's eyes, Eden had further let him down by not reserving his position when Attlee and other moderate Socialists had asked for India's participation. Instead Eden said:

... I invite the House to study it [the statement] and to observe, among other things, that it covers not only South-East Asia but also the Western Pacific, where we have the deepest and most intimate relations with our Commonwealth partners. I should very much like to see an arrangement which resulted in collective defence between them and us, and if possible more intimate strategic relations with them too.[84]

Douglas Dillon, then American Ambassador in Paris, recalled:

I was in Paris when Mr Dulles arrived from Washington via London, and he told me he had Mr Eden's agreement to move ahead in really helping the French and then the next day Mr Eden made some speech diametrically the opposite. Mr Dulles thought this was a complete breaking of faith ... I wasn't present at the conversation he had with Eden, so I don't know how the misunderstanding arose.

But it certainly was a very major one, and certainly it wasn't anything that was invented later by Secretary Dulles, because I was there in Paris and heard him. He came and spent the night with us before this came out, so I heard his first-hand report, thinking he had this agreement. Then the next day it all blew up . . . Certainly if the way Dulles described it to me that first day was accurate, and I am sure he thought it was, he was double-crossed by Eden. Or Eden changed his mind which I guess countries and people do from time to time. He may have persuaded Eden further than Eden wanted to be persuaded and he changed his mind the next day.

Even more vital is an entry in Shuckburgh's diary for 3 May:

According to what Dennis [Allen of the Foreign Office] says we are getting very near having cheated the Americans on this question of starting talks on SE Asian security. Dennis told Harold [Caccia] and me at lunch today that when Dulles was in London A.E. did indicate that we should be willing to start such talks at once, provided we were not committed to any action in Indo-China. The American record showed that, but ours was obscure on the point and A.E. has always denied it.

Shuckburgh had earlier recorded 'a divergence of opinion as to whether A.E. had agreed to the first meeting taking place before Geneva'. He added: 'Roger Makins seemed to be taking the American view that we *had* agreed and received sharp reprimands, drafted by A.E. himself . . .'[85]

Dulles was thus in large measure justified in feeling aggrieved. True, the divergence was partly caused by his having agreed to an imprecise formulation in the joint Anglo-American communiqué. But Eden surely knew that his remarks in Parliament would be unwelcome to Dulles, and that they would be seen by him as a unilateral move, made without warning, designed to permit only one interpretation of the Anglo-American communiqué. Why did Eden act in this way? Maybe he was to some degree consciously presenting not only Dulles but also his own Prime Minister with a *fait accompli*. Perhaps, as Dulles himself came to believe, he was under pressure from India. But the most plausible explanation is that he was trying to help the Leader of the Opposition who was facing grievous difficulties. Attlee and other Labour frontbenchers, under increasing criticism from their left, endorsed the Eden–Dulles communiqué subject only to various conditions. But Bevan, a member of the Shadow Cabinet, intervened in the debate and in effect repudiated his chief. 'Is the right hon. Gentleman aware,' he asked, 'that the statement which he made today will be resented by the majority of the people in Great Britain? Is he further aware that it will be universally regarded as a surrender to American pressure?' In his reply Eden probably felt obliged for the sake of bipartisanship to give Attlee some morsels of comfort in his struggle with the Bevanites and, above all, to avoid brutally rejecting the relatively 'doveish' sentiments expressed by him and by his moderate Labour colleagues. Understandable as such solicitide was, it may have constituted a major error. True, Attlee's hand was strengthened by Eden's conduct and Bevan resigned from the Shadow Cabinet on the following day. But the cost to Eden was high: he aroused the mistrust of Dulles and maybe also Eisenhower. It is arguable, moreover, that Eden's friendly gesture to Attlee also constituted, for good or ill, the final blow to the chances of an *international* anti-Communist intervention in Indochina.

Dulles retaliated by inviting nine countries to attend a meeting in Washington on 20 April to consider setting up a south-east Asia defence organization. The countries were those originally suggested by Eisenhower and hence did not include India. This was indeed, as one writer has claimed, 'diplomacy by *fait accompli*',[86] but it was Eden, not Dulles, who first used this method. Eden reacted vigorously: he immediately instructed Roger Makins, the British Ambassador in Washington, to inform Dulles that Great Britain would not take part. His message read:

Americans may think the time past when they need consider the feelings or difficulties of their allies. It is the conviction that this tendency becomes more pronounced every week that is creating mounting difficulties for anyone in this country who wants to maintain close Anglo-American relations. We, at least, have constantly to bear in mind all our Commonwealth partners, even if the United States does not like some of them.

To avoid a public quarrel, Dulles was compelled to retreat: the ten-power gathering was converted into a briefing session for the forthcoming Geneva Conference. He revealed his feelings to his sister: 'Eden has double-crossed me. He lied to me.'[87]

The two Foreign Ministers were thrown together again in Paris at a NATO Council Meeting between 22 and 24 April. No doubt there was some mutual recrimination. But Dulles evidently had so much confidence in the persuasiveness of his case that on 22 April he once again attempted to convert Eden to his plan for an early start to discussions about a regional security pact: he believed that this was the only way to stiffen French resolve and to give the West any bargaining counters at Geneva. Eden was unimpressed: he was determined not to alienate the Asian neutrals, both because they might be helpful in promoting a compromise on south-east Asia and because he feared their outright hostility to a prematurely launched plan for a regional pact.

On the following day discussions took a new form when the French received news that the fall of Dien Bien Phu was imminent. Hitherto they had been lukewarm about Dulles's plan for internationalizing their struggle, preferring instead to seek only American support in the form of an air strike on those besieging Dien Bien Phu. Now they panicked and agreed to accept all Dulles's ideas in return for action to save the fortress, which had to come within seventy-two hours.

Dulles was unenthusiastic about concentrating on Dien Bien Phu: he shared Eden's uncertainty about the measures, if any, that would enable it to be saved and also agreed with Eden that its strategic importance had been much overrated. But he realized that it had assumed a unique symbolic importance for Paris and that its fall might lead, however illogically, to a complete French withdrawal from Indochina. He was also now aware that a conditional offer of American help over Dien Bien Phu might be the means of involving France in a regional security arrangement and that the French could be used to put pressure on the British to the same end. There appears to have been a good deal of collusion between Dulles and the French in the following days and weeks either to force Eden's hand or to leave him with almost exclusive public responsibility for a Communist triumph in Indochina. Whether Dulles's main purpose was to draw in Eden or to saddle him with the blame is, however, a matter for debate. One American scholar has even argued that the American Secretary of State was strongly opposed to American involvement in the Vietnamese fighting and cynically used British reluctance to further his own views.[88] While this thesis is difficult to disprove, it involves acceptance of a view of Dulles as a consummate dissembler on a scale that none of his close associates has found plausible. More likely, he was the unbending anti-Communist that he appeared to be; he would personally have taken any risks to avoid loss of any territory or population to Communism; but he was unable to carry Eisenhower and Congress for such a line without some backing from Great Britain. Hence if he appeared to relish the prospect of placing blame for the victory of Communism on Eden, this was not done in a spirit of mere malice or selfishness but was based on a righteous belief that Eden did indeed deserve to be branded as an appeaser of Communism.

Probably in collusion with Bidault, Dulles staged a scene on 24 April for Eden's benefit. He offered to give a formal letter to the French Foreign Minister, undertaking to ask Eisenhower for an immediate American airstrike against the Vietminh besieging Dien Bien Phu if France consented to fight on. Bidault, after a show of reluctance, asked for the letter to be officially given to him. Now the question was whether the British would endorse American intervention. Eden certainly believed Dulles to be in earnest and was filled with foreboding. McDonald of *The Times* recorded the Foreign Secretary's impressions given to him a month later:

'According to my notes, Eden emphasized that at their Paris meeting on 22-4 April Dulles was in a fearfully excited state, saying that America was ready for action (he had, he said, authority from the President) and that all America was waiting for was agreement by Britain. [Admiral Arthur] Radford [Chairman of the Joint Chiefs of Staff] went further and started talking about bombing China to teach her a lesson once and for all. Dulles was present while Radford spoke, listening without any demur at all.' Walter Robertson, assistant secretary of state, was even more vehement and emotional than Radford. 'I was put on the spot,' Eden told me. Were we to risk war? He had replied to Dulles and the others as frankly as he knew ...[89]

Eden was probably less forthright in speaking to Dulles than this account would suggest. For Radford later recalled:

> For my part I think Eden was a rather weak sister. He gave us the impression in Paris – and I'm sure that Mr Dulles thought so too – for we talked about it after we saw him – that he was going to go along with us. When he went back to England and talked to Mr Churchill they backed out.

Bedell Smith's impression of Eden's approach was rather different but still less than entirely definite. He telephoned to Eisenhower the view that 'Eden has grave doubts that Britain would cooperate in any activity in that area.' And according to Shuckburgh, Eden merely said that 'he could not commit himself in any way but would fly home to consult'. Thus, while Eden certainly disliked the new American plan, the evidence suggests that he was somewhat diffident about engaging in face-to-face controversy with Dulles – just as he had been with Acheson. This gentlemanly trait was not appreciated or even understood in Washington. Even on his own testimony, Eden, instead of taking responsibility for definitely rejecting the American proposal, told Dulles that 'he was confronting British opinion with about as difficult a decision as it would be possible to find'. Here once again was the vague evocation of British 'opinion' as distinct from 'government' that he had first used with Mussolini in 1935. Vagueness in Paris was followed by decisiveness in London. For Eden forthwith returned to seek and receive full Cabinet endorsement for refusing Dulles's request. The formulation he and his colleagues agreed was:

1. We do not regard the London communiqué as committing us to join in immediate discussions on the possibility of Allied intervention in the Indo-China war.
2. We are not prepared to give any undertaking now, in advance of the Geneva Conference, concerning United Kingdom military action in Indo-China.
3. But we shall give all possible diplomatic support to the French delegation at Geneva in efforts to reach an honourable settlement.
4. We can give an assurance now that if a settlement is reached at Geneva, we shall join in guaranteeing that settlement and in setting up a collective defence in South-East Asia, as foreshadowed in the London communiqué, to make that joint guarantee effective.
5. We hope that any Geneva settlement will make it possible for the joint guarantee to apply to at least the greater part of Indo-China.
6. If no such settlement is reached, we shall be prepared at that time to consider with our allies the action to be taken jointly in the situation then existing.
7. But we cannot give any assurance now about possible action on the part of the United Kingdom in the event of failure to reach agreement at Geneva for the cessation of hostilities in Indo-China.

8. We shall be ready to join with the United States Government now in studying measures to ensure the defence of Thailand and the rest of South-East Asia, including Malaya, in the event of all or part of Indo-China being lost.

Evidence of unorthodox American pressure through France, Australia and New Zealand only served to stiffen Eden's determination not to waver from this policy and he so informed a despairing Bidault late on 25 April. Two days later Eisenhower recorded in his diary:

Latest reports from Foster Dulles indicate that the British have taken a very definite stand against any collective conversations looking towards the development of an anti-Communist coalition in South East Asia. Moreover, Eden has apparently gone to the Geneva Conference under strict instructions to press earnestly for a 'cease fire' in Indo-China, possibly with complete indifference to the complex decisions that the French and the Viet Namese will have to make. The only reason that we can visualize for such action is that the British are afraid that if the fighting continues we – and possibly other countries – might become involved and so tend to increase the danger, in the British opinion, of starting World War III.

The attitude of Britain in this respect is bitterly resented by Australia and New Zealand. It is entirely possible that these two countries will approach the United States to request that in company with them – and possibly with the Philippines, Thailand, France and Indo-China – we form a coalition to the complete exclusion of the British. This would be a very tough one for us, but I think that I would go along with the idea because I believe that the British government is showing a woeful unawareness of the risks we run in that region.[90]

Arriving in Geneva for the fateful conference, Eden found the atmosphere distinctly unpromising. The French were inclined to be defeatist; Dulles was cast down, reproachful towards the British,[91] and unwilling to speak to the Chinese; while Chou En-lai and his delegation from Peking were at first aloof and in no mood for compromise. Only the Soviets showed signs of being helpful. Eden accordingly approached Molotov and the two men succeeded in having themselves made co-chairmen. Throughout May and much of June little progress was made. But somewhat fortuitously a complete breakdown was avoided. Partly this was because Dulles went home on 3 May and left his more conciliatory Under-Secretary, Bedell Smith, in charge. Partly it arose from the failure of the French, after the fall of Dien Bien Phu, to agree terms with Washington for an armed American intervention in Indochina that Dulles otherwise conceivably might have brought about even without British approval. On 31 May, McDonald of *The Times* noted:

When I said we could thank our lucky stars that the Indo-China conference had not broken down three weeks before, at the height of the Anglo-American dispute over whether America should intervene, Eden said 'If it had, then I am convinced we would have been in World War Three by now.' Later talking further about the danger of war he said 'I suppose I ought not to think so much of Britain's position in all this – exposed as we are. But I do. I cannot help it.' Later still, referring to his talks with the Russians in Geneva, he said, 'It is the two countries likely to suffer most from bombing – ourselves and Russia – that are the most anxious to work out a settlement here in Geneva.'[92]

Shuckburgh's diary is also of interest for what it reveals of Eden's attitude towards Dulles and Molotov:

26 April 1954
A.E. is so anti-American today that it is hard to get him to look for positive ways of bringing Dulles to a more patient frame of mind.

30 April 1954
Dulles came round for 'half an hour alone' with A.E. before lunch, and was extremely grim. Said that nobody was supporting the US; nobody had said a word to defend them against Chou-en-lai's attacks; the alliance was nearly at an end; Asia lost; France finished etc. 'We have seen the best of our times . . . and the bond cracked between father and child' (? Lear) . . . He wants someone to make a speech, like his, attacking communism. I think one of us had better do it. A.E. says 'They would think in London I was mad.' . . . one major worry is the almost pathological rage and gloom of Foster Dulles, which we must really do something to allay. (Not easy; A.E. is fed up with Dulles, refuses to make concessions to his feelings, and almost resents seeing him.)

1 May 1954
. . . there is no doubt that Dulles and A.E. have got thoroughly on each others nerves, and are both behaving rather like prima donnas. Dulles is said to be irritated by the 'imprecision' of A.E.'s mind.

2 May 1954
A.E. had a terrible dinner with Dulles last night. After the ladies had left the table, he and Reading were left with Dulles, Bedell Smith, Merchant and Robertson . . . They all went for him, saying UK had let US down etc. Their new line is that they do not want us to put a single aeroplane or a single man or a single pound in; they know we are fully stretched (rather contemptuous he thought). All they want is that we should give our moral support to whatever they think it necessary to do to save Indo-China, and to agree to a 'declaration of common intention to combat communism in the Far East'. But what it is they propose to do, that we cannot find out . . . it seems to mean (A.E. and Reading certainly are convinced it means) taking over the direction of the war from the French. If we were to give our moral support . . . should we not be in effect approving the first steps to a third world war? That is what A.E. thinks . . . My own feeling is that we should be very cautious before we again turn down an American proposal . . . Unfortunately we are all steamed up against the Americans. Another thing; A.E.'s conviction is that all the Americans want to do is to replace the French and run Indo-China themselves. 'They want to replace us in Egypt too. They want to run the world.'

4 May 1954
. . . A.E. was cross with me because I drew his attention to the *Journal de Genève*, which says he is 'mediating' between East and West . . . His mood is that he is not

shocked at being told that he is mediating and rather resents our suggestion that it is wrong. He said, 'I am inside right, the Americans outside right, Molotov is inside left, Chou outside left.'

5 May 1954
... I joined A.E., Reading, Dennis [Allen] and Francis [Vallat] for the post-mortem [after a Soviet–British dinner]. They were in a state of some excitement, the dinner having been, they said, a great success and quite fascinating. I began to be sorry I had missed it until I realized the sort of success it had been. For Dennis was clearly shocked by the way A.E. had talked, and A.E. equally obviously knew it. He was in an exalté frame of mind, having had plenty to drink and being excited about the 'frank' talk with Molotov. It seems A.E. talked the whole way through dinner and for an hour afterwards, keeping up a most brilliant 'entertainment' they all said; but the theme was the middle position of USSR and UK with an implication that we deprecate the wildness of the Americans, (and Chinese), the hopelessness of the French. Rather an admission, it sounded, of the divisions in the Western alliance. A.E. recounted all this to us with the utmost satisfaction (though with frequent interjections like 'Have I done wrong?', 'Dennis thinks me a bad Foreign Secretary', 'The Foreign Office does not approve; you are so severe, dear', 'I really enjoy talking to Molotov; he has mellowed').

I myself, grumpy spoil-sport, could not really bear the mood, quite apart from what had been said at dinner, so I manoeuvred hard to get the others away and him to bed. Having achieved this at last, I went to see Dennis in his room, to ask him what had really happened. He said it had been pretty terrible. A.E. had certainly played up to Molotov mostly upon subjects which, though they seemed 'frank' and daring to embark upon, were in fact easy for Molotov to agree with. Hardly ever, except in a perfunctory and apologetic way, did A.E. touch upon the bad conduct of the other side. All the ills of the world, as Molotov was only too glad to confirm, came from the Americans. According to A.E.'s own account, he slipped in a passage intended to warn the Russians that if they don't get a settlement in Indo-China the US might get tough and there might be a world war. But Dennis fears that this was outweighed by the rest – which included an explanation of his visit to London from Paris, how he refused to undertake any commitment over Indo-China etc.: in fact, he went to the Bosom of Auntie Mol. I expect there will be some remorse in the morning.

Of course I dare say there is something in the idea that Molotov wants peace in Korea and a settlement in Indo-China. But why does he want it? I asked A.E. that, and he replied 'Because he is afraid what the continuation of this fighting may lead to. It may lead to a world war.' All right, then our policy should surely be to encourage that fear in Molotov's mind, not to allay it by exposing our determination to do nothing? ... A.E. cheerfully told Molotov his joke about Russia and UK being 'inside left and inside right', and says he enjoyed it very much. I'll bet he did: but he did not criticize his outside wing or show any divergence from them. A.E. seems now to be accepting the 'New Look' idea which he has been so roundly abusing in the PM ever since May 11th [1953]. When it is a question of Winston wanting to throw his arms round Malenkov, it is one thing. But when we ourselves are involved, and playing the beau rôle, it is a very different matter. These politicians are two-thirds prima donna.

14 May 1954

He [Eden] said he was very depressed about the state of the conference and not enjoying himself at all … I do not think it is really true. He is enjoying it in the fullest sense, because he is really running it, and recognized to be 'the King of the Conference' as the Chinese said. Nor do I think he really believes that World War III is at hand. He said that he had never been to so difficult a conference, and that he felt the situation was very dangerous; but when I said that I could not get the *feeling* of acute danger, he agreed. He thinks the Russians do not want war, and will have to prevent the Chinese from bringing one upon their heads. Of course he is influenced by the *universal* praise he is getting from British press for standing up to the Americans and keeping us out of war in Indo-China. The British people regard Indo-China as something remote and nasty like Czechoslovakia; they would react very differently, I dare say, if it were Egypt or Afghanistan. I have done my best in the last few weeks to paint in the other side of the picture, and to bring him back into relations with our only effective ally in the world.[93]

On 20 June the Conference adjourned partly to permit experts to explore details but also to enable the leading participants to return home without having to admit complete failure. Back in London, Eden faced renewed tension with Churchill. First, the Prime Minister had once more gone back on an offer to retire at the end of July. Seizing upon the international crisis he had written to Eden in mid-June informing him of this change of mind. Moran recorded Churchill as saying: 'I don't know if he has accepted it. He'd better.' The background to Churchill's ill-treatment of Eden in this respect is revealed in extracts from Shuckburgh's diary:

11 March 1954

A.E. summoned to PM at 12.00 to talk about 'the future of the Government'. Great excitement. He said he had been expecting it … On return, he told me as follows, strictly in secret … PM said he had decided to resign in May – or end of summer at the latest (depending on his health). His only concern is to hand over as smoothly and effectively as possible to A.E.

21 April 1954

He [Colville] told me the PM is *not* thinking of retiring at Whitsun … but 'might go at the end of the session *provided* he is not given any impression that he is being pushed'. In other words, no one is to say a hard word to him. Jock also said that the PM had been impressed with the way A.E. had faced a hostile House in defending him (W.S.C.) … and was more disposed on account of this to consider him fit to succeed. I expressed astonishment at this, and Jock added, 'Oh, but he has not been at all sure that the Government could hold together if he were to retire.' A.E.'s comment on what I told him of this was that Whitsun is the last date his colleagues will stand. If the old man doesn't go then, the Government will break up – several of them will resign. We shall see.

14 June 1954

… tonight I saw a letter from A.E. saying he has had 'a very depressing letter looking well beyond July!' … I thank God I have no further part in these death-bed agonies.

[Shuckburgh had been replaced as Principal Private Secretary to Eden by Anthony Rumbold in May 1954.][94]

There were also differences between Eden and Churchill over Anglo-American relations. The Prime Minister had acquiesced in Eden's early resistance to involvement in Indochina largely because of scorn for French colonialism and a belief that British efforts in Malaya would be prejudiced rather than advanced by a British presence in Indochina: he saw Malaya as being adequately cushioned from the Vietminh by Thailand. He was, moreover, aware of Attlee's continuing difficulties. For example, on 2 May Harold Wilson, then in the Shadow Cabinet, said:

Asia is in revolution and Britain has to learn to march on the side of the peoples in that revolution and not on the side of their oppressors. A settlement in Asia is imperilled by the lunatic fringe in the American Senate who want a holy crusade against Communism. Not a man nor a gun must be sent from Britain to aid French imperialism in Indo-China. Nor must Britain join or encourage an anti-Communist alliance in Asia.

But Churchill was also distressed by the eruption of Anglo-American ill-feeling and was much more prepared than Eden to sympathize with the wave of idealistic anti-Communism that the crisis in Indochina was clearly provoking in Washington. On 18 May Moran recorded him as saying:

'Dulles lays down what we must do if we are to hold the Communists, though he makes it sound terrible. But it is necessary that someone should stand up to them.

'The House was pleased at Anthony's appeasement. I like it up to a point, but only up to a point.'

He was eager, above all, to keep in touch with Eisenhower, both to prevent the issue of Indochina causing any permanent ill-feeling and in the hope once again of winning over the Americans to attending a summit with the Soviets or, if not, consenting at least to an Anglo-Soviet summit. Hence he eagerly grasped at a suggestion from the President that he should go to Washington late in June. Eden had resented this. On 2 June, Churchill, according to Moran, said:

'Anthony tells me nothing. He keeps me out of foreign affairs, treats them as a private preserve of his own. Now he doesn't want me to go to America. I don't mind. I'm ready to go alone.'

Again, on 15 June Moran recorded:

'... he [Eden] wanted to change all the arrangements that have been made with Ike. He said Dulles had been very difficult and had attacked him. They showed me the account of what had happened, but it had to be pointed out to me how it could be taken as an attack on Anthony ... I said I would not change my plans.'[95]

Eden clearly could not prevent Churchill from visiting Washington and decided that in that case he too must go. But on the eve of their departure, the Foreign Secretary made a provocative speech in the House of Commons – another instance of diplomacy by *fait accompli*. He chose first to outline his hopes for the resumed Geneva Conference: Cambodia and Laos would be independent and non-Communist; and Vietnam would be partitioned with the Communists. Then he urged that the result should be guaranteed, along the lines of the Locarno Treaties of 1925, by the United States, China, the Soviet Union, Great Britain, France and maybe other states including India. This was to ask the politically impossible of the United States: she would have to accept China as a co-guarantor and to endorse the creation of new Communist authorities in North Vietnam. He also unmistakably indicated that his proposed Locarno-type arrangements involving potential adversaries would be preferable to a NATO-type security organization confined to regional allies. He reaffirmed his belief in the wisdom of refraining 'from any precipitate move' towards the latter, whose 'relevance to current events must not be exaggerated'. 'It could be,' he added, 'a future safeguard but not a present panacea.'[96] The speech was received with dismay in the American press and constituted the worst possible backcloth to the British visit to Washington. It would seem that the aged Churchill may not have fully realized in advance the extent to which Eden was determined to give no ground to Dulles. For on the air journey the Prime Minister said plaintively to Moran: 'I hope Anthony won't upset them; they are so kind and generous to their friends.'[97]

Once in Washington, however, Churchill reasserted his authority and succeeded, with Eisenhower, in effecting a surprising degree of Anglo-American reconciliation. Even the two Foreign Ministers were brought together to some extent. On 26 June Eisenhower telephoned Dulles:

> ... he [Eisenhower] said he had deduced by bits of conversation from Anthony Eden, that Eden felt a lack of 'friendliness' that used to exist between Eden and Dulles. President suggested that by purely personal little things matters could be helped.

Moran's diary for the following day reveals the sequel:

> '... Eden must be back. Oh go and see. Christ! I hope they haven't quarrelled and killed each other,' he [Churchill] added with a grim smile. But he was not really amused at all; he was on edge about the result of Anthony's meeting with Dulles.
>
> The door opened. 'Can I come in?' It was Anthony's voice. Winston jumped up and advanced towards him with outstretched hands. 'Anthony, my dear, tell me what happened.' Before I withdrew I heard enough to know that the interview had gone well.[98]

This happy outcome owed more, however, to Dulles than to Eden. For the former had at last given up hope of securing a deal with the French involving any immediate American military intervention in Indochina. The Laniel Government had fallen and been replaced, on 18 June, by one led by

Pierre Mendès-France, who pledged himself to secure a settlement by 20 July or quit. At a press conference in London on 13 April Dulles had been asked with heavy irony if there was 'any compromise that might be offered' if the Communists did not simply agree to withdraw from Indochina. His dour reply had been: 'I had not thought of any.'[99] Now, two months later, he was compelled to recognize that the French would be fortunate to salvage freedom for Cambodia and Laos and obtain a partition of Vietnam. He accordingly reached agreement with Eden on a seven-point programme which he hoped the French would achieve on the assumption of a partition. In return for this compromise on Dulles's part, Eden agreed to the establishment of a study group intended to bring about a regional security arrangement; and he tacitly dropped his unrealistic plan for a Locarno-type guarantee of any Geneva settlement. Even so he was less willing than Churchill to conciliate the Americans on the issue of the recognition of Peking. Ambassador Makins wanted the British to issue a disclaimer when Senator William Knowland, leader of the 'China lobby', condemned the British for desiring to get Communist China into the United Nations. While Churchill agreed with Makins, Eden was adamantly opposed to the idea. 'It would be an intolerable position,' he insisted, 'if the FO had to make a statement every time Senator Knowland attacked Britain.'[100]

The other principal outcome of the Washington talks was Churchill's success in acquainting Eisenhower with his intention to visit Moscow on an exploratory mission without evoking any definite statement of disapproval. Eden was of course no less opposed to a Malenkov–Churchill meeting than he had been to a full-scale summit involving Eisenhower. But on the voyage back across the Atlantic in the *Queen Mary*, Churchill once again secured a partial submission after furious rows. Shuckburgh in London recorded his own and others' dismayed reaction in his diary:

5 July 1954
Andrew Stark showed me, to my consternation, a message which the PM has sent to Molotov from the *Queen Mary*, suggesting he go to Moscow with Anthony, for a top level meeting, *without* the Americans! Telegrams show that he completely ignored the Cabinet over this; sent the text 'private and personal' to R.A.B. [Butler], saying 'I hope you will agree', and just as R.A.B. .... was about to reply suggesting he wait to discuss it with colleagues at home, followed it up with another saying 'presume you have sent on my message; it does not commit the Cabinet'. So R.A.B., (feebly in my opinion) proposed a few minor changes and sent it on. So it is done. 'Anthony Eden agrees in principle.'

6 July 1954
Found in the FO that everyone who knows about this is as outraged as I am ... Selwyn Lloyd and Tony Nutting talk of resigning. Everyone feels A.E. has made a disgraceful compact with the old man ... A.E. always swore to me that the *one* thing he would not allow was a visit to Moscow without the Americans ...

7 July 1954

As soon as I got to the FO I went to see him [Eden], who had now returned ... He actually tried to put the blame on R.A.B. for not consulting the Cabinet colleagues. He also said he had been to see Norman Brook [the Secretary to the Cabinet] who had 'agreed that no power on earth will stop the old man doing this' – that salves his conscience.

12 July 1954

... I rang Salisbury to ask if he would see me ... Found him as indignant as I am. He thinks seriously of resigning, not so much on the issue itself as on the PM's underlying claim that he has the right to take major decisions of this sort without consulting Cabinet. S. says this is flat contrary to our constitutional system ... He is obviously deeply shocked by A.E.'s failure to stop it. 'Anthony has given way to the Prime Minister so often that it has become difficult for him to stand out on anything. He told me he had had a long tussle, but the old boy looked so old and pathetic, he hadn't the heart to say no.'

19 July 1954

A.E. is being rather clever about the Malenkov visit. He is sending telegrams from Geneva ... putting little grains of doubt and difficulty into the project. In particular he is stressing that there must be full Cabinet discussion (influenced no doubt by a long letter from Salisbury, who has made this issue grounds for resignation but is being persuaded to hold his hand until A.E. returns).[101]

But whether the resignations of at least Salisbury and Crookshank could have been avoided seems extremely doubtful had not the Soviets inadvertently ended the crisis by an unexpected *nyet*. Shuckburgh recorded on 28 July:

... the Moscow visit is off after a terrific struggle in Cabinet. Situation was saved by the opportune arrival of a most uncompromising Soviet note ... To be saved from our own embarrassments by a clumsy action on the part of the Soviet is quite like old Stalin times. I do not understand why Malenkov and Molotov have let us off so lightly.[102]

Meanwhile Eden had returned to Geneva. Here he found the Communists in a mood for compromise and he was even able to get on affable terms with the Chinese. The greatest difficulty he faced was the uncertain attitude of the Americans, who now had no senior representative at Geneva. Accordingly he and Mendès-France arranged to meet Dulles in Paris on 13 July. This proved to be a historic encounter. For Dulles opened the way to an Indochina agreement by consenting to send Bedell Smith back to Geneva and by undertaking not actually to oppose a settlement based on the Anglo-American seven points, though the United States would not of course join in any multilateral guarantee involving Peking. Dulles had not at first expected the French and the British to stick to the seven points. But in Paris he was agreeably surprised to find how resolute they had become. On 19 July he telephoned Eisenhower: 'British are taking pretty good line as to what they will do in case there's a break up. All prepared to organize for a collective defence of the area.'[103] For the Secretary of State this was the point at which a reconciliation with Eden was substantially achieved.

With Bedell Smith on hand, Eden was soon able to complete the Geneva negotiations. On 21 July final agreement was announced. Vietnam was partitioned at the Seventeenth Parallel, while Cambodia and Laos became independent and neutral states – a better result than had at one time seemed possible. All-Vietnam elections were due to be held within two years, though these unsurprisingly never took place. The American refusal to guarantee the outcome led other states to limit their obligations. Great Britain was thus spared any moral commitment to play a future rôle in Indochina. This was a significant contrast with Chamberlain's Munich settlement. Otherwise, however, there were some disturbing parallels for Eden as *Punch*, then edited by Malcolm Muggeridge, cruelly stressed with a cartoon of him returning from Geneva dressed like Chamberlain complete with an umbrella. Moreover, he had engaged in active and positive appeasement rather than the 'unheroic cunctation', which had been his own pre-war preference. And, like Chamberlain in 1938, he chose to speak optimistically about the result, though he never went so far as to refer to 'peace with honour'. This led one historian to make the judgement that 'time was to show that the pessimistic views of Dulles were more realistic than the optimism of Eden'. Privately, however, Eden, like Chamberlain before him, was aware that the settlement might prove to be a mere respite. For example, McDonald of *The Times* noted that he had 'few illusions';[104] and it is unlikely that he expected the all-Vietnam free elections, scheduled for 1956, to take place. He was, it is true, justified in taking pride in the technical diplomatic skills and patience which he had shown at Geneva. It is also easy to make a case on policy grounds for his willingness to act as a mixture of honest broker and negotiating ally: the French in the last resort turned out to prefer withdrawal to the continued drain on their resources; even the resolute Dulles had problems with Congress; the British themselves were militarily overstretched, with Malaya still a major concern; and, above all, British cities, unlike those of the United States, were obviously vulnerable to nuclear attack if the conflict should escalate into a world war. Nevertheless, Eden's rôle in facilitating a Communist advance of however explicable a character must surely have been to some degree unpleasing to one who less than three years earlier had offered these opinions:

... Let us make no mistake. The Communist assault on free and democratic thought is more formidable than was its Fascist counterpart of yesterday ... We had to re-arm: to oppose positions of strength to the use of force, wherever it might appear ... Already there must be serious doubts in the minds of any aggressor who might be tempted to dare a direct trial of strength. But there are parts of the world where it is not clear beyond doubt that open or concealed aggression will lead to such an issue between East and West. That is dangerous for us all. We can afford no breach in the dyke at any point . . . What of the Far East? In that vast area the threat of Communist advance and infiltration confronts us at many points . . . In Indo-China the French have been fighting a defensive battle with utmost difficulty . . . In Malaya, we, for our part, have been waging a long and bitter struggle against guerrilla forces. These positions must be held. It should be understood that the intervening by force by Chinese Communists in South-East Asia – even if they were called volunteers – would create a situation no less menacing than that which the United Nations met and faced in Korea. In any such event the United Nations should be equally solid to resist it.[105]

It is therefore ironic that claims that Eden had an *annus mirabilis* in 1954 should have to rest so largely on so ultimately unheroic a performance as Geneva represented.

Another alleged element in the *annus mirabilis* claim is the agreement reached with Egypt at this time. But here again Eden's achievement was far from universally popular and stood the test of time even less well than the Vietnam settlement. As has been seen, the removal of the Sudanese issue had greatly reduced the differences between London and Cairo. Now the withdrawal of British troops from Suez depended only on agreement about terms for their return in the event of an emergency. This did not prove easy to arrange. For example, Dulles failed in his attempt in 1953 to interest the Egyptians in joining a Middle East Defence Organization which could provide a face-saving justification for continuing British rights in the Canal Zone. Eventually, however, the Anglo-Egyptian issue narrowed down to whether or not an attack on Turkey or Pakistan should constitute grounds for a British return. Cairo gave no ground throughout 1953, but early in 1954 offered the compromise of allowing Turkey but not Pakistan to be covered by the terms of an agreement. Eden at first did not respond but he gradually came to the view that continued terrorist attacks on British installations made stalemate unattractive. He accordingly carried the Cabinet, with the rather surprising support of the Minister of Defence, Alexander, and the Secretary for War, Antony Head, for settling on the basis of Egypt's compromise offer. Churchill was unenthusiastic. In October 1953, according to Moran, he had said: 'I may have to say something in the Suez debate, but I shall put Anthony in front. It is his business. If he likes this policy of scuttle in Egypt he must defend it.' But towards the end of the year differences between Churchill and Eden resurfaced when it appeared that pro-Egyptian forces had won the Sudanese election. Shuckburgh's diary for 30 November is revealing:

News of the Sudan election having gone against the Umma, A.E. came into the office with a set face and started writing out his resignation. I quickly got Nutting along in order to try and get some discussion going before he did it, but A.E. said 'You can say what you like, I am going to do it' . . . it seemed to me like a pure manoeuvre which he had no intention of pressing . . . discussed it with Jock [Colville] and Pitblado . . . They doubted its sincerity, and thought the PM would have no difficulty in talking him out of it. I could not disagree, and so it proved, but A.E. came out from the interview convinced that the old man had said something new to him: 'I am tired, I am not enjoying office. It will not be long now before I hand over to you.' I do not believe he means a word of it. He just hypnotizes A.E. with these stories.

In the event, after the pro-Egyptian faction in Khartoum had suffered some crucial desertions, Churchill for a time softened his line. Hence a final crisis between him and Eden was once again averted. The Egyptian issue arose again, however, early in 1954. On 7 February, according to Shuckburgh: 'A very rude message to A.E. [then in Berlin] from the PM about the Israel–Egypt dispute on the Suez Canal. It is very clear that the PM is doing all he can to thwart agreement with Egypt over the base, and that Selwyn Lloyd is not playing straight with us.' Informed by Dulles that Eden was worried that 'Winston is going to be difficult' about the Egyptian question, Eisenhower sent an appeal to the Prime Minister on 9 February 1954:

> I am sure that when history looks back upon us today it will not long remember any one of this era who was merely a distinguished war leader whether on the battlefield or in the council chamber. It will remember and salute those people who succeed, out of the greatness of their understanding and the skill of their leadership, in establishing ties among the independent nations of the world that will throw back the Russian threat and allow civilization, as we have known it, to continue its progress. Indeed, unless individuals and nations of our time are successful – soon – in this effort, there will be no history of any kind as we know it. There will be only a concocted story made up by the Communist conquerors of the world.
>
> It is only when one allows his mind to contemplate momentarily such a disaster for the world and attempts to picture an atheistic materialism in complete domination of all human life, that he fully appreciates how necessary it is to seek renewed faith and strength from his God, and sharpen up his sword for the struggle that cannot possibly be escaped . . .

Whether the hero of the Battle of Britain and the author of the Fulton address welcomed being the recipient of such a sermon may be doubted. Nor did Churchill immediately respond to Eisenhower's appeal not to drive Egypt into Soviet arms. The subsequent fluctuations are apparent from Shuckburgh's diary:

1 *March 1954*
Cabinet on Egypt at 6.30, and after it A.E. rang me up to say he had a very bad time.

2 *March 1954*
He [Churchill] is . . . furious with the Chiefs of Staff for having written a paper urging agreement with the Egyptians and evacuation of the Zone.

3. March 1954
... Cabinet was easy, and the PM, he [Eden] says, was 'all milk and water', and said he was convinced of the need for a settlement with Egypt.

15 March 1954
A.E. still showing signs of indecision over Egypt ... He is like a sea anemone, covered with sensitive tentacles all recording currents of opinion around him. He quivers with sensitivity to opinion in the House, the party, the newspapers.

20 March 1954
... he [Eden] is beginning to find the unpopularity of his Egypt policy in his party too heavy a burden, and is seeking ways of abandoning it.

29 March 1954
Rioting in Egypt. Looks as if Neguib is losing out to Nasser ... A.E. and [Douglas] Dodds-Parker [Parliamentary Under-Secretary at the Foreign Office] are coming to the conclusion that Nasser is a man for us ... and that we ought to be ready for a quick agreement with them if they emerge at the top, and help them to keep power while we remove ourselves from the zone.[106]

Gradually Eden succeeded in winning over his colleagues to the idea of a deal with Nasser. And by the summer of 1954 even Churchill had reluctantly concluded that, with both the Chiefs of Staff and the Americans backing a 'scuttle' from Egypt, he must give Eden positive support. This he did in Parliament on 13 July. Head was sent to Cairo and on 27 July agreed with Nasser a document known as the Heads of Agreement. Nutting of the Foreign Office was then deputed to work out the details. A final settlement was duly signed on 19 October. All British troops were to withdraw from Egypt by 18 June 1956; while British civilian technicians were to remain for seven years to maintain installations which might be needed if British forces had to return. Such a return could only occur if an Arab state or Turkey should be attacked by an outside power other than Israel.

Eden defended this settlement in his memoirs. But he was clearly troubled by the argument that it constituted a precondition for his later confrontation with Nasser. His response was to point out that under the 1936 Treaty 'no British troops could have been on the canal in the autumn of 1956, for by then it would have expired'.[107] Strictly this need not have been the case. For the Treaty provided for an extension of the British occupation if both parties agreed or alternatively for arbitration on the issue if the Egyptians preferred that course. The British could thus have stayed beyond 1956 if they had won an arbitration victory or if the Egyptians had refused to go to arbitration. But in either case British relations with the Arab World, with the United States and with the New Commonwealth would have suffered. And terrorism would certainly have increased. The fact was that Eden, following Bevin, had been too liberal in his pronouncements when the prospects for agreement seemed remote for it now to be possible to turn back. But he had to pay a price. First, and most obviously, the British position in the Middle East was decisively weakened, with Cyprus proving a wholly unsatisfactory substitute in the absence of vast expenditure (which could not be afforded) to create adequate naval facilities. Secondly, he had to face a pressure group in Conservative ranks whose hostility to Eden's 'scuttle' was so intense as to constitute a major threat to the Government's survival if the Egyptian gamble should clearly be seen to have failed. The so-called Suez rebels, led by Captain Charles Waterhouse, held that the 1954 settlement was symptomatic not of any decline in British capabilities but of a loss of will and self-confidence. According to Churchill, Eden in the phase leading to the agreement with Nasser hated 'the Tory rebels more than the Egyptians'.[108] By 1956, however, Eden was to come face to face with the consequences of his policy of 1954. On the one hand, he could not accept the nationalization of the Suez Canal without risking the defeat of his Government at the hands of the Conservative Suez rebels and their backers in the Cabinet; on the other hand, he could not rapidly take effective action against Egypt because of the military weaknesses occasioned by the withdrawal to Cyprus. His promotion of the 1954 settlement thus made him the author of his own *Götterdämmerung*.

Another settlement achieved by Eden in 1954 was with Iran. As has been seen, Eisenhower and Dulles had initially shown more understanding than their predecessors of the British point of view and they had accordingly left the Iranians to struggle with economic adversity even at some risk that they would go Communist. It was the Americans, however, who finally found means to end the crisis: they were able through the good offices of the Central Intelligence Agency (CIA) to arrange for a right-wing coup against Mussadeq on 19 August 1953 when Eden was convalescing after his operation. It has been stated that Churchill approved CIA action which the more scrupulous Eden had earlier opposed.[109] Whatever the truth of this claim, Eden's policy of refusing to panic in the face of Mussadeq was widely seen as vindicated. By December 1953 diplomatic relations were restored with Teheran and in the following year negotiations ensued, culminating in complete agreement on 5 August 1954. A principal point of honour for Eden was achieved: the Anglo-Iranian Oil Company received £25 million in compensation for nationalization, to be spread over ten years. The rest of the settlement was less favourable to the British: they felt obliged to share their oil stake with various American companies. This decline of exclusive British influence in Teheran was thus Mussadeq's lasting achievement; but it was no gain for the West's enemies. Accordingly Eden could reasonably claim that the outcome was better than many had expected and constituted a delayed triumph over Acheson. It is possible, however, that he drew the wrong lessons from the affair. It may have led him in 1956 to suppose that similar resolve would pay against Nasser and, above all, that the Americans could again be won round to serving British purposes. If so, this proved to be a fatal miscalculation. He should have recognized how fortunate he had been in the Iranian case to have escaped the consequences of crossing Acheson; he should not have tempted fate by trying to outface his successor over Egypt. But such recklessness was probably inevitable from a man who had not fully come to terms with the extent of Great Britain's decline.

Eden's success over the Iranian issue was soon followed by another diplomatic achievement: reconciling Italy and Yugoslavia in October 1954. The two countries had long been at odds over the future of Trieste and an adjoining part of the Istrian Peninsula. The critical area had been temporarily split into two zones at the end of the war, Zone A being administered by the United States and Great Britain and Zone B being under Yugoslav control. Both Rome and Belgrade at times showed an inclination to claim both zones and hence armed conflict between them could not be ruled out. In 1948 the United States, Great Britain and France had indeed fully supported the extreme Italian claims without being willing to use force to achieve them. Once back in the Foreign Office Eden aimed to abandon the Western stand of 1948 and obtain both Italian and Yugoslav consent to a final settlement based substantially on Zone A going to the former and Zone B to the latter. In 1953 he accordingly sought Dulles's support. Dulles agreed in what may seem a surprisingly conciliatory line for so rigid an anti-Communist. But he was nevertheless more forthright than Eden in one respect: he wanted in the last resort to impose the partition solution on both parties.[110] Eden succeeded in resisting this approach. Instead he proclaimed the partition plan on 8 October 1953 and merely tried to gain the consent of both parties without any commitment to impose the plan. At first both Italy and Yugoslavia protested and Eden was the target of criticism in both countries. In Italy he became for a time what he had been two decades earlier: 'Porco' Eden. But by 1954 tempers had cooled and the partition solution now became the basis for negotiations in London. The ambassadors of the two parties, together with representatives of Great Britain and the United States, steadily eliminated most remaining detailed points of difference. The decisive pressure was in the end applied by the United States when Robert Murphy went to Belgrade and allegedly offered supplies of wheat and other inducements to Tito. But much of the credit clearly also belonged to Eden for boldly pointing the way to a solution a year earlier. Agreement was finally reached on 5 October 1954.[111]

Another significant achievement by Eden in his so-called *annus mirabilis* of 1954 was the resolution of the problem of German rearmament. Some commentators have even claimed that it constituted his finest hour. The necessity for his active diplomacy arose in August when Mendès-France informed him that without still more safeguards the French Assembly was unlikely to ratify the EDC plan. Neither the British nor any of their EDC partners were willing to reopen the debate on the terms. For, after all, the EDC had originally been a French idea and detailed negotiations had ended as long ago as May 1952. The French Government accordingly decided, after more than two years of hesitation, to put the matter to the vote. On 30 August the Assembly duly rejected the plan by 319 votes to 264.

Eden had long foreseen the likelihood that the EDC would suffer this fate and it is even possible that he had secretly recognized that such an outcome might open the way to a solution more congenial to him. He had nevertheless given no hint to any foreigner that he was other than a wholehearted supporter of the EDC plan or that he had any alternative in mind. This was wise, for as a result not only could he not be blamed for the Assembly vote but he was also ideally placed to try to offer a new initiative. Yet he had long given thought, together with his officials, to what alternative might be appropriate. Shortly after returning to the Foreign Office, for example, he spoke off-the-record to McDonald of *The Times*, who later recalled:

'If the European army plan fails,' said Eden ... 'then will be the time for Britain to bring forward an alternative plan.' ... Eden said that this alternative plan would be along the lines of a Shaef organization – meaning the inclusion of Germany inside a European base within NATO. That was in fact very much what he was to propose in his rescue operation of 1954.

Now in September 1954 he decided to suggest that the European base should be an expanded version of the Brussels Treaty of 1948 to be renamed the Western European Union (WEU). West Germany and Italy would be invited to join Great Britain, France and the Benelux countries, all except the British consenting to accept WEU verification of their agreed commitments and force levels. West Germany would in addition enter NATO on the basis of full sovereignty. Eden claimed that he thought of this plan in his bath; but its origin has recently been attributed to Christopher Steel of the Foreign Office.[112] Whatever the truth of this may be, the WEU project was to save NATO from disintegration.

Eden left London on 11 September to sound out reaction in Brussels (where he met the Benelux leaders), Bonn, Rome and Paris. Only in Paris did he meet with serious doubts. But even here Mendès-France was more forthcoming than would have been the case if he had been the outright neutralist that some in the British Foreign Office supposed. Certainly he did nothing to bolster the suspicion that he had earlier entered into a deal with Moscow involving Soviet help in achieving a face-saving settlement of the Indochina problem at Geneva in return for French sabotage of Western plans in Europe. The way thus now seemed open for Eden to call a nine-power conference in London to examine the details of his plan. If he had a major concern at this time it was not in fact the attitude of Mendès-France but that of Dulles. For the Secretary of State had seen fit to fly to Bonn to consult Adenauer on 16 September, the day Eden arrived in Paris. The Foreign Secretary's fear was that Dulles would try to isolate the French and seek to persuade Adenauer to favour an eight-power conference without them. But Dulles turned out to be relatively flexible about Eden's plan and agreed to consult him in London. This was a critical encounter. For it led to some meeting of minds and subsequently to close Anglo-American cooperation in pushing through the Eden plan. Dulles in effect wavered about insisting on the strong supranational features that had attracted him in the EDC scheme and concluded that, despite his own difficulties with Congress, the French had to be given one more chance to avoid neutralism. He accordingly agreed to support and attend a nine-power conference.

The London Conference opened on 28 September. Both Dulles and Eden, working in collusion, made decisive and skilfully timed interventions that succeeded in winning over Mendès-France. Dulles played his part by stressing his disappointment at the fate of the EDC but by conceding that 'if the hopes that were tied into the EDC can reasonably be transferred into the arrangements which will be the outgrowth of this meeting', he would 'be disposed to recommend to the President that he should renew a pledge comparable to that which was offered in connection with EDC'.[113] Then Eden sprang his surprise: other than in exceptional circumstances arising outside Europe, the British would maintain on the Continent four divisions and the Tactical Air Force for as long as the majority of WEU members desired it. This was the unilateral pledge that the French had vainly sought for so many decades. Eden made the most of it, using Churchillian rhetoric about 'ours being above all an island story'. The decision had not been lightly made by Eden or his colleagues. As has been seen, he had in 1951 and 1952 hated offering even the most modest concessions to France; in December 1953 he had told McDonald that it was 'insulting to be continually asked to re-pledge ourselves as if the old pledges were no good'; and only weeks before the London Conference he instructed Jebb, the British Ambassador in Paris, to tell Mendès-France that his request for a long-term, specific commitment was 'shop-soiled' and 'totally unacceptable'.[114] Eden's conversion came on the eve of the London Conference and was probably motivated by genuine fear of a recrudescence of an 'Asia First' philosophy in the United States. It is incidentally a measure of his sense of independence from Cabinet control, on which Kilmuir commented, that he considered the concurrence of Churchill was all that he needed. But the Prime Minister was now sufficiently conscious of constitutional proprieties to insist on this occasion that a Cabinet be called. Eden was duly authorized to make his offer but only after 'doubts were vigorously expressed'.[115]

Eden's historic offer transformed the atmosphere in the London Conference. It made French agreement to his plan a near-certainty, though

Mendès-France was at first rather ungracious in his immediate reaction and is said to have provoked a rare public outburst of Eden's temper.[116] Further details were worked out in Paris in late October. The French Assembly, after rejecting the agreement on 24 December, was persuaded, once Mendès-France had made the issue one of confidence, to accept a few days later. Was this, then, Eden's finest hour? Certainly it brought him universal acclaim among the statesmen and newspapers of the West. But the argument can of course be advanced that if he had been prepared to offer his historic commitment earlier instead of 'persistently and scornfully' rejecting such a course, he 'might have saved the EDC'.[117] In addition it is possible to maintain that Eden's offer was essentially meaningless. Moran quoted Churchill as follows: 'It can be cancelled at any time ... It does not mean anything. All words ... No one in their senses thought we could bring our troops home from the Continent ... We have always been better than our word. Never ... was the leadership of Europe so cheaply won.'[118] If it was as simple as that, it is tempting to assert that Eden's failure to grasp this earlier was indeed evidence of his lack of imagination and originality of mind – and of similar shortcomings in almost all members of the British élite since 1919. But to all these arguments there is the tenable rejoinder that Eden's initiative could not have been better timed, given that the French Assembly had a deep psychological need to reject at least once a European settlement involving the Germans.

Another important feature of the London Conference was the full restoration of harmony between Eden and Dulles. Dulles paid Eden fulsome tributes during the course of the Conference, and afterwards wrote privately:

As I leave, I want to express the great pleasure which I have had working here with you. You gave wonderful leadership to the Lancaster House Conference. In addition, we had important talks on other matters. I feel that we are, more than ever before, working closely together, both in terms of basic objectives and in terms of their implementation. We must keep this up.

Eden replied:

Thank you so much for your message. I cannot tell you how much I have valued your unwavering support during this critical week. I believe, like you, that we have made an historic step forwards. Without you it would have been quite impossible. Warmest regards.[119]

At the end of the year Dulles again sent a personal message to Eden on hearing the news of the French Assembly's final ratification of the settlement: 'I am sure we can both now have a more relaxed New Year's Day with even a mild bit of celebration. With best wishes.' He received the reply: 'And so say all of us. Anthony and Clarissa.'[120] Here, then, is some evidence that the Dulles–Eden relationship had survived the differences over south-east Asia without permanent damage. Without the Suez catastrophe of 1956, their cooperation over German rearmament might have been widely accorded at least as much retrospective importance as their earlier divergence over Indochina.

As Eden entered 1955 he could thus look back if not on an *annus mirabilis* at least on one that had been marked by many spectacular and portentous events. He had, moreover, been greatly moved in the autumn by having been made a Knight of the Garter, an honour in the personal gift of the sovereign. One subject, however, continued to depress him, namely his relationship with Churchill. For the Prime Minister, having said he would retire in July, had used the Indochina crisis to justify a postponement to the autumn. But by mid-August Moran was noting yet another change of mind:

'Last night I woke at three o'clock and lay awake for three hours ... I saw plainly outlined the most important and burdensome problem I have to solve – my relations with Anthony. I don't see why he wants to take over the dregs at the fag end of parliament – only one more session before the election – when nothing can be done ... I have told them that I am quite willing to go on for another year if they would like me to.'

At the same period Macmillan recorded in his diary:

... he had many times in the last few months told Anthony that he was on the point of 'handing over'. First he told him the Queen's return, that is May; then he said July; finally, in a letter, written on June 11th (which I had seen), he had categorically told Eden that he would resign the Premiership in September.[121]

In October Churchill was informed that much opinion at the Conservative Party Conference favoured an early change of Prime Minister. But his reaction was defiant: a major ministerial reshuffle. It must have been galling for Eden to have to read newspaper speculation that he might leave the Foreign Office not to become Prime Minister but to become a domestic policy supremo or Leader of the House. Valuable though such experience might have been to him, this would have involved the implication of his accepting a further extended period of Churchill's premiership. Understandably, this did not appeal to him and he accordingly stayed at the Foreign Office.

For Eden the breakthrough finally came early in 1955. The kingmaker was ironically to be Macmillan, with whom he had hitherto never been on the best of terms. The Minister of Defence had simply come to the conclusion that Churchill, having passed his eightieth birthday, was no longer capable of leading the country. As one of the Prime Minister's staunchest allies in earlier crises, his defection was decisive. In February 1955 Churchill accordingly informed Eden that he would definitely retire in April and he knew that this time he would not be allowed to go back on his promise. To Moran he pretended that he was anxious to give Eden his chance: 'If I dug in I don't think they could make me go. But I like Anthony so much and I have worked with him so long. And he wants to be Prime Minister terribly.' The reality was that he had been driven out by Macmillan. Moran himself was not deceived, for Churchill on other occasions betrayed different feelings about Eden: '... he [Churchill] spoke very sadly of political life. He had been hurt by the things Anthony had said lately.' Nor did the Churchillian loyalists ever forget Macmillan's 'treachery'. On 22 November 1956 Bracken told Beaverbrook: 'I can't forgive him his gross disloyalty to Churchill.'[122]

Eden was no doubt in an elated mood as he left London on 19 February for a tour of the Middle East and Asia that was to be his last major mission as Foreign Secretary. He began in Cairo where he entertained Nasser to dinner at the British Embassy. It was to be the only meeting between the two men and was not a success. Nasser thought Eden behaved like 'a prince dealing with vagabonds'. Eden thought Nasser 'a fine man physically' but otherwise was evidently not favourably impressed.[123] For Nasser bluntly rejected his idea that Egypt should join the so-called Baghdad Pact which had been publicly proposed by Nuri es-Said of Iraq with the support of Turkey. The scheme was in fact singularly ill-conceived, for no other Arab state was willing to join Iraq. Of other states only Pakistan, Iran and Great Britain subsequently participated. As will be seen, this was one regional pact that held little appeal for Dulles unless Eden should be successful in getting other Arab states, and especially Egypt, involved. This Nasser rejected adamantly, as he made unmistakably clear to Eden at their Cairo meeting. Their encounter also came at a time of intensifying Egyptian intrigues and propaganda broadcasts aimed at discrediting Great Britain's friends in the Middle East and, above all, Nuri es-Said.

Eden flew on to Pakistan for a brief visit before arriving on 23 February in Bangkok for a three-day meeting of the South-East Asia Treaty Organization (SEATO). This had been founded in Manila in the previous September when Eden had been preoccupied in Europe with the EDC crisis and was the rather anaemic body that had resulted from Dulles's quest before and during the Geneva Conference for a regional security pact. The British had played their part in its emasculation by insisting on the exclusion of Cambodia, Laos and South Vietnam. But Dulles's greatest problems had in the end lain at home where he and Eisenhower had concluded that Congress would not permit the Administration to have powers to use force in an emergency without being consulted. SEATO was therefore to be a mere shell in comparison with NATO. Dulles no doubt regretted this but does not appear to have thought that disproportionate blame should be apportioned to Eden.

Now in Bangkok Dulles and Eden came together to complete the detailed work on giving SEATO a permanent structure. Nothing, however, could be done to modify the fundamentally flawed framework and hence no serious arguments arose. A subject on which the two ministers did differ sharply was Formosa, which was not even a member of SEATO. Eden objected to Dulles's resolute stand in defence of Chiang's offshore islands of Quemoy and the Matsus, which, unlike Formosa itself, were vulnerable to shelling from mainland China. He also saw a danger that Chiang might overreact and attempt to catalyse an all-out American war with the Chinese Communists. His solution was to propose the withdrawal of Nationalist troops from Quemoy and the Matsus in return for a pledge by Peking not to use force against the islands or against Formosa itself. He was vague in the extreme about the means of ensuring that the Communist Chinese would keep their word. Such a one-sided bargain did not appeal to Dulles. He had earlier been strongly counselled to ignore British views by Robertson, his Assistant Secretary:

I have just read Eden's telegram to Makins which you handed to me a few minutes ago. The British apparently are determined to bend us to their will vis-à-vis the Chinese Communists. However unpopular the US position might be in London, the British position for us would be far more unpopular in the US. I suggest that political repercussions at home might be more difficult for us than disapproval by the British.[124]

Now in Bangkok Dulles spoke forcefully to Eden:

At the moment to pressure the Republic of China [Formosa] into the surrender of Quemoy and Matsu would (1) importantly increase the attacking capacity of the Chinese Communists by making available Amoy and Fuchow Harbours, the natural staging grounds for a sea attack; (2) greatly weaken the morale of the Republic of China on Formosa and increase the opportunity of Chinese Communist subversion; (3) probably increase the Chinese Communist intention to probe our resolution by putting it to the test of action.

In other words, further retreat would, in our opinion, both weaken the defensive capabilities of Formosa and increase the risk that that capability will be put to the test of battle.[125]

Eden was not won over and later, on 8 March, publicly criticized American policy in the House of Commons. Eisenhower was duly provoked to send another sermon to Churchill:

The conclusion seems inescapable that these differences come about because we do not agree on the probable extent and importance of further Communist expansion in Asia. In our contacts with New Zealand and Australia, we have the feeling that we encounter a common concern no less acute than ours; but your own government seems to regard Communist aggression in Asia as of little significance to the free world future ...

We must come to the point where every additional backward step must be deemed a defeat for the Western world. In fact it is a triple defeat. First, we lose a potential ally. Next, we give to an implacable enemy another recruit. Beyond this, every retreat creates in the minds of neutrals the fear that we do not mean what we say when we pledge our support to people who want to remain free. We show ourselves fearful of the Communistic brigands and create the impression that we are slinking along in the shadows, hoping that the beast will finally be satiated and cease his predatory tactics before he finally devours us. So the third result is that the morale of our friends crumbles . . .[126]

Dulles on this occasion was not, however, unduly disturbed by Eden's propensity to favour appeasement. For there was now no conference in existence at which Eden could act as 'honest broker' and Dulles was therefore at liberty to threaten the Chinese Communists along lines he judged best. His 'brinkmanship' proved to be successful. For Quemoy and the Matsus have never been evacuated by the Formosans and the Chinese have not seen fit to put American resolve to the test.

With the Bangkok Conference at an end, Eden now set out on his return journey. He first visited Burma, where he and his wife arranged to visit the Commonwealth Cemetary sixteen miles from Rangoon where his son, Simon, lies in a collective grave.[127] Next he flew to New Delhi where he was invited for the second time to address the Indian Parliament. India certainly mattered to Eden. He greatly valued her place in the Commonwealth and, at least until the Suez crisis, was anxious to consult Jawaharlal Nehru at least as assiduously as the leaders of the Old Dominions. At times he seemed almost as anxious to build a London–New Delhi axis as some of the utopian Bevanites in the Labour Party. This was certainly not an ignoble vision. But it was based on a delusion about the nature of British power and influence in the world. The reality of their economic situation probably made it foolhardy for the British to court Nehru and 'positive neutralism' without Washington's approval, which throughout the 1950s and even beyond was to be consistently withheld. Eden finally visited Baghdad to encourage Nuri es-Said in his lonely stand against Nasserite Arab nationalism.

Back in London, Eden had just a month to prepare to take over from Churchill, whom he had served so impatiently for fifteen years. His great day came on 6 April 1955. He drove to Buckingham Palace and kissed hands as Prime Minister to Queen Elizabeth the Second, the fourth sovereign under whom he had served as a Cabinet Minister. He had at last attained what Churchill described as 'the dream of his life'. 1955, not 1954, was surely his *annus mirabilis*.

Eden's first task on moving into Number Ten Downing Street was to announce his Cabinet. He chose to retain almost all of those who had served under Churchill and he kept to a minimum the shuffling of portfolios. No doubt he was conscious that a major reconstruction had been carried through by his predecessor in the previous autumn and also that sweeping changes now might provide ammunition for the Opposition in the General Election then in prospect. He did, however, require the retirement of two peers, namely Swinton and De la Warr. Both had served in Chamberlain's Cabinet and, though by no means extreme appeasers, neither had rallied to Eden's standard at the time of his resignation. Perhaps, then, the Prime Minister was paying off old scores.

The main difficulty for Eden in his Cabinet-making related not to former rivals from the 1930s but to his most loyal supporter in that period – Salisbury. Should he be given the Foreign Office? He had, after all, served there under Eden before February 1938 and he had been made Acting Secretary of State in 1953 during Eden's illness. Yet he was also a member of the House of Lords and hence, according to many, not a suitable choice in the post-war 'democratic age'. Again, it was argued that the House of Commons would no longer accept important statements on foreign affairs from a junior minister. In his memoirs Eden claimed that these considerations finally led him to reject Salisbury's claim.[1] If true, this revealed a singular willingness to conform to the dictates of the *Zeitgeist*. By contrast, Macmillan in 1960, shortly after the publication of Eden's account of his reasons for passing over Salisbury, jauntily disregarded conventional wisdom, now reinforced by the earlier decision, by giving the Foreign Office to Lord Home. The feelings of Eden, and still more those of Salisbury, may easily be imagined, especially as Macmillan had to survive an Opposition censure motion in which Eden's views were widely quoted.

Probably Eden had additional grounds for disregarding Salisbury's claims. Despite their long friendship, Salisbury might have proved too opinionated and too impulsive to make a good partner for the Prime Minister in a sphere where he had for so long held almost undisputed sway. For Salisbury's standing in society, his awareness of his place in history, and his sense of duty made him a potentially difficult colleague. The normal ambitions of the career politician did not motivate or restrain him. On the contrary, like his Uncle Robert, he was perhaps excessively conscious of his own integrity and this, together with some unconscious theatrical instincts, led him rather too often to contemplate resignation. Eden may therefore have had mixed motives for making him not Foreign Secretary but Lord President of the Council. Salisbury appears to have taken the setback in good part and he was to remain on affable terms with his chief. But, according to Macmillan, this did not prevent his twice threatening to resign during Eden's short premiership.[2] And in the Suez crisis, as will be seen, he played a decisive part in undermining the Prime Minister's position both by insisting that there be an early ceasefire and by his conduct in the byzantine domestic and international politics that followed. Nobody who knew the high-minded Salisbury has claimed that conscious pique at not obtaining the Foreign Office played any part in shaping his subsequent course. But his conduct suggests that he might have been even more troublesome to Eden had he actually become Foreign Secretary. In short, he was no longer temperamentally fitted to be Eden's subaltern.

If Eden wanted a loyal supporter at the Foreign Office, why then did he choose Macmillan? Was not Macmillan at least as assertive as Salisbury and not even a long-standing friend? And was he not a candidate for the premiership as Salisbury could not be? The answer may be that Eden intended Macmillan to be merely a stop-gap Foreign Secretary – but one of sufficient stature to seem tolerable to Salisbury. Once Salisbury had come to terms with his setback, Macmillan could be moved to another so-called great office of state and a loyal dependant of the Prime Minister could replace him. Certainly, whether planned or not, this was actually to happen before the end of 1955. But if Eden promoted Macmillan only to help deal with the Salisbury problem, he was taking a monumental risk. For once established in the top rungs of the administration Macmillan would not be easily dislodged. And at the same time his loyalty could never be counted on. In his handling of these top appointments, therefore, Eden was already storing up for himself later troubles. What may be doubted, however, is whether any significantly better solution was available to him.

Eden's full Cabinet list was

Lord President of the Council	Lord Salisbury
Foreign Secretary	Harold Macmillan
Chancellor of the Exchequer	R. A. Butler
Lord Privy Seal and Leader of the House of Commons	Harry Crookshank
Lord Chancellor	Lord Kilmuir
Minister of Defence	Selwyn Lloyd

Home Secretary	Gwylim Lloyd-George
Colonial Secretary	Alan Lennox-Boyd
Secretary for Commonwealth Relations	Lord Home
Secretary of State for Scotland	James Stuart
Minister of Labour	Sir Walter Monckton
President of the Board of Trade	Peter Thorneycroft
Minister of Housing and Local Government	Duncan Sandys
Chancellor of the Duchy of Lancaster	Lord Woolton
Minister of Education	Sir David Eccles
Minister of Agriculture	D. Heathcoat Amory
Minister of Pensions	Osbert Peake

Newcomers to the Cabinet were Lloyd and Home. Lloyd's appointment occasioned no surprise, for he had served as Minister of State under Eden at the Foreign Office and thus was thought to be a principal protégé. By contrast, the promotion of Home was unexpected, for he had been a most devoted Parliamentary Private Secretary to Neville Chamberlain. He was also an unreconstructed Municheer, unashamedly motivated by a loathing of Bolshevism, and a severe critic of the Churchill–Eden wartime policy of appeasing the Soviets over Poland. Eden could not, however, have imagined that he was helping to create a future Foreign Secretary and Prime Minister.

After announcing the composition of his Government, Eden now had to decide whether to call an early General Election or to delay it for up to eighteen months. By seeking an immediate mandate he ran the risk of appearing in the history books as Great Britain's shortest-lived Prime Minister in modern times. In 1963 Home, reincarnated as Sir Alexander Douglas-Home, faced a similar dilemma, and opted to serve until his time ran out. But Eden, unlike Douglas-Home, had a good chance of winning an immediate contest and he faced, moreover, the prospect of a deteriorating economic climate. Indeed, Eden took over at an ideal moment for an electoral appeal. The Churchill government had benefited from the terms of trade temporarily turning in Great Britain's favour and from the ending of the Korean War. It had thus been possible to remove many post-war restrictions. One historian has even claimed that the second Churchill administration 'was by a long stretch the most successful peacetime ministry that the country had seen since 1918'.[3] Certainly the austerity of the Attlee era had visibly departed. All rationing, for example, had ended by 1954, whereas when Labour had left office in 1951 some items were in as short supply as in wartime. The following table[4] is eloquent:

WEEKLY FOOD RATIONS

	July 1945	October 1951
Bacon and ham	3 oz.	3 oz.
Cheese	2 oz.	$1\frac{1}{2}$ oz.
Butter	2 oz.	3 oz.
Margarine	4 oz.	4 oz.
Cooking fat	1 oz.	2 oz.
Meat	1s. 2d. worth*	1s. 7d. worth*
Sugar	8 oz.	10 oz.
Tea	2 oz.	2 oz.
Chocolates and sweets	3 oz.	$6\frac{1}{2}$ oz.

*Prices had been increased twice during the period.

Possibly the Attlee Government, had it remained in office, would have been no less successful. But the Conservatives inevitably got the credit, deserved or not, for having ended rationing and controls. Indeed, the Conservatives' restoration of purchasing freedom was as strikingly evident a change in society as Labour's introduction of the Welfare State. Certainly no Government after those of Attlee and Churchill can boast any similar striking transformation in the lives of most citizens. Moreover, Churchill had succeeded in maintaining full employment and had thus largely devalued the Labour Party's chief asset in the previous General Election, namely fear that a Conservative Government would restore the 'Hungry Thirties'. Again, the Conservatives could boast that the number of private cars had increased by one third and that the number of television licences had risen from 1,031,095 to 4,580,725.[5]

Eden had yet another major advantage in 1955: the condition of the Labour Party. Attlee had chosen to remain Leader after his defeat in 1951 and was now seventy-two. Unlike Churchill, his long experience probably did not compensate in the electorate's eyes for his evident entry into old age. Moreover, he presided over a deeply divided party which early in 1955 came within one vote on its National Executive Committee of expelling Aneurin Bevan from membership. The impression was created that for many on both wings of the party a General Election would be a mere interlude in their principal business of fighting each other.

In the circumstances Eden thus required a little, but not much courage to act decisively. He accordingly announced on 15 April, nine days after kissing hands, that Parliament would be dissolved on 6 May and that a General Election would be held on 26 May. Before dissolution, however, the annual budget statement was to be made. This turned out to be the first of the many electioneering budgets of the post-war era. But precisely because it was the first, it may not have been widely identified as such by an electorate less cynical than it has subsequently become. With the balance of payments running into deficit, Butler reduced standard rate income tax from nine shillings to eight shillings and sixpence in the pound and removed 2,400,000 people from all liability. In addition, purchase tax on cotton goods was abolished. In his memoirs Butler himself characteristically quoted the elliptical verdict of the *Economist*, which was certainly no supporter of the Labour Party:

> Many people would have felt happier about the general balance of the Budget if the portion of the surplus to be given away had been put rather lower. But that the right figure, in all the political and economic circumstances, lies somewhere in the middle range between giving nothing at all away and eliminating the surplus altogether hardly admits of doubt. To have given nothing would have proved Mr Butler too much of an economist to survive in politics; to have given the lot would have shown him too much of a politician to have charge of the national economy.[6]

The Conservative election campaign was also helped by an unusually tranquil interlude in world affairs which seemed to reflect credit on Eden as the recent Foreign Secretary. For the first time in many years no major Communist offensive was capturing the headlines. And Eden had at last decided that a summit with the Soviets was desirable. The irony of this opportunism was not lost on Churchill, who remarked to Moran: 'How much more attractive a top-level meeting seems when one has reached the top.' And Kirkpatrick of the Foreign Office told Macmillan, his new master, that though personally sceptical about the value of a summit, he was resigned to the attempt being made. He added cynically that Eisenhower probably would not mind, since 'even the best friends must embarrass one another for electoral reasons'.[7] The Americans in fact behaved as he predicted, for they wanted to help Eden retain power, preferring him to a Bevanite-influenced Labour government. Dulles was as convinced as his President about this – more evidence that he felt no great personal animosity towards Eden. In Paris on 7–8 May Macmillan accordingly discussed details with Dulles and persuaded him to recommend to Washington a plan for a series of Foreign Ministers' meetings with a brief Heads of Governments' summit sandwiched between two of them. By 10 May Eisenhower had acquiesced. Molotov was presently sounded and it became clear that the Soviets would also agree – their formal assent being given on polling day, 26 May. The Labour Party had intended to issue an election poster calling for 'Top Level Talks Now'. This had to be altered to the less arresting 'Top Level Talks – Send Attlee'.

Another foreign policy development during the election campaign came on 15 May when in Vienna the Foreign Ministers of the United States, the Soviet Union, Great Britain and France signed a treaty with Austria involving her permanent neutrality and the withdrawal of occupation forces. Macmillan, Dulles, Molotov and Antoine Pinay saluted crowds of delighted Austrians from the balcony of the Belvedere. This was a unique occasion: the only time territory occupied by Communists has ever been voluntarily evacuated. It was also marked by the sight of Molotov and Dulles embracing each other. For Molotov, erstwhile business partner of Ribbentrop, such a gesture may have meant little. Whether Dulles found it so easy may be doubted. But to the watching British electorate the unmistakable impression was one of relaxation and a promise of enduring peace. Thus, while it is beyond doubt that most electors who changed their voting pattern in 1955 were, as always, more influenced by domestic than international developments, the Austrian State Treaty and the prospect of a summit must have helped to boost Eden's confidence.

Eden, accompanied by his wife, played an unusually active rôle in the General Election. He spoke extempore in most marginal constituencies, usually in outdoor meetings. According to one authority:

He reiterated the main themes in the Conservative manifesto, dwelling particularly on the government's achievements in foreign affairs ... He stressed the virtues of toleration and reasonableness and the perils of national disunity. He said nothing memorable but said it very well.[8]

The stress on foreign affairs need not surprise us, for only on this subject did he speak with real authority. The Conservative Party managers evidently realized this for two of their most utilized posters were one with the slogan 'For Peace through Strength' and one with a picture of the Prime Minister accompanied by the description 'Working for Peace'. One of the few issues to emerge during the election campaign itself was connected to overseas policy, namely whether the two-year National Service requirement should be reduced or abandoned. Labour Party spokesmen promised a 'review' which led many commentators to assume that at least a cut would be inevitable. But Eden refused to be drawn into an auction on the subject. With exaggerated dignity he stated that reduction would depend on 'progress with Soviet Russia' and that it would be 'criminal folly to weaken ourselves before the negotiations begin'.[9] In fact during his time as Prime Minister no cut in National Service occurred but his successor, Macmillan, abolished it altogether in 1957 without either a new mandate from the electorate or any 'progress' with the Soviets. Eden had, however, prepared the way for this move, principally by insisting while still at the Foreign Office

373

that in the nuclear age the Suez base should be given up. Thus the excessive dependence on nuclear weapons and the paucity of conventional capability that was to be a feature of the Macmillan era was the fulfilment and not the abandonment of Eden's approach to defence policy.

Eden also played a big part in election broadcasting in 1955. He appeared on television on 7 and 21 May and on radio on the 7th. According to the author of a study of the General Election of 1955:

> By common consent the greatest *tour-de-force* among the television broadcasts was the final one by Sir Anthony Eden. Without any tricks or visual devices he talked directly to the viewers for a quarter of an hour, speaking in a genuinely extempore fashion, summarizing the issues of the election, not attacking his opponents, but presenting the Conservative case with a confident, quiet reasonableness. He used no memorable phrases, he said nothing new and, as usual, he was more authoritative on foreign policy than on home affairs. But he won universal praise for the way in which he managed to convey a sense of calmness, optimism, decency and compassion.[10]

One leading Conservative who was not invited to appear on radio or television, however, was Churchill, who was not completely in retirement as he was seeking re-election to Parliament. Nor did Eden make any reference to him until faced with criticism for ingratitude in the *Manchester Guardian*. Churchill, according to Moran, was hurt.[11] At the time most observers accepted that Eden's motive for shunning his former chief arose from a need to be seen to have been re-elected on his own merits. But it is now obvious that there were also deep-seated reasons deriving from their troubled relationship in office.

The campaign in general passed off without serious incidents or more than routine party arguments. Smears, scares and sensations were almost wholly absent. Even the *Daily Mirror* could manage nothing more dramatic than a jibe at the difference in social class between the Prime Minister (pictured at Eton) and an ordinary secondary school pupil at the same age. Otherwise it was reduced to sneering at 'Miles and Miles of Eden Smiles'.[12]

The result of the General Election was a triumph for Eden. His own majority at Warwick and Leamington rose from 9,803 to 13,466. And nationally the Conservative majority over Labour increased to sixty seats. The popular vote gave the Conservatives 49·7 per cent against Labour's 46·4. This was the first time that the Conservatives had polled the largest share of the popular vote since 1935 and the first time a government had increased its majority for ninety years. It was thus a singularly impressive vote of confidence for the new Prime Minister.

Confirmed in office, Eden had no opportunity to bask contentedly in his success. For he at once faced a dramatic escalation in industrial strife. London busmen and dockworkers had been on strike for some time and may have contributed to the extent of Labour's defeat in the General Election. Now, on 29 May, only days after polling, the locomotive drivers (ASLEF) joined them, making the situation so grave that a State of Emergency had to be declared on 31 May. But the conciliatory charm of Monckton, the Minister of Labour, was to be shown to great advantage during June. First, ASLEF agreed on the 14th to call off their strike in return for a binding arbitration procedure. Then the TUC came into the negotiations with the dockworkers and eventually secured a settlement by 4 July. Eden, like Churchill, was prepared to allow Monckton to give way to strong unions to an extent that some orthodox economists believed damaging to the nation's best interests. But most union leaders were decidedly not extremists and were fully aware that there must be some limits set to their claims if inflation was to remain manageable. In this climate Eden examined ideas for introducing legislation to restrict the powers of trade unions but he did not press them in the face of the advice of the TUC.[13] Later more determined efforts by Harold Wilson and Edward Heath were unsuccessful, in the one case because proposed legislation proved unacceptable to the TUC-influenced Cabinet and in the other because the actual legislation was successfully flouted. Perhaps the time to put curbs on trade unions, if at all, was in the calm decade of the 1950s when the moderate leaders of the TUC would have presented only token opposition in contrast to that offered by some of their militant successors. But Eden had too little experience of home affairs and was insufficiently alarmed at the portents shown in the bout of strikes to contemplate making any fundamental changes. This was perhaps symptomatic of what one historian has referred to as his 'tendency to mark time' in domestic matters.[14]

Immigration provides another example of his neglect, benign or otherwise, of what was then a relatively minor problem but one that was destined to occasion his successors much more trouble. Churchill is said to have come to the conclusion in 1954 that unrestricted Commonwealth immigration must be halted and he ordered the preparation of appropriate legislation. He was also, incidentally, to be heard expressing sentiments in private about those whom he termed 'blackamoors' that had a distinctly racialist overtone.[15] Eden, by contrast, was unprepared for the controversy that closing the door to immigrants would have occasioned. Although he was greatly distracted during his premiership by problems in foreign affairs, he might in any case have shrunk from putting at risk his 'liberal' reputation in domestic politics. Moreover, as has been seen, he took seriously his own high-minded rhetoric about the unique character of the new multiracial Commonwealth. If in foreign policy matters he had been keen to please Nehru, he would scarcely have wished to offend him by introducing discriminatory laws relating to Commonwealth immigration. But had his premiership survived the watershed of Suez, in which his flirtation with New Delhi was decisively terminated, he might have reverted to a 'Little Englander' approach. As it was, immigration control was delayed until the 1960s.

It has often been claimed that Eden interfered in the work of his ministers in an erratic and inconsiderate fashion. The origins of this criticism probably lie in the recollections of only a small group of those with whom he had dealings. His principal Cabinet detractor appears to have been Kilmuir, who wrote in his memoirs of the Prime Minister's 'chronic restlessness', reflecting that 'no one in public life lived more on his nerves than he did'. Butler wrote more gently:

... the Prime Minister paid me the compliment of expecting me, more than the Chairman of the party, to be responsible for Conservative success in the country. I was therefore at the receiving end of those innumerable telephone calls, on every day of the week and at every hour of the day, which characterized his conscientious but highly strung supervision of our affairs.

Nigel Nicolson, a Conservative backbencher, went much further, though clearly not on the basis of first-hand experience:

Eden was a bad Prime Minister. For one thing, he could never leave his ministers alone. He was always fussing them, ringing them up in the middle of the night to ask them had they done this? Had they seen this in the newspapers? This showed in a lack of confidence, and worry, in ministers – senior ministers, and then junior ones, and from them it trickled down by the natural indiscretions you get in the lobbies and the smoking room in the House of Commons to the backbenchers.[16]

Plainly such rumours were not entirely unfounded. But there is a danger that they will be given disproportionate attention by historians and that insufficient weight will be given to those ministers who were not severe critics of his leadership or of his methods either at the time or in retrospect.

Eden's scope for undue interference in most ministries on the home front was certainly limited by his unfamiliarity with the details involved. And even if he had wished to break with the habit of a lifetime and immerse himself in domestic subjects, he could scarcely have done so during his short premiership because of the unavoidable and continuous pressures facing him in international affairs. Having been re-elected, he was at once compelled to concentrate on the Heads of Government summit arranged for Geneva from 18 to 23 July. Following the Austrian State Treaty and some relaxation of the rigours of Stalinism, hopes were high throughout the world of new agreements leading to a lasting peace. The promised first appearance in the West of the new Soviet leaders, Nikolai Bulganin and Nikita Khrushchev was seen as particularly auspicious. Eden, however, was probably less optimistic than the uninitiated masses. For he knew that the Americans were against the idea of any detailed bargaining at Geneva and that the key to any further reduction in tension in Europe was the future of

Germany, about which the Soviets and the West were as far apart as ever. In a sense, therefore, his principal purpose at Geneva was merely to contribute to the creation of a genial atmosphere that might serve in the eyes of the general public as an adequate substitute for concrete agreements. He no doubt also hoped to emerge from the summit with an enhanced reputation as a world statesman. He was, after all, much the most experienced of the Big Four and he might therefore have expected to receive the lion's share of the publicity. If so, he was to be disappointed. For already many commentators had recognized that the Soviet Union and the United States had become superpowers and that Great Britain was in a second tier together with the French. The re-emergence of France had in this respect damaged British standing in the world. As long as the world thought of summitry in terms of the Big Three of the wartime conferences, Great Britain's decline was partially masked; but the emergence of a Big Four served to draw attention to the new realities of the international power structure. Moreover, the Geneva Conference on Indochina in the previous year had given a false impression of continued British significance partly because Eden had served as a mediator and partly because the United States had chosen to play a minor rôle in the proceedings. In 1955, by contrast, the Americans were eager to play a full part and needed no mediator. Nor did they wish to encourage the idea that there was a 'special relationship' between Eisenhower and Eden. On 9 June Eisenhower and Dulles discussed an appeal from Aldrich, their Ambassador in London, that the President should visit Great Britain en route to Geneva. The President, recalling that Churchill 'was always trying to get him there on any pretext whatever' was cool about the suggestion. In any case he was determined that any visit to London would have to be matched by one to Paris[17] – clearly not what Eden had in view. In the event the idea was dropped. Eden might well have reflected on the extent to which he was the author of his own discomfiture. For, as has been seen, nobody had done more than he to resist the wartime policies of Roosevelt and Churchill that had tended towards ensuring that France did not re-emerge as a Great Power in the post-war world.

When Eisenhower arrived at Geneva in July 1955 he was rapidly accepted as the leader of the West; the British and the French were bracketed together as mere auxiliaries. This evidently delighted some of the Prime Minister's American critics. O'Connor of the State Department recalled with relish:

... at the Summit meeting, it was quite interesting. Eden had just married his second wife, who was much younger ... Mr [*sic*] Eden, I think, was quite interested in keeping his impression of glamour as much to her as to the public. He was obviously taking sun baths – or a sun-lamp – every day, because during the whole conference he was a blooming, vigorous tan. And he was quite chagrined, I think, because he didn't come out of the conference as the outstanding diplomat. All the advance press speculation had said, 'Well, Eden is so experienced, and Eisenhower hasn't been through these things before, and Eden's a good thing for the West.' Actually the Russians paid absolutely no attention to Eden whatsoever. And in the coffee breaks Eden would be by himself with his own group, while the Russians were surrounding Eisenhower, and the French were off having tea. And Eden just wasn't getting any play, nor did he end up getting much play in the press, because several of the proposals that Eisenhower made got the centre of the press attention.

I got the impression of a very proud and chagrined man on a personal basis.

The seating arrangements also favoured the Americans for they resulted in the Soviets speaking after the British and being followed in turn by the Americans. O'Connor continued:

The Russians were knocking them [the British] down, and we were knocking the Russians down ... And from a purely press and publicity point of view, it put us at a considerable advantage ... I came away with a very strong impression that Eden had been quite disappointed that he had not emerged as the star – had been rather overwhelmed, really, by Eisenhower both on position and on press attention. And certainly the Russians treated the British with calculated denigration, I would say. They obviously wanted to deal with us. And I think that was quite a blow to Eden.[18]

Whether Eden was quite so put out on this occasion may be doubted. But over a longer period in the mid-1950s the extent of Great Britain's decline was borne in upon him and upon many others in the British élite. It was to produce some remarkable reactions. But the most obvious, particularly in Conservative circles, was visceral jealousy of the United States.

At the Geneva Conference both Eden and Eisenhower produced a 'plan'. There can be no doubt, however, that the Americans' effort caught the world's attention more than that of the British and not only because they were more powerful. Eisenhower's was the so-called Open Skies Plan, publicly sprung without warning on his allies and on the Soviets alike. It was a device designed to overcome the deadlock in the interminable international disarmament talks that had arisen as a result of the unwillingness of the Soviet Union to permit teams of inspectors to have unfettered rights to verify compliance with any agreement. The President suggested that aerial inspection would be less vexatious but would provide adequate safeguards for at least some arms control measures. The British and the French warmly welcomed the plan, while Bulganin spoke with unexpected friendliness, declaring that 'it seems to have real merit' and that the Soviet Union 'would give it complete and sympathetic study at once'.[19] Nothing was to come of the Open Skies idea, at least not in Eisenhower's time, but for the duration of the Geneva Summit it held the world stage as something of glittering simplicity that might serve to end the arms race. Eden's plan, by contrast, was too complicated and too limited in scope to have any similar appeal; and it was received by the Soviets without enthusiasm. This was the idea that on either side of the demarcation line in central Europe zones of mutual inspection, initially of one or two hundred miles, should be established. There might also be scope for some de-militarization. This was one of the many plans advanced in the 1950s for mutual inspection perhaps to be accompanied by so-called disengagement. None entered the realm of practical politics and all were strongly disliked by Adenauer's government, whose support would have been essential to their success. Nor were the Americans impressed by Eden's Geneva Plan, which they thought much inferior to the previous so-called Eden Plan of 1954. Eisenhower in his memoirs dismissed his later idea in one sentence;[20] while Dulles seems to have seen little merit even in his own chief's scheme.

If Eisenhower overshadowed Eden at Geneva, it is not true, as O'Connor implied, that the Soviets were wholly indifferent to the British. On the contrary, the Soviets gave a dinner for them in which the Americans took no part. On this occasion Bulganin sounded Eden about the possiblity of his visiting Moscow where he had not been since the end of the war. But Eden said that it was the Soviets' turn to come to London and to his surprise Bulganin readily agreed. This duly led in the following spring to a full-scale Soviet visit.

The Geneva Conference achieved nothing concrete. Above all, no progress proved possible on disarmament or German reunification. The formal sessions were indeed largely as Macmillan characterized them in his memoirs: 'a great waste of time'.[21] But the general amiability, particularly outside the formal sessions, was seized upon by the world's press and was widely referred to as the 'Geneva Spirit'. This was an achievement of a sort and Eden made the most of it in his speeches at home in the aftermath of the Conference. And he stressed that the issues raised at Geneva would be discussed further in the autumn when the Big Four Foreign Ministers were due to meet. High hopes for concrete agreements were thus deferred rather than dashed.

The Geneva Conference also enabled Eden and Macmillan to hold private conversations with their American counterparts on subjects not on the formal agenda. One topic was Formosa, about which the Prime Minister tackled Eisenhower in vigorous fashion with particular reference to Quemoy and the Matsus. Hitherto, as has been seen, his efforts to push the Americans in the direction of surrender had been limited to dealings with the inflexible Dulles. He found the President rather more willing to listen. Both Eden and Macmillan accordingly persuaded themselves, probably mistakenly, that the subsequent lowering of tension between Chiang and the Communists was due in part to their words of warning having caused the Americans to urge Taipeh to see the offshore islands as outposts rather than strongholds.[22]

Less satisfactory were Eden's conversations with Dulles on the subject of the Middle East. The two men, as has been seen, had re-established

379

apparently cordial relations during the last months of 1954. And these had continued through the spring of 1955 when Eden succeeded to the premiership and won a General Election. On each occasion Dulles sent warm letters of congratulation. Eden's reply to the first read:

Thank you so much for your kind message. I have so much enjoyed our work together and I look forward to continuing our friendship. Clarissa and I send our best wishes to Janet and you.

To the second he replied:

Thank you so much for your kind message which I was glad to get. I am happy to feel that we shall be continuing our friendly working association.[23]

Now, at Geneva, sharp differences re-emerged over the Baghdad Pact. Eden and Macmillan maintained that Great Britain had joined the arrangement involving Turkey, Pakistan and Iraq at the instigation of the Americans and on the understanding that they, too, would join it. The Foreign Secretary, for example, wrote in his diary on 14 July: 'We had been left with the Turco-Iraqi pact, which the Americans started, and then ran out of.'[24] But Dulles did not accept this version of the origins of the Baghdad Pact. It would appear that in 1954 he had favoured the creation of an alliance involving the so-called Northern Tier of states along the southern borders of the Soviet Union. In particular, he had no objection to the formation of the Turco-Pakistani pact early in 1954; and envisaged that both the British and the Americans would give support to an expanded version. It was, if anything, the British who were hesitant at this stage, for, according to Loy Henderson of the State Department, they were anxious about the effect on India of their allying with Pakistan.[25] Moreover, both the Americans and the British seem to have been undecided about which other states to involve. They would have welcomed a Middle East Alliance comprising all Islamic states, Arab and other. But the long-standing attitude of Egypt made that unthinkable. So the practical question was whether the Turco-Pakistani Pact should be extended on a limited basis. The inclusion of just one more state, Iran, had its attractions. For in that case the Northern Tier would have consisted of all states along the southern borders of the Soviet Union from the Mediterranean to the Himalayas. Moreover, no Arab state would have been involved and hence the United States would have avoided complications with Israel and would not have appeared to Cairo to be establishing two camps among the Arabs. Yet Iran was so unstable and weak that including her in the Northern Tier might have overturned her government. While hesitating about the next step, Dulles suddenly found himself in March 1955 facing the *fait accompli* of the British joining the bilateral Turco-Iraqi pact, which had been forged a month earlier and to which at that stage the Americans had had no objection. The whole exercise was now seen in

Washington as a coup engineered by Eden in order to prolong British influence in Baghdad where his friend Nuri otherwise would face great problems in renewing the bilateral Anglo-Iraqi Pact of 1932. After entertaining doubts about joining the original Northern Tier, Eden had now suddenly become an enthusiast for the variant that had now emerged. The so-called Baghdad Pact of Turkey, Iraq and Great Britain was to be joined later in 1955 by Pakistan and Iran. By July, however, Dulles made it clear that he would go no further than to permit American observers to attend meetings of the Pact. Eden thereupon expressed surprise and dismay at this alleged backsliding. The fact was, however, that he had not sufficiently concerted his Middle East diplomacy with Washington. Dulles had not approved the creation of this particular multilateral regional arrangement involving only one Arab state, which was not incidentally contiguous to the Soviet Union. Iraq, moreover, belonged to the so-called Arab League, no other member of which volunteered to join the Baghdad Pact and two of which, Egypt and Saudi Arabia, had the strongest objections to Nuri and his link with Eden. Dulles felt he had no obligation to form an alliance with only a single Arab state, least of all one under exclusive British influence, in the face of opposition from Arab states that were closer to Washington than to London. To have done so would have been to risk antagonizing much of the Arab world and to have subordinated American interests to those of Great Britain. The fact that Baghdad, rather than Ankara, was to be the headquarters of the alliance only served to reinforce American reservations. True, Dulles was not blameless, for he had been too indecisive during 1954 and had thus allowed London, Ankara and Baghdad to present him with a *fait accompli*. But Eden's conduct was imprudent. For his Middle East policies rested on the assumption that he could afford to behave in a cavalier fashion towards Washington. His earlier success in outfacing the State Department over Iran had obviously gone to his head. But on this occasion he was involved in a far more complicated encounter. The stakes now were not just the fate of one small country on the edge of the Soviet Union, namely Iran, but the future of the whole of the Middle East. Hence even if they had wished to do so, the Americans could not have consistently responded in 1955 and 1956 with the largely passive acquiescence they had shown between 1951 and 1953. Clearly, then, there was merit in Dulles's little-known contention in April 1956 that Anglo-American differences in the Middle East really had their origins in Eden's conduct in 1954 and 1955. Addressing Washington newspaper correspondents in a private background session, he declared that the British 'had "perverted" *his* idea of a pact which would include only nations facing north, when they brought in Iraq, and in doing so had aroused the hostility of the other Arab nations'. Herman Finer wrote: 'The alleged "perversion" was declared by Dulles to be one among several mistakes made by the British in the Middle East and, he added ominously, "I say that charitably!".' Finer hinted that his view of the Baghdad Pact may have represented a later rationalization on Dulles's part and that he only became severely critical of the alleged 'perversion' when the extent of Arab hostility became clear.[26] There is probably a morsel of truth in this. But the case against Eden must be that he forged the Baghdad Pact without sufficient consultation with Washington and without an unambiguous promise of an American intention to join the particular version that he favoured. Hence at the Geneva Conference in 1955 he was faced with Dulles's refusal to participate.

Unwilling publicly to denounce the Baghdad Pact but equally unhappy about having to give it unequivocal praise, Dulles linked his attitude towards it to the question of the Arab–Israeli conflict and meanwhile allowed an American observer to attend Baghdad Pact meetings. He decided to draft a Peace Plan for the Middle East and to proclaim that only after a settlement had been reached would the United States contemplate actually joining the Baghdad Pact. He presumably hoped that Israel and Egypt would see this as giving them right to veto American adherence to the Pact which both countries disliked for different reasons. And of course he may have hoped that if an Arab–Israeli Peace Treaty did result the atmosphere in the region would be so transformed that a regional security pact linking all Arab states to the West would be in prospect. Eden was unimpressed by this somewhat devious American line. Kirkpatrick of the Foreign Office wrote to Macmillan on 20 August 1955:

> There is something in Mr Dulles which particularly irritates the Prime Minister. So you will not be surprised to hear that he is more than annoyed at Mr Dulles's latest antics.
>
> But my impression is that he has blown off steam and will not wish to provoke an open row with the Americans.
>
> The [American] draft statement is really not too bad and I am sure that our best course is to make the best of it.[27]

On 26 August Dulles made a vague public statement calling for fixed boundaries between Israel and the Arabs and regretting the plight of the Palestinians. Privately he canvassed a detailed scheme which contained the suggestion that Israel should offer to the Arabs two small triangles of territory in the southern Negev in return for a peace settlement. The United States would guarantee the resulting borders. The attraction to the Arabs would be that the two triangles would belong respectively to Egypt and Jordan and would be linked by a flyover. Under the flyover an Israeli-controlled road would lead to the Red Sea port of Eilat which Israel would retain. Thus Jordan and Egypt would ingeniously be given a common frontier without the Israelis having to surrender their outpost on the Red Sea. The plan was, however, unenthusiastically received in Cairo. According to his close associate, Mohammed Heikal, Nasser's reaction was scornful:

'The Arabs,' he said, 'will be on the overpass and the Israelis will be on the underpass. Well, all right, suppose an Arab was on the overpass one day and felt the call of nature and it landed on the Israeli car on the underpass ... What would happen? There would be war.'[28]

Nor did Israel take the idea of a peace settlement seriously. On the contrary, the hawkish David Ben-Gurion, having emerged from retirement to replace the moderate Moshe Sharett as Prime Minister, was sharply critical. Perhaps, then, the whole exercise was designed simply to enable Dulles to escape from the Baghdad Pact.

Meanwhile Eden was engaging in delicate negotiations about another area in the Middle East, Cyprus. The island had been transferred from Turkey to Great Britain at the Congress of Berlin in 1878. At that time the population was a balanced mix of Turks and Greeks. But after the First World War mass Greek immigration from Asia Minor caused a gradual shift in numbers to the disadvantage of the Turks. By the 1950s the Turks were outnumbered by four to one. And in this period independence was being given to many British colonies – most of them considerably less developed than Cyprus. Hence there grew up an understandable clamour for British withdrawal. But the matter was complicated by a demand among the Greek Cypriots not for independence but for fusion with Greece – known as *Enosis*. The fashionable view, said to be supported by 'world opinion', was that this constituted self-determination for the island's majority and hence could not be denied. But this was unacceptable no less in Turkey than in Great Britain. Both countries naturally emphasized their concern for the wishes of the Turkish minority, which was unalterably opposed to *Enosis*. But the unwillingness of political leaders in either London or Ankara to give serious consideration to the possibility of partitioning the island suggests that defence considerations were paramount. Turkey could not contemplate allowing the Greek government to have sovereignty over any part of an island so close to Asia Minor. And the British, as has been noted, had chosen Cyprus as their major regional base after the 1954 Agreement with Egypt. In theory Eden could have sought a settlement acceptable both to the Greek leaders in the island and to Athens but involving long-term British rights to bases. And if he had thus ignored the objections of the Turkish minority that would have been nothing unusual in the process of British decolonization – as is illustrated by the fate of many minority tribes in Black Africa. But there were two reasons which rendered it politically impossible for him to disregard Turkish feelings. First, Turkey might well have gone to war with Greece and, being the more populous state, would probably have triumphed – though at great cost to NATO. Secondly, and even more important, Eden saw Turkey as the key to his Middle East policy;[29] as has been seen, his Baghdad Pact coup had been largely engineered by Turkish Premier Adnan Menderes's initiatives. Inevitably, therefore, British policy on Cyprus was biased in the direction of Ankara.

During 1955 terroristic outrages by the pro-*Enosis* group known as EOKA spread throughout Cyprus. Much of 'world opinion' was hostile to London and Eden was only with difficulty able to prevent his country being indicted before the United Nations for resisting the principle of self-determination. He was, moreover, often faced with taunts that the Conservative Party was opposed to any changes in Cyprus not because of the undeniable communal difficulties involved but primarily because of the pressures of its diehard imperialist wing. On 28 July 1954, for example, at the time of the announcement of the withdrawal from the Suez base, Henry Hopkinson, Parliamentary Under-Secretary at the Colonial Office, had sought to appease right-wing rebels in Parliament anxious about the future of the replacement bases in Cyprus. He had hinted that the island would 'never' enjoy the rights of full self-government and self-determination and that 'the question of the abrogation of British sovereignty cannot arise'.[30] With the growth of terrorism and under pressure at the United Nations, Eden was obliged, in the summer of 1955, to retreat from this declaration: he accordingly summoned a conference in London to which he invited both Greece and Turkey. He must have known that the two countries would adopt diametrically opposed positions and that this would enable him to justify the British presence in less self-interested terms than in Hopkinson's blunt statement. The Turks, encouraged by Eden not only to attend but to be 'outspoken' in their opposition to *Enosis*, were naturally happy to oblige. But Greece was placed in a dilemma. While refusal to attend the London Conference would to some extent exculpate the British, their presence would constitute a tacit acknowledgement that Ankara had *locus standi*. The Greek-Cypriot leader, Archbishop Makarios, urged non-attendance on Athens. But after some hesitation, Greece accepted the British invitation.

After the opening ceremonies on 29 August, British tactics were to remain silent about the future and allow Greece and Turkey to state their positions. Only when the full extent of the divergence had been predictably established did Macmillan bring forward some ostensibly liberal proposals. A degree of autonomy would be granted to an Assembly which would have guaranteed representation for the minority community. Defence, foreign policy and internal security would, however, remain in British hands. The proposal for 'constitutional progress' enabled Eden to appear to have moved away from the illiberal statement of Hopkinson. It was not seen as that, however, by the Greek Cypriots. Makarios rejected the plan outright and EOKA organized an increase in terrorist acts. The reaction of the Greek government was more equivocal. While obviously unenthusiastic, they agreed to continue informal discussions with the British about the plan in the aftermath of the London Conference which broke up without agreement on 7 September.

Now that he had established a tenable moral justification for remaining in Cyprus for the present, Eden could risk introducing a policy of severe repression of the EOKA movement. Sir John Harding, the retiring Chief of the Imperial General Staff, was appointed Governor and he rapidly suspended normal civic rights. Soon hundreds of suspected terrorists were being detained without trial. Such developments were inevitably criticized by the Labour Opposition which was much influenced at this time by a neo-pacifist and anti-colonialist set of ethics. Dulles, too, was much tempted to strike a high-minded attitude. But in one of his not infrequent concessions to Eden's wishes, for which the latter unsurprisingly gave him scant credit in his memoirs, he arranged for the American-led bloc in effect to support the British line at the United Nations.

Eden's foreign policy was being conducted against a background of growing domestic problems. The effects of Butler's electioneering budget and Monckton's policy of condoning inflationary wage settlements began to show up in worsening trade figures. This was only a sharpening of a trend that had begun in Churchill's last months. But the importance of the trade figures had been greatly increased in the spring by Butler's ill-timed decision to introduce effective convertibility of the pound. Severe speculative runs against the currency were therefore in prospect. Influential elements close to the Bank of England canvassed the idea of allowing the pound to float. But Eden was subjected to American pressure at the Geneva summit, as a result of which he wrote this note to Eisenhower on 23 July:

It is not our policy to have the kind of floating £ which is now being talked about. Our aim must be the stability of sterling as an international currency, together with reasonable flexibility.

Widely or wildly fluctuating rates for the pound would be bad for world trade and sterling. Such a policy has never been part of our ideas.

We have kept the United States authorities fully informed about our ideas on eventual convertibility which have not changed. The Chancellor of the Exchequer has explained them to the Secretary of the US Treasury. We will continue to keep in close touch with the US authorities on our proposals.[31]

Accordingly Butler, unable to float the pound, introduced a mild credit squeeze and some public expenditure cuts on 25 July. By August he decided that more measures were required. Eden, who had only a modest comprehension of the subject, was deeply disturbed. He appears initially to have imagined that sustained growth could be combined with a convertible, non-floating, currency, inflationary wage settlements and a give-away budget. But having reconciled himself to the inevitability of deflationary action, he rather courageously favoured a formal autumn budget rather than the use of various regulators and government expenditure cuts. The shape of the budget, introduced on 26 October, was also much influenced by the Prime Minister. Most of the stimulus given in the spring was now cancelled. But whereas income tax had been reduced on the earlier occasion, the emphasis now was on increasing indirect taxes. This gave the Opposition a chance to argue that the Conservatives were redistributing wealth away from the working class. In particular, Gaitskell, the Shadow Chancellor, made a telling jibe about a 'pots and pans' budget, for these utensils were subjected to increased purchase tax. For Eden the need for a so-called 'stop' after years of sustained growth was most unwelcome, for inevitably unfavourable comparisons with his predecessor began to be made. No doubt Churchill had been fortunate in the timing of his peacetime premiership; no doubt some of his policies had contributed to the need for Eden's deflation; no doubt any Prime Minister would eventually have had to accept a 'stop' even if Butler's electioneering budget had never been. But the fact was that Churchill avoided the cyclical difficulties that all his successors have had to face. It was Eden's misfortune to be the first. For though his deflationary package was much less severe than many later ones, it made a deeper impression than most. Again, an autumn budget seemed at the time a portentous event, however commonplace it has subsequently become. It was in this respect that Eden was unlucky in the timing of his premiership. He might even have claimed that having to follow Churchill, in the domestic no less than in the international sphere, meant accepting a *damnosa hereditas*.

The autumn budget marked the beginning of a depressing few months for Eden. First, the Foreign Ministers Conference, which met in Geneva from 27 October to 16 November, failed to sustain the spirit of optimism engendered in the previous July at the summit. Next Eden had to endure sustained press hysteria about the two Foreign Office traitors, Donald Maclean and Guy Burgess. They had disappeared on 25 May 1951, when Attlee was still in office, and had been widely presumed to be in the Soviet Union. But only in 1955 was their presence in Moscow confirmed, when a Soviet defector, Vladimir Petrov, published his memoirs. Eden's Government accordingly produced in September 1955 a White Paper containing somewhat anodyne recommendations designed to tighten up security. The press seized upon the sensational features of the case: the way in which the missing diplomats' bizarre and disreputable conduct had been tolerated by a Foreign Office dominated by an 'old-boy network'; the alleged want of ministerial candour about the affair over a considerable period; the possibility of more traitors having escaped exposure, including a 'Third Man', said to have warned the defectors that they were about to be arrested; and the suspicion that Burgess's unconcealed homosexual affairs would not have been tolerated had there not been senior figures in the Foreign Office having the same inclination. Superficially, Labour should have been the more embarrassed of the two major parties, for the two defectors had achieved importance in the immediate post-war years. But by 1955 Bevin, Foreign Secretary until two months before their departure, was dead. So too was McNeil, who as a junior minister had furthered Burgess's career: he had died suddenly at sea on 11 October only weeks after the publication of the White Paper. Morrison alone on the Labour side was left to face the tide of scandal and rumour. This meant that Eden and his Conservative colleagues were in a more exposed position than would otherwise have been the case. For the main criticism shifted from Labour's former ministers to the 'Establishment' and to the Foreign Office as an institution. True, Eden had no responsibility during the immediate post-war years. But he was so much associated with the Foreign Office that any attacks on its integrity were bound to some extent to rub off upon him. Moreover, there was always the possibility – which did not materialize – that journalists might seek to link his name, however unfairly and however tenuously, with one or other of the missing diplomats. The kind of innuendo that could have resulted is suggested in a passage in the diary of Drew Pearson, the American 'muck-raking' journalist, dated 4 July 1951, which recorded that Burgess had been Eden's 'personal chauffeur' on the occasion of his visit to Washington in the spring of 1950.[32]

Eden was in the event spared any personal smears. But he faced a different kind of ordeal at question time in the House of Commons on 25 October. Marcus Lipton, a Labour MP, asked the Prime Minister whether he would 'move to appoint a Select Committee to investigate the circumstances of the disappearance of Burgess and Maclean in particular, and of the efficiency of Civil Service security arrangements in general'. Eden replied: 'No, Sir.' But then came Lipton's damaging supplementary: 'Has the Prime Minister made up his mind to cover up at all costs the dubious third man activities of Mr Harold Philby, who was First Secretary at the Washington Embassy a little while ago; and is he determined to stifle all discussion on the very great matters which were evaded in the wretched White Paper, which is an insult to the intelligence of the country?' Eden, reportedly looking shocked, could only reply with a limp negative.[33] For he had no decisive proof against Philby. Eventually Macmillan said: 'I have no reason to conclude that Mr Philby has at any time betrayed the interests of this country'[34] – an uncovenanted character reference for a man under deep suspicion and who was of course to make the Foreign Secretary look gullible whenever he chose to go 'home' to Moscow, as he eventually did in January 1963 during the last year of Macmillan's premiership.

Inevitably in the autumn of 1955 speculation and gossip were greatly increased by Lipton's ruthless use of Parliamentary privilege. Eden and his colleagues were accused of engaging in a cover-up and any response by them could only be muted. In due time, however, the press hysteria died down. And the matter was brought to a reasonably satisfactory conclusion in a temperate Commons debate on 7 November. Macmillan and Morrison set the tone by largely agreeing with one another and by deploring any suggestions that when officials were merely under suspicion the Rule of Law could be tampered with or that they could be presumed guilty until proved otherwise. Eden's speech was also well received. After proposing the establishment of a wholly private inquiry by a small group of Privy Councillors to examine the new security arrangements based on positive vetting, he concluded with a ringing peroration:

> British justice over the centuries has been based on the principle that a man is to be presumed innocent until he can be proved guilty. Are we going to abandon that principle? Perhaps, worst of all, are we to make an exception for political offences . . . I would never be willing to be Prime Minister of a Government which asked those powers of this House.[35]

It is perhaps surprising that Eden made no reference in his memoirs to this major Parliamentary success or indeed to any other aspect of the Burgess–Maclean Affair.

Another unhelpful development for Eden at this period was the retirement of the aged Attlee as Leader of the Labour Party. His successor, elected on 7 December, was Gaitskell. His relative youth and the publicity attending his selection was bound to benefit the Labour Party at least temporarily and this was shown a week later when a by-election at Torquay saw a fall of 9.4 per cent in the Conservatives' share of the poll. This was an unusually dramatic result by the standards of the immediate post-war era, though modest when compared with what has subsequently been seen.

Perhaps it was in an effort to overcome his followers' low spirits that Eden decided to reshuffle his Cabinet. On 20 December, Macmillan was moved to the Treasury; Butler became Lord Privy Seal and Leader of the House; Lloyd was promoted to the Foreign Office: and Monckton went to Defence. Crookshank and Woolton retired. New faces were Iain Macleod who became Minister of Labour and Edward Heath who was appointed Chief Whip. The changes were given a tepid reception and were judged in many quarters as unimaginative and too long delayed. Eden had wanted to act earlier and had indicated to Butler as early as September what he had in mind. But Macmillan had been reluctant to leave the Foreign Office. Already tension between Eden and Macmillan was growing. For they had had several differences of opinion about foreign policy, including the handling of the Middle East. And now Macmillan agreed to move to the Treasury only in return for a variety of undertakings from Eden, not least concerning the rôle of Butler.[36] Few Prime Ministers would have submitted to such impertinence from a subordinate and there is no reason to suppose that Eden did so without qualms. But Macmillan was a formidable figure with a considerable following among the restive backbenchers and Eden was probably just a little afraid of him. Indeed, it is a moot point whether he would have lasted longer as Prime Minister had he rid himself of Macmillan at the end of 1955 rather than allowing him to have supreme power in domestic policy. Bracken commented to Beaverbrook on 17 January 1956:

As there was every reason for getting rid of Macmillan from the Foreign Office it was inevitable that he should be parked on the Treasury. It is undoubtedly a desperation appointment, but our financial affairs are in a pretty desperate condition. You have more experience of British Government formation than anyone alive and so you need no telling of the difficulty of providing for an ambitious and potentially dangerous leading colleague. The Treasury was the only carrot that would have led Macmillan to go quietly from the Foreign Office.

Beaverbrook replied on 23 January: 'You will remember Macmillan served with me. He will do strange things and he will live to perpetrate a great deal of mischief.'[37]

The turn of the year brought no relief to Eden. For shrill press criticisms of his allegedly erratic and indecisive leadership reached a crescendo. Conservative newspapers like the *Daily Mail* and the *Daily Telegraph* were as scornful as their left-wing counterparts; while Randolph Churchill, son of the former Prime Minister, regularly wrote columns of personal venom in the *Evening Standard*. According to independent witnesses the last straw for Eden came when Donald McLachlan, deputy editor of the *Daily Telegraph*, wrote in a signed article in his newspaper: 'There's a favourite gesture with the Prime Minister. To emphasize a point, he will clench one fist to smash the open palm of the other hand, but the smash is seldom heard.' Butler was present when Eden read this and has testified that it 'drew a pained and pungent oath'.[38] Eden decided to confront the critics. First he issued a formal statement that rumours that he was about to resign were 'false and without any foundation whatever'. Then, speaking at Bradford on 18 January, he referred to cantankerous newspapers and declared: '... we were elected not for six or eight months, but for five years. It is on our record at the end of those years that we are prepared to be judged, and I intend – if God wills – to be there on that day.'[39] Some colleagues thought he had made a mistake in allowing the nation to see that he had been stung by criticism from quarters that should have been beneath his notice. And it does seem even in retrospect that he overreacted. Probably the explanation lay primarily in his life-long sensitivity to press comment. But it may also be that his years of expressing consensus views on foreign affairs had left him with a thin skin and somewhat unprepared for partisan politics at the top.

For Eden it must have come as a relief to turn once more to Anglo-American relations even though that meant grappling with Dulles. Together with Lloyd, he left for Washington on 25 January on the *Queen Elizabeth* for a major series of meetings with the Americans. Without doubt the Middle East was the most important item on the agenda. As has been seen, Dulles's attempts in August 1955 to promote a settlement between the Arabs and Israel had had little success. But in the absence of progress the Americans declined to supply Nasser with the modern arms for which he had long pleaded and with particular intensity since the success of a major Israeli strike against Gaza in the previous February. Egypt accordingly sought an alternative supplier in the Communist world: the Soviets were only too glad to seize the chance to gain influence in a region where they had previously been only marginally involved. True, Czechoslovakia took the formal responsibility but that deceived nobody. The deal was made public on 28 September. Dulles was disconcerted but this did not mean that he would now back the British and the Iraquis in the Middle East. His first instinct was to try to talk Nasser out of his new policy and hence a number of emissaries visited Cairo in the last months of 1955, notably George Allen of the State Department, Kermit Roosevelt of the CIA and, most importantly, Robert Anderson, formerly Secretary of the Navy, whose task was to try once again to promote a peace settlement with Israel.

Eden's reaction to Nasser's Czechoslovak arms deal was also rather muted. He, too, though in a different way from Dulles, adopted an essentially conciliatory policy. First, he tried to win favour in Cairo by making a public declaration about the terms for a Middle East peace settlement. Speaking at the Guildhall on 9 November, he went much further than Dulles in urging Israel to disgorge territory. He favoured a compromise between the armistice frontiers of 1949, which Israel desired, and the UN-recommended borders of 1947, which were more favourable to the Arabs. This plainly implied a larger loss of territory by the Israelis than the triangles in the southern Negev suggested by Dulles. Even Nasser praised Eden's initiative though he did not commit himself to accepting any particular solution. The Israelis, by contrast, were outraged and felt confirmed in their view that Eden was an extreme Arabist. They could not have anticipated that within a year they would be engaged with him in a common military enterprise! Eden also sought to please Nasser by actively canvassing the idea that the British and the Americans, together with the World Bank, should help to fund the construction of the Aswan High Dam which was seen as the key to future Egyptian prosperity. At this stage the Prime Minister evidently saw the Communist arms deal as a reason for increasing efforts to provide Western finance for the Aswan project rather than the reverse. As Nutting wrote: 'The alternative, he felt, was to let Egypt turn to Russia, as she had already done for arms. "And", he told me, "on no

account must we let the Russians into the Nile Valley.".'[40] Aldrich recalled
that on 21 October

Eden ... asked me to come to see him on a matter of greatest importance and
urgency. Eden told me that the emergency had arisen in connection with the
Egyptian proposal, namely that the Russians had offered to finance the dam ... Eden
feared this would give the Soviets a dangerous foothold in an area vital to the
interests of Great Britain. Eden was obviously greatly agitated. I think his physical
condition led to his being even more likely than he had been in the past to exaggerate
the urgency of any problem with which he was faced. He had a tendency to feel in
every case that a crisis had arisen which required immediate action. He asked me to
take up at once with Washington the question of whether the United States would
underwrite the obligations which Great Britain would assume in making such a
guarantee [of financing the dam].[41]

Dulles's initial response was cool, possibly because he was more sceptical
than Eden about the possibility that Moscow could afford to step in. But the
Prime Minister was determined to have his way and was evidently not
particularly scrupulous about putting pressure on Washington. George
Humphrey, then Secretary of the Treasury, recalled:

... Harold Stassen was at that time working on trying to have the British cut down
their sales to the Russians. And as I recall it, the first I heard of it was a kind of threat
from the British – that if we didn't help ... they were not going to abide by the strict
list we had with the Russians ... Well the first time it really came into the open for
me was the first meeting of the Cabinet, after the President came back ... the first
time the President had attended a Cabinet meeting in months ... He [Dulles] had a
cablegram from Eden which was – as it turned out afterwards – part of a series of
conferences and cablegrams ... that I'd never heard of. The cablegram was very
sharp ... demanding, practically – it was a kind of half demand and half threat – that
if we did not join them in building this Aswan Dam, that they would no longer
restrict their trade, and the fat would be in the fire ... It was left that Herb [Hoover.
Under-Secretary at the State Department] and I would meet with our great friends
Roger Makins and Bill Harcourt, and probe into this thing. And this was a proposal
by them as a partnership affair with Britain. I asked about what basis it would be on,
and it was just about what I thought – they'd take ten per cent, and we'd take ninety
per cent ... Dulles started out on the theory that this was something we ought to do
to help our relationship elsewhere ... Foster very gradually and very slowly came to
realize what we were up against.[42]

Yet British policy towards Egypt, still fundamentally conciliatory, was
subject to strange cross-currents. For Eden's desperate efforts to help with
the Aswan Dam were accompanied by actions bound to irritate Nasser.
Some concerned the Sudan, which was approaching complete independence following the withdrawal of British and Egyptian troops.
Difficulties arose on the method of arranging a formal constitutional
transition from the Anglo-Egyptian condominium. Egypt wanted to retain

hope of a union with the Sudan, whereas Great Britain sought to prevent this. Unscrupulous manoeuvring by both sides resulted. But the British, late in 1955, finally outmanoeuvred the Egyptians by encouraging the Sudanese Prime Minister to present them with a *fait accompli* which, in the absence of British or Egyptian troops, could not in practice be resisted. The tactic worked. But Nasser inevitably discovered that the British had engaged in sharp practice and this doubtless had repercussions on other aspects of the Anglo-Egyptian relationship. Humphrey Trevelyan, then Ambassador in Cairo, later recalled:

I had an understanding, whatever its value, with Nasser that we should not 'put each other in a corner' and I did not want to be the first to break it by going behind his back in a way which would quickly become known to him. The Foreign Office's reply opened with the sentence: 'I quite understand your position, but in life one must play the cards as they fall.' In Cairo we thought that was all right provided you were sure you had the highest trump in your hand.

... Nasser knew at once what had happened. He went over to the attack. Having decided correctly that I was trying to cheat him, he would no longer see me on Sudanese affairs ... We and the Egyptians had intrigued against each other and confidence was further eroded. I was naturally concerned with the effect of all this manoeuvring on Anglo-Egyptian relations and felt that we could have arrived at the same result with less damage to them if we had taken things more quietly.[43]

Another example of inconsistencies in British policy concerned the Baghdad Pact. In the spring of 1955, according to Trevelyan, Nasser had been informed that, in return for a cessation of propaganda by the Egyptians, the British would not seek to draw any other Arab state into line with Iraq – something neatly ignored by Lloyd in his later account, in which he merely mentioned the undoubted inaccuracy of Heikal's claim that he had personally given such a pledge when he had not in fact been at the Foreign Office at the relevant time.[44] Yet in December British policy was suddenly reversed. General Sir Gerald Templer, the Chief of the Imperial General Staff, arrived in Amman and sought to persuade the Jordanians to join. This split the Jordanian Cabinet; four pro-Egyptian Ministers resigned; and the pro-British majority felt obliged to resist any rapid agreement. The improbability of any change in Jordanian policy was further strengthened early in 1956 when pro-Egyptian riots were only with difficulty suppressed. Meanwhile Trevelyan had been instructed to tell the Egyptians that Templer's mission 'had not been to press Jordan to join the Pact'. The Ambassador later wrote: 'When I subsequently read General Templer's straightforward account, I could only conclude that what I had been told to tell Nasser about it was not a fair statement of the purpose of the mission.'[45] No diplomat should complain at being asked to lie for his country, for that is his profession. But if a lie is transparent, he is entitled to feel aggrieved – and in this instance Trevelyan evidently was. Moreover, Nasser now felt freed from his earlier commitment not to engage in all-out propaganda against British interests. The Americans, too, were displeased at consequences of the Templer mission. Ann Whitman, Eisenhower's private secretary, wrote in her diary on 16 December: 'President said about the Bagdad [sic] Pact "The British have never had any sense in the middle east." He also said that he was a little "afraid" of the results of the Bagdad Pact.'[46] The principal blame for all this British clumsiness both in Amman and Cairo lay not with Eden but with Macmillan, who initiated the Templer mission. At this stage the Prime Minister was still broadly in favour of seeking a *modus vivendi* with Nasser and hence Macmillan's motives in thus complicating matters invite speculation. Perhaps he was already seeking to lead the forces of the Conservative right, whose suspicious attitude to Eden dated from the Suez settlement of 1954. Whatever the truth of the matter, the Prime Minister was without doubt relieved when he left for Washington in January 1956 to have Lloyd and not Macmillan at his side.

Eden's approach to Nasser at the time of his Washington visit was curiously indecisive, though certainly more benign than Macmillan's would have been. He was, for example, not averse from reactivating the moratorium deal which the Templer mission had destroyed and indeed a month later Lloyd was to discuss this possibility with Nasser in Cairo. The Prime Minister was also apparently still willing to promote the Aswan project, which had been formally offered to Cairo on 16 December. But he now found that Dulles's mood had changed. According to Lloyd, 'We learned, I think for the first time, of doubts about the Aswan Dam project. Dulles told us that [Eugene] Black, of the International Bank, had said that his talks with Nasser were almost at breaking point. Black felt that the dam was too grandiose for Egypt's fragile economy and shaky political base.'[47] We may doubt whether this news was wholly welcome to Eden. Yet in his memoirs he stated that 'Anglo-American policies towards Egypt ... were at this time closely in accord' and he quoted a message he had sent to London from Washington:

We agreed that the future of our policy in the Middle East depended to a considerable extent on Nasser. If he showed himself willing to cooperate with us, we should reciprocate. The Americans thought that the present talks about the Aswan Dam with Mr Black might indicate his frame of mind. If his attitude on this and other matters was that he would not cooperate we would both have to reconsider our policy towards him.[48]

The degree of accord between the United States and Great Britain was, however, less complete than Eden chose here to argue. True, both countries were now doubtful about aiding Nasser. But in London fears of a break with Egypt rested primarily on uncertainty about Nasser's willingness to reduce his attacks on British interests in the Middle East. For the Americans, by contrast, as Lloyd at least realized, considerations of domestic politics and Treasury doubts about Egypt's financial condition were paramount. Eden had thus already begun to deceive himself about the degree to which the Americans might be persuaded to support narrow British interests. The Americans, on the other hand, could probably have done more, even at this stage, to undeceive him.

Obfuscation was also a feature of Eden's discussions with the Americans on two other Middle East issues. First, the problem of Saudi Arabia's claim to Muscat's Buraimi Oasis was the subject of inconclusive exchanges in which the full extent of the strength of American feeling against British support for Muscat was not made clear. Secondly, the Tripartite Declaration of 1950 was considered. This had envisaged the United States, Great Britain and France having the right to intervene to prevent any breaches of the Arab–Israeli armistice. But the Americans were clearly reluctant to make any contingency plans and gave the impression to Eden that the Declaration was practically a dead letter. Yet a formula was found for the official communiqué that did not quite close the door. Later in the year the British naturally claimed to be amazed that Eisenhower saw their Suez intervention as amounting to a unilateral tearing up of the Tripartite Declaration. Both sides, however, had probably been at fault in failing to clarify its real status at the Washington meeting.

A further issue arose at Washington, namely London's attitude to European unity. The background to this was a meeting of the Coal and Steel Community states in Messina, Sicily, during the previous June. Here, rather unexpectedly, a committee was established, under the chairmanship of Spaak of Belgium, to consider an ambitious programme for 'a common market, free from all tariff barriers'. Limited cooperation on communications, on power resources and on atomic energy were seen in London as understandable next steps in the 'European' project but a full-scale supranational common market was regarded as a utopian dream. The establishment of the Spaak Committee was rather seen as a mere sop to Belgian feelings. True, a British civil servant was sent as a representative to the Committee. But Eden and his Cabinet colleagues were understandably sceptical about its importance in the light of the demise of the apparently much less ambitious EDC project and the continuing reservations about supranationalism found in Bonn and, still more, in Paris. But towards the end of 1955 Franco-German relations suddenly improved, following the relaxation of tension over the future of the Saar and with the growing influence of the supranationalists in the new French government of the Socialist Guy Mollet. While still sceptical about the prospects for a full-scale common market, Eden now had at least to take the matter with some seriousness. The result was a British policy statement in December 1955 which dissociated London from an inward-looking, exclusive approach.

Even Macmillan reluctantly favoured this line and subsequently spent much of his time as Chancellor of the Exchequer in canvassing alternative plans for associating the Six in trade with Great Britain, the Scandinavian countries and the Commonwealth. This naturally implied the disappearance of all serious traces of supranationalism. Eisenhower and Dulles, however, were on the side of Spaak, as they made clear to Eden and Lloyd in Washington. For the Prime Minister this was an unwelcome though probably unsurprising development. Clearly the failure of the EDC had not sufficed to persuade the Americans that Great Britain ought after all to play a unique rôle as a bridge between North America and Europe. They continued to hold an unflattering opinion of Great Britain as a world power and as so-called Head of the Commonwealth and saw her long-term future as just one more element in a West European federation. For a man with Eden's relatively inflated view of his country's standing this was no doubt difficult to bear. At this stage, however, neither Eden nor his American hosts could have guessed that the Spaak Committee would within just over a year cause the signing by the Six of the Treaty of Rome.

Eden's visit to Washington concluded with separate addresses to the two Houses of Congress, which were most warmly received. It was probably no mere chance, however, that he made no reference to his country's European future but stressed instead the unique and evolving nature of the British Commonwealth. He next gave a lecture at Harvard University. Finally he journeyed to Ottawa for a two-day visit. He and Lloyd arrived back in London on 9 February.

The Prime Minister returned to a domestic scene even more sombre than before. First, on 14 February, in another disappointing by-election a Conservative majority of 5,542 over Labour at Taunton was reduced to 657. This represented a swing of more than 5 per cent to the Opposition – then considered to be of dramatic proportions. Other by-elections in the same period, at Gainsborough, Hereford and Walthamstow West, were equally discouraging. Even more worrying for Eden was an open quarrel with Macmillan, which had been in gestation even before the visit to North America. The ostensible cause was disagreement about measures to be taken to deal with an economy that had stubbornly failed to respond to Butler's autumn budget. Though apparently tempted by radical strokes such as floating the pound, the new Chancellor opted for an orthodox programme of deflationary measures. And, on 24 January, Eden and other Cabinet colleagues accepted the broad principle of further expenditure cuts and a rise in bank rate. But they doubted the need for any immediate action in advance of the normal budget, due in the spring; and Eden, in particular, objected to the Chancellor's plan for abolishing subsidies on bread and milk. The Prime Minister was no doubt conscious of his earlier pledges not to end food subsidies, and held probably correctly, that other measures would achieve the same economic objectives without a comparable cost to his popularity. On his return from North America, however, he faced a dramatic threat of resignation from Macmillan, who wrote to him on 11 February:

> I don't want to appear to threaten the Cabinet; I have never tried such tactics in all my service. But I would not like you to be under any misapprehension and afterwards perhaps blame me for not letting you know the depth of my feeling. I must tell you frankly that, if I cannot have your confidence and that of my colleagues in handling this problem which you have entrusted to me in the way that seems to me essential, I should not feel justified in proposing measures which seem insufficient for their purpose.

Eden avoided a personal encounter either at the Cabinet or face-to-face but chose to negotiate with his Chancellor through intermediaries. On 14 February Macmillan was told that the 'PM was absolutely determined not to give in on Bread or Milk'. 'In that case,' he retorted, 'he must get another Chancellor.' Faced with this threat Eden weakened, with perhaps fatal consequences for his future. He suggested a compromise and this was finally worked out for approval by the Cabinet on 15 February. In his memoirs Macmillan claimed, not unfairly, that the 'compromise' gave him 'four-fifths of my demands'.[49] Bread subsidy would at once be reduced from $2\frac{1}{2}$d. to $1\frac{1}{2}$d. a loaf with the rest to be abolished later; and the milk subsidy was to go completely in July as Macmillan had wished. The rest of the package, introduced on 17 February, was not at issue between Eden and Macmillan, but of course did nothing to please the electorate. Bank rate rose from $4\frac{1}{2}$ to 5 per cent; hire purchase deposits were increased; and public expenditure was to be cut. But for Eden the most significant point was that he had been defeated by Macmillan. He must have asked himself whether he should behave towards his colleague as Chamberlain had behaved towards him eighteen years earlier. To have done so would have given to his Conservative right-wing critics a formidable backbench leader and one, moreover, whose age – sixty – meant that he might be tempted to gamble all in a *kami kaze* attack designed to bring down the Eden government. Yet Macmillan was arguably to be no less a menace to the Prime Minister's position from within the Cabinet – and his victory over food subsidies gave him a psychological advantage for future encounters. The shrewd and well-informed Bracken grasped what was involved as is clear from what he wrote to Beaverbrook on the day that the Cabinet endorsed Macmillan's economic package:

> Your prophecy that your former Under-Secretary [Macmillan] would make trouble for Eden has been swiftly proved. He sent in his resignation yesterday on a cunningly contrived issue which would have gravely embarrassed his boss and would have given your former Under-Secretary the credit for being the only virtuous

and strong man in the government. A truce has been patched up, but how long it will last is anybody's guess.

Unfortunately he has given this man a job which puts him plumb in the middle of the political stage, and we may be sure he will make the fullest use of his nuisance value.

Beaverbrook replied:

Be sure that Macmillan will make trouble if he has the power. As long as he is kept in order he will be all right. When he gets up he will be all wrong.[50]

For Eden there was now little respite. Another major blow to British prestige in the Middle East came on 1 March. King Hussein of Jordan suddenly informed General John Glubb, the Commander of the Arab Legion, of his dismissal and insisted that he, together with two other leading British officers, must leave on the following day. Glubb Pasha had long been the symbol of British influence in Amman and hence this news was received by Eden with dismay. According to Nutting, who at this time was still close to his chief, the Prime Minister's initial instinct

was to telegraph personally to the King to say that if he persisted in removing Glubb our relations with Jordan would be at an end. This would have meant no more subsidy, no more British arms, the withdrawal of the force which we had moved to Jordan from the Canal Zone, and, of course, the removal of all remaining British officers from the Arab legion.[51]

But Eden was soon talked round into appeasing Hussein. He came to believe instead that Nasser should be blamed for Glubb's humiliation. Indeed, according to Nutting's testimony he now personally declared war on the Egyptian President, saying 'Nasser's got to go, it's either me or Nasser.' This led Nutting, in a possibly high coloured interpretation, to imply that Eden never subsequently wavered in his determination to destroy Nasser.[52] No doubt Eden did initially react as Nutting claims, but it seems probable that in the ensuing months his mood was subject to much fluctuation. After all, Nutting's own account reveals that his chief, always inclined to be hot-tempered, had at first contemplated taking extreme action against Hussein but in this case certainly had second thoughts.

Eden's principal difficulty in handling the coup against Glubb was in fact not how to deal with Nasser but how to avoid a further deterioration in his political standing at home. Having decided that the withdrawal of all remaining officers would be the only sanction to be taken against Jordan, he had to face what was bound to be a sullen Conservative Party in Parliament. He first made a low-key statement on 5 March. 'The House,' he conceded, 'will have heard with resentment and regret of the summary dismissal of General Glubb and two other senior officers of the Arab legion.' He also readily agreed to the Opposition's request for a full-scale debate at a later date. Then, however, he emphasized the more hopeful side of the picture: 'It is right to tell the House that the King of Jordan and the Jordan Prime Minister have told Her Majesty's Ambassador that they do not want any change to take place in Anglo-Jordan relations and that they stand by the Anglo-Jordan Treaty.' Eden's technique was only too reminiscent of that used by him in March 1936, when, it will be recalled, he had made the most of Hitler's friendly undertakings accompanying the remilitarization of the Rhineland. Many Conservative backbenchers deplored the absence of any firm commitment to take punitive action in Jordan. Patrick Maitland, for example, asked: 'Is my right hon. Friend aware of the very widespread anxiety and indignation about the matter and that there is a clamour, to put it no higher than that at the moment, for an emphatic reassertion of British interests in this area?' More ominously, Julian Amery, son-in-law of Macmillan, demanded whether the Prime Minister could 'at least assure us that we are not going to accept these reverses lying down and that something will be done to restore the general position in the Middle East?'. He reinforced this intervention with letters to *The Times*.[53]

On 7 March Eden faced the promised full-scale Commons debate and again his intention was to avoid provoking Jordan. He would therefore have been wiser to open the debate rather than wind up. For, as Nutting had warned him, it proved difficult to say little of substance after so much anxiety had been expressed in the day's speeches. True, he rebuked Nasser:

> To try to disrupt a treaty between Jordan and ourselves is utterly inconsistent with assurances of friendly relations. If the Egyptians generally want friendly relations with the Western Powers, they can be obtained, but not at any price. One way of ensuring that Egypt does not get them is to pursue a policy which, on the one hand, professes friendship and, on the other, incites hostility.

But on the question of Glubb he could only say:

> I must tonight tell the House bluntly that I am not in a position to announce tonight in respect of Jordan, though of other things I have more to say, immediate definite lines of policy which will inevitably be followed – I will tell the House why – because I am sure that to attempt to do so now, with such information as we have, would be not only premature, but probably dangerous to our own interests, more perhaps than to those of Jordan.[54]

A mere reading of *Hansard*, however, fails to convey the extent to which the speech was a disaster. For example, Nutting has written that it was 'a shambles'. He has also claimed: 'He really lost his temper in the House of Commons and made an appallingly bad speech. He allowed Dick Crossman to get under his thermostat, and he really blew it.' The loss of temper is not recorded in *Hansard* and may therefore have been an exaggerated perception on Nutting's part. But the testimony of other contemporaries confirms his verdict on the speech as a whole. Moreover, the newpapers on the following day were critical in the extreme, one journalist writing of the blow to Eden's shattered prestige being 'reflected in the silent devastated ranks ... behind him'.[55] And Drew Middleton of the *New York Times* wrote privately to Aldrich:

> I spent an hour in the House of Commons this morning talking to Tory MPs. My impression is that although they are profoundly gloomy about the state of the world and the state of their leadership, they are not now rebellious. That goes for the Suez group as well as the more moderate members. But I feel that another setback to British policy or to the home economy, coupled with any sign of indecision, will create an entirely new situation. I don't rule out the sort of rebellion that I watched in late April and early May 1940.[56]

Variants on this last appraisal were no doubt borne in upon Eden by his advisers. He may thus have concluded that, with Macmillan hovering menacingly above him, he simply might not survive another major setback. For example, fear of the Conservative 'jingoists' after the Glubb coup probably led him to take immediate and harsh steps in the deteriorating crisis in Cyprus. Following the predictable failure to reach agreement between Greece and Turkey on the island's long-term future at the London Conference of 1955, the British offered a degree of self-government on an interim basis and entered into discussions with Makarios to this end. A series of concessions was offered by London but all fell well short of the Archbishop's demands. Moreover, there was a gradual increase in terroristic activity from which Makarios was not sufficiently dissociated to satisfy the British. By March, hopes of an interim settlement having evaporated, Harding, the Governor, called for action to be taken against the Archbishop. Responsible ministers and officials in London favoured his expulsion from the island, whence he would presumably have gone to Athens. But Eden decided to go further and, apparently against the advice of Alan Lennox-Boyd, the Colonial Secretary, insisted that he be imprisoned on the Seychelles in the Indian Ocean. This drastic step was taken on 9 March, two days after the Prime Minister's feeble speech on the Middle East. The effect in Cyprus was to give Makarios the status of a martyr and hence greatly to facilitate the activities of EOKA: terrorist outrages were now to multiply dramatically. But at home Eden's move was extremely popular in his own party and in much of Fleet Street. He no doubt welcomed the opportunity to deliver a ringing speech on the subject to the Commons on 14 March.[57] With the frenzied cheers of his backbenchers resounding in his ears, he could thus reflect that he had for the moment ridden out the crisis caused by his prudent policy towards Jordan. But he had given decisive encouragement to primitive, nationalistic forces that were to present him with narrowed options later in the year. Nigel Nicolson, a moderate Conservative backbencher, who was acutely conscious of the growing mood of intolerance towards those twisting the lion's tail, recalled:

Eden arrested Makarios ... I was going to address some small meeting in my constituency ... So I announced it to an audience who were mostly unaware of what had happened. There was an instantaneous reaction; they rose to their feet, they cheered themselves hoarse and this was, of course, exactly what Eden had wanted ... I think it was really from this moment onwards that he felt his rôle to be that of the strong man who was going to speak up for England and for the empire, for this is what the Tory Party in the country really wanted.[58]

And Edward Boyle, then Financial Secretary to the Treasury, recalled a colleague having said of the Makarios move that 'Eden had unleashed certain emotions in the party which were dangerous, which could easily recoil on him in a few months' time.'[59]

Eden now had a relatively tranquil spring with the flood of criticism of his leadership temporarily dammed. Even the economic prospects seemed more hopeful. For Macmillan was able to present, on 17 April, a broadly neutral budget with no unpopular measures apart from an increase in tobacco tax. The case for an increase of sixpence on income tax, though carefully considered, was rejected. Most public attention focused on the introduction of Premium Bonds, a means of saving linked to gambling – a daring innovation made in the teeth of nonconformist hostility. With the benefit of hindsight, however, it may be doubted whether enough was done to strengthen the country's external economic position. Certainly after such a budget, the currency and the reserves were likely to remain in a frail condition for the foreseeable future – evidence either of Eden's lack of grasp of the economic base needed for the major foreign adventure which, according to Nutting, he already had in contemplation, or of the absence of any serious expectation that such an adventure would prove necessary.

April 1956 also saw the visit to Great Britain of Bulganin and Khrushchev, originally arranged at the Geneva summit in the previous year. Subsequent developments had not been so favourable as to make the visit uncontroversial. First, the so-called 'Geneva Spirit' had evaporated with the failure of the subsequent meeting of Foreign Ministers. Secondly, the Soviet leaders, during visits to India and Burma, had spoken in unusually vitriolic language about West European colonialism, not least that allegedly still practised by Great Britain. In the circumstances, therefore, some members of the Cabinet did not approve of the visit. Macmillan, in his memoirs, recalled this divergence but did not name the dissenting colleagues. But Beaverbrook's notes on a private luncheon meeting with him, held on 7 April 1957, are helpful: 'PM [Macmillan] spoke disparagingly of Salisbury. He declared that the Lord has resigned twice during Eden's Premiership. He mentioned Russian visit as such an occasion.'[60] Salisbury withdrew both his resignation offers, the other probably coming during the Suez crisis. But the significance of the one relating to the Soviet visit was that he was signalling to Eden and to his colleagues that in the future his conscience, always formidable, could not easily be stilled on account of loyalty arising from a long friendship. The Prime Minister's position was thus one of evident and increasing loneliness as he approached the testing time for the future of his administration.

The Soviet leaders' visit itself was a qualified success for Eden. They conducted themselves with affability and agreed to be seen a good deal in public. They made tours of London and Scotland; took tea with the Queen at Windsor; attended a variety of dinners and receptions; and in a piquant moment were introduced to the retired Churchill. The only discordant note was a public row at a Labour Party dinner where George Brown was outspokenly critical.

In general, the presence of the Soviet leaders in Great Britain for nine days was a remarkable development in itself, since Lenin and Stalin had for so long favoured the seclusion of Moscow. No doubt the visit to Great Britain, following that to Geneva, helped them to modify to some degree the simplistic and distorted picture of the capitalist world presented to them at home. And they in turn succeeded in projecting to the British people an image of the Soviet Union distinctly less forbidding than that in the last years of Stalin. For Eden, however, the main value of the visit was the opportunity for long and detailed discussions on a wide range of subjects. In particular, he came in retrospect to believe that he was able to impress upon his guests that Great Britain regarded her access to Middle East oil as a supreme national interest, for which she would fight if necessary.[61] This may have led the Soviet Union to keep a relatively low profile in at least the early stages of the Suez crisis.

After the Soviet leaders' departure an issue arose out of it that occasioned Eden much anger and embarrassment. This concerned the disappearance of Commander Lionel 'Buster' Crabb, a frogman who had last been seen in the vicinity of two Soviet destroyers located in Portsmouth harbour during the visit. The Soviet Union officially protested, after the return of Bulganin and Khrushchev to Moscow, about his alleged espionage activities. Eden dealt with the matter on 9 May by replying to a Parliamentary Question:

> While it is the practise for Ministers to accept responsibility I think it necessary, in the special circumstances of this case, to make it clear that what was done was done without the authority or the knowledge of Her Majesty's Ministers. Appropriate disciplinary steps are being taken.[62]

The result was a reorganization of the Security Services. In particular, Dick White, a civilian from MI5, replaced the retiring Major-General Sir John Sinclair as Head of the Secret Intelligence Service.

The coming of summer saw still more blows for Eden. First came more unfavourable by-election news: on 7 June at Tonbridge the Conservative majority fell from 10,196 to 1,602. Next, came a somewhat fractious

Commonwealth Conference, meeting in London between 28 June and 6 July, which revealed major differences of approach to international alignments, to nuclear weapons policy and to trade problems. Finally, on 26 July Nasser announced the nationalization of the Suez Canal. The great crisis of Eden's career was at hand.

XI

Suez

Nasser's proclamation of 26 July was in direct retaliation for the American and British cancellation of the Aswan Dam loan project, publicly announced during the previous week. Was Eden therefore a principal author of his own supreme crisis? Or did the main responsibility lie with the Americans? As has been seen, London had originally been more enthusiastic than Washington about the scheme. And as late as the Eisenhower–Eden summit at the beginning of 1956 the British had been marginally more inclined than the Americans to keep alive Egyptian hopes, even though Nasser would be required to mend his ways. The rôles were gradually to be reversed, however, after the dismissal of Glubb. Later in March Lloyd returned from a turbulent and depressing tour of the Middle East in a resolute frame of mind. Fearing that Nasser's next target would be the pro-Western regime in Libya, he had telegraphed to Eden from Tel Aviv: 'Must we go on with the dam?'[1]

Meanwhile, on 12 March, the Prime Minister had had a significant conversation with Mollet. The possibility of aligning their policies against Nasser was raised for the first time. Some in France, obsessed by Egypt's part in sponsoring rebellion in Algeria, already contemplated leading both Great Britain and Israel into a joint military venture against Cairo. True, Eden was at this stage still unwilling to abandon his long-standing anti-Zionist attitudes. Nevertheless the idea that Tel Aviv might in one way or another be used to serve British interests was now probably planted in his mind for the first time. But Eden, Lloyd and the British Cabinet as a whole still believed that Nasser could be tamed without military force providing only that the Americans could be persuaded to play their part. The Cabinet, meeting on 21 March, decided to approach Washington with a plan for isolating Egypt. The British would use Iraq as a means of overthrowing the Nasserite regime in Syria, while the Americans would work on the Saudis. In addition, various steps would be taken against Nasser, including cancellation of the Dam project. During the next three months the Americans moved into line with the British view that the Aswan deal should be cancelled but they did not otherwise do much to meet Eden's wishes. This failure to align British and American policies did not, however, stem from the absence of any shared assumptions about Nasser's character. Dulles told the British that 'he had almost come to the conclusion that Nasser was impossible and an enemy'.[2] And this verdict was certainly reinforced by Egypt's decision, on 16 May, to recognize Communist China. Eisenhower, too, drew sombre conclusions about Nasser as early as March. On the 8th he wrote in his diary:

... we have reached the point where it looks as if Egypt, under Nasser, is going to make no move whatsoever to meet the Israelites [sic] in an effort to settle outstanding differences. Moreover the Arabs, absorbing major consignments of arms from the Soviets, are daily growing more arrogant and disregarding the interests of Western Europe and the United States in the Middle East region. It would begin to appear that our efforts should be directed towards separating the Saudi Arabians from the Egyptians and concentrating, for the moment at least, in making the former see that their best interests lie with us, and not with the Egyptians and with the Russians ...

I am certain of one thing. If Egypt finds herself thus isolated from the rest of the Arab world, and with no ally in sight except Soviet Russia, she would very quickly get sick of that prospect and would join us in the search for a just and decent peace in that region.

On the 13th he wrote:

Late in the afternoon Mr Anderson returned from the Mid East, where he has been serving as my personal representative in an attempt to bring about some rapprochement between Egypt and Israel. This was the second trip he has made into this area.

He made no progress whatsoever in our basic purpose of arranging some kind of meeting between Egyptian officials and the Israelites. Nasser proved to be a complete stumbling block ...

It looks to me as though our best move is to prevent any concerted action on the part of the Arab States. Specifically I think we can hold Libya to our side ... and we have an excellent chance of winning Saudi Arabia to our side if we can get Britain to go along with us. Britain would, of course, have to make certain territorial concessions and this she might object to violently ... It is a very sorry situation.[3]

The President proved correct in doubting whether the British would help in buying off the Saudis. The Foreign Office saw merit in a scheme which would have involved the Saudis capitulating on the Buraimi issue but receiving in return access to the Persian Gulf. Eden vetoed it. He had long resented American influence in Saudi Arabia. On 15 September 1944 he had opposed the partition of Palestine because of the 'grave risk ... of losing to America the pre-eminent place we have always held, and which in our own strategic interests, including oil, we ought to continue to hold, in the Arab world'. 'There is no doubt in my mind,' he continued, 'that the Americans have thoughts of usurping that place, beginning with Saudi Arabia.'[4] No doubt he was also conscious of the rôle the Saudis had played in sponsoring the recent anti-British riots in Jordan and in offering to provide alternative funds for King Hussein if the British subsidy should be cancelled. Again, Macmillan and his followers would have condemned any compromise as further appeasement of Nasser. Nevertheless Eden's refusal to attempt to woo the Saudis was a blunder. For it ran counter to his fundamental aim of aligning himself with the Americans in a common policy against Nasser. Eisenhower's diaries clearly show that he was in a mood to put pressure on Cairo but that he saw Saudi Arabia as the key to success. That the Americans had significant oil interests there was not as decisive as that Saudi Arabia was a conservative state and hence a potential bulwark against Communism. She was also in a position to subsidize her friends on a unique scale. Eisenhower and Dulles judged that the West could not expect to retain influence and defend its interests in the Middle East if it simultaneously alienated both Egypt and Saudi Arabia. Iraq and Jordan were simply too weak and too impoverished to act as adequate satrapies for Western purposes. A further drawback was the total identification of the regimes in Baghdad and Amman with the British colonialist past. Hence, according to Lloyd, Dulles was 'determined to avoid any appearance of "ganging up" with' London.[5] Eden, however, rejected the American analysis. He continued to seek American support but only on his own terms – a vainglorious course for a junior partner with much at risk. The French soon drew an alternative conclusion from the Anglo-American impasse: they set about preparing for a showdown whose character and timing would be largely immune from American influence.

Early in May, at a NATO meeting in Paris, Dulles and Lloyd once again discussed the problem of Nasser. But their only common ground was that agreement on the Aswan Dam project was now 'most unlikely' and that it should accordingly be allowed 'to wither on the vine'.[6] Evidently Eden was now even keener than the Americans to rule out the scheme. Moreover, the American motivation was still in large part domestic in origin, in that Congressional difficulties were seen to be growing and Treasury doubts about Egypt's financial position remained strong. In these circumstances and in the absence of any Anglo-American agreement on other measures to be taken against Nasser, Eden's encouragement of the anti-Aswan policy was shortsighted. For when Nasser discovered what was intended – almost certainly several weeks before he was told officially – the British, not the Americans, would be the obvious targets for retaliation. Another example of Eden's failure to grasp the distance now separating him from the Americans allegedly came late in May. Believing that Nasser's recognition of Communist China was sure to have maddened Dulles, he is said to have suddenly proposed a melodramatic stroke. According to Kermit Roosevelt, he wanted the CIA to organize a coup against Nasser along the lines of the successful operation against Mussadeq three years earlier.[7] But displeased though Dulles was with Nasser, he recognized the difficulties involved in engineering a coup which would guarantee a more amenable successor and which would not simultaneously cost the United States support throughout the Arab world. The Prime Minister's suggestion was accordingly rejected.

Yet Eden was still far from ready to accept French advice to take on Nasser without regard to American views. He may thus have been only intermittently convinced of the inevitability of a final personal showdown with Nasser. This indecision was perhaps most strikingly illustrated when he allowed the withdrawal of the last British troops from Egypt to go ahead. Most departed late in March but a final 'tail' of officers remained until 13 June. The possibility of reneging on the Agreements of 1954 was entertained but eventually rejected. Lloyd's explanation is of interest: 'It would have exposed us to a charge of breach of faith. It would have been difficult to convince Middle Eastern countries that it had been justified by the provocation which we had received.'[8] This was of course exactly the kind of reasoning that underlay American policy towards Nasser throughout 1956. And it served as a greater constraint even on Eden, both before and after the nationalization of the Canal, than is often recognized.

The public cancellation of the Aswan scheme had the appearance of being an American action which the British subsequently supported. But did this involve the Americans, as Eden clearly believed, in any moral obligation to protect the British from all possible Egyptian reactions? As has been seen, the British had agreed with the Americans in May that the project was virtually dead but had urged it should be allowed 'to wither on the vine'. It has therefore on occasion been claimed that clumsiness on Dulles's part led to the cancellation taking a precipitate form – thereby increasing the American obligation to protect Great Britain from the consequences. The flaw here, however, is that Nasser had earlier learnt of the May decision, probably as a result of a leak through British-influenced Baghdad, and it was he, not Dulles, who was determined to bring matters to a head. He suddenly dropped all conditions which had been under discussion for months and required of the Americans an immediate decision. The policy of allowing the project 'to wither on the vine' was thus no longer feasible: Dulles was not to blame for this and hence rightly felt no special responsibility on that account to help Eden when Nasser retaliated.

Given the inevitability of the cancellation of the Aswan project, could Eden have averted Nasser's response? Perhaps he should have caused Lloyd to take a different line in his meeting in May with Dulles. British agreement to the cancellation could have been made conditional on a full alignment of American Middle Eastern policy with that of Eden. If this had been rejected by Washington, the British in July could have diverged from the American position, could have offered public sympathy to Nasser and could have undertaken to try at some future date to secure an American change of mind. Certainly this line would have made it difficult for Nasser to act immediately against the Canal. But this was not in practice a serious option for Eden. Domestic political constraints would have ruled it out even if his own attitude to Nasser had been more indulgent than it was. In any case the Prime Minister did not apparently even consider in advance any scenario involving the Canal.

On the evening of 26 July Eden held a dinner at Number Ten in honour of Iraqi visitors, including Nuri. Towards the end of the meal news was received of Nasser's speech in Alexandria proclaiming his coup. After most guests had departed the Prime Minister held immediate conversations with several members of his Cabinet, three of the four Chiefs of Staff, Templer, Lord Mountbatten, Sir Dermot Boyle, the French Ambassador, Jean Chavel, and the American Chargé d'Affaires, Andrew Foster, whose chief, Aldrich, happened to be on leave. Thus from the outset Eden sought to concert his policy not only with France but also with the United States. According to Lloyd, 'the Chiefs of Staff were asked for a speedy assessment of what military action was open to us'.[9] Foster was apparently present and his report to Washington may thus have been the first of several indications leading Eisenhower to conclude that Eden contemplated an immediate recourse to force. According to Christian Pineau, the French Foreign Minister, that is indeed what the Prime Minister would have preferred.[10] But at the Cabinet meeting, held on the following day, the Chiefs of Staff, now led by their Chairman, Sir William Dickson, insisted that any assault on Egypt would take weeks to prepare and would have to be an amphibious operation launched from distant Malta – strong evidence, incidentally, that Eden had not taken his rhetoric against Nasser in the previous March as seriously as Nutting had done. The Prime Minister accordingly made a virtue of necessity by offering to Eisenhower to align their policies with a view to putting diplomatic pressure on Nasser to back down. The Americans were invited to send a representative to London to meet with the British and with Pineau. But Eden added that 'my colleagues and I are convinced that we must be ready in the last resort, to use force to bring Nasser to his senses'. Lloyd later claimed that this reference to 'the last resort' constituted proof of a sincere desire for a peaceful outcome.[11] But it is also possible that, faced with a delay of several weeks, Eden merely wanted to give a superficial appearance of reasonableness in the hope of obtaining as favourable a climate of international opinion as possible for an attack on Egypt which he was unalterably intent on launching either because he was satisfied that she would never agree to retreat or even because he did not in any case wish to lose the chance of driving Nasser from power. The probability is, however, that for much of a fast-moving crisis he did not invariably have a fully thought-through position and accordingly pursued a somewhat erratic course. On 27 July, for example, he had a revealing off-the-record conversation with McDonald of *The Times*. He stressed the military aspect:

> 'The question was how soon we could move,' he [Eden] said. 'The military men had at first said it would take about a fortnight to perfect plans, but he had told them that was nonsense, and he must have them ready by Monday (this was Friday). They were sure, however, that forces could be moved quite quickly . . .'
> He agreed that we might have to depose Nasser, but said that the intended operation was not to occupy the base (he fully agreed it would be difficult to hold the base), but merely to secure the banks of the Canal. 'It might be done with a division and a half.'

The sense of urgency revealed here suggests that Lloyd's retrospective emphasis on the 'last resort' concerning the use of force was misleading. Yet Eden also told McDonald that he was open-minded about going to the United Nations; that he wanted to go forward with the French, the United States and the Dominions; and even that 'there was a real chance, if Nasser would take it, of getting an up-to-date agreement'.[12]

The same day, 27 July, saw several other developments. After Eden had made a brief statement to the Commons deploring Nasser's arbitrary action but otherwise reserving his position, Gaitskell spoke in vigorous terms about 'this high-handed and totally unjustifiable step'.[13] This may have raised the Prime Minister's hopes of bipartisan support for a robust response. On the same day he persuaded the Cabinet to establish an 'Egypt Committee' which was to manage the crisis on a day-to-day basis. Eden would serve as Chairman and its members were to be Lloyd, Macmillan, Salisbury, Home and Monckton. Butler was thus excluded – a move that significantly reduced the chances of the Prime Minister being subjected from the outset to weighty counsels of caution. The Cabinet also decided at its first full session after Nasser's coup to take a number of immediate counter-measures: Egyptian sterling balances held in London were frozen; British subjects in Egypt were to be advised to leave unless their presence was vital; and the export of arms to Egypt was banned. It was also determined that Great Britain would not base its approach to the crisis on the narrow international legal issue. Whether the Egyptians had been strictly entitled to repudiate obligations entered into in 1888 and recently reaffirmed was a matter for doubt. But in any case there could be no question of seeking a judgement from the International Court of Justice. For Egypt had not signed the Optional Clause and hence the Court could only have proclaimed that it had no jurisdiction. Nor, given the Soviet veto in the Security Council, did the Cabinet place reliance on the United Nations for the redress of their grievance; any future reference to the Security Council would in all probability be for the sake of appearances and even this was not to be contemplated until attempts had been made to win the support of the United States and the Dominions.

When the Suez crisis began Dulles was in Peru and declined to offend his hosts by returning to Washington immediately. Eisenhower accordingly instructed Robert Murphy, Deputy Under-Secretary in the State Department, to deputize in conferring with the British and the French in London. His brief was to 'see what it's all about' and 'to hold the fort'. He arrived on 29 July and immediately dined with Lloyd and Pineau. On the following day he lunched with Eden and dined with Macmillan. At all these encounters he heard robust declarations. But Macmillan made the deepest impression. For he indicated that military action was inevitable and might start in August. He added that 'Britain would not become another Netherlands.' Lloyd subsequently wrote of this 'intemperate talk' leading to a 'misunderstanding' of British policy.[14] Eisenhower was falsely led to conclude that Eden's reference to the use of force as 'a last resort' was meaningless and that Dulles must at once go to London if peace was to be preserved. Macmillan, on the other hand, later claimed that he had Eden's 'full acquiescence' to 'make full use' of the opportunity his dinner with Murphy presented. On 31 July the Chancellor wrote in his diary: 'It seems that we have succeeded in thoroughly alarming Murphy. He must have reported in the sense which we wanted, and Foster Dulles is now coming over post-haste. This is a very good development.'[15] It is possible, therefore, that Eden was at this stage using Macmillan to heighten the sense of crisis without fully confiding in his other Cabinet colleagues or even in his Foreign Secretary. But there is as yet no conclusive evidence to support Nutting's claim that at this time Eden sent Eisenhower a further 'very secret message saying that he had decided that the only way to break Nasser would be to resort to force without delay and without attempting to negotiate'.[16] Eisenhower, it is true, referred in his memoirs to having received secret messages through Murphy from both Eden and Macmillan.[17] Murphy, on the other hand, recalled in his memoirs only one message, namely Macmillan's. But even without a secret message from Eden, Eisenhower had heard enough from London to have reasonable grounds for fearing precipitate action. And the same reaction was found among the Dominions. On 1 August Hoover of the State Department informed Eisenhower that he had

told Prime Minister Menzies [then in Washington] last evening that we were very conscious about people talking of military action. Mr Menzies was also quite concerned. At lunch today he told Mr Hoover that he wired his Cabinet asking if they would agree to wire London. He agreed the threat of force was the worst possible thing right now. He said Mr Pearson is wiring London; he said that he felt sure that Nehru also would write.[18]

Menzies, subsequently a declaratory ally of Eden, need not have worried about Nehru. On 1 August the Indian Prime Minister said publicly in Bombay that Nasser's action was 'a sign of the weakening of European domination of Asia and the Middle East which has lasted more than a hundred years'.[19] Moreover, his attitude, and still more that of Menon, was subsequently to be unwaveringly sympathetic to Egypt throughout the crisis. Canada, too, was on Menzies's side in opposing early recourse to threats of force. Norman Robertson, her High Commissioner in London, had urged caution on the British in two meetings on 27 July and his conduct was warmly endorsed by Pearson. The Canadian Foreign Minister, together with Prime Minister Louis St Laurent, also expressed alarm at the contents of a message from Eden received on the same day. Pearson telegraphed to Robertson:

> I am deeply concerned at the implications of some parts of Eden's message; especially as I doubt very much whether he will receive strong support from Washington in the firm line which he proposes to follow. A talk which I have just had with the United States Ambassador here strengthens these doubts. Surely the UK Government will not do anything which would commit them to strong action against Egypt until they know that the US will back them.[20]

On the evening of 31 July Dulles arrived in London. He had been led to believe that military action was imminent and did not grasp at this stage that the British Chiefs of Staff had insisted on a lengthy delay in order that adequate preparations could be made. He thus felt obliged to offer Eden an exaggerated degree of declaratory sympathy and support in a desperate bid to secure at least a postponement of any military adventure. He was, moreover, no friend of Nasser and, in an ideal world, would not have been sorry to see him toppled. But he did not accept the desirability of a crude Anglo-French assault on Egypt in the prevailing circumstances. Nor was his reason merely that Eisenhower, facing the Presidential Election in November, wanted a period of calm in international affairs. To Dulles the nationalization of the Suez Canal seemed too insufficient a provocation and too unclear an issue in international legal terms to evoke the consensus of indignation in the non-Communist world which he judged a necessary precondition for Anglo-French military action and certainly for any American support of it. This did not mean that he ruled out force at some future date. He thought it possible, for example, that Nasser would take some additional action that would have the effect of giving Eden and Mollet a better case for taking military steps against him; he might arbitrarily close the Canal to vessels destined for Western Europe, or he might order Western European citizens to operate the Canal against their wishes. He also hoped that the bulk of maritime nations, if brought together, might collectively express such indignation and demand such assurances from Egypt that she might feel compelled to retreat. Nasser would thus lose face while the British and the French would gain a diplomatic victory. What Dulles could not see with clarity was any immediately practical course for the West which would absolutely ensure the replacement of Nasser by a more amenable successor. And that too was no less true of Eden and Mollet, though they were reluctant to admit it. But, unlike Dulles, they eventually proved willing to risk their reputations for the sake of a mere *possibility* that military action on their part would cause an indigenous Egyptian movement to overthrow Nasser. Eden certainly at no time planned to conquer all Egypt, set up a puppet ruler and remain in indefinite occupation of the whole country. It was precisely because Great Britain could not afford to continue to provide the manpower to defend even the Suez base against guerrillas that Eden had been led to adopt his appeasing policy in 1954. Two years later there was no question of taking on the much larger commitment involved in running the whole of Egypt. Hence the removal of Nasser was for Eden never more than an aspiration and the steps he eventually took to this end were probably only the desperate throes of a politician facing intolerable domestic pressures. In August, however, these pressures were less severe and immediate. He was thus able to go some way to meet Dulles. He in effect repudiated Macmillan's robust words to Murphy. Instead he would be satisfied with a diplomatic solution if one could be obtained, rather than insist upon a military assault and the toppling of Nasser.

Eden and Dulles, with half-hearted French concurrence, accordingly decided to summon an *ad hoc* conference of twenty-four maritime nations and this was duly announced on 2 August. Their object was to secure substantial support for a call for the Canal to be placed under international control. That Eden agreed to this so readily is evidence that at this stage he was aware of the risk of antagonizing world opinion. For the emphasis on internationalization was clearly a blow to the vested interests in both London and Paris which desired to see the Suez Canal Company's rights safeguarded. For example, Hankey, now a Director of the Company, argued that this refusal to demand the restoration of the *status quo ante* constituted a major blunder on Eden's part. Bowie of the State Department also noticed this pragmatic willingness to treat in cavalier fashion the only nominal victims of Nasser's coup. He later wrote:

While it might seem logically to follow that the Suez Canal should be restored to the Company, the remedy claimed was for its transfer to international control. The reasons were practical: first, a demand to reinstate the private Company would have alienated many newer nations, much more than would the creation of an international agency; for they would not have accepted any restriction on the general right to nationalize. Second, since the concession of the Company had only twelve years left to run, the same issues of Egyptian control would arise again when the legal case against it would be much weaker.[21]

Eden also yielded to Dulles in agreeing to defer any decision to ask the Suez Canal Company to urge its employees to leave Egypt.

Why did Eden go so far to fall in with Dulles's wishes? In his memoirs he stressed that Dulles had stated to Lloyd and Pineau that 'a way had to be found to make Nasser disgorge what he was attempting to swallow' and that these forthright words 'rang in my ears for months'. The Prime Minister also attached importance to Dulles's friendly reaction to his offer to inform him of British military preparations: 'It was preferable that the United States Government should not seek detailed information.' Towards the end of his life Eden, in an interview with a biographer of Dulles, went further:

He told Foster that he did not feel that a peaceful solution of the Suez crisis was possible, and that the only language Nasser understood was force. The British and French had already begun preparations to take back what belonged to them. The CIA station chief in London was trying to find out what those preparations were. Should Eden tell him – or should he tell Foster? Foster replied that he did not want to know. But, went on Eden, did Foster agree that what they were doing was right? Foster said he fully understood the Anglo-French point of view. The prime minister then said that neither the British nor the French governments would ask for military help of the United States when they 'took steps to restore the situation in Egypt' but would they be able to count on the moral support of the Americans? Foster replied that the British government could *always* count on the moral support *and* sympathy of the United States, and Anthony ... need have absolutely no qualms about that. Eden then said he thought the situation would come to a head some time in October – but was here interrupted by Foster, who told him firmly that he did not want to know anything about the Anglo-French plans. It would be better that way.

'So, of course,' Eden said later, 'one took good care not to inform him, officially or otherwise, when the time came.'

He added: 'Perhaps that was a mistake. It might have been better if one had sent a message, a personal message to Ike first before the balloon went up. I take the blame for that. I should have relied on the good sense and support of my old friend Ike. But I thought that he had been kept in touch with his Secretary of State. Foster misled me.'[22]

But was Eden really so misled either at the beginning of August or subsequently? His Foreign Secretary, for example, recalled the context in which Dulles spoke of possible use of force and about Nasser having to disgorge. Dulles stressed that Eisenhower wanted the British not to go 'through the motions of an international conference' but to make 'a genuine and sincere effort to settle the problem and avoid the use of force':

... force unless it was backed by world opinion would have disastrous results. Therefore, all efforts should be made to create a worldwide opinion so adverse to Nasser that he would be isolated. A genuine effort should be made to bring world opinion to favour the international operation of the Canal before force was used.[23]

Yet the use of force, when eventually resorted to, clearly did not have the backing of world opinion or even of a majority of the twenty-four states invited to the maritime nations' conference. True, Dulles at no time attempted to canvass support for such an approach. But even had he done so, he would probably have failed. Thus Eden's claim to have been misled early in August is unconvincing. Significantly, Pineau, who was also in London on the occasion of Dulles's crucial visit, made no comparable claim. On the contrary, the French consistently sought to persuade Eden that Dulles would do nothing to facilitate a military adventure.

Even less convincing is Eden's claim that Dulles's words about Nasser having to disgorge rang in his ears for months and that he took seriously Dulles's alleged wish not to be informed 'when the balloon went up'. As will be seen, Aldrich actually pressed for information about British military intentions on the eve of the Anglo-French invasion of Egypt and was intentionally misled. And if Dulles was somewhat opaque early in August, both he and Eisenhower subsequently made unmistakably clear their opposition to the use of force in the actual conditions prevailing during the ensuing months even if they never ruled out that circumstances might change. Bowie later recalled:

He [Dulles] did not really want to say explicitly that the use of force was out. He wanted to keep this as a possible threat to Nasser – as a sort of a danger which Nasser couldn't rule out – that he had to take account of – hoping that this might bring him to make a deal on terms which would be mutually satisfactory. But Eden kept using this as a device for trying to force Dulles to say that force would be used ...

... it was a sort of cat and mouse game, in which Dulles was constantly trying to manoeuvre the situation so that force wouldn't have to be used and that still a satisfactory solution could have been gotten. Eden was trying to manoeuvre the situation in such a way that the use of force would be legitimate, justified.[24]

Eden would thus have been wiser to allow some words of Neville Chamberlain, rather than those of Dulles, to ring in his ears: 'It is always best and safest to count on nothing from the Americans ...'[25]

While some will continue to argue that Dulles did, to some degree, mislead Eden at the beginning of August, it is no less plausible to argue that the Secretary of State also misled himself. For he believed that the chances of force being used had receded. On 1 August Hoover informed Eisenhower that he had had a message from Dulles that matters were 'not going badly' and that he seemed 'to be having luck on top, but may have troubles at the bottom level'. This may have reflected the relatively conciliatory tone adopted by Eden as compared with Macmillan, with whom he had spent an hour. The Chancellor wrote in his diary of this meeting:

I told Foster as plainly as I could that we just could not afford to lose this game. It was a question not of honour only but survival ... There was no other choice for us. I think he was quite alarmed; for he had hoped to find me less extreme, I think.[26]

That Dulles and Eden were on affable terms at this juncture is also evident from the testimony of William Macomber of the State Department. He drove away together with the Secretary of State on 2 August immediately after leaving the Prime Minister and was told by his chief, 'Antny – He [Dulles] always called Anthony Eden 'Antny' – said a strange thing to me just a few minutes ago ... Antny said I'm going to go down in history as one of the great foreign ministers.' Macomber noted that Dulles was 'sort of bemused by it': 'My gosh, it's strange that he said that.'[27] On 3 August, the day following his departure from London, Eden also spoke warmly of him to McDonald, who recalled:

'At first,' he [Eden] told me, 'the Americans had been slow in coming along. The Mediterranean was not such a direct interest of theirs, they tended to think that the Suez Canal was small compared to Panama, and of course they were busy with their elections (due November 6). He had frankly expected Dulles to be rather negative, but Dulles began and continued very well. The talks became better after he arrived. Undoubtedly the Americans' fear that we and the French might fly off the handle straightaway helped to bring Dulles nearer and faster to our point of view. At any rate, Dulles freely committed himself to the stand that the Canal should not be left in the sold control of Egypt and should be brought under an international authority.'

What if the conference failed? 'Nothing had been decided,' he said, 'except that each of the three powers (Britain, France, America) would then have full liberty of action to do whatever seemed necessary' ... there was not even a pledge of American moral support for Anglo-French action, but Eden obviously was now relying more than before on such moral support as a result of the three-power talks.[28]

This last sentence, incidentally, appears to contradict Eden's later alleged claim, mentioned earlier, that Dulles *did* pledge that Great Britain would 'always' have American moral support and sympathy even if force should be used.

While awaiting the maritime nations' conference, which at Dulles's insistence did not begin until as late as 16 August, Eden occupied himself by drawing up contingency plans for possible military action. On 2 August the Cabinet approved the recall of 20,000 reservists ostensibly in case the need arose 'to preserve British lives'.[29] At the same time it was agreed that if no peaceful solution could be found, force would ultimately be used. No member of the Cabinet protested. Hence it has been claimed that Eden was later able to quell dissent by referring back to this decision. Yet a good deal of question-begging was involved. For example, what kind of peaceful solution would be acceptable? And when and by whom would it be determined that this could not be secured? Perhaps, then, some later Cabinets were at least as decisive as that of 2 August. Nor did Eden on that day commit himself as irrevocably in Parliament as some commentators have supposed. True, he focused his criticism on Nasser as an individual. But he spoke in a relatively conciliatory tone. Indeed, in some respects Gaitskell adopted a more robust attitude. For example, the Leader of the Opposition said of Nasser's approach: 'It is all very familiar. It is exactly the same that we encountered from Mussolini and Hitler in those years before the war.' The tone of his intervention was indeed so firm that the Shadow Cabinet urged him to avoid a repetition. Instead he was asked to emphasize in future a little-noted reservation with respect to the use of force which had crept into his otherwise vigorous speech. This he did during the rest of the crisis. On the same day, 2 August, however, Gaitskell also had a private meeting with Eden at which no sharp differences appear to have emerged. Yet on the following day Gaitskell wrote to the Prime Minister in terms which a member of the Private Secretariat in Number Ten characterized as 'unsaying everything he said on Thursday'. But perhaps the two leaders had seemed to be close together on 2 August not only because Gaitskell was in a more militant mood than later but also because Eden was even at that stage by no means certain that he would be able to use force against Nasser without some further provocation. Gaitskell wrote in his diary later in August:

> I pressed him [Eden, in the private meeting on 2 August] once more on the use of force. There was not disagreement on the military precautions but I said, 'What is your attitude to be if Nasser refuses to accept the conclusions of the further conference?' As I recollect and so implied in what I subsequently wrote to him, he said, 'I only want to keep open the possibility of force in case Nasser does something else.' I must add, in fairness, that he claimed later that he had said that he only wanted to keep open the possibility of force *or* if Nasser did something else. But at any rate I certainly thought he said the first.

Thus Gaitskell's conduct was probably technically consistent throughout. Yet his initial rhetoric certainly served to reinforce public hostility to Nasser. The tone of his later criticisms of the British Government was accordingly all the harder for Eden to bear and may go far to explain the complete breakdown in relations between the two men in October and November. The *Economist* commented on 18 August with much justice:

> The Labour leadership has extricated itself with some delicacy from the charge of being allied with the Government's more belligerent supporters. Mr Gaitskell ... must now wish that he had laid more emphasis on the dangers of bellicosity in his speech on August 2nd, even though it included prudent qualifications in its support of the Government ... Mr [William] Warbey and some others appear to be virtually on Nasser's side and this group would be larger but for the fact that at least half the Labour MPs who would normally be instinctive members for Cairo are already instinctive members for Israel instead.
>
> The Labour leadership ... has avoided the dangerous precedent of being forced into these embraces. Its tactics have been simple. The shadow cabinet ... unanimously ... 'endorsed the speech of the leader ... on August 2nd' but with

'particular' emphasis on the points on which insufficient emphasis was in fact then laid.

... most Labour members will now follow the official line which proclaims – with a slight stretch of the imagination – that what he [Gaitskell] is saying now is what he has been saying all the time.[30]

On 5 August Eden sent to Eisenhower a revealing message which neither man saw fit to publish in his memoirs:

I do not think that we disagree about our primary objective ... to undo what Nasser has done and to set up an International Regime for the Canal ... But this is not all. Nasser has embarked on a course which is unpleasantly familiar ...

I have never thought Nasser a Hitler ... But the parallel with Mussolini is close. Neither of us can forget the lives and treasure he cost us before he was finally dealt with.

The removal of Nasser, and the installation in Egypt of a regime less hostile to the West, must therefore also rank high among our objectives. We must hope, as you say in your message, that the forthcoming conference will bring such pressures upon Nasser that the efficient operation of the Canal can be assured for the future. If so, everyone will be relieved and there will be no need of force. Moreover, if Nasser is compelled to disgorge his spoils, it is improbable that he will be able to maintain his internal position. We should thus have achieved our secondary objective ...

Our people here are neither excited nor eager to use force. They are, however, grimly determined that Nasser shall not get away with it this time, because they are convinced that if he does their existence will be at his mercy. So am I.[31]

The fall of Nasser was thus ostensibly Eden's secondary objective. He conceded, moreover, that such a result would be only probable rather than certain if international pressure led to a peaceful solution, which he nevertheless professed to prefer. The French were more unequivocal: they wished to mount a straightforward assault through Alexandria and Cairo with the clear aim of removing Nasser. Eden did not agree to this at a political level. But in the joint Anglo-French military planning the possibility of giving practical priority to toppling Nasser arose in an indirect form. For while the British were able to insist that the primary objective of any military expedition would be to secure the Canal, the French argued that the best way to achieve this would be to land at Alexandria and approach the Canal via the environs of Cairo – with probably fatal results for Nasser. Geography favoured the French case. Port Said was much further than Alexandria from Malta and Cyprus. Plainly speed was important – so much so that Eden had only reluctantly agreed to the insistence of the Chiefs of Staff that a simple airborne operation was too risky. But faced with a choice between landings at Alexandria and Port Said, Eden was hesitant. The French Task Force Commander, General André Beaufre, recalled that on 10 August he journeyed to London to be told by General Hugh Stockwell, later Supreme Commander in the Suez Campaign, that the

British military authorities had prepared a plan involving a landing at Alexandria but that this had been rejected on Eden's orders:

In his [Eden's] view the Canal was the political objective; a landing at Alexandria would be too indirect an approach and difficult to justify politically. On his side Stockwell considered that the Alexandria operation would allow us to debouch rapidly and in force and to reach Cairo well before any sizeable forces could be landed through Port Said. Moreover, Port Said is an island connected to the mainland merely by the Canal embankments; the break-out from a bridgehead there was therefore attended by considerable risk and, if the embankments were blown, we should be bottled up in Port Said for a prolonged period.[32]

Four days later, however, Beaufre was informed that Eden had finally been won over to the use of Alexandria.[32] This plan was known as 'Musketeer'. According to Stockwell, the operation was first fixed to commence on 15 September but later was advanced to the 8th.[33] All this, however, was contingency planning and does not prove that Eden was unalterably set on the use of force. Certainly, to the great dismay of most of the military planners, he did not adhere to the timetable he had fixed. As will be seen, the Alexandria expedition was repeatedly postponed and eventually abandoned.

Meanwhile the Lancaster House Conference of maritime nations had been held between 16 and 23 August. Twenty-two states participated. Eden, after attending the opening ceremony, left Lloyd in charge of the British case. From the outset Dulles played the leading rôle. He surprised Eden by the vigour with which he proposed a resolution that won the support of all except India, Indonesia, Ceylon and the Soviet Union. In essence he called for the Canal to be run by an international board whose duty would be to prevent its being used for political purposes against any user. A five-man committee was appointed to meet with Nasser with a view to obtaining his concurrence. Menzies, who had meanwhile pleased Eden by making a vigorous broadcast to the British people, was asked to head the mission.

Arriving in Cairo on 3 September, the team found Nasser evasive. He was not averse from discussing some aspects of the future of the Canal but not solely with the eighteen states which had supported the Menzies mission. He wanted to deal with a wider grouping which would include more anti-Western voices. He was also insistent on the unequivocal maintenance of Egyptian sovereignty. His hand was strengthened somewhat on 4 September when Eisenhower at a press conference stated that 'we are committed to a peaceful settlement of this dispute, nothing else'. But Nasser would probably not have acted differently even if the President had remained silent. Trevelyan, for example, believed that Menzies's mission was doomed from the outset. Menzies, on the other hand, blamed Eisenhower for undermining his chances of success and claimed in his memoirs that he rebuked the President while passing through Washington on his way home.[34] But, as has been seen, Menzies had originally reacted to Nasser's coup by agreeing with the Americans that 'the threat of force was the worst possible thing right now' and by undertaking to mobilize Commonwealth pressure on London in the contrary direction. The Americans continued to eschew threats of force, whereas Menzies, possibly because of Eden's personal appeals, had now adopted the declaratory position that Nasser must be got to disgorge by a policy of at least keeping him guessing about the possible use of force. To the Americans Menzies may now have seemed inconsistent. Certainly he made little impression on Eisenhower's resolve to discourage the use of force unless Nasser should go further and unless world opinion should alter. Yet Menzies may have been of some significance at the outset of the crisis in confirming the President in his inclination to adopt such an approach. Thus Eden's supposedly staunchest Commonwealth ally in the Suez crisis may on balance have done his cause more harm than good.

Eden was far from hopeful about the prospects of Menzies's mission and hence well before a final confession of failure was made he had given careful thought to his next moves. The French leaders and at least some members of his own Cabinet wanted the end of Menzies's mission to be followed by an immediate appeal to the Security Council. Eden anticipated that the Soviets would certainly veto any resolution supporting the eighteen-nation proposals. Yet if he could secure a large majority he might claim that he had the moral authority to take military action to require Egyptian compliance even in the face of a Soviet veto. But how much non-Communist support would he actually be able to count on? Here the United States was critical. Towards the end of August the French opposed a sincere reference to the Security Council unless the Americans agreed not only to support the eighteen-nation line but also privately promised to give subsequent diplomatic backing for the coercion of Egypt. Dulles would give no such pledge and further argued that reference to New York would be premature. Always more sensitive than his French colleagues to American and even general world opinion, Eden now wavered. He could fall in with the French suggestion that there should be immediate recourse to force without regard to the views of Americans or others – a policy that might possibly have been preceded by a merely token reference to the Security Council. Or he could conform to American wishes, namely to delay reference to the Security Council and wait for some favourable development to turn up. He chose the second course but perhaps only because he had not entirely abandoned hope that his luck would change. First, he knew that the Canal Company was poised to withdraw the bulk of its European pilots from Egypt. Many experts claimed that in their absence Nasser would be unable to keep the Canal open – thereby justifying intervention. Secondly, he clung to the belief that Eisenhower and Dulles might in the end adopt a tougher stance if Great Britain fell in with their wishes in not immediately going to the Security Council or using force. It seems doubtful, however, whether he can have expected that any increased American vigour would go so far as to encompass even tacit approval of military intervention in Egypt if Nasser should succeed in keeping the Canal open and offer no further provocation. In letters sent to Eden on 2 and 8 September Eisenhower left little room for doubt about this. On the 2nd he wrote:

As to the use of force or the threat of force at this juncture, I continue to feel as I expressed myself in the letter Foster carried to you some weeks ago. Even now military preparations and civilian evacuation exposed to public view seem to be solidifying support for Nasser which has been shaky in many important quarters. I regard it as indispensable that if we are to proceed solidly together to the solution of this problem, public opinion in our several countries must be overwhelming in support. I must tell you frankly that American public opinion flatly rejects the thought of using force, particularly when it does not seem that every possible means of protecting our vital interests has been exhausted without result ...

We have two problems, the first of which is the assurance of the permanent and efficient use of the Suez Canal with justice to all concerned. The second is to see that Nasser shall not grow as a menace to the peace and vital interests of the West. In my view these two problems need not and possibly cannot be solved simultaneously and by the same methods, although we are exploring further means to this end. The first is the most important for the moment and must be solved in such a way as not to make the second more difficult. Above all, there must be no grounds for our several peoples to believe that anyone is using the Canal difficulty as an excuse to proceed forcibly against Nasser. And we have friends in the Middle East who tell us they would like to see Nasser's deflation brought about. But they seem unanimous in feeling that the Suez is not the issue on which to attempt to do this by force. Under the circumstances because of the temper of their population, they say they would have to support Nasser even against their better judgement.

Six days later the President wrote again:

The use of military force against Egypt under present circumstances might have consequences even more serious than causing the Arabs to support Nasser. It might cause a serious misunderstanding between our two countries because I must say frankly that there is as yet no public opinion in this country which is prepared to support such a move, and the most significant public opinion that there is seems to think that the United Nations was formed to prevent this very thing ...

Nasser thrives on drama. If we let some of the drama go out of the situation and concentrate upon the task of deflating him through slower but sure processes ... I believe the desired results can more probably be obtained. Gradually it seems to me we could isolate Nasser and gain a victory which would not only be bloodless, but would be more far reaching in its ultimate consequences than could be anything brought about by force of arms ...

Of course, if during this process Nasser himself resorts to violence in clear disregard of the 1888 Treaty, then that would create a new situation and one in which he and not we would be violating the United Nations Charter.

I assure you we are not blind to the fact that eventually there may be no escape from the use of force.[35]

Only by tearing this last sentence out of its context, is it possible to argue that Eisenhower had not ruled out force as a means of settling the dispute over the nationalization of the Canal. Some further provocation to the West was a clear precondition in the President's mind. He also evidently still considered the crisis as an inappropriate vehicle for toppling Nasser, however desirable the objective. Thus Eden in conforming to American wishes must be presumed at this stage to have tacitly given way on these points. Faced with clear absence of support for use of force on the nationalization issue from the United States, from the Labour Party, from a minority in the Conservative Party and from the bulk of the international community including the Commonwealth, Eden was surely realistic in rejecting French suggestions in the opposite direction. He must have hoped, therefore, that a peaceful solution would give him at least a degree of face-saving comfort. So when Eden fell in with Dulles's next proposal for yet another conference, it was probably with such a modest aim principally in view. If meanwhile the Canal had to close or Nasser acted rashly that would be the optimum outcome and might reopen the possibility of using force – but he can scarcely have counted on any such development occurring.

The French deplored Eden's pusillanimous approach. The chances of a changed American attitude or of some new provocation from Nasser seemed in Paris to be insufficient to justify further delay. The time was rapidly approaching, according to French military advisers, when the weather would preclude a major amphibious operation. Moreover, the French recognized that each passing week would make it more difficult to gain even minimum international sympathy for an assault on Egypt on the issue of the nationalization of the Canal. But they had no choice other than to fall in with Eden's insistence on agreeing to Dulles's proposal for another conference. General Paul Ély, Chief of Staff of the Armed Forces, recalled that by 17 September 'the Suez affair seemed to me personally as very probably buried, and I had the feeling that any military intervention was no longer to be expected'.[36]

During the first half of September Eden also secured a revision of the Anglo-French military contingency plan. 'Musketeer' became 'Musketeer Revise'. An assault, if it ever took place, would be made on Port Said, not Alexandria. It was said to be feasible until the end of October. Explaining the reasoning behind the British Cabinet's decision of 11 September to endorse this new plan, Lloyd stressed in his memoirs that 'it was more flexible, fewer resources were required and there was less risk of civilian casualties'. But Ély made it clear that political, not military, motives were decisive:

This change of plan calls for some remarks: there were, no doubt, political reasons; the Franco-British intervention, if it began in the region of Alexandria, ran the risk of being considered by World opinion as an act of aggression against Egypt. Thus conceived, it would have been acceptable if it could have been started as early as July in immediate response to Nasser's coup. But as time passed and the affair became entangled in the delays of international procedures, it thereafter became preferable to take action on the Canal: thus the nature of the intervention would be modified and the campaign would be limited to a kind of police action, which was nevertheless capable of causing Nasser's fall, which was the true goal of the Allies.[37]

Beaufre and Stockwell also subsequently admitted that political reasons underlay the change of plan, which both, incidentally, regretted.[38]

With the advantage of hindsight it may also be contended that the switch from Alexandria to Port Said had the further benefit that it made a little more plausible the eventual Anglo-French intervention to separate the Israeli and Egyptian forces when fighting between them occurred at the end of the following month. But it is unlikely that this possibility was the decisive factor in leading Eden to approve 'Musketeer Revise' early in September. True, he and his Cabinet colleagues had from the outset of the crisis been conscious that Israel was in close touch with France and that an Israeli move against Egypt might conceivably be turned to Great Britain's advantage. But Eden was acutely conscious of the attendant risks. Above all, he knew that Lloyd and the Foreign Office were unalterably opposed to any formal alliance with Israel on the grounds that such a step would instantly destroy British standing in every Arab country. He also feared that an Israeli 'breakout' might involve war with Jordan as well as or instead of with Egypt. Hence Eden, possibly restrained to a degree by his Foreign Secretary, did no more in the early stages of the crisis than keep the Israeli card in reserve with no certainty in his mind that it would ever be played. Meanwhile France had to be kept in line. Lloyd recorded, for example, that on 24 August he agreed with Pineau that 'the Israelis should be discouraged from taking advantage of the situation'. Nor can Eden have been much encouraged to activate the Israelis when, on 3 September, Lloyd sounded out Pearson. The Canadian Minister of External Affairs recalled:

At one point in a fairly wide-ranging discussion of the canal crisis, he [Lloyd] rather wondered whether, if things dragged on, Israel might not take advantage of the situation by some aggressive move against Egypt. He seemed to think that this might help Britain out of some of her more immediate difficulties, but agreed with me when I said that the long-range results and, indeed, even the short-range results of such action would be deplorable and dangerous; that such action by Israel would certainly consolidate Arab opinion behind Egypt; that even Arab leaders who might now be worrying about Nasser's moves would have to rally behind him.[39]

The probability is, therefore, that the substitution of Port Said for Alexandria in the Anglo-French military contingency planning represented, so far as Eden was concerned, a hesitant retreat from, rather than a deliberate move towards, the brink of decisive action.

On 12 September Eden addressed a recalled House of Commons. He had originally intended to announce a reference of the crisis to the Security Council. But, having given way to Dulles, he now instead had to announce the convening of the conference which presently became known as the Suez Canal Users' Association (SCUA). The plan, rather vague in character, was that like-minded states should cooperate to assert their rights under the Convention of 1888. They might together hire pilots, collect dues and deal with Cairo on any disputed matters. Plainly, however, the Egyptian attitude would be crucial. Eden, conscious that this further conference would be unpopular with most of his backbenchers, added that if Dulles's scheme failed 'Her Majesty's Government and others concerned will be free to make such further steps as seem to be required either through the United Nations, or by other means for the assertion of their rights.'[40] This imprecise wording had been agreed with the Americans. Yet Eisenhower's earlier letters had surely made it clear that he did not favour the threat of force as a tactic in securing Cairo's cooperation with SCUA. The Prime Minister nevertheless was unprepared for this to be spelt out in public. He was thus distressed when on 13 September, the second day of the Commons Debate, Dulles in a Washington press conference said, 'We do not intend to shoot our way through. It may be we have the right to do so but we don't intend to do it as far as the United States is concerned.' He added that the Americans would in the last resort use the Cape route round Africa. Eden recalled:

It would be hard to imagine a statement more likely to cause the maximum allied disunity and disarray. The Americans having themselves volunteered that the new arrangements would be less acceptable to the Egyptians than the eighteen-power proposals, Mr Dulles proceeded to make plain at this juncture that the United States did not intend to use force, even though it had the right to do so. The words were an advertisement to Nasser that he could reject the project with impunity. We had never been told that a statement of this kind was to accompany the announcement of the Users' Club ... The Users' Club was an American project to which we had conformed. We were all three in agreement, even to the actual words of the announcement ... Such cynicism towards allies destroys true partnership. It leaves only the choice of parting, or a master and vassal relationship in foreign policy.[41]

This was a severe judgement on Dulles. But it may be that the Secretary of State saw no better way of trying to defuse the crisis. If Eden had wanted an excuse for inaction to give his restless followers, such a forthright statement from Washington might even have been helpful: he could put the blame on Dulles, much as Flandin had sought to place the responsibility on Eden for having to remain passive in the Rhineland crisis twenty years earlier. And there are signs that Eden was intermittently looking for a way out after hearing Dulles's statement. The Opposition, backed by a minority of

Conservatives, sought from the Prime Minister,who was due to wind up the two-day debate for the Government, a pledge that no force would be used without recourse to the United Nations. Given the general character of current world opinion on Nasser's act of nationalization, quite apart from the Soviet veto, such a pledge would have been tantamount to capitulating publicly to American insistence on a peaceful outcome. Macmillan recorded:

> Under all this pressure, PM naturally began to waver. On the other hand, the militant wing (Waterhouse–Amery) of the party might well turn nasty if he were to change his position too noticeably. Meanwhile, Foreign Secretary had moved the vote of confidence at 2.30 – in a fine speech – but Sir Lionel Heald (an ex-Solicitor-General) had declared himself unwilling to vote for the Government, and other Tories were following suit. There was a meeting at 6 p.m. Butler was for giving the pledge – 'no force, without recourse to UN'. I was for standing firm, 'What I have said, I have said.' If PM were to 'climb down' under Socialist pressure, it would be fatal to his reputation and position.[42]

Eden's choice was a compromise. He told the Commons:

> I want to deal with the question: would Her Majesty's Government give a pledge not to use force except after reference to the Security Council? If such a pledge or guarantee is to be absolute, then neither I nor any British Minister standing at this Box could give it. No one can possibly tell what will be Colonel Nasser's action, either in the Canal or in Egypt.
>
> Nevertheless, I will give this reply, which is as far as any Government can go: it would certainly be our intention, if circumstances allowed, or in other words, except in an emergency, to refer a matter of that kind to the Security Council.[43]

This went a long way to meet Dulles's wishes. For it meant that only in a new crisis would the British be able to use force. War merely to annul the nationalization of the Suez Canal was no longer practical politics. That this was not fully grasped at the time was due to the decision of Gaitskell to divide the House. He might instead have underlined Dulles's victory by withdrawing his motion and proclaiming his satisfaction with the Prime Minister's assurance about going to the Security Council except in an emergency. The Leader of the Opposition, possibly still unsure of his hold on his own party, next wrote to *The Times* stressing his worries at Eden's ambiguity on the question of force. Macmillan noted Eden's reaction: 'PM rang me about it, and seemed rather concerned. I said that I felt very relieved that Mr G. should take this line, as it entirely destroyed the argument that PM had "climbed down".'[44] All the same Eden had to some extent 'climbed down' and was conscious of it. But he was inclined at this stage to make the Opposition rather than the Americans his scapegoat in private conversation. McDonald recalled, 'Only once [in September] did I see Eden despondent. It was on September 13, the second day of the tense

Commons debate. "Poor country," he said, "how can we do anything when divisions are pressed so hard." Even Nutting grasped that Eden was no longer resolute for war:" ... Eden could not at this juncture see how it would be possible to use force, unless Nasser struck the first blow."'[45] Moreover, contrary to Nutting's supposition, Eden already knew at this time that the French now definitely favoured unleashing the Israelis. So it would seem that, though well aware of this possibility and showing increasing interest in it, he could not yet see how there could be British involvement in view of the risk of disastrous repercussions on British influence in the Arab world. He may even have been adhering to this line as late as 26 September when he met Pineau and Mollet in Paris. Moreover, General Moshe Dayan, the Israeli Chief of Staff, recalled:

> According to [Maurice] Bourgès-Maunoury [French Defence Minister], Pineau had told Eden before leaving [London on 21 September] that in such a situation [of British inaction] France might act alone – and even be aided by Israel. Eden's reply, according to Pineau, was that he was not opposed to this plan as long as Israel did not attack Jordan.[46]

The precise date on which Eden irrevocably determined to play a more direct part in turning the Israeli scenario into reality may indeed never be known with certainty. But the key probably lay in domestic Conservative Party politics during the early part of October.

Meanwhile the eighteen-nation SCUA Conference met in London between 19 and 22 September. Once again Dulles treated the participants to much robust oratory. But he did not retract his repudiation of 'shooting his way through the Canal'. And even on the issue of dues he indicated that American shipowners would only be invited rather than required to pay their dues to SCUA instead of Egypt. It is difficult, therefore, to understand why Lloyd wrote in his memoirs: 'I do not think that anyone who listened to him could have felt that if Nasser rejected the SCUA plan, and if the Security Council failed to obtain a solution, Dulles would do other than accept the use of force, even if the United States did not take part.'[47] So little faith did Lloyd and Eden in fact have that they, together with the French, referred the crisis to the Security Council on 22 September, immediately after the end of the SCUA Conference, without even giving precise advance notice to Dulles, who would have favoured further delay. The matter was duly scheduled for consideration on 5 October. But Eden probably did not appeal to New York with the clear intention of setting the stage for immediate recourse to force, and certainly not in the form of a straightforward response to Nasser's original coup. For the national and international climate continued to rule out for practical purposes any such *dénouement* so far as the Canal dispute was concerned. No doubt Eden was still hoping that Nasser would present him with some new provocation or pretext. But this still showed no sign of materializing. For example, the Egyptians had succeeded without serious difficulty in keeping the Canal in functioning order despite the departure of most European pilots. Thus Eden, probably with a heavy heart, went to the Security Council with the expectation that Great Britain's optimum course would be to try to negotiate a settlement. McDonald's testimony confirms this judgement: 'Throughout September I had many private talks with Eden and Selwyn Lloyd. Everything they said showed that they were hoping for a settlement at that time.'[48]

Towards the end of September Eden contemplated making a bizarre move to please the French. According to Nutting:

... Eden sent for me and told me to explore with the European experts at the Foreign Office whether there was any 'present' that he might take with him [to Paris] which would demonstrate our desire for Anglo-French solidarity ... To my astonishment he suggested that the Foreign Office should have another look at Churchill's offer of common citizenship for all British and French nationals, which was made in 1940 in a desperate effort to keep France in the fight against Hitler ... In the event nothing came of this strange notion.[49]

This was indeed a remarkable episode, suggesting growing desperation on Eden's part.

Eden's troubles multiplied dramatically in the early part of October. Above all, he faced a decisive move from Macmillan. The Chancellor, having spent from 20 September to 1 October in the United States, returned home in a belligerent mood. One historian has written:

He was anxious for action. He may have noticed on his return from the US a certain weakening of Eden's resolve, a new predisposition for negotiation. Eden probably missed his strong personality ... It was now, apparently, that Macmillan took the French line very strongly and threatened to resign unless, if the UN failed to accept British demands, force were used. He had, he said almost menacingly, 'taken soundings' in the Conservative Party – the Party Conference was a week off – which caused him to think that at least his own friends ... would not stand for a negotiated settlement.

The same writer claimed to have been told that the Chancellor's threat to resign is 'written down in the Cabinet minutes'. The recollection of William Clark, Eden's Public Relations Adviser, was a little less precise:

Towards the early part of October he [Macmillan] intervened in a Cabinet meeting (at which I was not present but which many of us heard about) to say that he did not see how, having gone to so much preparation of a military sort, he could continue to support a government which did not make use of that military preparation. This was a fairly clear, though reasonably polite, threat to resign if there wasn't military action.[50]

Simultaneously Eden received contradictory indications of the American attitude. From Macmillan he received encouraging news:

I [Macmillan] assured him [Eden] of my strong feeling that the President was really determined to stand up to Nasser. When I explained to him the economic difficulties in 'playing it long' he seemed to understand. He accepted that by one means or another we must achieve a clear victory.

Yet on 2 October Dulles made a public statement at a press conference pointing in the other direction:

The United States cannot be expected to identify itself 100 per cent either with the Colonial powers or the powers uniquely concerned with the problem of getting independence as rapidly and as fully as possible. There were, I admit, differences of approach by the three nations to the Suez dispute, which perhaps arise from fundamental concepts. For while we stand together, and I hope we shall always stand together in treaty relations covering the North Atlantic, any areas encroaching in some form or manner on the problem of so-called colonialism find the United States playing a somewhat independent rôle. The shift from colonialism to independence will be going on for another fifty years, and I believe that the task of the United Nations is to try to see that this process moves forward in a constructive, evolutionary way, and does not come to a halt or go forward through violent, revolutionary processes which would be destructive of much good.

He then said of SCUA: 'There is talk about teeth being pulled out of the plan, but I know of no teeth: there were no teeth in it, so far as I am aware.' Dulles's statement rather than Macmillan's report of Eisenhower's view was the more accurate representation of American policy. It is, moreover, possible that Macmillan was speaking with more than one voice. For though a 'fire-eater' in London, he had struck Eisenhower, at their meeting on 25 September, as 'far more reasonable on the Suez business than he had expected'.[51]

The noose was thus definitely tightening around Eden. A negotiated compromise with Nasser would probably lead to the resignation of Macmillan and perhaps of other Cabinet colleagues, to the Prime Minister being branded by many of his backbenchers as an appeaser and possibly even to a revolt culminating in the overthrow of the administration. Eden also had to expect the customary French recriminations. For example, while in Paris on 26 September he had sent this message to Butler:

My own feeling is that the French, particularly Pineau, are in a mood to blame everyone including us if military action is not taken before the end of October. They alleged that the weather would preclude it later. I contested that. Mollet, as I believe, would like to get a settlement on reasonable terms if he could. I doubt whether Pineau wants a settlement at all.[52]

On the other hand, Eden would have to face even more formidable risks if he launched a straightforward assault on Egypt after the passage of so much time. There might be threats of resignation from the other wing of the Conservative Party – led from within the Cabinet by Monckton, by Macleod and maybe even by Butler, who, as has been seen, had urged the offer of a pledge of no use of force without recourse to the Security Council. And a possibly decisive number of backbenchers might make common cause with the Labour Party, whose hostility to the use of force was now unmistakably clear. Moreover, much of the press and non-party élite opinion had gradually swung away from the bellicosity felt at the time of Nasser's coup. The moralistic and high-minded strand in British thinking about foreign policy had once again come to the fore. It must have been haunting for Eden, the beneficiary of such thinking in his earlier career, to reflect on its effect on such as Hoare and Neville Chamberlain. Certainly Eden can have had no illusions that if he took his country into war he would have to contend with significant domestic divisions and there was no recent precedent for such a venture. He also knew that he faced the hostility of the bulk of the Commonwealth and even the possibility of its break-up. And American disapproval had been foreshadowed in the private messages and public pronouncements of both Eisenhower and Dulles, though a self-deluded Eden may have clung desperately to the hope that they might not quite mean what they said.

Both capitulation and a straightforward assault had thus become overwhelmingly perilous options for Eden by early October. But did he have other alternatives? Only three possibilities remained. The first was that with American help a clear victory over Nasser might be achieved by nego-tiation. But the chances of this happening, never good, were further undermined on 2 October by Dulles's attack on colonialism and his declaration that SCUA had never been intended to have any teeth. True, this was not inconsistent with his public pronouncement in mid-September that the Americans did not intend to shoot their way through the Canal. But the deterioration in Eden's domestic position meant that the statement of 2 October was seen as a decisive turning-point in London. This was the moment when Eden, rightly or wrongly, saw chances of an honourable peaceful settlement disappear. McDonald recalled meeting him on 3 October:

I have never seen Eden so angry and so shocked. It was the colonial references he resented most. He was sincerely shocked that Dulles should so completely misunderstand this determination to have the Canal internationally controlled as to think he was reverting to colonialism. 'It was I who ended the "so-called colonialism" in Egypt,' Eden said. 'And look what Britain has done all over the world in giving the colonies independence.' He was desperately angry that Dulles, even if he had thought these things, should have come out publicly at such a critical time to impugn the motives of an ally: 'We have leaned over backwards to go along with him. And now look. How on earth can you work with people like that? It leaves us in a quite impossible situation. We can't go on like this.'

Nutting, too, saw Dulles's speech as a turning-point: '... I knew instinctively that this was for Eden the final let-down. We had reached breaking-point.'[53]

Eden was thus pushed towards a second alternative to capitulation or straightforward war for the Canal: the possibility of involving Israel. One historian has claimed that at this juncture, early in October, the matter was seriously discussed by Eden's colleagues:

A senior Cabinet Minister ... has confirmed that it was now that Eden revealed definitely that, in the words of another (and absolutely trustworthy) Minister 'the Jews had come up with an offer' to attack Egypt and so give Britain and France the chance at long last to launch Operation Musketeer. The matter came to the Cabinet probably on 3 October (the day Dulles's fatal 'teeth' remark appeared in the Press) and, though 'they didn't like it much', they did not oppose it. It seems likely that the possibility of an open alliance with Israel was raised but dropped.[54]

Lloyd had already departed for the Security Council and hence was not on hand to put the Arabist case against even indirect entanglement with Israel. Even so the Prime Minister had still not received and maybe had not even yet sought a Cabinet decision actually to unleash the Israelis. He certainly cannot have seen this option as being other than fraught with dangers. But it may by now have appeared to him to be marginally less 'unthinkable' than the other courses open to him. Above all, there was just a chance of being able to intervene under the cloak of high-minded peace-keeping and thereby cause divisions in the moralistic lobby at home.

There was, however, one further option for Eden: he could retire on grounds of ill-health and hand over the poisoned chalice to one of his not particularly loyal colleagues. On 5 October, while visiting his wife on hospital, he suddenly collapsed with a temperature of 106 degrees. This marked the beginning of the onset, in severe form, of the periodic fevers that had their origin in his bile-duct troubles of the early 1950s. He was able to return to his duties within a few days but was thereafter in uncertain health and in constant need of drugs. Possibly, then, the desperate character of the choices facing him at the beginning of October had caused this relapse. It might even have been a signal from his subconscious mind that the least unattractive course open to him was to quit. But he had won the Military Cross in the First World War and had deliberately resigned high office in 1938; he must be presumed to have been conscious, not without good reason, that he did not lack courage. This self-image no doubt played its part in ensuring that the option of resigning, at least at this stage, was excluded.

The next decisive turning-point for Eden came during the weekend of 13 to 14 October. On the thirteenth he addressed the concluding session of the Conservative Party Conference in Llandudno. From its first day the activists' mood had been overwhelmingly chauvinistic. Even Nutting had consented to make a fiery speech from the platform when Salisbury was taken ill. Eden was now expected to give further encouragement to the forces he had in part created by his treatment of Makarios and by his early public pronouncements on the Suez crisis, both in Parliament and in a dramatic broadcast on radio and television on 8 August. It would thus have taken much skill on his part now to lower the temperature in the Conservative Party, if indeed this could have been done at all. Eden had, however, just had from New York news, which some commentators have claimed might have given him just a change of doing so. For Lloyd in prolonged negotiations with Mahmoud Fawzi, his Egyptian counterpart, had reached agreement on Six Principles to govern a settlement. These were:

1. There should be free and open transit through the Canal without discrimination, overt or covert.
2. The sovereignty of Egypt to be respected.
3. The operation of the Canal should be insulated from the politics of any country.
4. The manner of fixing tolls and charges should be decided by agreement between Egypt and the users.
5. A fair proportion of the dues should be allocated to development.
6. Unresolved disputes between the Suez Canal Company and Egypt should be settled by arbitration.

Eisenhower, professing to be delighted by this breakthrough, proclaimed his confidence that 'a very great crisis is behind us'. Eden might have attempted to echo this view to his party activists. But he chose instead to inflame them further. And he tacitly repudiated Eisenhower's interpretation of the importance of the six points:

> President Eisenhower in his press conference on Thursday is reported to have said that you must have peace with justice, or it is not peace. I agree with those words. We should all take them as our text. That is why we have always said that with us force is the last resort, but it cannot be excluded. Therefore, we have refused to say that in no circumstances would we ever use force. No responsible Government could ever give such a pledge.

Probably Eden was correct in his belief that the six points were too vague to have much merit. True, Lloyd and Fawzi were due to meet again in Geneva at the end of October to try to arrange the details. But these were unlikely to be as satisfactory to the British as the SCUA plan, the Soviets having already vetoed a resolution presented to the Security Council containing a recommendation along such lines. Hence even Lloyd was insufficiently confident of the value of his achievement to express great confidence in a final outcome that could be presented as an Anglo-French triumph. And nothing less would any longer suffice to solve Eden's problem, now primarily domestic in nature in the form of the menacing figure of Macmillan. Thus neither lack of courage nor poor judgement led Eden to play up to the chauvinistic forces at Llandudno: he lacked any alternative that was both attractive and politically practical.

On the following day, 14 October, Eden took another fateful step. Together with Nutting, he received at Chequers two emissaries from Paris, General Maurice Challe and Albert Gazier (deputizing for Pineau). They now presented the British with a clear plan of action. Whether it was as much a surprise to Eden as to Nutting may be doubted. But the meeting nevertheless marked a major turning-point for the Prime Minister: he now grasped eagerly at an approach which he had hitherto kept at arms' length. Briefly, Israel would attack Egypt and move towards the Suez Canal. At this stage Great Britain and France would issue an ultimatum to both sides requiring them to allow Anglo-French forces to occupy the Canal in order to separate the combatants. Thus in Nutting's words, 'the two powers would be able to claim to be "separating the combatants" and "extinguishing a dangerous fire", while actually seizing control of the entire waterway and of its terminal ports, Port Said and Suez'. Challe personally had only contempt for Eden's need to have such an excuse for intervention:

> His anxiety was to have the appearance of not being the aggressor. The general hypocrisy required that one prepared more or less lame pretexts. They deceived nobody but certain persons pretended to believe them. As if the confiscation of the Canal was not enough.
> Thus I presented the pretext or rather the scenario that he awaited ...[55]

But relatively few of Challe's compatriots were susceptible to moralistic appeals in the context of the conduct of foreign policy and hence his government had no need to find a hypocritical pretext for defending the nation's narrow interests.

Eden could not, however, formally accept the French proposal at once, for he had to secure the acquiescence of at least some Cabinet colleagues. He accordingly told Challe that an answer would be provided on the following day. After the French visitors had left, Nutting, horrified at Eden's enthusiasm, urged that no early decision would be possible as the Foreign Secretary was still in New York. Eden met this argument instantly by recalling Lloyd by telephone. The Foreign Secretary duly arrived in London on the morning of 16 October to be informed by Nutting of what was afoot. According to Nutting, Lloyd's initial reaction was adverse. But over luncheon with Eden he was persuaded to adopt a more open-minded position.[56] That same afternoon Eden and Lloyd flew to Paris for discussions with Mollet and Pineau. Much has been made of the alleged effects of physical unfitness in shaping the Prime Minister's conduct at this period. But it was surely Lloyd, not Eden, who must be presumed to have been in no condition to make rapid decisions on matters of the utmost gravity. He arrived in Paris on Tuesday evening, having last had a normal night's sleep almost two days earlier and no doubt also suffering from the after-effects of a transatlantic flight. Though Eden had offered Lloyd the chance to delay departure to Paris for one day, the suspicion must remain that he tried to 'bounce' his Foreign Secretary into supporting the Challe plan by allowing him only minimum time for reflection and by effectively isolating him from the counsels of the doubters in the Cabinet and in the Foreign Office.

Once in Paris Eden and Lloyd entered upon discussions with their counterparts in conditions of extreme secrecy. All civil servants, even the British Ambassador, Gladwyn Jebb, were unceremoniously excluded. The Challe proposal was now examined. Lloyd's recollections suggest that there was still a certain amount of reserve on the British side: any Anglo-French collusion to instigate and aid an Israeli attack on Egypt was to be tacit rather than explicit. It may be, however, that Eden, behind the back of Lloyd, adopted a somewhat more forthcoming attitude than this. What is known is that Eden clearly indicated that, subject to his Cabinet's agreement, the British, like the French, would not operate the Tripartite Declaration of 1950 in favour of Egypt if Israel should attack. Nasser's earlier conduct, together with his attacks on the Declaration, were thought to be a sufficient moral justification for adopting this position. But, on the other hand, the British and the French could not be indifferent to the fate of the Canal and hence would have to occupy it both to safeguard it and to separate the combatants. This line might just have been acceptable to the Americans and others provided certain conditions had been fulfilled. First, the British and the French, if the safety of the Canal had really been their principal concern, had a duty to try to prevent the Israelis from attacking in the first place. This was of course not done. On the contrary, the French were already sending military aid rather than warnings to Israel and hence they were in effect instigating an attack whose consequences they would then piously use as a pretext for invading the territory of the victim. True, Eden was not apparently yet quite in this morally invidious situation – for he may not have been fully aware of the extent to which the French were involved in detailed collusion with Israel. Yet in another respect his position was as morally dubious as that of the French. For he should surely have insisted that the British and the French, as two parties to the Tripartite Declaration, had an obligation to share their current interpretation of its standing with the third party, namely the United States. This also was not done. Again, the contingency plan for separating the potential belligerents had the disadvantage for Eden that its implementation at any early date would occur before the chance of using force over the nationalization dispute had been formally ruled out. In this eventuality would Anglo-French spokesmen frankly admit to having intervened for more than one purpose; or would they claim that the particular threat which had been in the air since July was suddenly as redundant and irrelevant as the Tripartite Declaration; or would they by evading the point permit more than one interpretation to be placed upon their action? These questions should have worried Eden more than they apparently did on the occasion of his visit to Paris. But the desperate nature of his domestic problem caused him to take a reckless gamble that his position would in practice turn out to be just sufficiently defensible to confuse the critics. In contrast to Eden, Lloyd, not being Prime Minister, faced no clear threat to his political survival if nothing should be done about Nasser and hence was the least enthusiastic member of the Paris quartet. He showed repeated signs of hesitation in the ensuing days though he may have been too physically exhausted to discern the difficulties that would arise in defending the projected British rôle. Intellectual limitations may also have played a part in shaping his course. When, for example, he wrote his memoirs two decades later, he proved capable of making such a plaintive statement as:

It has frequently been suggested that there was something artificial about our declared intention to separate the combatants and stop the spread of hostilities. Our fear of damage to the Canal if there was fighting over the crossing places was genuine and well-founded.[57]

In the context of an account that is otherwise quite full and frank, this kind of apparently disingenuous claim is almost insulting to the reader. It could only have been written in its context by someone with an unusual capacity for self-deception or alternatively possessed of less than first-rate analytical powers. Signs of this same myopia in Lloyd can be seen in his conduct during the crisis itself.

On 18 October Eden called a Cabinet meeting. Beforehand Lloyd tried to express his doubts to Butler. The latter recalled:

I went straight to No. 10 where I found the Foreign Secretary, Selwyn Lloyd, in the lobby outside the Cabinet room. He seemed moved and, gripping my arm, described how he had got back from the UN early on the 16th and been immediately wafted to Paris in the wake of the Prime Minister ... it had been suggested that, if war broke out in the Middle East between Israel and Egypt, Britain and France should jointly intervene in the canal area to stop hostilities. Selwyn Lloyd seemed anxious about my own reaction. At that moment I was summoned into the Cabinet room.[58]

Eden had little difficulty in persuading his colleagues that in the event of an Israeli attack on Egypt, Great Britain could not be expected to come to Nasser's aid under the Tripartite Declaration. He further stated that the French should be informed and added 'that there was no reason why they [the French] should not tell the Israelis'.[59] This, it may be argued, was the first definite step by the Cabinet towards instigating an Israeli attack. In this context the reported views of an unnamed Cabinet Minister are of interest: 'The whole Cabinet knew about Israel from the beginning. The Israel thing would have come to the top of the pile only after no other pretext remained. The funny thing was, the Cabinet preferred this to a straight bash.'[60] Eden next suggested that in the event of an Israeli attack Great Britain and France should intervene to protect the Canal. Opposition came in surprising form from Butler. He recalled: 'I was impressed by the audacity of the thinking behind this plan but concerned about the public reaction. I wondered whether an agreement with the French and the Israelis, designed to free the Suez Canal and eventually to internationalize it, would not meet our objective ...'[61] This must have struck Eden as a deliberately unhelpful suggestion – one of many he had to bear from his senior colleagues. Butler, after all, had not hitherto revealed any enthusiasm for an assault on Egypt in the context of the Canal nationalization. He had, as has been seen, favoured capitulation to Labour demands that no force should be used without prior reference to the United Nations. Now, almost three months after Nasser's coup, he came forward as an advocate of a 'straight bash' against Egypt. He evidently also favoured open alliance with Israel – quite unnecessary if no indirect strategy was envisaged and in any case bound to be unacceptable to the Foreign Office because of the risk to general British interests in the Arab world. This last consideration forced Lloyd to lead the attack on Butler's approach to the advantage of Eden, whereas he might have been able to take a different line if Butler had openly backed the outright opponents of military action represented by Monckton. Lloyd's intervention was decisive in securing support for Eden. Hence not only had the majority of the Cabinet now come to prefer an indirect strategy to a 'straight bash' but the principal advocate of the 'straight bash', Butler, was also now probably seen by Eden as pursuing an indirect strategy of his own – the difference being that he himself, not Nasser, was the potential victim. Yet however insincere Butler's line must have seemed, his espousal of a line of criticism distinct from Monckton's ensured that at this stage the Prime Minister got his way. Eden, however, understandably felt no gratitude to Butler on this account. True, his overt Cabinet opponents were now divided into two camps. But this equally meant that in due time he could be subjected to a pincer attack. Moreover, while both Butler and Monckton bowed to the majority decision rather than resign, neither seems to have accepted defeat in a particularly loyal spirit. Butler merely bided his time before moving against Eden at the height of the military operation. Monckton for his part insisted on moving from the Ministry of Defence, accepting instead the post of Paymaster-General on 21 October. Two days later he is said to have explained to Aldrich that his move was motivated by his belief that the forthcoming war was 'a great blunder'.[62] Had Eden known of this he would surely have seen it as an act of outright treachery.

Meanwhile the French had been informed of the British Cabinet decisions of 18 October and had conveyed them to the Israelis. Eden must have hoped that nothing more would be required of him until official news of an Israeli attack reached him. He could then have intervened while maintaining that he had neither colluded with the Israelis nor had had foreknowledge that they would definitely strike. He would probably not have been widely believed and the Americans would have been entitled to complain about the unilateral repudiation of the Tripartite Declaration. But his opponents, whether in London or Washington, might have had no more than an unconfirmed suspicion of dishonourable conduct.

On 21 October, however, Eden received from Paris a message which effectively ended even this small chance that he might indefinitely sustain a 'not proven' defence against the charges of foreknowledge, incitement and collusion: the Israelis would not attack Egypt without more direct involvement by the British. Ben-Gurion, Dayan and Shimon Peres were due to arrive in Paris on the following day and insisted on seeing a British spokesman. Eden promptly discussed the matter with a small group of colleagues, namely Lloyd, Macmillan, Butler and the new Minister of Defence, Antony Head. It was decided that Lloyd should meet the Israelis in Paris. This was the moment when Eden crossed a line that ensured that his reputation will forever be stained by unanswerable accusations of having committed himself and his colleague to make public pronouncements of staggering mendacity and hypocrisy. This was surely the moment to have turned back from the Israeli scenario if that had been possible. But those who condemn him out of hand for not doing so have an obligation to say how he could hope to do so without a total loss of authority among his colleagues. A retreat to a peaceful compromise with Nasser was now even more politically unthinkable than it had been before Challe's *démarche*: almost every member of the Cabinet would have turned back to haggling over the Six Principles, oppressed by a deep sense of anticlimax. Equally unattractive, however, would be a 'straight bash' against Egypt. For, as has been seen, this would have brought instantaneous condemnation from the United States, from the bulk of the Commonwealth, from the United Nations and from the Opposition. True, hindsight suggests that it would probably have been no more unsuccessful than the course actually followed and would have been infinitely easier for Eden to defend with self-respect and honesty. Yet at the time he judged that while a 'straight bash' would meet with near-irresistible opposition, the more devious plan might just sufficiently succeed in confusing the issue to permit him to deliver a severe blow to Nasser's prestige and maybe even to topple him. Eden must have been aware, however, that in either the shorter or the longer run he would face disagreeable and essentially irrefutable charges of dishonourable conduct. He nevertheless chose to put his integrity at risk for the sake of marginally improving the chances of his perilous enterprise succeeding. Whether in so doing he was primarily motivated by fear of losing his place or by a profound and maybe unexampled sense of selfless patriotic duty will remain a matter for endless speculation. In either case, Eden's tragedy was that his gamble in the event was widely judged not to have succeeded, even to the limited degree that he himself claimed. Thus many will say that his decision to collude with the Israelis was worse than a crime, it was a blunder. Others may argue that he had no practical alternative: the luck that had been so much a feature of his early career had now decisively deserted him. Number 17 would not turn up in 1956 for Eden as it had done for Churchill in 1940.[63]

Eden's decision to single out Lloyd to meet Ben-Gurion was a move of some shrewdness. For it tied the hitherto hesitant Foreign Secretary closely into the plan just at the point when it was becoming an outright conspiracy. There was of course considerable piquancy in the political head of the Arabist Foreign Office being required to meet the Israeli Prime Minister. Clearly if Lloyd would do this, there was unlikely to be any sticking point for him. Hence Eden could thereafter count on the loyalty of at least one senior colleague. This did not mean, however, that Lloyd had become an enthusiast for what now had to be done. On the contrary, he made a less than favourable impression on both Ben-Gurion and the French leaders when he met them in great secrecy at a villa in Sèvres on the evening of 22 October. Ben-Gurion doubted British resolve and maintained that 'British prior action was a *sine qua non*' for a preconcerted Israeli strike. In particular, unless the British undertook to destroy the Egyptian air force at the outset of the fighting, he refused to contemplate moving in the direction of the Suez Canal – an obvious necessity if the Anglo-French intervention was to carry the slightest credibility but not otherwise of central interest to Israel. It was indeed the air factor that made British involvement essential for both Israel and France. For neither country had any adequate means of reaching Cairo to deliver a decisive pre-emptive air strike. The British were both beneficiaries and victims of these military facts. For they were able to use their indispensability to insist upon the devious strategy rather than the 'straight bash'; but they were unable simply to abstain from action with any confidence that the Israelis and the French would in any event obligingly check or topple Nasser – even if that course had held any attractions for Eden (and it probably did not). What Ben-Gurion brought home to Lloyd, however, was the extreme practical difficulty of reconciling the British desire for a high-minded pretext for intervention with the Israelis' need to protect their cities from air attack. For if the British delayed an air strike until the Israeli land forces had had the forty-eight hours said to be needed to reach the Canal, Haifa and Tel Aviv might already be in ruins. But if the British air strike came very near to the commencement of Israeli–Egyptian hostilities, the chances of persuading any intelligent observer that there had been no prior collusion would be much reduced. In any case there would have to be at least a short delay, during which the British and French Governments would be seen to go through the motions of consultation, and then a further delay to enable Egypt and Israel to consider the projected Anglo-French ultimatum. Lloyd now for the first time seemingly became conscious of the magnitude of this problem. He nevertheless at first insisted, according to Dayan, that no British air strike would be possible within forty-eight hours of the commencement of the Israeli assault. Ben-Gurion at this point was evidently inclined to call off the talks and return home. For as well as fearing air attacks on Israeli cities, he disliked the idea of being the recipient of the projected ultimatum. He further stated that, given the British attitude, 'Israel would not start a war against Egypt, neither now nor at any other stage.' But Dayan argued that if the Israelis dropped a paratroop unit behind the Egyptian lines, at the western end of the Mitla Pass, this might justify earlier British action to protect the Canal. Lloyd then suggested that thirty-six hours might in that case be a possibility. On the other hand, the Foreign Secretary was worried that the Israeli action might not be sufficiently vigorous. Dayan recalled:

> He simply urged that our military action not be a small-scale encounter but a 'real act of war', otherwise there would be no justification for the British ultimatum and Britain would appear in the eyes of the world as an aggressor. To this, Lloyd insisted, Britain could not agree, 'for she has friends like the Scandinavian countries, who would not view with favour Britain's starting a war'. I did not dare glance at Ben-Gurion as Selwyn Lloyd uttered this highly original argument. I thought he would jump out of his skin. But he restrained his anger, though not his squirming, and all I heard was the scraping of his chair.

Despite Ben-Gurion's distaste for what he called 'British duplicity', he thus tacitly indicated that he would fall in with Dayan's scenario provided the British gave way on the question of the forty-eight-hour delay.[64] Lloyd accordingly undertook to consult Eden and departed for home around midnight.

Next day, 23 October, Lloyd reported first to most members of the Cabinet's Egypt Committee and then to the full Cabinet. Whether he was totally frank with the latter may be doubted. He may not, for example, have admitted to having actually talked with Ben-Gurion. But he did indicate that an Israeli attack now seemed less likely – evidence that the Foreign Secretary at least was unenthusiastic about Dayan's plan. Eden, however, was less hesitant and during the evening of the same day decided to accept it. He was no doubt influenced to a degree by Pineau, who had arrived in London to put a more favourable gloss on Dayan's plan than Lloyd seemed likely to do. Lloyd once again capitulated to Eden and to salve his conscience penned a pitiful letter to Pineau. The French Foreign Minister recalled:

> ... I received a letter from Selwyn Lloyd from which I allow myself to extract a passage indicative of the state of mind of the British Cabinet.

'It must be clear, in view of what was said yesterday, that the United Kingdom did not ask the Israeli Government to undertake any kind of action. We only asked ourselves what our reactions would be in the case where certain events occurred.'

I took care not to show this letter to Ben Gurion and perhaps I was wrong.[65]

Lloyd had in fact been told that, owing to the vulnerability of Israeli cities, a British undertaking to eliminate the Egyptian air force was a *sine qua non* for any kind of substantial Israeli assault. Thus British willingness to offer this clearly amounted to an instigation of the Israelis. Moreover, the Foreign Secretary had also made it known that a precondition for British action was that the Israelis' attack, if it materialized, must include an otherwise unnecessary thrust towards the Canal. In these circumstances, for Lloyd subsequently to maintain privately to Pineau of all men that the British did 'not ask the Israeli Government to undertake any kind of action' was surely a transparent sophistry.

The following day, 24 October, British participation in further discussion at Sèvres was indicated. But Lloyd felt obliged to stay in London to answer parliamentary questions. Hence Eden decided to send at short notice Patrick Dean, Deputy Under-Secretary at the Foreign Office and not hitherto involved. According to Lloyd, Eden briefed Dean to discuss actions which might be taken in certain eventualities and to reaffirm that British forces would in no circumstances act unless there was a clear military threat to the Canal. Nobody present at Sèvres subsequently cast doubt on the punctiliousness with which Dean stuck to his instructions. Yet his presence may well have proved fatal to his career prospects. One historian has written:

Sir Patrick Dean acted as a loyal Government servant throughout. His conduct, which was entirely correct, was ill-requited. He had every expectation of becoming head of the Foreign Office. He was passed over, and the real reason, whatever justification may have been found, was his involvement in an episode of which the newly returned Labour Government [of Wilson] had deeply disapproved. Such treatment of a civil servant who simply obeyed orders can only be termed shabby. It could be a bad precedent if followed, and it could damage the whole nature of the relationship between politicans and those who serve them.[66]

Curiously, the Labour Party was more forgiving of Lloyd, raising no objection to one who had deceived the House of Commons becoming its Speaker.

Though Dean certainly did no more than carry out his instructions in the resumed meeting at Sèvres, he was placed in a dilemma when, at the end of the discussion, a text was produced. Lloyd wrote:

After a time quite unexpectedly a document was produced. It ... recorded the elements of the contingency plan which had been discussed, and the action which could be expected to follow them in given circumstances. Dean and [Donald] Logan [Lloyd's Assistant Private Secretary] had a word together about this development.

There had been no earlier mention of committing anything to paper and no reason to regard the document as anything other than a record of the discussion on which the three delegations would report. As that, Dean signed it.

Ben-Gurion, according to his diary, suggested that a protocol be prepared of the joint plan 'which will be signed by the three parties and which will be ratified by the three governments' and he added that the British delegates participated in the drafting. Dean was in no position, however, to ratify anything and he accordingly was only able to sign the document *ad referendum*. Perhaps, then, Lloyd was technically correct to describe the document as a 'record of discussion' rather than a protocol or an accord, though the contents and the fact that it was signed *ad referendum* indicated that actions might well flow from this mere 'record'. The following day, 25 October, however, Eden is said to have sent a letter to Mollet (who forwarded a copy to Ben-Gurion) containing the following: ' Her Majesty's Government have been informed of the course of the conversations held at Sèvres on 22–4 October. They confirm that in the situation therein envisaged, they will take the action decided ...'[67] Now the 'record of discussion' became something else, though Lloyd did not see fit to state this. Eden's letter of 25 October marked the point at which Great Britain definitely undertook to send what amounted to an ultimatum to Egypt if the Israelis first carried out their side of the plan. Few will surely quarrel with 'collusion' or even 'conspiracy' as appropriate descriptions of this arrangement.

The document drawn up at Sèvres had seven distinct articles. The first stated that Israel would launch a military action on 29 October and would aim at reaching the Canal on the following day. This reflected Eden's insistence on a clear military threat to the Canal being the essential prerequisite to British involvement. Thus if Eden had not actually incited the Israelis to attack Egypt, he had certainly incited them to appear to attack the Canal, which they would otherwise have ignored. The precision of the date of the Israeli attack in the 'record' of the Sèvres discussion is also important. Nobody present has queried that 29 October was unequivocally named. Yet Lloyd wrote of Dean reporting that '29th October was mentioned as the earliest possible date' for the Israelis. This vagueness was probably not accidental. For had Lloyd been more specific he would tacitly have exposed Eden, as will be seen, to the charge of having deceived the Cabinet. The choice of 29 October was also significant in the context of possible American reaction. With the Presidential Election due on 6 November, it represented a calculation that American hostility would be more muted during the campaign than after it. The expectation clearly was that concern not to alienate the Jewish vote would stay Eisenhower's hand – another reason, incidentally, for Eden's preference for Israeli involvement as distinct from a straightforward Anglo-French assault on Egypt. This decision was taken despite an alleged appeal from Eisenhower to Eden to delay any action until after the Election. Pineau is the principal source for this:

Eden communicated to us a confidential message received from Eisenhower. It was a truly astounding message in fact because it asked us to delay any operation until the American Presidential Election of 6 November. Thereafter he committed himself to forming a common front with us to obtain from Egypt a satisfactory arrangement of the Suez Affair.[68]

Eden did not find this vague American promise reassuring. In this he was no doubt justified. But an obvious corollary is that, having ignored Eisenhower's appeal, he could scarcely have felt much sincere moral outrage when the President retaliated with vigorous opposition. And the only basis for any surprise that Eden may have felt surely lay not in disillusionment concerning Eisenhower's basic views but rather in the degree to which he proved willing to disregard the pressures of the Zionist lobby.

The second and third articles of the plan laid down the steps which the British and the French would take after an Israeli assault: they would call on the Israelis and the Egyptians to accept a ceasefire, to withdraw from within ten miles of the Canal and, in the case of the Egyptians, to agree to the temporary occupation of key positions on the Canal by Anglo-French forces in order to guarantee freedom of passage through the Canal to the vessels of all nations until a final arrangement could be secured. If either Egypt or Israel failed to agree, within twelve hours, to this ultimatum, Anglo-French forces would take measures to ensure compliance. The Israelis understood that these would include a strike on Egypt's airfields in the early hours of 31 October.

Other articles completed the plan. Israel would be free to occupy the western shore of the Gulf of Aqaba and the islands of Tiran and Sanapir to ensure freedom of passage to her vessels approaching from the Red Sea. Israel undertook not to attack Jordan during the hostilities with Egypt – an eventuality that would have embarrassed Great Britain, obliged under the Anglo-Jordanian Treaty to defend Jordan. But if Jordan attacked Egypt, Great Britain would give the former no help. Finally, the whole plan was to remain entirely secret.

Meanwhile the British Cabinet had met again on 24 October. It is as yet unclear whether they were informed about the nature of Dean's mission and, above all, of the intention to give priority to the pretext of separating the Israelis and the Egyptians. It is certainly remarkable that, according to Lloyd, the Cabinet chose at this moment to reaffirm that the objectives of a military operation would be 'to obtain control of the Canal by landing an Anglo-French force after preliminary air bombardment; and to defeat Nasser, which would probably mean his downfall'. It is odd, too, that Eden should have declared that 'further talks with the French were necessary'.[69]

For he must have known that it had already been arranged for Dean to have such talks not merely with the French but also with the Israelis.

On the next day, 25 October, the Cabinet proceedings had greater relevance to Eden's actual intentions. Now he said that 'the Israelis were advancing their military preparations with a view to attacking Egypt, and the date might be 29th October'.[70] Even this, however, was not being wholly fair to the Cabinet. For Eden now knew from the 'record' signed by Dean, which he clearly did not circulate, that the date was definitely 29 October. Eden's conduct must thus be judged devious even towards his own colleagues. Yet if Eden concealed the exact degree of the collusion with and the incitement of Israel, he nevertheless involved the whole Cabinet in substantial foreknowledge of what was to happen. His basic argument was that in seizing the Canal 'it was better that we should seem to hold the balance between Egypt and Israel rather than to be accepting Israeli cooperation in an attack by us on Egypt'.[71] He thus appears to have hoped that this 'holding of the balance' might be credible. Yet the nature of the Sèvres plan made that highly improbable. First, the combatants were now only to receive twelve hours to consider the ultimatum – a brutally brief period. Secondly, the ultimatum would only relate to the Canal zone – a limitation that made nonsense of claims to be trying to prevent 'a forest fire spreading'. Moreover, the prior existence of the Anglo-French dispute over the Canal was bound to undermine belief in the disinterested character of an ultimatum limited only to that zone. Thirdly, the military measures provided for at Sèvres would affect Egypt alone. Article Three, for example, specifically referred to an air strike against the Egyptians only if they should fail to respond to the ultimatum. As Pineau later pointed out, no provision was made for comparable treatment of Israel 'in the case, obviously unlikely, that the Israeli army, exploiting its initial success, should wish to cross the prescribed limit'.[72] True, this particular written commitment was not intended to be made public, but in any event the uneven military treatment of the two adversaries was bound to be entirely evident. The stage had thus been reached, as one writer has put it, when the 'Israeli action was going to be perilously thin as a cover'.[73] But Eden now found himself in the position of Goethe's Faust: though he had freely taken one step in the direction of Ben-Gurion, in all his subsequent steps he was to be a slave of the first.

The crucial Cabinet of 25 October also gave thought to the matter of timing. Lloyd, for example, said that 'Israel's intervention in our dispute with Nasser had its disadvantages, but there was little prospect of any early opportunity to bring these issues to a head.'[74] This view was endorsed by Eden. For he knew that the French leaders had long maintained that the end of October was their effective deadline for action because of climatic conditions in the Mediterranean. The military advisers of both countries took the same line. And, in the British case, it was clear that reservists could not be kept in readiness indefinitely. But while the argument for bringing matters to a head was strong, this did not mean that action had to precede the American Presidential Election. Clearly, despite the climate, the operation could have been delayed for a further week without serious risk. But the Cabinet was evidently not led to consider this aspect of the timing – probably because Eden declined to make a frank admission that the precise date of the operation was something open to the British to determine in negotiation with the Israelis. Another feature of the Cabinet discussion was that no clear decision was made about the relationship between the projected operation to separate the combatants and the reaffirmation, made on the previous day, of the earlier intention to respond to the national-ization of the Canal by requiring its internationalization and in any military intervention to that end to seek also to overthrow Nasser.

The Cabinet of 25 October eventually ended with Eden getting such formal decisions as he requested. To some extent, therefore, all concerned share responsibility for what followed. True, Eden had been less than frank in his dealings with the majority of his colleagues. Nevertheless they had shown a disinclination to press him on detail and to insist on exploring all the implications of what had been proposed. Later, however, many of those who prior to the military operation had been willing to submit quietly to Eden's leadership were to act differently. If they did not quite behave towards him as their predecessors had towards Hoare in December 1935, they at least began to think for themselves in a way that they had not done in the last weeks of October. This in itself, as will be seen, was to be fatal to the Prime Minister's authority and left his enterprise in ruins. Eden, however, was probably his own worst enemy: his initial avoidance of explicitness left his colleagues too much scope to trip him up when the military operation was in progress. However devious his plan for dealing with Nasser, he revealed a touching naïvety in so lightly placing his future in the hands of ambitious colleagues whose loyalty to him was uncertain. Perhaps he did not realize that 'gentlemen' had to be watched at least as carefully as 'rug-merchants'.

Israeli mobilization followed on 27 October and this in turn caused a sharp increase in interest in Washington. The following day Dulles spoke to Eisenhower on the telephone about whether immediate evacuation of American subjects in Egypt should be arranged. These notes on their conversation have survived:

President asked Dulles if he thought that by starting [evacuation], would we exacerbate the situation?
Dulles replied that he does not think so. It may lead to some anti-American

demonstrations; and if the British strike it will lead to inference that we knew about it. But he thinks it will not basically make the situation more serious.

President said our statement today would take care of that one, because obviously we don't know anything about the British.

Mr Dulles asked if President got the information about the build-up around Cyprus ...

President said he just cannot believe Britain would be dragged into this ...

President asked have we taken any steps.

Mr Dulles said he had just talked to French Ambassador and British Chargé. They profess to know nothing about all this at all. The Britisher said he had some information that they had acted to warn the Israelis against attacking Jordan. But, he [Dulles] said, their ignorance is almost a sign of a guilty conscience in his opinion.[75]

Clearly, then, Eisenhower expected some military action but was unsure about its nature or even whether the British would be involved. He was also unclear about the likely timing of any assault. For Dillon, the American Ambassador in Paris, had earlier been led to expect that any action involving the French would be left until after the Presidential Election of 6 November. He recalled:

I guess I was the first person to learn of the plans for the military action and I reported it to the State Department some ten days before it began. This was reported to me confidentially by a member of the French government, who was not the Foreign Minister but who obviously knew what he was talking about. He reported it to me with the idea that it would be reported back home and that it would be a last chance for the United States to step in and take a strong position with Nasser, or there would be military action.

At the time I was told (I think there wouldn't have been any sense for telling me this, and the whole way this was done, unless this was true at the time) the military action was scheduled to begin a few days after our election – they wouldn't do anything before it. Something happened in the period in between – I've never known what – and that was speeded up by about a week.

... The British, at that time, when they were asked absolutely denied that there was any such thing in the wind. And for one reason or another I think our people were rather inclined ... to believe the British over the French at that time.

But they did take it seriously, to the point that they prepared a draft which I saw ... of a statement or a letter that President Eisenhower was going to write the night of the election as soon as he knew he was elected ... By the next day this would have been in the hands of all these countries, asking them to hold their horses and allow time for a new initiative by the United States ...[76]

The Israeli mobilization of 27 October, however, threw doubt on the timetable indicated by Dillon. On the evening of the 28th Aldrich accordingly sounded out Lloyd. Also present were Harold Beeley of the Foreign Office and Walworth Barbour of the American Embassy. Pressed about the possibility that the mobilization of the Israelis would lead to an attack on Egypt, Lloyd 'reiterated that the British government has no information to that effect whatsoever, but they were very much concerned about the Israelis attacking Jordan'. This was four days after the Sèvres Accord had expressly ruled out an Israeli attack on Jordan. Aldrich later commented: 'I have always taken the position, in spite of every evidence to the contrary, I am unable to believe that Mr Selwyn Lloyd deliberately misled me.'[77]

On the evening of the following day, 29 October, the Israelis launched their assault on Egypt. Eden was informed during the course of a dinner held in honour of Norwegian guests. He now embarked upon the preconcerted course. On the morning of the 30th a Cabinet was summoned and solemnly authorized the Prime Minister to make a statement to Parliament subject to agreement with the French. Mollet and Pineau accordingly flew to London for superfluous 'consultations' during the afternoon. Next, at 4.30 p.m., Eden told the Commons that the two combatants were being given twelve hours to fall back ten miles on either side of the Canal and to agree to Anglo-French forces temporarily occupying Port Said, Ismailia and Suez. If either party declined to comply, force would be used. He made no attempt to explain the by-passing of the United Nations and, more important, of the Tripartite Declaration. He merely stated that the British representative in New York would join his American counterpart in summoning a meeting of the Security Council; and noted that tripartite discussions between British, French and American representatives had taken place in Washington. He also made no reference to the long-standing British desire to reverse the July coup and secure the internationalization of the Canal.

Eden's treatment of the Americans on this crucial day was cavalier in the extreme. There was no British Ambassador in Washington, for Sir Harold Caccia, Makins's successor, was to cross the Atlantic by sea and was not to arrive until 8 November. Meanwhile the Chargé, John Coulson, was evidently given no significant message to convey to the Americans. In London, however, Aldrich could not be so easily ignored, for on the morning of the 30th he had managed to corner the Foreign Secretary. He no doubt drew attention to a message received overnight from Washington. Radford recalled its contents:

I received word that I was to be at the White House with Mr [Charles] Wilson [Secretary of Defense] at six o'clock [on 29 October] ... I believe – but I'm not sure – that Mr Dulles was there ... I am quite certain that Herbert Hoover was there. Anyway, it was a meeting between State, Defense and the President – a rather limited group. There was considerable discussion as to what we should do. The decision taken at that meeting, I thought, was a masterpiece. We sent to the British and the French – knowing that they were in cahoots to do something, but not exactly what – a message that we (the United States) would stand by our tripartite guarantees to defend the victim of aggression without naming who we thought that was. In other words (and this, as I understood the discussion, was done on purpose), if they wanted to come back and say 'Thank you very much. We certainly agree with you, and we think the Israelis are the victims', we could agree with them or disagree. If we disagreed, nothing could be done ... for at least three or four days. By that time the Israelis would have cleaned up on the Egyptians. I do not think we would have been too unhappy if that had happened.

... the French in Paris and the English in London received that dispatch by three or four o'clock next morning [Washington time], I'm sure ...[78]

Thus this message must have been discussed by Aldrich and Lloyd on the morning of the 30th. According to Aldrich's later recollection:

I asked Mr Lloyd what the British Government intended to do in view of Israel's action. He replied that he *thought Her Majesty's Government would immediately cite Israel before the Security Council of the United Nations as an aggressor against Egypt.* Believe it or not, that's what he told me that morning they were going to do, but he added that the French Prime Minister and the French Foreign Secretary were on their way to London for consultation and Her Majesty's Government would want to discuss with them before taking action, as they wanted to act in concert with the French. Moreover, he said, the British had shipping and cargo of great value in the Canal and it would be necessary to take this into consideration. In view of all this, Mr Lloyd concluded he could not tell me definitely what action the British would take until after the meeting which was to be held at once with the French, but that he would inform me about their decision immediately after luncheon. I then left Mr Lloyd and reported what he'd said to Washington by cable. At 1.30 p.m. Mr Lloyd's private secretary called Mr James Moffett, my private secretary, and said that Mr Lloyd would have to go directly to the House of Commons after luncheon, so could not see me then. However, Sir Ivone Kirkpatrick ... would see me at 4.45 and tell me exactly what had been decided.[79]

In Washington Dulles and Eisenhower discussed on the telephone the implications of the Anglo-French ultimatum which they had actually initially heard about from the press. The Secretary of State said that the twelve-hour ultimatum to Egypt was 'about as crude and brutal as anything he had ever seen'. He was distressed, too, that this should occur at a time when the Hungarian crisis was coming to a head. He was afraid that the West would be seen as 'in the same pasture as the Soviets'. Eisenhower also was angered: '... they are our friends and allies and suddenly they put us in a hole and expect us to rescue them'. He was particularly concerned about the decision to by-pass the Tripartite Declaration. Here he was inclined to blame Eden more than Mollet, for Dixon, the British Ambassador to the United Nations, had broken the news of this to his counterpart, Cabot Lodge, on the previous evening. Lodge had reported of Dixon, 'normally an agreeable fellow', that 'it was as though a mask had fallen off'.[80] The unsmiling British Ambassador stated that the Tripartite Declaration was 'ancient history without current validity'. Eisenhower told Dulles that he wanted Eden to know that 'we are a government of honour and we stick by it'. He stressed that the Prime Minister had not previously made his position known and hence that he had assumed that the British were just as in earnest as the Americans about the Tripartite Declaration.[81] Messages between Eisenhower and Eden now flowed back and forth across the Atlantic. But no ground was given on either side. A public breach between London and Washington was thus made inevitable. That same evening the Americans unexpectedly pressed for the immediate passing oa a resolution in the Security Council condemning Israeli aggression, demanding Israeli withdrawal and calling upon all members to refrain from the use or threat of use of force. Both Great Britain and France now used the veto. On the following day the Americans and the Soviets combined to raise the necessary vote on the Security Council to have the matter referred to the General Assembly – an extremely severe move by Washington that deeply shocked Eden.

For Eden the hostile American reaction was only one concern in the hectic days following the inevitable Egyptian rejection of the twelve-hour ultimatum. His first priority was to supervise the evolving military operation. For he faced unexpected difficulties. The first arose on the morning of 31 October. Though committed, under the Sèvres Accord, to commence the bombing of Egyptian airfields, he had overlooked the fact that during daylight hours many Americans were likely to be in the process of being evacuated and would thus possibly be at risk.[82] With minutes to spare Eden managed to get a message to Cyprus which halted the planned raids. It has been claimed that Eden said to Head: 'If you can stop these planes, I'll make you a duke.'[83] If so, it was to be a promise that was not honoured. A more serious broken promise, however, was that made to Israel. For it was now possible for the Egyptians to bomb Israeli cities. They did not in the event do so. But the Israelis cannot be blamed for having noted British inaction and hence for having reciprocated by giving priority to their own interests later in the crisis. Nor was even a night-time air attack mounted without hesitations in London. Eden was urged by his lukewarm military advisers to find technical excuses for further delay. But pressure from the French, fearing Egyptian air attacks on Algeria no less than on Israel, caused the bombing operation to go ahead during the night of 31 October/1 November.[84] Perhaps, then, Eden was already showing signs of indecision. On the other hand, to many observers he appeared at this stage to be calm and resolute.

Thursday 1 November was to be a grim day for Eden. For in the Commons the Opposition revealed the extent of its sense of outrage. Right and left united behind their leaders to condemn the Prime Minister. 'We are,' said James Griffiths, 'dishonoured.' Most Labour contributions merely reiterated this view with less economy. 'Collusion' was widely suspected despite

Lloyd's claims on the previous day that 'it is quite wrong to state that Israel was incited to this action by Her Majesty's Government' and, that 'there was no prior agreement between us about it'. But passions increased when Ministers sought to evade Opposition questions. For example, was the country at war? According to Eden, it was merely in a state of 'armed conflict', though this evidently did not mean that British forces who killed Egyptians would be guilty of murder – Geneva Convention privileges were claimed. Again, Eden aroused anger by stressing his 'high-minded' purpose:

Israel and Egypt are locked in conflict in that area. The first and urgent task is to separate those combatants and to stabilize the position. That is our purpose. If the United Nations were then willing to take over the physical task of maintaining peace in that area, no one would be better pleased than we. But police action there must be to separate the belligerents and to prevent a resumption of hostilities.[85]

The dissent on the Opposition benches became so heated during a speech by Head that the Speaker was obliged to suspend the sitting for half an hour – a step without precedent since 1924. To Eden the degree of Opposition hostility came as another serious blow, for news of it was bound to encourage his critics abroad. In the ensuing days, moreover, his ordeal in the Commons was to be regularly repeated. In this respect Butler, as Leader of the House, was less than helpful to him: he did little to limit Opposition opportunities to press their case. For Eden the strain was compounded by his lack of experience in facing a bitterly hostile Opposition: hitherto he had usually commanded a polite hearing for his bland contributions. He was also not physically well-equipped to face repeated interrogations in a highly charged atmosphere. Even more important was the frequent loss of sleep consequent upon his need to consult Dixon in New York, which was five hours behind London. This factor, rather than acute physical illness or a bad conscience, may account for unfavourable descriptions of his demeanour in the Commons. For example, J. P. W. Mallelieu, a Labour MP, wrote of his 'sprawling on the front bench head thrown back and mouth agape'. He continued: 'His eyes, inflamed with sleeplessness, stared into vacancies beyond the roof, except when they twitched with meaningless intensity to the face of the clock.'[86]

The evening of 1 November brought more trouble for Eden. For Dulles had decided to indict his allies in person at the General Assembly in New York. He delivered an impassioned sermon in support of a resolution demanding an immediate ceasefire. This was carried in the early hours of 2 November by sixty-four votes to five. The three colluding states were supported only by Australia and New Zealand. Dulles undoubtedly had mixed feelings about his rôle. He cannot have enjoyed acknowledging a breach with his principal NATO allies, particularly when the Soviets were facing a severe dilemma in Hungary. Nor did he necessarily relish the opportunity to attack Eden with whom his earlier relations, even during the

Suez crisis, had been less frigid than is usually supposed. A prominent American journalist, John M. Hightower, recalled:

> He [Dulles] was off and on with Eden. It all depended on whether Eden was doing what he wanted him to do . . . when it looked as if Eden was going along on a kind of Suez Canal solution in 1956 that Dulles favoured, Eden was a great fellow, generally referred to by Dulles's associates as 'Anthony'. When Eden got mixed up in the scheme to have the Israeli War to take over the Canal and so on he was known as 'Playboy' or 'the Nut' or something like that . . . by the way he was referred to you could judge the temperature of their relations.[87]

And Dulles was certainly no friend of Nasser. Yet his speech to the General Assembly left him with a deep sense of pride. He told one of his aides: 'If that had been my very last act on earth, it would have been exactly as I would have wished it. I would have liked it for my epitaph.'[88] The speech was a reaffirmation of his belief that the United States should be loyal to the Rule of Law in international affairs and hence to the Charter of the United Nations: 'If whenever a nation feels that it has been subjected to injustice it should have the right to resort to force . . . then I fear we should be tearing the Charter into shreds.' Some critics have doubted Dulles's sincerity. Herman Finer, for example, argued that 'he was afraid of a world war . . . and especially of the hostility of Arab–Asian people, much of it delinquent, unless the military actions were stopped at once'.[89] Others, not least in Great Britain, have seen commercial motives underlying ostensible American high-mindedness. But the Secretary of State himself, well aware of this argument, later wrote a defence now preserved in his papers:

> Our position is particularly subject to misinterpretation because we are unwittingly the beneficiary of the restraints and pressures which we exercise. When we urged the French to grant independence to the Associated States of Indochina, there was strong criticism that we were actuated by commercial purposes, and that American business would supplant the French in that area. Similar charges are being made in relation to Africa. Also there is strong sentiment in Britain and France that we are in effect backing our oil interests in the Middle East and otherwise trying to take over their positions. This is not the fact, but nevertheless to some extent a strengthening of the US position is a by-product of our supporting the principles in which we believe and restraining others of the free world . . . We also recognize that it is particularly difficult for some countries to accept the United Nations principles and to accept our backing them when we are living in a two-standard world where the Soviet–Chinese Communist bloc do not accept those principles. There is a sense that it is 'unfair' for us to seek to bring about compliance with principles which others ignore. This sentiment is felt in South Korea, Taiwan, Britain, France, Israel, etc.
>
> . . . We have confidence that adherence to sound principles will in the end prevail and that the Soviet–Chinese Communist world, which rejects such concepts as moral law, justice, the dignity of the individual, and so forth, will collapse. Already they are in deep trouble. Our task is to keep the free world sufficiently strong and

united in support of sound principles so that we will outlast the Communist world.[90]

Dulles was still in 1956 in some respects the same idealistic internationalist who had served Wilson in Paris in 1919. He might in the interim have become more sophisticated and made compromises with the requirements of *Realpolitik*. But at root he remained committed to a higher objective than merely promoting the narrow interests of his own career, party or country. Eden at times grasped this, finding it particularly distasteful to be indicted by one whom he later mocked as 'a preacher in politics'. It was also no doubt galling for him to reflect that he himself had constructed a good part of his own career on the basis of the skilful use of Wilsonian rhetoric – a case of full circle indeed.

During the early hours of 2 November the United Nations was the setting for a further move destined to complicate Eden's plans. Pearson of Canada seized upon the Prime Minister's offer in the Commons, repeated by Dixon in New York, to permit a UN force to take over the Anglo-French rôle of 'peace-keeping'. The Canadian Foreign Minister strongly supported the idea and began to organize with great speed the passing of a resolution to put it into effect. It is extremely doubtful whether Eden had made his offer in the expectation that any rapid response would be forthcoming. According to Lloyd's account, the relevant sentence in Eden's speech had been suggested following consultations in the Foreign Office. Lloyd did not, however, make it clear whether the implications were fully understood either by him or by his chief. But Eden's later conduct and, above all, his subsequent hostility to Pearson suggest that he did not expect his offer to be used as a means of getting the planned Anglo-French military operation halted immediately. Possibly he saw it merely as a harmless sop to reinforce the appearance of high-mindedness he hoped to create. But more probably he had been shaken by the extreme vigour of the reaction from the Americans, the Commonwealth and the Opposition, and hence needed to have some honourable escape route prepared for use in the period *after* the seizure of the whole Canal. On the other hand, the French, who had not been consulted about the UN force suggestion, were so alarmed at the new British demeanour and the speed of developments in New York that they decided to send Pineau to London on 2 November to review the position.

The military action against Egypt was now going more or less to plan. The bombing, after the delayed start, had been wholly successful in eliminating the Egyptian air force. The Israelis had captured most of Sinai and were established on the Mitla Pass. The main Anglo-French landing force in an impressive armada was sailing from Malta towards Port Said, where it was expected to arrive on 6 November. Meanwhile violently anti-Nasser leaflets were to be dropped on Egypt in the so-called aero-psychological phase of the conflict. Nevertheless the French were anxious to see amendments made to this original plan. The distance from Malta to Port Said lay at the root of their doubts. They contended that the policy of delaying the landing of troops until 6 November should now be abandoned, since international opposition was being mobilized more rapidly than had been envisaged. Now the Israelis had demonstrated the weakness of Egyptian military strength, could not airborne landings safely be authorized? Eden disagreed. He had at the outset of the crisis in late July favoured rapid use of airborne forces and had only reluctantly yielded to counsels of caution from the Chiefs of Staff. Now the risks were significantly less. But he failed to press the case on his military advisers with any comparable vigour. Possibly recollections of Arnhem and Crete were more clearly in his mind. Possibly, too, he was aware that if *in extremis* Israeli aid had to be summoned, charges of collusion would be even more strongly pressed. But the most plausible explanation of his hesitation is that he had begun to grasp for the first time the magnitude of the perils facing him and that in those circumstances he did not dare to add to these by exposing British troops to the slightest risk of mass slaughter. His morale, moreover, was at a low ebb on 2 November. He was about to lose his Public Relations Adviser, Clark.[91] And the resignations of Nutting and Boyle were also pending. Above all, Nasser had successfully defied both the British ultimatum and the bombing of his airfields. Eden's hopes that he would be toppled at the first 'splutter of musketry' had been dashed. Instead Nasser had pulled most of his troops back to Cairo and had sunk vessels in the Canal, thus effectively bringing about that closure which Eden's action had been ostensibly aimed to prevent. The Prime Minister may also have been aware – though this will probably never be firmly established – that a covert operation to have Nasser assassinated had been foiled.[92]

Pineau thus returned to Paris with no assurance that, given Pearson's activity, any further military action would be possible and hence with no confidence in Eden's reliability. Merely dropping leaflets for the next few days would in the French view be wholly inadequate. As Beaufre later wrote:

> The overriding error was acceptance of the idea of this long 'aero-psychological' phase. Militarily it was nonsense and politically a serious mistake. It was this which gave the whole operation the stamp of irresolution, all too faithful a reflection of the lack of determination shown by British opinion in general and Anthony Eden in particular.[93]

Similar feelings may have influenced Pineau to seek reinsurance with Washington. For on 2 November Eisenhower learnt from Dillon in Paris that the French Foreign Minister had outlined the whole history of the collusion with Israel. It is unlikely that Pineau told Eden that he had thus broken one of the terms of the Sèvres Accord. This had unfortunate consequences for Eden's subsequent relations with Washington. As Dillon recalled:

He [Pineau] said he thought that there shouldn't be any mystery, that we ought to know that it probably had been a mistake. But, anyway, this thing had been planned ...

Well, of course, right at the same time the British Government ... was telling Ambassador Aldrich that this had never been planned. Well this led to further disenchantment with the British, and particularly with Eden personally ...

This made our people ... feel that the French were wrong, but they were, at least, honest. The British, whom we felt ought to have been even closer to us, because of Anglo-American relations, were the ones who were not telling us the truth and deliberately misleading us and continued to do so after it was over. So that caused great bitterness ... against the British at that time. It caused us really to blame them.[94]

On Saturday 3 November Eden discussed the French plea for more rapid landing of troops in Egypt with his Cabinet colleagues and military advisers. He appears to have been in an indecisive mood and in the end shifted the main responsibility for a decision on to Head. The Minister of Defence was instructed to fly at once to Cyprus in order to assess the feasibility of the French plan. Thus Eden moved a little nearer Paris. At the same time, however, he sent a formal statement to New York laying down conditions for a ceasefire that gave encouragement to Pearson. During the night of 3/4 November the Canadian Foreign Minister steered through the General Assembly a resolution calling for and authorizing the establishment of a United Nations Emergency Force (UNEF). The voting was 57 to 1 with 19 abstentions. As one writer has put it: 'Peace was chasing war.'[95] And Eden was now wavering between the two.

Sunday 4 November was another vital day for Eden. It was to mark the last occasion on which he would show something of his earlier determination. He had three new developments to put to his leading colleagues. One was the UNEF resolution which could easily have been used to justify a cancellation of any landing of troops in Egypt. Secondly, he had to convey unwelcome news that Israel was apparently prepared to agree to an immediate ceasefire if Egypt would do so – a move not in the spirit of the Sèvres discussions. Thirdly, he had received from Head the opinion that an airborne invasion could safely be attempted on the following day, twenty-four hours before the armada would arrive from Malta. Before meeting the Egypt Committee, Eden spoke to Lloyd. Together they agreed that 'having got this far, it would be wrong to call off the operation'. They accordingly backed Head's recommendation. But they faced a major revolt for the first time. Butler seized upon the news that the Israelis were apparently prepared for a ceasefire. He recalled:

I took the line that were the news correct, we could not possibly continue our expedition. It had not been my idea to announce that we were going in to stop hostilities, but if they had already stopped we had no justification for invasion. This argument, which was backed by Lord Salisbury, seemed to nonplus the Prime Minister. He said he must go upstairs and consider his position. If he could not have united support, the situation might arise in which someone else might have to take over from him ... When Eden returned, a message came through from the Israeli Foreign Minister, Mrs [Golda] Meir, that there was to be no ceasefire. Tension round the table was immediately relieved and it was agreed that the troops should land.[96]

Evidently French pressure had now caused the Israelis to attach conditions to accepting a ceasefire. But for Eden there remained the ominous fact that Butler and Salisbury had revealed their essential willingness to question his leadership at a time when British forces were about to go into action. The Prime Minister himself saw that to some extent he was now hoist with his own petard. But the wooden literalness with which Salisbury in particular cited the original British pretexts as a means of obstructing any landing of troops represented a brutal *volte face*. Macmillan, too, was to show the first overt sign of entering upon a new phase of thinking for himself. Lloyd recalled: 'It was at this meeting that a report came in from Dixon that there had been some discussion in New York about oil sanctions. Macmillan threw his arms in the air and said, "Oil sanctions! That finishes it." Two of those present remember this.'[97] Moreover, even after news had been received that the Israelis were attaching conditions to a ceasefire some opposition remained to Eden's recommendation that the invasion take place on the following day. Five or six members of the full Cabinet favoured deferring action either indefinitely or at least for twenty-four hours to enable pressure to be put on Israel and to permit inquiries to be made about whether the projected UNEF could include British and French troops. Clearly Eden's authority was beginning to be eroded.

After some further hesitation Eden finally authorized the airborne attack. Challe, who had again come to London with Pineau to try to stiffen Eden, recalled:

After interminable discussions at Downing Street, Eden gave the order during the night of 4/5 November for all parachutists to jump. When we parted at about 3 a.m. on the 5th, Sir Anthony, putting his hand on my shoulder, said to me pleasantly, 'Well, general, we got there at last.' I replied, paraphrasing Mme Laetitia: 'Prime Minister, so long as it lasts ...' It was not to last forty-eight hours.[98]

On the following day Bracken felt able to write to Beaverbrook: 'The Socialists who thought Eden a charming milksop now hold him to be a blood-lusting monster. Vanity is a great toughener.'[99] The question now, however, was how long his toughness would endure.

On Monday 5 November the airborne assault thus took place, to be followed on the next day by the seaborne landings. Little resistance was encountered. Clearly the French view had been vindicated and Eden was seen to have been over-cautious. Now the Prime Minister's problem was how to resist world pressures for long enough to enable the troops to reach the southern end of the Canal, which had been his proclaimed objective at the beginning of the operation. Opinion in New York and Washington had been outraged by news of the landings, for it had been assumed that Pearson's resolution of 4 November would lead to at least a pause in Anglo-French action. Eisenhower, in particular, was furious at the interruption to his election campaign and at the deceit practised by Eden, as revealed by Pineau. Moreover, the President could not consult regularly with Dulles, who had suddenly been hospitalized for a cancer operation on 3 November. Determined to be seen to have authority in the Western world, Eisenhower accordingly brought overwhelming pressure to bear on 5–6 November. A run on the pound was allowed and probably encouraged to develop. Then, according to Pineau, on the morning of 6 November the President delivered a twelve-hour 'ultimatum' to Eden. This Eden accepted without consulting either Mollet or his own colleagues. The exact terms of the message, and indeed whether it was delivered by telephone or otherwise, is not known. But the effect on the Prime Minister was dramatic. The time in London was probably around 9.0 a.m. At 8.30 a.m. Eden had spoken on the telephone to Dixon envisaging occupying the whole length of the Canal within six further days, proof, if any be needed, that a threatening telegram from Bulganin on the previous day had had no decisive influence on him. An hour later Dixon received word that a ceasefire would be accepted. At 9.45 a.m. Eden met the Cabinet and told them that a ceasefire was essential. It would seem, however, that he made no mention of the personal 'ultimatum' from Eisenhower. Instead he allowed Macmillan to play the leading rôle in winning over his colleagues. The Chancellor, whose doubts had been voiced two days earlier, now insisted that the run on the pound could not be ignored. In his memoirs he referred to the speculation against sterling and heavy selling in New York:

How far this was due merely to the desire to avoid loss and how far this followed the lead of the United States Treasury it is hard to know. But certainly the selling by the Federal Reserve Bank seemed far above what was necessary as a precaution to protect the value of its own holdings. I would not have been unduly concerned had we been able to obtain either the money to which we were entitled from the International Monetary Fund, or, better still, some aid by way of temporary loan from the United States. The refusal of the second was understandable; the obstruction of the first is not so easy to forgive. We had a perfect right under the statutes to ask for the repayment of the British quota ... It was only while the Cabinet was in session [on the 6th] that I received the reply that the American Government would not agree to the technical procedure until we had agreed to the ceasefire. I regarded this then, and still do, as a breach of the spirit, and even of the letter of the system under which the Fund is supposed to operate. It was a form of pressure which seemed altogether unworthy.[100]

What the Chancellor did not do, however, was to explore the possibility of adopting temporary countermeasures against the Americans such as draconian exchange controls, freezing American assets or even a devaluation. Butler and Salisbury, on the other hand, merely reiterated their earlier arguments based on taking literally what the Cabinet had obviously earlier seen as only the ostensible grounds for intervention. This left only some junior members of the Cabinet with doubts about an immediate ceasefire: Head, Stuart and Peter Thorneycroft. Eden thus secured endorsement for a course that tacitly abandoned his original aims of at least internationalizing the Canal and maybe also toppling Nasser. He must have had a profound sense of defeat. But he was now intent not on victory but on mere survival. For though Eisenhower had probably delivered the *coup de grâce*, the conduct of some of Eden's principal colleagues had been so disloyal as to leave him with too little self-confidence to resist the President. It is difficult to be sure whether he resented most the conduct of Eisenhower, Butler, Salisbury or Macmillan. A political commentator, Hugh Massingham, later reported that Eden had said 'shortly before he disappeared into oblivion', 'I do not care who it [my successor] is going to be but I shall make absolutely certain that it isn't Rab. This man has never said a word against the policy in Cabinet, but my spies tell me that he has never stopped criticizing it when he has got into Downing Street.' But in his memoirs Eden wrote scornfully: 'There are always weak sisters in any crisis and sometimes they will be found among those who were toughest at the outset of the journey.'[101] It is hardly to be doubted that Macmillan and Salisbury were among the 'weak sisters' he had in view.

Having already decided to halt the operation, Eden at the end of the morning informed the French. He was, according to all French sources, unwilling to discuss the substance of the matter and left his allies with the choice of conforming or continuing alone down the length of the Canal. Mollet, possibly too loyal to 'perfidious Albion', agreed to a ceasefire. In return he secured from Eden only that the timing should be midnight rather than late afternoon. The Sèvres understanding was thus ruthlessly torn up by Eden. He had, moreover, yielded to Eisenhower without securing from him any undertakings about the future course of American policy. In his memoirs he wrote:

We would have taken a second, and maybe a third, look at the problem had we understood what was to come. We were ashore with a sufficient force to hold Port Said. We held a gage ... Out of this situation intelligent international statesmanship should, we thought, be able to shape a lasting settlement for the Arab–Israeli conflict and for the future of the canal. We had not understood that, so far from doing this, the United Nations, and in particular the United States, would insist that all the advantages gained must be thrown away before serious negotiation began. This was the most calamitous of all errors. Had we expected it to be perpetrated, our course

453

might have been otherwise, but we could not know. As it seems to me, the major mistakes were made, not before the ceasefire or in that decision, but after it. I did not foresee them.[102]

This lack of foresight, if true, can only be described as astonishing in one of Eden's experience. Could he possibly have been so naïve? Or did he perhaps lose his nerve on the morning of 6 November and recklessly throw away his negotiating position by failing to bargain an agreement to a ceasefire against pledges from Eisenhower of subsequent 'intelligent international statesmanship ... to shape a lasting settlement'? A more plausible explanation is simply that Eisenhower showed himself to be in no mood to bargain, with the result that Eden, under pressure also from some of his own colleagues, saw no rational alternative to unconditional capitulation. But whether naïvety, panic or calculation determined Eden's line, the prevailing mood in London was summed up by Salisbury: 'We have played every card in our hand, and we have none left.'[103] This has to be borne in mind when considering Eden's retrospective claim that 'the major mistakes were made, not before the ceasefire or in the decision, but after it'.

Similarly unpersuasive is Lloyd's alleged contemporary belief that 'we had as good a bargaining counter with twenty-three miles of the Canal as with the whole Canal'.[104] The whole world thought otherwise. Above all, many Conservative backbenchers were dismayed at the decision, which only served to reawaken their doubts about Eden's robustness. Now he was once again in danger of being dismissed as a 'charming milksop', possibly with the charm rather tarnished. Churchill, for example, commented to Moran on 26 November: 'I cannot understand why our troops were halted. To go so far and not go on was madness.' He was prepared to make some allowance, however, for the disloyalty of colleagues. On 6 December he mused, 'When things become known it will turn out, I think, that Anthony has been bitched, and that he wanted to go on and complete the military operation. When the Cabinet wouldn't let him he tried to resign, but they told him that he would split the Conservative Party.'[105] Eden might have strengthened his position if he had publicly hinted at his own reluctance to terminate the operation. But he was either too honourable or too shortsighted to act in this fashion. Above all, he chose to use in public the argument for halting which Butler and Salisbury had canvassed on 4 November. Even in his memoirs he wrote of one factor weighing more heavily than others in his mind: 'We had intervened to divide and, above all, to contain the conflict. The occasion for our intervention was over, the fire was out. Once the fighting had ceased, the justification for further intervention ceased with it.'[106] This was ironic in view of the distaste with which he had received this argument on 4 November. It also meant that Eden was committed in the aftermath of the ceasefire to emphasizing the threadbare fiction that there had been no collusion and no foreknowledge. He might have better pleased at least the majority of his own followers if he had stressed the iniquities of Nasser and the extent to which he had been checked. In this respect he was given a lead by Head who, whether through design or clumsiness, had said on 8 November, 'the Canal cannot and must not be solely the concern of the Egyptian Government. That is what all this has been about.'[107] That Eden did not feel able to do likewise probably sprang from fear of offending high-minded sections of British public opinion. But he should have realized that their respect was now beyond recovery, for his denials of foreknowledge were simply not sufficiently credible. If he wished to survive he now needed to throw off the tattered mask of noble internationalism and seek unambiguously to rally chauvinistic opinion to his side. This might not have prevented the Americans using overwhelming pressure to compel a retreat from Egypt but it would have enabled Eden openly to shift the blame for British humiliation on to Eisenhower. This would of course have been damaging to the cause of Western unity. But it might have strengthened Eden's own chances of political survival and would at least have ensured for him an enduring place in the hearts of the Conservative Right. He might even have launched Great Britain on a 'Gaullist' path ahead of France. As it was, he lacked the ultimate self-confidence to play the populist demagogue. He was thus destined after all to go out with a whimper.

The days after the ceasefire were ones of deep humiliation for Eden. On 7 November he had three telephone conversations with Eisenhower. On the first occasion the President was in a sunny mood. For on the previous day he had not only halted the Anglo-French operation but had also been re-elected President. He therefore readily agreed to Eden's request that he and Mollet be allowed to come at once to Washington. Eisenhower added that 'after all, it is like a family spat'. Eden was delighted with the news. He is said to have spoken at once to Mollet and stressed the wisdom of his decision to call a ceasefire: 'At last we can breathe again ... The spectacular re-establishment of a united Anglo-Franco-American front will offset the effect of the ceasefire. Our policy was sound.'[108] But within hours the President changed his mind. He was undoubtedly made aware by advisers in both the White House and the State Department that receiving the two 'aggressor' leaders would have a disastrous effect on American standing at the United Nations. He first telephoned Eden to ask whether possible disagreements about the character of UNEF might not lead them into 'a bad spot if we had to have a divided communiqué'. Eden's attempts to reassure him failed. For half an hour later Eisenhower called up again with a clear decision that the meeting could not take place. According to a writer who later interviewed Eden, 'this was the rebuff that wounded him most in the wake of the Suez débâcle'.[109]

Eden was reluctant to accept Eisenhower's *volte face*. In the ensuing days and weeks he repeatedly tried to get the decision reversed. But he only succeeded in further irritating the President. On the evening of his rebuff he sent a pleading telegram which only brought the reply that 'United Nations resolutions must first be carried out'. Four days later Eden tried again: 'M. Guy Mollet has told me of the letter which he has sent to you and asked me to support his views. As you know mine already I will only add that I am sure it would help the free world as a whole if we could meet as early as your plans allow.' On this message Eisenhower merely scribbled brusquely: 'No answer required.'[110] The President now ceased to have any direct dealings with the Prime Minister and remorselessly set about humiliating him. Probably he resented both the initial attempt to 'bounce' him into an early meeting and the subsequent persistence. But it may also be that he received fuller reports of the treatment of Aldrich and of the extent to which the British, in contrast to the French, were still lying to their ally about collusion with the Israelis. Above all, he now had time to reflect on Eden's ruthless exploitation of his own preoccupation with the Presidential Election – made all the more outrageous in view of the help he had given to Eden in the British General Election of 1955.

The consequence of the President's new attitude was recalled by Aldrich:

I myself was surprised at the vitriolic nature of Eisenhower's reaction to what happened. I think it was unstatesmanlike; indeed I think it was a dreadful thing, the way the United States Government permitted itself to act towards Eden because of pique or petulance ... the President just went off the deep end. He wouldn't have anything further to do with Eden at all. He wouldn't even communicate with him ... The problem was solved in a manner which never has been made public even now, although perhaps some people suspected it at the time ... Salisbury and Rab Butler and Harold Macmillan were willing to discuss with me the situation which had arisen between the United States and Great Britain and I became the channel of communication between them and Washington ... And for the period of time between the attack on Egypt to the time Eden retired and Macmillan became Prime Minister I would say that all important diplomatic exchanges in London between the United States and Great Britain took place between myself and those three members of the Cabinet. The meetings were confidential because it became necessary to by-pass the Prime Minister and the Foreign Secretary. After a few days of this procedure I decided I had to get direct authority from Washington to continue what I was doing, because I was having conferences with those three men that were entirely off the record and I had to assume that if they thought it necessary they would talk to Eden. Eden soon reached the point where he was incapable of assuming responsibility and it was perfectly obvious that he'd have to be superseded.

On another occasion Aldrich, in testimony which was not wholly consistent with that just cited, revealed that Churchill was also drawn into the President's clandestine dealings behind Eden's back:

... most of the relations between Great Britain and the United States, in London, in fact all of them went through me to Churchill. I used to have an appointment with him every Wednesday morning while he had breakfast in bed. Nobody knew anything about it. I finally got to the point where I insisted on having this made official, as far as I was concerned. I was afraid I might be getting into a position where both Dulles and Eden would be terribly upset by the fact that I was having these talks with Churchill.[111]

Some comments on Aldrich's testimony are here appropriate. First, while in some respects an *éminence grise* behind Salisbury, Macmillan and Butler, Churchill, according to a well-placed British source, did not have a central rôle.[112] Secondly, the initiative for the off-the-record conversations came from Washington, not from the three British Ministers.[113] Thirdly, Aldrich's instructions at least initially came from a quarter other than the State Department, presumably the White House. According to a well-placed American source, this irregular procedure caused the Ambassador some worry:

He was, of course, put in an embarrassing situation by the request for total secrecy and off-the-record handling of the conversations. In fact, despite his generally calm and collected nature, even in matters of great consequence, I can confirm that he seemed genuinely nervous as to where he was personally being led ...[114]

Next, it would seem that Aldrich was in error in supposing that all the off-the-record dealings went through him. This would be to underrate the importance of Humphrey, who had numerous telephone conversations with London. Probably Macmillan and Salisbury dealt primarily with Aldrich, while Butler was the main channel to Humphrey.[115] Finally, consideration must be given to Aldrich's statement that he 'had to assume that if they [the three British Ministers] thought it necessary they would talk to Eden'. Perhaps this 'assumption' was comparable to the one he claimed to have made, 'in spite of every evidence to the contrary', that Lloyd had not 'deliberately misled him'! In any case, testimony from more than one well-placed British source suggests that neither Eden nor Lloyd nor any civil servant learnt about the off-the-record dealings.[116]

Lloyd, though unaware of the way in which he was being by-passed, experienced at first hand the new American attitude when he arrived in New York on 12 November to take charge of the British delegation at the United Nations. He received little encouragement from Lodge and was curtly refused an interview with Eisenhower. On 13 November Eisenhower's Secretary recorded in her diary:

The President heard that Selwyn Lloyd wanted to see him. He said of course Mr Lloyd should see the Acting Secretary [Hoover], but remarked incidentally that he did think the State Department had a completely exaggerated view of the meaning that could be attached to seeing old friends. He said that the British and the French were trying to push the three-power meeting on the basis of planning for counteraction against the Soviets in the Middle East, forgetting that the Arabs thus would be greatly antagonized.

Colonel [Andrew] Goodpaster brought to the President's attention an article by Crosby Noyes, which apparently was written on information from the French Embassy, which suggests that the British and French are already in direct recriminations against one another as a result of the Suez affair. The President said that it had always been true that the British and French could not get along whenever they tried to combine forces, and he cited their animosity in World War II. Apparently there is a story to the effect that Eden told the French that Nasser would give up when news of the attack began, also he would give up when bombing began.[117]

Encouraged by these rumours of an Anglo-French rift, Eisenhower now made clear that his allies must withdraw unconditionally from Egypt. They would not be allowed to participate in or determine the composition of the UNEF; nor to clear the Canal; nor to bargain their withdrawal against a settlement of the original Canal dispute. To achieve this purpose Eisenhower had two instruments at hand: refusal of financial support for the ailing pound and denial of emergency supplies of oil which, following the closure of the Canal and the blowing up of various pipe-lines in the Middle East, were much needed both in France and Great Britain, where petrol rationing had had to be imposed. Economic sanctions were to be imposed but not proclaimed. Usually unsuccessful, they were decisive in coercing London. But perhaps this was in part because Eden faced more severe domestic difficulties than Mussolini or even Ian Smith. Above all, Macmillan. Butler and Salisbury had in effect deserted him. Even the Soviets were unable at this period to coerce the Hungarians other than by the use of armed force. In the British case, however, economic sanctions alone, as stated, sufficed to produce results for the overbearing superpower.

Eden, in a state of exhaustion and shock, allowed his colleagues to take the main responsibility for presenting to Parliament and to the country the disagreeable terms of capitulation. For on 21 November, citing doctors' advice, he announced that two days later he would fly, together with his wife, to Jamaica for a prolonged holiday at the home of Ian Fleming – a choice that occasioned much wry comment. He left Butler in nominal charge. On the eve of his departure, Bracken wrote to Beaverbrook:

This Government is, as you know, in a hell of a mess. Eden's illness is not diplomatic; he is suffering from exhaustion. But this doesn't affect his resolution and obstinacy.

Until a week ago [sic] Macmillan, whose bellicosity was beyond description, was wanting to tear Nasser's scalp out with his own finger nails ... Today he might be described as the leader of the bolters. His Treasury officials have put before him the economic consequences of the Suez fiasco and his feet are frost-bitten. You will remember that only ten days ago he declared that the financial cost of the Suez

Canal operation would be small. He now finds that it will probably wreck his credit restriction policy, as the cost of living is bound to go up through increases in commodity prices and transport costs. Furthermore there is a desperate shortage of diesel oil. Unless we can get supplies long distance buses ... will have to be laid up. But this is only one of many shortages that have impelled our Ministers to contemplate giving in to the United Nations' demand that they should bundle our troops out of Egypt without ceremony and in the face of the jeering minions of Nasser.

The Government may bring themselves to do this, but if they do there will be a tremendous yell of rage from a large section of the public which always wanted to scrag Nasser ... A big abstention in any Suez decision would bring down Eden's government as quickly as Chamberlain's was brought down.

The Government haven't yet decided to bolt ... But under Butler's chairmanship they are a dithering lot ...[118]

It is right to add, however, that Bracken's testimony at this period was not invariably reliable for he was not in a position to be aware of the full picture.[119]

Meanwhile Eden's lieutenants had made considerable progress in ingratiating themselves with Eisenhower. A White House record of a telephone conversation of 19 November between the President and Aldrich is eloquent:

Regarding the message he [Aldrich] sent after seeing Harold Macmillan [on the previous day] – the guess that Aldrich made is correct.

The President said he did not recall it just this second. (Later, we learned it was in the State Department, but not immediately delivered to the White House.)

Ambassador Aldrich said he guessed there was going to be a change. Will sent a message right off, giving President the details. He said Harold Macmillan is terribly anxious to see the President as soon as possible, but will spell that out too in his message.[120]

The gist of Aldrich's message may be gathered from a record of a telephone conversation between the President and Hoover:

The President inquired about the message to which Ambassador Aldrich referred. Mr Hoover received it today, said a copy was on its way over to Col. Goodpaster.

The 'guess' is that the Cabinet is completely to be reshuffled, and that Eden is going out because of sickness ...

Mr Hoover said it is very interesting, in that they [the British] are putting propositions up to us. They will either have to withdraw from Egypt and have their Cabinet fall – or else they will have to renew hostilities, taking over entire Canal. Mr Hoover's comment 'Obviously things are very much in the making there. I think this is one time to sit tight awaiting his [Aldrich's] further information.'[121]

Possibly the threat to resume hostilities was a final hesitant flirtation with a 'Gaullist' response on Eden's part, for, after his departure to Jamaica, nothing more was heard of it. But it is also possible that the Americans were being tacitly asked by Butler and Macmillan to lift economic sanctions and to secure tolerable terms from Egypt in return for a promise to capitulate to the United Nations and maybe also to overthrow Eden. Certainly on the following day, 20 November, the President appeared to believe that a bargain was possible – but one with Macmillan and Butler rather than Eden. His secretary recorded in her diary:

> Back in the office at 5.14 he had an appointment with Hoover and Humphrey regarding, primarily, the economic distress of the British Government. He called Ambassador Aldrich and gave him instructions to get in touch with Butler and MacMillan [sic] simultaneously, and tell them that they would have the necessary support from us. I think this means financial aid during the next couple of months.[122]

A White House summary of the conversation between Eisenhower and Aldrich reads:

PRESIDENT: We have been getting your messages, and I want to make an inquiry. You are dealing with at least one person – maybe two or three – on a very personal basis. Is it possible for you, without embarrassment, to get together the two you mentioned in one of your messages?

ALDRICH: Yes, one of them I have just been playing bridge with. Perhaps I can stop him.

PRESIDENT: I'd rather you talk to both together. You know who I mean? One has the same name as my predecessor at Columbia University Presidency [Butler]; the other was with me in the war [Macmillan].

ALDRICH: I know the one with you in the war. Oh yes, now I've got it.

PRESIDENT: Could you get them informally and say of course we are interested and sympathetic, and as soon as things happen that we anticipate, we can furnish 'a lot of fig leaves'.

ALDRICH: I certainly can say that.

PRESIDENT: Will that be enough to get the boys moving?

ALDRICH: I think it will be.

PRESIDENT: Herb [Hoover] probably will send you a cable later tonight. You see, we don't want to be in a position of interfering between those two [Butler and Macmillan]. But we want to have you personally tell them. They are both good friends.

ALDRICH: Yes, very much so. Have you seen all my messages? Regarding my conversations with them all?

PRESIDENT: Yes, – with at least two.

ALDRICH: That is wonderful. I will do this tomorrow?

PRESIDENT: Yes, first thing in the morning.

ALDRICH: I shall certainly do it. And I will then communicate with you at once. I can do it without the slightest embarrassment.

PRESIDENT: Communicate through regular channels – through Herb.[123]

What did Eisenhower have in view by 'things' happening 'that we anticipate'? That they may have included Eden's fall is suggested by a note in his secretary's diary for 23 November: 'Indications growing that Anthony Eden will not return as Prime Minister; he is off to Jamaica for a rest.' Even more eloquent is the record of a telephone conversation involving Eisenhower, Humphrey and Hoover on 26 November:

HUMPHREY: ... we got Rab [Butler] on the telephone ... He told a couple of encouraging things, and some suspicious. One encouraging thing: He was very grateful for picking up right where we left off. The principal thing he wanted was time. He said he has a difficult situation, and, if we could just not interfere with him – not have any more resolutions – he would appreciate it very much indeed. He wound up by saying we would hear from him as soon as he could get his affairs arranged.
   A bad thing: (And Herb was on the phone too; but can't decide whether this was for the record.) He said he had great confidence in Kasha [sic – Caccia, the new British Ambassador]. Also he heard from Anthony who had a good trip over. He then said he would carry on under those circumstances. (The President feels all this was for the record, since he was on the phone.)
   We have now reported back to Foster. He argues the thing for us to do is to keep our shirts on for a little bit. Herb will talk to Cabot [Lodge] and tell him to be as careful as he can, to let things rest for a few days now. They know exactly what our real attitude is – they now have it in their background.[124]

This record confirms Aldrich's testimony that Eisenhower wished to deal only with selected British personalities and that Lloyd and Caccia were not among them. It also suggests that Butler's apparent reference to Eden 'carrying on' was seen as a 'bad thing' by Eisenhower. Moreover, the President evidently saw Butler's line about Eden as inconsistent with views he had expressed on an earlier occasion. For otherwise Eisenhower and his two associates could have had no grounds for speculating whether Butler was speaking 'for the record, since he was on the phone'. Thus Butler, Macmillan and Salisbury must be presumed to have been seen in Washington as essentially disloyal to Eden. And they probably had the backing of Churchill who began to exchange private messages with Eisenhower on 23 November, the day of Eden's departure for Jamaica.[125] The way was now open for Eisenhower to seek someone in London prepared to play a rôle somewhat analogous to that of János Kádar in the aftermath of the Soviet invasion of Hungary. The President may well have considered that there was no apparent shortage of candidates.

It seems certain that Eden knew little or nothing of his colleagues' initial dealings with the Americans. Otherwise he would not have gone to Jamaica. He could not, for example, possibly have supposed that Washington would be led to believe that he would not return as Prime Minister. But this almost certainly happened. Humphrey's report on his conversation with Butler has already been noted. In addition, there is the testimony of a well-placed American source who was privy to Aldrich's communications with Washington: '... it was my definite understanding that when Eden took his first trip to Jamaica, there was no intention that he would return as Prime Minister. It was explained that this was an example of tactful British finesse.'[126]

The conduct of Macmillan, Butler and Salisbury may thus seem highly unusual. Whether it was 'unconstitutional is another matter. For, as A. J. P. Taylor has written in another context, 'in our flexible system, any practice is constitutional which is tolerated ...'[127] Of more interest is their motivation. Probably the three Ministers were, in varying degrees, genuinely alarmed at the deplorable condition into which Anglo-American relations had fallen. Even more important may have been the views they held or affected to hold about Eden's state of health, mental no less than physical. Of relevance in this connection are passages written many years later by a distinguished journalist, James Margach. He referred to the Cabinet meeting of 4 November, when for a brief period an Israeli acceptance of a ceasefire appeared imminent, and Butler and Salisbury were led to argue that the projected British landings at Port Said should be abandoned:

> Butler says that the debate 'seemed to nonplus the Prime Minister. He said he must go upstairs to consider his position.' In fact, the scene was much more moving. Eden was emotionally overcome. He broke down in tears and cried: 'You are all deserting me.' He was in total collapse, weeping unashamedly. Then he went upstairs to compose himself. For such is the agony of power when it denies you.[128]

This account is undoubtedly much exaggerated.[129] But that so experienced a journalist could take seriously gossip about a Prime Minister weeping in the Cabinet is itself revealing. It suggests that the three Ministers were able to justify their conduct to themselves and to one another in part on the grounds that Eden's mental condition, though not yet critical, might deteriorate and that he was in any case unlikely to be able either, on the one hand, to stand up effectively to the United States or, on the other hand, to give decisive orders to surrender to her. Their behaviour towards their highly strung chief may thus be to some extent explicable.

On 24 November the UN General Assembly passed by 63 votes to 5 a resolution censuring Great Britain and France and demanding the immediate withdrawal of their forces from Egypt. A Belgian amendment intended to delete the censure and permit gradual withdrawal was defeated by 37 votes to 23. Lodge abstained on the amendment and voted for the substantive resolution. This was of decisive importance, for if the Americans had supported the amendment they would no doubt have carried with them a sufficient number of their tame supporters to ensure its adoption. The President privately came to regret Lodge's move but he took no step to show remorse in his dealings with his allies in the ensuing days: unconditional compliance with UN resolutions remained his demand. In London Butler and Macmillan decided to yield despite the tabling of a Commons motion by over 100 Conservative MPs censuring the United States 'which is gravely endangering the Atlantic Alliance'. American aid was judged to be an overwhelming necessity, a case which Macmillan, once so bellicose, was now only too willing to canvass. The Chancellor recalled:

On the more immediate issues the American Government was now ready to assist us. It was, of course, a little wounding to feel that we were to be given a 'reward' for our submission to American pressure. Nevertheless, I was not foolish enough to refuse, even though the conditions were somewhat distasteful.[130]

One of the 'somewhat distasteful' conditions, tacitly or otherwise, may well have been the early departure of Eden. Another was certainly that the withdrawal of forces from Port Said would be carried out without delay. Lloyd informed the Commons on 3 December that this must happen and the operation was duly completed by 23 December.

Eden continued to rest in Jamaica. He acquiesced by telegram in the withdrawal of British troops. But he was still unaware of the dire threat to his leadership now materializing. On 7 December Bracken reported to Beaverbrook:

Macmillan is telling journalists that he intends to retire from politics and go to the morgue. He declares that he will never serve under Butler. His real intentions are to push his boss out of No. 10 and he has a fair following in the Tory Party. The so-called Canal die-hards think better of him than they do of Eden or Butler.

Eden has no intention of giving up No. 10. I should say he was the least rattled of all his Ministers. He writes cheerful letters from Jamaica and doesn't seem the least perturbed by all the storms that blow over him. There is nothing wrong with him physically, but he was very tired, hence his holiday.

If it was a mistake for him to go away at the present time (and I now think it probably was) I was one of the people who advised him to go. It shows you how poor an adviser I am! But as he told me that he fully intends to brazen this out, I thought he might as well get physically fit before facing the litter of problems that lie ahead.[131]

On his return to London on 14 December, however, Eden may not have received the support to which he felt entitled. According to Bracken:

Eden returned in high spirits which lasted for a few hours because scarcely had he arrived in Downing Street than a deputation led by Salisbury and Butler informed him that, while the Cabinet were willing to carry on under his leadership until

Easter, if it was then clear that his health was not fully restored they felt that a new head of Government would be necessary. If Churchill had had such a greeting from his colleagues he would have told them to go to the furthermost part of hell, but as you know very well, Eden has none of Churchill's pugnacity.[132]

But this cold reception alone was not enough to destroy Eden's resolve. Even more important was the attitude of his backbenchers. For he made two speeches on 18 and 20 December that were not attuned to the prevailing mood. On the first occasion he addressed the 1922 Committee. He was closely questioned, in particular, by Nigel Nicolson about his telling 'half truths' relating to alleged collusion and about his failure to invoke the Tripartite Declaration. On 'half truths' Eden offered a bland reply: 'Some – and if they existed at all, they were not serious or many in number – were necessary, and always are, in this sort of operation which demands extreme secrecy in its operation.' But on the Tripartite Declaration he was reduced to replying: 'I will have to look up your point about the Americans and the Tripartite Declaration. I haven't got it in my head.'[133] His second speech was to the Commons. He was first drawn into telling worse than a 'half truth', saying that 'there were no plans to get together to attack Egypt'. Later he added: '... there was not foreknowledge that Israel would attack Egypt.' But equally fatally he ended his speech, destined to be his last in the Commons, with these words: '... I would be compelled ... if I had the same very disagreeable decisions to take again, to repeat them.'[134] This was not what most of his followers wanted to hear. He obviously had not grasped the degree to which the premature ceasefire and the withdrawal of troops were now being regretted. This had been a final opportunity both to drop the pretence that his action had been designed to separate the combatants and also to blame the Americans for the subsequent British humiliation. In thus failing to modify his line he left himself at the mercy of his Cabinet colleagues and his relentless adversaries in Washington. He survived for less than three more weeks.

On 9 January 1957 Eden informed his Cabinet that ill-health had caused him to tender his resignation to the Queen. That he was not fully fit is beyond question. That he would have had to resign sooner rather than later is suggested by his subsequent medical history. But that he needed to quit so soon after the Suez débâcle has not been proved. For he was not compelled immediately to enter hospital but was able on 18 January to commence a long sea voyage to New Zealand. He had, moreover, even if pronounced unfit by his doctors, every incentive to struggle on in office for at least a few more months if only to establish that he had been able successfully to 'brazen out' the Suez crisis. There must therefore remain a suspicion that he was indeed a victim of Eisenhower's search for a compliant 'Kádár'. A series of letters between Bracken and Beaverbrook provides a clue:

23 January 1957 – Bracken to Beaverbrook
The main reason for Eden's departure is not the one circulated by politicians and the press. The reason is political, but as it involves a secret stuffed with dynamite I can't put it in a letter. This seems melodramatic but, alas, it is only too true and you will agree when you hear it. If Eden had been of tougher fibre he could, I am sure, have brazened it out.

29 January 1957 – Beaverbrook to Bracken
I can guess from your mention of political secrets, stuffed with dynamite, just what occurred. Political assassination has become a habit in Great Britain, for, of course, Churchill himself was a victim.

4 February 1957 –Bracken to Beaverbrook
The 'dynamite' I mentioned in my last letter is collusion, not assassination by colleagues. They were willing, of course, to stab. But our friend brought himself down and needless remorse unnerved him. Secret this![135]

It may well be that after his speech to the Commons of 20 December Eden feared that his mendacity would soon be exposed. For the broad facts of the British part in the collusion with Israel were now known in Washington as well as among a growing circle of potential critics at home. Moreover, Mollet and Pineau were being increasingly frank in telling their own compatriots that the real aims of the enterprise had been to capture the Canal and overthrow Nasser. Given that he was unwilling to speak with similar candour, Eden's early retirement was inevitable, for too many of his enemies were in a position at any time to reveal the true facts. Yet would he not equally have had to quit if he had belatedly imitated Mollet and Pineau? True, his French co-conspirators were not pilloried for behaving dis-honourably but only for failing to achieve their objectives – and other countries could be blamed for this. But three prosperous decades of high-minded posturing in British politics may have convinced Eden that large numbers of his compatriots would have reacted differently to the French. Could he possibly have hoped to survive, if, for example, it had become known that, despite the disclaimers of 'foreknowledge' and 'collusion', Lloyd had actually met Ben-Gurion at Sèvres only a week before the Israeli attack on Egypt? The fate of Hoare in 1935 provided a chilling precedent. Thus the reasoning that had originally led him to adopt a devious scenario in preference to a 'straight bash' may now have caused him to calculate that. lest worse befall, he must now quit on grounds of ill-health and thereafter refuse to elaborate on his implausible story. Given the attitude towards him of so many of his Cabinet colleagues, not to mention that of Mountbatten with his royal connections, he may have been wise.

XII

The Last Years

1957–77

After resigning the premiership Eden, accompanied by his wife, at once set out on a cruise. This took him to New Zealand via the West Indies. At first, despite short bouts of fever, he was hopeful that his health would recover. As he wrote to Bracken from New Zealand on 26 March:

Physically I am much better already. There has however been some trouble with these fevers. Cattell – who operated on me in Boston – has had the symptoms fully described to him by the Auckland doctor ... Cattell says he has no doubt fever is caused by *temporary* obstruction of bile duct, i.e. contraption he put in is not functioning perfectly. That it is only temporary is shown by short duration of fevers. Cattell wants to see me and rest here meanwhile. This seems to make sense, so we sail from here to Vancouver on 3 May, cross Canada by train, more restful for Clarissa to see the country, and fall in Cattell's clutches about the last week in May. I hate having to go to US just now, but it would be little use getting strong and then being knocked out by a bout of fever every two or three weeks. Cattell hopes an operation will not be necessary, so devoutly do we.[1]

This hope was quickly dashed. For on seeing his patient, who had to journey to Boston earlier than he had initially intended, Cattell decreed he must operate at once. Moreover, after the operation had been carried out on 14 April, Cattell's prognosis for the future was sombre. Clarissa Eden wrote to Beaverbrook on 18 May:

I think I ought to tell you a little about Anthony's health.

He was so exhausted and ravaged by the fevers which began last October, that he didn't have a fair start. However, as you know, he took the operation very well, and made a model recovery – but of course now he is terribly enfeebled and has relapses when he really feels like hell.

The doctors say they cannot predict if and when the same complaint will not start again. They think it pretty well inevitable that it will – maybe in months, maybe years.

When it does, the operation will have to be repeated. They say he will only be capable of leading a very quiet life, because of this threat.

At the moment, he will feel too weak to wish for anything else – and I suppose for months to come.[2]

Four days later she sent a further message:

What I meant to say in my last letter was that it looks as if – at least for some time –

Anthony will have to remain out of things. I think we owe it to you to tell you this – because you have been wonderful in supporting and helping him – and I wanted you to know the truth.[3]

Eden was now anxious to return home. Above all, he did not wish to stay in the United States longer than absolutely necessary, for he was acutely conscious of the political inappropriateness of his presence at a time when Macmillan was labouring hard to restore the 'special relationship'. To make matters worse, Dulles felt obliged to offer to visit Eden in hospital. This forced Eden to claim that he was too sick to receive anyone and would be spending his convalescence in Canada.[4] As he later wrote to Dixon:

I was so very sorry not to see you in Boston but I was very grateful for your offer to come. The trouble was that if I opened the door to any single visitor I would have had to see all who offered, including Foster Dulles – rather exhausting for a sick man![5]

Yet returning home also had its problems. On 23 January Beaverbrook had written to Eden:

Fear nothing for the future. Time will vindicate you. And when you return to London you will be received with gratitude and affection by the citizens.

But could this really be counted on? Clarissa Eden wrote doubtfully on 22 May:

Perhaps we are returning to England too soon? But I don't think we could go wandering round any longer, and we must sooner or later see how the land lies at home.[6]

In the event the Edens' return was largely a non-event. Neither plaudits nor abuse awaited them. They were allowed simply to retire to their cottage at Broade Chalke near Salisbury. Later in the same summer Beaverbrook lent them his home in Somerset, Cricket Malherbie – the first of many acts of personal kindness by one whom his biographer described as a 'foul-weather friend' to Eden.[7]

In the ensuing months and years Beaverbrook encouraged Eden to believe that his Suez policies had been sound and that a grateful nation would presently insist on his return. It is unclear whether this was a genuinely held opinion or whether he was consciously seeking to bolster the self-confidence of a sick and inevitably dispirited friend. On 24 March 1958, for example, Beaverbrook wrote to Eden, 'You will be back again in Whitehall where you are needed. The leaders of the Party have wrecked it. A task of reconstruction awaits you.' Eden replied, 'Thank you for what you write about politics. I can never shed what has been my life interest, but I cannot see how my part can be lively while these wretched attacks still lay me low every other week.' Eden thus only gradually came to terms with the permanence of his ill-health and with the absence of real evidence that he would ever receive the call of a grateful nation. But during the next few years the Edens' domestic arrangements became more settled. They first moved in 1958 to a larger house, namely Donhead House near Shaftesbury and then, a year later, to Fifield Manor at Pewsey in Wiltshire. They also began to spend their winters abroad. They went during the winter of 1959 to Acapulco, in 1960 to Antigua and finally in 1961 acquired a permanent home off St Vincent. Eden sent to Beaverbrook an idyllic picture of life on his island retreat:

> We ... like our new home very much, despite the difficulties of obtaining all supplies over a rough sea journey of nine miles from a not very well provided St Vincent.
> The weather is near perfect, the bathing is the best we have known anywhere, a little on the rough side, but we both prefer it that way.[8]

Another vital step for Eden in accepting that his life in active politics might well be over came with his decision, during 1958, to write lengthy and detailed political memoirs. The project finally ran to three volumes, two having originally been planned. The work occupied much of his time between 1958 and 1964. On Beaverbrook's advice he chose, probably unwisely, to work first on the 1950s. Thus *Full Circle* appeared as early as 1960. It is much the least satisfactory of his three volumes, though maybe also the most unconsciously revealing. Inevitably the level of documentation had to be restricted and many of the judgements suffered from too close proximity to the events. The treatment of Suez was naturally the section to which reviewers gave most attention. In this respect his account had the twin demerits, as has been seen, of lacking frankness about 'collusion' while simultaneously containing many somewhat unqualified verdicts on personalities. If he had written this volume in proper sequence, or, better still, left it until the late 1960s or beyond, he would have had to take more account of the revelations about 'collusion', which gradually became too numerous for him to have been able to ignore. And he might have found it easier to soften some of the more ephemeral expressions of rage at individual shortcomings which mar *Full Circle* much more than his other volumes. Above all, he might have arrived at a more equitable assessment of the relative delinquencies of Dulles and Eisenhower, for the President, still in office, escaped almost unscathed in *Full Circle*. But he would no doubt have argued that *Full Circle* was a vital tract for the times in a much more immediate sense than applied to his other volumes: the world could not wait for his message and, in any case, who could say how long he might live. Whatever the contemporary merits of these arguments, historians will surely judge his other volumes, *Facing the Dictators* and *The Reckoning*, by different standards and it seems likely that they will stand high among the political memoirs of the twentieth century. Perhaps not memorable for wit or style, they nevertheless have a solidity and a sombre spaciousness worthy of a politician of the first rank.

Memoir-writing certainly served to distract Eden from brooding unduly on the chances of a political comeback. But it was probably not until 1961 that he finally abandoned hope that he might return to the Commons. For only then did he decide, despite freedom from fever since 1959, to accept the earldom traditionally available to former Prime Ministers. Something of the anguish involved is apparent from letters received by Beaverbrook:

5 May 1961 – Clarissa Eden to Beaverbrook
... I am delighted you think Anthony should be an Earl. He feels it will be the irrevocable step – because he always thinks in the back of his mind that the miracle will happen and he will be well enough to go back to politics – which, of course, he won't.

3 July 1961 – Eden to Beaverbrook
In my last letter I mentioned that I had been giving further thought to joining the House of Lords ... I have now decided to go ahead and take the step. Had I been strong enough, I would have preferred to go back to the Commons, but I am quite sure that I am not and so is Clarissa, and what matters more, so are the doctors. This is not caution for fear of getting ill but simply the fact that I am sure my strength would not last for more than a few weeks. I do not propose to attend with any regularity, but I might make a speech or two there a year and do the same in the country ...[9]

Eden's evident hopes that he might stage a comeback clearly contain an element of pathos. But in having what might be termed a 'Chatham complex' he was not particularly exceptional. For such illusions are notoriously common among former Prime Ministers.

Eden was accordingly enobled as the Earl of Avon. He took his seat in the Lords on 26 July and spoke there occasionally in the ensuing years. Perhaps for the first time this restless and somewhat vulnerable figure could relax and come fully to terms with the life of a retired country gentleman. Unfortunately, however, fevers returned late in 1961 and were to haunt him for the rest of his life. Nor was he free from other ailments. In March 1962, for example, he had to have a growth removed from his chest. Yet during his remaining years he achieved a serenity of a kind. Devotedly cared for by his wife, he maintained a lively interest in domestic and international politics. And he could look back on a life of extraordinary interest and glamour, even if personal tragedies and restless temperament had not always allowed him to enjoy it to the full. In retirement, too, he consciously kept in good repair a limited number of intimate friendships. He did not, on the other hand, greatly miss London social life. For, as Randolph Churchill wrote, 'He is not at all what Dr Johnson called a "clubbable man". He is seldom seen in the smoking room in the House of Commons and except for his immediate entourage, much prefers the company of young men and women to that of his contemporaries.'[10] Yet to a favoured few Avon offered great charm. As Nigel Fisher recalled:

Although his whole life had been devoted to politics, it was by no means his only interest. He was a man of culture, well read and a delightful companion. He had beautiful manners and was the most courteous and considerate of men. Many who worked with him were struck by his concern for other people's feelings, and by his remarkable capacity for remembering names and faces, often long after the incident with which they were associated in his mind. Those who knew him best loved him deeply.

Another friend was Cecil Beaton, the photographer. He described in his diary for June 1967 how Avon marked his seventieth birthday:

There was quite an extraordinary atmosphere of joy and celebration in the pretty Georgian house at Alvediston that Clarissa and Anthony have recently bought. Despite his plastic duct and continuous fever, Anthony had reached seventy. It was his birthday and the events of last week [Israel's victory over Egypt] were a wonderful present. They have meant that, in principle, Anthony's much-criticized policy on Suez, and his distrust of Nasser, were correct. Clarissa, generally so cold and reserved, admitted this evening that she was 'stewed'. She was enchanting in her gaiety and, in an aside of happiness, said: 'I never thought Anthony would live long enough to see himself proved right.'

Anthony, sunburnt and wearing a marrow-coloured velvet dinner-suit, seemed the picture of health and radiance. He was surrounded by his loyal confrères, and a few members of his family. Bobbety Salisbury made a speech that was eulogistic but neither embarrassing nor sentimental. Oliver Lyttelton, whose desire to amuse has increased with the years to the extent that he is a real bore, made one funny joke. The evening was a great success. A surprising group: the Lambtons motored from London; Lord Scarborough came from Yorkshire; Nicholas and other young Edens; Lord Brooke; Ronnie Tree; Anthony and Dot Head and the Hoffs (Raimund von Hoffmannstahl and his wife Lady Elizabeth).

Nicholas handed round tulip-shaped glasses of Elizabethan Kümmel! This was real dynamite ... Bottles of champagne popped, and the gathering was very English, understated and poignant.[11]

Retirement, too, enabled Avon to devote attention to hobbies, old and new. Late in 1961 he decided to become a breeder of Hereford cattle. As he wrote to Beaverbrook, 'The Herefords are of course a gamble. If we are fortunate to breed anything worthwhile we shall recoup what we spend. If not, the beasts will go as beef, but I have been lucky enough to find a good man and I thought we would both have more fun this way.'[12] The experiment proved a success. And he was later, in 1970, delighted to be awarded a silver medal for breeding the best Hereford bull.[13]

Avon also took an increasing interest in the affairs of the University of

Birmingham of which he was Chancellor from 1945 to 1973. He duly charged the university with responsibility for preserving after his death his considerable collection of papers, which are now to be found in the university library, ironically placed in close proximity to those of his great adversary, Neville Chamberlain.

Apart from producing his political memoirs, Avon also wrote occasional pieces for newspapers and journals. In 1961, for example, he published in *Foreign Affairs*, the prestigious American quarterly, an article entitled 'The Slender Margin of Safety',[14] an appeal for 'Free World Unity': no doubt an ironic theme to the many Americans who judged him to have destroyed it in 1956. Again, in 1966 he wrote a short essay for Chatham House entitled *Towards Peace in Indochina*. Here he reverted to some of the ideas current in 1954. Above all, his message was that the Great Powers should 'guarantee the territories and the neutrality of Laos and Cambodia, offering the same option to South and North Vietnam'. He explained: 'the guarantees to be offered to North and South Vietnam, Laos and Cambodia should be joint and several, on the Locarno model, the guarantors having the right in certain conditions to act without waiting for unanimity should the terms of the agreement be violated'.[15] This scheme, needless to say, proved no more practical in the late 1960s than any of the other abortive proposals launched from many quarters. Avon's last publication was a delightful evocation of his early years, entitled *Another World*.[16] Casting aside the leaden prose and formal documentation of his volumes of political autobiography, he now showed an ability to write with charm and grace. His friends had always known that he possessed a lightness of touch usually concealed from the public. McDonald of *The Times*, for example, recalled: 'The gallant Sir Galahad of the public image frequently spoke heavily and often prosaically when on the platform whereas the hard-working professional spoke lightly, pithily, and with engaging modesty in private.'[17] Now these same qualities were fortunately captured for the public and for posterity in *Another World*.

The years of retirement brought their political trials. For it falls to few men to hold important Cabinet office under forty, to be Prime Minister under sixty and then to live for two full decades while the controversial events of their political lives gradually pass from the realm of current affairs and come up for judgement at various 'bars of history'. Had he been more reflective and whimsical, Avon might have got pleasure from the privilege, denied to most, of seeing what historians were already making of his life and times. But he appears mainly to have found the process irritating. He was, for example, enraged when in the early 1960s A. J. P. Taylor pioneered revisionist reflections in *The Origins of the Second World War* and, more importantly, he did not apparently even find Taylor's analysis intellectually stimulating. He wrote to Emrys-Evans complaining that he could not persuade the BBC to interview him on the contents of his memoirs unless he went to Lime Grove and added: 'But then A. J. P. Taylor, who does so much to encourage a revival of Nazism, is the hero of our TV programmes.'[18]

Still more disturbing for Eden was the flood of sensational revelations about two allegedly 'discreditable' episodes in his career, namely Suez and enforced repatriation. The first major blow came in 1959 with Randolph Churchill's *The Rise and Fall of Sir Anthony Eden*. This was remarkably well-informed on at least some aspects of 'collusion' and accordingly caused much speculation in the press and renewed Opposition calls for formal inquiries. But the damage Randolph Churchill could do to Eden's reputation was limited. For his whole book was marred by petulant and vindictive asides which were widely thought to reveal as much about the author as the subject. Above all, Randolph Churchill's jealousy of his father's long-standing colleague was wholly apparent and it was known in élite circles at least how socially 'impossible' he had been to both Eden and his wife. A much more damaging blow was struck by Nutting in 1967 in *No End of a Lesson*. He had of course resigned as Minister of State at the Foreign Office and had quit Parliament at the height of the Suez crisis but had hitherto offered no detailed justification. Various means may have been used to induce him to keep silent. At the time of the resignation Eden had said to him: *'Tout casse sauf l'amitié*. I hope, in spite of all this, that we shall see something of each other in the future', though in the event he steadily declined ever to meet him again.[19] Moreover, the Beaverbrook press would appear to have deliberately sought to intimidate him by revealing aspects of his private life.[20] By 1967, however, Nutting was ready to break his silence. But the long delay on his part, however honourable and constitutionally correct, deprived him of the chance to shape history. For had his authoritative revelations of 'collusion' come during the 1950s the political consequences would have been incalculable – by 1967 it was already largely a matter for historians. A year earlier, for example, the historian Hugh Thomas, son-in-law of Jebb, who as French Ambassador had been largely ignored during the Suez crisis, skilfully reconstructed the drama with considerable accuracy based on many private interviews and the collation of information that had been steadily appearing both in France and Israel.[21] Now was perhaps the time for Avon to speak out. But the tenth anniversary of the operation came and went with no elaboration on what had appeared in *Full Circle*. Towards the end of his life he had to face still more anxiety when Lloyd expressed his intention to produce a volume on Suez based on privileged access to official documents. This cannot have been particularly welcome to Avon but he could not prevent it. He did not live to see the work appear.

A no less vexatious series of revelations concerned enforced repatriation. The enactment of the Thirty Year rule in the late 1960s placed in the public domain wartime papers which Avon must not hitherto have expected to be made available during his lifetime. In particular, as has been seen, they revealed the ruthless nature of the bargain struck with Stalin during 1944–5. In 1974 Lord Bethell published *The Last Secret*, a sensational account highly critical of Avon personally. There followed a television documentary, press controversy and a debate in the House of Lords. Avon refused to make even the briefest comment. When the issue was before the Lords he was abroad. But his friend and former Parliamentary Private Secretary, Lord Allan of Kilmahew, claimed:

Had he been in this country, I have not the slightest doubt that he would have defied all possible advice and been in his place in your Lordship's Chamber tonight. As it happens, however, he is in America convalescing after a serious illness, and even then he considered making a special effort to get back for this debate, but was dissuaded from doing so.[22]

But this does not seem wholly plausible. For while he might have been insufficiently fit to attend Parliament he was certainly lucid enough to have granted interviews in his home. Indeed, he later made a lengthy television programme with Kenneth Harris of the BBC about his wartime recollections. But *The Last Secret* was simply ignored. It is not to be doubted that he was deeply hurt by the almost unanimous tone of moralistic outrage that arose in the media coverage. There were of course lines of defence open to him. But he might have found the kind of justification offered, for example, in the present volume almost more wounding to his self-image than some of the attacks. Probably, then, he saw silence as the only dignified and appropriate response. Yet it is ironic that the politician who had made so much of his reputation as a high-minded crusader in international affairs should have been haunted at the end of his life by shrill accusations that he had in effect committed a crime against humanity on a scale unmatched by any modern British statesman.

During the two decades of his retirement Avon clearly had little influence on the course of events. His successors in Downing Street did not see him as an elder statesman to be constantly consulted; and the managers of the Conservative Party made little attempt to associate him with their proceedings and campaigns. Yet his private opinions, expressed to close friends, may be thought to provide some guide to the essential philosophy and outlook which more than three decades in politics had fashioned. It is thus of some interest to the biographer. Such evidence as is at present available – much of it in the Beaverbrook Papers – reveals, above all, that he reverted in old age to the rather right-wing views with which he had entered politics in the 1920s. His life-style, too, was somewhat 'patrician'. For example, accompanied by his wife, he took a holiday in Antonio Salazar's 'reactionary' Portugal and could write afterwards without fashionable shame: 'We enjoyed Portugal very much and liked food, wine and people, and the general atmosphere of a hundred years ago.' It is not easy to reconcile this attitude of mind with that of the wartime 'progressive', whose then closest adviser had written disapprovingly of the United States that it was 'far more old-fashioned and anti-Russian than Great Britain – a hundred years behind us in social evolution'.[23] Avon's sympathy with 'liberal' causes was now scant. He was largely unmoved by rhetoric about strengthening the United Nations, decolonization, reversing the arms race and ending the exploitation of the Third World. He wanted to see the advanced countries of the West defend their interests in what he saw as an increasingly threatening world. He was at least as opposed to upstart dictators in the Third World as to the Communist autocrats in Moscow and Peking. Often he expressed deeply pessimistic views about the long-term future of the West and at times made short-term apocalyptic prophesies which, like those of most people, were more often wrong than right. Understandably, he foresaw particularly disastrous developments in the Middle East – at least in Nasser's lifetime. At times events appeared to justify his views. For example, in 1958 the Americans were compelled to intervene in the Lebanon; and the pro-British regime in Iraq was overthrown with his old friend, Nuri, brutally murdered. Yet Nasser did not in the event become quite the rampaging conqueror that he had at times appeared to fear. And even the Soviet presence in Egypt proved transient: Avon lived to see Nasser's successor, Anwar Sadat, expel the Soviets and align Egypt with the West. Again, the nationalization of the Suez Canal did not in itself prove disastrous. It was eventually to be closed again but as a result of the 1967 war, not Egyptian incompetence or anti-Western malice. In any case the second closure scarcely mattered. For larger tankers had been brought into service which were able to keep oil supplies flowing to the West by the Cape route. Only in the 1970s did the actions of the Organization of Petroleum Exporting Countries seem to bear out Avon's fears about oil supplies for the West. True, few in 1973 believed that his action in 1956 had much relevance. But his defenders will no doubt continue to claim that his policies concerning both Iran and Suez constituted a prophetic warning to the West that it might one day be crippled if it failed to guard its energy supplies. On 1 June 1956, for example, he declared: 'No oil, unemployment and hunger in Britain. It is as simple as that today.'[24]

Avon's pessimism, however, was not confined to the West's position in the Middle East. Most of all, he feared the consequences of continuing American pressure for rapid European decolonization. Samples of his thinking may be gleaned from extracts from letters to Beaverbrook:

April 1958
... I have the deepest sympathy with the French ... The trouble is that the Americans in their hearts, or rather those who are in control in Washington today,

are anti-colonial and do not really think that the French ought to be in Algeria, yet if Nasser is established there the flank of NATO is turned.

6 August 1958

I do not like what I read of Lebanon and Jordan and talk of withdrawal of American forces from Lebanon on a request which the new president will make as soon as he has a chance. These sudden gusts of improvization, which with Dulles pass for policy, are disastrous for the West. If this is one more of them, there will not be much left in the Middle East.

As for Cyprus, I do not think it has paid off to release Makarios without the promise on which we had previously insisted, that he should condemn violence. I think that Salisbury was right about this, but this letter is becoming a dirge.

16 January 1961

The world news I read as little as I can; it seems uniformly disagreeable. It is the age of triumph for the small bullies. The Queen, I read, is to see Makarios, on her way to India. I am only glad that the advice is not to see Nasser, who would no doubt ask for the Crown Jewels, when HMG would hastily comply with apologies for keeping them so long ... every good wish for 1961. May at least one bully get a bloody nose, but I don't expect so.

29 May 1961

... it seems that the fighting in Angola has been far heavier than I at least had understood. The African position darkens steadily yet we seem as far as ever from any agreed Western policy, which must make life unnecessarily comfortable for Khrushchev.

22 October 1962

The Chinese pressure on India will continue. The Communists did not capture Tibet for the scenery. Their purpose was the same as Mussolini's when he seized Albania, to dominate his southern neighbour, and Mao is a good deal more formidable than Mussolini ... I find Arabia intriguing. Nasser played the same part in Yemen as a few years ago in Baghdad. He wants, from a base in Yemen, to threaten Aden and infiltrate Saudi Arabia where lies the American oil he wants to control through a rebel Saudi Government. As we cannot defend the Persian Gulf without Aden, the stakes are high. Nasser may not have the means, but his opponents will have to be watchful and firm. Much hope of this?

16 December 1963

In international affairs I still deeply mistrust [Achmed] Sukarno, who is bent on destroying our friends in Malaysia. The Americans have some responsibility for this dangerous situation by the actions they took with UNO in forcing the Dutch out of Western New Guinea. This was an unscrupulous performance and has whetted Sukarno's already greedy appetite.[25]

In Conservative politics Avon's rôle was minimal. But he did take an interest in the replacement of Macmillan in 1963. He and Beaverbrook corresponded on the prospects in July 1963:

21 July 1963 – Avon to Beaverbrook
The Parliamentary Party appears to call for new leadership before the next General Election. In this I judge that it is right ...

Among the candidates, I prefer Quintin [Lord Hailsham] for courage and robustness and Enoch Powell for his flame of faith. But the second has not sufficient experience and following, and reluctantly I have to admit to some shortcomings in Quintin which we mentioned last month.

The third possibility is [Reginald] Maudling, who has brains and ability and kept his balance amidst the Common Market euphoria last autumn. He could make a sagacious Prime Minister. He would do well to get his weight down.

These are the counsels I propose to give in private to those who come to seek them.

28 July 1963 – Beaverbrook to Avon
I don't think that Macmillan can be unseated. There was no organization, no direction, no purpose and no common sense in his group of opponents.

If there had been an organized group they would have accomplished a good deal. They would have brought him down.[26]

But Macmillan quit in any case in October on grounds of ill-health. Avon now was, above all, anxious to see that Butler did not succeed:

10 October 1963 – Avon to Beaverbrook
I only set down that I wish Butler were a man I could respect. L.G. [Lloyd George] once called him 'the artful dodger', but if this is important in politics, it is also not enough.

14 October 1963 – Avon to Beaverbrook
The political situation is certainly lively. Each candidate has his failings and it may be my imagination, but it seems they are rather more conspicuous than usual. I cannot believe that Butler is the man for these times: he has too little faith for me and too much the habit of supporting one policy to one set of men and the opposite to another a few hours later.[27]

In the event Chamberlain's former Parliamentary Private Secretary, Home, was chosen. It seems unlikely that Avon played any part in producing this surprise – except in the indirect sense that his opposition to Butler may have added some weight to the many other influential Conservatives who were determined to prevent the succession of the heir-apparent.

Avon's views on the successive Conservative governments which held office until October 1964 were not particularly favourable. But privately he stood to the right rather than to the left of them. No longer was he, as in the wartime era, a Tory progressive. Still less was he tempted to desire the realignment of British politics in conjunction with Labour moderates; and, needless to say, nothing in the record of the Labour Government under Wilson served to push him back towards the left. On one issue, however, he supported Macmillan and his successors: he now accepted that Great Britain should join the European Economic Communicty (EEC). Never a fanatic on the issue and quite unrepentant about his own record in office, he nevertheless was prepared to sign messages and give television interviews favouring the various attempts that only came to fruition during the 1970s. He was undoubtedly disappointed at de Gaulle's decision to block British membership. But this did not mean that he did not understand de Gaulle's motives. On the contrary, they shared a distrust of American policies. After visiting Paris in 1961, he wrote revealingly:

I had a good talk with de Gaulle ... upon the world scene we found ourselves only too closely in agreement about its very sombre prospect. I told him that he had more influence with [President John] Kennedy than any other European and encouraged him to use it to get a closer coordination of Western policy. I think that he will try, but I have no doubt he feels some resentment, as we do, at the American outlook on colonial matters. His argument was that we understand that an evolution has to take place but we want to do it by our own methods and in our own time ... I do not think that in broad matters the present French administration wish to be in any way stand-offish. On the contrary, I think that they would value closer relations but think that we are so much tied up with the Americans that these things are hardly realizable.[28]

Here, then, is more evidence that had Avon remained Prime Minister after the Suez Crisis he might have developed into a British Gaullist.

In the autumn of 1976 occurred the twentieth anniversary of the Suez operation. There was, as there had been a decade earlier, some media coverage of the subject. But now Avon was not in so good a position, even if he had wished to do so, to offer reminiscences. For he was mortally ill with cancer. He spent the winter months in Florida as a guest of Harriman. Early in the New Year of 1977 he had a sudden relapse and, with the agreement of the Prime Minister, Callaghan, he was flown home to Wiltshire in an RAF VC-10. In the presence of his wife and son he was thus able to spend a last few days in the countryside to which he had for so long been devoted. It is said that some of the best-loved paintings in his collection of Impressionists were brought to his room for a final viewing – a fitting arrangement in the light of the solace they had been to him during difficult days in politics. He died on 14 January 1977. He was five months short of his eightieth birthday.

A simple funeral ceremony, attended by only a small circle of family and friends, was held at St Mary at Alvediston on 17 January. Avon was duly buried in the graveyard. Tributes were paid in the House of Commons followed by adjournment for the day. On 15 February a memorial service was held in Westminster Abbey. National leaders were present in large numbers together with diplomats from sixty-six countries.

Newspapers, radio and television, at home and abroad, gave much prominence to Avon's death and carried long obituaries. The emphasis in the media coverage was predictably on the Suez crisis. There was, by contrast, a dearth of penetrating analysis of his wider rôle as a world statesman over nearly three vital decades. The obituaries thus tended only too well to confirm the fears of one of his interim biographers who wrote two years before his death: 'The reputation he has built since 1923 remains identified with one event – the Suez crisis. It is a cruel fate, even by the harsh standards of politics, to be remembered by one failure and not by numerous achievements.'[29]

May we expect a kinder verdict in the coming decades? Certainly a greater sense of perspective should lead to less exclusive emphasis on the Suez Crisis. For Eden was born in the year of Queen Victoria's Diamond Jubilee when to all appearances British strength and influence in the world had never stood higher. By the year of his death, 1977, his country had sunk to the level of a second-rank power whose empire had vanished. She had, after many humiliations, been allowed to join a wider European Community and was numbered among its most impoverished members. Short of being conquered, a more precipitate decline would be difficult to imagine. Future historians will surely find endless fascination in this remarkable evolution. They are bound to analyse the rôle that prominent individuals played in speeding up or delaying the process. In this respect Eden will be more important than most twentieth century British states-men. For he was at or near the helm for more than two decades – and maybe the most decisive decades in his country's decline at that. As late as January 1938, for example, with Eden at the Foreign Office, Chamberlain could describe his country as 'a very rich and a very vulnerable empire'. By 1957, when Eden retired, the extent of that vulnerability had been ruthlessly exposed. Suez was but an episode, and maybe not a particularly important one, in this story of decline. Hence wider judgements of Eden's career are likely to emerge than those that focus sharply only on 1956. As Churchill generously and presciently said of Chamberlain in 1940:

... at the Lychgate we may all pass our own conduct and our own judgements under a searching review. It is not given to human beings, happily for them, for otherwise life would be intolerable, to foresee or to predict to any large extent the unfolding course of events. In one phase men seem to have been right, and in another they seem to have been wrong. Then again, a few years later, when the perspective of time has lengthened, all stands in a different setting. There is a new proportion. There is another scale of values.[30]

So, too, with Eden. With perspective Suez may come to seem a relatively unimportant event in and of itself, more symbolic than seminal, more an effect than a cause of national decline. For Suez had remarkably few consequences, favourable or otherwise. The Anglo-American 'special relationship' was soon repaired (with results not invariably welcome in London, as witness de Gaulle's veto on British EEC entry); the British standing in the Middle East continued to decline but it will remain debatable whether this would have been more or less rapid if Eden had not used force and to some extent checked Nasser; the British Commonwealth survived in recognizable form the era of Eden, though not that of Wilson; and at home the Conservative Party soon recovered its poise and went on to win a sweeping victory in the General Election of 1959. Perhaps only in helping to shape a new climate of opinion among British intellectuals was Suez of any lasting importance, and even this may have been of only limited significance. For the existing opinions of many on the left at least were, if anything, reinforced by Suez. As one historian has written:

In the Suez débâcle, both Eden and Gaitskell were prisoners of an illusion – the illusion of Britain's special mission to preserve peace, law and stability in the world.

It arose in the imperial era, when, with superb effrontery, the British tried to remake millions of Asians and Africans – not to mention Europeans – in their own image; tried to enforce on them, or persuade them into, a code of behaviour which, while in keeping with Britain's own interests, could be generalized as a solvent for the world's problems. The Labour Party inherited the idea, divested it of its imperialist trimmings, infused it with a moral fervour and tried to apply it to such post-imperialist institutions as the League of Nations, the United Nations and the Commonwealth of Nations. It was the White Man's burden all over again. The Suez crisis exposed its hollowness.

If anything the Labour Party's illusion ran deeper. The Tories' concept of their post-imperial responsibilities rested upon the illusion of power. Once that illusion was shattered, little remained of that concept; the way was opened to joining Europe. But the Labour Party's illusion rested on something that no mere harsh facts could dispose of. The old imperialist idea had been transposed into a dream of world brotherhood. It rested on the repudiation of power, the repudiation, in fact, of everything that goes to make up the real world. It was an imperialism with all the pain, the injustice, the cruelty and the oppression conjured out of existence by magic. It was the imperialism of the intelligentsia, both an atonement for past sins and a guarantee of status without tears.[31]

Otherwise the direct consequences of Suez were largely limited to Eden personally and his reputation. There were obviously many negative aspects. His judgement and integrity were alike assailed in many quarters. His claims to be a man of peace were shattered: he had clearly ceased to be eligible for a Nobel Peace Prize. His talent as a conference negotiator, demonstrated over many years, has been largely forgotten simply because he did not have his customary success during the conferences of 1956. Again, the accident of Suez and his resignation occurring within two years of his succeeding Churchill has led critics, perhaps unjustly, to see in this rapid process proof that Eden was 'qualified to serve as "adjutant" to a political leader of genius, but was temperamentally unfit to lead himself'.[32] But Suez paradoxically also had some advantages for Eden. He might otherwise have been much more associated in the public mind with the alleged blame for the failure to involve Great Britain in the making of the EEC. Again, with his ignorance of economics, his administration, had it lasted longer, might have been overwhelmed by what Macmillan called his 'little local difficulties'. Above all, media concentration on Suez has shielded Eden from much more searching criticism of the part he played before and during the Second World War.

The importance of Eden may thus be increasingly seen to lie in his conduct when Great Britain was still in every sense a front-rank power, that is in the period before the Soviet and American domination of the European continent had come about. In short, Eden could do nothing as Prime Minister of a second-rank power in the 1950s nearly so important for the future of the planet or his country as what he did or failed to do between his appointment as Foreign Secretary in December 1935 and, say, the Teheran Conference of 1943 by which time Great Britain had willingly surrendered the future of Europe and even perhaps her own fate as an independent state to two essentially extra-European superpowers. It has been argued here that Eden was far more responsible even than Churchill for halting Chamberlain's pursuit of 'appeasement' and his attempt to exclude the future superpowers from Europe. For the existence of Eden's sizeable group of left-wing Conservatives played a major part in causing the Cabinet to give the fateful guarantees to Poland in March 1939 and to seek, however half-heartedly, an alliance with the Soviet Union. It was also this group which formed the nucleus of the larger body of MPs whose hostility in May 1940 forced Chamberlain to resign and which in turn led to Churchill's historic premiership. And Chamberlain's death later in the year effectively ended the possibility of a reversal of policy.

The extent of the metamorphosis which these events represented is still by no means fully appreciated. At home it gave to the Labour Party a share in office which served as a springboard to full power in 1945. Eden thus helped to usher in the 'Social Democratic Age'. In world affairs, the ousting of Chamberlain was of even greater significance. It made it much less likely that the war would end with a compromise peace and ensured that in due time the Soviet Union would be warmly accepted as a worthy ally. Few in Great Britain at the time or since doubted that this transformation was overwhelmingly beneficial. Churchill and Eden are thus still widely held in high esteem for their respective rôles in the critical period. Eden's part is, however, usually denied sufficient recognition, partly because of Churchill's heroic public stance in the summer of 1940 and partly, it must be admitted, because of the overshadowing effect of Suez. In time the injustice will surely be corrected. On the other hand, some partisans of Eden may be less pleased by the impending flood of evidence, anticipated in the present work, revealing that his relationship with Churchill was anything but idyllic. For both men found it prudent to foist on the general public the contrary view during their lifetimes. And they had many abetters in thus misleading the nation. For example, Winant, the wartime American Ambassador in London, wrote in his memoirs in 1947:

> The personal relationship between the Prime Minister and Anthony Eden was as close and real as President Roosevelt's friendship for Harry Hopkins. Roosevelt and Churchill, each a great leader, single-minded in serving his country, understood that most men who crossed their doorsteps wanted something. Eden and Hopkins wanted nothing beyond being loyal to a leader and cause.

And Morrison referred in his memoirs, published in 1960, to an almost 'father-and-son' relationship between the two men.[33] Such verdicts will clearly be endorsed by posterity, if at all, with considerable qualification.

It must also be expected that the rôle of both Eden and Churchill in connection with pre-war 'appeasement' will be increasingly critically scrutinized. For evidence is gradually emerging which modifies the simplistic picture of the two men as models of heroic consistency: distinctions between 'appeasers' and 'anti-appeasers' in the Conservative Party were less sharp than has been popularly supposed. Yet some apologists for Eden and Churchill will no doubt resent the presentation of evidence in support of this thesis. It has been argued here, for example, that Eden initially formed a relatively favourable impression of Hitler; that he took a less vigorous line on Abyssinia than has often been supposed; that his policies on the Rhineland and the Spanish Civil War were substantially his own and not the result of Cabinet pressure; and that he adopted a less than thoroughgoing attitude in his opposition to Chamberlain after his resignation. But none of this should occasion surprise, for he was neither infallible in his prescience nor a saint in matters relating to his own advancement and survival. He was in short as much a professional politician as any of his colleagues – and perhaps none the worse for that. Yet when all this has been said and all the revisionist evidence has been sifted, the fact also remains that he did resign from Chamberlain's Government. For the man-in-the-street that surely was and is the important point. A major part of his long-term reputation will depend on whether he, and not Chamberlain, continues to be vindicated on the issue of pre-war 'appeasement'.

Today only a few specialist historians appear to believe that Chamberlain's policies were other than disastrous. Hence Eden's partisans still have good grounds for hoping that in due season he will come to be remembered at least as much for his vital and beneficent part in ending those policies as for his less successful exploits over Suez. But the possibility must also be faced that rather different views about Eden and Chamberlain may become fashionable as the extent of British decline comes to be fully realized. And what if the British place in the world should alter still more drastically and unfavourably in the coming decades? What, too, if the West as a whole should lose ground on a drastic scale to its totalitarian adversaries? Might there not then develop in Great Britain and the West what Churchill half predicted in his tribute to Chamberlain in 1940: 'a new proportion' and 'a new scale of values'?

Great Britain's decision to ally wholeheartedly with the Soviet Union against her various Fascist opponents was clearly of monumental significance. The Soviets rightly claim that the balance of world forces between 'differing social systems' has greatly altered in favour of the 'Socialist Camp' since 1941. The full consequences have still not become apparent and may not become so for many decades. The Soviets at least proclaim that the balance will continue to shift inexorably in their favour. If this should happen, it is possible that Eden will become increasingly subject to criticism in the West for his conduct between February 1938 and July 1945. For he played the most crucial rôle in reversing the traditional anti-Soviet line of Baldwin and Chamberlain. The former had said to Eden in 1936 that 'on no account, French or other, must he bring us in to fight on the side of the Russians'.[34] Yet, in just over three years following his resignation in 1938, that was precisely the policy which Eden, together with Churchill, had largely caused to be adopted. Thereafter the British Cabinet, dominated by them, acquiesced in the Soviets establishing a major bridgehead in Europe and publicly covered up for many Soviet crimes – Churchill with more forebodings than Eden. Moreover, even Great Britain itself might well have come into the Soviets' orbit. For had the Americans not come into the war six months after the Soviets, it might have been impossible to prevent Stalin from making himself master of the whole of continental Europe. The military involvement of the Americans owed little to the policies of Eden and Churchill. It was overwhelmingly the achievement of Hitler, who by his gratuitous declaration of war after Pearl Harbor rendered a long-term signal service, doubtless unintentionally, to the cause of Western liberal civilization in Europe. The post-war presence of the Americans in Europe has of course served to mask the extent to which the Churchill–Eden line involved the risk of the full-scale Bolshevization of the whole continent.

This leads to a further question. How could Eden of all men have so eagerly helped to push the world so much in a left-wing, even totalitarian left-wing, direction? Why did he not at least seek, as Churchill desired from as early as 1942, to prepare his fellow-countrymen for a possible future need to resist Stalin as well as the Fascist powers? Why did he not recognize that helping to build up Moscow as a major world force imposed a long-term threat to the survival of British power? Had he not begun his career as a 'diehard' Conservative condemning the first Labour Government's dealings with the Soviet Union and hoping that the British would not 'scuttle like flying curs' from their overseas domains and thereby make themselves 'a jibe in the mouth of every tavern-lounger from Marrakesh to Singapore'?[35] Did he not also as late as the 1950s show himself a bitter opponent of rising Third World nationalisms as typified by the 'rug-merchants', his scornful term for the Iranians. (Nasser's father-in-law actually was a rug-merchant!) Superficially at least, the middle phase of Eden's career with its radicalism and generosity to Moscow, might seem incompatible with these attitudes. But perhaps, as Randolph Churchill wrote of him in another context, he was after all 'a sphinx without a secret'.[36] The explanation may simply be that he stumbled into pursuing his pro-Soviet course above all because he had conceived a hatred of Mussolini – his 'anti-Christ'. All else flowed from this. On the Duce's account he quarrelled irrevocably with Chamberlain and this in turn drove him ever further to the left. He would flirt with political realignment in 1939 and would find himself during wartime anticipating with dismay the need in a post-war world to work with the bulk of Conservative MPs who had so signally failed to support him in 1938, and he accordingly expressed a private preference for the Labour Party. Above all, if Chamberlain and some of his followers contemplated compromise with one or more Fascist powers and shied away from cooperation with Moscow, Eden would take the other line, even though before February 1938 he had not been noticeably anti-German or pro-Soviet. Moreover, he was gratified and flattered to discover that it was at times surprisingly easy to work with Molotov, not only during the war, but even as late as 1954. And the line he took certainly had a good deal of popular support. Moreover, once the Second World War had begun in earnest he doubtless shared with his fellow-countrymen the belief that Hitler was the embodiment of evil. But the origins of his general outlook in the years after his quarrel with Chamberlain lay in no clear-minded analysis of the relative merits and demerits of conflicting ideologies or in any particular prescience about Hitler's aggressive and demonic potential. As one historian has perceptively written:

Eden's Italophobia was not rooted in any belief about – as he put it – 'forms of government, dictatorships versus democracies', for he remained to the day of his resignation an opponent of ideological blocs and an advocate of agreement with Hitler ... Eden's antipathy to Mussolini, like his rather xenophobic attitude to Japan ... was forged in a resentment against upstart have-not imperialisms poaching on traditionally English or 'white race' preserves and challenging Britain's historic control of the world's sea lanes. Reduced to its essentials, Eden's dispute with Italy was not: Shall fascism or democracy prevail? Rather it was 'who shall rule the Mediterranean?'[37]

This interpretation would also serve in part to explain the ease with which

Eden came to favour close alignment with Moscow: the Russians might be imperialists but, with expansionist traditions going back for centuries, surely not of the 'upstart have-not' variety. The same historian may also have discerned why he ignored Chamberlain's pleas to detach Rome from Berlin on grounds of the overstretched character of British military commitments:

> If there was one distinct trademark of Eden's approach to diplomacy, it was his willingness to use shows of force, often without considering their possible implications. He seems to have indulged the predilection to the end of his political career, as witness his behaviour in 1956. Chamberlain, by contrast, argued consistently that one must refrain from threats, displays of force etc., unless one was prepared to back them up to the hilt.[38]

It may be objected that Eden's attitude to Mussolini was more idealistically motivated than the foregoing analysis suggests. For had not Eden made his reputation in the early 1930s as a supporter of the League of Nations and had not Mussolini cynically destroyed it with his Abyssinian adventure? True, Eden was not as much of a Geneva zealot as has often been supposed. Nevertheless he certainly cannot be numbered among the League's enemies. Thus superficially it might seem that he had, after all, 'high-minded' rather than 'blimpish' grounds for hating Mussolini. Yet the distinction may be unreal. For the League was dominated by Great Britain and France and had been constructed on the basis of an Anglo-Saxon *Weltanschauung* and a British sense of good manners and 'fair play'. By contrast, during the last decades of his life, when the United Nations was developing along entirely different lines, Eden's enthusiasm for a world assembly waned rapidly – and not only because of the Suez affair. For Eden, as for many of his compatriots, support for 'internationalism' was thus a strangely inverted form of 'jingoism'. But once 'internationalism' and its institutions took on a line less compatible with British interests and with the noble Anglo-Saxon self-image, those who, like Eden, were at root simple patriots lost their faith. Italy's attack on the League aroused Eden's ire precisely because it was an upstart assault on something which he saw as an extension of the British 'way of life'. Eden's career, then, had after all a good deal of internal consistency.

Eden was thus at root essentially a 'conviction politician' with sturdy patriotism as the thread of belief running through his whole career. There remains, however, just a doubt whether excess of valour or some want of judgement as to the limits of British power did not on occasion lead him to favour imprudent courses to the possible detriment of causes he desired to serve; and whether in the post-war years his diehard unwillingness to subordinate British policies to those of the United States did not lead him, particularly at Geneva in 1954, to show paradoxical timidity just when military circumstances may for once have permitted the successful assertion of collective Western resolve at no great risk. In short, it is still an open question whether in the longer-term future he will be judged to have been wiser than his principal critics, Chamberlain and Dulles.

Notes

Abbreviations used

BD E. L. Woodward *et al.*, eds., *Documents on British Foreign Policy, 1919–39*, London
DDE Series Dwight D. Eisenhower Series (Eisenhower Papers, Ann Whitman File)
DDF Ministère des Affaires Étrangères, *Documents diplomatiques français. 1932–39*, Paris

HC Deb. *Parliamentary Debates, Official Report, House of Commons*
IS International Series (Eisenhower Papers, Ann Whitman File)
PRO Public Record Office, London

I *Early Years*, 1897–1931

1. Timothy Eden, *The Tribulations of a Baronet*, London, 1933, pp. 22–4.
2. Anthony Eden, Earl of Avon, *Another World, 1897–1917*, London, 1976, p. 31.
3. Lord Moran, *Winston Churchill: The Struggle for Survival*, London, 1966, p. 711.
4. Eden, *Another World*, p. 35.
5. ibid., p. 48.
6. Michael Howard, *The Continental Commitment: The Dilemma of British Defence Policy in the Era of the Two World Wars*, London, 1972, p. 100; Eden, *Another World*, p. 150; and Anthony Nutting, 'Another Eden', *Spectator*, 1 May 1976.
7. Margaret Blunden, *The Countess of Warwick: A Biography*, London, 1967, p. 275.
8. Tyler Abell, ed., *Drew Pearson: Diaries, 1949–1959*, London, 1974, p. 413.
9. *HC Deb.*, CLXIX, cols. 1678–9, 19 Feb. 1924.
10. Alan Campbell-Johnson, *Sir Anthony Eden: A Biography*, 2nd ed., London, 1955, p. 34.
11. Anthony Eden, *Places in the Sun*, London, 1926, pp. 111–12, 132–3.
12. *HC Deb.*, CLXXXIX, cols. 2088–94, 21 Dec. 1925.
13. Eyre Crowe to Austen Chamberlain, 12 Mar. 1925, Austen Chamberlain Papers, University of Birmingham, quoted in David Carlton, 'Disarmament with Guarantees: Lord Cecil, 1922–1927', *Disarmament and Arms Control*, III, 1965, p. 158.
14. Campbell-Johnson, *Eden*, 2nd ed., p. 58.
15. Chamberlain to D'Abernon, 19 Feb. 1926, D'Abernon Papers, British Library, Add. 48929, quoted in David Carlton, 'Great Britain and the League Council Crisis of 1926', *Historical Journal*, XI, 1968, pp. 357–8; and Chamberlain to Anthony Buxton, 30 Mar. 1926, Austen Chamberlain Papers quoted ibid., p. 364.
16. *HC Deb.*, CXCIII, cols. 1105–9, 23 Mar. 1926.
17. ibid., CC, cols. 2225–9, 8 Dec. 1926.
18. *Parliamentary Debates, Official Report, House of Lords*, LXIX, cols. 84–94, 16 Nov. 1927. See also David Carlton, 'Great Britain and the Coolidge Naval Disarmament Conference of 1927', *Political Science Quarterly*, LXXXIII, 1968, pp. 573–98.
19. *HC Deb.*, CCX, cols. 2160–65, 24 Nov. 1927.
20. Quoted in Arnold J. Toynbee, *Survey of International Affairs, 1928*, London, 1929, pp. 78–9.
21. *HC Deb.*, CCXXII, cols. 764–70, 13 Nov. 1928; and Anthony Eden, *Foreign Affairs*, London, 1939, pp. 16–17.
22. Cecil to H. A. St George Saunders, 28 Nov. 1928, Cecil of Chelwood Papers, British Library, Add. 51099, quoted in David Carlton, 'The Anglo-French Compromise on Arms Limitation, 1928', *Journal of British Studies*, VIII, 1968–9, p. 162.
23. See David Carlton, *MacDonald versus Henderson: The Foreign Policy of the Second Labour Government*, London, 1970.
24. *HC Deb.*, CCXXXVII, col. 2954, 16 Apr. 1930.
25. *The Times*, 6 Oct. 1930.
26. Cab. 16/102, PRO.

11 *Junior Minister in the Foreign Office, 1931–5*

1. The Earl of Avon, *The Eden Memoirs: Facing the Dictators*, London, 1962, p. 40.
2. FO 371/15490, PRO, quoted in Christopher Thorne, *The Limits of Foreign Policy: The West, the League and the Far Eastern Crisis of 1931–1933*, London, 1972, p. 151. See also James Barros, *The League of Nations and the Great Powers: The Greek–Bulgarian Incident, 1925*, London, 1970, pp. 124–5.
3. *HC Deb.* CCX, cols. 2160, 2163, 24 Nov. 1927.
4. *BD*, 2/IX, no. 216.
5. *HC Deb.*, CCLXII, cols. 917–20, 29 Feb. 1932, cols. 1085–6, 2 Mar. 1929, and cols. 359–62, 24 Feb. 1932.
6. Henry L. Stimson and McGeorge Bundy, *On Active Service in Peace and War*, London, n.d. (1949?), p. 96; and *BD*, 2/IX, no. 576.
7. Quoted in Reginald Bassett, *Democracy and Foreign Policy: A Case History: The Sino-Japanese Dispute, 1931–1933*, 2nd. ed., London, 1952, p. 211n.
8. Thorne, *The Limits of Foreign Policy*, p. 95n.
9. *BD*, 2/X, no. 545.
10. Thorne, *The Limits of Foreign Policy*, p. 360; *BD*, 2/XI, nos. 270 and 358; and *Manchester Guardian*, 1 Mar. 1933.
11. Ormsby-Gore to Baldwin, 1 Oct. 1933, Baldwin Papers, University of Cambridge Library; and *BD*, 2/XI, no. 371n.
12. *HC Deb.*, CCLXXXI, cols. 150–51, 7 Nov. 1933.
13. Eden to Baldwin, 10 Feb. and 9 May 1932, Baldwin Papers.
14. Salvador de Madariaga, *Disarmament*, London, 1929, p. 164.
15. See David Carlton, 'The Problem of Civil Aviation in British Air Disarmament Policy, 1919–1934', *Royal United Service Institution Journal*, CXI, 1966, pp. 307–16.
16. Avon, *Facing the Dictators*, p. 47.
17. Quoted in John W. Wheeler-Bennett, *The Pipe Dream of Peace: The Story of the Collapse of Disarmament*, London, 1935, p. 92.
18. Hodsoll to Hankey, 19 Sept. 1932 and marginal minute thereon by Hankey, Cab. 21/354, PRO.
19. MacDonald to Simon, 23 Dec. 1932 and Simon to MacDonald, 30 Dec. 1932, Simon Papers, FO 800/287, PRO.
20. Avon, *Facing the Dictators*, pp. 29–30.
21. Simon to Eden, 28 June 1934, Simon Papers, FO 800/289, PRO.
22. Avon, *Facing the Dictators*, p. 31.
23. DC(M)(32), 12th Conclusions, Cab. 21/379, PRO. See also Eden to Baldwin, 24 Feb. 1933, Baldwin Papers.
24. See Carlton, *MacDonald Versus Henderson, passim*.
25. Ramsay MacDonald Papers, 30/69/2/36, PRO.
26. DC(M)(32), 12th Conclusions, Cab. 21/379, PRO.
27. Murray to Cecil, 17 Mar. 1933 and Cecil to Murray, 20 Mar. 1933, Cecil Papers, Add. 51132.
28. *HC Deb.*, CCLXXVI, col. 615, 23 Mar. 1933.
29. Avon, *Facing the Dictators*, p. 37.
30. Eden to Simon, copy to Baldwin, 1 May 1933, Simon Papers quoted in Neville H. Waites, 'British Foreign Policy towards France regarding the German Problem from 1929 to 1934', unpublished London University PhD thesis, 1972, pp. 227–8.
31. CP 159(33), Cab. 24/242, June 1933, PRO.
32. DC(M)(32), 17th Conclusions, Cab. 21/379, PRO.
33. *HC Deb.*, CCLXXX, cols. 353, 371, 5 July 1933.
34. Avon, *Facing the Dictators*, p. 39.
35. DC(M)(32), memorandum 54, Cab. 21/379, PRO.
36. Eden to Hankey, 14 Sept. 1933, Cab. 21/380, PRO.
37. Eden memorandum, 20 Sept. 1933, MacDonald Papers, 30/69/1/531, PRO; and Cab. 23/77, PRO.
38. Avon, *Facing the Dictators*, p. 58; Eden to Simon, 18 Feb. 1934, Simon Papers, FO 800/289, PRO; and Eden to MacDonald, 18 Feb. 1934, MacDonald Papers, 30/69/1/547, PRO.
39. Eden to Baldwin, 21 Feb. 1934, Baldwin Papers; and Eden to Simon, 21 Feb. 1934, Simon Papers, FO 800/289, PRO.
40. Eden to MacDonald, 22 Feb. 1934, MacDonald Papers, 30/69/1/547, PRO.
41. Vansittart minute, 23 Feb. 1934, ibid.;

and Avon, *Facing the Dictators*, pp. 73–5.

42. See, for example, Gerhard Meinck, *Hitler und die deutsche Aufrüstung, 1933–1937*, Wiesbaden, 1959, pp. 52–86.

43. Dennis Bardens, *Portrait of a Statesman*, London, 1955, p. 134; and Avon, *Facing the Dictators*, p. 78.

44. Drummond to Simon, 29 Jan. 1934, Simon Papers, FO 800/289, PRO.

45. Avon, *Facing the Dictators*, p. 78; and *The Times*, 27 Feb. 1934.

46. Avon, *Facing the Dictators*, pp. 87–8; and DC(M)(32), 35th Conclusions, Cab. 21/388, PRO.

47. Avon, *Facing the Dictators*, p. 89.

48. Simon to King George the Fifth, 10 July 1934, Simon Papers, FO 800/289, PRO.

49. FO 371/17749, PRO.

50. ibid; and *HC Deb.*, CCXCII, col. 758, 13 July 1934.

51. Avon, *Facing the Dictators*, pp. 58, 95.

52. Lisanne Radice, 'Negotiations for an Eastern Security Pact, 1933–1936', unpublished London University PhD thesis, 1973, p. 156.

53. FO 371/18461, PRO, quoted in Bennet Kovrig, 'Mediation by Obfuscation: The Resolution of the Marseille Crisis, October 1934 to May 1935', *Historical Journal*, XIX, 1976, p. 206.

54. ibid., p. 215.

55. Simon to King George the Fifth, 26 Nov. 1934, Simon Papers, FO 800/289, PRO.

56. Hugh Seton-Watson, *Eastern Europe between the Wars, 1918–1941*, Cambridge, 1945, pp. 377–8.

57. *HC Deb.*, CCXCVI, cols. 213–14, 11 Dec. 1934.

58. Kovrig, 'Mediation by Obfuscation', loc. cit., p. 220.

59. *HC Deb.*, CCXCIII, cols. 619–20, 5 Nov. 1934; and Simon to King George the Fifth, 5 Nov. 1934, Simon Papers, FO 800/289, PRO.

60. Simon to Eden, 20 Nov. 1934, Simon Papers, FO 800/289, PRO.

61. Cab. 27/573, PRO.

62. Cecil to Eden, 7 Dec. 1934 and Eden to Cecil, 11 Dec. 1934, Cecil Papers, Add. 51083.

63. W. N. Medlicott, *Contemporary England, 1914–1964*, London, 1967, p. 349.

64. FO 371/19112, PRO.

65. *HC Deb.*, CCCV, cols. 207–25, 23 Oct. 1935; FO 371/19137, PRO, cited in Donald T. Rotunda, 'The Rome Embassy of Sir Eric Drummond, 16th Earl of Perth, 1933–1939', unpublished London University PhD thesis, 1972, p. 195.

66. Stephen Roskill, *Hankey: Man of Secrets* (3 vols.), London, 1970–74, vol. 3, p. 175.

67. Quoted in Angus Calder, *The People's War: Britain, 1939–45*, London, 1969, p. 32.

68. Interview with Dr Frank Hardie, President of the Oxford Union at the time of the 'King and Country' debate. But see also Martin Ceadel, 'The "King and Country" Debate, 1933: Student Politics, Pacifism and the Dictators', *Historical Journal*, XXII, 1979, pp. 397–422.

69. See, for example, Eden's correspondence with Cecil during 1935, Cecil Papers, Add. 51083.

70. See Martin Ceadel, 'The First British Referendum: The Peace Ballot 1934–5', *English Historical Review*, forthcoming.

71. *The Times*, 9 Jan. 1935.

72. Avon, *Facing the Dictators*, pp. 199–200.

73. ibid., p. 141.

74. ibid., pp. 153, 155, 157, 161.

75. ibid., pp. 162–3.

76. ibid., pp. 217–18; Roskill, *Hankey*, vol. 3, pp. 173–4; and Cecil to Baldwin, 6 June 1935, Cecil Papers, Add. 51080.

77. Avon, *Facing the Dictators*, p. 218.

78. *HC Deb.*, CCCIV, col. 613, 11 July 1935.

79. Avon, *Facing the Dictators*, p. 221.

80. Mario Toscano, 'Eden's Mission to Rome on the Eve of the Italo-Ethiopian Conflict', in A. O. Sarkissian, ed., *Studies in Diplomatic History and Historiography*, London, 1961, p. 152.

81. Avon, *Facing the Dictators*, pp. 234, 235, 244.

82. DO 114/66, PRO.

83. Cab. 23/82, PRO; and Frank Hardie, *The Abyssinian Crisis*, London, 1974, p. 135.

84. Cab. 23/82, PRO.

85. Avon, *Facing the Dictators*, pp. 260–1.

86. Hoare to Eden, 16 Oct. 1935, Templewood Papers, University of Cambridge Library, Tem. VIII: 3; cf. Avon, *Facing the Dictators*, pp. 281–3.

87. Cab. 23/82, PRO, and DO 114/66, PRO. See also J. A. Cross, *Sir Samuel Hoare: A Political Biography*, London, 1977, pp. 234, 237–40.
88. FO 371/19163, PRO, quoted in R. A. C. Parker, 'Great Britain, France and the Ethiopian Crisis, 1935–1936', *English Historical Review*, LXXXIX, 1974, p. 320.
89. Cab. 23/82, PRO.
90. Cab. 23/90B, PRO. For the view that backbench MPs, rather than public opinion in general, had a decisive impact, see Daniel Waley, *British Public Opinion and the Abyssinian War, 1935–6*, London, 1975.
91. FO 371/19168, PRO; Cab. 23/82, PRO.
92. Parker, 'Great Britain, France and the Ethiopian Crisis', loc. cit., p. 324.

III *Baldwin's Foreign Secretary, 1935–7*

1. *Not* the youngest since 'Lord Greville' [sic] in 1791 as claimed in Sidney Aster, *Anthony Eden*, London, 1976, p. 39.
2. J. W. Wheeler-Bennett, *Knaves, Fools and Heroes: In Europe between the Wars*, London, 1974, pp. 13–14.
3. Avon, *Facing the Dictators*, p. 218; Keith Middlemas, *Diplomacy of Illusion: The British Government and Germany, 1937–1939*, London, 1972, pp. 42, 96.
4. Avon, *Facing the Dictators*, p. 319.
5. ibid., pp. 295–7; and DO 114/66, PRO.
6. DO 114/68, PRO.
7. CP 5(36), Cab. 24/259, PRO; Cab. 23/83, PRO; and Avon, *Facing the Dictators*, p. 324.
8. CPs 10 and 52(36), Cab. 24/259 and 260, PRO.
9. DO 114/68, PRO.
10. Cab. 23/83, PRO.
11. Parker, 'Great Britain, France and the Ethiopian Crisis', loc. cit., p. 238.
12. W. N. Medlicott, *Britain and Germany: The Search for Agreement*, London, 1969, p. 32.
13. BD, 2/VI, no. 322.
14. FO 371/19885, PRO.
15. ibid.
16. Avon, *Facing the Dictators*, pp. 98–9.
17. FO 371/19885, PRO.
18. FO 371/19886, PRO.
19. FO 371/19885, PRO.
20. FO 371/19887, PRO.
21. CP 73(36), Cab. 24/261, PRO; and Avon, *Facing the Dictators*, p. 346.
22. *HC Deb.*, CCCIX, cols. 1812–13, 9 Mar. 1936.
23. See, for example, Maurice Baumont, 'The Rhineland Crisis: 7 March 1936' in Neville Waites, ed., *Troubled Neighbours: Franco-British Relations in the Twentieth Century*, London, 1971, p. 164.
24. FO 371/19891, PRO; cf. Avon, *Facing the Dictators*, p. 356.
25. Cab. 21/545, PRO; and Cranborne to Eden, 17 Mar. 1936, Cranborne Papers, FO 800/296, PRO.
26. Prem. 1/194, PRO; Cab. 23/83, PRO; and Pierre-Étienne Flandin, *Politique française, 1919–1940*, Paris, 1948, pp. 207–8.
27. Cab. 21/540, PRO, quoted in part in Lawrence R. Pratt, *East of Malta, West of Suez: Britain's Mediterranean Crisis, 1936–1939*, London, 1975, p. 39n, but *not* in Roskill, *Hankey*.
28. Nigel Nicolson, ed., *Harold Nicolson: Diaries and Letters, 1930–1939*, London, 1966, pp. 249–50.
29. Cab. 23/83, PRO.
30. Avon, *Facing the Dictators*, pp. 360, 362; and *HC Deb.*, CCCX, col. 1527, 26 Mar. 1936.
31. Cab. 21/545, PRO; Avon, *Facing the Dictators*, p. 366; and Nigel Nicolson, ed., *Harold Nicolson, Diaries and Letters, 1939–1945*, London, 1967, p. 56.
32. Cab. 23/83, PRO.
33. DO 114/68, PRO.
34. Cab. 23/84, PRO.
35. Lord Swinton, *Sixty Years of Power*, London, 1966, p. 166; Keith Feiling, *The Life of Neville Chamberlain*, London, 1946, p. 296; and Chamberlain to Hilda Chamberlain, 14 June 1936, Neville Chamberlain Papers, University of Birmingham Library.
36. See David Carlton, 'The Dominions and British Policy in the Abyssinian Crisis', *Journal of Imperial and Commonwealth History*, I, 1972–3, pp. 69–71.
37. Avon, *Facing the Dictators*, p. 388.
38. Thomas Jones, *A Diary with Letters, 1931–1950*, London, 1954, p. 231; and FO 371/20527, PRO, quoted in

Pratt, *East of Malta, West of Suez*, p. 42.

39. FO 371/20475, PRO, quoted in ibid., p. 39, but again curiously *not* in Roskill, *Hankey*.

40. Avon, *Facing the Dictators*, p. 441; Jill Edwards, *The British Government and the Spanish Civil War, 1936–1939*, London, 1979, pp. 18–19, 133; and United States Department of State, *Papers Relating to the Foreign Relations of the United States, 1937*, vol. I, Washington, DC, 1954, pp. 317–18. See also FO 371/21320, PRO, quoted in Pratt, *East of Malta, West of Suez*, p. 74.

41. A. H. Furnia, *The Diplomacy of Appeasement: Anglo-French Relations and the Prelude to World War II, 1931–1938*, Washington, DC, 1960, pp. 209–10.

42. FO 408/66, PRO; and Joel Colton, *Léon Blum: Humanist in Politics*, New York, 1966, pp. 241, 237, 242.

43. *DDF*, second series, III, no. 17. (Trans.)

44. Claude G. Bowers, *My Mission to Spain*, New York, 1954, p. 281; Léon Blum, *L'Oeuvre de Léon Blum* (7 vols.), Paris, 1954–65, vol. 4, p. 391; and *HC Deb.*, CCCXVI, col. 42, 29 Oct. 1936.

45. FO 371/20573, PRO; and Hugh Dalton, *The Fateful Years: Memoirs, 1931–1945*, London, 1957, pp. 95–6.

46. Hugh Thomas, *The Spanish Civil War*, 1st ed., London, 1961, p. 258; and André Géraud, *The Gravediggers of France*, New York, 1944, p. 433.

47. FO 371/20527, PRO. See also David Carlton, 'Eden, Blum and the Origins of Non-Intervention', *Journal of Contemporary History*, VI, 1971, pp. 48–9.

48. FO 432/2, PRO. See also *DDF*, 2/III, no. 108; and Carlton, 'Eden, Blum and the Origins of Non-Intervention', loc. cit., pp. 49–52. Cf also Edwards, *The British Government and the Spanish Civil War*, ch. 1; Glyn Stone, 'Britain, Non-Intervention and the Spanish Civil War', *European Studies Review*, IX, 1979, pp. 129–49; and Anthony P. Adamthwaite, *France and the Coming of the Second World War, 1936–1939*, London, 1977, pp. 43–5.

49. FO 371/20528, PRO; and Avon, *Facing the Dictators*, pp. 401–3.

50. Roskill, *Hankey*, vol. 3, p. 241n.

51. ibid., vol. 3, pp. 240–1.

52. FO 371/19949, quoted in Medlicott, *Britain and Germany*, p. 31.

53. Cab. 4/25, PRO; and Cab. 2/6, PRO.

54. Cranborne to Eden, 12 Nov. 1936, Cranborne Papers, FO 800/296, PRO; and Avon, *Facing the Dictators*, p. 425.

55. Medlicott, *Britain and Germany*, pp. 28–9; John E. Dreifort, *Yvon Delbos at the Quai d'Orsay: French Foreign Policy During the Popular Front, 1936–1938*, Lawrence, Kansas, 1973, pp. 163–6; Middlemas, *Diplomacy of Illusion*, pp. 110–12.

56. Avon, *Facing the Dictators*, pp. 427, 429.

57. See Carlton, *MacDonald versus Henderson*, pp. 163–73.

58. Trefor Evans, ed., *The Killearn Diaries, 1934–1946*, London, 1972, pp. 71–2.

59. For the view that the forging of the Rome–Berlin Axis was by no means inevitable as late as summer 1936 see Manfred Funke, *Sanktionen und Kanonen: Hitler, Mussolini und der Internationale Abessinienkonflikt, 1934–1936*, Düsseldorf, 1970.

60. Cab. 23/87, PRO; and Avon, *Facing the Dictators*, pp. 435–6. See also Maurice Cowling, *The Impact of Hitler: British Politics and British Policy, 1933–1940*, London, 1975, p. 165; and Edwards, *The British Government and the Spanish Civil War*, pp. 111–12.

61. Avon, *Facing the Dictators*, p. 445.

IV *Chamberlain's Foreign Secretary, 1937–8*

1. John Harvey, ed., *The Diplomatic Diaries of Oliver Harvey, 1937–1940*, London, 1970, p. 34; and Avon, *Facing the Dictators*, p. 445.

2. ibid., pp. 445, 452.

3. DO 32/128, PRO; and Rainer Tamchina, 'In Search of Common Causes: The Imperial Conference of 1937', *Journal of Imperial and Commonwealth History*, I, 1972–3, p. 82.

4. ibid., pp. 88–9; and Cab. 32/130, PRO.

5. Roskill, *Hankey*, vol. 3, pp. 280–1.

6. Harvey, ed., *Oliver Harvey 1937–1940*, p. 406.

7. Cab. 32/130, PRO.

8. Cab. 32/128, PRO.

9. ibid.

10. Correlli Barnett, *The Collapse of British Power*, London, 1972, p. 466.

11. Carlton, 'The Dominions and British

Policy in the Abyssinian Crisis', loc. cit., p. 77, n. 38.

12. DO 114/67, PRO.
13. Cab. 32/127, PRO.
14. Cab. 32/130, PRO. Tamchina, 'In Search of Common Causes', loc. cit., p. 83, asserts that there was a slight difference of view between Chamberlain and Eden on this matter but offers no evidence.
15. Cab. 23/88, PRO.
16. Harvey, ed., *Oliver Harvey 1937–1940*, p. 44.
17. Cab. 32/128, PRO.
18. ibid.
19. Cab. 2/6, PRO. See also Eden memorandum, 15 June 1937, Cab. 4/26, PRO.
20. Chamberlain to Ida Chamberlain, 4 July 1937, Neville Chamberlain Papers.
21. Prem. 1/276, PRO.
22. ibid.
23. Chamberlain to Hilda Chamberlain, 1 Aug. 1937, Neville Chamberlain Papers; and Neville Chamberlain Diary, 19–27 Feb. 1938, University of Birmingham Library.
24. Avon, *Facing the Dictators*, p. 453.
25. Roskill, *Hankey*, vol. 3, p. 265.
26. Prem. 1/276, PRO.
27. Chamberlain to Hilda Chamberlain, 6 Nov. 1938, Neville Chamberlain Papers quoted in Middlemas, *Diplomacy of Illusion*, p. 419; and Roskill, *Hankey*, vol. 3, p. 303.
28. Cranborne memorandum, 30 Aug. 1937, Cranborne Papers, FO 800/296, PRO.
29. Prem. 1/276, PRO.
30. ibid. See also Pratt, *East of Malta, West of Suez*, pp. 89–91.
31. For details on the Nyon Conference see Dreifort, *Yvon Delbos at the Quai d'Orsay*, ch. 4.
32. Chamberlain to Ida Chamberlain, 19 Sept. 1937, and to Hilda Chamberlain, 12 Sept. 1937, Neville Chamberlain Papers.
33. *HC Deb.*, CCCXXVIII, col. 595, 1 Nov. 1937. See also Avon, *Facing the Dictators*, pp. 506–8.
34. Harvey, ed., *Oliver Harvey, 1937–40*, p. 56; and Chamberlain to Hilda Chamberlain, 6 Nov. 1937, Neville Chamberlain Papers.
35. Chamberlain to Hilda Chamberlain, 24 Oct. 1937, Neville Chamberlain Papers.
36. Harvey, ed., *Oliver Harvey, 1937–1940*, p. 59.

37. Cranborne to Eden, 10 and 11 Nov. 1937, Avon Papers, FO 954/10, PRO; and Harvey, ed., *Oliver Harvey 1937–1940*, pp. 60–1.
38. Eden to Chamberlain, 16 Nov. 1937, Avon Papers, FO 954/10; and FO 371/21162, PRO, quoted in Roy Douglas, 'Chamberlain and Eden, 1937–38', *Journal of Contemporary History*, XIII, 1978, p. 105.
39. Harvey, ed., *Oliver Harvey, 1937–1940*, p. 62; and Avon, *Facing the Dictators*, pp. 513–16. See also The Earl of Birkenhead, *Halifax*, London, 1965, pp. 368–72.
40. Cab. 27/626, PRO.
41. Cab. 23/90A, PRO; and Chamberlain to Hilda Chamberlain, 5 Dec. 1937, Neville Chamberlain Papers.
42. FO 371/20702, PRO; Middlemas, *Diplomacy of Illusion*, pp. 43, 73, 115, 137; and Robert Skidelsky, review of Harvey, ed., *Oliver Harvey, 1937–1940*, in *Spectator*, 25 July 1970.
43. FO 371/20702, PRO. Suppressed in Cab. 2/7, PRO.
44. Prem. 1/276, PRO.
45. For details see Bradford A. Lee, *Britain and the Sino-Japanese War, 1937–1939*, London, 1973, p. 84.
46. Prem. 1/276; and Prem. 1/210, PRO.
47. Harvey, ed., *Oliver Harvey, 1937–1940*, pp. 85–6; and Prem. 1/276, PRO.
48. Cab. 23/90A, PRO; and Ian Colvin, *The Chamberlain Cabinet*, London, 1971, p. 81.
49. Harvey, ed., *Oliver Harvey, 1937–1940*, p. 416.
50. Prem. 1/210, PRO; and Iain Macleod, *Neville Chamberlain*, London, 1961, p. 210.
51. Prem. 1/259, PRO; and Neville Chamberlain Diary, 19–27 Feb. 1938.
52. David Dilks, ed., *The Diaries of Sir Alexander Cadogan, 1938–1945*, London, 1971, p. 37.
53. Lee, *Britain and the Sino-Japanese War*, p. 21.
54. ibid., pp. 94, 208.
55. William Roger Louis, *British Strategy in the Far East, 1919–1939*, London, 1971, pp. 244–5.
56. Lawrence Pratt, 'The Anglo-American Naval Conversations on the Far East of January 1938', *International Affairs*, XLVII, 1971, pp. 745–63; and Prem. 1/276, PRO.

57. Chamberlain to Hilda Chamberlain, 17 Dec. 1937, Neville Chamberlain Papers.
58. Neville Chamberlain Diary, 19–27 Feb. 1938.
59. Prem. 1/259, PRO.
60. Avon, *Facing the Dictators*, p. 525.
61. Cab. 27/623, PRO; Andrew Crozier, 'Prelude to Munich: British Foreign Policy and Germany, 1935–8', *European Studies Review*, VI, 1976, pp. 373–4; Prem. 1/330, PRO; Neville Chamberlain Diary, 19–27 Feb. 1938; Chamberlain to Hilda Chamberlain, 27 Feb. 1938, Neville Chamberlain Papers; Middlemas, *Diplomacy of Illusion*, pp. 139, 142–3; and Eden minute, 21 Jan. 1938, Avon Papers, FO 954/10, PRO.
62. Harvey, ed., *Oliver Harvey, 1937–1940*, p. 65; Avon, *Facing the Dictators*, p. 162; and Geoffrey McDermott, *The Eden Legacy*, London, 1969, p. 52.
63. Avon, *Facing the Dictators*, p. 569; Har-vey, ed., *Oliver Harvey, 1937–1940*, p. 78; and Prem. 1/276, PRO.
64. Dilks, ed., *Cadogan*, pp. 44–5.
65. Harvey, ed., *Oliver Harvey, 1937–1940*, p. 86; Ivy Chamberlain to Chamberlain, 16 Dec. 1937, Neville Chamberlain Papers; and Prem. 1/276, PRO.
66. Neville Chamberlain Diary, 19–27 Feb. 1938; and Malcolm Muggeridge, ed., *Ciano's Diplomatic Papers*, London, 1948, pp. 182–4.
67. Neville Chamberlain Diary, 19–27 Feb. 1938; Cab. 23/92 and Cab. 23/90A, PRO; and Middlemas, *Diplomacy of Illusion*, pp. 151–3.
68. Avon, *Facing the Dictators*, p. 486.
69. ibid., pp. 584–5.
70. Malcolm MacDonald to the author, 24 Jan. 1980.
71. Avon, *Facing the Dictators*, p. 579. See also Nicolson, ed., *Harold Nicolson, 1930–1939*, p. 323; and Harvey, ed., *Oliver Harvey, 1937–1940*, p. 93.

v *In the Wilderness,* 1938–9

1. Harvey, ed., *Oliver Harvey, 1937–1940*, pp. 117–18; Keith Middlemas and John Barnes, *Baldwin: A Biography*, London, 1969, pp. 1042–3; and John Harvey, ed., *The War Diaries of Oliver Harvey*, London, 1978, p. 143.
2. Feiling, *Neville Chamberlain*, p. 339.
3. Middlemas and Barnes, *Baldwin*, p. 1043.
4. *Documents on German Foreign Policy, 1918–1945*, series D, vol. I, London, 1949, no. 50.
5. Winston S. Churchill, *The Second World War* (6 vols.), London, 1948–54, vol. I, p. 221.
6. The Earl of Avon, *The Eden Memoirs: The Reckoning*, London, 1965, pp. 17, 31–2.
7. Martin Gilbert, *Winston S. Churchill*: vol. 5, 1922–1939, London, 1977, pp. 694, 696; John Ramsden, *The Age of Balfour and Baldwin, 1902–1940*, London, 1978, p. 366; and Churchill, *The Second World War*, vol. I, p. 201.
8. Avon, *Facing the Dictators*, p. 503.
9. FO 371/21131, PRO, quoted in J. W. Bruegel, *Czechoslovakia before Munich: The German Minority Problem and British Appeasement Policy*, Cambridge, 1973, p. 158.
10. Campbell-Johnson, *Sir Anthony Eden*, 2nd ed., pp. 159–60.
11. Halifax to Chamberlain, 12 Sept. 1938, Neville Chamberlain Papers, quoted in Middlemas, *Diplomacy of Illusion*, p. 328; *The Times*, 12 Sept. 1938; and Harvey, ed., *Oliver Harvey, 1937–1940*, p. 175.
12. ibid., p. 186; Avon, *The Reckoning*, p. 25; Nicolson, ed., *Harold Nicolson, 1930–1939*, p. 361; and Keith Robbins, *Munich, 1938*, London, 1968, p. 278.
13. Avon, *The Reckoning*, p. 26.
14. Robert Rhodes James, *Churchill: A Study in Failure, 1900–1939*, London, 1970, pp. 336–7.
15. Harvey, ed., *Oliver Harvey, 1937–1940*, p. 202.
16. HC Deb., CCCIX, cols. 77–88, 3 Oct. 1938.
17. ibid., CCCIX, cols. 359–74, 5 Oct. 1938.
18. Harvey, ed., *Oliver Harvey, 1937–1940*, pp. 212–13.
19. Feiling, *Neville Chamberlain*, p. 384.
20. Avon, *The Reckoning*, p. 30.
21. Neville Thompson, *The Anti-Appeasers: Conservative Opposition to Appeasement in the 1930s*, London, 1971, p. 187.

22. Eden to Baldwin, 30 Sept. 1938, Baldwin Papers, quoted in Roskill, *Hankey*, vol. 3, p. 386.

23. Harvey, ed., *Oliver Harvey, 1937–1940*, pp. 210–11.

24. Dalton, *The Fateful Years*, pp. 202–3.

25. L. S. Amery, *My Political Life* (3 vols.), London, 1953–5, vol. 3, pp. 299–300.

26. Harvey, ed., *Oliver Harvey, 1937–1940*, p. 221.

27. Basil Liddell Hart, *Memoirs*, vol. 2, London, 1966, p. 211; and Campbell-Johnson, *Sir Anthony Eden*, 2nd ed., p. 164; Harold Nicolson Diary, 15 Nov., 22 Dec. 1938 and 27 June 1939, Balliol College, Oxford; Avon to Nigel Nicolson, 12 June 1965, Harold Nicolson Papers, Balliol College, Oxford; and Avon to Emrys-Evans, 13 Aug. 1965, Paul Emrys-Evans Papers, British Library, Add. 58247.

28. Nicolson, ed., *Harold Nicolson, 1930–1939*, pp. 377–8, 382.

29. Harvey, ed., *Oliver Harvey, 1937–1940*, p. 236; and Nicolson, ed., *Harold Nicolson, 1930–1939*, p. 380.

30. Feiling, *Neville Chamberlain*, pp. 385–6; and Chamberlain to Mary Endicott, 5 Nov. 1938, Neville Chamberlain Papers.

31. Eden to Baldwin, 19 Dec. 1938, Baldwin Papers.

32. *HC Deb.*, cccxlv, cols. 458–62, 15 Mar. 1939; and Robert Rhodes James,

ed., *Chips: The Diary of Sir Henry Channon*, London, 1967, p. 186.

33. Cowling, *The Impact of Hitler*, p. 291. Cf also Simon Newman, *March 1939: The British Guarantee of Poland*, Oxford 1976, *passim*. He shows that Halifax played a decisive part but does not explore the possibility that his motivation was primarily party political.

34. Christopher Thorne, *The Approach of War, 1938–1939*, London, 1967, pp. 119–20; Eden to Chamberlain, 1 Apr. 1939, Neville Chamberlain Papers; and *HC Deb.*, cccxlv, cols. 2512–75, 3 Apr. 1939.

35. Harvey, ed., *Oliver Harvey, 1937–1940*, pp. 280–81.

36. *HC Deb.*, cccxlvii, cols. 1854–60, 19 May 1939.

37. FO 371/20702, PRO.

38. James, ed., *Chips*, p. 204. See also Gilbert, *Churchill*, vol. 5, pp. 1081–2, 1086.

39. Nicolson, ed., *Harold Nicolson, 1930–1939*, pp. 406–7.

40. Duff Cooper, *Old Men Forget*, London, 1954, p. 250.

41. Avon, *The Reckoning*, p. 62; and Nicolson, ed., *Harold Nicolson, 1930–1939*, p. 420.

42. Gilbert, *Churchill*, vol. 5, pp. 1107–8; and Harvey, ed., *Oliver Harvey, 1937–1940*, p. 280.

43. Avon, *The Reckoning*, p. 277.

VI *European War*, 1939–41

1. Chamberlain to Ida Chamberlain, 10 Sept. 1939, 5 Nov. 1939, 16 Mar. 1940; and Chamberlain to Hilda Chamberlain, 28 Oct. 1939, Chamberlain Papers.

2. Cab. 65/1, PRO; and Bruce to Robert Menzies, 8 Oct. 1939, in R. G. Neale, ed., *Documents on Australian Foreign Policy 1937–49*, vol. 2, Canberra, 1976, no. 270.

3. Cab. 99/1, PRO; and Cowling, *The Impact of Hitler*, p. 361.

4. Savage to Menzies, 5 Nov. 1939 in Neale, ed., *Australian Foreign Policy*, vol. 2, no. 326.

5. Cab. 99/1, PRO.

6. Bruce to Menzies, 8 Oct. 1939 in Neale, ed., *Australian Foreign Policy*, vol. 2, no. 270.

7. Harold Nicolson, Diary (unpublished), 27 Sept. 1939.

8. Avon, *The Reckoning*, p. 63.

9. Joseph T. Carroll, *Ireland in the War Years, 1939–1945*, Newton Abbot, Devon, 1975, p. 29.

10. Eden to Halifax, 20 Oct. 1940, Halifax Papers, FO 800/310, PRO.

11. Churchill to Halifax, 20 Oct. 1940, ibid.

12. Cab. 65/1, PRO.

13. Harold Nicolson Diary, 1 Oct. 1939 and 6 Jan. 1940; Harvey, ed., *Oliver Harvey, 1937–1940*, p. 326; and Avon to Nigel Nicolson, 26 May 1966, copy in Harold Nicolson Diary.

14. Joe Garner, *The Commonwealth Office, 1925–68*, London, 1978, p. 161; and Deneys Reitz, *No Outspan*, London, 1943, p. 255.

15. James, ed., *Chips*, pp. 244–7.
16. J. W. Wheeler-Bennett, *King George VI: His Life and Reign*, London, 1958, p. 444.
17. Avon, *The Reckoning*, p. 97.
18. Neville Chamberlain Diary, 9 Sept. 1940.
19. Montgomery Hyde, *Neville Chamberlain*, London, 1976, p. 164; and Beaverbrook Papers quoted in Paul Addison, *The Road to 1945: British Politics and the Second World War*, London, 1975, p. 101.
20. Neville Chamberlain Diary, 26 May 1940; and Cab. 65/13, PRO.
21. Dalton, *The Fateful Years*, p. 336.
22. Cab. 65/7, PRO; and Avon, *The Reckoning*, p. 112.
23. ibid., p. 118.
24. Cab. 65/13, PRO; and P. M. H. Bell, *A Certain Eventuality: Britain and the Fall of France*, London, 1974, p. 72, quoting FO 371/24310, PRO.
25. A. J. P. Taylor, ed., *W. P. Crozier: Off the Record: Political Interviews, 1933–1943*, London, 1973, p. 185; and Avon, *The Reckoning*, p. 107.
26. Neville Chamberlain Diary, 30 Sept. 1940.
27. Avon, *The Reckoning*, p. 145.
28. Hugh Trevor-Roper, ed., *The Goebbels Diaries: The Last Days*, London, 1978, p. 116.
29. Cab. 65/16, PRO.
30. Prem. 3/308, PRO.
31. Avon, *The Reckoning*, pp. 170–1.
32. Charles Cruikshank, *Greece, 1940–1941*, London, 1976, pp. 55–6; Churchill, *The Second World War*, vol. 2, p. 480; Avon, *The Reckoning*, p. 171.
33. Churchill, *The Second World War*, vol. 2, p. 505.
34. FO 371/29834, PRO, quoted in Martin van Creveld, 'Prelude to Disaster: the British Decision to Aid Greece, 1940–41', *Journal of Contemporary History*, IX, 1974, no. 3, p. 75.
35. Dilks, ed., *Cadogan*, p. 350.
36. Avon, *Facing the Dictators*, p. 188.
37. ibid., p. 192.
38. ibid., p. 196.
39. John S. Koliopoulos, *Greece and the British Connection, 1935–1941*, Oxford, 1977, p. 241; Alexander Papagos, *The Battle of Greece, 1940–1941*, Athens, 1949; Avon, *The Reckoning*, pp. 200–1; and Prem. 3/294/1, PRO (Dixon's record).
40. Prem. 3/294/1, annex 3, record 3, PRO.
41. ibid., record 4.
42. Koliopoulos, *Greece and the British Connection*, p. 241.
43. Cab. 105/2, PRO.
44. Sir Llewellyn Woodward, *British Foreign Policy in the Second World War* (5 vols.), London, 1970–76, vol. 1, p. 527.
45. Sir Pierson Dixon Papers in the possession of Piers Dixon.
46. ibid. See also Piers Dixon, *Double Diploma: The Life of Sir Pierson Dixon, Don and Diplomat*, London, 1968, pp. 71–2.
47. Sir Pierson Dixon Diary in the possession of Piers Dixon; cf. Dixon, *Double Diploma*, p. 64.
48. Dixon Papers.
49. Papagos, *The Battle of Greece*, pp. 323–4.
50. Avon, *The Reckoning*, pp. 214–15.
51. Dixon, *Double Diploma*, p. 68; and Churchill, *The Second World War*, vol. 3, pp. 86–7.
52. Dilks, ed., *Cadogan*, p. 359–60.
53. Cab. 65/21, PRO. See also Prem. 4/25/5, PRO.
54. Dilks, ed., *Cadogan*, p. 360; Woodward, *British Foreign Policy*, vol. 1, p. 536n.
55. Cab. 65/22, PRO.
56. Avon, *The Reckoning*, p. 242; and Prem. 3/294/1, annexes 12 and 13, PRO.
57. Dilks, ed., *Cadogan*, p. 361.
58. Avon, *The Reckoning*, p. 229.
59. King George the Sixth to Eden, 28 Mar. 1941, Avon Papers, FO 954/11, PRO.
60. Dilks, ed., *Cadogan*, p. 370.
61. Oliver Harvey Diary, 18 April 1941, British Library, Add. 56397.
62. Avon, *The Reckoning*, p. 241; and Martin L. van Creveld, *Hitler's Strategy, 1940–1941: The Balkan Clue*, London, 1973, Part Two.

VII *Global War, 1941–5*

1. Cab. 65/18, PRO.
2. Lord Boothby, *Recollections of a Rebel*, London, 1978, pp. 183–4.
3. Harvey Diary, 24, 15 Dec. 1941, Add. 56398.
4. Harvey, ed., *War Diaries*, p. 85.

5. Harvey Diary, 18 Sept. 1941, Add. 56398.
6. ibid., 6 Oct. 1943, Add. 56400; and Harvey, ed., *War Diaries*, p. 152.
7. Harvey Diary, 15 Jan., 6 June 1941, Add. 56397; and Harvey, ed., *War Diaries*, p. 152. See also ibid., p. 30.
8. Harvey, ed., *War Diaries*, pp. 39, 36.
9. ibid., pp. 21, 57.
10. Harvey Diary. 11, 18 Nov. 1941. Add. 56398.
11. Woodward, *British Foreign Policy*, vol. 2, pp. 53-4.
12. Harvey Diary, 6 Dec. 1941, Add. 56398.
13. FO 371/23556, PRO, quoted in Peter Lowe, *Great Britain and the Origins of the Pacific War: A Study of British Policy in East Asia, 1937–1941*, Oxford, 1977, p. 106.
14. Avon, *The Reckoning*, p. 311; and Cab. 65/23, PRO, quoted in Peter Lowe, 'Great Britain and the Coming of the Pacific War, 1939–1941', *Transactions of the Royal Historical Society*, XXIV, 1974, p. 55.
15. Halifax to Eden, 1 Dec. 1941, FO 371/27913, PRO.
16. FO 371/27883, PRO quoted in Lowe, *Great Britain and the Origins of the Pacific War*, pp. 257-8.
17. Avon, *The Reckoning*, p. 313.
18. Churchill, *The Second World War*, vol. 3, p. 539.
19. Craigie Report, 4 Feb. 1943 and Churchill to Eden, 19 Sept. 1943, FO 371/35957, PRO.
20. Donald Watt, *Daily Telegraph*, 15 July 1972.
21. Dilks, ed., *Cadogan*, p. 417.
22. ibid.
23. Harvey Diary, 13, 24 Dec. 1941, Add. 56398; Avon, *The Reckoning*, pp. 287-8; and Dilks, ed., *Cadogan*, pp. 419-20.
24. Harvey, ed., *War Diaries*, p. 77.
25. Prem. 3/399/7, PRO.
26. Dalton Papers, British Library of Political and Economic Science, quoted in T. D. Burridge, *British Labour and Hitler's War*, London, 1976, pp. 84-5; and Harvey Diary, 8 Jan. 1942, Add. 56398.
27. W.P. 48(42), Cab. 66/21, PRO; and Avon, *The Reckoning*, p. 319.
28. Cab. 65/29, PRO; Kenneth Young, *Churchill and Beaverbrook*, London, 1966, p. 235; and Beaverbrook to

Avon, 3 Mar. 1942, Avon Papers, FO 954/25, PRO.
29. Prem. 3/470, PRO, quoted in Elisabeth Barker, *Churchill and Eden at War*, London, 1978, p. 238.
30. Harvey, ed., *War Diaries*, p. 110; and Butler to Eden, 13 Mar. 1942, Avon Papers, FO 954/25, PRO.
31. Harvey Diary, 24 Mar. 1942, Add. 56398.
32. Prem. 4/32/9, PRO.
33. Cazalet to Eden, 17 Apr. 1942, Avon Papers, FO 954/25, PRO; and Harvey, ed., *War Diaries*, p. 118.
34. Duff Cooper to Eden, 22 Apr. 1942; and Nicolson to Eden, 24 Apr. 1942, Avon Papers, FO 954/25, PRO.
35. Harvie Watt memorandum, 24 Apr. 1942; and Eden to Churchill, 28 Apr. 1942, ibid.
36. Simon to Churchill, 8 May 1942, ibid.
37. Harvey, ed., *War Diaries*, p. 125.
38. Dilks, ed., *Cadogan*, p. 454; and Harvey, ed., *War Diaries*, p. 128.
39. Dilks, ed., *Cadogan*, p. 455.
40. Prem. 3/399/6, PRO.
41. Addison, *The Road to 1945*, pp. 134-5.
42. Eden to Churchill, 23 Mar. 1942, Avon Papers, FO 954/25, PRO.
43. Harvey, ed., *War Diaries*, pp. 25-7.
44. ibid., pp. 55, 87, 17-18.
45. ibid., pp. 94-5.
46. Harvey to Eden, 13 Feb. 1942, Harvey Papers, British Library, Add. 56402; Harvey, ed., *War Diaries*, pp. 95-6; and Harvey Diary, 16 Feb. 1942, Add. 56398.
47. Harvey, ed., *War Diaries*, p. 97.
48. Harvey Diary, 18 Feb. 1942, Add. 56398.
49. Avon, *The Reckoning*, p. 321; and Harvey, ed., *War Diaries*, p. 98.
50. Harvey, ed., *War Diaries*, p. 98.
51. ibid., p. 99; and Churchill, *The Second World War*, vol. 4, p. 80.
52. Harvey, ed., *War Diaries*, pp. 101-4; and Harvey Diary, Add. 56398.
53. Harvey, ed., *War Diaries*, p. 114.
54. ibid., pp. 149-50, 161, 164-6; and Avon, *The Reckoning*, p. 352.
55. Harvey, ed., *War Diaries*, p. 165.
56. Avon, *The Reckoning*, p. 351; and Charles de Gaulle, *War Memoirs: Unity, 1942-44*, London, 1959, p. 57.
57. Harvey, ed., *War Diaries*, p. 213.
58. Chester Wilmot, *The Struggle for Europe*, New York, 1952; Fitzroy Maclean. *Eastern Approaches*, London, 1949, pp.

402–3; Michael Howard, *The Mediterranean Strategy in the Second World War*,
London, 1968; and Richard M. Leighton, 'OVERLORD Revisited: An Interpretation of American Strategy in the
European War, 1942–1944', *American
Historical Review*, LXVIII, 1963,
pp. 919–37.

59. Harvey, ed., *War Diaries*, p. 229.
60. Henry H. Adams, *Harry Hopkins: A
Biography*, New York, 1977, p. 202.
61. Harvey, ed., *War Diaries*, p. 231.
62. Prem. 3/476/9, PRO; and Robert E.
Sherwood, *The White House Papers of
Harry L. Hopkins* (2 vols.), London,
1948–9, vol. 2, p. 714.
63. Avon, *The Reckoning*, p. 374.
64. William Roger Louis, *Imperialism at
Bay, 1941–1945: The United States and
the Decolonisation of the British Empire*,
Oxford, 1977, p. 200; and Sherwood,
Hopkins, vol. 2, p. 717.
65. For details see Louis, *Imperialism at Bay*;
Christopher Thorne, *Allies of a Kind; The
United States, Britain and the War against
Japan, 1941–1945*, London, 1978; and
J. E. Williams, 'The Joint Declaration on
Colonies: An Issue in Anglo-American
Relations, 1942–1944', *British Journal
of International Studies*, II, 1976, pp.
267–92.
66. Eden to Churchill, 29 Mar. 1943, Avon
Papers, FO 954/22, PRO; and Avon,
The Reckoning, p. 373.
67. Hopkins to Eden, 23 Apr. 1943, Harry
L. Hopkins Papers, Roosevelt Library,
Hyde Park, New York, Box 329.
68. HC Deb., CCCXXXVII, cols. 2082–7, 17
Dec. 1942.
69. Sherwood, *Hopkins*, vol. 2, p. 715; and
Eden to Harvey, Aug. 1941, Harvey
Papers, Add. 56402, quoted in Bernard
Wasserstein, *Britain and the Jews of
Europe, 1939–1945*, Oxford, 1979, p.
34.
70. For further details, both from view-
points extremely critical of British policy, see Wasserstein, *Britain and the
Jews of Europe*; and Nicholas Bethell, *The
Palestinian Triangle: The Struggle between
the British, the Jews and the Arabs,
1935–48*, London, 1979.
71. FO 371/34577, PRO.
72. Woodward, *British Foreign Policy*, vol.
2, p. 626n. Cf. E. L. Woodward, *British
Foreign Policy in the Second World War*
(one-volume edition), London, 1962, p.

204n. In this earlier, even more discreet
edition, Woodward wrote of the Foreign
Office eventually 'being unable to exclude the hypothesis that the responsibility for the Katyn massacres lay with
the Soviet authorities' and that the
Soviet Commission of Enquiry of January 1944 did 'not seem to the Foreign Office to provide evidence conclusive of German responsibility'.
73. Barker, *Churchill and Eden*, p. 249; and
Dilks, ed., *Cadogan*, pp. 520–21.
74. Dilks, ed., *Cadogan*, p. 523; Cab. 65/34,
PRO; Barker, *Churchill and Eden*, p. 249;
and Prem. 3/354/8, PRO.
75. Prem. 3/354/8, PRO.
76. *HC Deb.*, CCCLXXXIX, col. 31, 4 May
1943.
77. O'Malley memorandum, 27 May 1943
and Cadogan minute, 18 June 1943, FO
371/34577, PRO. See also Dilks, ed.,
Cadogan, p. 537.
78. *HC Deb.*, CCCIX, cols. 77–8, 5 Oct.
1938.
79. For details see Cmd. 6420 of 1943;
Avon, *The Reckoning*, pp. 257–8; and
Donald G. Bishop, *The Administration of
British Foreign Relations*, Syracuse, New
York, 1961, pp. 207–12.
80. Dilks, ed., *Cadogan*, p. 497; and Harvey
Diary, 19 Jan. 1943, Add. 56399.
81. Harvey, ed., *War Diaries*, p. 258.
82. Avon, *The Reckoning*, p. 382; Harvey,
ed., *War Diaries*, pp. 187, 250–51.
83. Harvey, ed., *War Diaries*, pp. 246, 249,
255, 257, 265.
84. ibid., p. 266; and Cab. 65/38, PRO. See
also Barker, *Churchill and Eden*, pp.
78–9.
85. Prem. 3/81/2, PRO, quoted in Barker,
Churchill and Eden, pp. 80–81.
86. Harvey, ed., *War Diaries*, pp. 273–4;
and Prem. 3/81/8, PRO.
87. Avon, *The Reckoning*, p. 398; and Prem.
3/181/8, PRO.
88. Harvey, ed., *War Diaries*, pp. 274–5.
89. For further details concerning the Washington Conference see Mark A. Stoler,
*The Politics of the Second Front: American
Military Planning and Diplomacy in Coalition Warfare, 1941–1943*, Westport,
Connecticut, 1977, pp. 92–6; and United States Department of State, *Papers
Relating to the Foreign Relations of the
United States, Washington and Quebec
Conferences, 1943*, Washington, DC,
1970, pp. 25–7, 193–5.

90. Henry L. Stimson Diary, Yale University Library, New Haven, Connecticut, reel 8, 14–29 Mar. 1943.
91. Stoler, *The Politics of the Second Front*, p. 98, based on Minutes of the Combined Chiefs of Staff.
92. Stimson Diary, reel 8, 4 Aug. 1943.
93. US Department of State, *Foreign Relations, Washington and Quebec, 1943*, p. 942.
94. ibid., pp. 966–7.
95. Harvey, ed., *War Diaries*, p. 288.
96. ibid., p. 304.
97. FO 371/33154, PRO, quoted in Elisabeth Barker, *British Policy in South-East Europe in the Second World War*, London, 1976, p. 134.
98. See above, p. 103.
99. W. Averell Harriman and Elie Abel, *Special Envoy to Churchill and Stalin*, New York, 1975, p. 245; and Prem. 3/114/2, PRO, quoted in Barker, *Churchill and Eden*, pp. 266–7.
100. Breckenridge Long Diary, Library of Congress, Washington, DC, container 5, 18 Nov. 1943; and Hull to Eden, 30 Oct. 1943, Cordell Hull Papers, Library of Congress, Washington, DC, reel 24.
101. Vojtech Mastny, 'Soviet War Aims at the Moscow and Teheran Conferences of 1943', *Journal of Modern History*, XLVII, 1975, p. 493.
102. Deane to Joint Chiefs of Staff, message no. 16983, 28 Oct. 1943, Military Archives, National Archives, Washington, DC.
103. Stimson Diary, reel 8, 28, 29 Oct., 4 Nov. 1943. See also Edward R. Stettinius Papers, University of Virginia Library, Charlottesville, Virginia, Box 237.
104. Harvey, ed., *War Diaries*, p. 317.
105. ibid., pp. 315, 317.
106. Moran, *Churchill*, p. 132; and Hopkins to Churchill, 24 Nov. 1943, Prem. 4/74/2/1, PRO.
107. William D. Leahy Diary, Library of Congress, Washington, DC, 3 Dec. 1943.
108. Moran, *Churchill*, pp. 136, 140–41.
109. Avon, *The Reckoning*, p. 429.
110. Churchill to Eden, 6 Oct. 1943, Prem. 3/399/6, PRO.
111. Churchill to Eden, 16 Jan. 1944; and Eden to Churchill, 25 Jan. 1944, ibid.
112. Anthony Polonsky, ed., *The Great Powers and the Polish Question, 1941–45:* *A Documentary Study in Cold War Origins*, London, 1976, p. 105n.
113. Dixon Diary; and Harvey, ed., *War Diaries*, p. 335.
114. Avon, *The Reckoning*, p. 439.
115. Barker, *Churchill and Eden*, p. 274. See also Elisabeth Barker, 'Some Factors in British Decision-Making over Yugoslavia, 1941–4', in Phyllis Auty and Richard Clogg, eds., *British Policy Towards Wartime Resistance in Yugoslavia and Greece*, London, 1975, pp. 22–5.
116. Dixon Diary, 16 Feb. 1944.
117. Dilks, ed., *Cadogan*, pp. 503, 608; and Dixon Diary.
118. Harvey, ed., *War Diaries*, p. 335; and Dilks, ed., *Cadogan*, p. 337.
119. Dixon Diary.
120. ibid., 3 July 1944; and Harvey, ed., *War Diaries*, pp. 346, 337.
121. Harvey Diary, 1 May, 21 Aug., 6 Sept. 1944.
122. Dixon Diary, 17 Apr. 1944; and Prem. 3/211/16, PRO, quoted in Barker, *Churchill and Eden*, pp. 276–7.
123. Dixon Diary, 12 July 1944; and FO 371/43772, PRO.
124. For further detail see Barker, *Churchill and Eden*, chs. 7 and 8.
125. Avon, *The Reckoning*, pp. 454–5.
126. Stimson Diary, reel 9, 22 June 1944.
127. Barker, *Churchill and Eden*, p. 112.
128. Quoted in Nikolai Tolstoy, *Victims of Yalta*, revised edition, London, 1979, p. 66.
129. Cab. 65/43, PRO.
130. Tolstoy, *Victims of Yalta*, pp. 67–9.
131. Barker, *British Policy in South-East Europe*, p. 140.
132. Tolstoy, *Victims of Yalta*, pp. 76–7.
133. ibid., pp. 77, 540.
134. Christopher Booker, *Spectator*, 18 Feb. 1978. For a critique of this article see David Carlton, ibid., 8 Apr. 1978.
135. Dilks, ed., *Cadogan*, pp. 597, 739; and Cadogan minute, FO 371/40444, PRO, quoted in Nicholas Bethell, *The Last Secret: Forcible Repatriation to Russia, 1944–7*, London, 1974, p. 28.
136. Cab. 65/43, PRO; and Selborne to Eden, 18 Aug. 1944, Selborne Papers, quoted in Tolstoy, *Victims of Yalta*, p. 80.
137. Avon, *The Reckoning*, p. 476; Stimson Diary, reel 9, Sept. 1944; and Dixon Diary, 16 Sept. 1944.
138. Moran, *Churchill*, pp. 193, 194.
139. Inverchapel Papers, FO 800/302, PRO;

and Churchill, *The Second World War*, vol. 6, pp. 196–7.

140. For further detail see Albert Resis, 'The Churchill-Stalin Secret "Percentages" Agreement on the Balkans, Moscow, October 1944', *American Historical Review*, LXXXIII, 1978, pp. 368–87.

141. Elisabeth Barker, 'British Policy towards Romania, Bulgaria and Hungary, 1944–1946' in Martin McCauley, ed., *Communist Power in Europe, 1944–1949*, London, 1977, p. 204.

142. Thomas Barman, *Diplomatic Correspondent*, London, 1968, pp. 175–6; and Churchill, *The Second World War*, vol. 6, p. 124.

143. For details see Barker, *Churchill and Eden*, pp. 290–91.

144. Dixon Diary, 10 Oct. 1944.

145. Prem. 3/364/8, PRO, quoted in Tolstoy, *Victims of Yalta*, pp. 92–3.

146. Moran, *Churchill*, p. 206; Cab. 65/51, PRO; and Dalton Diary, 23 Feb. 1945, quoted in Dilks, ed., *Cadogan*, p. 716.

147. Churchill to Eden, 8 May 1944, Avon Papers, FO 954/20, PRO; Churchill to Cranborne, 3 Apr. 1945. ibid.; and Moran, *Churchill*, p. 278.

148. FO 371/48193, PRO, quoted in Barker, *Churchill and Eden*, p. 294.

149. Churchill, *The Second World War*, vol. 6, p. 250.

150. Dixon Diary, 4 Dec. 1944. Cf. Churchill, *The Second World War*, vol. 6, p. 252.

151. Churchill, ibid.

152. ibid.

153. Dixon Diary.

154. Louis, *Imperialism at Bay*, chs. 29, 30.

155. Keith Sainsbury, 'British Policy and German unity at the end of the Second World War', *English Historical Review*, XCIV, 1979, p. 802.

156. Eden to Churchill, 28 Jan. 1945, Avon Papers, FO 954/20, PRO.

157. Churchill, *The Second World War*, vol. 6, p. 337.

158. William D. Leahy, *I Was There*, New York, 1950, pp. 315–16; and Churchill to Eden, 13 Mar. 1945, Avon Papers, FO 954/23, PRO.

159. *HC Deb.*, CDVIII, cols. 1267–1345, 1416–1516, 27, 28 Feb. 1945; and Nicolson, ed., *Harold Nicolson, 1939–1945*, p. 437.

160. Churchill to Eden, 19 Jan. 1945, Avon Papers, FO 954/23, PRO.

161. Churchill to Eden, 5 Mar. 1945, ibid.

162. Eden to Churchill, 5 Mar. 1945, ibid.

163. Churchill to Eden, 13 Mar. 1945, ibid.

164. Avon, *The Reckoning*, p. 525.

165. Cranborne to Eden, 9 Apr. 1945, Avon Papers, FO 954/20, PRO.

166. Dixon Diary, 3 May 1945.

167. Avon, *The Reckoning*, p. 536; and Dixon Diary, 4 May 1945.

168. Avon, *The Reckoning*, p. 545.

169. Moran, *Churchill*, p. 277.

170. Avon, *The Reckoning*, p. 551.

VIII *In Opposition, 1945–51*

1. Stettinius Papers, Box 247; and T. F. Lindsay and Michael Harrington, *The Conservative Party, 1918–1970*, London, 1974, p. 148.

2. *The Times*, 20 Dec. 1945.

3. Avon, *The Reckoning*, p. 554; and Trygve Lie, *In the Cause of Peace*, New York, 1954, pp. 11–12.

4. Cranborne to Emrys-Evans, 12 Feb. 1946, Emrys-Evans Papers, Add. 58240.

5. *HC Deb.*, CDXIII, col. 312, 20 Aug. 1945; Lord Butler, *The Art of the Possible*, London, 1971, p. 131; Avi Schlaim, Peter Jones and Keith Sainsbury, *British Foreign Secretaries since 1945*, Newton Abbot, Devon, 1977, p. 66; and Dixon, *Double Diploma*, pp. 195–7.

6. *HC Deb.*, CDXVI, cols. 614–15, 22 Nov.

1945; and CDXIII, cols. 316–18. 20 Aug. 1945.

7. ibid., CDXIX, cols. 1340–42, 21 Feb. 1946.

8. ibid., CDXIII, cols. 84–5, 16 Aug. 1945.

9. *The Times*, 6 Mar. 1946. See also Henry B. Ryan, 'A New Look at Churchill's "Iron Curtain" Speech', *Historical Journal*, XXII, 1979, pp. 895–920.

10. *The Times*, 6 Mar. 1946.

11. Cab. 128/5, 3 June 1946, PRO; and *HC Deb.*, CDXX, col. 761, 11 Mar. 1946.

12. Conservative and Unionist Central Office, *General Election, 1950: The Campaign Guide*, London, 1950, p. 348.

13. *HC Deb.*, CDXX, cols. 231–2, 236, 5 Mar. 1946.

14. Cranborne to Emrys-Evans, 14 Mar.

1946, Emrys-Evans Papers, Add. 58240.

15. Thomas to Emrys-Evans, 26 Mar. 1946, ibid., Add. 58242.

16. Thomas to Emrys-Evans, 22 Apr. 1946 and two undated letters, ibid.

17. Eden to Halifax, 8 Aug. 1946, Halifax Papers, Churchill College, Cambridge, A4.410.21.2; and Bracken to Beaverbrook, 16 Oct. 1946, Beaverbrook Papers, House of Lords Record Office, BBK C56.

18. J. D. Hoffman, *The Conservative Party in Opposition, 1945–51*, London, 1964, p. 138; and Aster, *Eden*, p. 92.

19. *The Times*, 19 May 1947.

20. Bracken to Beaverbrook, 7 Oct. 1946, Beaverbrook Papers, BBK C56.

21. Thomas to Emrys-Evans, n.d., Emrys-Evans Papers, Add. 58242.

22. The full text is in Anthony Eden, *Freedom and Order: Selected Speeches, 1939–1946*, London, 1947, pp. 419–24.

23. Bracken to Beaverbrook, 22 Sept. 1946, Beaverbrook Papers, BBK C56.

24. The full text of the Watford speech is in Eden, *Freedom and Order*, pp. 413–17.

25. *The Times*, 26 Sept. 1946.

26. *HC Deb.*, CDXXIII, cols. 701–08, 24 May 1946.

27. Eden to Halifax, 8 Aug. 1946, Halifax Papers, Churchill College, Cambridge, A4.410.21.2.

28. See Hassan Ahmed Ibrahim, 'The Anglo-Egyptian Treaty of 1936', unpublished London University PhD thesis, 1976.

29. James Stuart, *Within the Fringe: An Autobiography*, London, 1967, pp. 144–7. See also Alan Thompson, *The Day before Yesterday*, London, 1971, pp. 86–7.

30. Dixon, *Double Diploma*, p. 246.

31. Cranborne to Emrys-Evans, 9 Jan. 1947, Emrys-Evans Papers, Add. 58240.

32. Harold Macmillan, *Tides of Fortune, 1945–1955*, London, 1969, p. 287.

33. *The Times*, 21 Jan. 1947.

34. For American reactions to events in Hungary see United States Department of State, *Papers Relating to the Foreign Relations of the United States, 1947* (8 vols.), Washington, DC, 1971–3, vol. 4, p. 260 *et seq.*

35. Bruce Reed and Geoffrey Williams, *Denis Healey and the Politics of Power*, London, 1971, pp. 35, 25, 26, 51–4.

36. *Tribune*, 14 Feb. 1947.

37. Anthony Eden, *Days for Decision*, London, 1949, pp. 169–72.

38. *HC Deb.*, CDXXXVIII, cols. 1352–4, 12 June 1947; and FO 371/67179, PRO.

39. ibid., cols. 2236–7, 19 June 1947.

40. ibid., CDXXXVII, col. 1756, 15 May 1947.

41. ibid., CDXXXVIII, cols. 2236–7, 19 June 1947.

42. Eden, *Days for Decision*, p. 173.

43. *HC Deb.*, CDXLV, cols. 1468–70, 15 Dec. 1947.

44. Bardens, *Portrait of a Statesman*, pp. 268–9.

45. *The Times*, 1 May 1948.

46. Eden, *Days for Decision*, pp. 196–7, 217; and *The Times*, 18 Oct. 1948.

47. *HC Deb.*, CDLVII, cols. 20–21, 26 Oct. 1948.

48. See above, pp. 274–5; and Denis Healey, 'The Cominform and World Communism', *International Affairs*, XXIV, 1948, pp. 339–49.

49. *HC Deb.*, CDLVI, col. 81, 15 Sept. 1948.

50. ibid., CDXLIII, col. 20, 21 Oct. 1947.

51. Stuart, *Within the Fringe*, p. 178.

52. *The Times*, 9 June 1949.

53. Eden, *Days for Decision*, pp. 134–5.

54. *The Times*, 19 Feb. 1949.

55. ibid., 1 Mar. 1949.

56. Macmillan, *Tides of Fortune*, p. 287.

57. *The Times*, 13 June 1949.

58. ibid., 3 Dec. 1949.

59. H. G. Nicholas, *The British General Election of 1950*, London, 1951, pp. 133–4.

60. Bracken to Beaverbrook, 10 Jan. 1950, Beaverbrook Papers, BBK C57.

61. Macmillan, *Tides of Fortune*, pp. 193–6.

62. *HC Deb.*, CDLXXVI, cols. 1916, 2140–59, 26 and 27 June 1950.

63. *The Times*, 1 July 1950.

64. *HC Deb.*, CDLXXVII, cols. 584–5, 5 July 1950.

65. *The Times*, 26 Oct. 1950.

66. *HC Deb.*, CDLXXXI, cols. 1176–7, 1185–6, 29 Nov. 1950.

67. ibid., CDLXXXII, cols. 1451–3, 14 Dec. 1950.

68. ibid., CDLXXXI, cols. 1184–5, 29 Nov. 1950.

69. Bernard Donoughue and G. W. Jones, *Herbert Morrison: Portrait of a Politician*, London, 1973, p. 250.

70. *HC Deb.*, CDLXXXVII, col. 1954, 9 May 1951.

71. ibid., CDLXXXV, cols. 1767–70, 15 Mar. 1951.
72. Donoughue and Jones, *Herbert Morrison*, p. 503.
73. Quoted in *The Times*, 12 Oct. 1951.
74. *HC Deb.*, CDLXXXIX, cols. 752–3, 21 June 1951; and *The Sunday Times*, 24 June 1951.
75. *HC Deb.*, CDXC, col. 35, 9 July 1951.
76. *The Times*, 16 July 1951.

77. ibid., 7, 11 and 21 Aug. 1951. See also Anthony Eden, 'Britain in World Strategy', *Foreign Affairs*, XXIX, 1950–51, pp. 341–50.
78. *The Times*, 23 Oct. 1951.
79. Private information.
80. *The Times*, 8 Oct. 1951.
81. ibid., 11 Oct. 1951.
82. Law to Beaverbrook, 1 Jan. 1950, Beaverbrook Papers, BBK C214.

IX *Churchill's Foreign Secretary*, 1951–5

1. Sir Evelyn Shuckburgh Diary, in the possession of the diarist, 27 Oct. 1951; Wheeler-Bennett, *King George VI*, p. 797; and the Earl of Kilmuir, *Political Adventure*, London, 1964, p. 193.
2. John Colville in John W. Wheeler-Bennett, ed., *Action This Day: Working with Churchill*, London, 1968, pp. 107–8; Anthony Eden, *Full Circle: Memoirs*, London, 1960, pp. 247, 249; Moran, *Winston Churchill*, p. 559.
3. Shuckburgh Diary, 1 Apr. 1954.
4. Private information from an American source.
5. Shuckburgh Diary, 1952.
6. Shuckburgh Diary.
7. Lord Gladwyn quoted in Schlaim, Jones and Sainsbury, *British Foreign Secretaries since 1945*, p. 88.
8. Roderick Barclay, *Ernest Bevin and the Foreign Office*, London, 1975, p. 108; and Shuckburgh Diary.
9. Townshend Hoopes, *The Devil and John Foster Dulles*, London, 1974, p. 169.
10. Eden, *Full Circle*, pp. 63–4, 99, 256–7.
11. David S. McLellan, *Dean Acheson: The State Department Years*, New York, 1976, p. 358.
12. Livingston Merchant Recollections, Columbia University Oral Project, New York.
13. Iveragh McDonald, *A Man of The Times*, London, 1976, p. 135.
14. Eden, *Full Circle*, pp. 200, 21; and Dean Acheson, *Present at the Creation: My Years in the State Department*, London, 1969, p. 578.
15. McDonald, *A Man of The Times*, p. 133.
16. Moran, *Winston Churchill*, p. 355.
17. Eden, *Full Circle*, p. 19; and Acheson, *Present at the Creation*, pp. 603–4. See also memorandum on Acheson–Dulles–Franks conversation, 16 Jan. 1952; and memorandum on Acheson–Franks conversation, 24 Jan.

1952, Dean Acheson Papers, The Truman Library, Independence, Missouri, Box 66.
18. T. B. Millar, ed., *The Diaries of R. G. Casey, 1951–60* (London, 1972), pp. 72–3. See also memorandum on Acheson– Franks conversation, 6 June 1952; memorandum on Acheson–Menzies conversation, 20 June 1952; and Eden to Acheson, 2 Sept. 1952, Acheson Papers, Box 67.
19. See, for example, Victor Bator, *Vietnam: A Diplomatic Tragedy: Origins of U.S. Involvement*, London, 1967, p. 19.
20. Acheson, *Present at the Creation*, p. 599.
21. Moran, *Winston Churchill*, p. 362.
22. Acheson, *Present at the Creation*, p. 600. See also memorandum on Truman–Churchill–Acheson–Eden conversation, 5 Jan. 1952, Acheson Papers, Box 66.
23. Acheson, *Present at the Creation*, pp. 565, 564, 597.
24. Eden memorandum for Acheson, 4 Nov. 1951 and Acheson (Paris) to State Department, 10 Nov. 1951, Acheson Papers, quoted in McLellan, *Dean Acheson*, p. 390.
25. Acheson, *Present at the Creation*, p. 600.
26. McLellan, *Dean Acheson*, p. 390.
27. Gaddis Smith, *Dean Acheson*, New York, 1972, p. 343.
28. Acheson to Eden, 11 Apr. 1952 and Eden to Acheson, 18 Apr. 1952, Acheson Papers, Box 67, quoted in Acheson, *Present at the Creation*, pp. 605–6.
29. Moran, *Churchill*, p. 357.
30. Acheson, *Present at the Creation*, p. 594.
31. Moran, *Churchill*, p. 359.
32. Macmillan, *Tides of Fortune*, p. 217.
33. *HC Deb.*, CDLXXXIV, cols. 49–50, 12 Feb. 1951.
34. Macmillan, *Tides of Fortune*, p. 463; and Peter Calvocoressi, *Survey of Inter-*

national Affairs, 1951, London, 1954, pp. 79–80. See also as a corrective to Macmillan a letter by Lords Salisbury and Chandos (formerly Oliver Lyttelton), *The Times*, 12 Sept. 1969.

35. Eden, *Full Circle*, pp. 32–3.

36. McLellan, *Dean Acheson*, pp. 358–9.

37. Acheson, *Present at the Creation*, p. 596.

38. For long extracts from Eden's Gabriel Silver Lecture see Denise Folliot, ed., *Documents of International Affairs, 1952*, London, 1955, pp. 41–6. See also Eden, *Full Circle*, pp. 36–7.

39. *Time*, 23 Jan. 1952, cited in R. B. Manderson-Jones, *The Special Relationship: Anglo-American Relations and Western European Unity, 1947–56*, London, 1972, pp. 102–3. Italics supplied.

40. Pearson to Acheson, 15 Jan. 1952, and Acheson to Pearson, 23 Jan. 1952, Acheson Papers, Box 66.

41. Memorandum on Acheson–Franks conversation, 27 Jan. 1952, ibid.

42. For the background, see L. A. Fabunmi, *The Sudan in Anglo-Egyptian Relations: A Case Study in Power Politics*, London, 1960; and Eden, *Full Circle*, p. 230.

43. Anthony Nutting, *Nasser*, London, 1972, p. 35.

44. ibid, p. 40.

45. Peter Calvocoressi, *Survey of International Affairs, 1952*, London, 1955, p. 253. For the agreement of 1933, see Peter J. Beck, 'The Anglo-Persian Oil Dispute, 1932–33', *Journal of Contemporary History*, IX, 1974, no. 4, pp. 123–51.

46. Memorandum on Acheson–Franks conversation, 11 Aug. 1952, quoted in McLellan, *Dean Acheson*, p. 391; and Acheson, *Present at the Creation*, p. 680.

47. Memorandum on Acheson–Eden conversation, 20 Nov. 1952, Acheson Papers, Box 67; Acheson, *Present at the Creation*, pp. 682–5; and Dean Acheson Oral Recollections, Princeton Seminar, 1954, Truman Library, reel 2, track 2.

48. *Church Times*, quoted in Bardens, *Portrait of a Statesman*, pp. 287–8.

49. *HC Deb.*, D, col. 385, 7 May 1952; and Bethell, *The Last Secret*, p. 273.

50. Acheson, *Present at the Creation*, p. 700.

51. Eden, *Full Circle*, p. 22.

52. Lester Pearson, *Memoirs: II: 1948–1957, The International Years*, London, 1974, pp. 324, 326; and Shuckburgh Diary, 19 Nov. 1952. See also memorandum on Truman–Acheson–Eisen-hower conversation, 18 Nov. 1952, Acheson Papers, Box 67.

53. Pearson, *The International Years*, pp. 328–9; and Shuckburgh Diary, 22 Nov. 1952.

54. Dwight D. Eisenhower, *The White House Years: Mandate for Change, 1953–1956*, London, 1963, p. 142; and John W. Wheeler-Bennett and Anthony Nicholls, *The Semblance of Peace: The Political Settlement after the Second World War*, London, 1972, p. 620.

55. Shuckburgh Diary, Feb. 1953; Julius Holmes Recollections, Dulles Oral History Collection, Princeton University Library, Princeton, New Jersey; and Roderic O'Connor Recollections, ibid.

56. Eden, *Full Circle*, pp. 212–13.

57. *HC Deb.*, DX, cols. 1672–3, 3 Feb. 1953; and cols. 2061–2, 5 Feb. 1953. See also Hoopes, *Dulles*, p. 167.

58. Shuckburgh Diary.

59. Eden, *Full Circle*, p. 253.

60. Nutting, *Nasser*, p. 50. See also Mohammed Heikal, *Nasser: The Cairo Documents*, London, 1972, ch. 2.

61. Shuckburgh Diary, 5, 7 Apr., 5 June 1953.

62. Dixon Diary, 3 May and 20 June 1953.

63. Moran, *Winston Churchill*, p. 451; and Shuckburgh Diary.

64. Steering Committee Negotiating Papers, 3 and 6 Jan. 1952, Harry S. Truman Papers, The Truman Library, Independence, Missouri, Box 116; and Konrad Adenauer, *Memoirs, 1945–53*, London, 1966, p. 396.

65. Eisenhower to Churchill, 25 Apr. 1953 and record of an Eisenhower–Churchill telephone conversation 3 June 1953, Dwight D. Eisenhower Papers, Ann Whitman File, International Series, Eisenhower Library, Abilene, Kansas; Eisenhower Diary, 6 Jan. 1953, Ann Whitman File, DDE Series, ibid.; Shuckburgh Diary, 20 Nov. 1952; and Thompson, *The Day before Yesterday*, p. 105.

66. Shuckburgh Diary, 5 Oct. 1953.

67. Hoopes, *Dulles*, pp. 187–8; and Louis L. Gerson, *John Foster Dulles*, New York, 1967, p. 139.

68. Moran, *Winston Churchill*, p. 488; *HC Deb.*, DXX, col. 29, 3 Nov. 1953; and James, ed., *Chips*, p. 470.

69. Aldrich to Dulles, 6 Nov. 1953, Eisenhower Papers (IS).

70. Record of Eisenhower–Bedell Smith

telephone conversations, 6 and 7 Nov. 1953, ibid., (DDE Series).

71. Moran, *Winston Churchill*, p. 505.

72. Shuckburgh Diary.

73. McDonald, *Man of The Times*, p. 134; Notes on Bermuda, Dixon Papers; Eisenhower, *Mandate for Change*, pp. 244–5; Moran, *Winston Churchill*, p. 508; Merchant Recollections, Columbia University Oral Project; Robert Bowie Recollections, ibid.

74. Notes on Bermuda, Dixon Papers.

75. Eden, *Full Circle*, p. 58; Moran, *Winston Churchill*, p. 514; and McDonald, *Man of The Times*, p. 135.

76. Merchant Recollections, Columbia University Oral Project; O'Connor Recollections, Dulles Oral History Collection; and Eden, *Full Circle*, p. 63.

77. Merchant Recollections, Columbia University Oral Project; Shuckburgh Diary, 17 Feb. 1954.

78. See above, p. 288.

79. Bator, *Vietnam*, p. 48.

80. Eisenhower, *Mandate for Change*, pp. 346–7.

81. Bator, *Vietnam*, p. 68.

82. Eden, *Full Circle*, pp. 96–7.

83. ibid, p. 97.

84. For the Commons exchanges on the Anglo-American communiqué see *HC Deb.*, DXXVI, cols. 969–75, 13 Apr. 1954.

85. Douglas Dillon Recollections, Dulles Oral History Collection; and Shuckburgh Diary, 3 May and 16–19 Apr. 1954.

86. Bator, *Vietnam*, p. 69.

87. Eden, *Full Circle*, p. 99; and Leonard Mosley, *Dulles: A Biography of Eleanor, Allen and John Foster Dulles and their Family Network*, New York, 1978, p. 358. Mosley's general account of the quarrel between Dulles and Eden over Vietnam should be treated, however, with great caution. It is flawed, for example, by faulty chronology.

88. Robert E. Randle, *Geneva, 1954: The Settlement of the Indochinese War*, Princeton, 1969, esp. pp. 94–101.

89. McDonald, *Man of The Times*, p. 137.

90. Arthur Radford Recollections, Dulles Oral History Collection; Shuckburgh Diary, 24 Apr. 1954; Eden, *Full Circle*, p. 103; and Eisenhower Diary, 27 Apr. 1954.

91. Dulles messages to State Department,

Mike Gravel, ed., *The Pentagon Papers* (4 vols.), Boston, 1971, pp. 477–82, documents 36–9.

92. McDonald, *Man of The Times*, p. 136.

93. Shuckburgh Diary.

94. Moran, *Winston Churchill*, p. 556; and Shuckburgh Diary.

95. *The Times*, 3 May 1954; Eisenhower Diary, 27 Apr. 1954; and Moran, *Winston Churchill*, pp. 549, 553, 556.

96. *HC Deb.*, DXXIX, cols. 428–41, 23 June 1954.

97. Moran, *Winston Churchill*, p. 560.

98. Memorandum on Eisenhower–Dulles telephone conversation, 26 June 1954, Eisenhower Papers (DDE Series); and Moran, *Winston Churchill*, p. 566.

99. Hoopes, *Dulles*, p. 209.

100. Moran, *Winston Churchill*, p. 576.

101. Shuckburgh Diary.

102. ibid., 28 July 1954.

103. Memorandum on Eisenhower–Dulles telephone conversation, 19 July 1954, Eisenhower Papers (DDE Series).

104. W. N. Medlicott, *British Foreign Policy since Versailles 1919–1963*, London, 1968, pp. 307–8; and McDonald, *Man of The Times*, p. 137.

105. Folliot, ed., *Documents on International Affairs, 1952*, pp. 41–5.

106. Memorandum on Eisenhower–Bedell Smith telephone conversation, 9 Feb. 1954, Eisenhower Papers (DDE Series); Eisenhower to Churchill, 9 Feb. 1954, ibid. (IS); Moran, *Winston Churchill*, p. 478; and Shuckburgh Diary.

107. Eden, *Full Circle*, p. 261.

108. Moran, *Winston Churchill*, p. 515.

109. Anthony Sampson, *The Seven Sisters: The Great Oil Companies and the World They Made*, London, 1975, pp. 126–7.

110. Holmes Recollections, Dulles Oral History Collection.

111. For more details see John C. Campbell, ed., *Successful Negotiation: Trieste, 1954: An Appraisal by the Five Participants*, Princeton, 1976.

112. McDonald, *Man of The Times*, p. 132; and Schlaim, Jones and Sainsbury, *British Foreign Secretaries since 1945*, p. 101.

113. Eden, *Full Circle*, p. 168.

114. Lord Gladwyn, *Memoirs*, London, 1972, p. 273.

115. Eden, *Full Circle*, p. 167.

116. Richard Goold-Adams, *The Time of Power: A Reappraisal of John Foster Dulles*, London, 1962, p. 166.

117. Schlaim, Jones and Sainsbury, *British Foreign Secretaries since 1945*, p. 101.
118. Moran, *Winston Churchill*, p. 602.
119. Dulles to Eden, 3 Oct. 1954, John Foster Dulles Papers, Princeton University, Box 80; and Eden, *Full Circle*, p. 169.
120. Dulles to Eden, 30 Dec. 1954 and Eden to Dulles, 1 Jan. 1955, Dulles Papers, Box 80.
121. Moran, *Winston Churchill*, p. 590; and Macmillan, *Tides of Fortune*, p. 540.
122. Moran, *Winston Churchill*, p. 641; and Bracken to Beaverbrook, 22 Nov. 1956, Beaverbrook Papers, BBK C58.
123. Heikal, *Nasser*, p. 81; and Eden, *Full Circle*, p. 221.
124. Robertson to Dulles, 15 Feb. 1955, Dulles Papers, Box 91.
125. Dulles paper used in conversation with Eden, 24 Feb. 1955, ibid.; and Eisenhower to Eden, 29 Mar. 1955, Eisenhower Papers (DDE Series).
126. *HC Deb.*, DXXXVIII, cols. 157–63. 8 Mar. 1955.
127. Paul Gore-Booth, *With Great Truth and Respect*, London, 1974, pp. 215–16.

x *Prime Minister, April 1955–July 1956*

1. Eden, *Full Circle*, pp. 273–4.
2. Beaverbrook notes on a meeting with Macmillan, 8 Apr. 1957, Beaverbrook Papers, BBK C235.
3. Medlicott, *Contemporary England*, p. 522.
4. Conservative and Unionist Central Office, *The Campaign Guide, 1955*, London, 1955, p. 179.
5. D. E. Butler, *The British General Election of 1955*, London, 1955, p. 15.
6. Butler, *The Art of the Possible*, p. 178.
7. Macmillan, *Tides of Fortune*, pp. 587, 585. See also Moran, *Churchill*, p. 655.
8. Butler, *The British General Election of 1955*, p. 75.
9. ibid., p. 87.
10. ibid., p. 61.
11. Moran, *Churchill*, p. 658.
12. Butler, *The British General Election of 1955*, pp. 103–4.
13. Lord Birkenhead, *Walter Monckton: The Life of Viscount Monckton of Brenchley*, London, 1969, p. 300; and Eden, *Full Circle*, pp. 286–7.
14. Medlicott, *Contemporary England*, p. 537.
15. *Daily Mail*, 1 Feb. 1978; and Moran, *Churchill*, pp. 651–2.
16. Kilmuir, *Political Adventure*, p. 308; Butler, *The Art of the Possible*, p. 184; and Thompson, *The Day before Yesterday*, p. 121.
17. Record of Dulles–Eisenhower telephone conversation, 9 June 1955, Eisenhower Papers (DDE Series).
18. O'Connor Recollections, Dulles Oral History Collection.
19. Eisenhower, *Mandate for Change*, p. 521.
20. ibid., p. 517.
21. Macmillan, *Tides of Fortune*, p. 618.
22. ibid., p. 630; and Eden, *Full Circle*, pp. 308–10.
23. Eden in Makins to Dulles, 13 Apr. and 29 May 1955, Dulles Papers, Box 91.
24. Macmillan, *Tides of Fortune*, p. 632.
25. Loy Henderson Recollections, Dulles Oral History Collection. See also Waldemar J. Gallman, *Iraq under General Nuri: My Recollections of Nuri al-said*, Baltimore, 1964, p. 60.
26. Herman Finer, *Dulles over Suez: The Theory and Practice of his Diplomacy*, London, 1964, p. 18.
27. Macmillan, *Tides of Fortune*, p. 634.
28. Heikal, *Nasser*, p. 64.
29. Eden, *Full Circle*, p. 414.
30. *HC Deb.*, DXXXI, col. 508, 28 July 1954.
31. Eden to Eisenhower, 23 July 1955, Eisenhower Papers (IS).
32. Pearson, *Diaries, 1949–1959*, p. 172.
33. *HC Deb.*, DXLV, col. 29, 25 Oct. 1955.
34. ibid., col. 1496, 7 Nov. 1955.
35. ibid., col. 1610, 7 Nov. 1955.
36. Macmillan, *Tides of Fortune*, pp. 692–4.
37. Bracken to Beaverbrook, 17 Jan.; and Beaverbrook to Bracken, 23 Jan. 1956, Beaverbrook Papers, BBK C58.
38. Thompson, *The Day before Yesterday*, p. 122; and Butler, *The Art of the Possible*, p. 183.
39. Thompson, *The Day before Yesterday*, p. 123; and *The Times*, 19 Jan. 1956.
40. Anthony Nutting, *No End of a Lesson*, London, 1967, p. 23.
41. Winthrop Aldrich Recollections, Dulles Oral History Collection.
42. Herbert Hoover, jr, and George Humphrey Recollections, ibid.

43. Humphrey Trevelyan, *The Middle East in Revolution*, London, 1970, pp. 21–2, 25.
44. ibid., p. 56; Selwyn Lloyd, *Suez, 1956: A Personal Account*, London, 1978, p. 31; Heikal, *Nasser*, pp. 82–3.
45. Trevelyan, *The Middle East in Revolution*, p. 57.
46. Ann Whitman Diary Series, Ann Whitman File, 16 Dec. 1955, The Eisenhower Library, Abilene, Kansas.
47. Lloyd, *Suez*, p. 41.
48. Eden, *Full Circle*, p. 335.
49. Harold Macmillan, *Riding the Storm, 1956–1959*, London, 1971, p. 13.
50. Bracken to Beaverbrook, 15 Feb.; and Beaverbrook to Bracken, 21 Feb. 1956, Beaverbrook Papers, BBK C58. The former letter is misdated in Andrew Boyle, *Poor Dear Brendan*, London, 1974. p. 335.
51. Nutting, *No End of a Lesson*, p. 28.
52. Thompson, *The Day before Yesterday*, p. 124; and Nutting, *No End of a Lesson*, passim.
53. *HC Deb.*, DIL, cols. 1709–13, 5 Mar. 1956; and *The Times*, 5 and 7 Mar. 1956.
54. Nutting, *No End of a Lesson*, p. 32; and *HC Deb.*, DIL, cols. 2228–9, 7 Mar. 1956.
55. Nutting, *No End of a Lesson*, p. 32; Thompson, *The Day before Yesterday*, p. 124–5.
56. Middleton to Aldrich, 9 Mar. 1956, Winthrop Aldrich Papers, Baker Library, Harvard Business School, Cambridge, Mass., Box 222.
57. *HC Deb.*, DL, cols. 402–19, 14 Mar. 1956.
58. Thompson, *The Day before Yesterday*, p. 125.
59. ibid.
60. Macmillan, *Riding the Storm*, p. 96; and Beaverbrook notes, 7 Apr. 1957, Beaverbrook Papers, BBK C235.
61. Eden, *Full Circle*, p. 358.
62. *HC Deb.*, DLII, col. 1220, 9 May 1956.

XI *Suez, July* 1956–*January* 1957

1. Lloyd, *Suez*, p. 58.
2. ibid., p. 60.
3. Eisenhower Diary, 8 and 13 Mar. 1956.
4. Nutting, *No End of a Lesson*, p. 42; and Cab. 95/14, PRO, quoted in Michael J. Cohen, *Palestine: Retreat from the Mandate: The Making of British Policy, 1936–45*, London, 1978, pp. 154–5.
5. Lloyd, *Suez*, p. 61.
6. ibid., pp. 68–9.
7. Kennett Love, *Suez: The Twice-Fought War*, London, 1969, p. 216.
8. Lloyd, *Suez*, p. 66.
9. ibid., p. 75.
10. Christian Pineau, *1956, Suez*, Paris, 1976, p. 81.
11. Eden, *Full Circle*, p. 428; and Lloyd, *Suez*, pp. 85–6.
12. McDonald, *Man of The Times*, pp. 142–4.
13. *HC Deb.*, DLVII, cols. 777–80, 27 July 1956.
14. Robert Murphy, *Diplomat among Warriors*, London, 1964, pp. 461–5; and Lloyd, *Suez*, pp. 75, 91.
15. Macmillan, *Riding the Storm*, pp. 104–5.
16. Nutting, *No End of a Lesson*, p. 48.
17. Macmillan, *Riding the Storm*, p. 664.
18. Record of Eisenhower–Hoover telephone conversation, 1 Aug. 1956. Eisenhower Papers (DDE Series).
19. Love, *Suez*, p. 364.
20. Pearson, *The International Years*, p. 227.
21. Roskill, *Hankey*, vol. 3, pp. 636–7; and Robert R. Bowie, *Suez, 1956*, London, 1974, pp. 23–4.
22. Eden, *Full Circle*, pp. 437–8; and Mosley, *Dulles*, p. 412.
23. Lloyd, *Suez*, pp. 98–9.
24. Robert R. Bowie Recollections, Dulles Oral History Collection.
25. Chamberlain to Hilda Chamberlain, 17 Dec. 1937, Neville Chamberlain Papers.
26. Record of Eisenhower–Hoover telephone conversation, 1 Aug. 1956, Eisenhower Papers (DDE Series); and Macmillan, *Riding the Storm*, p. 106.
27. William Macomber Recollections, Dulles Oral History Collection.
28. McDonald, *Man of The Times*, p. 145.
29. Trevelyan, *The Middle East in Revolution*, p. 107.
30. Philip M. Williams, *Hugh Gaitskell: A Political Biography*, London, 1979, esp. pp. 421–2; William Clark, 'Suez: An Unofficial Chronicle', *Listener*, 22 Nov. 1979; *Economist*, CLXXX, 1956, p. 547.

Cf also Robert Rhodes James, 'Hugh Gaitskell and Suez', *Listener*, 13 Dec. 1979.

31. Eden to Eisenhower, 5 Aug. 1956, Eisenhower Papers, quoted in Love, *Suez*, p. 394.

32. André Beaufre, *The Suez Expedition, 1956*, London, 1969, pp. 28–9, 34.

33. Hugh Stockwell, 'Suez: Success or Disaster?', *Listener*, 4 Nov. 1976.

34. Trevelyan, *The Middle East in Revolution*, p. 99; Robert Menzies, *Afternoon Light: Some Memories of Men and Events*, London, 1967, pp. 167–8.

35. Eisenhower to Eden, 2 and 8 Sept. 1956, Dwight D. Eisenhower, *The White House Years: Waging Peace, 1956–1961*, New York, 1965, pp. 666–71.

36. Paul Ély, *Mémoires: II: Suez ... Le 13 Mai*, Paris, 1969, p. 112, (Translation supplied.)

37. Lloyd, *Suez*, p. 135; and Ély, *Suez ... Le 13 Mai*, pp. 104–5. (Translation supplied.)

38. Beaufre, *The Suez Expedition*, p. 50; and Stockwell, loc. cit.

39. Lloyd, *Suez*, p. 20; and Pearson, *The International Years*, pp. 231–2.

40. *HC Deb.*, DLVIII, cols. 1–15, 12 Sept. 1956.

41. Eden, *Full Circle*, pp. 483–4.

42. Macmillan, *Riding the Storm*, p. 125.

43. *HC Deb.*, DLVIII, cols. 302–8, 13 Sept. 1956.

44. Macmillan, *Riding the Storm*, p. 127.

45. McDonald, *Man of The Times*, p. 148; and Nutting, *No End of a Lesson*, p. 63.

46. Moshe Dayan, *Story of My Life*, London, 1976, p. 155. See also Peres diary quoted at secondhand in Geoffrey Warner, ' "Collusion" and the Suez Crisis of 1956', *International Affairs*, LV, 1979, pp. 230–31.

47. Lloyd, *Suez*, p. 144.

48. McDonald, *Man of The Times*, p. 147.

49. Nutting, *No End of a Lesson*, pp. 67–8.

50. Hugh Thomas, *The Suez Affair*, London, 1967, pp. 98, 230 n.88; and Clark, loc. cit.

51. Macmillan, *Riding the Storm*, p. 135; and Ann Whitman Diary Series, 25 Sept. 1956.

52. Lloyd, *Suez*, p. 151.

53. McDonald, *Man of The Times*, p. 149; and Nutting, *No End of a Lesson*, p. 70.

54. Thomas, *The Suez Affair*, p. 96.

55. Nutting, *No End of a Lesson*, p. 93; and

Maurice Challe, *Notre Révolte*, Paris, 1968, p. 27. (Translation supplied.)

56. Nutting, *No End of a Lesson*, pp. 97–8.

57. Lloyd, *Suez*, p. 174.

58. Butler, *The Art of the Possible*, p. 192.

59. Lloyd, *Suez*, p. 177.

60. Love, *Suez*, p. 370.

61. Butler, *The Art of the Possible*, p. 192.

62. Love, *Suez*, p. 447.

63. See above, p. 166.

64. Lloyd, *Suez*, p. 182; Dayan, *My Life*, p. 181; and Pineau, *1956, Suez*, p. 136.

65. Pineau, *1956, Suez*, p. 137. (Translation supplied.)

66. Lloyd, *Suez*, p. 187; and Robert Blake, 'Anthony Eden' in John P. Mackintosh, ed., *British Prime Ministers in the Twentieth Century: II: Churchill to Callaghan*, London, 1978, p. 101.

67. Lloyd, *Suez*, p. 188; Michael Bar-Zohar, *Ben-Gurion*, London, 1978, p. 243; and Warner, 'The Suez Crisis', loc. cit., 236–7.

68. Lloyd, *Suez*, p. 188; and Pineau, *1956, Suez*, p. 124.

69. Lloyd, *Suez*, pp. 187–8.

70. ibid., p. 189.

71. ibid.

72. Pineau, *1956, Suez*, p. 151. (Translation supplied.)

73. Keith Kyle, 'Suez: What Really Happened', *Listener*, 11 Nov. 1976.

74. Lloyd, *Suez*, p. 189.

75. Record of Dulles–Eisenhower telephone conversation, 28 Oct. 1956, Eisenhower Papers (DDE Series).

76. Dillon Recolllections, Dulles Oral History Collection.

77. Aldrich Recollections, ibid.

78. Radford Recollections, ibid.

79. Aldrich Recollections, ibid.

80. Record of Dulles–Eisenhower telephone conversation, 30 Oct. 1956, Eisenhower Papers (DDE Series).

81. ibid., See also Eisenhower, *Waging Peace*, p. 679.

82. Trevelyan, *The Middle East in Revolution*, p. 115.

83. Love, *Suez*, p. 521.

84. Challe, *Notre Révolte*, pp. 29–30; and Ély, *Suez ... Le 13 Mai*, pp. 158–9.

85. *HC Deb.*, DLVIII, cols. 1569, 1631–53, 31 Oct., 1 Nov. 1956.

86. Quoted in Russell Braddon, *Suez: Splitting of a Nation*, London, 1973, p. 119.

87. John M. Hightower Recollections, Columbia University Oral Project.

88. Hoopes, *Dulles*, p. 379.
89. Finer, *Dulles over Suez*, p. 395.
90. Dulles Memorandum, 6 Dec. 1956, Dulles Papers, Box 106.
91. Thompson, *The Day before Yesterday*, p. 139, alleged that Clark was sent 'on his way with a flying inkpot'. This Clark has denied. (Letter to present writer, 20 Nov. 1979.) Another alleged victim of Eden's inkpot-throwing was Liddell Hart – also during the Suez crisis. In 1978, however, Eden's widow and Sir Frederick Bishop, Eden's Private Secretary in 1956, cogently expressed their disbelief. Mosley, *Dulles*, p. 409; and *Sunday Telegraph*, 11, 25 June, 9 July 1978.
92. Chapman Pincher, *Inside Story: A Documentary of the Pursuit of Power*, London, 1978, p. 90.
93. Beaufre, *The Suez Expedition*, p. 63.
94. Eisenhower, *Waging Peace*, p. 84; and Dillon Recollections, Dulles Oral History Collection.
95. Terence Robertson, *Crisis: The Inside Story of the Suez Conspiracy*, London, 1965, p. 195.
96. Lloyd, *Suez*, p. 205; and Butler, *The Art of the Possible*, p. 193.
97. Lloyd, *Suez*, p. 206.
98. Challe, *Notre Révolte*, pp. 30–31. (Translation supplied.)
99. Bracken to Beaverbrook, 5 Nov. 1956, Beaverbrook Papers, BBK C58.
100. Lloyd, *Suez*, p. 209; Dixon, *Double Diploma*, pp. 271–3; and Macmillan, *Riding the Storm*, p. 164.
101. *Sunday Telegraph*, 28 Aug. 1966; and Eden, *Full Circle*, p. 557.
102. ibid., p. 558.
103. McDonald, *Man of The Times*, p. 153.
104. Lloyd, *Suez*, p. 209.
105. Moran, *Churchill*, pp. 709, 710.
106. Eden, *Full Circle*, p. 557.
107. *HC Deb.*, DLX, col. 262, 8 Nov. 1956.
108. Note on Eden–Eisenhower telephone conversation, 7 Nov. 1956, Eisenhower Papers (DDE Series); and Finer, *Dulles Over Suez*, p. 438.
109. Love, *Suez*, pp. 644–5; Sherman Adams, *Firsthand Report: The Story of the Eisenhower Administration*, New York, 1961, p. 260; and Mosley, *Dulles*, p. 428n.
110. Eden, *Full Circle*, p. 563; and Eden to Eisenhower, 11 Nov. 1956, Eisenhower Papers (IS).
111. Aldrich Recollections, Dulles Oral History Collection; and Winthrop Aldrich Recollections, Columbia University Oral Project.
112. Private information.
113. Private information from a well-placed British source.
114. Private letter to the present writer, 7 June 1979.
115. Private information from a well-placed British source. Cf. also Butler, *The Art of the Possible*, p. 195.
116. Private information.
117. Ann Whitman Diary Series, 13 Nov. 1956.
118. Bracken to Beaverbrook, 22 Nov. 1956, Beaverbrook Papers, BBK C58.
119. Comment from a well-placed British source.
120. Record of Aldrich–Eisenhower telephone conversation, 19 Nov. 1956, Eisenhower Papers (DDE Series); and Aldrich desk diary, 18 Nov. 1956, Aldrich Papers.
121. Record of Aldrich–Eisenhower telephone conversation, 19 Nov. 1956, Eisenhower Papers (DDE Series).
122. Ann Whitman Diary, 20 Nov. 1956; and record of Aldrich–Eisenhower telephone conversation, 20 Nov. 1956, Eisenhower Papers (DDE Series).
123. Record of Aldrich–Eisenhower telephone conversation, 20 Nov. 1956, Eisenhower Papers (DDE Series).
124. Ann Whitman Diary Series, 23 Nov. 1956; and record of Humphrey–Eisenhower telephone conversation, 26 Nov. 1956, Eisenhower Papers (DDE Series).
125. Churchill to Eisenhower, 23 Nov. 1956, Eisenhower Papers (IS).
126. Private letter to the present writer, 7 June 1979.
127. A. J. P. Taylor, *Rumours of War*, London, 1952, pp. 163–4.
128. James Margach, *The Abuse of Power*, London, 1978, p. 113.
129. Private information from a well-placed British source.
130. Macmillan, *Riding the Storm*, p. 177.
131. Bracken to Beaverbrook, 7 Dec. 1956, Beaverbrook Papers, BBK C58.
132. Bracken to Beaverbrook, 23 Jan. 1957, ibid., BBK C59.
133. Thomas, *The Suez Affair*, p. 214.
134. *HC Deb.*, DLXII, col. 1518, 20 Dec. 1956.
135. Beaverbrook Papers, BBK C59.

XII *The Last Years, 1957–77*

1. Eden to Bracken, 26 Mar. 1957, Beaverbrook Papers, BBK C17.
2. Clarissa Eden to Beaverbrook, 18 May 1957, ibid.
3. Clarissa Eden to Beaverbrook, 22 May 1957, ibid.
4. Dulles to Eden, 18 Apr. 1957; and Eden to Dulles, rec. 24 Apr. 1957, Dulles Papers, Box 115.
5. Eden to Dixon, 17 May 1957, Dixon Papers.
6. Beaverbrook to Eden, 23 Jan. 1957; and Clarissa Eden to Beaverbrook, 22 May 1957, Beaverbrook Papers, BBK C17.
7. A. J. P. Taylor, *Beaverbrook*, London, 1972, p. 813.
8. In Beaverbrook to Eden, 24 Mar. 1958; Eden to Beaverbrook, 25 Mar. 1958, Beaverbrook Papers, BBK C17; and Eden to Beaverbrook, 16 Jan. 1961, ibid., BBK C18.
9. Beaverbrook Papers, BBK C18.
10. Randolph S. Churchill, *The Rise and Fall of Sir Anthony Eden*, London, 1959, p. 19.
11. Nigel Fisher, *The Tory Leaders: Their Struggle for Power*, London, 1977, p. 82; and Richard Buckle, ed., *Self Portrait with Friends: The Selected Diaries of Cecil Beaton, 1926–1974*, London, 1979, p. 384.
12. Eden to Beaverbrook, 19 Aug. 1961, Beaverbrook Papers, BBK C18.
13. *Radio Times*, 19–25 Oct. 1974.
14. Anthony Eden, 'The Slender Margin of Safety', *Foreign Affairs*, XXXIX, 1960–61, pp. 165–7.
15. Anthony Eden, Earl of Avon, *Towards Peace in Indochina*, London, 1966, p. 39.
16. Avon, *Another World*.
17. McDonald, *Man of The Times*, p. 75.
18. Avon to Emrys–Evans, 6 Aug. 1963, Emrys–Evans Papers.
19. Nutting, *No End of a Lesson*, p. 123.
20. Leon D. Epstein, *British Politics in the Suez Crisis*, London, 1964, pp. 106–7.
21. Thomas, *The Suez Affair*.
22. *Parliamentary Debates, Official Report, House of Lords*, CCCLXIX, col. 321, 17 Mar. 1976.
23. Avon to Beaverbrook, 4 Oct. 1963, Beaverbrook Papers, BBK C18; and Harvey, ed., *War Diaries*, p. 85.
24. *The Times*, 2 June 1956.
25. Beaverbrook Papers, BBK C17 and 18.
26. ibid., BBK C18.
27. ibid.
28. Eden to Beaverbrook, 18 May 1961, ibid.
29. Aster, *Anthony Eden*, p. 165.
30. Feiling, *Neville Chamberlain*, p. 323; and *HC Deb.*, CCCLXV, col. 1617, 12 Nov. 1940.
31. Robert Skidelsky, 'Lessons of Suez' in Vernon Bogdanor and Robert Skidelsky, eds., *The Age of Affluence, 1951–1964*, London, 1970, pp. 188–9.
32. John Grigg, *Spectator*, 30 Oct. 1976.
33. John G. Winant, *A Letter from Grosvenor Square*, London, 1947, p. 66; and Lord Morrison, *An Autobiography*, London, 1960, p. 200.
34. Jones, *A Diary with Letters*, p. 231.
35. *HC Deb.*, CLXXXIX, cols. 2088–94, 21 Dec. 1925.
36. Churchill, *Rise and Fall of Eden*, p. 18.
37. Pratt, *East of Malta, West of Suez*, pp. 86–7.
38. ibid., p. 83.

Sources and Bibliography

1. Unpublished Primary Sources

Records of the Cabinet Office (Cab.), Public Record Office (PRO), London.

Records of the Dominions Office (DO), PRO.

Records of the Foreign Office (FO), PRO.

Records of the Prime Minister's Office (Prem.), PRO.

Military Archives, National Archives, Washington, DC.

Dean Acheson Papers, The Truman Library, Independence, Missouri.

Winthrop Aldrich Papers and Desk Diary, Baker Library, Harvard Business School, Cambridge, Massachusetts.

Avon Papers (FO 954), PRO.

Baldwin Papers, University of Cambridge Library, Cambridge.

Beaverbrook Papers, House of Lords Record Office, London.

Cecil of Chelwood Papers, British Library, London.

Neville Chamberlain Papers and Diary, University of Birmingham, Birmingham.

Cranborne Papers (FO 800), PRO.

Sir Pierson Dixon Papers and Diary in the possession of Piers Dixon.

John Foster Dulles Papers, Princeton University Library, Princeton, New Jersey.

Dwight D. Eisenhower Papers and Diary, The Eisenhower Library, Abilene, Kansas.

Paul Emrys-Evans Papers, British Library, London.

Halifax Papers (FO 800), PRO.

Halifax Papers, Churchill College Library, Cambridge.

Harvey Papers and Diary, British Library, London.

Harry L. Hopkins Papers, The Roosevelt Library, Hyde Park, New York.

Cordell Hull Papers, Library of Congress, Washington, DC.

Inverchapel Papers (FO 800), PRO.

William D. Leahy Diary, Library of Congress, Washington, DC.

Breckenridge Long Diary, Library of Congress, Washington, DC.

Harold Nicolson Papers and Diary, Balliol College, Oxford.

Sir Evelyn Shuckburgh Diary, in the possession of the diarist.

Simon Papers (FO 800), PRO.

Edward R. Stettinius Papers, University of Virginia Library, Charlottesville, Virginia.

Henry L. Stimson Diary, Yale University Library, New Haven, Connecticut.

Templewood Papers, University of Cambridge Library, Cambridge.

Harry S. Truman Papers, The Truman Library, Independence, Missouri.

Ann Whitman Diary, The Eisenhower Library, Abilene, Kansas.

Columbia University Oral Project, Columbia University Library, New York. Recollections by: Winthrop Aldrich; Robert R. Bowie; John M. Hightower; and Livingston Merchant.

Dulles Oral History Collection, Princeton University Library, Princeton, New Jersey. Recollections by Winthrop Aldrich; Robert R. Bowie; Douglas Dillon; Loy Henderson; Julius Holmes; Herbert Hoover, jr, and George Humphrey; William Macomber; Roderic O'Connor; and Arthur Radford.

Princeton University Seminar, 1954: Oral Recollections of Dean Acheson, The Truman Library, Independence, Missouri.

2. Published Primary Sources

Abell, Tyler, ed., *Drew Pearson: Diaries, 1949–1959*, London, 1974.

Blum, Léon, *L'Oeuvre de Léon Blum* (7 vols.), Paris, 1954–65.

Command Papers, London, various dates.

Dilks, David, ed., *The Diaries of Sir Alexander Cadogan, 1938–1945*, London, 1971.

Documents on German Foreign Policy, 1918–1945, London, various dates.

Evans, Trefor, ed., *The Killearn Diaries, 1934–1946*, London, 1972.

Folliot, Denise, ed., *Documents on International Affairs, 1952*, London, 1955.

Gravel, Mike, ed., *The Pentagon Papers* (4 vols.), Boston, Massachusetts, 1971.

Harvey, John, ed., *The Diplomatic Diaries of Oliver Harvey, 1937–1940*, London, 1970.

— *The War Diaries of Oliver Harvey*, London, 1978.

James, Robert Rhodes, ed., *Chips: The Diary of Sir Henry Channon*, London, 1967.

Jones, Thomas, *A Diary with Letters, 1931–1950*, London, 1954.

Millar, T. B., ed., *The Diaries of R. G. Casey, 1951–60*, London, 1972.

Ministère des Affaires Étrangères, *Documents diplomatiques français, 1932–1939*, Paris, various dates.

Muggeridge, Malcolm, ed., *Ciano's Diplomatic Papers*, London, 1948.

Neale, R. G., ed., *Documents on Australian Foreign Policy, 1937–1949*, Canberra, various dates.

Nicolson, Nigel, ed., *Harold Nicolson: Diaries and Letters, 1930–1939*, London, 1966.

— *Harold Nicolson: Diaries and Letters, 1939–1945*, London, 1967.

Parliamentary Debates, Official Report, House of Commons, London.

Parliamentary Debates, Official Report, House of Lords, London.

Taylor, A. J. P., ed., *W. P. Crozier: Off the Record: Political Interviews, 1933–1943*, London, 1973.

Trevor-Roper, Hugh, ed., *The Goebbels Diaries: The Last Days*, London, 1978.

United States Department of State, *Papers Relating to the Foreign Relations of the United States*, Washington, DC, various dates.

Woodward, E. L., *et al.*, eds., *Documents on British Foreign Policy, 1919–1939*, London, various dates.

3. Books and Articles by Anthony Eden, Earl of Avon

Places in the Sun, London, 1926.

Foreign Affairs, London, 1939.

Freedom and Order: Selected Speeches, 1939–1946, London, 1947.

Days for Decision, London, 1949.

Memoirs: Full Circle, London, 1960.

Memoirs: Facing the Dictators, London, 1962.

Memoirs: The Reckoning, London, 1965.

Towards Peace in Indochina, London, 1966.

Another World, 1897–1917, London, 1976.

'Britain in World Strategy', *Foreign Affairs*, XXIX, 1950–51.

'The Slender Margin of Safety', *Foreign Affairs*, XXXIX, 1960–61.

4. Studies of Eden

Aster, Sidney, *Anthony Eden*, London, 1976.

Bardens, Dennis, *Portrait of a Statesman*, London, 1955.

Barker, Elisabeth, *Churchill and Eden at War*, London, 1978.

Broad, Lewis, *Sir Anthony Eden*, London, 1955.

Campbell-Johnson, Alan, *Sir Anthony Eden: A Biography*, London, revised ed., 1955.

Churchill, Randolph S., *The Rise and Fall of Sir Anthony Eden*, London, 1959.

McDermott, Geoffrey, *The Eden Legacy*, London, 1969.

Rees-Mogg, William, *Sir Anthony Eden*, London, 1956

5. Secondary Studies

(a) BOOKS

Acheson, Dean, *Present at the Creation: My Years in the State Department*, London, 1969.

Adamthwaite, Anthony P., *France and the Coming of the Second World War, 1936–1939*, London, 1977.

Adams, Henry H., *Harry Hopkins: A Biography*, New York, 1967.

Adams, Sherman, *Firsthand Report: The Story of the Eisenhower Administration*, New York, 1961.

Addison, Paul, *The Road to 1945: British Politics and the Second World War*, London, 1975.

Adenauer, Konrad, *Memoirs, 1945–53*, London, 1966.

Amery, L. S., *My Political Life* (3 vols.), London, 1953–5.

Barclay, Roderick, *Ernest Bevin and the Foreign Office*, London, 1975.

Barker, Elisabeth, *British Policy in South-East Europe in the Second World War*, London, 1976.

Barman, Thomas, *Diplomatic Correspondent*, London, 1968.

Barnett, Correlli, *The Collapse of British Power*, London, 1972.

Barros, James, *The League of Nations and the Great Powers: The Greek–Bulgarian Incident, 1925*, London, 1970.

Bar-Zohar, Michael, *Ben-Gurion*, London, 1978.

Bassett, Reginald, *Democracy and Foreign Policy: A Case History: The Sino-Japanese Dispute, 1931–1933*, London, 1952.

Bator, Victor, *Vietnam: A Diplomatic Tragedy: Origins of U.S. Involvement*, London, 1967.

Beaufre, André, *The Suez Expedition, 1956*, London, 1969.

Bell, P. M. H., *A Certain Eventuality: Britain and the Fall of France*, London, 1974.

Bethell, Nicholas *The Last Secret: Forcible Repatriation to Russia, 1944–7*, London, 1974.

— *The Palestinian Triangle: The Struggle between the British, the Jews and the Arabs*, London, 1979.

Birkenhead, Earl of, *The Life of Lord Halifax*, London, 1965.

— *Walter Monckton: The Life of Viscount Monckton of Brenchley*, London, 1969.

Bishop, Donald G., *The Administration of British Foreign Relations*, Syracuse, New York, 1961.

Blunden, Margaret, *The Countess of Warwick: A Biography*, London, 1967.

Boothby, Lord, *Recollections of a Rebel*, London, 1978.

Bowers, G. Claude, *My Mission to Spain*, New York, 1954.

Bowie, Robert R., *Suez, 1956*, London, 1974.

Boyle, Andrew, *Poor Dear Brendan*, London, 1974.

Braddon, Russell, *Suez: Splitting of a Nation*, London, 1973.

Bruegel, J. W., *Czechoslovakia before Munich: The German Minority Problem and British Appeasement Policy*, Cambridge, 1973.

Buckle, Richard, ed., *Self Portrait with Friends: The Selected Diaries of Cecil Beaton, 1926–1974*, London, 1979.

Burridge, T. D., *British Labour and Hitler's War*, London, 1976.

Butler, D. E., *The British General Election of 1955*, London, 1955.

Butler, Lord, *The Art of the Possible*, London, 1971.

Calder, Angus, *The People's War: Britain, 1939–45*, London, 1969.

Calvocoressi, Peter, *Survey of International Affairs, 1951*, London, 1954.

— *Survey of International Affairs, 1952*, London, 1955.

Campbell, John C., ed., *Successful Negotiation: Trieste, 1954: An Appraisal by the Five Participants*, Princeton, NJ, 1976.

Carlton, David, *MacDonald versus Henderson: The Foreign Policy of the Second Labour Government*, London, 1970.

Carroll, Joseph T., *Ireland in the War Years*, Newton Abbot, Devon, 1975.

Challe, Maurice, *Notre Révolte*, Paris, 1968.

Churchill, Winston S., *The Second World War* (6 vols.), London, 1948–54.

Cohen, Michael J., *Palestine: Retreat from the Mandate: The Making of British Policy, 1936–45*, London, 1978.

Colton, Joel, *Leon Blum: Humanist in Politics*, New York, 1966.

Colvin, Ian, *The Chamberlain Cabinet*, London, 1971.

Cooper, Duff, *Old Men Forget*, London, 1954.

Cowling, Maurice, *The Impact of Hitler: British Politics and British Policy, 1933–1940*, London, 1975.

Cross, J. A., *Sir Samuel Hoare: A Political Biography*, London, 1977.

Cruikshank, Charles, *Greece, 1940–1941*, London, 1976.

Dalton, Hugh, *The Fateful Years: Memoirs, 1931–1945*, London, 1957.

Dayan, Moshe, *Story of My Life*, London, 1976.

de Gaulle, Charles, *War Memoirs: Unity, 1942–44*, London, 1959.

de Madariaga, Salvador, *Disarmament*, London, 1929.

Dixon, Piers, *Double Diploma: The Life of Sir Pierson Dixon, Don and Diplomat*, London, 1968.

Donoughue, Bernard and Jones, G. W., *Herbert Morrison: Portrait of a Politician*, London, 1973.

Dreifort, John E., *Yvon Delbos at the Quai d'Orsay: French Foreign Policy During the Popular Front, 1936–1938*, Lawrence, Kansas, 1973.

Eden, Timothy, *The Tribulations of a Baronet*, London, 1933.

Edwards, Jill, *The British Government and the Spanish Civil War, 1936–1939*, London, 1979.

Eisenhower, Dwight D., *The White House Years: Mandate for Change, 1953–1956*, London, 1963.

— *The White House Years: Waging Peace, 1956–1961*, New York, 1965.

Ély, Paul, *Mémoires: II: Suez ... Le 13 Mai*, Paris, 1969.

Epstein, Leon D., *British Politics in the Suez Crisis*, London, 1964.

Fabunmi, L. A., *The Sudan in Anglo-Egyptian Relations: A Case Study in Power Politics*, London, 1960.

Feiling, Keith, *The Life of Neville Chamberlain*, London, 1946.

Finer, Herman, *Dulles over Suez: The Theory and Practice of his Diplomacy*, London, 1964.

Fisher, Nigel, *The Tory Leaders: Their Struggle for Power*, London, 1977.

Flandin, Pierre-Étienne, *Politique française, 1919–1940*, Paris, 1948.

Funke, Manfred, *Sanktionen und Kanonen: Hitler, Mussolini und der internationale Abessinienkonflikt, 1934–1936*, Düsseldorf, 1970.

Furnia, A. H., *The Diplomacy of Appeasement: Anglo-French Relations and the Prelude to World War II, 1931–1938*, Washington, DC, 1960.

Gallman, Waldemar J., *Iraq under General Nuri: My Recollections of Nuri al-said*, Baltimore, 1964.

Garner, Joe, *The Commonwealth Office, 1925–68*, London, 1978.

Géraud, André, *The Gravediggers of France*, New York, 1944.

Gerson, Louis L., *John Foster Dulles*, New York, 1967.

Gilbert, Martin, *Winston S. Churchill: V: 1922–1939*, London, 1977.

Gladwyn, Lord, *Memoirs*, London, 1972.

Goold-Adams, Richard, *The Time of Power: A Reappraisal of John Foster Dulles*, London, 1962.

Gore-Booth, Paul, *With Great Truth and Respect*, London, 1974.

Hardie, Frank, *The Abyssinian Crisis*, London, 1974.

Harriman, W. Averell, and Abel Elie, *Special Envoy to Churchill and Stalin*, New York, 1975.

Hart, Basil Liddell, *Memoirs* (2 vols.), London, 1966.

Heikal, Mohammed, *Nasser: The Cairo Documents*, London, 1972.

Hoffman, J. D., *The Conservative Party in Opposition, 1945–51*, London, 1964.

Hoopes, Townshend, *The Devil and John Foster Dulles*, London, 1974.

Howard, Michael, *The Continental Commitment: The Dilemma of British Defence Policy in the Era of the Two World Wars*, London, 1972.

— *The Mediterranean Strategy in the Second World War*, London, 1968.

Hyde, Montgomery, *Neville Chamberlain*, London, 1976.

James, Robert Rhodes, *Churchill: A Study in Failure, 1900–1939*, London, 1970.

Kilmuir, Lord, *Political Adventure*, London, 1964.

Koliopoulos, John S., *Greece and the British Connection, 1935–1941*, Oxford, 1977.

Leahy, William D., *I Was There*, New York, 1950.

Lee, Bradford A., *Britain and the Sino-Japanese War, 1937–1939*, London, 1973.

Lie, Trygve, *In the Cause of Peace*, New York, 1954.

Lindsay, T. F. and Harrington, Michael, *The Conservative Party, 1918–1970*, London, 1974.

Lloyd, Selwyn, *Suez, 1956: A Personal Account*, London, 1978.

Louis, William Roger, *British Strategy in the Far East, 1919–1939*, London, 1971.

—*Imperialism at Bay, 1941–1945: The United States and the Decolonization of the British Empire*, Oxford, 1977.

Love, Kennett, *Suez: The Twice-Fought War*, London, 1969.

Lowe, Peter, *Great Britain and the Origins of the Pacific War: A Study of British Policy in East Asia, 1937–1941*, Oxford, 1977.

McDonald, Iveragh, *A Man of The Times*, London, 1976.

Maclean, Fitzroy, *Eastern Approaches*, London, 1949.

McLellan, David S., *Dean Acheson: State Department Years*, New York, 1976.

Macleod, Iain, *Neville Chamberlain*, London, 1961.

Macmillan, Harold, *Riding the Storm, 1956–1959*, London, 1971.

— *Tides of Fortune, 1945–1955*, London, 1969.

Manderson-Jones, R. B., *The Special Relationship: Anglo-American Relations and Western European Unity, 1947–56*, London, 1972.

Margach, James, *The Abuse of Power*, London, 1978.

Medlicott, W. N., *Britain and Germany: The Search for Agreement*, London, 1969.

— *British Foreign Policy since Versailles, 1919–1963*, London, 1968.

— *Contemporary England, 1914–1964*, London, 1967.

Meinck, Gerhard, *Hitler und die deutsche Aufrüstung, 1933–1937*, Wiesbaden, 1959.

Menzies, Robert, *Afternoon Light: Some Memories of Men and Events*, London, 1967.

Middlemas, Keith, *Diplomacy of Illusion: The British Government and Germany, 1937–1939*, London, 1972.

Middlemas, Keith and John Barnes, *Baldwin: A Biography*, London, 1969.

Moran, Lord, *Winston Churchill: The Struggle for Survival*, London, 1966.

Morrison, Lord, *An Autobiography*, London, 1950.

Mosley, Leonard, *Dulles: A Biography of Eleanor, Allen and John Foster Dulles and their Family Network*, New York, 1978.

Murphy, Robert, *Diplomat among Warriors*, London, 1964.

Newman, Simon, *March 1939: The British Guarantees of Poland*, Oxford, 1976.

Nicholas, H. G., *The British General Election of 1950*, London, 1951.

Nutting, Anthony, *Nasser*, London, 1972.

— *No End of a Lesson*, London, 1967.

Papagos, Alexander, *The Battle for Greece, 1940–1941*, Athens, 1949.

Pearson, Lester, *Memoirs: II: 1948–1957, The International Years*, London, 1974.

Pincher, Chapman, *Inside Story: A Documen-*

tary of the Pursuit of Power, London, 1978.

Pineau, Christian, *1956, Suez*, Paris, 1976.

Polonsky, Anthony, ed., *The Great Powers and the Polish Question, 1941–45*, London, 1976.

Pratt, Lawrence R., *East of Malta, West of Suez: Britain's Mediterranean Crisis, 1936–1939*, London, 1975.

Ramsden, John, *The Age of Balfour and Baldwin, 1902–1940*, London, 1978.

Randle, Robert E., *Geneva, 1954: The Settlement of the Indochinese War*, Princeton, NJ, 1969.

Reed, Bruce and Williams, Geoffrey, *Denis Healey and the Politics of Power*, London, 1971.

Reitz, Deneys, *No Outspan*, London, 1943.

Robbins, Keith, *Munich, 1938*, London, 1968.

Robertson, Terence, *Crisis: The Inside Story of the Suez Conspiracy*, London, 1965.

Roskill, Stephen, *Hankey: Man of Secrets* (3 vols.), London, 1970–74.

Sampson, Anthony, *The Seven Sisters: The Great Oil Companies and the World They Made*, London, 1975.

Schlaim, Avi, Jones, Peter and Sainsbury, Keith, *British Foreign Secretaries since 1945*, Newton Abbot, Devon, 1977.

Seton-Watson, Hugh, *Eastern Europe between the Wars, 1918–1941*, Cambridge, 1945.

Sherwood, Robert E., *The White House Papers of Harry L. Hopkins* (2 vols.), London, 1948–9.

Smith, Gaddis, *Dean Acheson*, New York, 1972.

Stimson, Henry L. and Bundy, McGeorge, *On Active Service in War and Peace*, London, n.d. (1949?).

Stoler, Mark A., *The Politics of the Second Front: American Military Planning and Diplomacy in Coalition Warfare, 1941–1943*, Westport, Connecticut, 1977.

Stuart, James, *Within the Fringe: an Autobiography*, London, 1967.

Swinton, Lord, *Sixty Years of Power*, London, 1966.

Taylor, A. J. P., *Beaverbrook*, London, 1972.

Thomas, Hugh, *The Spanish Civil War*, 1st ed., London, 1961.

— *The Suez Affair*, London, 1967.

Thompson, Alan, *The Day before Yesterday*, London, 1971.

Thompson, Neville, *The Anti-Appeasers: Conservative Opposition to Appeasement in the 1930s*, London, 1971.

Thorne, Christopher, *Allies of a Kind: The United States, Britain and the War against Japan*, London, 1978.

— *The Approach of War, 1938–1939*, London, 1967.

— *The Limits of Foreign Policy: The West, the League and the Far Eastern Crisis of 1931–1933*, London, 1972.

Tolstoy, Nikolai, *Victims of Yalta*, revised ed., London, 1979.

Toynbee, Arnold J., *Survey of International Affairs, 1928*, London, 1929.

Trevelyan, Humphrey, *The Middle East in Revolution*, London, 1970.

van Creveld, Martin L. *Hitler's Strategy, 1940–1941: The Balkan Clue*, London, 1973.

Waley, Daniel, *British Public Opinion and the Abyssinian War, 1935–6*, London, 1975.

Wasserstein, Bernard, *Britain and the Jews of Europe, 1939–45*, London, 1979.

Wheeler-Bennett, J. W., *King George the Sixth: His Life and Reign*, London, 1958.

— *Knaves, Fools and Heroes: In Europe between the Wars*, London, 1974.

— *The Pipe Dream of Peace: The Story of the Collapse of Disarmament*, London, 1935.

— ed., *Action This Day: Working with Churchill*, London, 1968.

Wheeler-Bennett, J. W. and Nicholls, Anthony, *The Semblance of Peace: The Political Settlement after the Second World War*, London, 1972.

Wilmot, Chester, *The Struggle for Europe*, New York, 1952.

Winant, John G. *A Letter from Grosvenor Square*, London, 1947.

Woodward, E. L., *British Foreign Policy in the Second World War* (one-volume ed.), London, 1962.

— *British Foreign Policy in the Second World War* (5 vols.), London, 1970–76.

Young, Kenneth, *Churchill and Beaverbrook*, London, 1966.

(b) ARTICLES

Barker, Elisabeth, 'British Policy towards Romania, Bulgaria and Hungary, 1944–1946', in Martin McCauley, ed., *Communist Power in Europe, 1944–1949*, London, 1977.

— 'Some Factors in British Decision-Making over Yugoslavia, 1941–4', in Phyllis Auty and Richard Clogg, eds., *British Policy Towards Wartime Resistance in Yugoslavia and Greece*, London, 1975.

Baumont, Maurice, 'The Rhineland Crisis: March 1936' in Neville Waites, ed., *Troub-*

led Neighbours: Franco-British Relations in the Twentieth Century, London, 1971.

Beck, Peter J., 'The Anglo-Persian Oil Dispute, 1932–33', Journal of Contemporary History, IX, 1974.

Blake, Robert, 'Anthony Eden', in John P. Mackintosh, ed., British Prime Ministers in the Twentieth Century: II: Churchill to Callaghan, London, 1978.

Carlton, David, 'The Anglo-French Compromise on Arms Limitation, 1928', Journal of British Studies, VIII, 1968–9.

— 'Disarmament with Guarantees: Lord Cecil, 1922–1927', Disarmament and Arms Control, III, 1965.

— 'The Dominions and British Policy in the Abyssinian Crisis', Journal of Imperial and Commonwealth History, I, 1972–3.

— 'Eden, Blum and the Origins of Non-Intervention', Journal of Contemporary History, VI, 1971.

— 'Great Britain and the Coolidge Naval Disarmament Conference of 1927', Political Science Quarterly, LXXXIII, 1968.

— 'Great Britain and the League Council Crisis of 1926', Historical Journal, XI, 1968.

— 'The Problem of Civil Aviation in British Air Disarmament Policy, 1919–1934', The Royal United Service Institution Journal, CXI, 1966.

Ceadel, Martin, 'The "King and Country" Debate, 1933: Student Politics, Pacifism and the Dictators', Historical Journal, XXII, 1979.

Crozier, Andrew, 'Prelude to Munich: British Foreign Policy and Germany, 1935–8', European Studies Review, VI, 1976.

Douglas, Roy, 'Chamberlain and Eden, 1937–38', Journal of Contemporary History, XIII, 1978.

Healey, Denis, 'The Cominform and World Communism', International Affairs, XXIV, 1948.

Kovrig, Bennet, 'Mediation by Obfuscation: The Resolution of the Marseille Crisis, October 1934 to May 1935', Historical Journal, XIX, 1976.

Leighton, Richard M., 'OVERLORD Revisited: An Interpretation of American Strategy in the European War, 1942–1944', American Historical Review, LXVIII, 1963.

Lowe, Peter, 'Great Britain and the Coming of the Pacific War, 1939–1941', Transactions of the Royal Historical Society, XXIV, 1974.

Parker, R. A. C., 'Great Britain, France and the Ethiopian Crisis, 1935–1936', English Historical Review, LXXXIX, 1974.

Pratt, Lawrence, 'The Anglo-American Naval Conversations on the Far East of January 1938', International Affairs, XLVII, 1971.

Resis, Albert, 'The Churchill–Stalin Secret "Percentages" Agreement on the Balkans, Moscow, October 1944', American Historical Review, LXXXIII, 1978.

Ryan, Henry B., 'A New Look at Churchill's "Iron Curtain" Speech', Historical Journal, XXII, 1979.

Sainsbury, Keith, 'British Policy and German Unity at the End of the Second World War', English Historical Review, XCIV, 1979.

Skidelsky, Robert, 'Lessons of Suez' in Vernon Bogdanor and Robert Skidelsky, eds., The Age of Affluence, 1951–1964, London, 1970.

Stone, Glyn, 'Britain, Non-Intervention and the Spanish Civil War', European Studies Review, IX, 1979.

Tamchina, Rainer, 'In Search of Common Causes: The Imperial Conference of 1937', Journal of Imperial and Commonwealth History, I, 1972–3.

Toscano, Mario, 'Eden's Mission to Rome on the Eve of the Italo-Ethiopian Conflict', in A. O. Sarkissian, ed., Studies in Diplomatic History and Historiography, London, 1961.

van Creveld, Martin, 'Prelude to Disaster: The British Decision to Aid Greece, 1940–41', Journal of Contemporary History, IX, 1974.

Warner, Geoffrey, ' "Collusion" and the Suez Crisis of 1956', International Affairs, LV, 1979.

Williams, J. E., 'The Joint Declaration on Colonies: An Issue in Anglo-American Relations, 1942–1944', British Journal of International Studies, II, 1976.

(c) UNPUBLISHED DISSERTATIONS

Ibrahim, Hassan Ahmed, 'The Anglo-Egyptian Treaty of 1936', London University PhD thesis, 1976.

Radice, Lisanne, 'Negotiations for an Eastern Security Pact, 1933–1936', London University PhD thesis, 1973.

Rotunda, Donald T., 'The Rome Embassy of Sir Eric Drummond, 16th Earl of Perth, 1933–1939', London University PhD thesis, 1972.

Waites, Neville H., 'British Foreign Policy towards France regarding the German Problem from 1929 to 1934', London University PhD thesis, 1972.

Index

516

Eccles, Sir David, 370
Economist, 372, 415–16

Eden (Robert) Anthony (later Earl of Avon)
Family life: birth, 11; parents, 11–12, marries Beatrice Beckett, 15; separation and divorce from Beatrice, 15, 270; children, 15; death of elder son, 257–8; marries Clarissa Churchill, 318
Books: Another World, 11–13, 471; *Place in the Sun,* 17–18; *Foreign Affairs,* 26; *Full Circle,* 468–9, 472; *Facing the Dictators,* 468–9; *The Reckoning,* 468–9; *Towards Peace in Indochina,* 471
Ill-health: heart trouble (1935), 64; ulcer (1945), 257, 259; ulcer (1951), 298; operation (1953), 327–8, 330; during Suez crisis, 428, 430, 458, 462, 464–5; in retirement, 466–9; death, 477
Military career: 12–13
Political career: contests Spennymoor, 14; selected to contest Warwick and Leamington, 14; successful in General Election (1923), 14; maiden speech (1924), 15–16; re-elected in General Election (1924), 16–17; becomes Parliamentary Private Secretary to Locker-Lampson, 17; Imperial tour (1925), 17–18; Parliamentary Private Secretary to Austen Chamberlain (1926–9), 19–26; and League Council crisis (1926), 21–2; critical of Lloyd George, 22, 24, 25–6; and Anglo-French compromise on arms limitation (1928), 25–6; in Opposition (1929–31), 26–7; relationship with Baldwin, 26–7, 71–2; serves on CID sub-committee (1931), 27; becomes Parliamentary Under-Secretary in the Foreign Office, 28; relationship with Simon, 29, 37–8; and Manchurian crisis, 29–34; and World Disarmament Conference, 34–52; visits Paris (September 1933), 42–3; becomes Lord Privy Seal (1934), 44; visits Paris, Berlin and Rome (1934), 44–9; and Marseilles crisis (1934), 53–4; and Saar crisis (1934–5), 54–6; fundamental attitudes to Abyssinian crisis and League of Nations, 56–62, 66–9; visits Berlin (1935), 62; visits Moscow (1935), 62–3; visits Warsaw and Prague (1935), 64; enters Cabinet (1935), 64; visits Rome and Paris to canvass Zeila Plan, 65–6; and sanctions against Italy, 67–8, 72–4, 83–6; and Hoare–Laval Plan, 68–70; becomes Foreign Secretary (December 1935), 70; and Rhineland crisis, 74–83; and Spanish Civil War, 86–93; and rearmament, 93–5; and

'appeasement', 95–6; and Gentleman's Agreement, 96–7; and Montreux Convention, 97; and Anglo-Egyptian Treaty (1936), 97–8; relationship with Chamberlain (1937–8), 100–131; and Imperial Conference (1937), 102–6; and Germany (1937), 102–4, 114–17; and defence policy (1937), 113, 115–19; and Roosevelt initiative (1938), 119–23; and colonial restitution to Germany (1938), 123–4; resignation, 124–33; relationship with Churchill, 135–6, 200–206, 294–7, 329–30, 350, 353–4, 356–7, 364–5; and Czechoslovak crisis (1938), 134–42; caution after Munich crisis, 142–9; visits United States (December 1938), 146–7; changed attitude to Soviet Union (1939), 149–50; outbreak of war and acceptance of Dominions Office, 150–52; serves at Dominions Office during 'Phoney War', 153–60; and succession of Churchill, 161–3, 258–60, 266–7, 271, 283–4; serves at the War Office, 163–70; visits Middle East (1940), 167–70; restored to Foreign Office, 170; mission to Middle East and Balkans (1941), 171–82; and wartime alliance with Soviet Union, 183–7, 191–9; and Far East (1940–41), 187–91; wartime clashes with Churchill on methods of running the war, 200–206; and post-war future of France, 207, 218–21, 225, 238–9; and Mediterranean strategy, 208–9, 221–4, 228–31; visits Washington (1943), 209–13; and Katyn crisis, 214–16; as Leader of the House, 206, 216–17, 234–6; and 'enforced repatriation', 239–42, 246–7, 251; and post-war future of Germany, 211, 225, 243, 248, 258; and consideration of post-war Soviet frontiers and spheres of influence, 194–5, 199, 231–3, 237, 242–58; considers becoming Viceroy of India (1943), 217–19; attends Moscow Foreign Ministers' Conference (1943), 225–30; and development of Cold War (1945–51), 260–62, 265, 269–70, 272–3, 275–7, 279–81, 286–8; and the shaping of the Opposition's domestic policy, 267–8, 281–2; and the Opposition's policy on European unity, 278–9, 282–3, 285–6; and Attlee Government's handling of Iranian crisis (1951), 289–90, 292; again becomes Foreign Secretary (1951), 294; relationship with Butler, 296–7; relationship with Acheson, 301–2, 307, 316–17, 323; relationship with Dulles, 300–301, 323–4, 336, 338, 342–8, 354–5, 363–4;

as Foreign Secretary (1951-5), 294-367 *passim* (*see also* Egypt; European Defence Community; Indochina; Iran; Korean War; Western European Union); becomes Prime Minister (1955), 367; constructs Cabinet (1955), 368-70; wins General Election (1955), 370-74; and domestic policy (1955-6), 374-6, 385-6, 389, 395-6, 400-401; and Geneva Summit Conference (1953), 376-82; and origins of Suez crisis, 380-83, 390-94, 397-9, 402; and Cyprus crisis, 383-5, 399-400; and Burgess-Maclean scandal, 386-8; Cabinet reshuffle (December 1955), 388-9; visits Washington (January 1956), 390-95; and visit of Bulganin and Khrushchev (1956), 400-401; and Suez crisis, 403-465; resignation, 464-5
Eden, Beatrice, 15, 130, 185, 259, 271
Eden, Clarissa (later Countess of Avon), 219, 318-19, 363, 367, 373, 377, 380, 428, 466-70, 504
Eden, John, 12
Eden, Nicholas (brother of Anthony), 13
Eden, Nicholas (son of Anthony, later 2nd Earl of Avon), 15, 278, 470
Eden, Sir Robert, 213
Eden, Simon, 15, 250; death of, 257-8, 367
Eden, Sybil, 12
Eden, Timothy, 11-12
Eden, William, 11-12
'Eden Group', 135, 143, 145, 153, 157, 161
Egypt: and Anglo-Soviet Treaty (1936), 97-8; Eden visits (February 1940), 160; Eden visits (October 1940), 168; Eden visits (February-March 1941), 172-3, 179-80; attempted renegotiation of Anglo-Egyptian Treaty of 1936, 194-6, 270; Eden criticizes Morrison's policy towards (1951), 288-9, 292; British relations with (1952-3), 299-300, 303, 305-6, 314-15, 325-7, 340-41; British relations with (1954), 348, 356-9; Eden visits (1955), 365; and origins of Suez crisis, 380-83, 390-94, 397-8, 402; and evolution of Suez crisis after nationalization of Canal, 403-65, 470, 474
Eire, 158-9
Eisenhower, Dwight D., 219, 228-9, 291; as Supreme Commander of NATO, 309-11; relations with Great Britain while President, 300-301, 323, 327, 332-6, 345-7, 351-2, 354, 357, 365-7, 377-9, 385, 391, 393, 395, 403-65 *passim*
Elizabeth II, 297, 330, 364, 367, 401, 464, 475
Elliot, Walter, 128, 130

Ély, Paul, 420-21
Emrys-Evans, Paul, 135, 144, 157, 260, 265-6, 269, 271, 471-2
Erskine, Sir George, 314
Erskine Hill, Alexander, 202
Estonia, 183; *see also* Baltic States
Europe, movement for unity of, 272, 278-9; Eden's interest in reviving Anglo-French union project (1956), 425; British application to join European Economic Community, 476-7, 479-80; *see also* Schuman, Robert; European Defence Community; Western European Union; Spaak, committee chaired by
European Advisory Commission, 227
European Defence Community (EDC), Plan for, 308-14, 317-18, 334, 336-8, 360-63, 394-5
Evans, Sir Horace, 327-8
Evening Standard, 389

Farouk, King of Egypt, 314-15, 325-6
Fawzi, Mahmoud, 429
Finer, Herbert, 381-2, 447
Finland, 160, 183, 186, 191-2, 232, 270
Fisher, Sir Nigel, 470
Flandin, Pierre Étienne, 49; and Abyssinian and Rhineland crises, 74-83, 422
Fleming, Ian, 458
Focus Movement, 139
Formosa, 303, 340, 366-7, 379
Foster, Andrew, 407
France: and Geneva Protocol, 19, 186, 194, 200; and Locarno Treaties, 20; and League Council crisis (1926), 20; and compromise with Great Britain on arms limitation (1928), 24-6; and World Disarmament Conference, 34-52; and Marseilles crisis (1934), 52-4; and Saar crisis (1934-5), 54-5; and League of Nations, 57-8; and Abyssinian crisis, 53, 58, 61, 66-70, 72-4, 83-6; and Rhineland crisis, 74, 76, 80-83; and Spanish Civil War, 86-92; and Nyon Conference, 109-10; Ministerial visit to London (November 1937), 114-15, 118; and Munich crisis, 137-8, 142; and possibility of compromise peace (October 1939), 154-5; Eden visits (November 1939), 160; fall of (1940), 163-5; Anglo-American discussions about postwar future of, 206-7, 218-21, 238-9; Churchill and Eden visit (1951), 302, 310; Eden visits (1952), 313; and Bermuda Conference (1953), 336-7; and Berlin Conference (1953), 338; and Geneva Conference (1954), 347, 352-5; and Austrian State Treaty (1955), 373; and Geneva

461, 463
Jancović, Radivoje, 181
Japan, 96, 102, 116–17, 156, 186; and
    Manchurian crisis, 29–34; and approach
    of Pearl Harbor, 187–90; atomic bombs
    used on (1945), 258; and post-war peace
    treaty, 303–4
Jebb, Sir Gladwyn (later Lord Gladwyn), 298,
    431, 472
Jews, wartime fate of, 212–13, 240
Jones, Thomas, 86
Jordan, 304, 475; Templer mission to,
    392–3; and dismissal of Glubb (1956),
    397–9; and Suez crisis, 405, 421, 424,
    439, 442–3
Journal de Genève, 348
Joynson-Hicks, Sir William, 17

Kádár, Janos, 461
Katyn massacre, 213–16
Kennedy, John F., 477
Khrushchev, Nikita, 376, 400–401, 475
Kilmuir, Lord, *see* Maxwell Fyfe, Sir David
King, Mackenzie, 154
'King and Country' debate, 60
Kirkpatrick, Sir Ivone, 298, 372, 382, 444
Knowland, William, 353
Knox, Sir Geoffrey, 55
Korean War, 286–8, 290, 299, 302–3, 318,
    335–6, 338, 340, 356, 370; and armistice
    negotiations (1952), 319–23
Koryzis, Alexander, 171, 176
Kovács, Béla, 273, 275

Lambton, Lord, 470
Lampson, Sir Miles (later Lord Killearn), 98
Laniel, Joseph, 336, 352
Laos, 328, 341, 352–3, 355, 471
Lascelles, Alan, 297
Latvia, 183, 196; *see also* Baltic States
Laval, Pierre, 49, 197; and Marseilles crisis
    (1934), 52–3; and Abyssinian crisis, 53,
    58, 61, 66–70, 72–4
Law, Andrew Bonar, 132
Law, Richard (later Lord Coleraine), 135,
    202–4, 235, 293
League of Nations, 20–22; and Marseilles
    crisis (1934), 53–4; and Saar crisis
    (1934–5), 54–5; Eden's attitude towards
    (1935), 56–62, 484; Special Assembly
    (1937), 105
League of Nations Union, 19–20, 56–61, 93
Leahy, William D., 230, 252
Lebanon, 475
Leeper, Sir Reginald, 249
Lenin, V. I., 401
Lennox-Boyd, Alan, 369, 399

Libya, 403–4
Liddell Hart, Sir Basil, *see* Hart, Sir Basil
    Liddell
Lie, Trygve, 260
Lindley, Sir Francis, 33
Lindsay, Sir Ronald, 122–3
Lipton, Marcus, 387
Lithuania, 183; *see also* Baltic States
Litvinov, Maxim, 63
Llandudno, Conservative Conference at
    (1956), 428–30
Lloyd, Lord, 139
Lloyd, Selwyn, 108, 327, 329, 353, 357; and
    Korean war armistice negotiations (1952),
    320–22; becomes Minister of Defence
    (1955), 369–70; becomes Foreign Sec-
    retary (December 1955), 388; accom-
    panies Eden to Washington (January
    1956), 390–95; and Suez crisis, 403–65
    passim
Lloyd George, David, 22, 24–6, 31, 132,
    167, 202, 476
Locker-Lampson, Sir Godfrey, 17, 19
Locarno Treaties (1925), 19–20, 56–61, 93
Lodge, Henry Cabot, 444, 457, 461–3
Logan, Sir Donald, 437–8
London Conference of Maritime Nations
    (August 1956), 411–12, 414, 416–17
London Conference of Suez Canal Users'
    Association (September 1956), 422, 424,
    426
London Conference on Cyprus (1955),
    384–5
London Conference on Western European
    Union (1954), 362–3
Londonderry, Lord, 35, 42
Long, Breckenridge, 227
Longmore, Arthur, 172–3
Lumley, L. R., 19
Lwow, 254–6, 252
Lyttelton, Oliver (later Lord Chandos), 205,
    470
Lytton, Lord, 33

MacArthur, Douglas, 287
McDermott, Geoffrey, 124
McDonald, Iveragh, 301–2, 336–7, 345–6,
    347–8, 355, 361–2, 408, 414, 423–5,
    427, 471
MacDonald, James Ramsay, 167; forms first
    Labour Government, 15; forms second
    Labour Government, 26; forms National
    Government, 27; gives Eden post in For-
    eign Office (1931), 27; pro-American,
    33–4; and World Disarmament Confer-
    ence, 36, 46, 49; attends Stresa Con-
    ference (1935), 64; resigns premiership